NIKKI BRADFORD

THE WELL
WOMAN'S
SELF HELP
DIRECTORY

PUBLISHED IN ASSOCIATION WITH

Marie Stopes
·WOMEN'S·HEALTH·CLINICS·

||| · PARRAGON · |||

To my husband Peter for putting up with me while I wrote this book; and my son Ben, with whom I was pregnant at the time – and who taught me more about the practicalities of pregnancy, childbirth and breastfeeding than any adult expert ever could have done.

This edition published 1996 for
Parrallel Books
Units 13-17 Avonbridge Industrial Estate
Atlantic Road
Avonmouth, Bristol BS11 9QD
by Diamond Books
77-85 Fulham Palace Road
Hammersmith, London W6 8JB

First published in Great Britain by
Sidgwick & Jackson Limited

Copyright © 1990 by Nikki Bradford
Illustrations/line drawings by Rick Sullivan

ISBN 0-75251-821-6

Printed in Great Britain

Contents

Acknowledgements

I'd like to thank the following experts for their patience, their time and their knowledge, which have proved so invaluable in writing this book:

Dr Beth Alder, Senior Lecturer and Researcher at Queen Margaret College in Edinburgh;

Helen Axby, Director of Clinic Services at Marie Stopes Clinics;

Beverley Beech, Chairwoman of the Association for Improvements in the Maternity Services (AIMS);

Dr Michael Brush, Consulting Biochemist at St Thomas's Hospital, London, and Co-chairman of the Premenstrual Society;

Dr Sarah Creighton, Research Fellow at St George's Hospital, London;

Professor Michael Chapman, Head of Obstetrics and Gynaecology at Guy's Hospital, London;

Professor Ian Cooke, Head of Obstetrics and Gynaecology at the Jessop Hospital for Women in Sheffield;

Paul Entwistle, Fertility Researcher and Fellow of Liverpool University;

Dr Bob Etheridge, Consultant Gynaecologist at the North Middlesex Hospital, London;

Dr Glynn Evans, Head of the Micology Unit at Leeds University;

Dr Jason Gardosi, Senior Registrar and Lecturer at University Hospital in Nottingham;

Dr Jack Glatt, Director of the Infertility Advisory Centres in Birmingham and London;

Dr Grant Harris, Consultant Gynaecologist at the Lewisham Hospital, London;

Dr Michael Kamm, Consultant physician at St Mark's Hospital for Diseases of the Rectum and Colon, London;

Angela Kilmartin, Cystitis expert and Author;

Maxine Korn, Information Services Co-ordinator of Cancer Link;

Dr Chenni Kumur, Consultant Psychiatrist at the Institute of Psychiatry in London;

John McGarry, Consultant Obstetrician at the North Devon District Hospital;

Dr Vanessa Mooney, of Marie Stopes Clinics and the Amarant Trust;

Dr Karina Reynolds, Research Fellow at the John Radcliffe Hospital, Aylesbury;

Dr Diana Riley, Consultant Psychiatrist at St John's Hospital, Aylesbury;

Dr Adam Rodin, Senior Registrar in Gynaecology and Obstetrics at Farnborough Hospital;

John Shepherd (and his secretary, Carol Bartleman), Consultant Gynaecologist Specializing in Oncology at St Bartholomew's and the Royal Marsden Hositals in London;

Annette Spence, Psychosexual Counsellor at Marie Stopes Clinics;

Maggie Thom, Consultant Obstetrician and Gynaecologist at Guys Hospital, London;

Dr Anne Szarewski, Clinical Assistant in Colposcopy at the Royal Northern Hospital, Clinical Assistant in Genito-Urinary Medicine at St Thomas's Hospital (both in London) and Family Planning Doctor at Marie Stopes Clinics;

Jenny Underwood, Research Fellow at St Mary's Hospital Medical School, London;

Helen White, Director (for the north of England) for the Continence Advisory Service; and

Chris Williams, Senior Lecturer in Oncology at Southampton General Hospital and Medical School.

Thanks also to The Family Planning Association's bookshop – Healthwise – and its manageress, Carmel McDonnell;

The National Childbirth Trust (especially Shirleyanne Seel);

The Royal College of Midwives (especially Greta Balfour); and

Mary McKoane, Senior Midwifery Tutor for Harringay, London.

Also to my editors, Libby Joy and Karen Hurrell, for their support and encouragement, and to Laura Swaffield, for her assistance on several of the chapters.

Complementary therapist contributors

Acupuncture
Dr Yu graduated as a doctor at the Charing Cross
Hospital in London, before returning to the Far East to
specialize both in acupuncture, and in obstetrics and
gynaecology. A Master of Acupuncture in both China
and Japan, he practises at three clinics in London:
Camden, Hampstead and Kentish Town. He is also the
Director of the Academy of Chinese Acupuncture,
advisor in Acupuncture to the Institute of
Complementary Medicine, and advisor to the Association
of GPs in Natural Medicine.

Aromatherapy
Dr Lunney trained at the Medical School of San Andreas
University at La-Paz in Bolivia, before coming to Britain
and working as a registrar in Pathology at the Mount
Vernon, Northwood and Harefield Hospitals in London.
A former NCT breastfeeding counsellor, she is also a
graduate of L'Institut des Sciences Biomedicales in
France and of the London School of Aromatherapy. She
has her own aromatherapy and colour therapy clinic
called 'Vida', in Stevenage, and another at Stevenage
Leisure Centre.

Chiropractic
Susan Moore is past President of the British
Chiropractic Association and has her own clinic in
Birmingham. She is also the author of two books:
Alternative Health: Chiropractic (Optima) and *New Ways
to Health: A Guide to Chiropractic* (Hamlyn).

Nutrition
Dr Howell has a PhD from London University in
Health Education, and is a nutritionist and
psychotherapist, with his own clinic (the Candida and
ME Clinic in Templecombe, Somerset). He also
practises at Harley House, in London. Dr Howell
practises lymphatic drainage and colonic irrigation
therapy, has written twenty-four books and was voted
Complementary Practitioner of the Year in 1989.

Homoeopathy

Dr Khanna graduated as a doctor from Punjab University Medical School, and subsequently worked all over the world – in India, Nigeria, Iran and America – before moving to Britain to practise medicine at University College Hospital and the Whittington Hospital in London. She is qualified in both Classical and Complex Homoeopathy. At her clinic in Richmond (The Richmond Clinic), she also practises clinical nutrition, clinical ecology, oxygen ozone therapy and neural therapy.

Medical herbalism

Mark Evans is Past President for the National Institute of Medical Herbalists, and practises in Bath and Bristol. He is also a writer and has co-authored several books including *Alternatives in Healing* (Macmillan) and is Principal of the Bath School of Massage.

Osteopathy

Steven Sandler is the Director of Osteopathic Practice at the British School of Osteopathy, where he set up the first (and only) osteopathic clinic for expectant mothers in the UK. He also has his own practice in Chingford and has written two books, both called *Osteopathy*, one published by Optima and one by Hamlyn.

Introduction

No matter what is wrong with you, somewhere out there there is a doctor, therapist or self-help strategy that can help you. The only problem can be tracking down the right one.

That's where this book comes in. It aims to point you in the right direction to find the health professionals you need in both the orthodox medical establishment and in complementary medicine; to put you in touch with the best support groups – giving their names, phone numbers, addresses and what they can offer; and to explain which self help and preventative measures really will either stop you being ill in the first place or help you recover as fast as possible.

I wrote the book because I know – both from bitter personal experience and from answering hundreds of letters from *Essentials* and *Good Housekeeping* readers – that if you are ill, you are vulnerable. You may be rather scared. You do not always have either the confidence or the energy to insist on your health rights, to argue with doctors who say there is nothing the matter with you, nothing which can be done, when you reckon there is. Nor do you generally have the strength to shop around, endlessly knocking on doors and asking questions all on your own, hoping to find someone who can help.

What you do want is support, practical assistance, a bit of sympathy and the correct health professional to help you when you're ill, whether your problem is unexplained infertility, recurrent thrush or cystitis, a difficult menopause or pre-menstrual tension that just won't quit. Turn these pages and they'll tell you WHO to ask, WHAT your options are, WHERE to look for help and WHICH telephone numbers to ring. And that's 90 per cent of the battle.

The new three-pronged approach to getting better

If you have a persistent health problem one approach on its own is often *not* enough to get rid of it. You may find instead that you need to do battle with it from two or even three different angles all at the same time, which means using:

1. ordinary orthodox medicine (usually in the form of drugs or surgery);
2. a good self-help strategy including practical ways that *you* can reinforce the treatments you are getting to make the most of them;
3. the right complementary therapy (such as homoeopathy or acupuncture), used together with orthodox medicine.

That is why each section in this book covers these three areas. It explains what orthodox medicine can offer you, including what is likely to be causing your problem, the available – and new – medical treatments that can help and where to go to get them.

It also tells you whether complementary therapy can help, and if so which ones are likely to be the most useful for your particular problem. Plus an idea of what the therapists concerned will do, and where to find one.

It gives advice on, and suggestions for, self help. What you personally can do off your own bat, while receiving treatment from therapists and doctors, to maximize your chances of a quick and complete recovery. Plus how to try and avoid the problem in the first place, stop it coming back again – and what your other options are if the treatments offered to you aren't a success.

There is an alphabetical HELPLINES section at the end of each chapter, listing the self-help and support groups that exist for each condition or problem, as well as a list of general medical or help organizations at the back of the book. Support groups can be more comforting than any health professional or official organization as they are run on a charitable or voluntary basis, by other women who have had your problem themselves, know very well how you feel – and what may help. See also SETTING UP A SUPPORT GROUP. It also lists useful addresses of relevant equipment manufacturers, counselling services, where to go for cosmetic surgery, relaxation classes or hypnotherapy, companies supplying drugs and supplements, etc., which you may find useful.

Good general sources for help
If you don't seem to be getting anywhere with your GP or local hospital, try:

1. *The Medical Advisory Service* (081 994 6477)
Run 10 a.m.–10 p.m. Monday to Friday, by trained nurses, this is a help- and information-giving charity which can tell you what treatments are available for a vast range of health problems (from heart disease to endometriosis) and how to get them – both on the NHS and in the private sector. It will also advise you if you are having difficulties getting a referral to a specialist or obtaining a specific sort of treatment.

2. *Self-help and support groups*
There is at least one for just about every women's health problem you can imagine – sometimes several. They are run on a charitable basis, usually by those who have experienced the problem themselves, and have medical advisors who will include some of the very best and most sympathetic doctors in the relevant area. The Post-Natal Depression Association, for instance, is backed up by several of the leading doctors and psychiatrists in the field; the National Association of Pre-Menstrual Syndrome can put you in touch with the pioneer doctors who specialize in treating pre-menstrual difficulties.

Please see HELPLINES for the groups available. Either the associations themselves, or their medical advisors, will be able to answer many of your questions (normally by post). They can usually also recommend a good specialist in your part of the country if you are having difficulty finding, or being referred to, one.

3. *The Good Doctor Guide*, by Martin Page (Sphere, 1989)
It is the only consumer's directory in existence which actually lists some of the top London specialists in many different areas of medicine, from dermatology and cardiology to plastic surgery. These include obstetrics, gynaecology,

paediatrics and cancer treatment. It is not exhaustive, does not deal with other areas of the country, but at least it gives you a starting point. If these specialists themselves cannot help you, they are very likely to know one of their colleagues who can. It was compiled by asking the doctors' former patients which specialists they rated highest – and why.

PRIVATE MEDICINE DIAGNOSIS:
* It is worth knowing that while most of these specialists work in the Harley Street golden square mile of medicine in London, many have NHS hospital posts too, and you can be referred by your GP (if he or she is willing) from anywhere in the UK to see them on the NHS, though recent NHS reforms have made this harder now.
* It is also worth knowing that if you do have the money (£40 to £50 for a first private consultation) you can, in practice, refer yourself to a specialist privately, if you have to – though officially a specialist prefers a GP's referral note for private appointments, too.

A private appointment means that you get seen fairly promptly (usually within a week or two), and that you don't need your GP's blessing or recommendation to do so. An NHS appointment with the same consultant would be free but the waiting lists could be anything from weeks, even to months in some areas, if the queues are long and yours is a 'chronic' (i.e. been going on a long time, and not life-threatening) rather than an 'acute' (urgent, possibly life-threatening) problem.

WHAT YOU GET PRIVATELY is an expert diagnosis and advice – quickly, and at your own request. Many people will pay for this, so that having found out just what the problem is and what the treatment should be – if they need it – they are perfectly within their rights to return to their GP with this diagnosis *in writing*, and to ask to go back into the NHS free system again.

4. Women's Health Concern
Send an SAE to PO Box 1629, London W8 (071 938 3932). This is a charity run by trained nurses which can give advice on all areas of women's health (it specializes in PMT and the menopause) and suggest where you will find any further expert medical help you may need.

5. Women's Health Information and Reproductive Rights Centre,
52 Featherstone Street, London EC1 (071 251 6580)
This charitable organization has data banks and computers with details on all sorts of women's self-help groups countrywide. It can advise women with health problems where to seek expert help and send you background information.

6. The Regional Health Information Service,
Freephone (0800 665544)
This has a large computer database of countrywide self-help and support groups for almost every health problem imaginable, and can provide you with the relevant names, addresses, telephone numbers and information on what they offer and details of hospital waiting lists.

Abortion

What is it?

Abortion describes the removal – or expulsion – of a developing embryo or foetus to end a pregnancy. There are two different types of abortion. One is brought about artificially, perhaps at the mother's own request because her pregnancy is unwanted, perhaps because doctors have detected that the developing foetus is abnormal in some way.

The second is 'spontaneous' abortion – meaning a miscarriage. Many pregnancies end spontaneously (abort) in the early weeks after conception. Birthright, the appeal arm of the Royal College of Obstetricians & Gynaecologists, which funds a great deal of research into women's health, estimates that between 40 and 60 per cent of pregnancies miscarry early. Many of them do so before the woman even knows she is pregnant, so all she is aware of is a period that might be later and heavier than usual. (See MISCARRIAGE, page 297.)

You may also hear the term 'threatened abortion', when a pregnancy is showing some warning signs of ending by itself: i.e. a threatened miscarriage (see MISCARRIAGE page 297). You may also hear 'miscarriage' which happens repeatedly called 'habitual' or 'recurrent' abortion. Another term, 'incomplete abortion', describes an abortion or miscarriage when part of the womb's contents is left behind (see **Retained products of conception**, below, page 19).

You are most certainly not alone if you have had, or are seeking, an abortion. The latest official figures from the Office of Population Censuses & Surveys (OPCS) 1989 show that one in five confirmed pregnancies are now ended by a legal abortion.

What is the law?

How late can an abortion be carried out?

If a severe foetal abnormality has been detected, or serious health complications are likely if the woman continues her pregnancy, the new legal limit is up to 24 weeks (six months), but there are extensions available if there is severe foetal abnormality, or if the pregnancy would cause permanent injury to the mother's health if it were allowed to continue. For an abortion requested by the mother for other reasons (such as personal choice, other family commitments or financial considerations) the new practical time limit is 24 weeks. Only a limited number of places have the necessary licenses to perform terminations so late in pregnancy.

The later the termination, the more potential health risks there are for the woman, and the more upsetting the procedure is, both for her and for the nursing staff. As a result, women who are more than 20 weeks pregnant will find it increasingly difficult to get an abortion. (See HELPLINES, page 25: **Late Terminations – Who Can Help?**)

Whose authority do you need?

Under the 1967 Abortion Act you need *two* doctors to sign the green-coloured form (often just referred to as the Green Form) giving their consent for the operation. Though it is not yet law, there are moves afoot that only one doctor should need to sign a woman's abortion consent form if she is less than 12 weeks pregnant. The doctors are allowed to give four commonly used reasons for agreeing to an abortion.

1. If continuing your pregnancy would 'present a greater risk to your life than if the pregnancy were terminated'. This would mean that you were suffering from a potentially life-threatening condition associated with your pregnancy, such as eclampsia (see PREGNANCY PROBLEMS, page 360).

2. If continuing your pregnancy would mean 'more of a risk to your physical or mental health than if it were terminated'. This would be given as the reason for termination if you did not want to have a baby – perhaps for personal, career or financial reasons – and that having it would cause a deterioration in your physical and/or mental health.

3. If continuing the pregnancy would mean 'more of a risk of injury to the physical or mental health of existing children in your family than if the pregnancy were terminated'. This reason would be given if, for instance, a woman was short of money and living space, and already had demanding young children to care for.

4. If there was a risk that the child would be born with a serious handicap. This reason might be used if an ante-natal test (such as an ultrasound scan or amniocentesis) had indicated the foetus had a serious abnormality, such as spina bifida, and the woman decided because of this that she no longer wanted to continue her pregnancy.

Finding out if you are pregnant

Pregnancy testing: home kits

Home use kits are available over the counter for as little as £6.99 from major chemists like Boots. Many of them can be used to detect pregnancy as little as a day after a missed period should have started. They work by checking for a hormone called Human Chorionic Gonadatrophin (HCG) in your urine. HCG is the hormone your body starts producing as soon as you become pregnant.

But be careful how you use them. Although the manufacturers say the tests are 99 to 100 per cent accurate, a study carried out in America by the National Medical Center and the George Washington University made an important observation. Using two different home test kits on 200 women's urine samples, they showed that if the tests were done by trained lab technicians they were indeed 99 per cent accurate. But tests done by 'untrained personnel' (i.e. ordinary people) were wrong in up to 12.5 per cent of cases. So follow the instructions very carefully, and do another test three or four days later. (Most kits come with a back-up for this.) It may also be an idea to wait a few days after a missed period was due to start, rather than to do the test the day after.

Pregnancy testing: your GP or clinic

Your GP could do a pregnancy test for you for free on the NHS (although it would take a few days to get the results back). So might your family planning clinic, who can often give you the results at the end of the day if you take your urine sample first thing in the morning. Some chemists also offer pregnancy testing services (ask at the pharmacy counter).

What to do if you are pregnant

If you have confirmed that you are pregnant, have been able to think about it carefully, and decide that you do not want to continue the pregnancy, go and see your GP immediately. Explain that you wish to be referred to a consultant gynaecologist for a termination. If, for whatever reason, your own GP seems reluctant to refer you or appears to be taking too long to do so, remember that he or she is *legally obliged* to refer you to another doctor who *will* give your request the proper consideration.

You can also refer *yourself* – no GP note needed – to a private clinic or charity, such as Marie Stopes, the British Pregnancy Advisory Service (BPAS) (see HELPLINES), or to a private gynaecologist.

If you run into problems and no one seems to be doing anything to help you, contact one of the organizations listed in HELPLINES for advice immediately. Do not let the matter drag on once you have come to your decision. The later an abortion is carried out, the more health risks it may carry, the more distressing it can be for you, and the harder it is to get one.

If you decide you *do* want to continue your pregnancy, but there is a problem – perhaps you are single or have little money and are worried about being able to afford to have a child – it might help to speak to your social worker (your GP can put you in touch) or one of the help organizations listed in HELPLINES under **Continuing the Pregnancy**.

How to get an abortion: the legal options
Your GP

He or she may be the first person you consult and should be able to arrange for a free NHS abortion if the circumstances are appropriate (see **Whose Authority Do You Need?** page 13). If, for any reason, he proves unhelpful or tries to persuade you to change your mind when you have already made a considered decision, firmly point out that a GP is legally obliged to refer you to another one who *will* make arrangements to help you. Establish whether or not you are going to get help from your GP *right in the beginning*. This is much better than waiting for weeks, only to find out that no help is forthcoming.

Your family planning clinic (FPC) is also able to arrange a free NHS abortion, if the circumstances are appropriate. They will inform your GP themselves, unless you ask them not to. Referral to an NHS hospital often depends on the area in which you live. If facilities are not available at your local hospital ask about being referred to another district.

Your local family planning clinic

If you regularly attend a family planning clinic, this is a family planning problem, so make an immediate appointment with them. Even if you do not already belong to a FPC you can seek help from one. (Look them up under 'F' in the Yellow Pages, or ring the Family Planning Association's HQ in London

14

– see HELPLINES – for your nearest one.) FPCs are run by the NHS so their services, and the terminations they arrange, may be free, although they will also sometimes recommend a private or charitable clinic (see below).

It may be, though, that if you are a new patient and not already on their lists they may not be able to help you. Their resources are getting stretched as there have been so many cut-backs. (A quarter of all UK Health Authorities have either cut back FPC resources (or are considering doing so) by up to 50 per cent over the past four years due to lack of government funding.) However, if you explain to the clinic Advice Sister that you need urgent counselling about a termination she will always be able to refer you for help.

Free charitable organizations
Organizations such as the Brook Advisory Centres can offer counselling, advice and referrals for NHS and private sector abortions, but they are only for young people under 25 (see HELPLINES).

Charitable clinic groups
Clinics such as Marie Stopes, the British Pregnancy Advisory Service and the Pregnancy Advisory Service (see HELPLINES) do charge low fees. Counselling, arranging a termination at a licensed nursing home and a check-up afterwards costs between £200 and £400. But they can often arrange a staggered payment of fees for women who do not have enough money to pay all at once and are always willing to discuss financial problems on a one-to-one, confidential basis.

A private gynaecologist
Generally, gynaecologists' charges for arranging a nursing home termination are controlled by the Department of Health and remain at around £300 to £400. Fees for the operation, an overnight stay at a clinic or hospital, meals and drugs, should be 'all in'. But it is a good idea to double check – just to make sure your bill does not end up bigger than you had been led to believe.

Technically speaking, you would need to be referred to a gynaecologist by your GP, just as you would for any other specialist. In practice, however, you can often ring up and make an appointment yourself as a new patient, then discuss your situation when you get there. You might well have to wait between a week and six weeks, as good gynaecologists can have long waiting lists, so ask to be kept informed of any appointment cancellations. If time is very much of the essence, ring around a bit to establish who can see you soonest.

FINDING A GYNAECOLOGIST the best way is by word of mouth recommendation or through your GP. If no one you know can suggest anyone and you don't feel you can ask your GP because it is due to his uncooperative attitude that you are having to look for a private gynaecologist in the first place, try:
1. Contacting your local private hospital (under 'H' in the Yellow Pages, where they often have display advertisements). Explain that you are looking for a private gynaecologist and ask if they can recommend anyone who has a clinic or works at their hospital. Having got a name ask to speak to that doctor's secretary and request an appointment (they will often see patients both at the hospital and in their own private practice).

2. Contacting the charitable help organizations (see HELPLINES) or a general medical help charity like the Medical Advisory Service (081 994 6477) (see INTRODUCTION). Ask them how to find a good private gynaecologist and they should be able to point you in the right direction.

Approaching a private clinic or a nursing home direct
Abortions are actually carried out at these private clinics and nursing homes if they are not done in NHS hospitals (the NHS uses beds at homes and clinics belonging to the Pregnancy Advisory Service, BPAS and Marie Stopes). Sometimes a free NHS referral for a termination will be done at one of these clinics which are licensed to carry out terminations and have specialist staff working there. See HELPLINES for telephone numbers and addresses or look under 'C' for clinics in the Yellow Pages. It may be worth phoning several and shopping around a little to get the feel of the clinic first before making a definite appointment.

Note: at any clinic, NHS or private, you can arrange to be seen by a woman doctor, and you can refer yourself direct.

Waiting lists and how to avoid them
If you have made up your mind that you wish to end a pregnancy, naturally you'll want to arrange for this as soon as possible. Unfortunately there can be delays – either because your GP is anxious not to refer you for an abortion or because you live in an area where there are long queues for terminations. This might be because of underfunding, because terminations are given low priority or because hospital doctors are reluctant to perform them.

The first wait is after you have obtained your referral to a hospital consultant gynaecologist from your GP. A week or two is common, but it may be three or even four weeks before you can get to see that gynaecologist. He will be the second doctor to sign your Green Form (your GP is the first). Your own signature goes on the notes when you are admitted to the hospital or clinic for your termination.

To try and cut down distressing delay:
1. Ask your GP how long you must wait to see the consultant. If it is more than two weeks, ask whether your GP could perhaps phone any other consultants to see if their waiting lists are shorter.
2. Ask the consultant when you get to see him how long the waiting list is for a termination at the hospital. (Some hospitals contract out terminations to private charitable nursing homes and pay the costs themselves, to avoid undesirable delays.) To save even more time, try ringing his/her secretary for this information.

If the queue is too long for you, go back to your GP and ask for a private referral if you can afford it, or refer yourself. If you cannot afford it, contact one of the charitable associations (see HELPLINES) which offer loan or staggered payment schemes.
3. If your GP does not take steps on your behalf when you first go and explain you want an abortion (e.g. ringing a hospital, referring you to a gynaecologist, and signing your Green Form), ask why. If it transpires that he/she is unwilling

to help, go to another GP in the same practice (if there is one), or change your GP (you are within your rights to do so, without having to explain why), or ask if he/she can refer you to another GP – immediately – who will be able to give your request the proper attention.

Should your GP try to delay or dissuade you once you have made your decision, you should also report him to your Family Practitioner Committee (the receptionist will have the address) and the local Community Health Council (the receptionist is also likely to have this address too; if not, call up Directory Enquiries). If he has behaved this way towards you, it is likely that he will do so with other women seeking abortions, unless he is reprimanded by the relevant authorities.

How it is done: methods of abortion
Early termination
These methods all involve slightly different ways of removing the contents of your womb and are usually used up to four and a half months. Different hospitals and clinics use slightly different methods, and have varying time limits for the different techniques.

Vacuum Aspiration (Suction Abortion) is suitable for use in the first three months of pregnancy (the first trimester) and can be carried out under local anaesthetic. Providing that certain criteria are met, it is possible to have this as an outpatient. The cervix (neck of womb) is opened using special rods following which a small flexible tube is passed via the vagina into the uterus. This is connected to a syringe or suction pump which gently sucks out the lining of the uterus including early foetal material. A small metal instrument, a curette, may be used to scrape the inside of the uterus to ensure that it is empty once the aspiration has been completed. This method keeps the potentially damaging opening of the cervix to a minimum, thus reducing the risk of an incompetent cervix (see **Incompetent cervix**, page 19).

D&E (Dilatation – of the cervix – and Evacuation – of the womb) is normally used from the thirteenth week of pregnancy and can be used up to the twentieth. This involves gentle stretching of the neck of the womb using special rods and a combination of the suction technique described above and the use of surgical instruments to remove the products of conception. A curette is also used at the end of a D&E. This procedure is normally carried out under general anaesthetic and requires an overnight stay in the hospital or clinic.

D&C which stands for Dilatation – of the cervix – and Curettage – the method used to remove the womb's lining with an instrument called a curette, is a similar procedure. A curette is a slim surgical scraper. This technique is also used to treat or diagnose gynaecological problems (like heavy menstrual bleeding) and to investigate fertility problems (see also MENOPAUSE, HYSTERECTOMY and PERIOD PROBLEMS). A D&C might be used to end an unwanted pregnancy up to about 18 weeks.

Late termination
For a number of doctors, an abortion carried out after 12 weeks pregnancy is 'late'. For others it is anything over 16 weeks – and for some, 20 weeks or more.

But some women have menstrual cycles so irregular that they cannot be sure of their pregnancy until later than this. Others get no signs of pregnancy for many weeks, even months. Occasionally a woman continues to have apparent 'periods' while actually in the first few months of pregnancy (see PREGNANCY PROBLEMS, **Bleeding in Pregnancy**, page 362). Others get stuck in waiting lists or delayed by unhelpful GPs. These are all reasons why some women, through no fault of their own, may be 20 or more weeks pregnant before they have their termination.

INDUCING AN EARLY LABOUR is the usual method of termination for abortions after about 20 or 22 weeks. This can be very upsetting, both for the woman and the staff involved. Labour has to be induced because after 16 weeks or so the walls of the womb are thinner and can puncture more easily if a curette instrument is used. An artificially induced labour would probably mean staying in hospital for two or three days.

An induced labour to end a pregnancy has all the emotional and physical stresses of an ordinary labour. It is brought about by injecting either hormones called prostaglandins (which make the womb contract), or a saline solution, into the sac of amniotic fluid surrounding the foetus. This is done via your abdominal wall, or passed in via your vagina. You would then need to wait for labour to begin (anything from a couple of hours to a day). The contractions might be quite painful, so ask for painkilling drugs. Sedation is usually given.

It is a good idea to get a close friend or relative to collect you from the hospital or clinic afterwards, and to take a few days off work.

A 'TWO-STAGE' D&E, done under general anaesthetic, is used in some clinics, such as Marie Stopes, for women who are over 20 weeks pregnant, unless the foetus has developed too far for this. The first stage involves inserting a dilating substance (based on seaweed) into the cervix. This swells when it comes into contact with your normal body fluids, very gently opening the cervix over the next 24 hours. This reduces the risk to the delicate tissue here; dilating the cervix mechanically could cause some damage.

On the second day, after another general anaesthetic, the contents of the womb are removed by D&E through the newly opened cervix.

HYSTEROTOMY is another method. This is rather similar to a Caesarian section but is only rarely used – when the woman cannot have labour contractions induced for a late (16 to 28 weeks) termination. The reasons for this might be an allergy to prostaglandins or saline solution (unlikely), extensive scarring of the womb wall from a previous caesarean which might not be strong enough to withstand the contractions of induced labour, glaucoma (which causes raised pressure in the eyeball) or asthma, which could be controlled with steroids.

The medical risks
Careful, professional, legal abortion is a very safe procedure. But illegal abortion does carry greater risks, not least because it is unlikely to be carried out by professional medical staff in the best possible clinical conditions. If you

do have an illegal termination and feel unwell afterwards (see the warning signs for the risks listed below) you might be unhappy about seeking help from your GP. However, potential complications can be dangerous. Infection, for instance, can, if not treated, eventually lead to scarring of the Fallopian tubes and even infertility. If you do feel you need some help and cannot approach your own doctor, call up one of the help organizations. Their trained counsellors will be only too happy to advise you, and suggest where you can get sympathetic treatment.

Risks from legal abortion, though very small – and lower than those from illegal abortion – include:

INFECTION: there is about a one per cent risk of this. The infection (which is a risk in *any* operation, not just an abortion) may begin in the womb or vagina. If not diagnosed and treated promptly, it might progress up the Fallopian tubes causing salpingitis (see **salpingitis** and PELVIC INFLAMMATORY DISEASE). This can result in scarring of the thread-thin tubes as they heal. Subsequent blockage can cause infertility, as the egg could no longer travel down the Fallopian tube to the womb to be fertilized. (See INFERTILITY, page 250.)

Warning signs include:
* pain in your lower back;
* continuous period style cramping pains;
* abdominal pain and tenderness;
* swelling in the lower abdomen;
* bad smelling vaginal discharge;
* a high temperature (fever);
* discomfort or pain when you have intercourse;
* continual tiredness;
* blood spotting.

If you develop any of these, go straight to your doctor or back to the clinic where you had the operation. Pelvic infections, caught early, can be very effectively treated with complete rest and antibiotics. But a long term infection (even if it's a 'low level' one that grumbles quietly along with a little abdominal discomfort and backache) can be hard to detect and to get rid of.

RETAINED PRODUCTS OF CONCEPTION means that small pieces of placenta or foetal material have been left behind in your womb, and may cause infection. This happens in less than 0.5 per cent of all abortions but would need a D&E or D&C procedure.

Warning signs include:
* passing large blood clots in subsequent periods;
* abdominal pain or cramps;
* additional lower backache when you have your periods (especially if you never used to get any).

These symptoms usually show up within 2 to 3 weeks of the abortion.

INCOMPETENT CERVIX means that the os (the small canal that leads up into the womb from the middle of the cervix) has been damaged by the dilation part of the termination. As a result, it is no longer able to stay closed under pressure. If you become pregnant again the growing weight of the foetus presses down on it and forces it open, resulting in a miscarriage during the second three months.

If this condition is recognized, by manual internal examination, it can be treated with a surgical stitch or band across the cervix to keep it closed, inserted soon after you conceive. There is, however, a controversy amongst doctors as to how helpful this really is. A large national medical trial is going on at the moment to find out for sure (see INFERTILITY, page 250; MISCARRIAGE, page 297; and HELPLINES).

The later the termination and the more often terminations are carried out, the more risk there is of developing an incompetent cervix.

However most gynaecologists agree that one or two early terminations will make little difference. But they begin to be a bit more concerned if a woman has had more than three early abortions, or a couple of much later ones.

POSSIBLE PERFORATION (PIERCING) OF THE WOMB WALL is extremely unusual, but may cause heavy bleeding. It might be caused by the curette scraping too hard against the wall of the womb, or accidentally piercing a hole in it.

HAEMORRHAGE is even rarer and is treated as an extreme emergency. It can happen very occasionally if, for instance, some amniotic fluid gets into the bloodstream and makes it more difficult for it to clot.

STENOSIS OF THE OS (hardening of the inside of the os) is another potential complication. It may result in more painful periods because your normal menstrual blood flow cannot pass through it so easily, and this can cause painful cramps as the womb contracts harder to expel its lining. This can happen in about one per cent of cases. If you do find that your periods are more painful after a termination it might be worth asking your GP if your cervix could be very slightly – and gently – dilated, to soften the os once again.

CONTINUING PREGNANCY might occur if the termination is carried out in the first 7 weeks of pregnancy (though in less than one per cent of cases). It happens when not all the womb's contents are removed, and the minute embryo is left still attached to the womb's wall – where it will continue to grow. Symptoms would be the same as for any other pregnancy and would not wear off: continuing morning sickness; tender or swollen breasts; etc.

After an early termination it is therefore a good idea to do a pregnancy test four to six weeks later, just to put your mind at rest if you are worried. If your pregnancy has indeed continued, contact the clinic or doctor who arranged your initial operation for you immediately to sort out a repeat if you still wish to end your pregnancy.

Aftercare – recovering quickly
Recovery times
Even for early abortions it is best to take two or three days off afterwards if you can (more if you feel you need it). Everyone's rate of recovery from operations,

even minor ones, is different. Theoretically you could go back to work after only 24 hours. The later your termination is, the more time you will need to rest.

Emotional recovery may take a lot longer. If you find you need someone sympathetic to talk to and cannot discuss your abortion with your friends or partner, there are many good counselling organizations who would be happy to try and help you (mostly on the telephone). See HELPLINES, **Post-abortion counselling**.

Your periods
They should return in six to eight weeks, and should not be any heavier or more painful than before. If they are heavier, if you are passing clots, or if you have cramps or abdominal pain which you never had before, go back to your doctor or clinic. Get a thorough check-up to ensure there are no problems, or to get them corrected if there are (see Medical Risks above). It is best to use soft sanitary towels or pads instead of tampons for your first period, to ensure there is no risk of a tampon introducing any infections into the still-healing Os or womb.

For very early termination – up to nine weeks – you might find there is no bleeding at all after the operation, yet you seem to have a light period three or four days later. This is because bleeding inside the womb after a vacuum aspiration is very slow, and the blood tends to collect there until the womb contracts to expel it. Passing large clots several times, a couple of days apart or more frequently, means there is slow but steady internal bleeding which is not tailing off as it ought to. If this happens, get a check-up.

For later terminations of 13 weeks or more, you may find your breasts remain a bit swollen and tender for a few days. It helps to wear a firm, well-fitting bra and take aspirin. You may also find that your nipples start leaking a little clear fluid (pre milk or colostrum). This is quite normal. As long as you do not squeeze your nipples, which stimulates them to make even more, this will stop within a few days. It may help to wear small, soft pads of tissue in your bra for a while, to soak up this liquid.

Starting your sex life again
It is advisable to avoid intercourse (and even manual stimulation *inside* your vagina) for about three weeks, so as to avoid the risk of infection. Gentle manual or oral stimulation on your clitoris would not carry an infection risk.

Likelihood of vaginal infections
You may be more prone to vaginal infections like thrush for a while (see Thrush). This is because the presence of even a small amount of blood there gives bacteria, fungi and viruses a perfect environment.

Your contraception
THE PILL: start taking it again the day after your operation.

IUD: you can have one put in, if you wish, at the same time as the termination if

21

you are up to 12 weeks pregnant, or six weeks later if you are more than 12 weeks.

DIAPHRAGM: you may be sore and have a bit of muscle tension around your cervix for two or three months after an abortion. So you might want to leave using a diaphragm for a while and use an alternative method (like a condom). It is also a very good idea, when you do begin to use your diaphragm again, to be re-checked by your GP or family planning clinic as the size you now need might be slightly larger.

The future

THE ABORTION PILL (known as RU 486, Mifepristone) is now available in Britain at about 100 of the 300 clinics licensed to carry out abortions. Because the NHS is still being rather disorganized about offering medical termination (RU486) as an alternative to surgical abortion (i.e. using an operation) some GPs are unaware nearby hospitals do actually have it so if you are interested insist they ask around properly for you.

If you are being stonewalled, contact the drug's makers Roussel (see HELPLINES) to check availability in your area.

The abortion pill works by bringing about a heavy period to end an early pregnancy. It cannot be used if you are more than 9 weeks pregnant. You would have to go to a clinic as an out-patient (no hospital stays) for three appointments.

1. To take a dose of 'anti progesterone' tablets, which stop progesterone from doing its job of maintaining your womb lining in place. Both the lining, and the tiny developing foetus, would be shed (as if you were having a late, heavy period). You would be kept under observation for about four hours, then allowed to go home if there were no complications.

2. The next day you would have another appointment at the clinic to receive a dose of prostaglandins (hormones which make your womb contract) to ensure the womb expels all its contents.

3. Your final appointment, the day after, would be a check-up to ensure your womb lining had been completely shed. In trials, RU 486 has been 95 per cent totally successful. But in five per cent of cases there was additional bleeding, or a D&C operation was necessary because some products of conception had been left behind.

Plus points are that you would not need an operation or anaesthetic; that it is a simple, non invasive way to end a pregnancy; and that you would not have to wait for a bed at a clinic or nursing home, so you could probably have an abortion without some of the usual delays. Minus points are that it must be done before you are 9 weeks pregnant, and there is a small chance that it might not work properly, so you would need a D&C or D&E.

Complementary therapy

Complementary therapies tailor their treatments very much to the individual: the precise nature of the treatment you receive will vary, depending on your medical history, symptoms, lifestyle, etc. The following information indicates the *sorts* of things a therapist is most likely to do or recommend. Do not be surprised if they feel you need something slightly different. This section is meant purely as an indication of likely treatments; it is not meant as a DIY guide to the medical uses of the different complementary therapies.

Certain therapies can help women suffering unpleasant symptoms – depression, infection, pain and lack of libido – after a termination of pregnancy.

Acupuncture
Specific acupuncture points are selected to counteract the individual symptoms. Likely symptoms to work against: depression and infection. Using other points encourages natural production of the body's own pain killing and/or libido-increasing chemicals.

Aromatherapy
Aromatherapy is especially good for treating some or all of the problems following an abortion. Essential oil of rose is one of the most useful 'female' oils, but it is expensive, so the aromatherapist is likely to use another single oil, or blend of oils, chosen with the individual patient's problems in mind.

Oil of bergamot relaxes and uplifts. Essential oil of lavender is relaxing and antiseptic. Essential oil of ylang ylang is aphrodisiac. Essential oil of clary sage enhances oestrogen output. The oil (or oils) may be used in a full-body massage, in the bath or in a room humidifier – or even in all of these ways.

It's worth mentioning here that certain oils used in aromatherapy may cause a miscarriage. They should not be used if there is a possibility that you might be pregnant.

Clinical nutrition
Adrenal tissue concentrate, Vitamin B complex and pantothenic acid all help the body deal with stress, which is usually a strong factor in depression. The amino acid, tyrosine, can also help to relieve depression. Chlorophyll and histidine help with lack of libido. Fenugreek tea helps to detoxify the body by stimulating the lymphatic system, thus reducing infection.

Homoeopathy
Homoeopathy offers Ignati, Calc-carb, and Pulsatilla (among other things) for depression following abortion. China helps weakness due to loss of blood.

Homoeopathy is very much based on a full understanding of your mental and emotional make-up, which is assessed along with any physical symptoms before remedies are suggested. Thus, depression could be treated with many different remedies. For instance: Natrum Mur would be used if you don't like being at the seaside, you like being alone, you are normally a rather timid and nervous person, and you feel tired; Belladonna would be used if you feel agitated, have colicky pains in your lower abdomen, have lost your appetite and suffer from exhaustion; sepia (a good general remedy for many female complaints) might be used if you feel severe pain and want to be alone – as well as suffer from depression.

Medical herbalism
The choice of remedies depends very much on individual circumstances – but medical herbalism has much to offer. Treatment is aimed at restoring normal body functions, and helping the patient with mental and emotional distress.

Abortion helplines

British Pregnancy Advisory Service (BPAS)
HQ – Austy Manor, Wooton Wawen, Solihull, West Midlands B95 6BX
  (056 42 3225)
Non-profit-making charity with branches countrywide – ring HQ for your nearest
  centre. Provides counselling and can arrange a medical or surgical abortion.

Brook Advisory Centres
HQ – 153A East Street, London SE17 (071 708 1234)
Centres countrywide – ring HQ for your nearest one. Brook is for women under
  25. Services, except a small fee for a pregnancy test, are free. Staff can counsel
  and advise you, and refer you for either a free NHS abortion or a private one.

The Irish Womens Support Group (071 251 6580) in London, and ESCORT in
  Liverpool (the latter affiliated to the National Students Union) are both
  befriending services offered to Irish women who have to come over to England
  for their terminations. They can help organize your visit to the clinic in question,
  meet you off your boat or plane, even put you up for the night in their own
  homes, and will stay with you if you wish during your clinic visit.

The Family Planning Association
HQ – 27–35 Mortimer Street, London W1 (071 636 7866)
Can advise on the location of your nearest family planning clinic.

Marie Stopes Clinics
 HQ – Marie Stopes House, 108 Whitfield Street, London W1 (071 388 0662/2585)
Marie Stopes Centre, 10 Queens Square, Leeds (0532 440685)
Marie Stopes Centre, 1 Police Street, Manchester (061 832 4260)
A registered charity, it counsels on abortion and can arrange pregnancy termination.

Pregnancy Advisory Service
11–13 Charlotte Street, London W1 (071 637 8962)
A registered charity which counsels on abortion and can arrange surgical or medical
  termination.

Ulster Pregnancy Advisory Association
719A Lisburn Road, Belfast 9 (Belfast 381345)
Pregnancy counselling and, where necessary, further assessment in England
  (terminations are not legal in Ireland).

Late termination – who can help?
The following organizations have some access to nursing homes which have licences to
  perform abortions up to the 24th week of pregnancy, if necessary:

Brook Advisory Centres, British Pregnancy Advisory Service, Pregnancy Advisory Service, Marie Stopes Clinics (see above for addresses).

Continuing your pregnancy

If you have problems – either financial or personal – the organizations previously mentioned can put you in touch with advisory bodies who can help you. The following can also help:

Citizen's Advice Bureau
Look in the telephone directory under 'C' to locate your nearest branch. Can advise on local mother and baby groups, housing benefits and facilities in your area.

Gingerbread
HQ – 35 Wellington Street, London WC2 (071 240 0953)
Nationwide self-help groups for one-parent families; contact HQ for the branch nearest you.

Let Live Association (Not affiliated to LIFE)
(071 828 3824) Lines are open from 10 a.m. to 10 p.m. on weekdays and weekends.
LLA has a network in the Greater London and Essex areas. Staffed by a mix of volunteers, social workers and nurses, it can offer counselling, accommodation and other practical support to women who wish to continue their pregnancy – plus advice on adoption, should it be required.

Lifeline (Not affiliated to LIFE)
1st Floor, Ruskin Building, 190 Corporation Street, Birmingham (021 233 1641)
Branches countrywide, contact HQ for branch nearest you. Advice for single parents on local mother and baby homes; practical help with baby clothes and equipment; advice on adoption, if required; help with accommodation.

LIFE
HQ – 188–120 Warwick Street, Leamington Spa, Warwickshire (0926 311667)
Can arrange for accommodation during pregnancy; helps liaise with social services to obtain a place to live after baby is born; helps with adoption; gives counselling.

National Council for One-Parent Families
255 Kentish Town Road, London NW5 (071 267 1361)
Advice on housing, social security benefits and other practical matters for single, pregnant women.

Post-abortion counselling

If you need someone to talk to afterwards, the following groups can help:

Pregnancy Advisory Service, British Pregnancy Advisory Service, some of the Brook Centres and Marie Stopes Clinics. (A small charge may be levied if you had your termination elsewhere.) The following organizations can also help:

LIFE
(Address and telephone number above)
Offers face-to-face or telephone counselling, free from most branches.

The Post-Abortion Counselling Service
340 Westbourne Park Road, London W11 (071 221 9631)
Fees are low, on a sliding scale, for up to 10 sessions.

SATFA (Support After Termination for Foetal Abnormality)
29–30 Soho Square, London W1 (071 439 6124)
Support and advice for those who are facing, or who have had, a termination because
an ante-natal test detected an abnormal foetus.

NOTE: MORNING AFTER or 'Emergency' contraception may also be an option
if you feel you have just taken a risk with unprotected intercourse – or if there
was a problem with the contraception you used such as a sheath splitting or
being dragged off the man's penis during intercourse. You could go to hospital
casualty or to your own GP for either a) the IUD to be inserted (this is thought
to prevent pregnancy by stopping any fertilized egg implanting in the womb
lining) and can be used up to 5 days after the risk was taken, or b) the Morning
After Pill, which can be used up to 72 hours later.

Further reading
Coping with Abortion by Alison Frater and Catherine Wright (Chambers)
Mixed Feelings by Angela Neustatter and Gina Newson (Pluto Press)
Experiences of Abortion by Denise Winn (Optima)

AIDS

Women *are* at risk from AIDS. It is a dangerous myth that AIDS is something that happens mostly to gay men. In Africa, where it probably first developed, it is almost exclusively a heterosexual disease.

Women do in fact catch the HIV virus which leads to AIDS, more easily than men, say experts like Dr Ali Kubba, consultant gynaecologist at St Thomas Hospital, London – partly because their vaginal lining offers a larger surface area of mucous membranes for absorption of the virus than those on the head of a man's penis. But research from many sources shows that most heterosexuals (men and women) are not doing much to protect themselves – and, there are other ways to catch AIDS apart from sex.

What is it?
AIDS means Acquired Immune Deficiency Syndrome. The virus that causes it damages the body's immune system so badly that all kinds of normally harmless infections are able to run riot. Two, in particular, are seen as signs that AIDS is present – an unusual type of pneumonia called pneumocystis carinii (PCP) and a virus-related skin cancer called Kaposi's sarcoma.

The virus blamed for AIDS is called HIV (Human Immuno-deficiency Virus). Some researchers (notably Peter Duesberg, virologist at the University of California) suggest that it isn't solely, or even mainly, to blame – but this is controversial. There is, however, much attention focussing on this new theory. If HIV is not the cause of AIDS, then there is still much research to be undertaken. Mainstream theories are, however, based on the belief that AIDS is the result of the HIV virus.

If you are infected with HIV, the medical term is 'HIV-positive' (HIV+). It is not the same thing as having full-blown AIDS. You are probably infectious, but your health may be fine for many years to come. There is no evidence yet that everyone who is HIV+ goes on to develop AIDS. So far, about 30 per cent of HIV+ people have done so.

Latest official figures for the UK (at the time of writing) are: a total of 6,463 have so far been diagnosed with AIDS. Of these, 466 were women.

For every person with AIDS, there are probably 25 to 100 who are HIV+ (i.e., not yet ill – but probably infectious). Estimates vary – see **Symptoms** below. In December 1992 the official estimated number of people in total in the UK with the HIV infection was 16,640. Some 2,370 of these were women – rising rapidly from 1,807 women with HIV in 1991, and showing just how real the threat of HIV is for us right now.

Who is at risk?
HIV is found in body fluids and secretions: blood (including menstrual blood), semen, vaginal secretions, urine, faeces and breast milk. It is also found in sweat and saliva (in very small, fragmented quantities, so these two fluids are not seen as infection risks). To infect someone new, the HIV virus has to get

27

into their bloodstream directly, because it soon dies if it is not in someone's body. The most likely ways for it to gain access are:

* infected semen entering an unprotected vagina or rectum;
* infected body fluids entering your bloodstream via a cut, graze or tiny abrasion on your skin. It can also enter by an injection with an infected needle; *or* by receiving an infected blood product – say a blood transfusion for an accident victim or blood clotting agents for a haemophiliac;
* a mixture of any of these – say a man is infected by an injection, and then has sex with you;
* It is a myth that you can contract the HIV virus from a toilet seat – unless you sit on a patch of *very recently* spilt, infected fluid or faecal matter, and the virus it carries enters your body via a cut or graze.

Doctors have until now been reluctant to make a guess at how likely you are to contract the HIV virus if you come into contact with infected fluids (either through lovemaking or looking after/treating someone with the virus). However, a report in America's medical journal, *The New England Journal of Medicine*, in 1989, suggested that the risk is slightly below one per cent each time.

All women are now at risk, but it is greater for those who:
* have a partner who is a haemophiliac;
* have sex in a Third World country;
* have a blood transfusion in a Third World country (see HELPLINES);
* have a partner who is bisexual;
* have a lot of sexual partners;
* have a job which brings them into contact with other people's body fluids: doctors, nurses, dentists, ambulance staff, beauticians who pierce clients' ears, paramedics, prostitutes and, to some extent, policemen;
* have a social life which brings them into contact with possible sources of infection, e.g. injecting drugs using shared equipment;
* have a sexual partner who has any of the above risk factors – or who did so at any time over the last 10 to 15 years.

How soon does HIV+ turn into AIDS?

AIDS can lie dormant for many years, leaving its carrier HIV+, but symptomless – and possibly unaware that they are infected. Contact with the person who infected you need not therefore have been recent.

Initial estimates of how long it took HIV+ people to develop AIDS were five to 10 years. Now work with 112 HIV+ haemophiliacs at London's Royal Free Hospital and School of Medicine suggests that three-quarters of them are likely to develop AIDS within 15 years.

So if you know you are infected you should consult the existing support and advisory organizations (see HELPLINES, page 38) and get medical advice for how to take the very best care not to infect others, while living as full and normal a life as possible. If you take the best possible care of your own health (see HELPLINES, page 38) you may well have many comparatively healthy years ahead.

Symptoms

In general terms it is more sensible to talk about HIV infection than AIDS. AIDS is only the final, fatal stage of three possible stages. The symptoms for the various stages are as follows:

1. HIV+: you will have no outward symptoms at all, but
* you can infect other people;
* within about 12 to 16 weeks (it can be sooner or even longer), your body produces antibodies against the HIV virus (see **The HIV test**, below). (There are two schools of thought about the HIV+ antibodies: some experts think that the number of people who have the virus is up to 10 per cent greater than estimated because they never produce antibodies at all; some think 95 per cent of HIV+ people produce antibodies within six months and that HIV infection without detectable antibodies is uncommon – less than 1 per cent);
* the antibodies don't fight the virus, but they can be detected;
* this stage may last for several years with no illness at all;
* The Terrence Higgins Trust estimates that 'most' people infected with HIV will eventually go on to develop AIDS but nobody knows the long-term picture, because AIDS is such a new disease;
* even if you don't develop AIDS, however, somebody you infect might;
* the health of HIV+ people depends partly on the state of their immune system before HIV was contracted and partly on how well the body is cared for in terms of nutrition, exercise, low-stress living, immune-system boosting and the many other health-enhancing tactics in existence (see HELPLINES) once you have got it.
* HIV virus makes women more vulnerable to severe, continual thrush; and cervical cancer.

2. ARC – AIDS Related Complex: a stage recognized by some (not all) authorities:
* heavy sweating at night;
* diarrhoea;
* fever;
* weight loss;
* extreme tiredness.

3. AIDS itself can have many symptoms, depending upon which 'opportunistic infections' are taking advantage of your lowered immunity. The most common are:
* symptoms listed under ARC above;
* fever, a dry cough, breathing problems (from PCP to other lung troubles);
* a white rash and swelling in the mouth, genitals and elsewhere (from thrush – see VAGINAL THRUSH);
* purple marks on the skin (Kaposi's sarcoma);
* headaches, fits and confusion (various diseases affect the brain);
* yellow skin and swollen and painful joints (from hepatitis B);
* eye infections (various);
* painful blisters from herpes (see SEXUALITY TRANSMITTED DISEASES).

The HIV test

If you are worried about HIV, you may want to take a test to see if you have

HIV antibodies. There are a number of places you can go to be tested. (See also HELPLINES.)

* GPs are supposed to arrange testing for anyone who wants it, but they have been given no special funds or training, and might not be the ideal person to approach. Consult your GP if you trust him.
* If you are pregnant, many ante-natal clinics offer you the option of testing.
* You can be tested at any STD clinic for free and you do not need a GP's referral note. See SEXUALLY TRANSMITTED DISEASES for more information on these clinics. (The Terrence Higgins Trust (see HELPLINES) thinks STD clinics are the best place to go.)
* You might also like to try a private clinic (look in your local press for advertisements). Costs and standards vary, however, and follow-up counselling (very important) may be sketchy.
* *Don't* give blood if you are doing so just to get an HIV test. The blood donor service isn't really geared up to counsel you properly.

The future: The PREM machine test. This is a new device which can detect immediately whether someone has been infected with HIV, and it can detect traces of the virus in the bloodstream, instead of the usual tests which can only be done after several weeks. Traditional tests look for antibodies which your body has produced against the disease. This machine is currently being tested at a limited number of AIDS clinics.

THE ADVANTAGES OF THE TEST ARE THAT:
* if you get the all-clear, it is reassuring;
* if you don't get the all-clear, at least you know you are a risk to other people, and can take responsibility for protecting them;
* if you don't get the all-clear, you can also start looking after yourself as well as possible to try and stay symptom-free for as long as you can. You are now prone to opportunistic infections, possibly to AIDS, and you can adopt the ideas in the **Self help** section, below;
* if you don't get the all-clear, and you are pregnant, you can decide whether to continue the pregnancy.

THE DISADVANTAGES OF THE TEST ARE THAT:
* knowing you are HIV+ can be traumatic – testing centres have a counselling service (both for before and after the test) to help you cope;
* you will have to decide whether to tell other people – this can cause havoc in personal relationships;
* you may be asked whether you have had the test by employers and insurance companies – and discriminated against if you say yes, or if you say no and they find out later that you have. For women, the risk of being asked is, in fact, almost unknown. STD clinics do have a confidentiality rule to protect you, but you should ask what their policy is before you take the test;
* if you are HIV+, whoever tests you will want to tell your GP so that you get the right care and he or she can take precautions to avoid being infected – and not every GP has a perfect record of confidentiality: again, try and check;

* remember, it can take 3 to 6 months (sometimes more) to produce antibodies, so you can't trust an all-clear unless you are tested *at least* sixteen weeks after you last took a risk; and some people take longer to produce antibodies – a few still have not produced any since research began in the early 1980s.

If you are HIV+

If you are HIV+ you may want a lot of support. All good testing agencies must provide full counselling both before and after the test and you can expect sympathetic treatment. You may be referred to the 'contact tracer' at the STD clinic if this is relevant (see SEXUALLY TRANSMITTED DISEASES, page 438) – here, you can expect enormous sympathy and discretion. You should also contact at least one of the many self help organizations (see HELPLINES, page 38) which are often run by people who are in exactly the same situation as you.

But there are also some special medical facts about women and HIV.

* HIV makes certain cancers more likely to develop, so normal, regular screening tests, such as cervical smear tests, are more important than ever.

* You may well want an extra effective contraceptive to prevent pregnancy, or you might possibly consider sterilization (see CONTRACEPTION, page 155). Also, IUDs, although effective, might not be suitable because they make you more vulnerable to pelvic infections – the last thing you want, as your immunity is already weakened. Whatever method you use, you will also need to practise safe sex, including the sheath (see below), to avoid infecting your partner.

* If you do get pregnant, you may want to consider an abortion. Make sure you discuss the pros and cons fully with your doctor, your partner or a professional counsellor – or anyone who you feel could help you come to a decision you would be happy with (see ABORTION, page 12).

* If you have a baby, it has a chance of becoming HIV+ in the womb (through the placenta). Research from Britain's Institute of Child Health in 1992 suggested that for babies whose mothers had HIV before the birth, 14 per cent of those babies later developed AIDS. If the infection was caught by the mother after the baby's birth, the risk was 29 per cent.

You will find that the birth itself involves a lot of protective equipment, to prevent staff being infected by your body fluids.

* If you find you've become HIV+ after giving birth, you will probably be advised not to breastfeed (the virus is present in your milk, and babies' intestines are more vulnerable than adults'). The extent of the risk from breast milk is unknown as yet, but you may well find you prefer to play safe.

Pregnancy and AIDS

If you are not HIV+ but are worried about any risks associated with being pregnant or having a baby there are some things you need to know.

* Donors for artificial insemination are now carefully screened, so if you want to get pregnant this way you are safe – if you stick to reputable sources like the British Pregnancy Advisory Service or an NHS clinic (see HELPLINES).

* You won't have to worry about HIV infection if your baby is offered milk

31

from the health authority milk bank. All milk is now pasteurized, which kills the virus.

* The Department of Health has decided to carry out routine HIV antibody testing of the blood samples taken at some ante-natal clinics (information on which ones is not available). The samples will be collected anonymously, so you won't be told the result. The idea is to monitor the spread of HIV in the population.

You may not like that idea, and it is causing arguments among health professionals in the UK. You have a right to refuse this test and, if you do, you should be treated without discrimination.

* If you do want to be tested, and to know the result, you can ask for a test at your ante-natal clinic.

If your child is HIV+

Some children are infected with HIV by their parents. Others by outside factors such as treatment for haemophilia. (The latter danger is over, as all blood products used in haemophilia care are now heat-treated.)

A child with HIV can lead a fairly normal life. The treatment and self help (see below) is the same for children as for adults. But there are a few specific things to look out for with children.

* Obviously safe sex isn't an issue, but rough games which draw blood are not confined to adults, so look out for cuts and grazes on the children. Cover any such abrasion with plasters immediately after cleaning them, and be careful that none of the blood comes into contact with any cuts or abrasions on your or anyone else's body. (See **Self help**, below.)

* Small children are more free with their body fluids than adults (nappies, toilet training, dribbling, etc.) so you will have to take extra care they don't pass on the virus.

* HIV+ children also need extra protection against infections (their immune system is weak, remember).

* People who deal with your child day-to-day will need to be warned of the dangers: the nursery nurse, the head teacher, the class teacher and/or the school nurse, as appropriate.

* Make it quite clear that this is confidential information and not for everyone's ears. Ignorant people can be frightened – and cruel.

* Your local education authority (look in the phone book) can advise you on local policies towards HIV+ children (and partners), as can many of the helplines, such as Positively Women.

For detailed advice, consult the Haemophilia Society or one of the other groups listed in HELPLINES.

Treatment

There is, as yet, no vaccine against HIV, and no known cure for AIDS. But much research is going on, so people with AIDS are being offered all kinds of experimental treatments. There are three basic approaches in the research:

1. To keep the body (and mind) as healthy as possible, to build up the immune system to fight the HIV virus. Immunity-boosting drugs (e.g. Interferon) are

32

sometimes tried. Most ideas on this, however, are discussed in **Self help** and **Complementary therapies**, below, and are based on boosting the immune system by every possible means and cultivating a positive attitude.

This is worth doing whether you are merely HIV+, or are showing signs of ARC or AIDS. It is the newest trend in treatment and, many experts feel, the most hopeful.

2. To control the symptoms of opportunistic infections as they come along. These are the normal treatments given to anyone with these infections (e.g. pain-controlling drugs as necessary, nystatin cream and pessaries for thrush, good nutrition for weight loss and diarrhoea, radiotherapy for severe Kaposi's sarcoma, good basic hygiene and skin care for diarrhoea and all infections, drugs like pentamidine and septrin for PCP – often in spray form).

3. To try to attack HIV itself. Most commonly used for this is AZT (azidothy-midine), also called Zidovudine and Retrovir. The advantages are that it seems to control symptoms and to prolong life in people with AIDS. However, a major study of both French and British people with the virus published in 1993 suggested AZT seemed not to be so useful in preventing people with HIV infection going on to develop AIDS. The disadvantage is that the side effects can be severe (fatigue, nausea, headaches, liver damage, anaemia bad enough to need blood transfusions), but they occur more often in the AIDS patients who are very ill.

Alternatives

An alternative to AZT worth knowing about is called AL 721. It is being tried out at St Mary's Hospital, London, and is a mix of fats derived from egg yolks. Its advantages are that it seems to boost the immune system and reverse some symptoms, it doesn't have side effects and it is available on NHS prescription.

The disadvantages are that it is not yet proven to work – by the required extensive medical trials – and that not all doctors have heard of it, least of all GP's, so you may have to press for it. (It is made by Ethigen Corporation, distributed in the UK by Penn Pharmaceuticals.) The news on treatments changes almost day by day and there is a lot of controversy. Find out all you can from the groups listed in HELPLINES, page 38, as they will have much of the up-to-date information and (if you are receiving any treatment) your doctor.

Self help

The best form of self help is to protect yourself against getting HIV in the first place.

1. Know your sexual partner(s):

* people with haemophilia are treated with blood products, and some have been infected by contaminated blood through delay in getting a heat-treatment programme started – is your partner a haemophiliac?

* obviously, the more sexual partners you have the more likely you are to run into someone infected by HIV;

* if your sexual partner(s) has a lot of partners, the risk duly increases;

* some women feel they are safe because they have not slept around – but you have to be sure your partner doesn't, and that neither of you has done so in the last ten to fifteen years;
* unfortunately, partners don't always tell you everything;
* more men than you might think have, or once had, gay sex (while exploring their teenage sexuality, for instance);
* AIDS can take years to show up, so high-risk sex could have taken place a long time ago;
* high-risk sex is: (i) sex in a high-AIDS country (the USA, the Middle East, Africa, the Caribbean and South America); (ii) sex with a prostitute (male or female); (iii) anal sex – which can tear the rectum and makes it easy for HIV to penetrate; and (iv) sex without a condom with new or casual partners.

2. Know the risks from blood:
* people who inject drugs (e.g. heroin) should *never* share equipment with others. Does that affect you – or your sexual partner? Schemes to provide clean needles are rare in the UK, but find out the possibilities through an organization listed in HELPLINES;
* check with ear-piercers, acupuncturists, dentists etc. that they use (preferably) disposable needles, and/or disinfect instruments, either by auto-claving or in bleach. Both these simple methods work 100 per cent;
* don't share anybody's razor (skin gets nicked) or toothbrush (plenty of people have bleeding gums);
* blood transfusions are risky in some Third World countries (in the UK, all donated blood is screened for HIV antibodies, although there are a few rare cases of infection). If you are ill enough to need an emergency transfusion, however, its benefits far outweigh any risk. If a transfusion is planned ahead (e.g. you are due for surgery) you may choose to 'bank' supplies of your own blood in advance (see HELPLINES, page 38);
* if you're in a high risk profession or caring for a child or an adult with HIV or AIDS (see **Who is at risk?** above), remember that infected body fluids can endanger you only if they get through your skin, so: (i) cover any cuts with a waterproof plaster; (ii) wear plastic gloves if you have lots of cuts, or eczema; (iii) don't let any spills come near your mouth or nose, where they can be absorbed through unbroken skin; (iv) clean up spills at once (gloved hands) with ordinary household bleach diluted with water (1 measure of bleach per 10 measures of water) – this is completely effective, nothing more elaborate is needed; and (v) get more detailed advice from your professional organization.

3. Know what *is* safe:
* it is perfectly safe to donate blood – all equipment used is disposable.
* fresh blood (and other body fluids, like plasma) carry a risk. But the HIV virus is, in fact, quite frail and doesn't live for long outside the human body. If you know somebody with HIV or AIDS:
* saliva contains only fragments of virus, and isn't thought to be a risk;
* the Royal College of Nursing says that 'ordinary, domestic contact' (washed tea-cups, touching, dry kissing, hugging, sharing towels and so on) carries no risk at all;
* with things like soiled, blood-stained or sweaty sheets, use your judgement.

Don't handle them with unprotected cuts on your hands. Disinfect them with ordinary domestic bleach and clean in a very hot wash. This works perfectly well.

Safe sex
If you are unsure about your partner, you need to practise safe sex. The basic rule, as always, is to prevent *any* body fluids (semen, menstrual blood, other blood, urine or faeces) getting through your skin. So:
* don't do anything which breaks the skin;
* cover any cuts you've got with a waterproof plaster;
* above all, prevent all contact between body fluids and the inside of your mouth, vagina or rectum, where skin is more absorbent because it is thin and has a rich blood supply, even if it is intact; so:
* use a sheath for contraception (caps and diaphragms only stop semen getting past your cervix – they don't stop it getting into your vagina);
* if you practise mutual masturbation, don't let semen get into any skin breaks, or your vagina or rectum – elsewhere on your body, it is safe: 'On, not in' is the rule;
* practise other forms of no-risk sex: (i) caressing any body part away from the penis, vagina or rectum; (ii) using sex toys (vibrators etc.) as long as they are not shared; and (iii) self masturbation;
* be aware of low-risk sex: (i) oral sex (fellatio or cunnilingus) – but make sure neither of you has mouth ulcers or bleeding gums, and that you can trust a male partner to withdraw before an orgasm by fellatio, so you do not swallow his semen; (ii) kissing – although deep 'French' kissing is thought by some experts to carry a small risk; and (iii) using your fingers in your partner's vagina or rectum – but make sure jagged fingernails etc. don't cause damage;
* know about high-risk sex: (i) vaginal or anal sex without a sheath, or using a sheath carelessly (see CONTRACEPTION); (ii) vaginal sex during your period; (iii) anything that draws blood or pierces the skin; and (iv) sharing sex toys.

It can be tricky bringing up the question of safe sex and/or using a sheath if you are just starting a romance. Your best bet is to bring up the subject in general conversation, well before things get intimate (something along the lines of: 'Isn't it awful, this AIDS business . . .'), to prepare the ground and sound out likely reactions. It helps, too, to rehearse possible conversations in your head, so you are not thrown by an unexpected reaction.

There is some good news, however. The *New England Journal of Medicine* has released the results of a study which suggests that the likelihood of acquiring the HIV virus from a carrier, from just one sexual encounter, is less than one per cent. This is obviously reassuring for anyone who has had one risky encounter, but all the more reason to practise safe sex in the future.

If you are HIV+
A book can't tell you the half of what you want and need to know. There are several very helpful support groups for women, and other mixed-sex groups, whose activities vary from emotional support to exchanging information about

new 'underground' forms of treatment. You don't ever have to be alone. (See HELPLINES, page 38.)

There are also support groups for friends and partners of people who are HIV+, or who have AIDS – very important. (See HELPLINES, page 38.) Cancer support groups can give excellent advice, too – AIDS has certain aspects in common with cancer (and can cause certain types of it, like Kaposi's sarcoma). (See CANCER HELPLINES.)

People with HIV and AIDS are starting to demand more control over what happens to them, and the right to try treatment ideas for themselves. This is a good idea in itself. If you feel in control, your more positive emotional state can have strong effects on your immune system.

Complementary therapies and self help ideas (used alone or in conjunction with orthodox medicine) do seem to help – sometimes better than conventional treatments. HIV+ people have remained symptom-free for years; even people with full-blown AIDS are finding sometimes their symptoms improve, or disappear. It is very much up to the individual to find out exactly what her individual problems are (e.g. nutritional deficiencies) and to explore the many body treatments and therapies available, to find which ones feel right for them. Get expert and sympathetic advice, via HELPLINES. Basic tactics include:
* good nutrition;
* meditation;
* relaxation;
* massage;
* mental imagery work (visualization);
* aerobic exercise;
* yoga;
* getting lots of emotional support;
* sorting out worrying problems with your job, your finances, your accommodation, your relationships, using the specialist advice available through HELPLINES;
* not getting too tired or stressed;
* guarding yourself against infections.

Complementary therapy
Complementary therapies tailor their treatments very much to the individual: the precise nature of the treatment you receive will vary, depending on your medical history, symptoms, lifestyle, etc. The following information indicates the *sorts* of things a therapist is most likely to do or recommend. Do not be surprised if they feel you need something slightly different. This section is meant purely as an indication of likely treatments; it is not meant as a DIY guide to the medical uses of the different complementary therapies.

Complementary therapy cannot prevent or treat the AIDS virus. However, alone or in combination, several therapies can be used to strengthen the immune system and decrease vulnerability to infection, both for full AIDS sufferers and people who are HIV+. Distressing symptoms can be alleviated to some extent.

Acupuncture

The acupuncturist will select points which suppress pain and discomfort; promote an appropriate anti-inflammatory effect; and stimulate production of antibodies against infection. The specific points and the length of treatment will depend on the patient's individual problems; treatment might continue for up to twelve months.

Aromatherapy

Lymphatic massage using highly anti-infective and immunomodulant essential oils, such as the oil of the Melaleuca family (for example, tea tree), helps boost the immune system, thus making it less vulnerable to opportunistic (piggy-back) infections. Treatment for thrush, for example, might be needed every day for two to three weeks, with local bathing; for skin disorders, bathing or local application twice a week for perhaps four weeks, reinforced by visits to the therapist once a fortnight for two or three months. The aromatherapist can also offer oil of thymus vulgaris as either a mouthwash or for local application, for mouth ulcers.

Clinical nutrition

To help you resist infection and generally strengthen the immune system itself, a clinical nutritionist will prescribe a daily dose of cod liver oil to enhance the thymus gland (the main organ of the immune system). Plus: a two-month course of valine, tryptophan and phenylalanine (amino acids essential to the production of antibodies); daily doses of phosphatidyl choline to help repair nerves and produce neurotransmitters to counter nerve symptoms; Vitamin E to protect against damaging body chemicals called free radicals; co-enzyme Q10, to increase activity of macrophages (infection fighting cells); and Vitamin B15 (to attract oxygen to the blood). Also, a rectal or colonic irrigation (a bit like an enema), can be followed by an acidophilus implant placed in the rectum, to restore colon health.

For those who are HIV+, a vitamin and mineral supplement will help boost activity in the immune system and stimulate production of infection-fighting lymphocytes and antibodies. This will include: Vitamin A, Vitamin E, Vitamin C, folic acid, Vitamin B6, Vitamin B5, zinc, iron, manganese, magnesium, selenium, bioflavonoids, GTF (a fan of Gemomium) chromium and copper.

For those suffering from mouth ulcers, and/or thrush, a vitamin supplement (A, B, B1, B2, B5, B6 and C), plus a yoghurt and cider vinegar (diluted) mouthwash, will help. Vitamins A and C, with B complex and pantothenic acid, will aid skin repair and regeneration.

Homoeopathy

Combined with other natural therapies such as clinical nutrition and medical herbalism, homoeopathic remedies can help strengthen the immune system and make the body more resistant to infection. Echinacea augustifolia and Echinacea purpurea are used.

Homoeopathy also has remedies to offer for symptoms like mouth ulcers (Heparsul, etc.) and skin disorders and thrush (Natrum Mur or Borax). The most suitable remedy will be chosen according to the patient's particular problem or combination of problems. Of special value is 'the constitutional remedy', a remedy chosen after a full review of your weaknesses and strengths – mental, emotional and physical (in that order).

Medical herbalism

By enhancing resistance to infection and strengthening the immune system, medical herbalism offers help both to AIDS sufferers and those who are HIV+. Especially effective are Echinacea and/or garlic, taken with nutritional supplements and a generally healthy diet. These stimulate lymphocyte activity to clear the body (Echinacea), inhibit viral action and improve the action of gut flora (garlic).

For specific symptoms, such as skin complaints, dandelion or burdock help to eliminate toxins and improve skin nourishment via the circulation. To mouthwash or gargle, using tincture of myrrh as an antiseptic astringent, helps mouth troubles.

Aids helplines

AVERT (Aids Virus Education and Research Trust)
PO Box 91, Horsham RH13 7YR (0403 210202): leaflets and advice for women
  with AIDS and HIV, on pregnancy, childbirth, breastfeeding, the care of an
  HIV+ child and much more.

Body Positive Group
PO Box 493, West Kensington, London W14 0TF (071 373 9124). Lines are open
  from 7 to 10 p.m., daily. Runs a group for HIV+ women.

British Medical Association Foundation for AIDS
BMA House, Tavistock Square, London WC1H 9JP (071 383 6345)
The foundation is a registered charity which promotes education and understanding
  of all aspects of HIV infection and AIDS.

Bristol Cancer Help Centre
Grove House, Clifton, Bristol, Avon BS8 4PG
The pioneering cancer help centre opened by HRH Prince Charles.

Cancer Link
46A Pentonville Road, London N1 9HF (071 833 2451)
This is not an alternative/holistic centre, but provides general information,
  counselling on all aspects of all types of cancers, and can put you in touch with
  supportive groups and sources of practical help.

The National Federation of Spiritual Healers
Old Manor Farm Studio, Church Street, Sunbury on Thames (0932 783164)

Gay Bereavement Project
Unitarian Rooms, Hoop Lane, London NW11 8BS (081 455 8894)

The Gay Medical Association
BA/GMA, London WC1N 3XX

The Haemophilia Society
123 Westminster Bridge Road, London SE1 7HR (071 928 2020)

The Lantern Trust
72 Honey Lane, Waltham Abbey, Essex EN9 3 BS (0992 7149000)
A charity organization which runs courses for the sufferers and carriers of AIDS,
    ARC and HIV.

London Lesbian and Gay Switchboard
BM Switchboard, London WC1N 3XX (071 837 7324)

London Lighthouse
(071 792 1200)
The aim of the groups is to provide a safe and supportive environment in which to
    discuss and explore the issues arising from the situation sufferers from AIDS, ARC
    and HIV find themselves in.

Mildmay Mission Hospital
Hackney Road, London E2 7NA (071 739 2331)
This is the first place in Britain to have a special facility for women and children
    with AIDS, so families can stay together.

National Advisory Service on AIDS
(0800 567123) A free and confidential helpline for those concerned about AIDS or
    drug abuse. There are additional lines available in a variety of languages:
Cantonese: (0800 282446) from 6 to 10 p.m., Tuesdays
Punjabi, Bengali, Hindi, Urdu, Gujerati: (0800 282447) From 6 to 10 p.m.,
    Wednesdays
Arabic, English: (0800 282447) From 6 to 10 p.m., Wednesdays
Afro-Caribbean: (0800 567123) From 6 to 10 p.m., Fridays

National AIDS Helpline
(071 387 6900)
Call for details of specific local helplines. Or send SAE to NAM Publications, PO
    Box 99, London SW2 1EL.

Northwest Thames Regional Health Authority
40 Eastbourne Terrace, London W2 4QR (071 723 8904)
Suppliers of a leaflet entitled 'The HIV Test and Your Pregnancy', which answers
  common questions about HIV testing, including the disadvantages of testing.

Positively Women
333 Grays Inn Road, London WC1X 8PX (071 837 9705)
An organization run by women for women with HIV, ARC and AIDS. They offer
  fortnightly support groups, counselling advice, and information for women with a
  positive diagnosis. (Moving soon, will have new number.)

The Terrence Higgins Trust
BA/AIDS, London WC1N 3XX (071 831 0330)
The trust provides a number of different counselling and support services. In
  particular, there is a women's support group, which is a weekly self-help/support
  group for women who have AIDS, ARC and HIV.

Further reading
The Truth about AIDS by Dr P. Dixon (Kingsway Publications)
Safer Sex: A New Look at Sexual Pleasure by P. Gordon and L. Mitchell (Faber)
AIDS: A Guide to the Law by Dai Harris and Richard Harris (Tavistock/Routledge)
Living with HIV in Self and Others by Richie McMullen (GMP Publishing)
Women and the AIDS Crisis by D. Richardson (Pandora)
Understanding Aids by Dr J. Starkie and R. Dale (The Consumer's Association)
Caring for Someone with AIDS, edited by Richard Yelding (Hodder)

Positive Partners, and Positively Children
(071 738 7333); for women whose partner or child(ren) are affected by the HIV
  virus.

Benign breast problems

What breasts are made of

Your breasts are made up of one third mammary glands – the small lobes blooming at the end of the network of milk-carrying ducts which branch away from the nipple like the leaves of a tree – and two thirds fatty tissue, wrapped around this network of glands and ducts, which gives the breast its soft, rounded shape and contributes a good deal to its size.

Both fatty tissue and glands are enclosed in a smooth envelope of skin which stretches around and underneath them, and upwards to the neck and chest in a fan-shape, supporting the breasts. This fan of skin acts like a natural bra, and is itself supported by another fan shape, this time made up of three muscles called the pectoral muscles – plus another small muscle called the platysma, which runs from the upper chest, past the collar-bone and neck, to the side of the mouth and chin.

By exercising these muscles to keep them toned, you can make sure that they do a better job of supporting the weight of your breasts and that your bust keeps as upstanding a shape as possible. However, building up these muscles

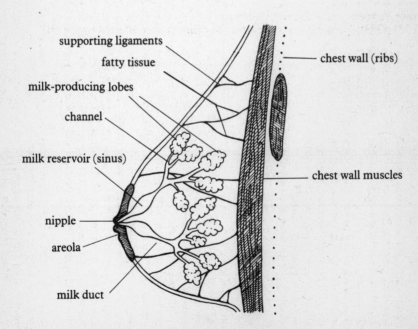

Side view of the breast. (*Adapted from* Breast Cancer: The Facts *by Michael Baum*)

41

Breast problems and their treatment

Problems, symptoms and causes

ABSCESSES. An abscess starts as an infection in the breast tissue itself (as opposed to a duct) which produces swelling, pain and redness. If left untreated for too long it can become a pus-filled abscess.

Abscesses are caused by bacterial infections. On top of redness, pain and 'throbbing' you may get a temperature, too. The bacteria usually get into the breast via a crack on the edge of your nipple (e.g. during breastfeeding). It has no connection with cancer.

BENIGN MAMMARY DYSPLASIA (BMD) and CYCLICAL BREAST PAIN also known as fibrocystic disease, chronic mastitis, fibroadenosis or, as it often goes with certain parts of the menstrual cycle, it may be referred to as CYCLICAL MASTALGIA. This is lumpiness and tenderness (may include small or large cysts – fluid filled sacs – too). It usually affects both breasts and is worst in the outer, upper 'quarter' of the breast area. It varies in severity according to which part of your menstrual cycle you are in. It is most often found in women in their twenties and thirties.

The likeliest cause is that the hormones prolactin and oestrogen are over-stimulating the breast tissue; particularly since it varies with your cycle and disappears after the menopause. It is commoner, too, in women who have irregular periods, or no children.

Medical help

Antibiotics are the treatment, but if the area is throbbing, pus will already have formed, so it will be too late for antibiotics to help. You may need an operation under general anaesthetic to release the pus. Sometimes it is possible to draw off (aspirate) the contents of an abscess with a needle and then to use antibiotics to kill the infection causing it.

There are several drugs which can help by acting on your hormone output:
* Danazol, which works for about 7 out of 10 women, although it can have unpleasant side effects like weight gain, skin and hair greasiness or hair growth in unwelcome places;
* Tamoxifen, which works by blocking out the production of oestrogen, will help about 8 out of 10 women. It has side effects for many, such as menopausal-style hot flushes, nausea and irregular periods. But if the dose is kept low only about 20 per cent get these. It is usually given for three months;
* Bromocriptine acts by reducing your production of prolactin, the milk-making hormone, and is effective for 9 out of 10 women. Its side effects include dizziness, headaches and nausea, but these can be reduced if you begin taking very low doses and work slowly up to higher ones;

Self help

* If the abscesses are painful and tender to touch, warm flannels or a warm hot-water bottle can be temporarily soothing.
* Aspirin can help with inflammation and pain (use its soluble form, as it is gentler on the stomach), but seek your GP's advice about taking it long term.
* Cool compresses may also be soothing. Try putting layers of damp men's cotton handkerchiefs in the freezer, interleaved with polythene to stop them freezing into a lump. They are malleable and will wrap exactly around the area, unlike ice packs.

* Essential fatty acid supplements can help and have very few side effects, even when taken in the high doses required – about six 500 gm capsules a day for 12 weeks are recommended. Occasionally the high doses lead to nausea or headaches. EFAs affect the way our hormones function, which is why they are also helpful for pre-menstrual syndrome (PMS). Available from health food shops in the form of evening primrose oil, (or – much cheaper – from your GP – as 'Efamast').

* Eat less saturated animal fat by cutting down on dairy products like butter, cream, cheese and full fat yogurts. Go for soya or semi-skimmed milk, fat reduced cheese or cottage cheese, and spreads high in polyunsaturates instead of butter. Saturated fats are thought to interfere with the way our bodies utilize essential fatty acids to make hormones.

* Progestogen, which is an artificial form of progesterone which balances out any excess oestrogen that is overstimulating your breasts – and is taken in the second half of your menstrual cycle;

* The Combined Pill (contains both oestrogen and progestogen), whose synthetic hormones balance out the effect of the oestrogen you are making naturally, and so has a protective effect against BMD and, reduce your chance of getting it by between 50 and 75 per cent. May also help reduce the symptoms of BMD for women who already have it.

* Vitamin B6 and B1 (50 to 100mg) supplements can sometimes benefit as it is thought to help the body use the essential fatty acids it gets as food or food supplements, which is why it is often prescribed for PMS.

* Avoid eating too much sugary sweet food because it is possible that high sugar levels lead to higher levels of the hormone insulin, which controls our blood sugar, and this can have a similar effect on breast tissue as oestrogen does.

* Always wear comfortable and supportive bras. American sportsbras, which partially flatten the breast against the chest wall, rather than styles which make you 'carry all before you', can support a large bust as well as making it look smaller. Getting professionally fitted is a must, too (see HELPLINES).

BREASTS TOO BIG. Possibly hormonal, possibly hereditary, but some women's breasts grow excessively in puberty and do not seem to know when to stop. If you are very overweight the extra fatty tissue deposited around your breasts can make them uncomfortably large, too.

Cosmetic surgery to reduce the size of your breasts is done by taking away a symmetrical wedge of breast tissue and fat. The nipple and areola have to be moved too, which can produce loss of sensation in your nipple, and you would not be able to breast feed afterwards. All surgery leaves scars, but they would be slim ones that would fade a fair amount in the year after the operation.

The operation would mean a general anaesthetic and about four days in hospital. You can have such an operation on the NHS if your breasts are causing you physical problems such as backache, poor posture, infections of the skin under the breast, or serious mental distress. The waiting lists vary but may be up to four years. A private operation would cost around £3,500 to £4,000 (see HELPLINES), but if the surgeon felt it would help and there were no medical reasons why you should not have a breast reduction, you could have an operation within a couple of weeks.

Problems, symptoms and causes

BREASTS TOO SMALL. Again, the reason may be hormonal, hereditary or simply that your body shape is naturally small-breasted. Some women report that after breast feeding their breasts get smaller. This may be because breastfeeding uses up the body's fat stores, including those that give the breast much of its shape and size (the fat deposits usually return after a few months if you are eating well).

CYSTS. This is a balloon-like capsule filled with fluid that forms in one of the breast's ducts or milk-producing lobes. Most cysts are small and appear in groups, some may be bigger and felt as a smooth lump which moves about under your skin. They are most common in women in their twenties to thirties (but may occur later), and in women who have not had children. Cysts have no link with cancer.

DUCT ECTASIA. This is a very common reason for breast pain, especially for women in their forties and fifties. Besides pain, it can cause a

Medical help

The higher dose Combined Pill contains small amounts of oestrogen and may make your breasts a size or so larger, as oestrogen is the hormone that makes breast tissue active. But most Pills prescribed today would have little effect, as they are usually as low a dose as possible.

A breast augmentation cosmetic operation would help (rarely available on the NHS, it costs about £2,000 to £2,500 to have done privately). It is the most common private cosmetic operation, and involves placing a strong bag of silicon gel (which feels soft and malleable like a natural breast) under your existing breast tissue via an incision in the armpit, or low down on the breast or around the nipple. It usually means a couple of days in hospital, but not always a general anaesthetic. One drawback is the possibility of fibrous tissue forming around the silicon bag, but if it does it can be broken down by a firm hand squeeze from the surgeon on your follow-up visit. Silicon bags can however mask cancer spots.

Sometimes cysts will burst and disappear of their own accord. They will usually be treated by aspiration: gently inserting a surgical needle and drawing off the fluid in them, in the same way as a blood sample might be taken.

If the problem keeps on recurring, you may be given Danazol.

Early on this can be treated with certain types of antibiotics, but if it has become quite advanced the drugs would make little

Self help

* Exercises to develop the pectorals and platysma will help make the most of what you naturally have by encouraging your breasts to stand up more firmly (see HELPLINES).
* Subtly padded and underwired bras and swimwear help. But cosmetic creams, especially the 'hormone' creams you still see in the classified ads section of magazines will not.

* If the cysts are painful and tender to touch, warm flannels or a warm hot-water bottle can be temporarily soothing.

* Aspirin can help with inflammation and pain (use its soluble form, as it is gentler on the stomach), but seek your GP's advice about

nipple retraction. The discharge is usually watery but may be coloured by a little red blood – or appear greenish brown from old blood.

It is caused by the milk ducts filling with milky fluid, becoming blocked, then inflamed. This produces hot, red, painful areas on the breast but it is a benign condition and it has no connection with cancer.

condition to settle down of its own accord. Very occasionally, if there is persistent discharge and pain, the problem might be treated surgically.

* Cool compresses may also be soothing. Try putting layers of damp men's cotton handkerchiefs in the freezer, interleaved with polythene to stop them freezing into a lump. They are malleable and will wrap exactly around the area, unlike ice packs which are less precise.

DUCT PAPILLOMAS. These are benign little tumours, which appear in the ducts as small, wart-like bumps. They may, if not removed, sometimes become malignant. Their cause is uncertain but it is probably hormonal, as they do not occur in women who have had their menopause. The first sign of a duct papilloma is generally a little red blood coming up through the nipple.

They would be removed surgically by a minor operation, although you would need a general anaesthetic.

Nil.

FAT NECROSIS. A hard knock can cause this condition by breaking open fat cells in the breast (it would have to be a hard bump, the sort that causes bruising). The body doesn't recognize the fatty material released from the burst fat cells as 'self' and behaves as if it were a foreign substance, producing a lot of scar tissue. This forms into a hard lump and when it contracts, as scar tissue will, it puckers the skin above by pulling on it, causing skin dimpling.

This is where the 'blows on the breast can give you cancer' scare stories came from, but Fat Necrosis has no connection with cancer. In fact, after a blow on the breast, this is often the first time a woman feels around her breast, perhaps discovering lumps that were already there and undetected.

Most people would remember a blow on their breast which was hard enough to cause bruising and burst fat cells, so doctors can usually be sure that this is what has caused the problem and will leave it alone. If, however, there is the slightest doubt about it, a lump should be surgically removed.

Nil.

FIBROADENOMA (a solid lump). Sometimes called a 'breast mouse' because it can be moved around so easily underneath the skin, this is a benign breast tumour – an overdivision of cells which have formed a lump. It is not going to turn malignant (cancerous). It may be anything from pea-sized to an inch or so across, and inside it is solid white tissue.

HAIR AROUND THE NIPPLES. This can be caused by the same sex hormones as produce pubic hair on the rest of the body – or by any hormonal disturbance.

Drugs will not help, so fibroadenomas are either left and watched to see if they will disappear the way they came, or removed surgically, depending on how big they are. The operation can be done under local anaesthetic and need not mean an overnight stay in hospital. This will not interfere with breastfeeding.

Some combined oral contraceptive pills can help by stimulating the liver to make more binding protein to 'mop up' any excess male hormone going round in the bloodstream.

Some drugs (e.g. Spironolactone) stop male hormones acting on the hair follicles to produce thicker hairs (but side effects can include tiredness and depression). Steroids have also been used effectively.

The drawback with all these drugs is that the hairiness will recur to some extent when you stop taking them. Also, hair's response to drugs is slow as a hair's life cycle is 6 to 9 months and the drugs will only affect newly growing hair. It will not make a difference to what's already there.

If the hair has appeared suddenly, check with your doctor that there is no underlying hormonal problem. If the hair growth is extensive and has appeared in other places, like your face or abdomen, they may want to do a blood test to check for levels of the male hormone testosterone.

* Reduce or cut out your coffee intake. High levels of caffeine have been linked, in some studies, to fibrous breast lumps.

* Bleaching. Use facial hair bleach for such a sensitive area, and do a skin patch test first.
* Waxing. Efficient, and hair does not even start to come back for a couple of weeks, but it is painful if done around the nipple.
* Plucking. Can be painful, so widen the entrance to the hair follicles first by laying on a hot flannel so that the hair comes out without having to pull too hard. Dab with cool water and maybe a little antiseptic cream (something very mild like Savlon) to prevent any infection afterwards.
* Cutting off the hair at its base or shaving can encourage tougher growth and has to be done every few days, but is painless.
* Electrolysis is the only permanent method but may be a bit painful on such a sensitive area. However there are some electrolysis methods which hurt less (see HELPLINES) and many women feel it's well worth it to get rid of the hair for good. If you have been plucking it out, the hair root may be a bit twisted and it can be hard for the electrolysis needle to reach and cauterize the hair root bulb. It may therefore take two or three attempts.

will not make any difference to the actual size of your breasts, although making them stand up more pertly may make them seem larger.

Breast problems
It is thought that tens of thousands of women every year go to their GP with a breast problem – and that many more suffer in silence from aching, tenderness, benign lumps and bumps and other difficulties. However, it is also encouraging to know that:
* Up to 90 per cent of all breast lumps are benign. (See BREAST CANCER, page 68, for what to do if your lump is not.)
* There is seldom any connection at all between breast cancer and benign breast disease (a lump that is not cancerous and will never become so).

Quick checklist of breast symptoms
Many disorders and diseases of the breast have similar symptoms; some share symptoms and others will produce different signs in different women. The vast majority do not mean you have cancer – a symptom is just a sign that *something* is wrong. It is very unlikely to be cancer and may well be something fairly small or easily put right.

Symptoms	*Problem could be*
CHANGES IN SIZE	Big cyst, large fibroadenoma, phase in menstrual cycle, pregnancy; occasionally cancerous.
DIMPLED SKIN	Duct ectasia, fat necrosis; occasionally cancerous.
ENLARGED LYMPH NODES	An infection which has nothing to do with your breast (e.g. mumps or glandular fever); or mastitis, fat necrosis, duct ectasia, an abscess; cancer can also produce this symptom.
INFLAMED AREA	Duct ectasia, occasionally a cyst or duct papilloma, mastitis, abscess; occasionally cancerous.
INVERTED NIPPLES	Many women have inverted nipples anyway, and the nipples concerned are perfectly normal and healthy. However, if a nipple suddenly becomes inverted it may occasionally indicate duct papilloma or, more likely, duct ectasia. Very occasionally cancerous.
LUMPINESS IN GENERAL	Often due to certain phases of your menstrual cycle, multiple small breast cysts, or BMD.
LUMPS IN BREAST	Cyst, fibrous breast disease, fibroadenoma, BMD, duct papilloma, duct ectasia, absess, fat necrosis; occasionally cancerous.
NIPPLE DISCHARGE	Overproduction of Prolactin (the milk-making hormone) in pregnancy, changes in your hormone levels during menstrual cycle, or after an abortion or miscarriage, mastitis; sometimes a cyst, duct papilloma, duct ectasia; occasionally cancerous.

47

PAIN IN YOUR BREASTS   Fluctuating hormone levels during menstrual cycle, cysts, abscess, mastitis, fat necrosis, duct ectasia; *very* rarely indicates cancer. See PMS chapter.

Checking your breasts

Do this every month at the same time (just after your period has finished, say three days later, is ideal as any natural cyclical lumpiness will have calmed down by then). If you notice anything that is unusual for your breasts – and you know best what is normal for them and what is not – don't delay in getting checked by your GP. Remember that if there is a problem it is far more likely to be one of the benign breast problems which can usually be put right quickly and easily – not cancer. But just in case it is something more serious, the sooner it is diagnosed the simpler and more effective any treatment will be.

Step one: looking things over
* Undress to your waist and stand in front of a mirror, arms comfortably at your sides.
* Look for any changes in the size of your breasts, any lopsidedness, any difference in the way your nipples look, any discharge from your nipples, any dimpling of your breast skin, any veins standing out more than usual.
* Raise your arms above your head and turn from side to side, looking at your breasts from different angles to see if there is anything out of the ordinary.

Step two: feeling your way
* Lie down on your bed with your head on a pillow. Tuck your right arm behind your head comfortably (see diagram ii).
* Using your left hand, fingers flat and held close together, use the flats of the fingers (not the tips) to feel around your breast in a closing spiral, moving your fingers gently in small circles, checking for any small lumps or anything unusual (see diagram below).
* Finally, with your right arm back down by your side, check under your armpit for lumps and bumps too.

And that's all there is to it – just a quick two or three minutes a month which could save you a good deal of trouble, and reassure you regularly.

Checking your breasts.

Complementary therapy

Complementary therapies tailor their treatments very much to the individual: the precise nature of the treatment you receive will vary, depending on your medical history, symptoms, lifestyle, etc. The following information indicates the *sorts* of things a therapist is most likely to do or recommend. Do not be surprised if they feel you need something slightly different. This section is meant purely as an indication of likely treatments; it is not meant as a DIY guide to the medical uses of the different complementary therapies.

Certain therapies can help with specific breast conditions, such as abcesses and cystic mastitis. They are also useful in treating cyclic breast pain associated with menstruation or with the menopause.

Acupuncture

The therapist will use acupuncture points which increase the production of antibodies, increase the strength of resistance to infection and promote the recovery process. This is good for both breast abscesses and cystic mastitis, and can also help balance hormone levels.

Aromatherapy

Breast abcesses are treated by improving the patient's immunity and destroying the pathogenic bacteria. Aromatherapy can also deal with inflammation. Essential oils with bacteria-killing and healing properties include rosewood, geranium and palmarosa.

The same oils can be used to treat infection in cystic mastitis; the hormonal problem is treated with clary sage. Encouraging the lymphatic flow and circulation aids reabsorption of small cysts. Specific treatment will differ from patient to patient, depending, however, on individual needs.

Clinical nutrition

A clinical nutritionist is likely to advise women with cystic mastitis to avoid caffeine (tea, coffee, chocolate and cola drinks) and (if your orthodox doctor agrees) reduce asthma medication. All of these can cause toxins to build up in the lymph vessels.

Treatment may include daily doses of Vitamin E, which is anti-toxic, and fenugreek tea, which breaks down toxins in the lymphatic system and encourages its flow.

Homoeopathy

Homoeopathy offers a number of treatments, according to the nature of the condition. In very early, acute stages, aconite; for a developed abscess, Hepar sulph; when there is hardening, Phytolacca; left-sided, with swelling, pain, hardening, often associated with uterine troubles, Cimicifuga; when the breast is hot with streaks radiating – red, pulsating pains which are worse with touch or movement, Belladonna; when the whole breast is hard, painful, tense with stitching pains, Bryonia.

Clearly, careful consultation is important to find out exactly what the problem is.

Medical herbalism

Fully developed breast abscesses respond to hot compresses of herbs, such as marsh-mallow or slippery elm. Taken internally, remedies such as Calendula or cleavers can improve lymphatic drainage. Garlic helps the system to resist infection.

Medical herbalism is unlikely to be of major value to cystic mastitis, but individual cases may respond to treatment with Calendula or sweet violet. A therapist can advise.

49

Benign breast problems helplines

Bras
All John Lewis plc department stores have trained fitters in their lingerie departments who will fit you in private, for no extra charge.

Breast screening
You can refer yourself for private screenings – available from private medical insurance companies like BUPA. You can also be referred on the National Health Service, either by your own GP or by a doctor from one of the charitable well woman clinics, like Marie Stopes. (They can also refer you for a private screening.)

Costs for private mammograms are between £50 and £60 – but always be sure to find out when your results are due, and chase them up. Speak to a doctor when you receive them, if you want them explained fully. If there is a problem, call up one of the cancer help associations, which are staffed by trained nurses and can answer queries on benign breast disease as well as cancer. The following addresses should be of help:

BUPA
HQ – 300 Grays Inn Road, London WC1 (071 837 6484)
Clinics countrywide, contact HQ for the nearest clinic to you.

Cancer Link
17 Britannia Street, London WC1 (071 833 2451)

Marie Stopes Clinics
In London, Manchester and Leeds. (See GENERAL HELPLINES at the back of the book for details.)

The Breast Care Helpline
(0628 481333); help and advice.

Cosmetic surgery
There are a number of cowboy cosmetic surgery clinics around, so it's a good idea not to choose a clinic by looking in the classified advertisement section of the magazines. Ask your GP if he can recommend a good cosmetic surgeon (a qualification in general surgery – FRCS – is not enough).

Alternatively, check the *Good Doctor Guide* for possible names (see page 10), or ask your GP to write for a name to:

British Association of Plastic Surgeons
c/o The Honorary Secretary, 35 Lincoln's Inn Fields, London WC2

If you get really stuck, try The Medical Advisory Service (081 994 9874), a charity run by nurses, which offers information on all aspects of medical care, both private and NHS.

Electrolysis
TAO Electrolysis
Info from: 5 Sloane Street, London SW1 (branches countrywide) (071 235 9333)
A nationwide chain of clinics that specialize in electrolysis and train their own
  therapists. Contact HQ for the branch nearest you.

Sylvia Lewis Clinic
HQ – 108 New Bond Street, London W1
A gentler method of electrolysis, developed by electrolysist, Sylvia Lewis, in
  conjunction with University College, is practised countrywide by therapists she has
  trained. It may be more suitable for an especially sensitive area, like that around the
  nipple. Send SAE with covering note to HQ for your nearest Sylvia Lewis therapist.

Essential fatty acids
Available in capsule form as Evening Primrose Oil (Boots and Holland & Barrett have
their own brands, or try brands like Britannia Health, at health food shops), or as
Blackcurrant Seed Oil (available at the same places; look out for brands like Lanes
GLA). EPO can be expensive if bought in health shops so save money by asking
  for it from your GP: a brand called EFAMAST is now on prescription for
  cyclical breast pain.

Nutritional advice
For advice on cutting down on things like saturated fats and sugars, without a boring
diet, your GP may be able to refer you to a community or hospital dietitian on the NHS.

The British Nutrition Foundation
52 to 54 High Holborn, London WC1 (071 404 6504)
This centre can put you in touch with a trained dietitian (trained for at least 3
  years).

National Association for Pre-Menstrual Syndrome
PO Box 72, Sevenoaks, Kent TW13 3PS (0732 459378)
Advises women on all aspects of PMS, including breast discomfort. They advocate
  treatment with natural progesterone, and also keeping the blood sugar constant, to
  avoid symptoms such as anxiety and mood swings, by eating complex
  carbohydrates (such as bread) every three hours pre-menstrually.

Women's Nutritional Advisory Service (formerly the PMT Advisory Service)
PO Box 268, Hove, East Sussex BN3 1RW (0273 771366)
Advice for coping with PMS problems, including breast discomfort, by changing the
  food that you eat and by taking mineral and vitamin supplements.

There are five specialist clinical centres on the NHS dealing particularly with breast
  problems (e.g. pain, lumpiness) see pp 427 for list if you want your GP to refer
  you.

Further reading
Disorderly Breasts by Sarah Boston and Jill Louw (Camden Press)
A Woman's Guide to Breast Health by Cath Cirket (Grapevine)
The Breast Book by consultant surgeon, John Cochrane, and Dr Anne Szarewski
  (Optima)
The Woman's Cancer Book by Carolyn Faulder (Virago)

Breastfeeding difficulties

If you do decide you want to breastfeed, as any health professional will tell you, your colostrum (pre-milk) and milk are the perfect foods for a new baby. However, some them are so pro-breastfeeding that they can make mothers who do not wish to, or who give up because of difficulties they cannot solve (perhaps they are so tired that their milk supply is insufficient), feel guilty. They shouldn't. Millions of babies have grown up perfectly well on formula milk, too, after all. And if you do have such trouble with breastfeeding that it is causing you distress – which you are communicating to your baby – it might be better to call it a day and bottle feed instead.

The benefits of breastfeeding are, however, that your colostrum and milk contain antibodies which can protect your baby from infections, together with all the nutrients he will need for the first four to six months of life. There are other plus points to breastfeeding, which health professionals often forget to mention as they are so anxious to impress on new mothers these two major health benefits of breastmilk.

* Breast milk is always available and it is free. You won't need to spend either money on buying infant formula feed, sterilizers and bottles, or time on mixing and warming up these feeds, washing and sterilizing bottles and teats.

* Breastfeeding is a gentle and rewarding way for you and your baby to get to know and love each other and will help the bonding process between you.

* Breastfeeding is a good way to help you get your figure back faster. Feeding 'fully' – i.e. on demand, day and night, as your baby's sole source of nourishment – uses up to 1,000 calories a day. And this can make satisfying inroads on 'pregnancy pile-on' – the fat stores laid down by your body during your pregnancy, which are easiest to lose in the first couple of months after the birth, after which they become harder to move.

* Breastfeeding helps your stomach get flatter quite quickly. Your womb, throughout pregnancy, has expanded from the size of a small muscular pear to something large enough to hold a baby, the placenta and amniotic fluid – quite a difference in volume. But the hormone oxytocin, which is involved in the 'let-down reflex' – the process by which your baby's suckling stimulates the release of milk from the milk ducts in your breasts – also acts upon your womb, causing it to contract and tighten, and so hastening its shrinkage back to its former compact size.

* Breastfeeding can be a good form of natural contraception if you do it *fully*. This might be especially useful if your religion frowns on the use of artificial contraceptive devices. Another hormone involved in milk production, prolactin, suppresses the body's production of oestrogen. Without oestrogen you will not be ripening an egg cell for ovulation. And no egg means no more babies

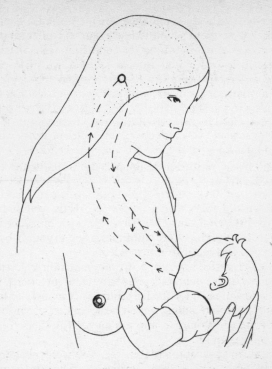

Milk is released from the breast when it is stimulated by the 'let-down reflex' (which can be triggered by anything from just thinking about breastfeeding to hearing your baby's cry). It is set off by the brain's pituitary gland which receives stimulation from the sucking and sends out a hormone called oxytocin – and it is this that makes the muscles surrounding your milk-producing glands squeeze out milk.

until the brakes are taken off your oestrogen production by stopping – or reducing – breastfeeding. Full breastfeeding is 98 per cent effective at preventing pregnancy (about the same as a diaphragm or an IUD). But if you want to be completely on the safe side, use an effective method of artificial contraception like the progesterone-only Pill instead. And beware of leaving too-long gaps between feeds, or skipping night feeds (when the most prolactin is released). Full means breast for EVERY feed – no bottles at all.

* Breastfeeding can be very effective at sending babies to sleep. This is partly due to the closeness and comfort it gives – but there's more to it than that. Recent Swedish studies have shown that breastmilk actually contains tiny quantities of a compound similar to benzodiazepine (the tranquillizer).

Who is doing it?

Around 60 per cent of mothers have at least one try at breastfeeding their babies. But there is a lack of support and encouragement – perhaps due to staffing levels, so that the hospital midwives are too rushed and busy to give all the help you need. Or different people tell new mothers different things so they get conflicting advice which is ultimately confusing. This means you often receive inadequate help with initial problems which, with friendly guidance, could have been sorted out easily. As a result many do not try breastfeeding again and only a quarter of mothers will still be breastfeeding four months later. But according to the World Health Organization, 97 per cent of women are physically able to feed their babies if they wish to do so.

How breastfeeding works

The milk in your breasts gets from the breast's milk-producing cells into your baby's mouth in the following way.

Any new mothers who are having initial difficulties with breastfeeding may find the following Four-Step Plan helps:

1. *Place a big soft pillow on your lap supporting the baby's weight so that your arms don't start aching and getting stiff (tension will transfer itself to the baby);*
2. *When offering your breast, turn his **whole** body towards you, not just the head;*
3. *Get as much of your nipple in his mouth as possible, and as much of the areola (especially the lower bit) as you comfortably can. And as you do, draw him towards you welcomingly. Even if your nipples are sore or your breasts tender, try not to wince or pull away when he latches on or the message he gets will be confusing ('Feed here – but I'd rather you didn't');*
4. *Try 'swapping' babies with a breastfeeding friend – her baby will know what to do, and it will show you you can do it; your friend can show your baby how to feed.*

1. STIMULATION, which can be anything from the sound of your baby crying or thinking about feeding your baby, to the warmth and sucking of your baby's mouth on your breast. The stimulation messages are transmitted to the pituitary gland.

2. THE PITUITARY GLAND (sometimes called the body's Master Gland because it controls so many things) receives these stimulation messages and then releases a hormone called oxytocin.

3. OXYTOCIN acts on the tiny muscles surrounding the milk-producing cells in each breast. They already contain milk, and the oxytocin causes the muscle tissue around them to contract, squeezing your milk from the milk glands into the reservoirs behind your nipples. You may feel this reflex at work as a tingling in your breasts and nipples, even as sharper little needle-like pains, or you may feel nothing at all. It may also produce what midwives call 'afterpains' in your womb for a few days as the oxytocin helps this contract efficiently back to its former size, but these will not continue for long.

Breastfeeding is natural, but . . .

Breastfeeding is natural, but that does not mean that it always comes instinctively. It is more of a gentle skill, which mother and baby can learn together – with a bit of help and support from all around them, from partner and father to local breastfeeding counsellor. Like any new skill, it does take a bit of practice, so don't be discouraged if you do not find it easy immediately. Keep at it, and ask for help (SEE HELPLINES) as soon as possible because most breastfeeding problems can be solved quite easily and quickly if you decide you really do want to feed your baby yourself.

The medical and self help advice for breastfeeding difficulties is the same, as a GP would refer a woman having breastfeeding problems to a specialist counsellor such as the community midwife or local NCT group for one to one help and advice, or offer similar advice himself or herself. A GP would not treat any of the problems we list here with drugs, and if the difficulties persisted, might well suggest giving up breastfeeding and opting for bottle feeding instead.

Breastfeeding problems and how to help

Problem	Symptoms and causes	Medical and self help
ACHING, FULL BREASTS	Usually due to engorgement, of which there are two types: primary and secondary. * Primary is caused by increased blood pressure and opening up your milk ducts. If you try too hard to regiment the intervals between feeds and to limit the length of feeds, as opposed to feeding 'on demand' for as long as your baby seems to want, you will probably get engorged. You may feel as though you have a temperature and your breasts might feel hard, lumpy and swollen. * Secondary is when your breasts seem to be making too much milk. Engorgement can sometimes lead to MASTITIS if not dealt with.	Feeding more often and for longer periods can help. It is also worth asking your midwife or local breastfeeding counsellor (see HELPLINES) to make doubly sure that your baby is latching on properly to your breast and is therefore able to take plenty of milk from it. If he cannot, this means too much is left behind, causing over-fullness. Cold compresses between feeds and warm compresses at the start of a feed help too. Speak to your midwife or breastfeeding counsellor about how often and when you are feeding your baby to see if a change in your breastfeeding pattern might help. If the engorgement is in the early days of your breastfeeding, when the rush of blood to your breasts is making them feel very hard and full, let your baby suckle at them fairly often to help relieve the pressure. The leaves of a cabbage, placed in the fridge to get cold, rolled with a rolling pin to crush them slightly so they release the enzymes they contain, then placed over your breasts under your bra are also, surprisingly, soothing for engorged breasts as you wait for your milk to come through. If your breasts are too full for your baby to latch on to properly, or the milk is coming in a large gush and choking him a little, express some by hand before you start each feed.

BLOCKED DUCT (a small red lump on the breast or a white spot on the nipple)

This can be caused by not letting the baby choose when to stop feeding, by missed or hurried feeds or by a segment of the breast not being emptied properly.

Feed from the affected breast first. You can encourage 'unblocking' by sitting in a warm bath, soaping your breasts to make them slippery and then using your fingers or a wide-toothed or Afro comb to smooth the lump towards your nipple, gently.

BREASTS: SMALLER AND LESS FIRM

After having breastfed for a few months your breasts may become smaller, as breastfeeding uses up the body's fat stores, including those which help give the breast its shape. (Breasts are two thirds fat, one third milk glands.) Its initial loss is most noticeable in the areas where it is less tightly 'packed', i.e. around the collar-bone, face and breasts. A rapid increase in breast size can cause them to sag after they return to normal if they are not adequately supported *all* the time.

The shaping of fat should return after 9 to 12 months after you have stopped breastfeeding if you are eating well. Protect the shape and 'free standing' firmness of your breasts by wearing a really good maternity bra (see HELPLINES) all the time if your breasts seem to need it, from around the 6th or 7th month of pregnancy – as well as day and night while you are establishing breastfeeding.

Bust exercises to strengthen the two sets of muscles supporting them (the pectorals and the platysma), done all through pregnancy and breastfeeding might help too.

CAESAREAN DELIVERY

One in nine births is by Caesarean. If it is carried out under general anaesthetic instead of an epidural it may take time for both you and your baby to come round properly. The baby may be sleepy at first and not suckling very well, so he will need very short, frequent feeds till this wears off. Also his weight, slight as it is, on your abdomen where your stitches are may be very uncomfortable, but with careful cushioning and positioning you can still breast-feed very successfully.

Use a large light pillow to cushion your abdomen, or a light polystyrene-filled baby sack like the Snugglesac (see HELPLINES). Also the 'American Football' hold is helpful – his legs tucked back under your arm on the same side that he's feeding from; or try feeding lying down comfortably supported by pillows. The Caesarean Support Network and your midwife will be able to offer you plenty of advice and help too (see HELPLINES).

Problem	Symptoms and causes	Medical and self help
CONFLICTING ADVICE	Though there may be more than one way to tackle a problem, it can be very confusing if several well-meaning people offer you breastfeeding advice – all of it slightly different – and very disheartening.	Pick one person you like and trust: your hospital or community midwife or local breastfeeding counsellor, your mother or a close friend who has breastfed, and stick with what they suggest instead of taking bits of advice from several different sources (unless you feel entirely confident using hints from different people).
EXPRESSING MILK	Many mothers find commercial hand-operated breast pumps rather difficult to use; and also find expressing milk a bit problematic at first.	A hired electric breast pump, which simulates the action of a baby suckling, is often easier to use (see HELPLINES). Ask a counsellor to show you how to use one then practise with it – as you would with any new gadget – and keep going back to your counsellor with any difficulties until you feel happy with the device. Expressing sitting in a hot bath makes the milk flow more freely (use a handpump or your own hands, not an electric pump). And you can often collect a lot of milk at each feed time by just wearing a plastic breast shield (shaped like a closed flying saucer with a pouring lip at the top and a hole to insert your nipple through) on your nipple, held in place by your bra when feeding the baby from the other nipple. Suckling often stimulates *both* nipples to produce milk – so this way you can catch the milk not being drunk and save it in a sterile feeding bottle in the fridge for 2 or 3 feeds until you have enough for a full feed later, perhaps given by your partner, at night.
INVERTED NIPPLES	Nipples come in all shapes, colours and sizes and because they contain muscle tissue they usually become erect when you are breastfeeding, sexually excited or plain chilly. Sometimes due to a very minor abnormality they will not protrude but that doesn't mean you cannot breastfeed.	Nipples will often become erect during pregnancy on their own. If yours remain inverted, it can help, from your fifteenth week of pregnancy, to wear small breast shields of rubber, glass or plastic over your nipple, under your bra, gradually building up the length of time you wear them. They are not uncomfortable, and work by producing a gentle suction to pull the nipple upwards and outwards.

You can also try the Hoffman Technique: placing a finger either side of your areola and stretching the nipple twice a day throughout pregnancy.

MASTITIS (red patches on the breast; temperature and 'flu-like feelings)	Can be caused by a blocked duct not being cleared (not infective) or a bug entering the breast tissue (perhaps via the baby's nose – infective), usually during a stay in hospital. In case your mastitis is not being caused by an infection (and most of the time it is not), try encouraging any lumpy areas of your breast to drain by stroking them towards your nipple, and expressing milk (some women find this easier in a warm bath or shower) can help. Try this before accepting the usual broad spectrum antibiotic treatment and waiting 12 to 24 hours to see if it improves. You should also treat, as for a blocked duct.
MILK: LACK OF	This is the main reason why mothers give up breastfeeding. But you can usually tell if your baby *is* getting enough milk: * if he has 6–8 really wet nappies per 24 hrs * if he is gaining 4–7oz a week or 1lb a month * if he is feeding eight or more times in every 24 hrs (this applies to breastfeeding, not bottle) * if he seems healthy, has a good skin colour, is filling out, and is alert, active. Things that can reduce your milk supply are: * supplementing your baby's milk with juice or water * giving your baby a dummy * wearing nipple shields * rigidly scheduled feeding times * shortening feed times * tension and tiredness and overactivity on your part To help increase your milk supply: * try and feed frequently * offer both breasts at each feed (although some babies only fed from one breast at a feed – do make sure you offer the other breast) * only give your baby breast milk * avoid dummies and bottles * drink lots of liquids and eat a good diet * get plenty of rest and quiet * strong sucking by the baby will mostly empty a full breast in only 10 minutes. But since the first milk to come out is thinner and more thirst quenching, and the later milk richer, it is important that the baby feeds for that 10-minute period to ensure he's getting both sorts.

Problem	Symptoms and causes	Medical and self help
	* not eating enough nutritious food (you also need plenty of carbohydrates: the one time in your life when you can eat more without getting fatter – up to 1,000 extra calories a day) * smoking and some medication * some oral contraceptives can affect milk production and quality (ask your doctor or family planning clinic). The progesterone-only Pill (POP) is the one recommended if breastfeeding * not drinking enough liquids – try and drink lots every time you are thirsty.	
MILK: 'SPURTING' FROM YOUR BREASTS	This may happen if you become sexually excited and if your breasts are caressed, as well as when your baby cries or you think about feeding him. It is very normal but some couples can find it a bit disconcerting at first.	To prevent a gush of milk immediately, cross your arms and press the heels of your hands firmly against your nipple and areola. As an added precaution you could make love after you have fed your baby recently, or express some of the milk from your breasts beforehand if you and your partner find this a problem. Breast pads can also absorb any sudden spurts and leaks (carry a supply about with you and change them as soon as they become damp).
MILK: WON'T START FLOWING	This can be a common problem when you first begin to breastfeed but it rarely lasts for long. Usually the colostrum, which is your baby's very first natural food, will begin to appear in response to his suckling as soon as he shows an interest in it after delivery. (The hormones involved in the delivery of the baby and placenta get it going.) It changes to a whitish-blue milk in 2 to 4 days. If the flow won't begin it is possible that there are still some small pieces of placenta in your womb (ask the obstetrician).	If it won't start flowing at all, warm compresses like hot flannels or a covered warm hot-water bottle help, as does sitting in a warm bath with the water level up over your breasts, or lying on elbows and stomach in the bath dangling your breasts in the warm water. An electric breast pump (available in hospital or from NCT counsellors (see HELPLINES) may also help. Also make sure you have plenty of peace and quiet when you begin to breastfeed. Try some of the relaxation exercises you learned during your pregnancy classes. Check your feeding position.

NIPPLES, CRACKED

Keep the nipple and areola area softened with oil but free from dampness. Rubbing in the rich, fatty 'hind-milk' which flows towards the end of a feed helps too, as it moisturizes.

Kamillosan cream, which contains Calendula and is available from major chemists like Boots, is also helpful. Put it on each feed, after drying the nipple gently with cotton wool or soft tissue. It also helps to change breast pads as soon as they get wet or damp. And, when taking the baby *off* your nipple, gently insert your little finger into the corner of baby's mouth to break the suction if he is still gripping it.

Damp breast pads which are keeping the nipple wet may be responsible (especially those with plastic backing which keeps in wetness – Eveflow have non-plastic backed ones). (See also **Sore nipples** below.)

NIPPLES, SORE

If it is actually painful and makes you wince, it may well be that the baby's mouth is not quite positioned properly on your nipple: ask your breastfeeding counsellor to help. Ignore advice about getting 'all your areola in the baby's mouth'; if your areolas are fairly large this is physically impossible! Try and get the bottom part in, with your baby's bottom lip curled back and down. You could also try 'Resting and Expressing': not breastfeeding directly but expressing milk instead for your baby's feeds for a couple of days. See also **Cracked nipples**, above.

The action of a baby suckling for up to half an hour on each one at two or three hourly intervals can make your nipples a bit sore until they get used to it. This tenderness should disappear after 2 to 3 weeks. If, during your pregnancy, you think your nipples areola looks at all dry, try some of the above-listed moisture creams.

SLEEP, LACK OF

If you can encourage your baby to accept your milk from a bottle as well as your breast, perhaps your partner could do one night feed, e.g. the last one before retiring for the night (say at midnight or 11.30 p.m.). You could go to bed after your 10 p.m. feed and have four uninterrupted hours until 2 a.m. or so. Or, though 'mixed feeding' (bottle and breast) is frowned upon by purists, the practicalities of the matter are that one bottle feed out of, say, eight feeds in 24 hours is unlikely to do the baby any harm (though some say it *can* upset their digestion, watch carefully to see if it does).

This is a problem every new mother faces no matter how she feeds her baby, because babies have tiny stomachs when they are very young so cannot take much at a time and need very frequent feeds. The frequency depends on your baby, as they are all different, but this will mean anything from every two hours to every four. Intervals between 'on demand' feeds vary though – and may be longer at night.

Problem	Symptoms and causes	Medical and self help
		So if you cannot express enough for a night feed and badly need some unbroken sleep, consider your partner giving the baby a small bottle feed of formula milk. The earlier a baby is introduced to a rubber teat – and to occasional formula milk – the more easily they tend to accept it. Often this is done in hospital where the nurses can, on request, take the baby into the night nursery for a few hours to give you some sleep and either give the baby expressed, or a small amount of formula, milk.

Warning: *increased* amounts of mixed feeding will reduce your milk supply as it will lessen the baby's sucking on your nipple, which is what stimulates milk production. If in doubt, speak to your health visitor.

It also helps if you can snatch naps during the day and sleep or doze whenever your baby does. It is encouraging to know that many babies are sleeping through the night after as little as three months.

Also, the hormones released when you breastfeed tend to make you sleepy, so going back to sleep again may be less of a problem than you thought.

Why not take your baby into bed with you and allow him/her to feed whilst you nap at the same time? |
| 'TIED' TO YOUR BABY | If you are his sole source of nourishment it could mean that you cannot leave your baby for more than two or three hours at any one time.

Further, breast milk is easier for babies' immature digestive systems to deal with than formula milk, which takes them longer, so breastfed babies do tend to need to be fed more often. | With a little pre-planning, and by getting your baby used to accepting your own expressed milk from a bottle from another trusted person (e.g. a regular babysitter, mother's help, nanny, your husband, your mother), you can most certainly disappear for an evening out, half a day's shopping or an outing whenever you like. But as the way the baby strafes milk from your nipple with his tongue and the way he sucks it from a bottle teat differ, it will initially take a bit of practice and patience to get him used to both – |

but the earlier you start the more likely the baby is to accept it (see **Lack of sleep**, above). You might also find your baby will not accept milk via a bottle from you even with practice but will from a babysitter, partner or your mother.

But get breastfeeding established, so that it is easy and no fuss for either of you, before trying milk in a bottle given by another person, or the baby will get confused.

When you go out, do look for the Babycare symbol, which shows somewhere you can breastfeed and change your baby in comfort.

VAGINAL DRYNESS

No one usually tells mothers who intend to breastfeed that the additional prolactin your body produces to help make your milk can have the additional effect of suppressing oestrogen production. This means that while you breastfeed, your vagina will be dryer than usual, which may make lovemaking less comfortable.

This only lasts while you are breastfeeding and your vaginal secretions will return to normal after you stop. This side effect can be dealt with easily by using a bland lubricant like KY jelly, applied before you make love. Consider using a tiny bit around your vagina and labia every day anyway as dryness makes the area a bit more prone to infections like thrush.

Complementary therapy

Complementary therapies tailor their treatments very much to the individual: the precise nature of the treatment you receive will vary, depending on your medical history, symptoms, lifestyle, etc. The following information indicates the *sorts* of things a therapist is most likely to do or recommend. Do not be surprised if they feel you need something slightly different. This section is meant purely as an indication of likely treatments; it is not meant as a DIY guide to the medical uses of the different complementary therapies.

Acupuncture

Acupuncture can help about fifty per cent of women who have difficulty starting the flow of milk at the beginning of breastfeeding. For women who have insufficient milk for the baby's needs, the right acupuncture points can increase the absorption of materials needed for milk production. Points which increase the necessary hormone activity, plus acupressure and perhaps dietary advice, are also useful.

Aromatherapy

Essential oil of lavender works to help increase the let-down reflex, which establishes breastfeeding. It is also an antiseptic and will aid healing of small cracks or soreness on the nipples, if diluted in oil and applied directly. The baby will not be affected. Women with insufficient milk may find essential oil of jasmine or aniseed will increase milk production and, at the same time, help them relax. Your individual needs *must*, however, be assessed by a qualified therapist.

Clinical nutrition

Breastfeeding mothers need a diet which includes four to six ounces of protein daily. High-protein drinks mixed with apple juice may be suitable.

For those having difficulty in establishing milk flow, the nutritionist may recommend cider vinegar and honey, and a reduction in intake of Vitamin B6 (B6 tends to contract the mammary ducts). A supplement containing Vitamins A, B12 and C, iron and kelp can help milk production. Breastfeeding mothers should not smoke.

Homoeopathy

Homoeopathic remedies for breastfeeding difficulties are prescribed according to the reason for the problem. For example, if no milk appears after the first day, Agnus castus is prescribed; if the flow starts and suddenly stops, asafoetida is suitable. If milk decreases due to anger, chamomila is used; if the cause is shock, aconite. Tincture of arnica can be applied to painful, swollen nipples, but if the nipple skin is broken or cracked, Calendula should be used. Painful nipples when feeding can be helped by Croton Tig; general feeding difficulty by Phellandrium.

Medical herbalism

Possible remedies to encourage milk flow include goat's rue, fennel or chaste tree. These can also be used to increase the amount of milk produced, once the flow has started – goat's rue increases both the volume of milk and the proportion of milk solids; chaste tree has an effect on hormone levels.

Sore or cracked nipples respond to Calendula ointment, which soothes and heals.

Osteopathy

Some of those who have difficulty in establishing a flow of milk might find that manipulation in the thoracic spine will encourage the let-down reflex, by removing blocks in the sympathetic nervous system.

Breastfeeding helplines

Association of Breastfeeding Mothers
Sydenham Green Health Centre, 26 Holmshaw Close, SE26 4TN (081 778 4769)

BLISS (Baby Life Support System)
17–21 Emerald Street, London WC1N 3QL (071 831 9393)
They can advise, help and support with all aspects of caring for premature babies, including breastfeeding or feeding them with your own breast milk by some other method.

Caesarean Support Network
2 Hurst Park Drive, Huyton, Liverpool L35 1FT (051 480 1184)
Offers information and help on all aspects of a Caesarean delivery, including the most comfortable ways to breastfeed, so that the baby is not pressing down on the stitches in your abdomen. Will supply several books and leaflets, including 'Breastfeeding After a Caesarean'.

La Leche League
LLL GB, Box No. 3424, London WC1 3XX (071 242 1278)
Information, encouragement and local support groups and counsellors for women who wish to breastfeed. Counsellors can often help you over the phone, and will also visit you in your home.

National Childbirth Trust (NCT)
Alexandra House, Oldham Terrace, London W3 6NH (081 922 8637)
Organize a network of ante-natal classes and breastfeeding counsellors who will advise over the telephone or come directly to your home. NCT also hire out electric breast pumps, several helpful leaflets and publications on breastfeeding. They supply the MAVA range of pregnancy and nursing bras, as well as nightwear whose front opening designs make breastfeeding easier at night. Ring for a catalogue – local counsellors can often come and fit you at home.

Specialist products and services
Egnell Ameda Limited
Freepost 6424, Taunton, Somerset, TA1 1BR (0823 336362)
Manufacturers of an electric breast pump and a battery-operated breast pump, which is small enough to carry around with you.

Evenflow
The Mentholatum Company, Longfield Road, Twyford, Berkshire RG10 9AT (0734 340117)
Produce 'Natural Mother' breast pads (approximately £2.50 for 48), which contain no plastic backing which might keep in dampness and lead to sore nipples.

John Lewis plc department stores carry a good range of nursing bras. Trained saleswomen will professionally fit you (free of charge) in the privacy of a cubicle, to ensure you get exactly the right size after your baby is born.

Further reading
Breastfeeding Your Baby by Sheila Kitzinger (Dorling Kindersley)
Breast is Best by Dr Andrew Stanway (Pan Books)
The National Childbirth Trust and La Leche League also have very useful leaflets on specific aspects of breastfeeding difficulties and how to solve them. Contact them by telephone or by post (see above for details).

Cancer

What is it?

Cancer is a disease of the cells. Instead of growing, dividing and reproducing in the usual orderly, controlled way as and when they need to, somehow the process gets out of control and the biological brakes stop working properly, so the cells *carry on dividing*, and develop into a lump called a tumour.

Tumours can be either benign or malignant. A benign tumour's cells will *not* spread to other parts of the body and they are not cancerous. A malignant tumour's cells *are* cancerous as they *may* spread to other parts of the body if they are not prevented from doing so by medical treatment.

The make-up of the cells in a malignant tumour is a little different from those found in a benign tumour because a malignant tumour's cells have actually changed slightly from their original form. Tiny deposits of these changed cells can, if not stopped, spread beyond their original place and invade surrounding tissue. They can also get to other parts of the body, carried in the blood and lymphatic systems, to set up secondary tumours called metastases. Doctors can tell what sort of tumour it is by analysing cells taken from it, under a microscope.

Although cancer sounds like one single disease, it is not. There are actually more than 200 different types, all with different names, different causes and different treatments.

Usually these treatments involve: SURGERY – removing the cancer and the area around it; RADIOTHERAPY – killing the cancer cells with strong doses of X-rays; or CHEMOTHERAPY – killing cancer cells with drugs. Sometimes they will be used singly, sometimes all together.

One drawback about radiotherapy and chemotherapy is that they can destroy the beneficial disease-fighting cells (white blood cells) along with the cancer cells – leaving you more vulnerable to infections for a while.

But there are also two other brand new and very promising types of treatment.

GROWTH FACTORS are chemicals which control the growth of cells. They encourage them to start growing – and they stop them when the time is right. Scientists in several different places, including Manchester University, are working on using growth factors to stimulate the body to make more disease-fighting white blood cells. If used during chemotherapy or radiotherapy, these could help balance out the way white cells get killed. This would alleviate one of the major side effects of current cancer treatments.

MONOCLONAL ANTIBODIES are the other piece of good news in cancer treatment. These 'cancer bullets' or 'magic bullets', as they have often been called, are parts of cells which are made radioactive and are attracted, like a magnet, to a particular type of cell in the body (e.g. liver cells). When they reach, for example, the liver cells, the radioactive part then destroys the diseased liver cell without affecting any other body cells. They are a good way of delivering a dose of chemotherapy precisely where it is needed, and without affecting any other areas of the body in the process.

CONTINUOUS, HYPERFRACTIONATED ACCELERATED RADIOTHERAPY is a variation in the administration of radiotherapy. The usual way to give radiotherapy is in a series of once a day, four- or five-day sessions, for about four to six weeks. Breaks in between each session allow the rest of the body to recover. Now, however, work is going on at some major hospitals, like the Mount Vernon in London, where doctors are giving long, uninterrupted sessions of radiotherapy, for twelve consecutive days, three times daily. The dose given in the thirty-six sessions is equivalent to a dose given once a day, five times a week, for four weeks. Each session lasts almost the same length of time as it would if it were given once a day (about 30 seconds), with no breaks. The results seem to be good, as the cancer cells get less chance to recover between sessions. Initial work is being done with lung cancer, and some head and neck cancers.

Breast cancer

Please see WHAT IS CANCER? on pages 67–68 for further details on the nature of cancer, the way it behaves, and encouraging news of the successful new treatments being developed to fight against it.

What is it?
Breast cancer is a malignant growth in the tissues of the breast. Different names are given to it, depending on which type of cells within the breast it develops from (see **Medical terminology**, page 72). The commonest kind, adenocarcinoma, grows from the milk-producing glands (milk lobes, see the diagram on BENIGN BREAST PROBLEMS). Around one in 12 women is likely to develop breast cancer at some time in her life. But it is very much a curable disease and can be detected in its earlier stages either by your examining your own breasts every month or by a breast X-ray called a mammogram which can find even the smallest lumps that an examination by hand cannot.

Who is at risk?
According to Cancer Link, the following categories of women are thought to be most at risk from breast cancer, women who:
* have a history of breast cancer in their immediate family, e.g. mother, aunt, sister (see HELPLINES, the Family Breast Cancer Clinic);
* start their periods young;

* have a late menopause;
* are on, or have taken, a high oestrogen ('high dose') Pill. These have mostly been phased out now and women are offered the new lower dose ones instead. If you are still on one, ask your doctor why and request a lower dose;
* have a history of breast cysts (Canadian study, 1992);
* have had benign breast disease such as cysts or fibroadenosis;
* are childless;
* eat a high animal fat, high protein, high carbohydrate diet;
* bottlefeed their babies, if they have them, rather than breastfeeding them. Breastfeeding seems to have a protective effect, probably because prolactin, produced during breastfeeding, suppresses oestrogen production and oestrogen has a stimulating effect on breast tissue;
* are overweight;
* are over the age of 40, when the risk increases;
* are white, white women being more at risk than other races;
* are of higher social class;
* are long-term Pill users. There has been a vast amount of controversy over the past twenty years as to whether Pill use in general affects women's predisposition towards breast cancer. It's thought not that the Pill causes breast cancer but that it may aggravate early cancer that is already there or strengthens a person's existing predisposition towards breast cancer. The most recent study (by the Medical Research Council, the Imperial Cancer Research Fund and the Cancer Research Campaign, in 1989) suggested that a woman runs a greater risk of developing breast cancer under the age of 36 if she has been taking the Pill for four years or more. Her chances, say the survey, go up by an additional 40 per cent if she's been taking the Pill (high dose or lower dose) for four to eight years and under the age of 25.
* women with silicon gel breast implants (controversial).

Symptoms and detection
For 90 per cent of women the first sign of breast cancer is a small lump in the breast or armpit. In nine cases out of every ten, the lump will prove to be benign (a benign tumour, fibrodema or cyst) rather than cancer. But for that one case in ten, it will be cancerous. The sooner the lump is detected the easier it will be to diagnose and treat, so try and get into the routine of checking your breasts every month for the early signs of potential trouble.

Checking your own breasts
While examining your breasts, don't only look for lumps and bumps. The overall checklist for symptoms is:

THE BREAST
* Changes in shape or size
* Enlarged veins
* Thickened looking areas
* Dimpling or squashiness of the skin
* Any ulceration on the skin

THE NIPPLE
* Unusual discharge of any sort, other than that which you may have around period time anyway (some women have a small amount of clear discharge from their nipples)
* Nipple turning inwards (inverting)
* Lumps, thickening or swelling

THE ARM/ARMPIT
* Swelling in your upper arm
* Swelling or lumps in the armpit

The upper outer 'quarter' of the breast and in the armpit tends to be the place where tumours appear the most often (about 50 per cent of the time), followed by the nipple area (about 20 per cent).

Mammograms
The medical method of lump detection is by mammogram, a sort of breast X-ray, which can detect very small changes in the breast long before you could see them or feel them.

If you are aged between 50 and 64 the Department of Health is now offering them free every three years. If you are not in this age group, but are concerned because you have a family history of breast cancer, or many of the other predisposing factors, try and have regular mammograms anyway if you possibly can. Your GP may recommend you for free ones if you explain that you feel you are at risk. If you cannot get one on the NHS, ask your GP or the Women's National Cancer Control Campaign (WNCCC) (see HELPLINES) if they can recommend a screening centre near you. Prices are from around £60 to £120. Women over sixty-five can also have free mammograms, but are not 'called up' as often.

Mammograms involve gently flattening the breast as far as possible between two X-ray plates to take the required picture. This can be uncomfortable for some women, and it may not be suitable for women with very firm breasts (e.g. women under 35) or very small breasts.

What happens if you find a lump?
Get the best treatment available – as fast as possible.

Go to your GP immediately, say you have found a lump by examining your breast yourself and ask either to be referred to a hospital, where the specialists can do a mammogram, or have the lump 'aspirated'.

A MAMMOGRAM will confirm the pressure of the lump, and get a clearer idea of its shape and size (for older women over 35).

ASPIRATION is a test which uses a fine needle to draw some of the cells or fluid out of the lump, so it can be sent off to a laboratory for analysis.

Do not be fobbed off by vague reassurance, such as being told it is 'probably' a benign breast problem like mastitis. It probably is, but it is your right to insist on being properly checked out.

Should your GP be unwilling to refer you to a hospital for a proper medical examination, phone one of the help associations like BACUP (British Association of United Cancer Patients) or CancerLink (see HELPLINES) for advice.

Alternatively, if you have enough money – around £60 to £120 – you could choose to have an investigation (a mammogram or an aspiration of the lump) carried out immediately and privately by a private hospital. Again, the help associations could tell you how and where to find a suitable one.

THE CHRONOBRA is a new way to check for pre-cancerous breast lumps. Currently being developed at Glasgow University, it is literally a bra with heat sensors that use differences in temperature within the breast to detect pre-cancerous areas, which can then be treated before they become a problem.

The private route
If you need to find a private centre to do a lump aspiration or mammogram for you, or if your GP is unwilling to arrange one on the NHS, the following strategy should help.
1. Call the WNCCC, CancerLink, BACUP or one of the private medical insurance companies such as AMI, PPP or BUPA listed in the phonebook.
2. Say you have a breast lump needing investigation and ask them for the telephone number and address of a private hospital in your area where you can get a mammogram or aspiration done.
3. Ask to speak to the hospital administrator, who usually handles things like details of costs for tests and operations, and who can put you through to the person who can make you an immediate appointment.
4. Request an immediate appointment.
5. When you go for your test, ask when the results will be ready (if specially requested they can be in two or three days). Ask for the name of the doctor who will give you the results, explain them to you and advise on any further action you may need to take.
6. Ring on the appointed day and ask to speak to the doctor concerned. Discuss your results, and ask for a copy of them to be sent to you that day so you have them in writing.
7. If the result is that you do have a cancerous lump, ask the doctor to refer you back into the NHS system immediately or return to your GP the next day, with a copy of your results, and ask him to refer you to an NHS surgeon. It is your right to do this, as cancer treatment is classed as emergency treatment and therefore qualifies for high priority on the NHS.

Your test results and what they mean
If you see a copy of your results from a test done on the NHS, or when you see the results from your private test, they will describe – if you have a cancerous lump – what type of tissue the tumour is in and how far advanced it is. It helps to understand a bit about the terms that might be used. It is always a good idea to ask for a copy of your results, whether they are from an NHS or private source, as you may want to discuss the treatment or options with one of the help associations, or seek a second opinion.

Remember, if you do have a problem, then the success rates for operable

71

early (Stage One) breast cancer are excellent – some 90 per cent of women are alive and well ten years after such an operation, though the survival rate does begin to fall for the later stages of the disease.

Medical terminology written on your results
Words meaning the type of tissue the cancer is in:
* Carcinoma: in the lining tissue of the lobes of the breast;
* Adenocarcinoma: in the gland tissue of the breast;
* Sarcoma: in the muscle tissue surrounding the breast;
* Some types of breast cancer are called 'oestrogen dependent', meaning they are affected by the amount of oestrogen in your body.
   Words which explain how advanced the cancer has become:
* Stage One: the tumour is inside the breast, but not 'fixed' to the muscle wall of the chest (you can move it with your fingers). It may also affect the skin of the breast;
* Stage Two: There are cancerous cells in the breast; also small lumps which feel like hard peas around the armpit area (or in the neck), which can be moved about under the skin with the fingers (these mean the lymph nodes there are affected too);
* Stage Three: The lump in the breast has become 'fixed' to the muscular wall of the chest – you cannot move it about with your fingers. There are small lumps under the armpit meaning the lymph nodes there are affected, and the skin of the breast may also be invaded and ulcerated;
* Stage Four: The breast lump is fixed to the chest wall; there are fixed lumps under the armpit, meaning the lymph glands there are affected; also the lymph nodes around the neck, and above the collar-bone may be affected; and the skin may be ulcerated.
   Terms meaning 'size of the lump':
* T1: less than 2cm across;
* T2: between 2cm and 5cm;
* T3: 5cm or more;
* T4: a tumour of any size which has become far enough advanced to attach itself to the chest wall and not be movable by the fingers.

Terms explaining the state of the lymph nodes:
* N0: no enlarged ones;
* N1: some enlarged affected ones in the region associated with the breast on the same side of the body as the breast tumour, but they can be moved about underneath the fingers;
* N2: the lymph nodes are fixed in position and cannot be moved about;
* N3: there are fixed, affected lymph nodes under the arm, above and below the collar-bone, and the arm might be swollen up.
   Terms for whether cancer has spread to other parts of your body or not:
* M0: it has not;
* M1: it has.

RESULT READING. If, for instance, your results said 'Stage One, T1, N1, M0'

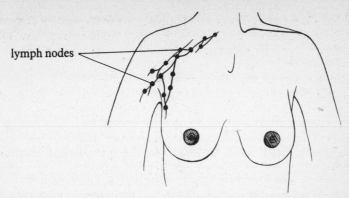

lymph nodes

Diagram of the breasts, showing where the lymph nodes are. If they feel lumpy or hard, see your GP.

you would know this meant, when translated: 'The tumour is a very early one. There is a lump in the breast, some swollen affected lymph nodes on the same side under the armpit, but the tumour is less than 2cm across and cancerous cells have not spread to any other parts of the body.'

The treatments
The next step is surgery to remove the cancerous cells, possibly followed by radiotherapy, chemotherapy or hormone therapy; or a mixture of all three, to make sure the problem does not return. The exact mix of treatments depends on what sort of lump you have.

Some women prefer to place themselves entirely in their doctors' hands and let them make the decisions. Others may prefer to become more involved with the decision making about their treatment. If you would prefer the latter, ask your doctor about the sort of treatment he plans for you – and why. Write down a list of questions you would like to ask – and the answers you get to them. It is only too easy to forget certain things if you are getting a lot of important information at once, or to forget to ask something you especially wanted to know when there is so much to check on. No matter how small something seems, if it is bothering you – do ask.

IS THIS REALLY NECESSARY? Perhaps you are not happy about the treatment suggested for you. Maybe the doctor is recommending a radical mastectomy and you are not entirely convinced this is necessary. You are entitled to a second opinion. Either ask the surgeon to recommend you to someone else, or ask your GP to do it.

Unless the tumour is progressing unusually rapidly or is extremely advanced, you do have time for this. Another week or so will make no difference to the eventual outcome of your operation and it may well be worth a few more days to ensure that you are satisfied with the treatment being suggested.

If you need someone to talk to at this stage, take the details of your test results and telephone one of the help associations (e.g. BACUP or Cancer

Link, see HELPLINES) which are staffed by specialist medical personnel (such as nurse counsellors) who are experts in this area. You may also like a chat with one of them after you've got your second opinion and are weighing up what each of them has said to you.

It is usually not a bad idea either to think about the recommendations given to you by the consultants for a day or two, before making your decision.

A CONSENT FORM must be signed once you are happy that the treatment being suggested is the best one for you. Then the doctors can proceed. Make sure you fully understand what you are signing – ask for advice, if you feel you would like it, from one of the cancer help associations. There have been alarming stories of women who went into the operating theatre thinking it was just for a biopsy, only to come out again without a breast, because the surgeon decided to act straight away. To avoid any possibility of this you can request that any operations be done in two stages: first the biopsy, then, if found to be necessary after its results are known, a further operation a few days later, arranged with your full consent and knowledge. This gives you time to adjust to the idea or seek a second opinion if you wish to.

Surgery
Fortunately most breast surgery is minimal these days, as surgeons are much more concerned than they used to be about saving a breast if at all possible, rather than completely removing it. But remember, all operations need your consent, even if they are something minor like a biopsy. None of the following operations should be done without your written consent. Before the scheduled operation discuss with the surgeon what will happen if they find evidence that a more radical operation is necessary. Make sure they will not do it then and there, but will wait for a few days, having obtained your official consent first.

BIOPSY is where a small piece of your breast tissue is taken for very close examination while you are under general anaesthetic, to determine more about the sort of cancer you have and the sort of treatment which would help you the most.

LUMPECTOMY is the usual sort of operation for early stage breast cancer. It means removing the breast lump itself, together with some of the tissue around it. It is possible to do this for many women now, and because it takes away the least amount of breast it leaves the best cosmetic result.

SEGMENTECTOMY is a bit like a lumpectomy, but it means taking away more of the breast tissue so it will show more, especially in women who have quite small breasts. For larger breasted women it usually leaves a pretty good appearance and the site of the operation will not be too noticeable.

MASTECTOMY is the removal of the whole breast in women for whom the two more minimal operations above are not suitable. If you are advised to have a mastectomy and are not convinced that it is entirely necessary, or wish to

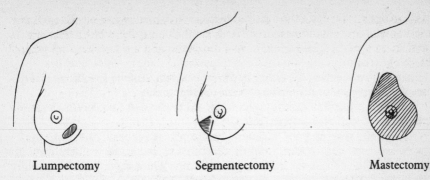

Lumpectomy   Segmentectomy   Mastectomy

Most breast surgery is kept to a minimum these days – the first two operations, Lumpectomy and Segmentectomy, are far more common than Mastectomy.

explore other possibilities which may mean saving more of your breast, you are entitled to get a second opinion (see *Is this really necessary?*). There are two types of mastectomy: i) a simple mastectomy, when only the breast tissue is removed; and ii) a radical mastectomy, meaning that the muscles on the chest wall underneath the breast are taken away too.

With any of these operations, from a lumpectomy onwards, the surgeon may also need to remove some of the lymph glands from under your arm.

After the operation you may need one or more of the following treatments to help make sure the tumour never returns.

Irridium wire treatment
Suitable for: treating an area where a smaller tumour used to be. Fine, radioactive wires are inserted carefully through the area to help kill any remaining cancer cells at the site. These wires are removed after a couple of days, and afterwards you might still have some conventional radiotherapy.

Conventional radiotherapy
Suitable for: treating cancer in specific areas. These are powerful X-rays which can kill cancer cells if they hit them during their vulnerable growing phase.

Taken as: several short bursts of four or five times a week, spread over a few weeks to help make sure all cancer cells are eliminated.

Side effects: include redness and soreness, and sometimes 'weepiness' of the skin in the area being treated, tiredness, itching in the area being treated, temporary loss of underarm hair, small red marks on the skin due to burst blood vessels and one breast sometimes becomes firmer than the other one.

Afterwards: you will receive a full check-up a few weeks after your radiotherapy treatment has been completed – usually after about 4 to 6 weeks – to see if you will need further treatment. If it has been effective, you will be asked to come back for regular check-ups to ensure the problem has not returned.

Chemotherapy
There are forty or fifty different types of chemotherapy drugs for cancer. Some

of them have unpleasant side effects, some a few, some none at all. They can be used singly or in combination with each other, and the sort of side effects depend on the types, and the mix. Ask the doctor about side effects before you begin the treatment, so you can take steps to alleviate any there may be.

Suitable for: treating the entire body, rather than just one specific site, if the cancer has spread, or may have spread, to other areas.

Taken as: injections and/or tablets once every three or four weeks, depending on the type of drug and its dose.

Side effects may include sickness, vomiting, temporary hair loss, burning when you pass water, mouth ulcers, and increased vulnerability to infection as the body's white blood cells (the one which fight infection) will be temporarily affected by the anti-cancer drugs.

Afterwards: you will have a check-up which may be a straightforward physical examination – the most usual approach – but may also involve a bone scan, and sometimes a liver scan or brain scan to ensure the cancer has definitely not spread elsewhere. Then check-ups six weeks later (when any chemotherapy side effects should be wearing off), and at two to three month intervals for the first year, then at six to nine month intervals for a further two years – and finally just one check-up each year, to ensure all is still well.

Hormone therapy
It is often given for ovarian, uterine and cervical cancer in the form of Hormone Replacement Therapy (HRT) if (as is often the case) the treatment involves surgery to remove the ovaries, and has brought on an early menopause. (See CERVICAL CANCER, CANCER OF THE OVARY, CANCER OF THE UTERUS and MENO-PAUSE.) For breast cancer, hormone therapy is used rather differently. Not as HRT but as a cancer fighting treatment in its own right.

Suitable for: cancers which are 'oestrogen dependent', where oestrogen actually encourages the tumour to grow. Other forms of hormone can be given which block oestrogen production in the body and stop it feeding the tumour.

Taken as: tablets or (usually) injection. Tamoxifen is the most common one given. Bromocriptine is also given occasionally, as it blocks the production of yet another hormone called Prolactin. Prolactin is produced when women are breastfeeding, but it is also made by the body in times of stress – for instance, when a woman is facing breast cancer surgery – and it, too, can affect the growth of cancer cells of certain types.

An alternative substance called aminoglutethamide also blocks oestrogen formation, and is best used for post-menopausal women who are still producing a little oestrogen, but not as much as pre-menopausal women. Another way of permanently stopping oestrogen production is to give the ovaries a small dose of radiation. But, unlike the drug methods, this is not reversible and will bring on a premature menopause in younger women, so it is an option that needs to be carefully discussed with your doctor and, if you wish, one of the professional counsellors at a help association.

Side effects. Drugs like Tamoxifen have the fewest, causing 'only' menopausal-style dryish skin and hot flushes in some of those treated. Removing or irradiating the ovaries would have all the effects of an early menopause if you have not already had yours naturally, and this may be especially distressing for women who were hoping to have children.

Afterwards: you would usually be on a hormonal programme for two years or more, with check-ups every 6 months.

New: The Imperial Cancer Research Fund is running a trial to use Tamoxifen as a cancer-*preventing* measure.

What about breast reconstruction?

Many women feel after breast surgery that they do not want any more medical treatment on the breast. Others are reminded of the operation and their illness every time they get undressed, and find it causes problems within their sexual relationships. Reconstructing as lifelike a breast and nipple as possible is a solution (results can be very good indeed). Some surgeons are happy to do this when they perform a mastectomy. Others are not happy about giving a woman an implant because they feel it will make detecting any recurrence of the cancer very difficult. Research by a team of specialists in St Louis, in America, suggests that silicon gel can mask developing breast tumours. They found, however, that other substances, such as peanut and sunflower oil, did not obscure detection when scanned. They are now wondering if breast implants of liquid with similar properties to living tissues might be a better option.

* For a lumpectomy or segmentectomy: often the area removed is so small that it can be carefully stitched up and little difference will be noticeable.

* For a simple mastectomy: some of the breast's skin and nipple will be left in place to cover the implant – a strong bag of silicon gel which is soft, malleable and feels, when placed under the breast skin, just like a natural breast. The implants come in many different sizes to suit your personal requirements.

If there is not enough skin left, skin grafts can be taken from other parts of your body – or the existing skin could be slowly stretched until it can comfortably cover a silicon implant. It is also possible to reconstruct a nipple to look much the same as the one you still have on your other breast.

Fat from the abdomen or bottom may also be grafted into the breast, instead of using an implant, to reconstruct its soft, rounded shape.

Scars from the operation will be visible, but they fade a certain amount after the first few months, becoming paler, and will eventually become more difficult to see.

Breast reconstruction after mastectomy operations is free on the NHS. For further information, contact the Breast Care and Mastectomy Association or one of the cancer help groups (see HELPLINES). For updated information on the most recent breast reconstruction techniques it may also be useful to contact the Phoenix Appeal, a charity set up in 1989 to fund and carry out research into new ways to improve plastic and reconstructive surgery, including work on rebuilding breasts. (See HELPLINES.)

Reconstruction is not suitable for every mastectomy patient (e.g. someone who has had advanced cancer).

Self help

Please see SELF HELP FOR CANCER on pages 98–102 for advice and information on coping with cancer and its treatment.

Cervical cancer

Please see WHAT IS CANCER? on pages 67–68 for further details on the nature of cancer, the way it behaves, and encouraging news of the successful new treatments being developed to fight against it.

What is it?
Cervical cancer (CC) is cancer of the neck of the womb (you may be able to feel your cervix with your finger, as a rounded bump at the far end of your vagina). Of all the types of cancer in existence, this is the easiest one to detect very early on. You can do this simply by having regular smear tests to check for the very first signs of cell changes in your cervix. These can indicate the possibility of a problem there, even before it even gets the chance to turn into cancer.

Who is at risk?
The following things can increase your chances of developing cervical cancer:
* having several pregnancies;
* smoking;
* beginning to make love young (under the age of 15 or 16);
* having your first baby in your teens;
* using a high oestrogen pill. (These are not often prescribed these days, so if you are on one ask your doctor why, and request a change to a low dose Pill);
* your age. The older you are, the more likely you are to develop it. Around 75 per cent of women who do so are over 35, but it is becoming increasingly common in younger women, too. In the late 1960s about 10 per cent of the women who developed cervical cancer were under 35. Now the figure is nearer 25 per cent;
* certain viral infections in the genital area, like herpes and genital warts, are thought to be a factor. Three out of four of us do carry these viruses (though far fewer have any symptoms). But three out of four do not get cervical cancer – so they are possibly just one contributing factor among many. A number of experts do feel there is a connection between genital infections and CC. It is suggested that these viruses might themselves be causing some minor cell changes which could, if left unchecked, go on to turn into more substantial cell changes – and then, eventually, turn into the sort of changes associated with cancer.
* having many different sexual partners. The bad news about these viruses is that these doctors also feel that the more male sexual partners a woman has, the greater her chances of coming into contact with a viral genital infection, introduced into her vagina by her partner's penis. The good news is that the Imperial Cancer Research Fund is working to develop an anti-genital-warts vaccine (though it's not yet available), and that barrier methods of contraception like the condom and diaphragm offer considerable protection, too.

78

Symptoms

Most women do not have any. However, some may notice any of the following:
* bleeding in between periods (if you are still having them);
* bleeding from your vagina at any time (if you are no longer having periods);
* bleeding after intercourse.

Irregular bleeding has many other causes apart from the beginnings of cervical cancer. But it is still important to get this symptom checked out thoroughly by your doctor, so you can establish what is causing it.

Preventing it

Smear tests

You can detect cervical cancer very early on indeed, at the stage of the smallest of suspect changes in your cervical cells, by having frequent, regular smear or 'pap' tests. The earlier you can spot it, the milder – and more successful – the treatment is.

HOW OFTEN? At the moment the Department of Health recommends that women between 20 and 65 have a test every five years. Most clinics and GPs try to do them every three years. However this may not be often enough to protect you fully because:

1. It is possible for the slight and very early cell changes (called CIN 1; see **Medical terms** below) to seem to develop within a year into CIN 3 (more noticeable changes needing prompt treatment), although it is usually not as quick as this. This may be because a previous smear has missed something.

2. There are suggestions that there is a sort of cervical cancer younger women are developing which is more 'aggressive' (i.e. fast moving) than before. Again, this may be because a previous smear missed something: so a woman may seem to have progressed from having slight cell changes to having more serious ones, very rapidly – when in fact the problem has been developing at the 'normal' rate all along and was just not detected.

3. Smear tests themselves are not always as accurate as they should be. Studies from London's Royal Northern Hospital have suggested that in the often understaffed and overworked NHS cytology labs, where smear tests are sent to be checked out, there is around a 30 to 40 per cent 'false negative' rate (i.e. missing something like an early cell change) or missed things like 'inflammatory' smears or early cell changes which could eventually, if not checked, lead to cervical cancer. ('Inflammatory' means that there is a small infection in your cervix – perhaps one so small that you have no symptoms for it and were not even aware of it.)

Therefore, to be on the safe side have a smear done every 18 months, so if anything *is* missed it won't have much time to develop into something more serious. Or you could have one yearly on the same day each year. Your GP or FPC will probably be able to give you one free every three years on the NHS. If you are in a high-risk group they may well be persuaded to give you a test every 18 months. If they will not do so, it is possible to get a smear test done privately at a charitable screening clinic (see HELPLINES) from as little as £15.

To further reduce the risk of anything potentially important being missed when you have a smear test there is a new check, called cervicography, which some clinics offer too (see HELPLINES). This involves taking a medical photograph of your cervix after having it swabbed in mild vinegar solution, which makes any abnormal areas show up far more clearly. It is painless, needs no anaesthetic and can be done in conjunction with an ordinary smear test. It only has a 'false negative' rate (i.e. something's been missed) of 3 per cent. The drawbacks are that it is not available on the NHS, it costs around £25 and is so sensitive it has a 'false positive' rate (i.e. it detects a problem when there isn't one) of 25 per cent.

Your test results and what they mean

1. Always chase up your results after you have had a smear test. Do not assume no news is necessarily good news. Results have been known to get lost on their way to the lab, or on the way back, and yours may be one of them. Ask the clinic who did the test for you to give you a likely date when the results should be back and ring on that day to check. Keep ringing back if necessary until you get the results.

2. Get things in writing. Ask for your results, or for details of the findings, to be sent to you in a letter. Do not make do with 'They're OK' from the receptionist on the telephone. Having them in writing in front of you will be invaluable if you wish to discuss them with another doctor, clinic or help organization.

This is especially important if you go for a private test. Some private screening clinics do not follow up their service very well (i.e. they do not bother to explain your results to you properly or advise you on any further action needed – such as appropriate treatments and where to get them).

3. Make sure you understand what has been written on your results form, and are quite happy about it. If you are concerned about something make an immediate appointment to discuss your results fully with your own doctor (you can do this even though you had the tests done privately).

4. If you are still none the wiser after discussing your results, call up one of the help associations. They are specially trained to answer queries, and will be very happy to do so (see HELPLINES).

Medical terms: on your results form

When it is sent back to you you might find the form has been extensively filled in, using some of the terms given below. You might also see the words 'Negative', 'Positive' or 'Abnormal' scrawled across it. This can be worrying if it is either of the last two – but they are extremely unlikely to mean you have cervical cancer. 'Abnormal', for instance, may well just mean you have a small infection in your cervix. And 'Positive' could mean anything from a very early pre-cancerous cell change to 'Carcinoma in Situ', meaning many changed cells in one place. This is a condition that is not yet cancerous but it requires immediate treatment to make sure it does not become so.

NEGATIVE 'all's well'. Other terms, which also mean negative, or which may have been written on the form as well, include:

* CERVICAL EROSION/ERODED CERVIX: this is a harmless condition, common if

you are pregnant or taking the Combined Pill. It just means that the soft 'columnar' or glandular cells, which are usually tucked away in the cervical canal that leads up into your womb, are turning up on the outside of the cervix instead. Because they are soft, and have a good blood supply, they 'break' easily and may cause blood spotting after making love. You can treat this easily with Cryotherapy.

* SCANTY OR INADEQUATE SMEAR: means the smear sample was too small to be used for testing; that it had dried up by the time it got to the lab; or that it was a bit too dry when taken (if, for example, you have passed your menopause and have less vaginal secretions than before). You need another.

* ENDOCERVICAL OR ECTOCERVICAL CELLS seen: this just means they found the cells they wanted to test.

* NO ENDOCERVICAL OR ECTOCERVICAL CELLS seen: means they did not find the cells they needed to test. You should go back and have another smear test done. They might use a cytobrush – looking like a surgical mascara brush – which is better for collecting the cells required.

* BORDERLINE: Not quite normal but too mild to need to be called CIN 1. Will need watching though.

ABNORMAL could mean anything from an infection (which perhaps you never realized you had) or CIN 1 (the earliest cell changes, which could eventually lead to cancer if untreated), to Carcinoma in Situ. The form may explain itself further – if the test has discovered an infection – with the words:

* INFLAMMATORY SMEAR/VIRAL SMEAR/ATYPICAL CELLS seen. All these terms refer to the fact that there is a small infection there that needs treating. This has caused very minor cell changes, which should disappear when the infection is treated with drugs. Your clinic or GP will probably recall you in about three to six months to make sure the trouble has cleared up.

* HPV: has nothing to do with HIV or AIDS. It stands for Human Papilloma Virus (or genital warts). This can be transmitted sexually but may also lie dormant for years and be nothing whatsoever to do with your present partner. Any actual warts can be treated by freezing the area or by applying chemical paint; but they may return, as it is not possible to treat the virus itself.

POSITIVE will usually be explained further (see terms below). The severity of the condition depends on how marked the changes in the cervical cells are, and how deeply they have spread into the skin covering of the cervix. You may see the following terms to describe the situation:

* CIN 1/MILD DYSPLASIA/MILD DYSKARYOSIS: means very slight cell changes, affecting only one third of the thickness of the cervix's covering layer. A clinic may leave this to see if it will resolve on its own. You should be asked to go back to the clinic or GP who did the test within 3 to 6 months to make sure it has cleared up, and, if it has not, be given appropriate treatment.

* CIN 2/MODERATE DYSPLASIA/MODERATE DYSKARYOSIS: means moderate changes in the cervix's cells, going deeper than CIN 1 – two thirds of the cervix's covering layer will now be affected. It should always be treated, and promptly.

* CIN 3/SEVERE DYSPLASIA/SEVERE DYSKARYOSIS: means substantial cell changes, affecting the full thickness of the cervix's covering layer, but still 'pre-cancerous' (i.e. not cancer yet). It will always be treated as soon as possible. CIN 3 is also sometimes called Carcinoma in Situ, but they both mean very similar things, and treatment for both should be immediate.

There are two further categories: MICRO INVASIVE, which means the condition is cancerous but only just, and has spread only a very little way into the cervix. This can often be treated with just a cone biopsy. There is also INVASIVE cancer (see **Treatment for cervical cancer** below). Do not feel that cancer of the cervix always means some form of hysterectomy. In its early form (Micro Invasive), it is not necessary.

The treatments for pre-cancerous cervix problems
Before you have any treatments, you will have an investigation procedure called a colposcopy, where a doctor takes a much closer look at your cervix using a form of medical microscope, then removes a small piece of cervical tissue with tweezers and takes it away for careful analysis. This does not need an anaesthetic, and you can have it done as an out-patient.

Depending on the results of the analysis, the doctors will then go ahead with the treatment most appropriate for you. CIN 1 (if treated), CIN 2 and CIN 3 may all be dealt with by any of the following.

Cryotherapy
Cryotherapy freezes the abnormal cells with a special probe. It is done on an out-patient basis and does not need an anaesthetic. It is suitable for CIN 1 (if treated) and CIN 2.

Laser treatment
This treatment uses lasers to remove abnormal cells from your cervix. You need no general anaesthetic for this either, and it can often be done on a day-patient basis. It is suitable for CIN 1 (if treated), CIN 2 and CIN 3.

Electrodiathermy
This means using a high-temperature probe to kill any abnormal cells. It needs to be done under a general anaesthetic, so you would usually stay in hospital overnight, though some clinics now do it on a day-patient basis. It is suitable for CIN 1 (if treated), CIN 2 and CIN 3.

Cone biopsy
This operation, which is carried out under a general anaesthetic and usually means a short stay in hospital, can be a method of diagnosis and also a treatment in itself. It involves removing a cone-shaped section of the cervix for examination, taking away all the abnormal cells there in the process. The cervix will usually regenerate and regain its former rounded shape following a cone biopsy.

This operation may weaken the cervix a little and affect its ability to remain shut during a pregnancy, keeping the developing foetus safely inside. You may

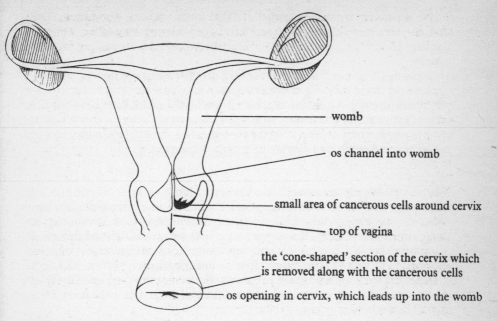

womb

os channel into womb

small area of cancerous cells around cervix

top of vagina

the 'cone-shaped' section of the cervix which is removed along with the cancerous cells

os opening in cervix, which leads up into the womb

What a Cone Biopsy involves:

require a few stitches when you do become pregnant, to help the cervix stay closed against the growing weight of the baby.

The treatment for cervical cancer

If the cell changes in the cervix have progressed far enough, the condition will have become cervical cancer rather than a CIN stage or Carcinoma in Situ. There are many very effective ways to treat this, but first the doctors need to see what stage of development the cancer has reached, so as to pick exactly the right treatment. They classify the stages of cervical cancer like this:

* Stage 1: cancer is just in the cervix (see also MICRO INVASIVE) cancer, above;
* Stage 2: it has progressed past the cervix itself, possibly into the vagina;
* Stage 2a: it has spread upwards to the outer casing of the womb (parametrium);
* Stage 2b: it has reached the connective tissue of the womb;
* Stage 3: it has spread to the pelvic wall, and perhaps also to the lower third of the vagina;
* Stage 3a: it has reached the pelvic wall.

TESTS WHICH CAN BE DONE to check how far the condition has spread. You may have any – or several – of the following tests:

* Blood tests to check how well the liver and kidneys are working;
* A chest X-ray;
* Pelvic ultrasound to measure exactly the size and position of the cancer;

* An examination under anaesthetic (EUA) which allows a surgeon to examine you very thoroughly internally, without causing you any discomfort. They will usually do a D&C to get a sample of the cells from your womb lining, to check them;
* A pelvic CT or CAT Scan to build up a detailed picture of the size and exact position of the cancer (see CANCER OF THE OVARY, page 88);
* An Intravenous Urogram to show up any abnormalities in the kidneys or urinary system (see CANCER OF THE OVARY, page 89);
* A Lymphogram to check for any problems in the lymph nodes of your abdomen and pelvis (see CANCER OF THE OVARY, page 89).

Surgery
Surgery physically removes cancerous areas, plus any areas which may also have been slightly affected. For Stages 1 and 2 (unless it is at the very early Micro Invasive stage) this usually involves removing the womb, cervix and, if it has progressed to there, the upper part of the vagina too. If your cancer has developed beyond Stage 2 you will need surgery, to remove any of the areas affected. This would probably involve the Fallopian tubes, ovaries, part of the vagina and the lymph nodes in the pelvis, as well as the womb and cervix. At more advanced stages, any other organs affected would have to be taken away, too.

Most women are able to go home about 10 days after their operation. You may need some extra practical help at home, or someone professional to talk to about any worries you may have. Get advice from your hospital social worker while you are still in hospital (the nurses will ask her to come and see you while you are in bed if you let them know). There are also several excellent trained helpline organizations like BACUP and CancerLink (see HELPLINES) who will be very happy to help you over the phone or to send someone round to see you at home.

You will have a check-up about six weeks after the operation.

If you have had a hysterectomy (removal of womb), see HYSTERECTOMY, page 225, for information on how to overcome the problems which may be associated with the operation, how to recover as quickly as possible, helpful exercises, ways to make lifting and carrying easier, going back to work and beginning lovemaking once more.

WILL THE OPERATIONS AFFECT MY SEX LIFE? You might have heard many old wives' tales about what a hysterectomy may do to your sex life. But generally speaking they are untrue. Most women welcome affection, love and cuddling *especially* at this time and enjoy close physical touch and contact with their partner. Couples will often seek advice about resuming their sex life again, too.

The truth is that, unless the whole of the vagina has had to be removed, which is extremely unlikely, the operation will make no difference to your ability to have sexual intercourse or any other forms of sexual stimulation, nor to your enjoying it as much as ever. The part of the female sex organs that gives the most intense pleasure is the clitoris, and this will not have been touched by surgery. Also, the most sensitive part of the vagina is the outer two thirds

84

furthest away from the cervix, and this also usually remains untouched. The area that is generally removed is the cervix itself and the top of the vagina (perhaps the upper third or, in some cases, two thirds) with the far end carefully stitched up. The operation in no way affects a woman's ability to have an orgasm either.

Fortunately, because the vagina is made of folds of stretchy skin, and also because it lengthens and swells when you are sexually aroused, the fact that it is shorter than it used to be when unaroused makes very little difference to having intercourse. However, the more that has been removed the more gentle a male partner would need to be, especially at first.

If the area of vagina remaining is fairly small, and if you or your partner might welcome any further advice or information, you can get help from an association called SPOD (the organization to aid the Sexual and Personal Relationships of People with a Disability). Don't be put off by their name. Though you are most certainly *not* disabled, it may be helpful to speak to sympathetic professionals (just over the phone if you wish) about the many ways in which you and your partner can still continue to enjoy a very satisfying physical relationship together.

Radiotherapy
This may be given either before surgery or after surgery for cervical cancer. It can be used internally or externally, depending on the size and position of the tumour.

GIVEN EXTERNALLY your treatment will be very carefully planned and it may mean a few visits to the X-ray department before the doctors decide exactly where to target the X-rays to kill the cancer cells. Marks will be drawn on your skin to show the radiotherapist exactly where to direct the rays, and the treatment will probably be given as a series of three- to five-day sessions.

GIVEN INTERNALLY an applicator like a tampon, containing a radioactive substance, will be inserted up through your vagina so it rests next to your cervix. It is put in place under a general anaesthetic and you stay in hospital while it is left there for a few days, delivering its high dose of radiation exactly where it is needed most – at the site of the cancer itself – without being weakened by having to go through the abdominal wall.

Sometimes an implant containing a very high dose of radiation will be used instead, but left in place for only a few hours, rather than a few days.

Side effects include redness and soreness where the radiation comes into contact with the skin, possible slight scarring of the vagina which may cause some initial problems when you resume intercourse later on, a burning sensation when you pass water, tiredness and diarrhoea.

Suitable for targeting a specific area very accurately.

Chemotherapy
This treatment uses drugs to kill cancer cells and is suitable for use after surgery, not as a 'first line of defence' treatment, in case the cancer has spread,

or may spread, to other areas. It is given as injections or pills, over varying periods of time.

There are many different types of anti-cancer drugs, some of which have side effects, some of which have none. They may be given singly, or as a combined anti-cancer cocktail. The side effects depend on the type of drugs you are taking, and in what combination. Please ask your doctor to tell you exactly which drugs you will be taking and what side effects you can expect from them, so you can take measures to minimize any unpleasant side effects as far as possible.

Side effects may include a sore mouth and mouth ulcers, tiredness, hair loss (it grows back later), nausea and vomiting, a temporary reduction of the normal blood cells in your body which makes you more vulnerable to infections for a while, anaemia and bleeding. Most of these side effects can be offset with other drugs such as antibiotics, anti-sickness drugs, and possibly blood transfusions if your normal cell count drops too low.

Hormone treatment
With cervical cancer this is not an anti-cancer treatment, but is used to offset potential side effects of treatment. If your ovaries need to be removed, or you have extensive radiotherapy and have not yet been through your menopause naturally, you will unfortunately do so now.

A natural menopause takes place when the ovaries gradually slow down, then stop producing oestrogen around your late forties or early fifties. If you no longer have ovaries to make the oestrogen, you will experience the menopause early, with its symptoms of hot flushes, dry vagina and dry skin. However, if you do experience menopausal problems, there is no reason why you should have to put up with them until they go away (this might take months or even years). Instead it is possible to replace the oestrogen your body is no longer making for itself with Hormone Replacement Therapy (HRT). This can combat all the menopausal symptoms, so if you wish to take it and continue it until the age at which you would have reached your menopause anyway – or, as many women now do, beyond that almost indefinitely – discuss it with your doctor. Check if there is any medical reason why you should not do this, and, if there is not, find out how to go about receiving expert HRT treatment for as long as you wish. (See MENOPAUSE, page 276 for further details.)

Self help
Please see SELF HELP FOR CANCER on pages 98–102 for advice and information on coping with cancer and its treatment.

Cancer of the ovary

Please see WHAT IS CANCER? on pages 67–68 for further details on the nature of cancer, the way it behaves, and encouraging news of the successful new treatments being developed to fight against it.

What is it?
The ovaries are small oval organs about the size of a pair of kidney beans, positioned roughly level with your navel, about two to three inches on either side of it (see diagram on page 95). They manufacture the female sex hormones oestrogen and progesterone, and once a month, either one or the other of them will release an egg which, if fertilized at the right time, will develop into a baby.

Cancer can occur in one of these ovaries, and occasionally it may do so in both.

Who is at risk?
Doctors are not sure exactly what makes one woman more likely to develop cancer of the ovary than another, but suggestions include:
* women who have never had children;
* women who are sub fertile;
* women for whom there may be a hereditary link between mother and daughter;
* women over 50 who have had their menopause.

On the other hand women who are on the Pill, or who have taken it, are less likely to develop ovarian cancer.

Symptoms
Most women with cancer of the ovary have no symptoms at all for some time, and often are unaware there is a problem until the disease is quite well advanced. When symptoms do occur they include:
* a bloated feeling in the stomach, and (often) feeling as if you do not want to eat much because of it;
* vague indigestion and sickness;
* a swollen abdomen due to a buildup of fluid by-products called ascites produced by the ovarian cancer cells. This usually happens in the more advanced stages;
* persistent constipation or diarrhoea;
* loss of appetite;
* weight loss;
* pain in the lower abdomen;
* occasional shortness of breath due to an accumulation of fluid in the chest (again this would mean the condition is quite advanced);

* occasionally, unusual bleeding from the vagina (between periods, if you are still having them).

Detection
Before ovarian cancer can be treated it must first be detected, and its seriousness assessed. These are the detection methods that would be used to see if you have definitely got it (your symptoms may have many other causes) and how developed it is. In fact the majority of lumps do turn out to be benign ovarian cysts, not cancerous growths (see BENIGN BREAST PROBLEMS, page 41). The cysts can often be removed leaving the ovary in place, depending on their size and whereabouts.

General examination
At the first sign of trouble, make an appointment to see your GP, who will do an internal vaginal examination to check for swellings and abnormalities. If you have any, he or she will immediately refer you to hospital where one or, if necessary, several of the following tests will be done.

Ultrasound
This is the test you would be most likely to have. It is a good way to see the shape and size of any swellings or lumps on your ovaries, but it is not very accurate when it comes to telling whether the lumps are harmless cysts or cancer.

Ultrasound uses sound waves to build up a picture of the inside of your pelvis and abdomen. Your bladder needs to be full to get a clear picture, and the scan is done by passing a small microphone-like device over your stomach.

You might have one or more of the following, too, though they are not so routine.

CAT scan
Sometimes called a CT scan, this is a sort of 3-D X-ray where several pictures are taken of the ovaries from different angles. The images are then fed into a computer to give a detailed picture of everything inside your pelvis and abdomen. CAT stands for 'computerized axial tomography'.

On the day of your scan you'll be asked not to eat or drink anything for about four hours, then you will be given a special liquid to drink, which shows up on X-rays. A similar liquid will also be passed into your back passage, and a tampon, soaked in the liquid, inserted into your vagina. All this ensures as clear a picture as possible.

Barium enema
This is an enema with barium in it, which shows up on an X-ray screen as it passes through your bowel, so the doctors can check if there are abnormal areas, and ensure any potential cancer has not spread. You may be asked to eat a light diet for a couple of days before having this done at the hospital. The day before the test you might also be given a laxative and asked to drink plenty of

liquids. For two or three days afterwards you may be constipated and need laxatives. You will also notice your stools are whiteish from the barium mixture.

Lymphogram
This is done to check whether or not the ovarian cancer has spread to the lymph nodes. The test is split into two parts:
1. At the hospital X-ray department an oily substance containing blue-green dye is injected into the lymph vessels. These form a network like the blood system all over your body, and are fed from lymph nodes or glands situated in various places, such as the folds of the groin, under the armpits and in the neck. The liquid passes through the nodes in your abdomen and pelvis, and its progress can be followed on an X-ray to see if it meets any obstacles or abnormalities on its journey. These might suggest small tumours blocking its way.
   The dye's colour can give your skin a slight greenish tinge (your urine may also be blue-green coloured) which may persist for days, even weeks. You might also experience some side effects such as flu-like symptoms and swelling in your legs immediately afterwards (sit with your legs raised and do not drive yourself home from the appointment).
2. You return for more X-rays and an intravenous urogram (see below), which takes about an hour.

Intravenous urogram
This is done to check for any abnormalities in your kidneys, bladder or urinary tract and it is carried out by having a dye mix injected into your bloodstream. From here it goes via your kidneys, and doctors can watch its progress on an X-ray screen to see if anything unusual shows up. The dye may make you feel a bit hot and flushed for a few minutes, but the feeling gradually disappears.

Fluid aspiration
If there is a build-up of fluid in your abdomen the hospital will want to check it to see if it is ascites fluid produced by cancer cells. A doctor will numb a small area on your abdomen with local anaesthetic, draw off some of the fluid with a syringe through your stomach wall, and take it away for examination under a microscope.

Laparoscopy
This is done under a general anaesthetic and means an overnight stay in hospital. The laparoscope is a thin, flexible micro telescope device which can be inserted into your abdomen via a small cut. It will enable doctors to have a very clear, close-up view of your ovaries when looking for signs of trouble there, and to take a small piece from one or both of them for examination in a lab (a biopsy).
   It is important to discuss with your surgeon before this operation what he or she will do if there are signs of cancer. He should undertake not to remove either or both of your ovaries then and there. It is not possible to be 100 per cent

sure that a growth is cancerous until the results of the biopsy come back from the lab, so this should never happen; but the fact remains that, on occasion, it has. It is important, therefore, to stress that should removal be necessary there ought to be a gap of a day or two between finding the cancer and taking away your ovary(ies). No operation should ever be done without your informed consent. This is especially important for younger women who have not yet begun a family but who wish to. No ovaries means no eggs – and therefore no babies – plus a sudden and premature menopause.

The future

Much of the new research work into ovarian cancer is looking into new ways of detecting it as soon as possible. One promising new method involves looking for the presence of a particular protein called CA125 which can be present 80 per cent of the time if there is an ovarian cancer there.

Another method looks at the image of the blood supply flowing through ovaries, on a scanner screen. The areas where the blood flow is restricted or blocked – often by a tumour – show up clearly on the screen as a different colour. This is called 'transvaginal colour flow imaging'.

The stages of ovarian cancer

For women who have ovarian cancer which has remained around the ovaries and not spread elsewhere, the chances of complete recovery and survival are good; they become less so as the disease becomes more advanced. This is how the extent of the cancer would be described by doctors:

* Stage 1a: there is a growth on one ovary;
* Stage 1b: there is a growth on both ovaries;
* Stage 1c: ascites, the liquid by-products from cancer cells, are present in the abdomen;
* Stage 2: cancer has spread from the ovaries to the pelvis;
* Stage 3: cancer has extended to the abdomen;
* Stage 4: secondary cancers (metastases) have appeared outside the abdomen area, in places such as the lungs.

The treatments

Surgery

The first line of treatment is surgery. How extensive this will be depends on how far the problem has progressed, but it usually involves removing both ovaries, the Fallopian tubes and the womb (a hysterectomy). In some mild cases, especially where the woman wants to have children and only one ovary is affected, only one ovary and the Fallopian tube leading to it would be removed, so she can still be fertile.

The surgeon may also take samples of tissue from any nearby lymph glands, either to make sure they are clear, or remove some as part of the treatment if they have been affected, too.

Sometimes information about the size and the spread of the cancer only becomes available during the operation. So it is very important to discuss the possible options beforehand with your surgeon, as no operation should be done without your consent (see **Laparoscopy**, above).

90

If the cancer has spread to the bowel, the piece affected can be removed and the two ends carefully rejoined.

Physically, the effects of the different types of operation are as follows.

REMOVAL OF A SINGLE OVARY: none.

REMOVAL OF BOTH OVARIES AND FALLOPIAN TUBES: generally, woman who have ovarian cancer will have already had their menopause – but this operation will mean a premature menopause for women who have not yet experienced it naturally. Side effects such as dry skin, dry vagina, hot flushes and perhaps decreased sexual desire, can all be treated with HRT if necessary (see MENOPAUSE, page 276).

REMOVAL OF OVARIES, FALLOPIAN TUBES, WOMB AND CERVIX (neck of the womb): for women who have not yet had their menopause this will mean a premature one whose effects can be alleviated with HRT (see above and HYSTERECTOMY, page 225).

AFTER A HYSTERECTOMY you may need a drip to replace lost body fluids and a catheter to drain the urine away from your bladder for a couple of days, and perhaps a draining tube to remove any extra fluid trying to collect around the wound itself.

Most women are well enough to go home about 10 days after the operation (see HYSTERECTOMY for information on some of the best and quickest ways to recover from the operation). You may feel, too, that you need some extra practical help at home, or someone professional to talk to about how you feel about the operation. If you feel you might, have a word with the hospital social worker before you are discharged: many are trained counsellors. (See also HELPLINES for all the support organizations who will also be glad to help you.)

IF YOU HAVE AN ACTIVE SEX LIFE. Women are usually advised to wait at least six weeks after surgery before having intercourse, to allow the wound to heal. If you feel loving, but are not yet ready to have intercourse as such, gentle manual or oral sex with a caring and emotionally supportive partner can be comforting and satisfying for both of you. Many women have no problem at all resuming an active sex life after a hysterectomy but others feel they need more time. Because the operation has removed some – or all – of the reproductive organs, it is natural to worry that it might have made a difference to your sexual identity. Younger women especially may find it hard to accept the implications of a hysterectomy, particularly if they had wanted children.

It can help enormously to discuss the way you feel not only with your partner, but with a trained counsellor, with one of the help groups or with a local support group of other women who have experienced the same thing, recovered well from it, but are able to understand very well indeed how you may be feeling. (See also HYSTERECTOMY and CERVICAL CANCER, pages 225 and 78.)

Chemotherapy
After your operation the hospital should want to follow up to see how you are

recovering, and to check for any recurrence of the cancer. The follow-up treatment can take the form of chemotherapy, radiotherapy or, sometimes, both.

There are 40 or 50 types of chemotherapy drugs, which may be given singly or in different combinations to treat the 200 or more cancers which exist. All of these drugs have different side effects, some of which are minor, some unpleasant.

Suitable for: treating the entire body rather than one specific site, if the cancer has spread to other parts of the body.

Given as: injections or tablets. A new way of giving chemotherapy is also being developed, in which the drugs are injected directly into the abdominal cavity as a sort of chemotherapy internal wash. This is called Intra Peritoneal Chemotherapy, and means any tumours (including the tiny 'seedling tumour' variety which may be multiple and quite widely scattered about) can be bathed well in a solution of anti-cancer drug. Side effects include discomfort, sickness and sometimes infections, all of which can be alleviated with drugs.

Between bouts of chemotherapy you will have rest periods of a few weeks to allow your body to recover from the side effects of the treatment. The number of chemotherapy courses you will have depends on what type of tumour(s) you have and how advanced they have become – as well as how well your body is responding to the drugs. Chemotherapy can be given as an out-patient treatment, but it may also mean spending a few days in hospital, depending on what sort of drugs you are being given.

Side effects can vary so much that you should ask the nurse at the oncology unit, or the oncologist himself, about the effects of the ones you are taking, so you can take steps to help offset them. But they can include nausea and vomiting, temporary hair loss, sore mouth and mouth ulcers, lowered resistance to infection, and tiredness, as the drugs can temporarily reduce the number of normal cells in your blood, too. During chemotherapy you will have your blood tested regularly. You will be given a blood transfusion if the normal cells in it are especially depleted, or antibiotics to help cope with any infections.

Check-ups: four to six weeks after all the courses of treatment have finished, to make sure they were effective. If they were not, more treatment will be given. If the original treatment was successful, however, your next check-up would probably not be for three months and then every three months for a year, then every six months for the next two years, to ensure the problem does not come back – or to catch it quickly if it does.

Radiotherapy
This is not given so often now for ovarian cancer, but involves high doses of powerful X-rays to kill the cancer cells when they are in their vulnerable growing stage. Treatment takes place in the hospital's Radiotherapy department and the first visit will be taken up with targetting exactly which area(s) need treating. Before the initial exploratory X-rays are taken a tampon will be placed in your vagina; and a liquid which shows up on X-rays passed up inside your rectum in the same way as an enema would be given (see **Barium enema**, page 88). This will give a very clear picture of what is happening in your pelvis

and abdomen. When the doctor is satisfied that the exact place and size of the tumour has been found, he will draw marks on your skin to show the radiographer exactly where the X-rays must be targetted.

Suitable for: cancer in a specific place.

Taken as: a series of treatments in several short bursts of a few days each.

Side effects can include redness and soreness where the X-rays hit your skin, nausea, dry vagina, tiredness, diarrhoea, cystitis and loss of pubic hair if the treatment area is low down on your abdomen (it grows back afterwards).

Hormone treatment
This is not a part of anti-ovarian cancer treatment as such (in the sense that the others kill cancer cells), but it is often used to offset the effects of having your ovaries removed and the premature menopause this brings if you have not yet had your menopause naturally. (See MENOPAUSE for further information on HRT.)

Self help
Please see SELF HELP FOR CANCER on pages 98–102 for advice and information on coping with cancer and its treatment.

Cancer of the uterus

Please see WHAT IS CANCER? on pages 67–68 for further details on the nature of cancer, the way it behaves, and encouraging news of the successful new treatments being developed to fight against it.

What is it?
The uterus (womb) is about the size and shape of a small pear, and made mostly of muscle. Its upper roundish part is the uterus proper, and the area just at the top of the vagina is the cervix or neck of the womb (which you may be able to feel as a smooth bump). The womb's lining, which sheds each month as a period bleed in women who have not had the menopause, is called the endometrium – and this is the area where cancers of the uterus usually begin.

The death rate from uterine cancer is low because it is very slow-growing and usually stays within the womb itself, rather than tending to spread easily to other parts of the body, as some cancers can. Two thirds of women with uterine cancer recover completely.

Who is at risk?
It is more common in women who:
* are between 50 and 70 years old. Only 20 per cent of uterine cancers happen to women who have not yet had their menopause;

* are overweight. This is because fat is one of our body's storage areas for oestrogen, which can influence the growth of some forms of uterine cancer;
* have had a late menopause – the oestrogen their ovaries produce will have affected their bodies for longer than in women who have an earlier menopause;
* have high blood pressure;
* have not had children (the risk is only slight);
* have diabetes;
* have had 'unopposed' Hormone Replacement Therapy (HRT). This means the sort of old-fashioned HRT that was given in the 1970s, and consisted of oestrogen only – without the balancing effect of extra progesterone. Oestrogen *plus* progesterone (opposed HRT) is the way it is given today;
* have had tamoxifen, the drug often given to women after surgery for breast cancer to stop it coming back. This *may* increase the risk of uterine cancer;
* are of certain races and living in particular areas. For instance if you are white and living in South East England you are 28 times more likely to develop it than if you are Nigerian. No one fully understands what environmental or dietary factors may be causing the differences.

Symptoms
Symptoms for uterine cancer may include the following:
* bleeding in between periods, for women who have not yet had their menopause;
* vaginal bleeding at any time, for women who have had their menopause;
* abdominal pain and discharge from the vagina (though this is not common, and may suggest the cancer problem is well advanced);
* a swollen womb, which can be detected by an internal examination from a doctor.

Doctors can tell how far it has developed by taking some cells from the womb lining by a D&C operation, then examining them closely in a laboratory, or by doing an exploratory laparoscopy operation (using a form of medical telescope while you are under a general anaesthetic) to have a close look at the area.

Detection
A D&C (dilatation and curettage)
This enables doctors to take a closer look at what's happening in the womb lining. If the problem is at a very early stage (Stage 1) it may also be all that's needed to cure it.

A Laparoscopy
This uses a medical microscope in the form of a thin flexible fibre optic tube, inserted either via the vagina and cervix or through a small incision in the lower abdomen, to see exactly what is going on inside your womb. This is not a treatment in itself, merely an exploratory measure.

The stages of uterine cancer
These are how the different stages of uterine cancer are described by doctors:
* 0: there are cancerous cells in the womb lining;

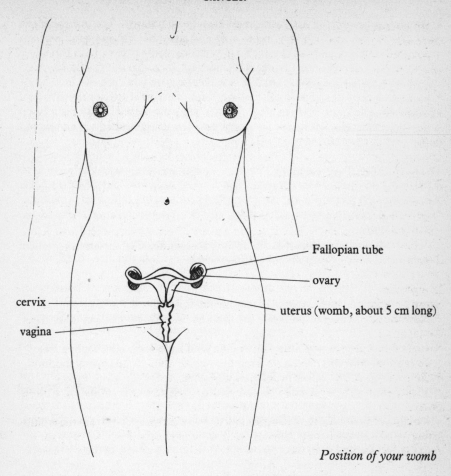

Position of your womb

* Stage 1: there is a tumour there, but it measures less than 8cm across, and it is inside the womb;
* Stage 1a: the tumour measures more than 8cm across, and it is filling up the womb cavity.
* Stage 1b: the tumour has reached the cervix;
* Stage 2: the cancer has spread past the cervix and into the vagina;
* Stage 3: the cancer has spread to the bladder, rectum, and/or lymph nodes around the groin or pelvic area.

The treatments
Surgery
A HYSTERECTOMY: is the removal of your womb and cervix, plus Fallopian tubes, and often ovaries as well. It would be used for Stages 1, 1a and 1b, where the cancer has stayed in the womb and has not spread beyond it. If the woman has not yet had her menopause, removing the ovaries means that she will go

through a premature menopause immediately afterwards. The menopause's side effects can include dry skin, a dry vagina, hot flushes and perhaps decreased sexual desire, all of which can be successfully treated with HRT (see MENOPAUSE, page 288 for further information). (See also HYSTERECTOMY and CERVICAL CANCER, pages 225 and 78, for its effect on your sex life.)

A new method of removing the womb-lining instead of the womb with heat treatment (called Endometrial Resection) is being pioneered. It can be done on a day patient basis, is far less traumatic and leaves the outside of the womb intact (see HYSTERECTOMY, page 225).

WILL THIS AFFECT MY SEX LIFE? There are a lot of old wives' tales about sex after a hysterectomy and cervix removal. Most women need love and affection at this time *especially*, and enjoy the close physical contact of cuddling and touching. They and their partners often seek advice about resuming their sexual relations, too.

The truth is that physically, the operation will make no difference whatsoever to your ability to have sexual intercourse as much as you like – or to enjoy it as much as ever.

The part of the female sex organs which gives us the most pleasure is the clitoris, and this is left completely untouched. The most sensitive part of the vagina is the outer two thirds, and this, too, usually remains untouched, even if the very top part may sometimes be taken away with the cervix at the top of it. If this is necessary, the far end of the vagina (nearest the womb) will be carefully stitched up.

Initially that will shorten the vagina a little. But it is lined with folds of stretchy skin and it lengthens and swells when you are sexually aroused anyway, so this does not create any problems when you resume intercourse. If more than a third of the vagina has had to be removed this will perhaps mean your partner needs to proceed especially gently at first, until it stretches.

This sort of operation does not affect your ability to have an orgasm either.

MORE EXTENSIVE PELVIC SURGERY may be necessary if the cancer has spread to other parts of the pelvis such as the bladder and rectum, and it could include removing more of the vagina, part of the rectum and several lymph nodes, as well as the areas taken away in a hysterectomy. This sort of surgery is called Pelvic Exteneration.

The side effects are the same as for a hysterectomy (see above) though depending on the extent of the surgery, it may mean that you and your partner have to adapt your love making around it. Much depends on the operation you need, so it would be helpful to speak to your specialist, and to one of the self help and support advisory services (see HELPLINES) so you can decide what is best for you personally. If the rectum is involved, it may make a difference to the way you empty your bowels (see HELPLINES).

Radiotherapy
This involves using powerful doses of X-rays to kill the cancer cells when they are at their most vulnerable 'growing' stage. It may be done before you have

your operation to shrink the tumour – in fact, in 50 per cent of cases this proves to be enough to clear up the cancer altogether. Or it may be done afterwards, as an extra back-up measure to try and ensure the cancer does not come back. Radiotherapy can be given internally, or externally.

INTERNAL RADIOTHERAPY will be done using a vaginal implant containing some radioactive material called Caesium. If you are having this before surgery, in order to try and shrink the tumour first, it will be placed, like a tampon, high up inside your vagina while you are under general anaesthetic. It will then be left there for about three days to deliver its cancer-killing radiation right where it is needed most.

If you have internal radiotherapy after surgery, this will also be done under general anaesthetic. A slim, hollow, plastic rod containing a narrow rod of radioactive material will be slid gently into the place where the womb used to be and left there for a few days to kill any cancer cells which could be lingering in the area. You would need to stay in bed in hospital with a catheter to drain your urine during this time.

Side effects can include soreness in the vagina and rectum, diarrhoea and cystitis, and may last for several weeks after your treatment has ended. There is also a risk of scar tissue forming in the area.

EXTERNAL RADIOTHERAPY only takes a few minutes each time and may be given in a series of bursts 4 to 5 days long, continuing over a period of up to six weeks.

The treatment is given at the hospital's radiotherapy department, and involves taking X-ray pictures to work out the exact position of the tumour first. This might include having a tampon soaked in barium (which shows up on X-rays) placed gently in your vagina. When the doctors are satisfied that they have pinpointed its exact shape and size and where it is, they will draw on your skin to show the radiographer precisely where to target the treatment.

Side effects can include soreness in the vagina and rectum, diarrhoea and cystitis, which may continue several weeks after your treatment has finished.

Hormone therapy
Some types of uterine cancer can be successfully treated with progesterone tablets.

Side effects should be checked with your specialist, as there may be none at all. It will depend on how your body reacts.

Chemotherapy
This is not usually used for uterine cancer, unless the hospital has tried other treatments first and found they have not worked.

Side effects vary a lot, depending on which drugs have been used. They range from sickness, hair loss and fatigue to diarrhoea and being more vulnerable to infections.

Jet washing
This is a new treatment often used in America but not widely available in the

UK yet, and it is an alternative way of doing the same job as a D&C does when it removes the lining of the womb. (This may help in itself, but is largely a diagnostic technique.)

It might be used when doctors suspect the possibility of a very early form of cancer of the endometrium starting. Jet washing, as its name suggests, involves using high-pressure water jets instead of a D&C instrument to remove the womb lining. Its advantages over a D&C are that your cervix would not have to be dilated very far, so it would not need a general anaesthetic and could be done on a simple daycare basis.

There are no side effects.

Self help

Please see SELF HELP FOR CANCER on pages 98–102 for advice and information on coping with cancer and its treatment.

Self help for cancer

After surgery

AFTER A MASTECTOMY avoid stretching and lifting during your recovery period (check how long with your doctor, as the time span varies). Then begin daily gentle exercises, which the hospital physiotherapist will show you, to ease your muscles and ligaments back into use. The Breast Care and Mastectomy Association has information on additional exercises for women who have had all types of breast surgery, also advice on swimwear, nightwear, lingerie and artificial breast shapes (see HELPLINES).

AFTER A HYSTERECTOMY exercises like gentle pelvic tilts and knee rolling can help strengthen your stomach muscles from the very first day after the operation. Then, when you have had your stitches removed, you can move on to other gentle ones such as 'hip hitching' and head raising. (See HYSTERECTOMY, page 225, for advice on exercises, dealing with wind and other side effects, how best to cope with lifting, returning to work and doing housework.) The Hysterectomy Association and the Association of Chartered Physiotherapists in Obstetrics and Gynaecology have additional information on exercises, ways of walking and standing which may be very useful (see HELPLINES).

After radiotherapy

Problem	*Self help*
ITCHING SKIN around area treated	* Bathe the area with cotton wool or lint soaked in a very mild solution of sodium bicarbonate (check this is all right with the radiographer first, as sometimes they prefer you not even to wash the area during treatment). Measurements are 1 teaspoon sodium bicarbonate in a tumbler of water that has been boiled and left to cool. * You could also take very diluted salt baths (warm, not hot), but again – check with the radiographer first. See also **Soreness** below.
ACCUMULATION OF WASTES from destruction of cancer cells	* This can make you feel unwell. Drink lots of plain liquids to help the kidneys eliminate increased wastes.
SORENESS around area treated	* If it is your breast and/or armpit, wear a large soft man's cotton handkerchief over the area to stop bra straps and cups rubbing. Hold it in place by Micropore tape (not elastoplast, as the zinc in it will react with the radiation from the radiotherapy treatment). * Wear very soft, loose-fitting cotton clothes, perhaps with raglan sleeves. * You may also wish to go without a bra for a while. * If the area treated is your stomach, pelvis and abdomen wear loose dresses rather than skirts or trousers with waistbands, which may rub the irritated area; also very loose cotton pants, or bikini briefs that do not come over the area treated. See also **Itching skin** above.
TIREDNESS	* Get as much rest as you feel you need, especially if you are working as well as going to hospital treatment appointments. The trekking to and fro will tire you. Do not necessarily expect to be back to your old energy level for a few months after the treatment ends. Remember also that the treatment may well go on working in your body for up to several weeks after your sessions end, and can initially make you feel worse. * Arrange lifts or taxis wherever possible; take afternoon naps; if you feel like returning to work, do so part time until you feel stronger. * Ask social services about additional help in the house while you recover; or enlist friends, family or (if you can afford it) a cleaning person to help take any pressure off you.

BURNING URINE/CYSTITIS (see CYSTITIS, page 182)	* This can be helped by drugs – ask your doctor. Some over-the-counter treatments are also pretty good – and cheaper than prescriptions. * Drink lots of plain liquid to dilute your urine.
DIARRHOEA	* Eat binding foods such as eggs if you feel you can. If not, ask your radiographer for anti-diarrhoea drugs and a diet sheet that will enable you to follow a really gentle, bland eating programme. * Your anus may be sore from the diarrhoea so it can help to rinse the area, pat it dry and apply a gentle cream like Savlon or zinc oxide each time you empty your bowels.
DISCHARGE after internal radiotherapy	* Use soft sanitary pads, not tampons.

After chemotherapy

Problem	*Self help*
SICKNESS	* The hospital will be able to give you anti-sickness drugs. You may also find that Sea Bands help. These are small elasticated wristlets with a plastic stud on the inside worn at the base of both wrists. The stud presses on the acupressure point called the Nei Kwan, and can reduce feelings of sickness by affecting the middle ear (which contains mechanisms for controlling things like balance and nausea). Trials have shown that they are between 70 and 80 per cent effective at reducing sickness associated with chemotherapy (see HELPLINES).
LOSS OF APPETITE	* If you don't feel up to eating, high nutrition drinks containing protein, vitamins, fat, minerals and carbohydrates such as Complan and Build-Up (from the chemist) can be a great help. * After your treatment has finished and you begin to feel your appetite returning it may be helpful to eat 'stodgy' high-calorie foods for a while. Many are fairly bland but will help you regain lost weight.
HAIR LOSS	* Though this is only temporary, it can be very upsetting. Fortunately it is possible to get some very good-looking wigs (which do not have a give-away 'wiggy' appearance) on the NHS. Wig bars at major department stores like Selfridges can be useful for experimenting to see what suits you best. A shop called Hair Raisers in London specializes in real hair and good-quality fake hair wigs, and though they usually supply the hairdressing trade they are happy

to help private customers. (See HELPLINES for free mail order catalogue.)
* Soft scarves twisted African or gypsy style around the head can look very good too, as do soft towelling turbans.

SORE MOUTH, mouth ulcers   * Careful oral hygiene helps, as do regular medicinal mouthwashes (ask your radiographer for advice).

In general

You might well feel especially low when your treatment comes to an end. Suddenly the activity of the last few weeks stops, and the medical attention and encouragement from hospital staff ceases. It might feel as if there is nothing much left for you to do now but go home and worry about the problem recurring. Every ache may seem like a warning that the trouble has started up again (especially the ones you get in the middle of the night when everyone else is asleep).

* TALK to friends, family – let them know how you are feeling.

* CONTACT a Helpline for an informed but friendly and sympathetic ear.

* RING UP A SUPPORT GROUP formed by other people who have had, and recovered from, cancer. It may be very helpful and comforting to talk to people who know exactly how you feel and understand from personal experience. One of the Helplines could put you in touch with your nearest group, or put you in contact with another woman who's had a similar operation to yours, on a one-to-one basis.

* SEEK COUNSELLING. If you can't ask for extra support and advice now, when can you? You may be especially worried about the effect that a hysterectomy or the loss of a breast could have on your relationships. Many women are worried that their partners might reject them physically and yet most find their fears are unfounded, and that working through the problem with a partner in fact brings them closer together than ever.

* GIVE VENT TO YOUR FEELINGS, be they anger ('Why me, anyway?') resentment, fear, guilt ('If I hadn't . . . maybe this would not have happened'), withdrawal and isolation ('Just leave me alone please'), uncertainty ('Will the cancer come back?') and sense of loss (if your womb or breast was removed).

* PRACTISE RELAXATION. It is *deep* relaxation techniques which can be very valuable – not just sitting down and putting your feet up with a cup of tea in front of the TV. A hypnotherapist or yoga teacher could show you how to do this easily and effectively, as could specialist relaxation classes (see HELPLINES). Do the relaxation exercises every day.

* VISUALIZATION TECHNIQUES involve literally visualizing or 'seeing' yourself feeling better. Many experts are now convinced that it can prove very helpful for people with cancer, or for those who have had it and are actively doing all they can to stay well. Groups such as New Approaches to Cancer and the Bristol Cancer Help Centre both recommend and teach visualization. Again, a hypnotherapist, yoga teacher or a spiritual healer (see HELPLINES) could teach you visualization quite quickly, and it would be up to you to practise it yourself at home – best done together with the relaxation techniques.

* SPIRITUAL HEALING. A growing number of doctors take the mind/body connection so seriously that there are currently many hospitals running controlled trials to see if healing really does help. These are notably pain clinics like the Walton Hospital's in Liverpool, arthritis clinics such as the Leeds General Infirmary's, and AIDS programmes – including the ones running at St Stephen's and St Mary's Hospitals in London, plus several centres specializing in cancer treatment. According to the Confederation of Healing Organizations (the umbrella body for registered healers) the initial results are most encouraging.

If you decide to go to a healer check with the National Federation of Spiritual Healers for a properly registered person in your area (see HELPLINES). Healing is a very calming and pleasant experience, involving the placing of the healer's hands on you; the use of what they say is another source of power. The healing energy or power passes from its source through them. Some refer to that power as God, others as the 'power of nature' or *chi*, 'life force', or just plain 'energy'. It can be tapped into and passed on to you, to help your body mobilize its own healing defences. Many healers do not charge any money, others can charge up to £10, £15 or £20 a session.

* FOOD. If you find you have lost weight during your treatment you may want to build yourself back up with high carbohydrate stodgy foods. But when you are back to near normal weight slowly try and change the way you eat so that you are doing so as healthily as possible. Gradually move over to eating more lean meat, fish, cheese, eggs, salads, raw vegetables and raw fruit, wholemeal products like wholemeal bread and pasta. Consider careful mineral and vitamin supplements too. It may be helpful to ask a nutritionist about this – your GP can refer you to an NHS one – as a tailored programme would be far more use to you than a box of pills off the shelf at random.

* PREMATURE MENOPAUSE. See MENOPAUSE, page 276 for information on HRT and CANCER OF THE OVARY and CANCER OF THE UTERUS, pages 87 and 93, when cancer treatment might result in premature menopause.

Complementary therapy
Complementary therapies tailor their treatments very much to the individual: the precise nature of the treatment you receive will vary, depending on your medical history, symptoms, lifestyle, etc. The following information indicates the *sorts* of things

a therapist is most likely to do or recommend. Do not be surprised if they feel you need something slightly different. This section is meant purely as an indication of likely treatments; it is not meant as a DIY guide to the medical uses of the different complementary therapies.

Complementary therapists in the UK make no claims to cure cancer or to prevent its recurrence after treatment. What certain therapies do claim to do is *help* the body fight the disease, and *help* prevent or slow down its return after orthodox treatment. And certainly they can lessen many of the unpleasant symptoms associated not just with cancer but with its treatment.

If you want to try complementary therapy, tell your doctor in advance. The complementary practitioner should also discuss with you what orthodox treatment you've received or are going to receive. This is important in order to prevent a mismatch of orthodox and complementary medicine which might make problems worse – instead of improving them.

BREAST, CERVICAL, OVARIAN AND UTERINE CANCERS
Acupuncture
Acupuncture at appropriate points can help relieve pain. Reports from China indicate that acupuncture has, by promoting the production of the body's own anti-cancer substances, slowed or reduced the growth of cancers in up to twenty per cent of cases. This research has not been replicated in the UK. Chinese acupuncturists also claim that acupuncture boosts the body's immune system to speed the healing process after surgery (in thirty per cent of cases).

The use of anti-depression points and tranquillizing points has been very successful in combating fear and depression in cancer patients.

Some of the unpleasant side effects of orthodox chemotherapy and radiotherapy can be reduced by acupuncture. These include sickness, tiredness, lack of appetite, and lowered resistance to general infection.

Aromatherapy
Aromatherapy can provide help and support for cancer patients – with certain provisos. Essential oils should not be used during, or immediately after, chemotherapy. And massage may speed the spread of cancer cells through the lymph and circulatory systems.

So, for people with cancer in the early stages, aromatic bath blends or room aerosols (with an air pump) are the best treatment. They help you relax and induce a sense of well-being.

For patients in the terminal stages of cancer, aromatherapy massage is of great benefit – again, for relaxation and well-being. Aromatherapy is widely used in hospices.

Essential oils which help fight fear and depression include rose, bergamot and geranium.

Oils to use in the bath to help relieve symptoms of tiredness and lack of appetite after chemotherapy or radiotherapy might include rosemary, bergamot, sandalwood, neroli, melissa. Fennel and chamomile may help nausea. The aromatherapist would blend these oils to meet the patient's individual needs.

Clinical nutrition
Amino acids (parts of proteins) can be very useful. Cancer pain can be helped by daily doses of phenylalanine, a natural painkiller. Tryptophan, also in daily doses, activates the pineal gland which produces serotonin, a brain hormone which reduces pain.

Phenylalanine, tryptophan, cysteine, glutamic acid, and valine all taken together, can help reduce or slow the growth of cancer, both by fighting the cancer cells and by stimulating antibodies.

Reducing foods containing serine (wild game, pork, luncheon meat, duck, cottage cheese, wheat germ, sausages and turkey) also helps to strengthen the immune system.

To help restore the immune system after surgery, vitamins (including the B complex) and minerals (including calcium and zinc) can be taken in combination.

Sickness, tiredness, and lack of appetite (after chemotherapy or radiotherapy) and skin soreness (after radiotherapy) can all be helped by the clinical nutritionist, who will choose the right substances to meet each individual patient's needs.

Homoeopathy

Homoeopathy, in combination with other therapies, can be of great use in detoxifying and stimulating the immune system. But it's very important only to have experienced prescribing by a qualified homoeopath.

Certain remedies can be offered, individually or combined as a complex remedy, to activate the body's defence mechanisms – for example, Galium aparius, Galium album, Sempervivum tectorum, Clematis, Echinacea and augustifolia.

For specific cancers, other remedies are prescribed: for breast cancer, Lachesis or Cimicifuga, together with remedies for hormonal dysfunction (such as Senecio fuchsii, Ignatia, Marjorana and Nux maschata). For uterine cancer, Phosphorus, Apis mellificia, Lapis alb., Lachesis, Cimicifuga or Caltha Palustris. For ovarian cancer, Lachesis. For any of these cancers, the homoeopath might also use a cancer 'nosode' which is a disease product used in high potency.

Medical herbalism

A medical herbalist can help relieve the symptoms of cancer and its treatment, and encourage the body to fight the disease. But any treatment given will need to be specially adapted, for instance to work alongside any orthodox medical treatment being used.

This is the case, for example, with pain relief. Herbal remedies are available, according to the nature and location of the pain.

The general approach of the medical herbalist to try to slow or reduce the growth of tumours is to improve elimination, cleanse the system, and at the same time boost vitality and the immune defences. Useful remedies include sweet violet, cleavers, Echinacea, red clover and burdock. Echinacea is also of help in promoting healing – it enhances resistance to disease, and improves the immune system.

Depressed and fearful patients benefit from treatment with St John's wort, which is an anti-depressant and acts as a nervous restorative.

A medical herbalist can also help patients suffering the side effects of chemotherapy or radiotherapy. Ginger or peppermint, for example, relieve nausea and settle the stomach. Vervain or rosemary act as gentle tonics, with mild stimulating effects on the liver; ginseng is a more powerful stimulant and tonic, which helps to counteract the stress of treatment.

If the site of radiation treatment is sore, Calendula ointment or lotion promotes healing and is anti-inflammatory.

Echinacea, and possibly garlic, improve resistance to both bacterial and viral infection, and make the immune system and the white blood cells function better.

General treatment to improve health, circulation and nutrition, plus, perhaps, rosemary or nettle applied directly, will improve thinning or falling hair.

Cancer helplines

Breast cancer
Much of the advice and information is common to all forms of gynaecological cancer; however, the following adresses are especially relevant to helping women overcome breast cancer and its results. Please see the 'Cancer in General' helplines at the back of this section for more detailed cancer helplines.

The Breast Care and Mastectomy Association
26A Harrison Street, London WC1 (071 867 1103)
Information and support for women facing breast surgery. They have a network of
   volunteers nationwide, who offer one-to-one or group support.

The Family Breast Cancer Clinic
Royal Free Hospital, Pond Street, London NW3
Specializes in assessing women's risk of developing breast cancer, if someone in
   their close family has had it. NHS-run, so ask your GP to refer you.
Aspect (0843 596732) for info. on side effects of Tamaxifen treatment.

Further reading
Body Image, Sexuality and Cancer, published by Cancer Link.
The Woman's Cancer Book by Carolyn Faulder (Virago)
Mastectomy by Nancy Robinson and Ian Swash (Thorsons)
Coping with Breast Cancer by Betty Westgate (The Breast Care and Mastectomy
   Association)

Cervical cancer
Please see the **Cancer in General** section on page 106, as the basic information for all the different forms of cancer is detailed there. There are, however, some associations specifically relevant to cervical cancer, which may be helpful:

The Abnormal Smear Group
(0602 731 778)
Advice, information and support for women who have had smear tests whose results
   were abnormal in some way. (Send SAE plus £1.)

The Hysterectomy Support Group
c/o 3 Lynne Close, Greenstreet Green, Orpington, Kent (081 856 3881)
Advice and information on local support groups. Literature and information sheets
   available. Or contact 071 251 6580 (WHRRIC) for HSG details.

Marie Stopes Clinics
In London, Leeds and Manchester. See GENERAL HELPLINES, page 480 for details.

Cytoscreen
(081 868 2423) Budget cervical smear screening service: charges only £7 a smear to
   you if you send the test via your own GP. Run by the President of the British
   Association of Cytologists and available to women countrywide who want more
   frequent smears than they are offered on the NHS.

Women's National Cancer Control Campaign
1 South Audley Street, London W1 (071 499 7532)
Provides information about cervical cancer screening services, advice on results and
  treatment, and a helpline with trained counsellors to help you deal with your
  problems.

Further Reading
Body Image, Sexuality and Cancer, published by Cancer Link
Cervical Cancer by Dr Jane Chomet and Jukian Chomet (Thorsons)
The Women's Cancer Book by Carolyn Faulder (Virago)
Cervical Cancer and How to Stop Worrying About It by Judith Harvey, Sue Mack and
  Julian Woolfson (Faber)
Menopause: The Best Years of Your Life? by Ada Khan and Linda Hughey Holt
  (Bloomsbury)
Cervical Smear Test: What Every Woman Should Know by Albert Singer and Dr Anne
  Szarewski (Optima)
Thorson's Guide to Medical Tests by Joanna Trevelyan and Dr David Dowson, with
  Ruth West (Thorsons)
Experiences of Hysterectomy by Anne Webb (Optima)
The National Directory of Alternative Aid, by Michael Williams (Health Farm
  Publishing)

Cancer in general
Association of Chartered Physiotherapists in Obstetrics and Gynaecology
c/o Chartered Society of Physiotherapists, 14 Bedford Row, London WC1
  (071 242 1941)
Advice and literature on recovering from operations such as hysterectomy and
  mastectomy.

BACUP Cancer Help (British Association of United Cancer Patients)
121–123 Charterhouse Street, London EC1 (071 608 1661; outside London,
  Freephone 0800 181199)
Advice and support from trained nurse counsellors on all aspects and all types of
  cancer. Can put you in touch with local support groups and befrienders. Literature
  is available.

Breast Care and Mastectomy Association
(071 807 1103)
Information and support for women about to have, or who have had, breast surgery.
  There is a network of volunteers countrywide, offering group or one-to-one
  support. Advice and literature on swimwear, lingerie, nightwear and breast
  prostheses – as well as on breast reconstructive surgery.

Cancer Link
17 Britannia Street, London WC1 (071 833 2451)
Nurse counsellors offer support, advice, information and literature on all types and all
  aspects of cancer. They can also put you in touch with local support groups and
  supply literature.

Cancer Aftercare and Rehabilitation Society
21 Zetland Road, Redland, Bristol, Avon (0272 427419)
Countrywide volunteer network to support and comfort cancer patients and their
    families and friends. Information on all subjects relation to cancer including
    financial benefits and practical aids.

Cancer Help Centre
Grove House, Cornwallis Grove, Clifton, Bristol, Avon (0272 743216)
Offers a programme of healing for people with cancer, working on all levels – the
    body, mind and spirit – and aims to encourage a positive mental attitude in people
    with cancer.

Hysterectomy Support Group
c/o 3 Lynne Close, Greenstreet Green, Orpington, Kent (081 856 3881)

The Womens National Cancer Control Campaign
(071 729 2229) a campaigning and advice charity with helpline.

The Ulster Cancer Foundation
40–42 Eglatine Avenue, Belfast (0232 663281).
Offering information by telephone on all aspects of cancer, as well as training courses
    for people setting up support groups.

The Women's Health Concern
See GENERAL HELPLINES, page 480.

Specialist products and services
Hair Raisers (Wigs and Toupees)
(081 965 2500)
Specialist wig-makers, both mail order service and catalogues available.

Hypnotherapists
Contact The Association of Qualified Curative Hypnotherapists
10 Balaclava Road, Kings Heath, Birmingham (021 441 1775)
This association will supply the names of properly trained and qualified practitioners
    in your area.

Sea Bands Ltd.
(0455 251020)
Ring to enquire about direct mail order, or your nearest stockist. Major Boots
    branches carry them at about £8 per pair.

Spiritual Healing
Contact the National Federation of Spiritual Healers
Old Manor Farm Studio, Church Street, Sunbury on Thames TW16 6RG
    (0932 783164)

Can put you in touch with a healer near you, who can come to your home, if you wish.
    Many healers do not accept payment for their help.

Yoga
Contact The British Wheel of Yoga
1 Hamilton Place, Boston Road, Sleaford, Lincs
Send SAE with covering note to ascertain your nearest qualified teacher.

Further reading
The Woman's Cancer Book by Carolyn Faulder (Virago)
Please see **Further Reading** for Hysterectomy on page 238 and for Menopause on
 page 296, if relevant. Also see **Further Reading** for specific cancers, above.

Childbirth

Where to have your baby?

In theory you have the right to choose any hospital you wish in which to give birth to your baby. In practice it is not so easy, because:

1. It is safer to stick with one close to home so you do not have to travel too far when you go into labour – if you live in Leeds it is not really practical to choose one in London, no matter how good it is.

2. Some hospitals, notably the busy top teaching hospitals, have started imposing restrictions on which mothers they will accept. They may turn down a woman who lives outside their 'catchment area'.

3. Because of the government policy of hospital closures there is sometimes little choice, as there may be only one maternity unit in your area (usually a consultant unit). The choice could be between booking into that, booking a home birth or travelling a fair distance to another maternity unit.

But in an ideal area the choices open to you are:

Domino delivery

What is it? Domino stands for DOMiciliary midwifery (home midwifery) IN and OUT (DOM-IN-O). It means your local midwife will look after you all the time, both for ante- and post-natal care, and in hospital.

When you go into labour, she comes to see you in your home and decides when to transfer you to hospital, where she assists you during the birth. After 6 to 18 hours she takes you home again. Then she visits daily for 10 days after the birth; in some areas she visits you once a week for 3 weeks.

Information: from your local Director of Midwifery Services at the local consultant unit at the hospital (ring the unit administrator if in doubt).

Cost: free on the NHS.

GP unit birth

What is it? The GP (trained in obstetrics) carries out your ante-natal care, and is present at the birth if possible. GPs often leave the actual delivery to the community midwives, who are experts in normal deliveries. Births in GP units have generally lower rates of intervention (forceps deliveries, induced and accelerated births, use of drugs) than ordinary consultant units.

Information: for a GP birth you have to book your care and delivery with your local GP. If your own doctor cannot provide obstetric care and is not involved with a local GP unit, you can sign on temporarily with another one just for the pregnancy, birth and post-natal care, then return to your own GP afterwards. You would need to carry on going to your own GP for health matters not associated with your pregnancy (for instance, if you caught a throat infection). Your GP may be able to recommend someone to you. If not, write to your

District Nursing Officer (get the address from your GP's receptionist). Once you have found someone who does such unit deliveries, see him and ask if he can take you on. Your own GP should be very happy to help you in this. If it does cause a problem, change your doctor.

If you are refused a GP unit place on the grounds that you are a 'high risk' mother and you feel this is unfair, check with a help organization such as AIMS (Association for Improvements in the Maternity Services) and the NCT (National Childbirth Trust) (see HELPLINES), or with a doctor or midwife outside your area and get help in arguing your case.

Cost: free on the NHS.

Home birth

What is it? Giving birth in your home, attended by a midwife. You have the right to give birth at home, attended by a midwife, even if the baby is your first. The decision and responsibility rest with you alone, by law. Women are, in fact, frequently discouraged from having a home birth (only one in 50 does so in the UK) on the grounds that hospital births are far safer. Yet studies done by Dr Marjorie Tew of Nottingham University Medical School, suggest that the reverse is true. Her figures showed that the death rate of babies for 'low risk' mothers giving birth at home was 5.2 per 1,000 compared to 17.9 in hospital. 'Moderate risk' mothers scored a 3.2 per 1,000 rate of baby deaths, compared with 32.2 in hospital.

An American study compared 1,046 women giving birth at home with a carefully matched group of women in hospital, and found that home labours were longer but hospital births had nine times as many episiotomies, three times as many Caesareans, twenty-one times as many forceps deliveries, three times as many post-partum haemorrhages, four times as many newborn babies developing infection and seventeen times as many cases of babies with breathing distress.

It is your baby, and your responsibility to weigh up the pros and cons. Should anything go wrong, hospitals may be the safest places to be – but many women also find the atmosphere and security of their own homes very important and reassuring. If you do decide on a home birth, you do not need your GP's approval. This is how to get a home birth, if you are satisfied it is a safe option for both you and your baby:

Information: Speak to your GP, explaining you would like a home birth. If he is unable or unwilling to help, ask to be recommended to another GP who is more sympathetic to your request. Failing that, ask the Society to Support Home Confinements or AIMS (see HELPLINES) if they know of a helpful doctor in your area. Remember, too, that if you are already booked into a hospital, you will need to write to them and cancel your booking. Alternatively speak to your midwife (you can contact her via the area's Director of Midwifery Services, DMS).

If you still have no luck, write immediately to the Director of Midwifery Services at your District Health Authority (under 'H' for 'Health' in the Yellow Pages telephone directory). Explain you would like a home birth, that your GP (give his name, and the address of the clinic) is unable to help and that you wish the Director to help you make the necessary arrangements for a midwife to look after you during your pregnancy and to attend the birth. Also tell them that you accept full responsibility for a birth at home. Keep a copy of this letter.

If you have the energy, write too to your local MP and Community Health Council so they will know there is a demand for home births in their area.

If, when you meet your midwife, she does not seem to approve of the idea of your having a home birth, ask the DMS to find you another midwife.

Cost: Free on the NHS. You can have a home birth attended by a private independent midwife, too, though you would have to pay (see **Independent midwife home birth**, below.

Consultant unit birth

What is it? These are usually at major hospitals, and there may be as many as half a dozen consultants at each unit. Consultants do not all have exactly the same ideas about ante-natal care and delivery, so the consultant you are given could make a difference to the treatment you receive.

Generally you have your regular ante-natal check-ups with one of the registrars on the consultant's team (called a 'firm') and it is not unusual never to see the consultant in charge at all. A variant on this, which is becoming popular, is to have your ante-natal care shared between your GP practice and the consultant unit. Ask your GP if this is done in your area, or ring your Community Health Council (under 'C' or 'H'). A midwife at the hospital, whom you may or may not have met before, will deliver your baby unless there is a complication. If there is, a registrar, or even the consultant obstetrician responsible for you, will be called in to help. This is the most usual way to have a baby in the UK.

Information: To find out about the policies towards pregnancy and labour at particular local hospitals, so as to choose the one which may best suit you, ask your GP or health visitor for information. Failing that, write to your local Community Health Council (found under 'C' in the phone book or 'H' for 'Health' in the Thomson local directory). They monitor hospitals and health centres for patients and bring out regular reports on services, including maternity care, so they should be able to help.

Cost: Free on the NHS.

Independent midwife home birth

What is it? This is paying privately for a midwife who has set up an independent practice. She looks after your ante-natal care, delivery at home and post-natal care for a flat fee. Independent midwifes (IM) work all over the country, but most of them are in and around the London area.

Information: You should inform your GP that this is what you wish to do, but you do not need his permission. Your GP or health visitor *may* know a good independent midwife, but you may have more luck if you ask the Association of Independent Midwives (see HELPLINES) if there are any in your area.

Once you have contacted an independent midwife, see if she sympathizes with the way you wish to give birth, and that she feels that it would be perfectly

111

safe for you. Often IMs are very sympathetic towards natural childbirth and have left the NHS because they did not feel happy with its policies on maternity care and labour. If you feel the midwife is not the person you wish to have caring for you, find another in the same way you contacted the first.

Independent midwives are registered with the Midwifery Supervisor of each health district they practise in. Your midwife will inform the MS of your pregnancy and that you are under her care.

Cost: approximately £500 to £1,000, depending on the area (London is at the upper end of the scale).

Private hospital birth

What is it? Having your ante-natal care, childbirth and post-natal care looked after by a senior or consultant obstetrician in a private hospital. Your environment will be more comfortable and luxurious than in an NHS hospital, and there will be little of the queuing, waiting and sometimes production-line approach to ante-natal care often seen at overcrowded NHS units.

You will probably have a private room and have more say in the way you wish to give birth – but there are generally more interventions. Also, the quality of care will not necessarily be better than in an NHS hospital; it is just that there are more staff who therefore have more time to give to you. The consultant looking after you will probably be at your delivery, unless you request otherwise.

A cheaper form of private care is becoming increasingly popular: a no-frills room (no wallpaper, pretty curtains or colour TV and telephone, but often better food – sent down by a hospital's private wing if it has one) off an NHS maternity ward. You will be looked after by the NHS nurses and midwives who staff the main maternity ward.

Information: Private hospitals are not officially monitored in the same way as NHS hospitals are. This means that getting to hear of bad or good practice and policies is often a matter of word of mouth, as is consultant choice. As to the consultant's own competence, a general rule of thumb (though there are exceptions) is that he should have held, or be holding, a post as a consultant as an NHS hospital as well as working privately.

You can refer yourself to a private consultant if you prefer not to go through your GP – although your GP will like to know that this is what you are doing.

Health Insurance companies such as BUPA should be able to advise you of private maternity units in your area – in private hospitals, and private wards of NHS hospitals. But it will be up to you to check them out. Make an appointment with the hospital administrator for someone to show you around the unit and ask as many questions as you can about the care they provide and facilities they offer. Also, perhaps see two or three units that sound promising before making up your mind, so you can compare the attitude of their staff, the atmosphere, price and facilities.

Check especially for back-up facilities in case your baby needs special care for a while after it is born – some private hospitals do not have special care units and your baby would have to be transferred to the nearest special care unit with available space.

Cost: Private hospital administrators can all send you a comprehensive price sheet which details the cost of everything you will need, from regular ante-natal check-ups (around £50 for the first and £40 for subsequent ones) to the cost of any necessary blood tests, ultrasound scans (approximately £50 each), delivery charges and anaesthesia costs (e.g. an epidural is around £175 to £250), with meals, other drugs, dressings etc, all added in on top. Ask, too, for an all-in approximate figure based on a normal delivery, ante-natal care, plus four or five days' stay (or however long you wish) and one post-natal check up. It will be from around £2,500 upwards. If they appear vague about this, or are unwilling to suggest even an approximate figure, be wary – you could end up with an expensive surprise when you get your bill.

According to the Oxford National Perinatal Epidemiology Unit, only about one per cent of births are private, partly because you cannot generally get private insurance for childbirth unless there are specific complications. On average, the intervention and Caesarean rates at private maternity units is double that of the average NHS hospital.

VISIT THE BIRTH PLACE having decided where to have your baby. If it is your first baby, or if you or your partner feel apprehensive about the birth in any way, it may help considerably to get to know the place where you are going to give birth beforehand so that it becomes familiar and more reassuring to you. Ask if you can see round the labour ward, look around the labour or delivery suite for a while, get chatting to the staff there, even familiarize yourself with the layout a bit – for instance, the toilets and bathrooms, the TV/sitting room if there is one, the nurseries where babies sleep if their mothers feel like a break from them, and so on.

What happens in labour and childbirth
Labour is divided into three stages:
1. The first stage, where your womb's contractions slowly dilate the cervix until it is wide enough to allow your baby's head to pass through;
2. The second stage, where the baby's head passes into the lower part of your birth canal (vagina), pushed along by ever strengthening and ever more frequent contractions of your womb. Then its body passes down your vagina and out into the world;
3. The third stage, where your womb continues to contract to expel the placenta as well.

Labour lasts from about 8 to 24 hours, varying from woman to woman. An average is 12 hours for a first-time mother, and six hours (anything from two or three to twelve) for mothers having subsequent babies.

EARLY SIGNS OF LABOUR INCLUDE:
* persistent lower backache;
* your womb contracting painfully – as opposed to Braxton-Hicks contractions, hardening your abdomen for 10 to 20 or 30 seconds, then relaxing again repeatedly, at ever closer intervals;
* passing the plug of protective mucus which has been in your cervical canal

since the beginning of your pregnancy, protecting the entrance to your womb from any infection. It may be slightly bloodstained;
* your 'bag of waters' breaking open. You will feel a gentle gush or slow leak of the amniotic fluid pass from your vagina. However, this may not happen until far later in the labour, or may not mean that you are *in* labour.

Stage one
In the first stage of labour the contractions may be as far apart as every half an hour, lasting perhaps 10 seconds. As labour progresses they become increasingly frequent and last longer.

Your womb begins to contract increasingly strongly and frequently to do two jobs.
1. To 'take up', or to shorten the cervical canal.
2. To dilate your cervix slowly, until it is open wide enough to allow the baby's head to pass through it and into your vagina for delivery. The midwife or doctor will check at regular intervals to see how dilated the opening circle of the cervix has become. It will need to reach about 10cm eventually.

WHAT DOES IT FEEL LIKE? Because every woman has a different pain threshold and labour progresses in different ways, reactions to labour will vary. Some recall labour as a hard physical effort but not all that painful; others remember their labours as being very painful indeed. But whatever you experience, hospitals have the facilities to cope with any problems which may arise, from feeling excessive pain to a labour which is progressing too slowly and exhausting you.

The discomfort or pain which women experience in the first stage has often been described by them afterwards as an almost 'passive pain' which they tried to relax into. It is then that the most help comes from massage, warm soothing baths, rocking and circling the pelvis, changing positions and walking around and moving about frequently, as the body helps the cervix to widen so the baby can start being pushed out.

The pain of a contraction resembles a very bad period pain and can appear in the lower abdomen, lower back or even down the side of a thigh. It is different from other sorts of pain because, as many women say, though it feels familiar because of its similarity to severe menstrual cramps it is different because it has regular breaks in it. If you slam your hand in a door it hurts sharply and continuously. A contraction begins gently, builds up to a climax of pain, then dies away – which women say makes it easier to cope with – and then there is a rest period to gather yourself together to cope with the next one. Towards the end of labour the rest periods become very short.

The other thing which makes this type of pain 'different' is the amount of natural calming painkillers (a form of opiate called endorphins) which the body produces in huge quantities when a women is in labour, again helping her cope far better than one could with an ordinary type of discomfort.

Second stage
Second stage pain comes when women are encouraged to actively push or 'bear

114

down' to help the baby's passage down through their birth canal and across the perineum (though the uterine contractions are usually so very powerful by now that extra active pushing by the mother is not always strictly necessary). This has been described as a more 'active' pain that you can try and work with, rather than relax against. Your contractions will not be as painful as they were during the first stage but as the perineum expands for the baby's head to pass through it, you will feel a profound stretching, sometimes described as 'like a Chinese burn' or a 'splitting, tearing sensation'. Others have described it as 'almost orgasmic'.

As your body enters its second stage of labour the contractions change subtly and you have a great desire to help push the baby out. As the first stage changes over to the second (the transition) you may well feel sick, and it is not unusual to actually be sick. Many women also feel at this point (though temporarily) that they have had enough, and become very upset or negative for a while; and this is when encouragment from your midwife or partner can make all the difference.

By now the contractions are happening once every two to three minutes, lasting around a minute each as the baby's head and body are pushed down your vagina, past the perineum and out through the vagina's entrance. Babies are usually born forehead first, then nose. This stage of labour usually lasts anywhere between 30 minutes and a couple of hours.

Third stage
Your womb carries on contracting powerfully (sometimes with the help of the injection of a drug – see **Intervention**, below). The midwife or doctor may help the placenta out by pulling gently on it whilst pushing your womb upwards and backwards with a hand on your stomach wall (but not if you did not have Syntometrine, a drug which speeds up the placenta's expulsion).

Preparation for childbirth
'Labour, without getting your mind and body into training for it, is like being told to run the London Marathon at 30 seconds notice,' says Stephen Sandler, director of the British School of Osteopathy's osteopathic practice division, who has set up the only osteopathy maternity clinic in the UK. 'With training you can take it right in your stride. Without, you'll be lucky if you get half way round without becoming exhausted.'

Ante-natal classes
Classes teach you (and your partner if you wish) about the process of labour, explaining what happens, when and why. They suggest ways of coping with pain, explain what you can expect at the hospital, show you how to have a comfortable pregnancy and labour, and most teach the basics of babycare (bathing, changing etc.) and breastfeeding, too. They are free, and run by your local health authority, held at health centres, the larger GP practices and the hospital where you are booked to have your baby (if you have chosen a hospital birth). The National Childbirth Trust (NCT) and Active Birth Movement hold their own classes, too, which are fee-paying (see HELPLINES).

Exercise

Three times a week can help keep you supple, build up your stamina for labour, and taking care of the baby afterwards, plus help keep your weight and blood pressure down (putting on too much weight is responsible for all sorts of pregnancy problems from stretchmarks to flatter feet). Exercise has also been shown to reduce the likelihood of pre-eclampsia (see PREGNANCY PROBLEMS, page 360) *and* it will keep your muscles toned (to avoid post-pregnancy flop).

Ante-natal classes will teach you helpful exercises. There will be such classes attached to your hospital ante-natal clinic or at your local health centre or GP practice (if it is a fair-sized one), all of which are free. The National Childbirth Trust, the Active Birth Movement and yoga teachers also hold helpful classes (see HELPLINES) but you will have to pay separately for these. Prices are from around £2 a session. You can usually begin the classes as early in your pregnancy as you wish – women often go from their fourth month onwards for as long as they feel they can manage.

If you are doing a particular sort of exercise regularly anyway, it is usually considered safe to continue with most forms of exercise for about five months, and that includes jogging, dance, aerobics and riding. But check first with your doctor or midwife to make sure. Otherwise swimming is an excellent option. As it is not weight bearing and can be slow, gentle and steady, it can be continued right up to the last moment. In fact, when many pregnant women reach the last heavy months of pregnancy they feel more comfortable in the water than out of it. An organization called Splashdance (specializing in water exercises in swimming pools) may be useful if you get bored with just swimming (see HELPLINES).

PELVIC FLOOR EXERCISES are vital. The baby's increasing weight pressing down on this sling of muscle means that one in three women have stress incontinence problems after the birth. Pelvic toning can much reduce the risk. (See INCONTINENCE, page 239, for a full description of the exercises concerned. See also **Incontinence** in PREGNANCY PROBLEMS, page 360.)

Body maintenance

Taking steps to help avoid problems – everything from back trouble to stretchmarks – while you are pregnant beats trying to repair any damage afterwards (see PREGNANCY PROBLEMS, page 360).

BACK PROBLEMS are due to changes in posture and rapid increase in body weight. Help stop any problems developing by having regular visits to an osteopath or chiropractor. (The British School of Osteopathy has an expectant mother's clinic in London which only charges £11 a session.) Unless you are having real problems, you would probably need to go once every month or so from about the sixth month of pregnancy.

OTHER COMPLEMENTARY THERAPIES can prevent many different sorts of difficulty, or at least minimize them.

Medical herbalism, for instance, suggests drinking raspberry-leaf tea (available from herbalists such as the Culpeper's and Neal's Yard chains, also in tablet form from Heath & Heather at health food shops – or from a professional medical herbalist). (See **Medical herbalism** in PREGNANCY PROBLEMS.) It helps tone up the womb's muscles so that your contractions will be stronger and more efficient, making for a briefer labour.

Aromatherapy and *Clinical Nutrition* used together can help prevent stretch marks forming (see PREGNANCY PROBLEMS pages 360 and 376).

Homoeopathic preparations like Cholophyllum can help reduce the risk of bad bruising and substantial bleeding during labour (see **Homoeopathy** in PREGNANCY PROBLEMS).

Check out complementary treatments and what they can offer early on in your pregnancy as many need to be continued for several months leading up to your delivery to be really effective. (See also all **Complementary therapy** in CHILDBIRTH and PREGNANCY PROBLEMS.)

Sex

Some women feel no desire for sexual intercourse, or any other sort of lovemaking during their pregnancy. Others feel an increased desire for it. Others again find in the early weeks of pregnancy their libido drops, then recovers in the second trimester, receding again in the third. Everyone is different. Changes in sexuality are normal, as is no change, during a pregnancy.

Though women with a history of repeated miscarriages may be advised to avoid intercourse until the pregnancy is well established (say until the third or fourth month), it is exceptionally unlikely that even the most vigorous lovemaking could harm the foetus or displace a healthy pregnancy. The baby is very well protected from any thrusts of the penis inside your vagina by its cushioning sac of amniotic fluid.

You may find though that the positions which make especially deep penetration possible (such as astride a male partner) are uncomfortable, and also that the missionary position squashes your stomach too much. So experiment a bit to see what is most pleasurable and comfortable for you both as the pregnancy progresses – lying on your side with your bottom fitting snugly into your partner's lap ('spoons' position) is one that many women say they find the easiest. And an active sex life for as long as you wish it is, in fact, good for toning up the pelvic muscles, says John McGarry, consultant obstetrician at the North Devon District Hospital.

Diet

It is important to eat well, taking in plenty of fresh fruit and raw vegetable dishes, wholefoods like wholegrain rice, pastas and wholemeal breads, high protein foods such as soya products, meat and cheese and eggs, and plenty of liquids. (See HELPLINES for helpful books on diet in pregnancy, and for how to contact a nutritionist for expert advice specifically tailored to your individual needs.)

It is also important to eat small amounts regularly (every two or three hours), as during pregnancy your blood sugar level drops faster than usual, leaving you feeling faint and wobbly.

During labour midwives recommend eating a light meal early on, then just sipping a high calorie drink like Lucozade or nibbling glucose tablets to keep your energy levels up.

How to have your baby
Having decided *where* to have your baby (i.e. at home or in hospital etc), the next stage is to decide *how* you would like to have him or her and to locate a hospital which would be sympathetic. If, for instance, you want to go for a natural non-interventionist childbirth (with the option of pain relief and full back-up if you find that it is necessary after all) ask the Natural Childbirth Trust (NCT) (see HELPLINES) or your local health visitor to suggest a local hospital with sympathetic consultants.

Your birthplan
This is a good way of communicating your wishes – in writing – so they can be attached to your notes for future reference. Keep a copy and take it with you when you go in to have your baby, so that you or your partner can refer the staff to it if necessary. According to John McGarry, a consultant obstetrician at the North Devon District Hospital, about one in ten women now makes a birthplan – but all but 10 to 15 per cent concentrate solely on the method of delivery and labour. The period following the birth is just as important. So try and decide what you want immediately afterwards, as well as during, to give you and your baby the calm and peace to recover and get to know each other.

AIMS makes the following suggestions. You'll need security (someone with you as a birth partner whom you trust and who gives you confidence) and the continuous and reassuring presence of a good midwife. Also peace, calm and the confidence in your own ability to give birth to your baby without drugs or intervention if possible. These conditions may be a bit hard to come by in a crowded, busy hospital. Speak to your local natural childbirth group about the best ways to go about this, and try to involve the hospital staff in your choices.

Drawing up a birthplan helps you to sort out in your own mind what you feel is important, and what you would and would not be happy with. Show it to your consultant, senior registrar and midwife and discuss it with them to ensure that what you would like to do is possible with the facilities they have – and acceptable to them. If they disagree with some things that are important to you, consider changing hospital/midwife/consultant. Talk to AIMS or the Maternity Alliance (see HELPLINES) for advice on this. It is best not to do a birthplan too late in pregnancy (e.g. about 5 to 6 months or before) so that if you do need to change to a different hospital or method of care (e.g. go for a home or domino delivery rather than a consultant unit one) there will be plenty of time to organize it.

Some birthplan points to think about
(See the text on the following pages for more details about points 1 to 7 below. For **After delivery** see page 136 and for **Breastfeeding** see BREASTFEEDING DIFFICULTIES, page 52.)

1. PEOPLE PRESENT AT THE BIRTH: Who would you like (or prefer not) to be there apart from the midwife: your partner? A friend? Would you object to student midwives or a student doctor being there to watch and learn?

2. MEDICAL INTERVENTION. How do you feel about the different forms that are often practised during childbirth, like: episiotomy, forceps delivery, labour acceleration, Caesarean section? Which ones, if any, would you wish to avoid if at all possible? Which would you have no objection to?

3. DELIVERY. Who would you like to deliver your baby: a doctor, the midwife? Would you mind a student doctor or midwife doing it under supervision if there were no complications?

4. PAIN KILLING METHODS. What would you prefer to use (in order of preference: from gas and air, to acupuncture, hot baths or showers, or hypnotherapy)? Check if you have the option of an epidural if you feel you need one when the time comes.

5. MONITORING. How do you feel about foetal monitoring, and the different techniques used?

6. POSITIONS FOR LABOUR. Would you wish to be free to move about as much as possible, try squatting, being on all fours? Say which you would prefer, check what you will need and ask if it means bringing extra things with you (e.g. huge cushions) or whether the labour ward has them. Would you feel happier if the lighting were dimmer, if you were allowed to play gentle music? Check practical details, e.g. is there anywhere to plug a cassette recorder in?

7. DELIVERY POSITIONS. Are there any which you feel would especially suit you?

8. AFTER DELIVERY. Do you want to hold your baby immediately or would you prefer it washed and wrapped comfortably in a blanket first? Do you want the baby's cot next to you or taken to the nursery so you can sleep? How many visitors do you want, how soon, and who would you be glad (and not so glad) to see?

9. BREASTFEEDING. Do you want to feed your baby yourself, or would you prefer to bottle feed? If you do, say so, and also say if you would appreciate plenty of help if it proves necessary, especially if you are a first-time mum. Breastfeeding may be natural, but it is not always as easy as you are led to believe and may take a bit of perseverence (see BREASTFEEDING DIFFICULTIES).

Note. Be prepared to be a bit flexible. The birthplan represents what you would like ideally if there are no problems with the birth: if there are you may need to modify them at the time.

Natural childbirth, for instance, is not something you can 'get' or 'have' in the same way that you might book a particular sort of summer holiday, although the way other people refer to it ('Are you going to have a natural childbirth then?') makes it sound a bit like it. If there are problems it simply might not be possible.

For instance, you might have practised and planned to spend your first stage walking about, using warm baths, massage, position changes and breathing control only as pain relief, and wanted the second stage to be delivery in the hanging squat position held by your partner and with no drugs for pain relief – but, in the end, your labour was accelerated by an oxytocin drip, your contractions were weak and erratic, and you needed to have an epidural because your labour was exhaustingly long.

It helps to be as flexible in your approach towards natural childbirth as you are towards the rest of your birthplan, and take the attitude 'I'll do it this way if I possibly can', rather than 'I'm going to feel very disappointed, and as if I have failed in some way, if I don't have a natural childbirth'.

Because every woman's labour and pain threshold are different, and because labours do not always go to plan, you may find you do need some extra help you weren't planning to have. But that doesn't mean you have 'failed' in any way whatsoever. Everyone manages labour the best way they can, and it might help a bit to remember that the teachings of natural childbirth classes are very helpful, positive guidelines to help women find the best way for *them*. The classes offer you plans of action, some invaluable techniques and new options for coping. But they need not be rigidly stuck to.

1. Partners and others

If you would like a husband, partner or friend to stay with you all through the labour, check that the staff will not ask them to leave for any reason. When things get stressful you may need their comfort and support the most. It is important to have someone with you who can help explain what you need or want during labour, and who can see that, where possible, the staff respect the wishes set out in your birthplan, and help you relax.

A 'partner' can be a husband, boyfriend, friend, your mother or sister, the teacher from your active birth classes – anyone who you want to be there. And while it is now common to have your male partner present, some women feel they would rather not and prefer to be left just with the midwife or doctor instead – it is completely up to you.

Student doctors and midwives may be present at the birth, unless you state otherwise, as part of their learning process.

2. Intervention

One way to check out a hospital's birth policies (whether NHS or private) is to look at its figures for intervention – i.e. forcep deliveries, Caesarian sections, episiotomies etc – and to check its rates against the national average. The lower the rates, the better. If they are higher than average this may be because the consultants there are a bit too ready to interfere with a birth when it is not really necessary, *or* that the unit is at a big major teaching hospital and it gets more than its fair share of problem births referred to it which *need* more interventions than straightforward births.

Figures on intervention rates are hard to get nationally as they vary from region to region, hospital to hospital – and even from consultant to consultant in the same hospital. However, the National Perinatal Epidemiology Unit at Oxford, which gathers such figures, estimates the national averages as follows:
* 11 per cent for Caesareans (4 per cent of which are 'elective', i.e. planned in advance);
* 17.5 per cent for inductions, i.e. inducing labour to begin artificially (contractions tend to get strong and frequent rapidly instead of building up gradually – which means they can be more painful);
* 10.7 per cent for forceps deliveries and vacuum extractions to pull the baby out. They usually need an episiotomy, too (see below);
* about 40 per cent for episiotomies (this figure varies from 90 per cent in some units to as low as 10 per cent in others countrywide).

TO FIND OUT WHAT A HOSPITAL'S INTERVENTION POLICIES ARE you can try the following:
i) Ring up the labour ward itself, ask to speak to a senior sister there and ask.
ii) Ask the director of midwifery services at the hospital (the switchboard will put you through).
iii) Ask your local Community Health Council (CHC) (in the telephone book under 'C' – or see HELPLINES) if you cannot get a more specific answer than 'We do not carry out interventions unless they are necessary'. Definitions of what is necessary, and when, are much open to interpretation by different people.
The CHC should be able to get you these figures (it is part of its job to monitor hospital practices, including those for the maternity services). If the hospital will not give the figures to the CHC you might perhaps regard them a bit warily – if their care really is good, they should have no qualms about revealing such data.
iv) As intervention rates can differ between consultants at the same hospital, if you like the hospital and its staff, check out the figures for another consultant there if the figures for one are a bit high. (There will be as many as three or four in big hospitals to choose from.) If they are lower for the second, ask to be put under his care instead.
The following are the sort of things you want to know a hospital's policy on:

WATERS BROKEN ARTIFICIALLY. Would you agree to this when you are admitted? Ask yourself if this is what you would want.
The membranes of your baby's amniotic sac are most likely to rupture of their own accord at 4 a.m. because the level of hormones in your bloodstream is at its lowest then. Having your waters broken artificially to help begin labour increases the chances of infection. Some hospitals would only wait 12 hours after the waters have broken to see if labour starts of its own accord, before accelerating it artificially, some have a policy of waiting up to 24 hours.
Dr Jason Gardosi, senior registrar at Nottingham University Hospital, feels that the bag of unbroken waters during part of labour is very helpful as it gives a large, even area to press down against the cervix and so help dilate it more gently. Left to themselves, he reckons that 75 per cent of women would

naturally reach full dilation without their waters breaking (this figure is also confirmed by a recent South American study). When the waters break (especially if made to do so artificially) it can speed up labour very dramatically. This may be due to the hormones contained in the amniotic sac's membrane tissue.

ACCELERATING OR INDUCING LABOUR. How would the hospital do this; and at what point would they feel it was necessary? AIMS figures suggest that if the figures are higher than 10 per cent for first-time mothers – and they are the ones who generally receive higher levels of intervention – maybe the hospital is doing this too often. Because they are strong contractions, and tend not to have the slow gentle build-up of natural labour, they can hurt more.

A labour is usually accelerated either by: a) placing a prostaglandin pessary in the vagina next to the cervix; or b) placing an oxytocin drip in the woman's arm to deliver this hormone directly into her bloodstream. The latter especially tends to produce strong contractions which do not build up and die away like natural contractions, but start suddenly and violently, and finish quite suddenly, too, so induced labour will often require an epidural.

Doctors will usually try option a) (often twice, five hours or so apart), before resorting to option b).

STARTING YOUR OWN LABOUR. If you are overdue and fed up with waiting, this is sometimes possible. Sexual intercourse (if you feel up to it) can start off labour naturally and gently as the prostaglandins in semen make your womb contract. You can also trigger the production of another helpful hormone, called oxytocin, by stimulating your own breasts – which also encourages your womb to contract. John McGarry suggests stripping to the waist and standing in front of a basin of warm water; using a soft flannel or sponge, soak it in water and allow the liquid to trickle down over your breasts, especially your nipples. Try and do this for 20 minutes a day, six times a day. Dr Adam Rodin, senior registrar in obstetrics and gynaecology at Farnborough Hospital suggests a curry, caster oil or a long walk. Visualization (imagine your cervix gently opening perhaps) can help.

SHAVING AND ENEMAS. These used to be routine practice (shaving the pubic area and giving a standard enema), but most hospitals now recognize that these things are not necessary. Enemas only now tend to be given if constipated. It also adds to the risk of infection and the hair regrowth can be uncomfortably itchy for weeks. Enemas only now tend to be given if constipated.

EPISIOTOMY. What is the hospital's episiotomy rate; do they do it routinely? Episiotomy is a cut (or cuts) made in the perineum (see diagram on page 243) which is the area of skin and muscle between your anus and vagina. This needs to stretch to allow the baby's head and body to come out. If it is not able to stretch wide enough, the baby may get stuck or the area may tear. Small tears heal easily and are preferable to episiotomy cuts, but large ones can be a problem to heal and painful so doctors and midwives are anxious to avoid.

Episiotomies may also be done if the medical staff think your labour is going a bit too slowly in the second stage, when the baby's head is trying to push past your perineum. Unfortunately the definition of 'too slowly' varies considerably, so it may be a case of 'standard time's up' rather than allowing the area to stretch naturally in its own time – as long as the baby is not in distress.

Avoiding an episiotomy: sometimes they are unavoidable. However, the following can help reduce the likelihood of your having one:

* check the episiotomy rate for the consultant you are under (if having a hospital birth). Either ask him directly, or call your local Community Health Council or Director of Midwifery Services to see if they know. You could also casually ask a junior registrar on that consultant's 'firm': they might well know, as the consultant's method of practice usually dictates that of his or her junior staff;

* try massaging the perineum with olive oil every day during the last three months of pregnancy – it may help it stretch more easily;

* practise stretching positions which require your legs to be wide apart, or your knees open, all the way through pregnancy: e.g. sit in the tailor or lotus/half-lotus position whenever possible; sit with your back supported and legs straight but stretched wide on the floor;

* use any variant of the squatting position during labour and delivery (including birth cushion);

* ask your midwife to use a hot compress on your perineum during the delivery stage of labour to soften the tissue there and help it stretch more easily.

* practise pelvic floor exercises daily especially when you release the muscles in your vagina after 'pulling up' (see INCONTINENCE, page 239) which can help you get used to the idea of 'letting go' and 'opening up' to make room for the baby's descending head;

* try visualization exercises – seeing the area in your mind's eye as soft and stretching, opening widely and easily.

If the thought of an episiotomy worries you, discuss it fully with your midwife or doctor on your ante-natal visits and ask what steps they can take to help you avoid one unless absolutely necessary.

3. *Who do you want to deliver your baby?*

i) Say whether you wish to be delivered by the midwife alone (plus a doctor, should potential complications arise) and whether you would object to a medical student or midwifery student doing it (or even being present).

ii) Would you mind being stitched up (after an episiotomy cut) by another doctor or midwife? It is not advisable, bearing in mind that this is a very sensitive part of your anatomy, and badly stitched cuts can make the area uncomfortable for many months (or even permanently).

4. *Pain relief*

You can choose from the following methods of pain relief (assuming they are all available).

SEDATIVES are rarely used now, but if they are, they will be given in small doses early on in labour to help keep you calm and relaxed (their use in the present day is, however, very rare). They will often make you slightly sleepy. Common tranquillizers and sedatives include diazepam and promazine hydrochloride. If you actually fall asleep you might wake up feeling confused and not able to get to proper grips with the progression of your labour. They can affect the baby's breathing too.

ANALGESICS affect the pain centres of the brain, dulling or numbing pain signals.
i) Pethidine (which midwives often, confusingly, call a 'sedative') is one such drug. It is given as a matter of course in the first stage of labour at some hospitals. It can have side effects such as a sense of unreality (it is a narcotic drug) and sickness (this can be alleviated with other drugs). It does not seem to work for everyone. It can also make your baby sleepy when it is born as the drug crosses the placenta. Meptid or Pethidus is a similar drug, but it is thought that it may affect your baby less.
ii) Gas and air (such as entonox, a mix of nitrous oxide gas and oxygen) you inhale yourself when you want it via a gas mask. The best time is just before the peak painful bit of a contraction. It can make you feel light headed, and even somewhat drunk, and is described by John McGarry as 'the equivalent of four double gins'. It wears off fast, but does affect the baby and, even if it doesn't work for you very well, can give you something concrete to do during a contraction. It is best used during the first stage of labour, rather than during the second stage when you will need your wits about you to push.

ANAESTHETICS blank out your conscious perception of pain and are the best way to get a 'pain-free' labour.
i) A general anaesthetic will only be necessary if you have an emergency Caesarean. It puts you 'out' completely but usually makes you feel rather sick when you come round (see **A Caesarean** below).
ii) A local anaesthetic (Pudendal Block), is delivered via injection into the perineum when you have an episiotomy cut, or when your cut or tear is stitched up. It might also be used if you need a forceps or (less usual) vacuum extraction delivery because the baby has got a bit stuck.
iii) Epidural anaesthesia is delivered by an injection given by a fully qualified anaesthetist. It is done by having a tiny hole made in your back between two of the lower vertebrae so that a hollow needle carrying a tube can be threaded carefully into the epidural space between your spinal cord (which is carrying the pain signals from your womb up to your brain) and its covering membrane. This is secured, with a small length protruding from your back, and then the anaesthetic fluid is injected into the tube. More anaesthetic fluid is added about every two hours, or as necessary.

The procedure takes about 20 minutes. It can give total pain relief and loss of feeling from the waist down (hence it can be given for a Caesarean instead of a general anaesthetic) or, if lower doses are used, it can deaden the pain to a great extent. Occasionally, though, some areas get 'missed' (see below), and you may still feel pain in a specific place or places.

Epidurals can be a great boon if the contractions are too painful for you to manage any longer, or if they are tiring you out too much, you are exhausted and only part of the way through your labour. They are also very helpful for women with high blood pressure (see below).

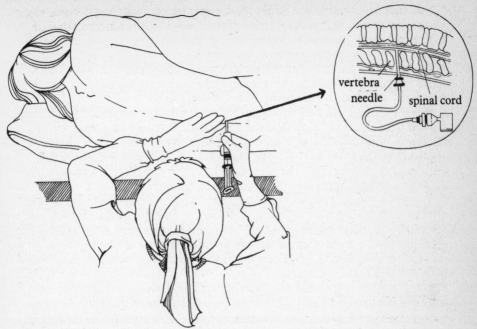

vertebra
needle
spinal cord

Epidurals can offer complete pain relief from the waist down, but leave you alert so you can enjoy the experience of giving birth to your baby. You need to have a medically managed birth, though (with a drip, a foetal heart monitor, and perhaps a catheter). Epidurals can be used for a Caesarean delivery, if it is not an emergency. (Inset) The anaesthetic is injected into the spine next to your spinal cord, via a needle and tube. This will not hurt as the area is deadened first.

An epidural does not affect your mind at all and leaves you fully awake and alert to enjoy the experience of your baby being born. There are some drawbacks however.
★ You usually have to remain lying on your side and keeping still, partly so as not to pull out the needle and partly so that the epidural can be topped up as necessary if it begins to wear off too soon, or is not strong enough to mask later contractions as they become more powerful. So no walking around. (You will probably find your legs are numb, too, which would make walking difficult, anyway.)
★ You cannot really change positions for labour and delivery which may be one reason why women who've had epidurals tend to suffer more back problems for months after the birth. But you *can* sit on a birth cushion (if you are helped onto it and supported at your back) or sit in a supported squat.
★ You need an intravenous drip in your arm because an epidural can make your blood pressure drop. (This is useful if you have high blood pressure as a result of pregnancy, or naturally anyway.) You may also feel a bit dizzy or sick as your blood pressure drops; this wears off fast after the epidural is removed.

* You may possibly have a headache for several hours after the birth (not usual), and in some cases suffer from severe intermittent headaches for years.
* You will probably need a catheter in your bladder as you will not be able to feel when you need to pass water. But you can ask to try a bedpan first, instead.
* There is a possibility that the epidural will only numb one side of your body. If this happens, the anaesthetist will adjust the position of the needle's angle in your back or, if necessary, remove and re-insert it again.
* While epidurals can be a total pain block, deadening everything below the waist if used to deliver high doses of anaesthetic into your back (e.g. as for a Caesarean with an epidural instead of a general anaesthetic), they may 'miss' segments of the lower part of your body and this means you might still feel some pain in certain areas. The procedure for remedying this is as above, but it may mean another small area just gets 'missed' instead.
* There is a greater possibility of an episiotomy and forceps delivery, as it is difficult to feel when to push during the second stage (though the midwife can tell you by checking on the monitor you are attached to when a contraction is coming up). To try and avoid this, an epidural is often allowed to wear off partially, or even totally, in the second stage so you can feel when to push your baby out with each contraction.
* Many women are afraid of paralysis with an epidural, thanks to some alarming media scare stories. It *has* happened, but the chances are very tiny indeed (Dr Gardosi puts them at 'one in a million'). You usually regain feeling in your lower half 4 to 6 hours later, though you may feel a bit numb for part of the day after delivery.
* An epidural can occasionally affect a baby, making it a bit jittery or sleepy for up to six weeks.
* Check that, if you think you might like an epidural, the hospital you are going to has 24-hour cover by an anaesthetist (many do not). If it does not, you may want to ring other maternity/labour units in the area.
* Do not leave it to the last minute to have epidural relief. It can take from a few minutes to a couple of hours to find an anaesthetist who may have to come from another hospital. And the device itself takes about 20 minutes to set up and perhaps another 10 to work. That may not sound like much but if you are in a lot of pain it can seem like a very long time.

TENS MACHINES are a method of stimulating and using the body's own natural pain-killing chemicals, called endorphins. TENS stands for Transcutaneous Electrical Nerve Stimulation and you operate the small cigarette-packet-sized machine yourself as and when you feel you need pain relief. TENS is best used for the first stage of labour. For best results, use as soon as the pains start rather than waiting until they become more severe.
The machine has two pairs of small electrodes, which you attach to your lower and upper back with tape. By pressing the lever on the machine (which you can carry in your hand or put in your dressing-gown pocket) you can turn on the electrical impulse it generates. This feels like a tickling, electronic 'buzzing' on your skin. It works by stimulating your endorphins to kill the pain and also by partially blocking out pain signals on their way up the spine to the

brain. It is also used in pain relief clinics for people suffering from chronic conditions like back pain or arthritis.

This is a mobile form of pain relief, so you can continue to walk around with it or assume any position for labour that you want.

It does not work for every woman. Studies (such as those in Sweden where it was invented) show that 44 per cent of women found it very helpful as a pain killer, 44 per cent thought it was moderately good and 12 per cent said it was no good at all.

Many hospitals now have TENS units but there is no guarantee that your labour ward will have one free when you want it. You can hire your own from companies called Spembly Medical and Pulsar Obstetrics (see HELPLINES). It is important to learn to use the machine before you go into labour, so ask if you can practise on it when you go for an ante-natal appointment, or practise at home (or in ante-natal class) if you are hiring one yourself.

ACUPUNCTURE. According to Christina Mcausland, acupuncturist and founder of Acupuncture for Childbirth, acupuncture for pain relief in labour involves using tiny acupuncture needles at the relevant sites in your ears (if you want to be able to move around), or in your hands and feet, and then stimulating the needles by wiring them up to a very mild electrical current from a mobile generating unit. 'Electro acupuncture', as this form of acupuncture is called, is very good for things like speeding up labour or making contractions stronger and more frequent. 'It can also work well as a method of pain relief by reducing, rather than completely blotting out, the pain,' she explains. 'It helps for about one in three women by taking the edge off the sensations to help them cope.' (See **Acupuncture**, below, for more details.)

As the consultant you are under is responsible for you, you need to obtain his permission to bring an acupuncturist with you to help you in labour. You should also discuss it well beforehand with any other staff likely to be there, as the acupuncturist will be working as part of their team. It is a good idea to visit the acupuncturist you choose two or three months before the birth, so you can get to know each other. If your consultant will not give his permission, change to another more sympathetic one. You could also consult your local CHC about any maternity units in the area who do accept complementary therapists.

Because helping women in childbirth can be a lengthy business, not all acupuncturists will be willing to assist you. Call their professional associations (see HELPLINES), and ask if they can suggest anyone; ring up the therapists they mention and discuss the matter over the phone; then visit them to see if you like, trust and feel totally comfortable with them. It is important to make sure they have experience in this form of acupuncture and have given pain relief to other women during childbirth; also that they are properly qualified and have membership of one of the professional associations. Their fees are likely to vary from between £100 to £175 for attending the birth. (Ask if it is possible to meet other mothers they have treated.)

Acupuncture is without side effects if done correctly, either for the mother or baby. Many women have found a sympathetic practitioner is a great support and comfort during the birth.

HYPNOTHERAPY involves attaining a very calm, relaxed state (similar to the way you feel just before you drop off to sleep) and using the power of your mind to help control physical pain. According to senior hypnotherapist Marissa Peer, for some women it helps enormously. Pain, fear and physical tension are closely linked, and according to Dr Gardosi 'one of the best methods of pain relief is indeed to feel calm, relaxed and confident'. These are things which hypnotherapy can help you achieve.

You would probably need about six sessions with your hypnotherapist to learn how to relax and soothe yourself and to practise certain visualization techniques (literally 'seeing' yourself calm, without pain and relaxed). These will cost you anything from £15 to £40 a session (usually lasting an hour). It would also be very helpful for the therapist to be able to come to hospital with you – having obtained co-operation from the consultant and staff first – when you go into labour. Consult your local CHC if you have difficulty finding a sympathetic maternity unit.

Hypnotherapy can work very well for some women, especially during the first stage of labour (it has no effect on other women). It has the added plus of being something you know you can do to help yourself when you need a weapon to fight the pain, rather than something you are given passively (like a drug).

See HELPLINES for where to contact a hypnotherapist. Ask their professional association if they can suggest anyone in your area who has experience of helping women through childbirth and then telephone them to explain what you want, go to see them if they sound receptive. Ensure that you like and trust them, that they have experience of this sort of thing, and that they are properly qualified. Ask if it is possible to speak to any other mothers they have treated.

BREATHING CONTROL is taught in most hospital ante-natal classes, and in natural childbirth classes. You learn different levels of breathing to help you relax, calm yourself and control your body during labour. If this is the only method of pain relief you want to use, explain it to the consultant and staff in your birth plan when you meet them. This is often done together with the physical relaxation techniques you learn during childbirth classes. These involve tensing and relaxing your body, so you can learn to let your womb contract without the rest of you tensing up.

* deep breathing is calming, good for the beginning and end of contractions;
* light breathing is fast, shallow and short, for the middle peak of a contraction;
* featherlight breathing is panting, to prevent yourself pushing down too soon during the transition phase between labour's first and second stages, when contractions are coming strong and fast.

5. *Monitoring*

Women will usually be given a 'tracer' foetal monitor when they first come into the hospital in labour, to check that the baby's heartbeat is normal. After that it will be monitored about three times an hour. This does not mean you have to

128

keep being strapped up to a complicated machine while lying flat on your back. The staff can put a listening-in device on your stomach so it will not restrict you if you are moving around. (Lying flat on your back during labour can cause foetal distress in itself as the weight of your womb squashes back on major pelvic blood vessels trying to bring blood to the placenta.) This also prevents the baby monitor from being inadvertently left on.

It may also be possible to listen to the baby's heartbeat, to make sure it is not in trouble, by using a special (if a bit old fashioned) instrument like a stethoscope, called a foetascope. This, used by an experienced midwife, is thought to be very effective – and using one like Sonicaid *you* can hear the baby's heartbeat, too.

A 1989 report in the *Journal of the Royal Society of Medicine* listed six out of eight medical trials which showed electronic monitoring was no more help than listening intermittently with a foetascope to check on the baby's heartbeat. Some hospitals now have small monitoring units which can be strapped to the mother's leg so she can still move around a bit rather than having to lie flat on her back, but these have a scalp electrode fitted to the baby's head.

6. *Labour positions*
Do you want to be able to move around freely and adopt whichever positions feel most comfortable to you during your labour – and to deliver the baby in whatever position you choose yourself? Or are you happy to be guided by the midwife and doctor in this? It is important to say which you would prefer in your birthplan. In fact, AIMS quotes one eminent obstetrician, Dr Roberto Caldeyro-Barcia, as saying that there is only one position worse than lying on your back for delivery – and that's hanging by your heels from a chandelier.

The positions can include just about anything you feel comfortable with, including going down on all-fours, being curled archwise over a big pile of large cushions (ask if the hospital has any or whether it is best to bring your own), standing leaning forwards against your partner so he can massage your back, or swaying from side to side while being supported, sitting leaning over a chair back, squatting between your partner's knees, being supported under your arms and against your back. Other positions recommended by active birth teachers and many midwives include the standing squat and the supported squat, which are suitable for labour *and* delivery. The variations are many. The following diagrams show some of them, and some of the possible delivery positions, too.

Essentially *anything* that keeps you upright rather than lying down means gravity is working for you, rather than against you, to help the baby down, and also to help ensure a good blood supply to your pelvic area. Active Birth and NCT classes can help show you the positions, or try them at home using a birth book as a guide. It helps to practise with your partner, or on your own, before you go into labour so you feel totally familiar with them – or they may go right out of your head just when you need them.

7. *Delivery*
Are there any positions you would prefer? Tell the staff in your birthplan.

There are many positions for the first and second stages of labour – you might want to practise them with your partner beforehand (2–3 weeks?) to see which one feels the most comfortable. Unless you have a medically managed labour (involving lying down at all times and being closely monitored), you will be free to choose the positions which instinctively feel the best to you at the time. Discuss this with your doctor or midwife beforehand, explaining that you want to be free to move about as much as possible.

a) **Lying on side**, *one leg raised for delivery (second stage)*
b) **Half-kneeling, half-squatting** *for delivery*
c) **The hanging squat**: *you can walk around between contractions, and then bend knees to be supported during them*
d) **Supported squatting**: *can be used for the first stage of labour, or second stage (delivery)*
e) *Practising the* **all-fours position** *for delivery*

i) A birthing stool is a very traditional way of giving birth but a study carried out at Northwick Park Hospital in London in 1986 by obstetrician Mike Turner suggested the birth stool or chair might produce higher rates of tears and after-delivery bleeding. Another study by Glasgow Royal Maternity Hospital also found increased blood loss was likely with stools, and an American report suggested that prolonged pushing in this position could make the vulva swell extensively. However, some women do find these chairs comfortable; they keep you working with gravity and keep you upright

ii) Squatting gives you the advantage of gravity, and helps your pelvis open up more, relaxing its soft tissues so that that vital extra bit of room is created for the baby's head to pass through the dilated cervix. However, without extensive practise and good natural childbirth training, prolonged squatting can be far too tiring for most women in Western cultures.

There is now a device called the birth cushion which supports the woman in an upright squatting position. It consists of a wedge of foam rubber with a V-shape cut out of the centre, placed in a light aluminium frame with padded arm handles. The woman sits on it in a supported squat, so her bottom sinks down into the lowest part of the wedge and her thighs take her weight – supported on the upwards slope of the foam wedge along the sloping sides of the V-shape. Her birth canal area is left free and exposed at the point of the V, and to help her push effectively she can grip the arms of the frame for leverage. The birth cushion can be used on a delivery bed and with an epidural if required.

It was devised by Dr Gardosi, and in a trial in 1988 on 427 first-time mothers at Milton Keynes General Hospital (half using the cushion, half not), he found that the cushion users had half the expected number of forcep deliveries, a third fewer perineal tears and a shorter second (pushing) stage of labour than non-users. The only disadvantage seemed to be more labial tears, but as they were smaller they healed easily and did not need stitching.

Several major hospitals already have the cushion. If your chosen one does not, you can hire or buy one. See 'Gardosi Birth Cushion' entry in HELPLINES.

Or contact the company for some literature and medical papers on its use, show them to your consultant and suggest he may find it useful, and that you would like to try it yourself. To save money, some women in the same ante-natal class may club together in groups of 2 or 3 to buy one (as long as their due dates are not all the same!) or buy one and sell it on at a reduced rate to the labour ward afterwards.

iii) A supported squat, on the bed or floor, is one supported by your midwife or partner or both (see diagram d, page 130). The 'hanging squat' is a variation on this when your partner or midwife holds you semi-standing, supporting you under your armpits.

iv) A semi-upright position, leaning back against your partner for support, can be comforting, but it can also reduce the size of the birth canal widthways, as the position does not allow the coccyx to move backwards to widen the pelvic area.

v) Lying on your back is not a good position. You don't have the benefit of gravity for helping you push, your pelvis is not in a position where it can widen as far as possible, and it may cause foetal distress with the weight of your womb pressing back on blood vessels leading to the placenta. However, it may be necessary if you need to have full electronic foetal monitoring, where a belt is strapped around your middle and a small electrode clipped over the baby's head so that your contractions and its heartbeat can be recorded on a computer printout.

Foetal monitors increase the amount of equipment surrounding a birth and mean that the staff may begin to pay rather more attention to what the machine says, than to you. It also means that they will be far more aware of small changes, so they can be likely to intervene rather than letting the labour take a natural course. There are more Caesarean deliveries where a foetal monitor has been used during labour.

vi) In water: a delivery method pioneered by obstetrician Michael Odent at his clinic in France, combining it with natural childbirth. Warm water supports the mother in labour and can be very soothing and comfortable. Also when the baby is born underwater it comes from one warm, watery environment (the amniotic fluid in the sac which has protected it for the last nine months) to another. It is argued that this is a far gentler way to introduce the baby into the world. It is, however, also argued that water births are anything but natural.

You could also use it as a method of soothing pain, and calming yourself, during labour's first stage only.

Few hospitals in the UK have the facilities for a delivery in water – and no NHS hospitals which I have been able to find. However, it is possible to stay in an ordinary warm bath – if the staff are willing, and if it has been disinfected properly – during the first stage of labour, if your waters have not broken (if they have, there is an increased risk of infection in a much-used hospital bath). But you would probably have to get out for the second stage, when the baby is actually delivered.

It is possible to hire a collapsible birthing tub (which looks not unlike a deep paddling pool) to take with you to the hospital. It comes with its own water heaters to keep it at a constant temperature and costs from around £30 a week to borrow. Phone up and speak to the Active Birth Centre in London (see HELPLINES). Check with the hospital first to get their agreement and arrange th : best way to get it sterilized.

Possible problems in labour
If a woman's pregnancy and her progress during labour are carefully and sensitively monitored, the risk of problems during labour is cut down enormously. Many potential difficulties can be spotted early. However, the following *can* occur – though according to John McGarry less than 10 per cent of women today experience complications.

Prolonged labour
By definition this is one which lasts for 24 hours or more. The 'normal' length of labour is 12 to 18 hours for a first baby and 6 to 12 for a second. The problem is often deciding when labour has actually started.

Labour's progress is monitored by checking how far your cervix is dilated – the rate is somewhere around 1cm an hour if all is going well. By the time it has reached 10cm it is wide enough to allow the baby's head to stretch the opening further and pass down the vagina. Delay is usually for one of three reasons.

1. Problems with the way your uterus is contracting (perhaps not strongly enough or not often enough). This can be treated with drugs. (See also **Aromatherapy**, **Acupuncture** and **Medical herbalism**, below).

2. The baby is in a difficult position such as bottom first (breech) or face forward (occipito posterior, chin pointing forwards). It is often possible to

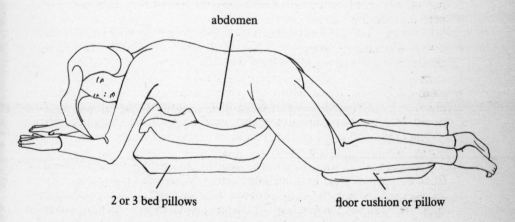

abdomen

2 or 3 bed pillows　　　　　　　　　floor cushion or pillow

The position recommended by John McGarry, consultant obstetrician at the Royal Devon Hospital, for encouraging a baby in the breech position (bottom downwards, instead of head downwards) to turn around into a better position for delivery of its own accord. Only remain in this position for as long as you feel comfortable.

133

rotate or move the baby by hand to encourage it into a better position for delivery. If this is not possible, there are other methods to aid delivery such as suction (vacuum extraction or ventouse), an episiotomy cut to widen the birth canal exit, forceps or (if all else fails) a Caesarean.

3. Failure of the placenta to appear of its own accord in the third stage of labour. When the baby has been born the placenta needs to be expelled before the cervix closes up. Occasionally it may need a very gentle tug (extremely carefully done) or (in about three per cent of cases) a general anaesthetic so that it can be removed by surgery.

Foetal distress

This means that the baby is becoming short of oxygen for one reason or another, and distress can be detected by checking the baby's heartbeat regularly. It should be between 110 and 160 beats a minute – higher or lower suggests a problem.

Sudden violent movements made by the baby (as if it were turning over and over) or the presence of a substance called meconium (thick green matter from in the baby's rectum and usually passed only after delivery) in the amniotic fluid, can also be signs of distress and may be accompanied by heartbeat abnormalities.

Reasons for foetal distress include:
* too-frequent contractions of the uterus (which can obstruct the blood supply to the placenta), this may also occur while being induced by a drip;
* the umbilical cord becoming twined around the baby's neck, or compressed between the baby and the womb;
* the baby's head being squashed tightly into your pelvis, or coming down too quickly.

If the baby is in severe distress the medical staff will make sure it is delivered as soon as possible, by Caesarean if the cervix is not yet fully dilated or via suction (ventouse) or forceps delivery if it is.

Heavy bleeding in the mother

When the uterus has delivered the baby and the placenta, it will contract, and when it has contracted it will stop bleeding. The baby suckling immediately at your breast helps this process.

Actual haemorrhages are very rare now, but remember that oxytocin produces double the rates of post-partum haemorrhaging. They can be stopped with drugs, such as syntocinon or ergometrine, which encourage the womb to contract fully and are given by injection. Massaging the uterus through the abdomen wall helps, too. Injections or tablets of Vitamin K (clotting agent) may also be given. Problem bleeding might be caused by small parts of the placenta left behind in the womb. This could also cause infection, so it should be dealt with immediately.

A small amount of bleeding may come from the site of an episiotomy before it is carefully sewn up. This can be controlled by pressing the area firmly until it can be stitched.

A Caesarean

This means delivering the baby surgically via an incision in the mother's abdomen, rather than via her vagina. Rates vary hugely around the world – in Rio de Janeiro Caesareans can amount for up to 90 per cent of deliveries. The USA has a rate approaching 25 per cent – many clinics there actually advertise the Caesarean option so women will ask for it on the grounds that it is 'safer', painless and will keep the vaginal passage as tight as it always was (referred to as 'keeping your tubes honeymoon fresh' by one Florida private clinic). In the UK the rate is nearer 10 per cent. It rose substantially in the 1970s and is now levelling off in most areas.

HOW IT IS DONE. Either under an epidural or a general anaesthetic. The latter is more likely if the procedure is an emergency one, as an epidural takes time to set up and 15 to 20 minutes to take effect, plus possible extra time to locate an anaesthetist, who is not always readily available.

If it is carried out under general anaesthetic, you will naturally remember nothing at all about the procedure. Some women feel strange waking up and being handed a baby they are told is theirs, without any knowledge of its having been delivered. They may even fear that the child might not be theirs after all. Ask the staff, or a partner, if someone can take a picture of the baby being lifted from your abdomen as 'proof', if you feel this might be something that could worry you.

Under an epidural, you can stay awake and be given the baby to hold immediately it is lifted from your womb (usually after a paediatrician has checked it over). A screen is set up across your waist, the epidural is given (see Pain Relief, page 123) and a drip put into your arm. The doctor will make a neat five- or six-inch cut just above your pubic hair-line, suck out the amniotic fluid (which you will hear) and lift out the baby, pressing down on your stomach. You will then be given an injection to speed up the expulsion of the placenta and will be able to hold the baby and put it straight to your breast (if you wish) while this is happening, and while the cut is stitched. The delivery takes only 10 to 15 minutes; the careful stitching up afterwards nearer 30 (your womb wall and stomach wall have to be sewn separately).

AFTERWARDS you stay in bed for a day, and then are encouraged to get up and start moving around and doing post-natal exercises. The cut will be sore and you might have a headache from the epidural as well (ask the staff for painkillers). Most women feel fine after a week or so and are allowed home after about 6 to 8 days (and often less).

Breastfeeding can be painful as the baby rests on your stomach – try cushioning the area with a soft light pillow or a light polystyrene-filled bag like the Snugglesac (see HELPLINES). If you feel dissatisfied or distressed by the Caesarean in any way, speak to your consultant about it or get in touch with one of the Caesarean self help groups (see HELPLINES).

WHY IT IS DONE. An emergency Caesarean is needed for:
* labour problems such as foetal distress;

* a cervix which will not dilate far enough;
* a very long labour which has exhausted you and may be endangering your baby;
* a placenta which has become detatched from the womb wall and will no longer be able to keep the baby supplied with oxygen via the umbilical cord.

You might also have an 'elective' Caesarean (planned in advance) for any of the following reasons:
* if the baby is especially big or if you are expecting more than one;
* if you have a womb infection or vaginal infection such as active herpes;
* if there is Rhesus factor incompatibility between you and the baby;
* if the placenta is positioned at the bottom part of the uterus (placenta praevia) and might obstruct the baby's exit;
* if you have pre-eclampsia, heart disease, high blood pressure;
* if your baby needs to be delivered early or is in a breech position and cannot be turned – often an obstetrician will be able to encourage it to turn around beforehand (according to John McGarry it is often possible to do it yourself, very gradually), while some breech babies and twins are born by normal vaginal delivery.

To encourage the baby to turn round try lying on your front, kneeling on one cushion with two or three more under your stomach, elbows bent and chin on the floor. The pressure, though gentle, is persistent and will often encourage a breech baby to change its position (see diagram iv).

'ONCE A C SECTION, ALWAYS A C SECTION'?: This is no longer true. In the past if you had had your first baby by Caesarean, it used to follow that future babies would also be delivered this way, too. Now obstetricians are becoming far more sympathetic towards encouraging women to give birth vaginally if they wish to try it after *one* Caesarean. They monitor the progress of the labour very carefully to ensure, amongst other things, that the site of the former Caesarean's scar (which will be weaker than the surrounding tissue) does not rupture.

Discuss with your consultant whether the conditions favour a vaginal birth next time. If you are not happy with his response, get a second opinion (ask your GP to refer you to another consultant, or ask the first consultant if you might discuss the matter with one of his colleagues). Contact the Caesarean Support Network (see HELPLINES) which provides information, help and encouragement for women who have had a Caesarean, and wish to try a vaginal delivery.

8. *After delivery*
It is tempting to concentrate only on what you would like for the labour part of your stay in hospital or your home confinement. But the few days immediately after the birth itself are just as important to the wellbeing of you and your baby. If you are going into hospital, state on your birthplan the sort of post-delivery conditions you would prefer.
i) See **After Delivery** and **Breastfeeding** on page 119.
ii) Visitors: It can be exhausting to be deluged with well-meaning relatives and

friends all anxious to meet the new baby. If you think this might be a bit much for you both, say that you want two or three days (or however many you prefer) with your partner as the only visitor, or instruct your partner and the hospital about who you would like to see.

iii) When you go home with your baby you will need to have thought about who you want to be around to help you (and who you'd rather not have around for a bit, too). Tell your partner so that he can be there for you, or ask a good friend or parent to come and help you out for a while and to fend off eager relatives and other visitors. You will need the benefit of a few days or weeks in a quiet, calm home environment.

Your physical recovery
Everyone's rates and powers of recovery vary considerably. Much depends on getting enough rest, on performing post-natal exercises religiously (the physiotherapist will show you these in hospital) and on the skill of the midwife or doctor attending your birth. See POST-PREGNANCY PROBLEMS, page 393; see also **Acupuncture**, **Medical herbalism**, **Aromatherapy** and **Homoeopathy**, below, for what complementary therapies can do to help. Many of them are most helpful for reducing bruising and soreness and for rebalancing the hormonal system.

It may take a while to feel completely 100 per cent again – partly thanks to the additional demands the new baby places on your energies. Maggie Thom, consultant at Guy's Hospital in London, estimates that many women won't feel fully back to their old selves for about a year, so a slow but steady recovery is perfectly usual. Please do not feel discouraged if you do not feel physically and mentally terrific by the initial six-week post-natal check-up. Few women do.

STITCHES (from an episiotomy or a natural tear). Stitches to repair an episiotomy can take anything from 10 days to several weeks to heal. Natural tears tend to heal faster, but the time is still variable. Usually soluble thread is used for the sewing, so the stitches will have 'melted' away on their own after about 10 days, leaving the area neat and repaired but probably still tender for a while.

The following things will help if your stitches are hurting.
* Adding half a cupful of salt to your bath and soaking in it once or twice a day (this also helps the healing process).
* Adding a strong herbal tea to the bath and soaking in it once or twice a day. Take equal measures of uva ursa, comfrey and shepherd's purse herbs, mix them up together in a big plastic bag and use a good handful in a couple of pints of boiling water. (These are available from the Culpepers and Neal's Yard chains and from Baldwins of Walworth Road – see HELPLINES.) Leave it to stand and steep for 10 to 15 minutes, then add it to your bathwater. While you are in hospital you can borrow a large catering teapot from the ward kitchen (if the nurses will let you) to make it in. Or ask someone to make it daily at home and bring it in a lidded container or a bottle each day. You can also add the herbs direct to the bath, but this can be messy to clear up afterwards.
* If it hurts to pass water because your stitches sting painfully, take a glass of water into the lavatory and pour it gently down over your perineum area as you

urinate. Or if there is a bidet (there often will be in maternity ward loos) turn on the water flow, sit across the bidet so that the stream of water is directed across your lower region and perineum, and urinate. (You must clean the bidet thoroughly afterwards.) Some women also find it convenient to pass water in the bath just before they get out. If you haven't got a bidet the showerhead in the bath will have the same effect – but don't turn the water on too hard.

The following measures will help speed the healing process.

* Keep the stitched area very clean and dry. Wipe from front to back after going to the lavatory. Wash the area afterwards by pouring a glass of water down it or spraying water from a showerhead or bidet over it. Dab dry with cotton wool to avoid the stitches getting 'soggy' (which can encourage infection). Dry the area with a hairdryer with the setting on 'cool' (a towel may be abrasive, not dry the area completely and also spread infection).

* Comfrey tea (cooled) poured over the area also helps, as do many herbal and homoeopathic remedies (see **Medical herbalism** and **Homoeopathy**, below).

Do not put creams on the area (e.g. Savlon or Arnica cream) unless directed by a doctor, though antiseptic and healing they, too, will make the area soggy and encourage infection).

BLEEDING. The womb is raw inside where the placenta was attached to its wall, so it will take about 10 days to heal. For about five of these the blood will be red, then it becomes reddish brown, then brown, then it tails off altogether. Use very soft pads (not tampons) as sanitary protection.

CONSTIPATION. You may find you are constipated after childbirth, and if you have any temporary haemorrhoids from pushing during the second stage of labour (or which appeared during your pregnancy) this can be very uncomfortable. Ask the nursing staff for mild laxatives (Lactulose is very helpful and will not affect the baby's bowels if you are breastfeeding).

If you have any stitching around the rectum passage or anus, do not be afraid that straining a bit to empty your bowels will burst them – it is very unlikely to do so but the worry of that can make some women 'hold on' to the contents of their bowels and thus become even more constipated. Check with the doctor or nurses if you are concerned.

WEAKENED PELVIC FLOOR. Do pelvic exercises again each day as soon as you feel ready (see INCONTINENCE).

POST-NATAL EXERCISES to tone up your stomach muscles. Again, start as soon as you can (ask to see the hospital physiotherapist or midwife about the best ones. Pregnancy or childbirth books will also describe suitable exercises.

SEX AFTER PREGNANCY. Mention any problems at your six-week check-up and see POST-PREGNANCY PROBLEMS, page 393.

Complementary therapy

Complementary therapies tailor their treatments very much to the individual: the precise nature of the treatment you receive will vary, depending on your medical history, symptoms, lifestyle, etc. The following information indicates the *sorts* of things a therapist is most likely to do or recommend. Do not be surprised if they feel you need something slightly different. This section is meant purely as an indication of likely treatments; it is not meant as a DIY guide to the medical uses of the different complementary therapies.

The various complementary therapies can greatly help to prepare you for the physical and mental stresses of labour, to withstand pain in the first, second and transitional stages of labour itself, and to alleviate problems which may later arise because of the birth process.

If you want to have a complementary therapist present during the birth – at home or in hospital – you must negotiate with the orthodox medical staff (midwife and/or doctor) for permission. The therapist may have helpful information about this. Some therapists are also able to suggest methods of self help. Ask for advice.

Acupuncture

Acupuncture at selected points, which help to produce anti-depressant and calming substances in the body, can help prepare you for labour in the days before it begins.

Throughout labour, pain control through acupuncture techniques alone works well for most women and can continue throughout the first and second stages. Acupuncture controls the pains of contractions without suppressing the contractions themselves.

After childbirth, acupuncture may help to speed your recovery from trauma and injury in the genital area, and to fight infection. Acupuncture, combined perhaps with acupressure and dietary advice, can be useful in helping your body to regain flexibility and mobility. The treatment will probably continue for up to three months, depending on your individual needs.

In the longer term, acupuncture at the hormonal balance points can help your hormones return to normal levels after birth. Treatment may last between two and six months.

Aromatherapy

For two to three weeks before the expected date of birth, aromatherapy is useful to help you to cope with increasing physical discomfort, emotional disturbance and feelings of anticipation.

Ideally, weekly body massage with a combination of essential oils of lavender, melissa, bergamot, rose and neroli, among others – individually blended for you and used with an individually devised bath blend – helps prepare your body and mind for the coming event.

In the first stage of labour, lower back massage – with specially blended oils of lavender, melissa, clary sage, jasmine and rose – for ten to fifteen minutes every half hour, helps relax your muscles, increase your pain threshold and has a pain-reducing effect. These analgesic essential oils are also anti-spasmodic, sedative and calming. They offer a measure of pain relief for almost every woman, and can be used alone.

In the second stage, the therapist may choose to use lower back massage, foot massage, or face, scalp, neck and shoulder massage, with the same individual blend of oils. To a large extent, this massage helps with the pain of contractions.

After childbirth, local applications of a blend of healing and analgesic oils – three or four times daily for two or three weeks – will help heal any cuts, tears and soreness around your perineum, labia and vagina.

THE WELL WOMAN'S SELF HELP DIRECTORY

Massage with personal blends of anti-infectious oils, such as tea tree and rosemary, can act both directly and indirectly on the immune system to fight off infection.

Massage with individual blends of oils can help restore muscle tone and physical flexibility during the months after childbirth, invigorating your body and mind. Extremely gentle massage of your abdomen and lower back with specialized techniques and oils can help your womb contract in the weeks after birth, thereby reducing pain and tenderness.

Stretched, flabby skin and stretch marks can also respond to aromatherapy.

Chiropractic

Chiropractic therapy helps to prepare your body for the mechanical stress of labour. You can be treated by a chiropractor for backache and pain throughout pregnancy – up until just hours before labour. As your pregnancy progresses, the types of manipulation may vary, to adjust to the changing shape of your abdomen.

Because your enlarged abdomen puts greater strain on your lower back, and because the relaxation of the pelvic ligaments in some women makes the lower back unstable, pregnancy can make an existing back problem worse – or start a new one. Appropriate manipulation can prevent or minimize this problem.

You should seek a consultation with the chiropractor within six weeks of childbirth, to check for any weakness in your spine or pelvic area. If a problem has already manifested itself, then help should be sought immediately. Chiropractic therapy can reduce strain and tension in your soft tissue and restore normal joint mobility.

Soft-tissue massage and spinal manipulation can also help restore physical flexibility, and can sometimes help indirectly with such problems as constipation or tenderness in your abdomen, because it affects your nervous system as a whole.

Homoeopathy

The homoeopathic approach to childbirth is to prepare you for delivery by stimulating the tone of your uterus in the final week, using Caulophyllum. Painful and difficult labour may respond to different remedies, according to the exact nature of your problems. Some of these include; Chamomila, Coffea or Gelsenium; and possible preventatives are Gelsemium, Cimicifuga or Caulophyllum. If labour contractions are ineffective, possibilities include Nat. Mur. or Nux. Vom. For excessive fatigue, Arnica is useful; if it is accompanied by fever after labour, the remedies are Kali-carb or phyrogenium. There are a number of remedies for pain.

Back ache after the birth responds to various treatments, according to the type of pain, but a good general remedy is Rhus-tox.

A prolapsed womb responds to Podophyllum; anaemia after childbirth may be treated with Cinchona or a combination of Calc. Phos. and Ferr. Phos.

Bladder problems after labour can also be treated – Causticum if it's hard to urinate, or Sepia if it's hard to control it. If your abdomen remains swollen, Sepia, Colocynth and Podophyllum can help.

Medical herbalism

To prepare your body for the stresses of childbirth, a medical herbalist will offer a combination of advice on diet, exercise and relaxation techniques, together with internal treatment taken for several months before the birth, such as raspberry-leaf tea (this acts as an astringent tonic to your uterus, toning its muscles for labour).

During labour, lemon balm or raspberry leaf ease the process by gently calming and relaxing your body without interfering with the contractions. Medical herbalism does not always, however, offer direct relief from pain, so think about other methods.

After childbirth, the medical herbalist can suggest remedies to help the healing process and to promote the return to normal of your ligaments, muscles and skin, etc. But any internal treatment must be considered with great care, as it may affect the hormonal balance or be passed on to your baby via breastmilk. It is essential to have a careful consultation with a qualified medical herbalist – who may prefer to suggest external remedies like herbal baths and compresses coupled with exercise and dietary advice.

Osteopathy
Osteopathy is a safe and effective way of assessing you throughout your pregnancy, and then treating you so that your muscles are in the best possible shape for labour – making labour itself shorter and easier.

Through advice on posture and specific exercises – individually designed for you, and usually given once a week at first, then less often as you progress – the osteopath prepares your body to perform its birth-giving task.

A post-natal check of mother and baby after six weeks can diagnose and/or treat any residual mechanical problems arising from a difficult birth.

Childbirth helplines

Association of Independent Midwives
c/o 65 Mount Nod Road, Streatham, London SW16 (081 677 9746)
A network of midwives who work privately – ante-natally at your own home, and post-natally – for a fixed fee. About half of the midwives are in Greater London.

AIMS (Association for the Improvement of Maternity Services)
c/o Beverley Beech, Chairwoman, 121 Iver Lane, Bucks (0753 652781)
Offers support, advice and information (on the telephone and in a series of booklets) about your maternity options and rights. Send SAE with a covering note.

Continence Line
(091 213 0050)
For totally confidential advice from trained nurse counsellors on continence difficulties, including those following childbirth.

Active Birth Centre
HQ – 55 Dartmouth Park Road, London NW5 1SL (071 267 3006)
Runs one- to four-day courses on natural childbirth techniques. Teachers nationwide; contact HQ for your nearest centre. They supply extensive literature on the subject and offer support and advice to women who want to try to have a natural childbirth. Classes run from approximately £15 for one day to £60 for four. Rent collapsible birth pools.

Association of Chartered Physiotherapists in Obstetrics and Gynaecology
c/o Association of Chartered Physiotherapists, 14 Bedford Row, London WC1
  (071 242 1941)
Offers advice and information on exercises to correct postural and continence
  problems associated with pregnancy.

Association of Qualified Curative Hypnotherapists
10 Balaclava Road, Kings Health, Birmingham (021 441 1775)
One of the professional hypnotherapists' organizations that can put you in touch with
  a properly qualified practitioner in your area.

BLISS (Baby Life Support System) 17–21 Emerald Street, London WC1
  (071 831 9393)
Provides life support equipment for premature babies to hospitals countrywise. They
  have informative publications for parents whose baby is on a life support system,
  plus a support group – Blisslink – for parents whose babies are premature.

Caesarean Avoidance Support Scheme
Poplar Farm, Silverleys Green, Halesworth, Suffolk IP19 0QJ
Advice and support for those wishing to avoid Caesarean delivery – as well as contact
  with women all over the UK who have successfully carried out vaginal delivery after
  a previous Caesarean section.

Caesarean Support Network
2 Hurst Park Drive, Huyton, Liverpool L36 17F (051 480 1184)
Support from a contacts network, meetings or over the telephone – as well as
  encouragement and advice for those who have undergone Caesarean section
  previously and wish to try for vaginal delivery next time. Send SAE.

Expectant Mothers Clinic
British School of Osteopathy, 1–4 Suffolk Street, London SW1 (071 930 9254)
The only osteopathy clinic in the UK to cater specifically to the postural problems
  etc., which pregnant women experience. It is possible to see an advanced student –
  or a fully qualified practitioner – so prices are much lower (from £12) than if you
  went to an osteopath at a private clinic. The clinic can also teach partners massage
  techniques to help alleviate back pains during the first stage of labour.

Foresight (Association for the Promotion of Preconceptual Care)
28 The Paddock, Godalming, Surrey (0483 427839)
To achieve the healthiest possible pregnancy, this society gives advice on diet, vitamin
  and mineral supplementation and ways to offset the effects of pollution on you and
  your partner's systems, several months before you conceive. Foresight has
  practitioners countrywide and charges for initial visits vary from £10 to £80, with
  extra charges for allergy or infection tests. Send SAE.

Gingerbread
HQ – 35 Wellington Street, London WC2 (071 240 0953)
Offers help and support to single mothers and one-parent families through a nationwide self-help support-group network. Contact HQ for details of the group nearest you.

Healthrights
344 South Lambeth Road, London SW8 (071 274 4000)
Researchers and advisors on all aspects of healthcare, in particular, maternity. Information on services is available by post or by telephone.

Maternity Alliance
59–61 Camden High Street, London NW1 (071 837 1265)
Organization which campaigns for improvements in social and financial support for pregnant women and parents with babies. They will supply advice and information about healthcare, provision and legal rights, as well as financial support systems available.

National Childbirth Trust
HQ – Alexandra House, Oldham Terrace, London W3 (071 992 8637)
With classes promoting ante- and post-natal preparation and care nationwide, NCT prepares expectant mothers and their partners for the birth and labour process. Relaxation techniques, exercises, breastfeeding advice – and a wide range of informative books, pamphlets, and a mail-order service for maternity nightwear, underwear (including pregnancy and breastfeeding bras) and breastfeeding apparatus – are just some of the many services offered.

National Council for One-Parent Families
255 Kentish Town Road, London NW5 (071 267 1361)
Advice for single parents and single, pregnant women.

Society to Support Home Confinements
Lydgate, Lydgate Lane, Wolsingham, Ship Aukland (0388 528044)
Supports and gives information to women who wish to have their birth at home but are having difficulty with the arrangement. (Send SAE)

Pre-Eclamptic Toxaemia Society (PETS)
Ty Iago, High Street, Llanberis, Gynned, Wales (0286 872477)
A support and self-help group for mothers who have developed PET. They also look at possible causes and avoidance tactics as well as preparing a newsletter.

SANDS (Stillbirth and Neo-natal Death Society)
28 Portland Place, London W1N 3DE (071 436 5881)
Support, friendship and counselling for the parents and family of a baby who has died at birth, or shortly afterwards. Support is offered to recent victims – or many years after the event. They will also visit you in hospital following labour.

TAMBA: Twins and Multiple Births Association
PO Box 30, Little Sutton, South Wirral L66 1TH (051 348 0020)

Specialist products and services
Birthways Inc.
Redmond, Washington, USA (0101 206 881 5242)
Supply 'empathy belly' – available by post. Telephone or write for details.

Natural Pregnancy Oils
55 Dartmouth Park Road, London NW1 1SL (071 267 3006)
Pure oils for pregnancy and labour supplied by mail order.

TENS machine rental
Try Medicare (071 228 2577) or TENS Rental (0256 64192).
If you want to ensure you have a TENS unit when you need it, it's best to rent one
   (costs from around £30 for 4 weeks or about £90 to buy).

Gardosi Birth Cushions
Are soon to be mass produced so they cost £90 instead of the current £250 if you
   want to buy one and share it with another pregnant woman friend whose dates
   aren't the same as yours – but many hospitals now have one. Call Caroline Ray,
   The Perinatal Research and Monitoring Unit, Queens Medical Centre
   (Nottingham University Hospital), Nottingham NG7 2UH (0602 709211)

Further reading
Active Birth by Janet Balaskas (Unwin Hyman)
New Active Birth by Janet Balaskas (Unwin Hyman)
The Active Birth Partner's Handbook by Janet Balaskas (Sidgwick & Jackson)
Natural Pregnancy by Janet Balaskas (Sidgwick & Jackson)
Who's Having Your Baby? A Health Rights Handbook to Maternity Care by Beverley
   Beech (Camden Press)
Childbirth for Men by Herbert Brant (Oxford University Press)
Pregnancy and Childbirth by Sheila Kitzinger (Penguin)
Birth Over 30 by Sheila Kitzinger (Sheldon Press)
Herbs for Pregnancy and Childbirth by Anne McIntyre (Sheldon Press)
Eating Well for a Healthy Pregnancy by Dr Barbara Pickard (Sheldon Press)
Birth Reborn by Michel Odent (Fontana)

Constipation

What is it?

Constipation means hard, infrequent stools – 'infrequent' being defined as every three or four days only and 'hard' as being so firm that they feel pebble-like, and are difficult and painful to pass.

It is a very common complaint, especially for women and for older people: one study found, in fact, that 20 per cent of older people had it to some extent, compared with 8 per cent of middle-aged people and only 3 per cent of young people. Men seem to have less of a problem.

It may be especially prevalent in women because bowel movements can be affected by changes in their hormone levels – which take place every month in women who are having periods, as well as during and after pregnancy, and during the menopause. Stress, and the hormones associated with it, may also be a factor, especially with women who have families and work (between half and two thirds of all married mothers have jobs).

Who is at risk?

Women are more likely to suffer from constipation if they fall into one or more of the following categories (and see **Causes**, below, for more detail). Women who:

* don't have enough fibre in their diet and eat a lot of refined and processed foods (instant meals, take-aways, sweets, cakes, pastries, biscuits, convenience foods) and too little fresh fruit, vegetables and whole grains (wholemeal bread, pulses, beans). But just to complicate matters, many people who do eat 'enough' fibre can get constipated too, suggesting that fibre-lack is not, as is often thought, the main reason for constipation;
* take little exercise or lead a sedentary life – working in an office, driving to and from work;
* have a history of gynaecological problems and operations, and other abdominal operations, such as appendix removal and exploratory operations around your stomach and bowel;
* are pregnant;
* are under stress;
* are elderly;
* have irritable bowel syndrome (IBS) – sometimes called irritable colon;
* drink very little liquid.

Summary

Constipation can be triggered off by:
1. anything which reduces the amount of water in your bowel (fever, sweating, not drinking much);

Causes	Medical help	Self help
AGE. If you are elderly certain medications you may be taking (e.g. drugs for high blood pressure or heart problems) could be responsible for aggravating constipation.	Ask your GP if he thinks anything he is prescribing might have this effect and if there are alternatives.	* Make sure you are eating properly if you are cooking for yourself (plenty of fresh vegetables and fruit, and high-fibre foods, and not too many instant meals and refined foods). * Try and take some exercise if your life is fairly sedentary. (Organizations like EXTEND have information on exercise facilities and local classes for older people; see HELPLINES.) * See HELPLINES for where to go for advice for problems specifically related to the elderly.
FEVER depletes the body's supplies of water so the bowel tries to conserve it by reabsorbing water from the faeces, making them harder and more difficult to pass.	None, other than some medication (aspirin or paracetamol) to bring down the fever.	* Drink as much liquid as you can (not coffee or tea as they are diuretic and encourage water loss).
GYNAECOLOGICAL PROBLEMS (including pelvic inflammatory disease, endometriosis, gynaecological operations and period problems). All these problems may temporarily alter the balance of hormones in your system. Gynaecological or other abdominal operations can also cause temporary damage to the nerves which make your bowel work, or produce temporary spasm in the abdominal and pelvic areas, which can affect the normal movements of your bowel. Some women suffer regularly from constipation before a period, but there is debate as to whether the rise in progesterone is really great enough to be causing this. It may be that women are particularly sensitive to hormone changes.	Nil, other than prescription of mild laxatives, if necessary. If you regularly suffer from constipation before a period you could ask your GP for a supply of mild laxatives for that time.	* If the problem is the result of an operation drink plenty of liquids and take mild laxatives until it rights itself. * If your constipation is related to your menstrual cycle change your diet to include more laxative or fibre-rich foods during the second half of your cycle, or take a prescribed fibre supplement then.

help.

sometimes called irritable colon. This is a blanket term for a wide variety of bowel complaints, all of which involve stomach pain and fluctuation between diarrhoea and constipation. IBS could mean that the nerves which usually make your bowel work are out of 'fine tuning,' so the bowel isn't receiving the messages it needs to push food and waste along.

* Avoid taking too many laxatives and treat yourself by some of the other self help suggestions given here (as well as a small amount of laxative agents).
* Reduce the stress in your life – at work and at home – if you can (see **Stress**, below).
* Use a hot-water bottle to help control any painful stomach spasms.
* See HELPLINES for details of where to get information on IBS and its management.

LACK OF EXERCISE. Any kind of movement helps reduce constipation by stimulating the nerves which 'drive' the bowel to function.

Your GP might suggest some laxatives to be taken for a short while and advise you to get some exercise.

If this presents a problem because you are elderly and/or not as mobile as you would like to be, there are associations who can help you (see HELPLINES).

* Take as much exercise as you can, even if it is only walking or – if you are housebound – moving from room to room. Any movement helps.

LACK OF FIBRE. More fibre is usually the first thing a GP might suggest for constipation. Fibre in food bulks out stools, making them softer and giving them more mass for the bowel muscles to push along; it also retains and absorbs water, making stools softer and easier to pass without discomfort.

Your GP may prescribe fibre supplements like Fibrogel, or bulking agents to be added to food or taken alone. He would also recommend an improvement in your diet to include more high-fibre foods (especially whole grains). But don't persist if it does not seem to be helping: Leeds University's major study in 1991 noted that lots of fibre doesn't always help and tried excessively could even do more harm than good.

* Eat plenty of fibre in your diet – fresh vegetables, especially green leafy ones (preferably eaten raw or lightly steamed), peas, beans and sweetcorn; fruit, especially bananas and fruit in its skin (scrub it well first); and 'whole' foods like unrefined carbohydrates such as wholemeal bread, brown rice, wholemeal pasta; wholegrain cereals such as oats and high-bran cereals like All Bran or Bran Hearts.
* High-fibre food has the added advantage of making you feel full without having to eat as many calories as usual because it is not absorbed by the gut but passed straight through. It can be very helpful in a weight-reducing or weight-maintenance plan as well.
* Try linseed (from health food shops) mixed with cereal or salads.

Causes

LACK OF LIQUID. Liquid softens waste matter and makes it bulkier and easier for the muscle to pass it out.

PREGNANCY. The additional amounts of progesterone required for a healthy, successful pregnancy have the result of relaxing all muscles and ligaments. This is to allow the birth canal and cervix to be as flexible as possible, to make room for the baby to pass through.

But the action of the progesterone is not selective – it acts on all muscle tissue, including the smooth muscle of the bowel, whose function is to contract and help waste matter pass down its length. The faeces is not 'massaged' so efficiently, therefore, and can become stuck, later becoming compacted and hard as the bowel absorbs its water content. This tends to mean that you empty your bowels less often because of the discomfort and the slow rate at which the waste is passed along (see PREGNANCY PROBLEMS, page 360)

Also, levels of the hormone motilin drop when you are pregnant, which also slows down the workings of the bowel.

Medical help

Nil

Unfortunately you can't alter the levels of progesterone in your body as this hormone is helping to maintain your pregnancy. However, your GP may give you some mild laxative and recommend laxative foods (such as prunes or figs for breakfast, or liquorice during the day).

Self help

* Drink a litre and a half a day, if you can, of plain spa or mineral water, fruit juice and water cordials, semi-skimmed or skimmed milk and herb teas.
* Do not drink too much tea or coffee. They are diuretic and will encourage your body to eliminate water via your kidneys and urine.
* A cup of coffee in the morning, however, can often help stimulate a bowel movement (as can a cigarette, but this is not a reason to take up smoking!).

* Eat a sensible diet.
* Take plenty of exercise.
* Drink lots of liquid.
* See also **General self help**, below.

STRESS hormones like adrenalin interfere with the bowel's nerve messages and produce abdominal muscle tension, restricting the gut.

Your GP may suggest relaxation training – visualization, self-hypnosis, breathing control and massage – see HELPLINES.

If the tension is severe he may prescribe mild tranquillizers (some of which are addictive, so they must be viewed as short-term treatment, i.e. up to about four weeks only).

* If possible, try to reduce the amount of stress in your life.
* Delegate more work to others, at home and in the office.
* Avoid situations you know to be stressful (like doing your supermarket shopping at off-peak times or early in the morning on Saturday).
* Consider relaxation classes or taking up regular exercise which also has an anti-stress effect (see HELPLINES).

USE OF LAXATIVES. Excessive use of laxatives and purgatives (many milder brands can be bought over the counter in the chemist) may, if taken for long, make the bowel lazy, because it becomes so used to being stimulated to work by artificial means that it stops responding to the body's natural reflexes. It may eventually come to rely on purgatives in order to work.

Your GP would suggest that you stop using purgatives and turn to high-fibre foods and natural laxatives instead.

* Eat foods that are good natural laxatives like a bowl of tinned figs or prunes.
* If you need a snack, try nibbling dried prunes or figs or liquorice.
* Chop dried prunes or figs into your morning cereal or stew them as a compote.
* After your bowels have returned to normal give them a break from the laxative foods and rely on fibre, extra drinks and exercise to keep things running smoothly. (Dried fruit or sweetened fruit in tins can be very calorific.)

2. anything which cuts down the bulkiness of the matter passing through your bowel (a diet high in heavily-processed foods and low in fibre);
3. anything that changes your hormonal balance, especially anything that alters the amount of *progesterone* in your body (pregnancy/menstrual cycle);
4. anything which affects the nerves which drive the bowel to work (abdominal or gynaecological operations, IBS or excessive laxatives).

Chronic Constipation.
Some women suffer from constipation which does not respond to any treatment and can cause considerable pain and discomfort.

Surgery to remove a portion of the colon might be the answer, but it should be seen as a last resort. In up to a third of patients it can produce chronic diarrhoea instead. Try all the self help advice (see also **General self help**, below) before resorting to surgery. Consultant gastroenterologist Peter Whorwell at Manchester's Withington Hospital uses gentle 'gut directed' hypnosis on intractable constipation problems.

General self help
In addition to the self help for specific causes of constipation, given above:
* Do not sit on the loo for hours straining to empty your bowels. Do not read when you are on the lavatory either, as this increases the time you spend there, and it also relaxes the muscles around your anus. Coupled with repeated straining, that encourages piles (enlarged veins like varicose veins around the anus) which can be very uncomfortable and itchy. This may sound like conventional wisdom, but a study done at the famous John Radcliffe Hospital in Oxford in 1989 looked at the early morning habits of 100 men and women with piles and found half the sufferers did in fact admit to spending six minutes or more reading on the lavatory, straining intermittently.
* When you feel the urge to empty your bowels, visit the lavatory immediately if possible, rather than trying to 'hang on'. Try and do so each morning. It is easy to forget, or to feel you do not have the time, if you lead a busy life and have to rush every morning. But it helps retrain your bowel to respond to its normal reflexes.

If you are 'hanging on' because of fear of pain or discomfort treat the cause of that pain. Dietary changes may be sufficient, or a temporary course of laxatives. (See also what to do if you have a small anal tear or fissure, below.) The longer you associate emptying your bowels with feeling pain, the more it will reinforce your constipation.
* If you have a small anal tear or fissure which opens up and bleeds a little red blood each time your bowels are emptied, it is important to keep it very clean so that it heals fast and does not become infected by the waste that passes across it. Hard stools can cause such a small tear, as can anal sex (which needs good lubrication from something like KY Jelly or a natural body lubricant like saliva, and also requires gentle penetration so as not to harm the anal passage).

So each time you pass stools, wash the area afterwards with warm water, pat dry with toilet paper and apply a little gentle antiseptic cream such as Savlon, which will not sting but will help prevent infection. If it does not heal within a few days, seek advice from your GP.

* Colonic irrigation may be helpful for loosening impacted bowel matter and giving the colon (large bowel) a direct internal spring clean, as long as you do not have any medical complications which make interference with your colon inadvisable. Colonic irrigation involves passing warm water, via a small tube, up into your colon, then allowing it to flow back out again via the tube for disposal. It is not at all uncomfortable (many people find it very pleasant and calming).

Costs for colonic therapy vary from £30 to £50 a session; it is not available on the NHS. You should usually need only one or two sessions to deal with ordinary constipation: be a bit wary if the therapist suggests a course of six or ten. Check that the therapist is:

a) properly qualified (contact the Colonic International Association, see HELP PLINES, for your nearest therapist);

b) using fully disposable parts to ensure there is no risk of infection – sterilization of equipment is *not* enough; and

c) using practice rooms which have the required proper plumbing facilities and drainage system to dispose of the waste immediately and hygienically. (A temporary receptacle for waste, such as a covered surgical container, is not good enough.)

If in doubt as to whether colonic therapy would be safe and suitable for you, ask your GP. Suggest your GP refers your question to a specialist gastro-enterologist, if he seems at a bit of a loss.

Complementary therapy
Complementary therapies tailor their treatments very much to the individual: the precise nature of the treatment you receive will vary, depending on your medical history, symptoms, lifestyle, etc. The following information indicates the *sorts* of things a therapist is most likely to do or recommend. Do not be surprised if they feel you need something slightly different. This section is meant purely as an indication of likely treatments; it is not meant as a DIY guide to the medical uses of the different complementary therapies.

The most satisfactory, long-lasting and gentle remedy for constipation is an improved diet, coupled with exercise and general attention to your lifestyle. Any complementary therapist who is consulted about troublesome constipation is likely to offer advice in all these areas, besides more immediate help based on their own professional expertise.

Acupuncture
Constipation may respond to acupuncture treatment.

Aromatherapy
Full-body massage – undertaken by a qualified therapist – with an individual blend of essential oils such as rosemary and lavender may help increase intestinal movement. The therapist may also teach you some self-massage techniques for daily use.

Clinical nutrition

Diet changes likely to be suggested are as follows. Avoid white flour, white rice, sugar (white or brown) and laxatives. Reduce red meat, milk, fried food, tea, coffee, cocoa, alcohol. Have wheat or oat bran, natural sauerkraut, rice bran, figs, prunes, prune juice, green leafy vegetables, celery, uncooked fruit, apples, garlic. Refined foods, coffee, tea, fried foods tend to cause constipation because they lack fibre and have an adverse effect on healthy bowel flora.

Useful supplements include B complex, Magnesium, Brewer's yeast, cod liver oil, psyllium husks, inositol, Vitamins A and C, and betaine hydrochloride. Magnesium is needed to increase muscle tone and peristalsis (movement of waste via muscle contractions). B complex is helpful in reducing stress, which may be a factor. Inositol is normally synthesised in the colon but may be lacking due to wrong bowel flora.

Cod liver oil helps movements and absorption/utilisation of calcium. Psyllium husks provide bulk fibre, which aids peristalsis. Betaine hydrochloride helps the intestines break down meat protein, thus reducing any putrefaction which might be taking place.

Vitamins A and C are likely to be deficient. Colonic irrigation is advisable, followed by a rectal implant of healthy bowel flora.

Homoeopathy

There are several remedies, according to the exact problem: opium for 'lazy bowels'; Silica for stools low in the rectum but still hard to pass; Alumin or Nitric acid for stools which result in bleeding; Bryonia when stools are large, hard and dry no matter how much fluid you drink; Nux Vomica or Aesculus when the rectum never feels quite empty after a bowel movement; and various others.

Medical herbalism

Dietary advice is most valuable, but gentle laxatives – for example, dandelion root – may be prescribed. Consult a practitioner for individual treatment.

Osteopathy

Osteopathic treatments applied to the supporting structure of the large intestine might help.

Constipation helplines

British Digestive Foundation
3 St Andrew's Place, London NW1 4LB (071 387 3534)
Part of the British Society of Gastroenterology, this charitable organization has many
  useful booklets, including two on Diarrhoea and Constipation, and another on
  Irritable Bowel Sydrome. Send a SAE for answers to specific queries, including
  travellers' advice.

British Nutrition Foundation
15 Belgrave Square, London W1 (071 235 4904)
Can put you in touch with a private nutritionist in your area, who can prepare a diet
  with special anti-constipation features. Your GP could also refer you to an NHS
  dietitian, should he/she feel it necessary.

The Candida and ME Clinic
93 Cheap Street, Sherborne, Dorset DT9 3LS (0935 813257)
Send SAE for details of colonic irrigation.

The Colonic Irrigation Association
26 Sea Road, Boscombe, Bournemouth BH5 1DF
Contact this association for details about colonic irrigation and local therapists.

The Hale Clinic
7 Park Crescent, London W1N 3HE (071 631 0156)
Provides details of, and practises, colonic irrigation.

Gut Reaction
c/o Voluntary Action Sheffield, The General Office, 69 Division Street, Sheffield:
  help group for IBS sufferers; one major symptom of which is constipation.

Institute of Optimum Nutrition
5 Jerdan Place, London SW6 (071 385 7984)
Can put you in touch with a nutritionist in your area – if you want personalized dietary
  advice. They train their nutritionists for two years, rather than the three required
  for NHS dietitians.

(National Association of) Disablement Information and Advice Lines
St Catherine's Hospital, Tickhill Road, Doncaster DN4 8QN (0302 310123)
This association supplies a wealth of advice and addresses about exercising if you are
  elderly – the best sports (swimming is excellent), and where special classes and
  sessions are held.

National Association for Pre-Menstrual Syndrome
(Guildford 572 715)
Telephone this association for advice on hormonal and dietary treatment for all
aspects of PMS, including constipation.

The Women's Health Concern
See GENERAL HELPLINES, page 480.

Women's Nutritional Advisory Service
See GENERAL HELPLINES, page 480.

Specialist products and services
Aquacise
HQ – 0255 436932
Phone for nearest class. Exercise in water by qualified swimming instructors and
lifeguards. Suitable for pregnant women.

Association of Qualified Curative Hypnotherapists
10 Balaclava Road, Kings Heath, Birmingham B14 7SG (021 441 1775)
To ensure your hypnotherapist is properly qualified, contact this association.

British Wheel of Yoga
1 Hamilton Place, Boston Road, Sleaford, Lincs (0529 306851)
For details of your nearest yoga or relaxation classes, telephone HQ.

Extend
Penny Copple, 1A North Street, Sherringham, Norfolk NR26 8LJ (0263 822479)
Send SAE for information on special classes, held by well-qualified teachers, which
help you exercise, improve mobility and suppleness, if you are elderly.

Health and Beauty Exercise
HQ – Walter House, 418–422 The Strand, London WC2R 0PT (071 240 8456)
Contact HQ for details of your nearest exercise/mobility class.

Relaxation for Living
HQ – 29 Burwood Park Road, Walton on Thames, Surrey
Hold relaxation classes countrywide; contact HQ for the class nearest to you.

IBS and chronic constipation sufferers: Write to Dr Peter Whorwell at Withington
Hospital, Manchester (061 445 8111) to find out which other units in the UK are
now doing the gut directed hypnosis treatment, as a few more hospitals now are.

Contraception

There is a wider choice of contraceptive methods available today than ever before, plus some very promising research both into completely new methods and into making improvements on the ones we already have. However, the perfect contraceptive does not exist yet. They still all have their pros and their cons, because:

* No method is 100 per cent effective in preventing pregnancy.
* Few are 100 per cent safe for the health of the user and/or future pregnancies.
* Few are 100 per cent convenient to use.
* Those which score 100 per cent on one count will fail to score 100 per cent on another.

So finding the right method for you will involve a lot of decisions, some of them on quite intimate matters. Some couples can find a method which is absolutely ideal for them – but your eventual choice is most likely to be the method which is simply the least disadvantageous.

The first step is to list the kind of questions which may be important to you in deciding which method to use:

For instance, if getting pregnant would be a total catastrophe at the moment, you might choose a method which is very effective, despite the fact that it may have some side-effects. You might even use more than one method at once.

If you (or your partner) hate the thought of sex which isn't totally spontaneous or if your partner doesn't like the idea of your using contraception at all – you won't want a method which has to be applied when you're just about to make love.

Also, your own medical history will make certain methods more of a health risk for you than they would be for another woman.

Points to consider
1. Does the method have a good record for preventing pregnancy?
* The figures for each method are usually quoted as percentages or 'woman years', i.e. a method that is 97 per cent effective means that if 100 women use it for a year, three will get pregnant.
* Effectiveness rates, also, may be given in two version: the ideal and the realistic. The first is the effectiveness if the method is used **exactly** according to instructions, every time a couple makes love. Unfortunately, there are times when this does not happen. Cautionary new figures on *actual* failure rates, as opposed to 'in ideal usage' failure rates are: oral contraceptives, 6.2 per cent; condoms, 14.2 per cent; diaphragms, 15.6 per cent; spermicides only, 26.3 per cent; there are no figures for IUDs (AGI Institute of New York, 1989). The

second is the average effectiveness when used by real-life couples who some-times forget or can't be bothered. You know yourself what kind of partner(s) you have, and whether contraception will be taken seriously on every occasion.

2. How fertile are you?

The answer to this question may help you make a decision on effectiveness (see above).

* Some couples, for instance, seem to be super-fertile, and know they have to be super-careful.

* The trouble is that, unless you've had pregnancies before, it is impossible to know – especially as you may be more fertile with one partner than with another. (See INFERTILITY, page 250.)

* One factor you *can* take into account, however, is your age: fertility is at its peak for women at around 24 to 27 years, and declines very slowly from around 28 to your early 30s; it then begins to drop more rapidly (see INFERTILITY, page 250).

3. What stage have you got to in your child-bearing years? How important is it to avoid pregnancy right now? And how important is it to make sure your future fertility is not compromised?

* Some family planning experts divide their clients into 'delayers' (women who have not yet started a family), 'spacers' (women who have one or more children and probably want more – but not yet) and 'stoppers' (women who have completed their family). One could add 'nevers' (women who don't want children at all).

* You could assume that spacers, and some (but not all) delayers, might not be too upset if they got pregnant, and so might choose the method which they prefer, even if it is less effective than some others. Stoppers and nevers, on the other hand, want to be as sure as possible that they won't conceive – and won't mind if their method makes it more difficult (or impossible) to conceive later on.

4. What side-effects (if any) does the method have? Are they worth it?

Again, this is something that depends on the individual. For instance:

* Early research on the IUD seemed to show that older women suffered less from heavy periods when using an IUD. Later, it emerged that they had just as much heavy bleeding – but complained of it less, because the convenience and effectiveness of the method was more important to them.

* Again, heavier periods may not bother you too much if your normal periods are very light, but could be totally unacceptable if you already bleed heavily every month.

5. Does the method carry known risks to health? How serious are they? Are you in one of the high-risk groups? (See **Which method?**, below, for details.)

* You have a little flexibility here because you can control some of the health risks yourself. For instance, if you like taking the pill, you should give up smoking and may want to consider nutritional supplementation (see **The Pill**, **dietary deficiences**, below).

6. Is using a certain method of contraception (or using contraception at all) against your religion, your personal beliefs – or your partner's?

* Roman Catholics are officially not supposed to use anything but natural methods (see **Natural family planning**, below), although many do.
* Buddhism carries no duty to 'be fruitful and multiply' (many Buddhist leaders support contraception).
* Orthodox Judaism does – although certain contraceptive methods are possible – and other forms of Judaism are much more liberal.
* Modern Islamic legal opinion tends to allow contraception – but not types which can't be reversed (like sterilization).
* If your partner has strong beliefs about contraception which you don't share, you may decide to look after your own contraceptive needs without consulting him. You will obviously want a method which is undetectable. Family planning is a confidential health service, and you don't legally need your partner's consent to have it. If necessary, you also have the right to insist that your own GP is not informed.
* If religion and contraception are causing you problems it may be helpful to discuss contraception with a sympathetic priest or with a counsellor. You should get detailed advice on exactly which methods (if any) are acceptable in your own religion – it can be quite complicated. The Catholic Marriage Advisory Service, and the Jewish Marriage Council may also be able to help – and despite their titles you do not have to be married to get advice from them (see HELPLINES).

7. How pleasant is the method to use?
* Tastes vary – both in sexual practice and in contraceptive method. This is important, and you may need all your courage to explain something like this to a doctor who is convinced he has found just the right method for you. If you (or your partner) don't really like a certain method, you are unlikely to use it (not often enough, anyway) to make it effective. For instance, some women don't like the 'messiness' of using spermicidal creams and jellies, or methods which involve touching their own genital area. Others may not wish to interrupt the love-making process by stopping so their partner can put on a sheath, or waiting for a spermicidal pessary to take effect.

8. Does this method fit in with your lifestyle?
This question covers all sorts of things. For instance:
* If you make love at unpredictable times, in unpredictable places, you might not want something like a diaphragm because you'd have to carry it, and spermicidal jelly, round with you all the time.
* If you have to make love in secrecy, a diaphragm or packet of sheaths in your handbag might be indiscreet.
* If you tend to forget things, you might not remember to take a Pill every day.

9. Who controls the supply of the method?
* Some methods (sheaths, spermicides, female sponges etc.) can be bought over the counter, and it's nobody's business but yours.
* Others (like the Pill and the IUD) you can get only from a doctor.

10. Who controls the use of the method?
* Some methods (like withdrawal, or the sheath) depend on the man. Other methods (the Pill, the IUD etc.) are under the control of the woman. How

reliable is your partner, and is he as keen as you are to prevent a pregnancy?
* How reliable do you feel you are, come to think of it?
11. Do you have a sexual relationship with just one man – or more than one?
The answer to this question will affect your choice in several ways.
* It will govern various things already covered under 'lifestyle' above (convenience, discretion and so on).
* It will make you more likely to choose a method which is under your own control.
* You will run a greater risk of catching some kind of infection – so it might be a good idea to choose a method which gives some protection from infections (such as the sheath or the diaphragm).

Where to go for family planning help
You have quite a choice of places to go for advice and help. All have advantages and disadvantages.

Local shops
This is the simplest way to get contraceptives – but the range of methods available is correspondingly small.
* Thanks to all the worries about AIDS, you can buy condoms in quite a lot of shops – sometimes from slot machines (in clubs, bars, pubs – and some fashion clothes shops too).
* Chemists have condoms, sperm-killing (spermicide) products to place in your vagina and the 'female sponge' ('Today') to place over your cervix. (Ask for the pharmacist, not just a shop assistant, who will be able to give you a certain amount of advice.)

Your GP
Most GPs offer some kind of family planning service. Modern GPs (trained after around 1974) have some basic training in the subject.
* Family planning supplies are free on the NHS – whether you are married or single – although GPs do not supply condoms.
* There is specialized post-graduate training in family planning, both for doctors (JCC or FPA) and for nurses (FPA or ENB), so ask if anyone at your GP practice has these certificates.
* GPs without this training are most likely to offer you the Pill and least likely to offer you something that needs careful fitting – like the diaphragm or the IUD. However, your GP may refer you to a family planning clinic if you wish to discuss these methods – ask for a referral.
* Diaphragms and (especially) IUDs do take training and skill to make the fitting as comfortable as possible and the result effective. Even if the GP or nurse who does the fitting is trained in family planning, experience counts for a lot – this is a manual skill, which can be built up only through practice. So pluck up courage and ask how many fittings he does on a regular basis.
* If your GP doesn't specialize in family planning – or do family planning at all – you can ask him to refer you to a GP who does, while the first still takes care of all your other health needs. Or simply change GP. To find one who specializes

in contraception, call up your local Community Health Council (see HELP-LINES).
* If you prefer to keep the fact that you are using contraception very private, if your GP is your family doctor, he will know your family – which may be a disadvantage. On the other hand, other people in the waiting room won't know why you've called in, which won't be the case if you're seen at the family planning clinic.

Family planning clinics
Look in the phone book under 'family planning' to find one. Many were once run by the Family Planning Association, and were taken over by the NHS in 1974. (If you cannot find one, call up the FPA in London and ask where your nearest one is – they will be able to tell you – see HELPLINES.)
* Anyone – male or female, married or single – can go to these clinics and receive supplies free (including condoms).
* If they prescribe a family planning method which has some bearing on your health (i.e. the Pill, IUD, sterilization) the practice is to inform your GP so that (i) the clinic knows there is no medical drawback you haven't told them about, and (ii) the GP can maintain a complete record of factors affecting your health. If you don't want your GP informed for any reason, make this very clear. The clinic is obliged to respect your wishes.
* Family planning clinics have some advantages over GPs: (i) staff are certain to be specially trained and experienced; and (ii) because there are more staff, you have more chance to pick and choose – to have a woman doctor, for instance.
* The disadvantage is, like all NHS facilities, FPCs are hard-pressed and subject to cuts, so you may have long waits and possibly hurried consultations.

Domiciliary family planning
If it's hard for you to get out – you're disabled, say, or you have to look after an elderly or disabled dependent – it might be possible to have a doctor or nurse visit you at home. Ask your GP, or local Community Health Council (look in the phone book under 'C' or see HELPLINES.) However, these services are few and far between.

Private or charity services
The Family Planning Association still has a few clinics it runs itself. So do other charities like Marie Stopes Clinics and (especially for young people) Brook Advisory Centres. Find them in the phone book or through the HELPLINES section. Most of them also offer related women's services, like cancer screening, psycho-sexual counselling and pregnancy termination.
* These clinics have very much the same advantages as NHS family planning clinics (trained staff etc.) plus, almost certainly, a more unhurried and personal service.
* The disadvantage is that all (except Brook) have to charge a fee to make ends meet, both for consultations and for supplies, although it is kept low (for

example, Marie Stopes Clinics charge £20 for a routine visit, plus the cost of supplies).

Miscellaneous
Contraceptive services may well be provided by other people, such as well woman clinics, ante- and post-natal clinics, health visitors and hospitals. Find out as for family planning clinics. Or you could choose a private gynaecologist.

Young people and contraception
* Brook Advisory Centres are specially for people under 25. Find your nearest in the phone book, or contact headquarters (see HELPLINES).
* Some family planning clinics (both NHS and charity) run special sessions for young people.
* If you're under 16, and therefore not legally old enough to have sex, doctors are obliged to encourage you to tell your parents. They are not strictly entitled to force you to tell, and they are not certainly entitled to tell your parents themselves.

But the BMA (the GP's professional body) is a bit lukewarm on this, so confidentiality is not 100 per cent guaranteed. Clinics (both NHS and private) put a much higher priority on your rights, so your confidentiality is safer there.

Which method?
METHODS THAT DON'T WORK. An enterprising sperm can cope with all kinds of obstacles so you are *not* safe if:
* you are having sex for the very first time;
* your periods appear to have recently halted due to the menopause;
* you wash or douche afterwards;
* you have sex during or just after your period;
* the man withdraws his penis before he ejaculates;
* the man ejaculates near – but not in – your vagina.
The main reasons are:
* sperm can swim a long, long way;
* they can stay alive inside you for two or three days – waiting for you to ovulate, for instance, and you don't always ovulate mid-cycle anyway;
* sperm can get into your vagina via fingers, etc;
* there are some sperm in the lubricating fluid the penis produces before ejaculation. And even if your periods have ceased, you *might* still ovulate for a while, irregularly, for a few months after it seems that your menopause has begun.

METHODS THAT WORK. Roughly speaking, birth control methods fall into two groups:
(i) 'barrier' methods, which physically prevent sperm reaching the female egg to fertilize it;
(ii) methods which interfere with the body in some way to prevent it from supporting a pregnancy. So far, all these are for women only.

Breastfeeding

The female body isn't over-keen to get pregnant again while a new baby is still being nourished. So if you're breastfeeding, this can act as a contraceptive.

Disadvantages: it works only if you're (i) doing it 'fully': about every two to three hours, day and night (i.e. 'on demand'), and (ii) using no other form of feed for the baby at all; and (iii) protection drops if you are supplementing with formula milk, early solids or juice or if you miss even one or two feeds. But remember, even though breastfeeding suppresses periods, you might just be ovulating sometimes so don't assume no periods means you cannot get pregnant.

Advantages: (i) with all these conditions fulfilled, breastfeeding is about 98 per cent effective; (ii) there is no risk to your health; (iii) there is no interference with love-making; and (iv) it is a method acceptable to all religions. (See BREASTFEEDING DIFFICULTIES, page 52.)

Male condom (sheath)

The man puts it on his erect penis (*before* he enters your vagina, not halfway through love-making – there are sperm in the penis's lubricating fluid). Or you put it on for him. The sperm are safely trapped inside.

Advantages: (i) used properly, they are pretty effective – about 95 per cent; (ii) you can buy condoms easily and cheaply, without seeing a doctor; (iii) you can keep your own supplies handy; (iv) there is no risk for your health – if by any chance you're allergic to the rubber they're made of, you can get brands like Durex Hypo-allergenic; and (v) they help protect you from infections and sexually transmitted diseases (including AIDS) – especially useful if you have more than one sexual partner. Many condoms are impregnated with a spermicide (nonoxynol-9) which – in the test-tube, at least – kills the HIV (AIDS) virus. If you dislike the smell of rubber, try Mates' peppermint condoms.

Disadvantages: (i) many men don't much like using condoms because whatever the manufacturers claim, they do dull sensation; (ii) many women aren't keen either, although you may have some fun experimenting with ribbed or 'tickler' brands – more fun for the woman than the man, though; and (iii) it can be awkward asking a man to use one.

Tips:

* only buy condoms labelled with the British Standards kitemark – quality can't be guaranteed with anything else;

* choose a condom with a teat at the end (this holds the sperm better – but squeeze out any air in it before it's put on);

* handle with care – tear the packet at the edge, not in the middle, and watch out for jagged finger-nails etc.;

* make sure the man withdraws his penis soon after orgasm, before it goes soft again, and keeps the condom in place with his hand so it doesn't slip – otherwise sperm can escape into your vagina;

* If it won't flush away neatly – wrap it in loo paper to weight it down.

* use a new condom *every* time you make love, not just at each love-making session;

* many condoms have a lubricant – but if you need extra lubrication, use

something designed for the purpose (like KY jelly, from the chemist), oil-based lubricants (like Vaseline) will rot the rubber within minutes. So will oil-based spermicidal pessaries, like Rendells and Genexols.

Diaphragm or cap

There are various shapes and sizes with various names like Dutch cap/ diaphragm (the most common type), vimule, Dumas/vault cap. These may have a small spring in the rim. With expert help you choose the right size to fit over your cervix and seal out sperm.

You put it in before you have sex (several hours before, if that's more convenient and you want to start making love without fiddling about with it – e.g. before going to bed or before going out for the evening) and put spermicidal jelly on both sides. You keep it in for at least six hours *after* sex – sperm can stay alive a long time. Then you hook it out with your finger. Remember that spermicide has a time limit and needs to be topped up (check the instructions on your particular brand).

Advantages: (i) used properly (i.e. every time with enough spermicide) it is 98 per cent effective; (ii) it is under the woman's control; and (iii) it carries no risk to health, unless you're allergic to rubber, in which case you can't use it.

Disadvantages: (i) it has to be properly chosen and fitted; (ii) you have to have it handy for when you make love – which might be inconvenient unless you always make love at home and/or can plan your sex life carefully; (iii) it can be awkward to insert, especially if it is covered with slippery jelly, or if you've had a few drinks – the ones with springs can ping right across the room; (iv) some men say they can feel it when they make love; (v) things can get rather messy/smelly during prolonged love-making bouts, since it has to stay in six hours each time you make love and you must keep the spermicide topped up; and (vi) according to american urologist Larrian Gillespie, a too-large cap can press on your bladder or urethra and constrict the strong flow of urine which acts to flush out the system and keep it free from infection – worth bearing in mind if you suffer from cystitis or other recurring infections (see CYSTITIS).

Tips: * putting it in may take some learning – it will help to practise, at first, at times you don't *need* to use it;
* if the cap makes *you* feel uncomfortable, you need a re-fit;
* if looser vaginal muscle tone is a problem, try the cervical cap instead.
* you may need a re-fit from time to time – e.g. if you've lost or gained more than 7lb, given birth or had a miscarriage or abortion;
* if these are taken care of, you can buy supplies in Boots;
* rubber can perish and caps can get damaged in other ways, so you must get a new one at least once a year and follow the instructions you're given about washing it and storing it – in particular, avoid heat and damp and regularly check for any tiny holes in it by holding it up to a strong light;
* be very careful, for the same reason, with lubricants and spermicidal pessaries (see under **Tips** for male condoms);
* if it does not slip into place accurately first time, it can get very slippery all over when covered in spermicide and harder to insert. If this happens, wipe it dry, reapply the spermicide in the cap vault and edge and start again.

Putting a condom on

womb

Diaphragm in place

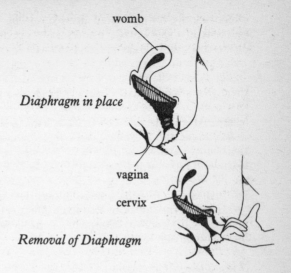

vagina

cervix

Removal of Diaphragm

*The Sponge: This is soft
and circular, and made
of polyurethane foam.*

Female sponge

This is a soft, foam rubber circle with a dimple in the middle, impregnated with a spermicide, which you fit over your cervix like a cap (it has a cord for easy removal). You use each one just once, and keep it in for 24 hours after lovemaking. You can put it in up to 24 hours before lovemaking.

Advantages: (i) you can buy them at the chemists (they're called Today Sponges); (ii) one size fits everyone; and (iii) most women find them easier and pleasanter to use than conventional caps.

Disadvantages: (i) it is only 75 per cent effective, so is suitable only for women over 46 or those who wouldn't mind too much getting pregnant; and (ii) it can disintegrate inside you – not dangerous but tiresome to remove all the bits; (iii) it can be expensive if you need to use contraception often.

★ *Tip*: some women find these sponges are difficult to remove; the best way is to bear down, as if you're having a baby and a bowel motion simultaneously.

Spermicides

These kill sperm. They are best used in conjunction with another method, such as the condom or cap. Spermicides come in various forms – creams, jelly, pessaries (tablets), foams, or a square of papery-looking material called a C-film. They have to be placed high up in the vagina, near your cervix, to be most effective. Some (especially the foams) have a special applicator to help you reach the right spot.

All spermicides have some kind of time factor. Pessaries need time to melt inside you, so you have to wait after you have put them in. All types are

163

effective only for a limited period, so you can't put them in a long time beforehand and you have to add some more during long love-making sessions. *Don't* wash, bath or douche straight after sex – you'll wash out the spermicide too, and some sperm will still be there, ready to move in.

Advantages: (i) you can buy spermicides at the chemists (you can also get them from doctors and clinics); (ii) there is no risk to your health; and (iii) spermicides which contain nonoxynol-9 (read the label) may help protect against AIDS; this kills the virus, at least in test-tube conditions.

Disadvantages: (i) some people find them messy to use. The time constrictions can be awkward; (ii) you (or your partner) may be allergic to one of the ingredients (try swapping brands if either of you gets any irritation); and (iii) used alone, they are not very effective (30 per cent effective) for young women, but may be suitable for women in their late forties.

* *Tip*: spermicides can lose their effectiveness if they linger on the shelves too long. Check sell-by dates when you buy and renew your personal stocks if they become out of date.

Natural family planning

Sometimes called the rhythm method or, less encouragingly, 'Vatican roulette', this makes use of the woman's normal menstrual cycle.

About 14 days before periods, the ovaries produce an ovum (egg), which is capable of being fertilized for about two days. The danger period is longer than that, however, as sperm can survive in the body for about three days. So that makes a total of about five days (often marked up to seven to be on the safe side) in every month when you are most likely to get pregnant. The rest of the month is considered the 'safe period', when hopefully you might be able safely to make love without using contraception at all.

The trick, of course, is to find out exactly which seven days you have to avoid – the days around ovulation. About a third of women feel a little pain when they ovulate (towards the side of the body – whichever side the ovary producing an egg that month is on). Many women, however, have to look for rather more subtle signs.

There are three methods for detecting ovulation.

(i) Your temperature drops very slightly when the egg is released, and then gets slightly higher (up to 1°F) and stays higher. You need a special, sensitive fertility thermometer and you need to take your temperature every morning (before you get up or eat or drink anything). This method gives you fewer safe days than the other methods, but is probably the most effective.

(ii) The quality of your vaginal secretions changes around the time of ovulation. The mucus becomes clear and slippery – a bit like raw egg white – in order to allow the sperm through; some women just feel a bit of extra wetness. You have to abstain from sex as soon as your mucus changes, and not have sex again until your mucus has been back to normal (or you're dry-ish again) for about four days.

This is sometimes called the Billings method, after the doctor who invented it. Used alone, it is less effective than the temperature method (about 85 per cent effective).

(iii) The calendar method: this is the most complicated. You have to find out *exactly* what your cycle is by keeping records for at least six months and preferably a year – cycles can vary quite a lot, even in women who think they are very regular. Once you have these records to work from you identify your safe and unsafe periods according to a set formula. This is the most awkward and – because women don't always ovulate according to formula, or even at the same time each month – the least effective method (about 50 per cent effective).

Some women use two or all of these methods at once, to be as sure as possible.

Advantages: (i) you don't have to use contraception or interfere with your body's workings in any way; (ii) you don't have to do anything at the time you make love; (iii) there is no risk to your physical health; and (iv) for some couples with religious reasons (such as Roman Catholics), it is the only method they can use.

Disadvantages: (i) it is the least effective method available; (ii) it takes a lot of calculation and work; (iii) you need very careful teaching – preferably one-to-one personalized tuition by an expert – see HELP-LINES; (iv) all kinds of things can distort the body signals you are looking for, including: upsets to your menstrual cycle from travel, illness or stress; changes of temperature or mucus caused, again, by illness, stress or any medication you might be taking; (v) it often isn't possible to isolate just seven unsafe days to avoid, so you may have to abstain for half or more of the month; and (vi) this kind of thing can cause a lot of tension and stress.

Tips: women who should *not* use natural family planning (unless they have no other choice):
* women with irregular periods;
* women who have just had a baby (irregular periods);
* women around the time of menopause (same reason again);
* women (or partners) who can't, or don't want to, give up penetrative sex for much of the time;
* women who are anything less than super-organized.

Note: Natural family planning methods (or, in modern marketing terms 'Green Contraception') can in fact be 97 per cent effective.

Furthermore, the trend is now towards using not just one way of pinpointing ovulation, and steering clear of it – i.e. temperature-taking, noting mucus consistency or chart-keeping, but *both* temperature and mucus check methods together in a new, and a far more successful approach. It is called MULTIPLE INDEX or SYMPTO THERMAL system, where each indicator double-checks the other.

It is not unusual these days either to triple-check the most fertile days of your cycle, when in doubt, using an ovulation predictor kit like Clearplan (expensive, but a good back-up if you are not sure).

The idea that natural family planning methods were only 80 per cent safe came from a misinterpretation of a huge World Health Organization trial, carried out in five different countries (including New Zealand, The Philippines and India) in 1981. The WHO studied the fortunes of 725 couples and found 15 per cent conceived either because they, or their partners,

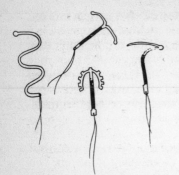

IUD (the intrauterine device or coil): This is a small device, made of plastic with copper, put in the woman's womb by a doctor. Once in place it works for several years and stops any fertilized egg from settling there. Not a first choice method for young women.

deliberately broke 'the rules'. Three and a half per cent conceived because they had not quite understood the rules, and the rest because they'd done everything properly, yet the natural method still failed them.

Remember also, that breast feeding (see breastfeeding difficulties, page 52) done fully is 98 per cent effective as a contraceptive method, and that withdrawal (especially popular with older women in the forty to forty-nine year age group, and used by some 500,000 in the UK alone) are also natural methods, but the latter is only 25 per cent effective.

The IUD

This stands for intra-uterine device, meaning that it goes inside your uterus, sometimes called IUCD (intra-uterine contraceptive device), or loop, or coil.

IUDs are made of plastic and/or copper. It is very small (the illustrations show its actual size), but the non-pregnant uterus is very small inside, too, so the IUD more or less fills it up. Nobody is quite sure how it works except that a foreign body in the womb somehow stops the fertilized egg implanting in the womb lining. Although the copper versions certainly make use of the fact that copper, leaking out steadily, has a contraceptive effect in itself.

There are new thoughts on the way IUDs work, from the Leicester Royal Infirmary. Until now it was believed to produce a very, very early abortion of the small fertilized bundle of cells. This has worried some women who are opposed to abortion. James Drift, from LRI believes that IUD's may somehow block the passage of the sperm through the womb cavity, so they cannot get to a fallopian tube. Another theory is that the womb usually secretes substances like proteins which help the sperm travel along, but that an IUD puts paid to this, making it harder for the sperm to reach the egg.

IUDs come in various shapes. They have to be inserted by a trained person, who will first give you an internal examination to find out exactly which way your uterus lies – they vary. Using a special 'inserter tube' the IUD is then pushed gently through the cervical canal and into your uterus – where it springs into shape and settles in.

This is seldom completely painless, although reactions vary from 'a bit like a period pain, for a few moments' to 'severe cramps'. Sometimes the cervix shuts in protest and has to be dilated with a special device – not particularly painful, alarming though it sounds.

You may feel faint or wobbly or even tearful afterwards; the pain may or may not persist; you will certainly be encouraged to rest for a while before you leave. You might like to have somebody come and meet you. You are protected from pregnancy as soon as the IUD is in.

Partly because they have to go through the cervical canal, IUDs at one time were used only for women who had had a child – making the canal a bit bigger. However, the new and smaller copper devices can be used by most women.

Once in place, the IUD does its job with no more attention from you. Each IUD has a thin plastic cord which remains threading out of the cervical canal and into the vagina. This makes it easy for you to check it is still there.

A non-copper IUD can stay in place for up to ten years, depending on the type. Copper versions, however, have to be replaced about every three to five years, again depending on the type, because the copper gets used up. Having an IUD removed is usually easy and painless.

It is possible to get pregnant with an IUD in place. One danger is ectopic pregnancy (see ECTOPIC PREGNANCY, page 194) – if you think you're pregnant see a doctor *at once* to make sure this hasn't happened, it could be very dangerous. The other danger is of miscarriage: if you are pregnant the doctor will remove the IUD, but once you've had it removed you still have a 25 per cent chance of miscarriage. If your pregnancy continues, however, there is no evidence that it risks being abnormal – you have exactly the same chance of a normal baby as a woman who was not wearing an IUD.

Advantages: (i) once the IUD is in, you're protected against pregnancy straight away and you don't have to do anything further about contraception (except make sure from time to time that it is still in by feeling for the nylon threads of the IUD's tail at the top of your vagina, and turn up for regular check-ups); and (ii) it is a very effective method – about 98 per cent. But note that effectiveness statistics do vary from doctor to doctor, so make sure you get somebody really experienced to fit it.

Disadvantages: (i) insertion varies from OK to quite unpleasant – another reason to make sure your doctor is experienced; (ii) there is a very slight chance that the insertion could perforate your uterus; (iii) periods may become heavier and more painful; (iv) sometimes the man can feel the IUD's threads when you make love – but it's not a good idea to trim them, and they soften after a while; (v) sometimes the IUD turns round and pulls the thread up with it – leaving a painful little bristle sticking out which can spike a male partner's penis; (vi) some doctors feel that IUDs work by preventing a fertilized ovum from implanting in the uterus – in other words, a sort of very early abortion, an idea you may not like; (vii) apart from the risk of pregnancy and miscarriage, there is a risk of ectopic pregnancy (see ECTOPIC PREGNANCY). This seems to be because the IUD somehow slows down the journey of the fertilized egg from the Fallopian tube into the uterus – until it has grown too big to get in; (viii) IUDs also carry a risk of infection because the threads provide a handy route into the uterus for bacteria (etc.). Jason Gardosi, registrar at St Mary's Hospital in London, is working towards a thread-less IUD which may solve that problem – see HELPLINES; and (ix) some IUDs do at present get 'lost', and prove difficult to remove, if you decide you want to get pregnant, but help is available – see HELPLINES.

You should definitely not have an IUD if: you have a current pelvic infection, or a past history of frequent pelvic infection; you may be pregnant; you have current cancer in the reproductive system (IUDs do not cause cancer, but they might make it worse).

You should discuss your choice very thoroughly if: you have heart disease or kidney disease (an infection might do you a lot of harm); a previous history of ectopic pregnancy; untreated anaemia or very heavy or painful periods (because of the heavier, more painful periods caused by IUDs); you are allergic to copper (this, obviously, applies only to copper IUDs); you are on anticoagulant drugs – you may bleed extra-heavily; you are on steroids (these cut down inflammation, so you might not be able to tell if you've got an infection).

* *Tips*: keep a watchful eye open for symptoms of infection and ectopic pregnancy (see chapters on ECTOPIC PREGNANCY, PELVIC INFLAMMATORY DISEASE, page 322 and SEXUALLY TRANSMITTED DISEASES, page 438);
* look out, too, for pain and/or bleeding during sex – it could be a sign the IUD is starting to come out, so get it checked;
* IUDs do sometimes come out, but if you can't feel the thread don't panic – it may just have been swept up into the uterus because the IUD has turned around. But you *must* check with your doctor: to make sure the IUD really is still there, and because it *may* be a sign the IUD has perforated your uterus – very rare, but dangerous if neglected.
* Make a note of the name of the IUD you've been fitted with – in several years' time you may have lost touch with the prescribing doctor and if you need to know what type you have (if there's a health scare about a particular type, for instance) the only other way to find out will be to have it removed.
* ask to be checked for hidden infections (especially chlamydia) before an IUD is inserted. If there is an infection, an IUD might carry it further into your reproductive system.
* take a little extra care removing tampons. When being pulled out, they might help displace an IUD by dragging against its tail string.

The Pill (oral contraception)
This induces – artificially – the kind of hormone changes that take place during pregnancy. While a woman is pregnant, she doesn't get pregnant a second time. Her extra production of the two hormones oestrogen and progesterone take care of that, in various ways.

Early versions of the Pill contained quite high levels of hormones; today's Pills have much lower doses but are just as effective. Some Pills contain synthetic versions of both hormones; others just have progesterone. So, basically, there are two types of Pill, but the one prescribed in the vast majority of cases (about 98 per cent) is the combined Pill. It has both oestrogen and progesterone.

THE COMBINED PILL. There are three versions: monophasic (21 pills which are the same strength all through the month); biphasic (21 pills in two different

168

strengths); and triphasic (21 pills in three different strengths). With each of these, you get a seven-day break, during which you are probably going to bleed (although it won't be a 'proper' period because you haven't ovulated). There is also the 'every day Pills' – 21 hormonal tablets and 7 blanks – so effectively you take one every day (no potentially confusing gaps in tablet taking). The two brands which have this format are Logynon and Femodene ED. You still have your period (withdrawal bleed) during the 7 days you are taking the dummy pills.

The idea of the bi/tri-phasic versions is to mimic more closely the hormone changes of the normal menstrual cycle, which makes it possible to use lower doses overall. Obviously, you have to take these in the right order – follow the instructions on the pack.

Some different brands are identical in their formulation, and clinics may not want to stock every single one all the time, so at some point you may be prescribed what seems to be a different pill – but it isn't.

Advantages: (i) it is very effective – virtually 100 per cent if taken properly; (ii) very little trouble to use – unless you have a bad memory; (iii) does not interfere with love-making; (iv) may have some positive side-effects, like putting an end to PMS or heavy periods; and (v) *suppressing periods*: it is also possible to use the hormones of the Pill continuously to avoid having periods for up to two or three months. This may be a welcome thought for some women who get sick and tired of their monthly bleeds and simply want a short break from them for once, or it may be helpful if you have a special romantic weekend or a honeymoon booked when your period is due and you feel menstruating would spoil it.

However, this is an option with some brands of Pill (but *not* with the 'every day Pills' as seven tablets in each pack are blanks) and not with others, and you will need expert advice as to how to use them. The Family Planning Association says most clinics would regard this as a perfectly reasonable request and be happy to help you, but recommend that you do not suppress your periods (which on the Pill are actually withdrawal bleeds, not true periods) too often in this way.

Disadvantages: these are still being hotly debated. Massive research projects go on and on. The Pill, after all, dates back only to the 1960s, so doctors still don't know enough about the really long-term effects. A proper evaluation of the Pill would have to balance up *all* the different reports. Taking any one on its own is bound to distort the picture: think of the way the media still hypes any new report on long-term risks.

Remember that, the next time there is news of a big scare story. *Don't* stop the Pill until you've discussed the story with your doctor – if there really is a risk, a few more days on the Pill won't make it worse, and you could get pregnant in the meantime if you suddenly stop taking it.

How the combined Pill works. The main action of the combined Pill is to stop you ovulating altogether: and no egg means no pregnancy. It is the oestrogen component which does this, although it is kept as low as possible (often as low as 20 mcg, compared to 100–150 mcg in the earliest Pills). The idea is to prescribe the lowest oestrogen dose Pill which works for you (i.e. stops you ovulating). Breakthrough bleeding is the chief sign that you need a higher dose – so don't forget to report it.

You definitely should not take the combined Pill if you have any health problems: certain cancers (e.g. of the breast) which thrive on oestrogen; any history of thrombosis (blood clots); or a recent history of liver disease or sickle cell anaemia. All these conditions are potentially fatal, and oestrogen encourages them.

Note: there is no evidence that the Pill *causes* any cancer – just that it can encourage certain types to grow if you are already predisposed to the disease or have the very earliest stages of cancer already, and if they are the type that thrive on the oestrogen the Pill contains. If you have any family history of breast cancer, or other indications that cancer might be a risk for you, this should be covered when a medical history is taken. Also, cancer checks (e.g. breast examination, smear tests) are part of the standard routine at all family planning clinics.

* *Tips*: this is a good reason for going to specialist family planning clinic rather than a GP – GPs have to keep up to date on all aspects of health, while family planning doctors can concentrate on getting a really in-depth knowledge of contraceptive health risks, and they have their own associations and information sources to check out the details;

* remember that long-term studies on cancer, now being published, include data from the days when the oestrogen content of the Pill was *much* higher than it is now;

* if you have any worries at all, about cancer or anything else, make sure you discuss them fully with the doctor. Don't be afraid he will think you are silly. It is his job to make sure you are completely happy with the method chosen. If you're not happy with the way you are treated go elsewhere – there is plenty of choice (see **Where to go**, above);

* see the sections on CANCER in this book – especially BREAST CANCER, page 68.

Discuss your choice very thoroughly if you have any of these: amenorrhoea (periods stopped) past or present (see PERIOD PROBLEMS, page 332); irregular periods; very scanty periods; a recently treated hydatidiform mole; severe migraine; diabetes; epilepsy; anxiety; depression; anorexia nervosa; high blood pressure; high blood fat level; structural heart disease; a family history of heart disease or stroke; you are over 35; you smoke; you are breastfeeding; you are overweight; you are due to have major surgery; you are not certain that you are not pregnant; you are young and your menstrual cycle is only just established.

All these conditions can combine rather badly with the kind of side effects sometimes associated with the Pill; so you and the doctor need to know just how many risk factors you have, and which ones, to calculate which brand of Pill is best for you (and, indeed, whether you should be on the Pill at all).

Side effects.

You won't necessarily get any of these at all, but be on the lookout – it is easy to feel vaguely unwell but fail to make the connection with the Pill that might be causing it.

If you're just starting a new Pill, it is not a bad idea to make a quick note every day of any symptom you've got, whether it seems to be connected with the Pill or not. Then you can make sure everything's checked out at your follow-up appointment, and any patterns will show up clearly. Some side effects can be handled by changing your brand of Pill to one with a different dosage of either oestrogen or progesterone.

Note: it is impossible to list in this book every possible side-effect that has ever been known to happen. So note everything that's happened to *you*, and ask about it.

* Amenorrhoea. You won't be having 'proper' periods when you're on the Pill, since you're not ovulating, but a total blank in your seven-day break may encourage your body to lose the habit of periods completely. This might possibly be a risk to your future fertility after you come off the Pill (this isn't certain). Possible Pill change: more progesterone.

* Breakthrough bleeding. Unexpected bleeding outside the break may indicate you're a bit borderline in the non-ovulation stakes. Possible Pill change: more progesterone. Breakthrough bleeding may also indicate missed Pills, late Pills, or something interfering with the Pill's absorption. It is also a common 'settling down' problem with being on the Pill, or changing Pills, and often subsides after 2 to 3 months.

* Heavy periods. Possible Pill change: more progesterone.

* Loss of interest in sex. This may return once your hormone cycles have adjusted to the new Pill – unless, of course, it is to do with unresolved feelings. Possible Pill change: less progesterone.

* Raised blood pressure (especially if you're a smoker and/or over 35 and/or already have raised BP). You'll have your BP taken at every six-month appointment. Possible Pill change: to progesterone-only Pill – see below.

* Weight gain (partly because of the change in body metabolism, partly from a tendency to retain fluids). This is similar to what happens to some women in pregnancy. Both these factors are supposed to wear off after your body adjusts to the Pill – but for some women, they don't. It can make breasts uncomfortable, too. Possible Pill change: less oestrogen, less progesterone. For water retention alone: less oestrogen.

* Headaches (mostly caused by progesterone withdrawal during the seven-day break, so potentially curable by taking extra progesterone then). True migraine is different – possible Pill change is to *reduce* progesterone, or stop taking the Pills completely.

* Nausea (this usually wears off after the first month. If not, experiment with changing the time of day you take the Pill). Possible Pill change: less oestrogen.

* PMS. Plenty to be done here (see PRE-MENSTRUAL SYNDROME, page 411). Possible Pill change: less progesterone.

* Darker skin patches on your face, called chloasma. This looks like a sort of patchy sunburn on the forehead and cheeks, and happens to some pregnant women, too. Unlike the pregnancy sort, however, it takes ages to fade – years sometimes. So watch out for signs. Effects will be minimized if you screen your face from the sun (hat, sunblock cream, etc.). But you may have to give up the Pill.

* Acne. Possible Pill change: less oestrogen. Minovlar, Minilyn and Dianette are brands which actually improve acne for many people (Dianette is marketed as an acne cure; its contraceptive effect is extra).
* Depression and/or stress. These could be connected with any mixed feelings you might be having about taking the Pill at all. For instance, are you being pressurized because the Pill is so convenient – for your partner? Do you long for a baby? Is all well in your relationship? Are you worried by the 'Pill scare' stories in the media? If so, you need to discuss your worries at the clinic, or seek counselling for your emotional problem (see HELPLINES).

On the other hand it might be a direct physical side effect. Vitamin B6 often helps the depression, and good nutrition in general can be important. Possible Pill change: less progesterone.
* Thrush (Candida albicans) – see VAGINAL THRUSH, page 453.
* Thromboembolism. This one is rare, but serious. A blood clot forms in the leg, which may break off and travel to the lungs, causing sudden death, or to the heart and/or brain, causing a heart attack and/or stroke. The same thing can happen in pregnancy, for the same reason – oestrogen makes the blood thicker and stickier. Obviously the danger is increased if you already have related risk factors like high blood fats, smoking, high BP, obesity. An extra risk factor is being laid up on complete bed rest, which makes blood more sluggish. Ask your doctor if you should stop the Pill. If you have limbs in plaster there may be the same kind of danger – ask the doctor.
* Dietary deficiencies. The Pill affects the whole body, so it is not surprising that it interacts with your nutritional chemistry. Some effects are welcome: since periods will usually become lighter, for instance, so your iron status should get better. The Pill also tends to raise your absorption of calcium, which is no bad thing for women (see OSTEOPOROSIS, page 311).

Other dietary effects are a bit more complex: (i) blood levels of copper and Vitamin A will tend to rise – so don't take supplements of these without advice, because both can be toxic in excess and copper also adds to the (rare) risk of blood clots; (ii) potassium and Vitamin C, however, go down because they're used up faster (but if you take a daily C supplement of more than 400mg of Vitamin C you'll increase the activity of oestrogen and therefore get more side effects from the Pill); (iii) Vitamin B12 levels go down, this time because absorption decreases – more of a problem for strict vegetarians/vegans, who may already be short of it; and (iv) there is a whole list of nutrients for which the Pill may create a raised requirement: Vitamins B2 and B3, biotin, folic acid, choline, manganese and zinc.

Note: Supplement-popping at random is a bad idea – all these nutrients work together in complex ways and taking extra of a few only, and in the wrong quantities, might make an existing imbalance even worse. But do get specialist nutrition advice (see HELPLINES) if you have stubborn side effects that nothing else seems to explain.

What stops the Pill working?
* The lowest dose Pills have barely enough oestrogen to stop ovulation – so it is vital to take them at the same time every day or the anti-ovulation effect wears off. (If you travel across time zones a lot, take care!)

If you have left it more than 12 hours, take one Pill straight away and carry on – but take other contraceptive measures for at least seven days. If you forget more than one, check on the Pill packet's instruction sheet or get advice from your doctor. And expect maybe a week of 'breakthrough bleeding'.

The worst Pills to miss are the Mini-Pill or Progesterone-only Pill (POP) which need to be taken at the *same time* each day – or, if you are taking a Combined Pill, the ones at the beginning or end of the pack, because that extends the finely-calculated seven-day break and maximizes the chance that you will ovulate. If you're a forgetful type you are not an ideal POP candidate – instead ask to have a Pill with no seven-day break and/or – as an absolute last resort – a brand with a higher content of oestrogen (50mcg), which damps down ovulation more thoroughly. High oestrogen doses are never a good idea, however.

* Certain drugs can also interfere with the effectiveness of the Pill. It is well worth checking on this with the doctor, any time you're prescribed a drug, or with the chemist, any time you buy something over the counter. (They are supposed to remember to check this themselves with women – but nobody's perfect). Among the main culprits are: antibiotics (e.g. ampicillin); barbiturates; sedatives and tranquillizers (e.g. Chlorpromazine, Meprobamate); some analgesics/anti-inflammatories (e.g. Phenacetin, Ethylmorphine, Phenylbutazone); anti-histamines (e.g. Chlorcyclizine).

* There is some evidence, says Dr Gillian Cardy of the National Association of Family Planning Doctors, that no meat in the diet increases the risk of ovulation if you're on one of the lower oestrogen pills – breakthrough bleeding is a danger sign.

* One more thing: vomiting and/or diarrhoea can make the Pill go straight through you without being absorbed – as bad as not taking it at all. If you get 'holiday tummy' your romantic holiday might be ruined, so a pessimist will pack an alternative contraceptive method, just in case.

Apart from the Combined Pill . . .

THE PROGESTERONE-ONLY PILL, called the POP or Mini-Pill. Because it contains no oestrogen, it has fewer side-effects, on balance. But, for the same reason, it doesn't always stop ovulation so it is not as effective as the Combined Pill.

It works by mimicking the effects of the extra progesterone produced by the body during pregnancy to prevent a further pregnancy – basically changes to the cervical mucus, the lining of the uterus and the Fallopian tubes which make them more hostile to sperm or to a fertilized egg.

You take them every day, without a break, and taking them at the same time every day is extra important (early evening is best). If you can stick to this rigid timetable, the Mini-Pill is almost as effective as the Combined Pill (98 per cent).

The Mini-Pill is recommended for women who aren't ideal for the Combined Pill – smokers aged over 35, for instance, or women who should not take oestrogen because they have other risk factors. Only about 2–3 per cent of Pill takers use the Mini-Pill.

Reading the section above on the Combined Pill will be a good guide to how the Mini-Pill may affect you, if you just concentrate on the comments on progesterone. For some women, the Mini-Pill causes breakthrough bleeding, or makes periods very unpredictable, or peter out completely. So, if you do get pregnant (unlikely) you may not notice the most obvious sign of it.

If you forget a POP Pill, take one as soon as you remember and then carry on (this may mean you take two Pills in one day. If you were more than three hours adrift, take other precautions for at least two days. Side effects include nausea and occasionally, ovarian cysts.

IF YOU'RE OVER 30. It's been traditional to discourage women over 30 or (more usually) 35 from taking any kind of Pill, because a report by the Royal College of GPs in 1977 found they had an increased risk of heart trouble with the Pill. But this is now out of date, says Dr Ali Kubba, gynaecologist with the Marie Stopes and Margaret Pyke centres. The main factor, the RCGP found when they looked at the evidence again in 1981, was smoking.

If you don't smoke (or gave up at least two years ago), have normal blood pressure and have no family history of heart trouble, Dr Kubba says even the Combined Pill is OK until age 45 or so – the oestrogen dose is now so low, compared to the type of Pills the RCGP was studying. Or try the POP.

THE MALE PILL. Work has been going on to develop various Pills for men which halt sperm production, ever since the Pill was thought of. So far, none has been adopted because of initial side effects including impotence and others such as: greasy skin and weight gain. A new version of the Pill, using a lighter dose of synthetic testosterone, called Primoteston, has had better results in a multi-country World Health Organization trial – and it's still going on. In surveys, however, only seven out of ten women said they would trust their partner to take it. Male volunteers to try the latest version (no guarantee it is effective) are being sought by Dr Fred Wu at the Medical Research Council's reproductive biology unit at Edinburgh University.

Injectable contraceptives
Sometimes, the Pill's effects are introduced into the body as an injection of a high dose of progesterone. Commonest types are Depo Provera and Nori-sterat. The effects last about three months, and can't be reversed during this time. It is used for women who can't manage to take the Pill every day, for whatever reason.

Sometimes it is used regularly for long-term protection. Most often, it is used just once, for those who need to be completely protected for a limited time – because they've just had a rubella vaccination, for instance, which would damage any pregnancy. Since the injection itself would harm any foetus, it is usually done during a period, to make sure you're not pregnant.

Advantages: (i) it is very convenient; and (ii) very effective (over 99 per cent).

Disadvantage: while the official line is that this method carries very little risk to health, some researchers disagree strongly. Symptoms alleged include: menstrual problems (heavy or irregular or continuous bleeding); delay in getting pregnant afterwards; irregular periods; water retention leading to headaches and breast discomfort, and all kinds of symptoms usually associated with the Pill – with the added problem that you can stop taking the Pill, but with injectables you can only wait for them to wear off.

If you're offered this method, find out more – the WHRRIC (see HELPLINES) has some useful publications.

New
VAGINAL RING. Now being developed is a ring placed in the vagina, which releases low doses of both oestrogen and progesterone and is removed one week in four to allow a period. To find out more, contact the Margaret Pyke Centre (see HELPLINES). Another version uses only progesterone, which thickens the cervical mucus so sperm cannot get past.
Coming soon: another type of ring (releasing progestogen only to thicken the mucus protecting the entrance to the womb around the cervix) will be available from family planning clinics, too. You can put it in or remove it (it must be replaced within the hour or the protective effect is lost) yourself. A new one will be required every 3 to 4 months. It is suitable for women of all ages, and does not interefere with breastfeeding. Side effects include possible spotting between periods, nausea, and occasional ovarian cysts. Further information is available from Roussel labs, who will be making it in the UK.

FEMALE CONDOM. Called the Femidom, this is a new method. It is a sort of sheath-shape, but larger, made of very fine material that looks a bit like clingfilm, with a springy ring at each end to keep it in place. You put it inside you – it covers the outer genitals, too (and dulls sensation a bit, but should protect against infection). You need to practice using it a little (as with the diaphragm) – three practice go's recommended. Guide the penis into your vagina carefully or it may push down the side of the device. Some couples complain they can hear the Femidom 'rustling' as they make love. As effective as the male condom against pregnancy and STDs.

ON TEST. London's Hammersmith Hospital is trying out an implant (Capronor) which goes under the skin in your arm and releases a steady (but low) dose of progesterone hormone – available, maybe, in 1994.
Vaccine: There is also a birth control 'vaccine' of another pregnancy hormone called chorionic gonadotrophin, being given early trials by the World Health Organization in Australia and the USA.
Also: new IUDs which offer extra protection as they are impregnated with progesterone; biodegradable womb implants; longer lasting ordinary implants; and hormonal nasal sprays, and Pills that are taken only once a month.

Morning-after contraception
There are two things you can do *after* you've had unprotected sex, to stop you getting pregnant.
(i) An IUD can be inserted, which will work possibly by stopping a fertilized

egg implanting in the womb – and, of course, will mean you're protected for the future, too. Doctors won't insert a morning-after IUD more than five days after you took the risk (many won't do it after three). After that, it's too late.

(ii) You can be given a high dose of oestrogen, which will stop ovulation. This must be done as soon as possible – at the very latest, within 72 hours of the unprotected sex. This is called the morning-after Pill.

Advantage: it is thought to be about 97 per cent effective.

Disadvantages: (i) you may feel sick; and (ii) it has all the possible side-effects of the Combined Pill, so it is particularly bad news for women who react badly to oestrogen (see **The Combined Pill**, above). No doctor will be willing to do it at the drop of a hat – still less, to do it more than once.

Sterilization

If you're quite sure you don't want any more children (or any children at all), and especially if you're youngish and face many years of having to use contraception, sterilization may be a good option. It can be done for men or for women.

But you do have to be sure. Afterwards you can't change your mind. Both procedures involve cutting or sealing off the relevant body tubes (Fallopian tubes in women, sperm ducts in men). It is sometimes possible to join things up again (and indeed, it is not unknown for tubes to join up again all by themselves). But the chances are only 30 to 60 per cent success for women depending on when/how the sterilization was done. Sterilization is thought of as permanent.

You will be thoroughly counselled to make sure you've thought it through (especially if you're young and/or not in a steady relationship) because all doctors know of heart-breaking cases where people *did* change their minds afterwards, and were shattered to find it was too late.

So you'll have to face up to some hard questions. What if something happened to your children – would you want more? What if this relationship breaks down and one of you wants to have a new family with somebody else? Try and take plenty of time, preferably months, not weeks, to think it over carefully first.

That done, you have two basic choices: male or female sterilization.

MALE STERILIZATION, otherwise called vasectomy, is a simple procedure, and involves only a local anaesthetic. A small incision is made in the scrotum and a piece of the vas deferens (the tubes which carry sperm to the penis for ejaculation) is brought out and either cut or heat-sealed. There are two tubes, so (except with certain techniques) two incisions are made. Usually there's a bit of bruising and discomfort for a day or two, but nothing worse (tight underpants keep things more comfortable). Dressings may be needed until there is full healing (one or two weeks at most).

In future, sperm will still be produced but they'll be reabsorbed harmlessly

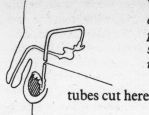

Vasectomy (male sterilization). This involves a minor operation in which the tubes carrying the sperm to your penis are cut and tied. Vasectomy doesn't affect your sex life. You still enjoy sex and climax, but your semen no longer contains sperm.

tubes cut here

tubes cut here

Female sterilization: This means that the tubes carrying the egg to the womb are cut and blocked. It's not as simple as vasectomy because the tubes are harder to reach. The woman still has periods, still enjoys sex and climaxes, but she cannot conceive.

Sterilization: This is a very effective, permanent form of family planning if you're absolutely sure you don't want any more children.

by the body. There will still be the same amount of semen ejaculated (sperm form only a small part of the total) and everything will still feel the same. However, male sterilization is not an immediate contraceptive, as there will be some sperm in existing stocks of semen and it will take 10 or more ejaculations to become sperm-free. The man will have to have two to four sperm counts until this reaches zero and in the meantime you'll still need protection.

Advantages: (i) it is a much simpler and safer operation than the female version; (ii) it is also more effective (the rate is one failure in several hundred cases). The risk of the tubes rejoining is very low, and usually happens early so it will be picked up at the sperm count stage. The risk of later rejoining is tiny (one in several thousand) once there's been a zero sperm count to prove it's worked; and (iii) there are no long-term effects on health.

Disadvantages: (i) there is slight danger of infection or inflammation, treated successfully with antibiotics; (ii) some men don't feel masculine any more if they are no longer fertile – make sure this is thoroughly explored during counselling; and (iii) reversing the operation may not be possible – the success rate is 30 to 60 per cent at best and you will need a specialist in micro-surgery. Get advice from agencies like BPAS, Marie Stopes or the National Association for the Childless.

FEMALE STERILIZATION is almost invariably done under a general anaesthetic – something which always carries a slight risk – plus a stay in hospital and some post-operative pain. The tubes in question here are the Fallopian tubes, where conception takes place. The method used in most cases is laparoscopy (see description in ENDOMETRIOSIS, page 203, for full details), and the tubes are

177

heat-sealed, clipped tight or have a section cut out (about 3–4 cm) and the ends closed off. You'll need to rest for a few days after leaving hospital.

Advantage: very effective, although not as effective as vasectomy – between one and six women per thousand become pregnant again, usually within two years of the operation.

Disadvantages: (i) there is increased risk of ectopic pregnancy (see ECTOPIC PREGNANCY); (ii) there is a risk of major or minor complications after the surgery (about 4 per cent), although these will almost certainly be picked up while you're still in hospital and can be treated; (iii) there is a risk (about 15 per cent) that you'll get heavier periods afterwards, although in many cases this won't be a direct result of the operation but because you've given up using the pill, which has made you get used to lighter periods; and (iv) you may feel less of a woman if you can no longer get pregnant – explore this thoroughly during counselling.

THE FUTURE. Methods are being developed, for both sexes, which involve inserting a sort of chemical plug in the tubes. This has a much higher chance of being reversible later, but is not yet available in this country. Also being tested on animals, in India, are copper implants in the male scrotum, which have the same contraceptive effect as the copper in an IUD.

Complementary therapy
Complementary therapies tailor their treatments very much to the individual: the precise nature of the treatment you receive will vary, depending on your medical history, symptoms, lifestyle, etc. The following information indicates the *sorts* of things a therapist is most likely to do or recommend. Do not be surprised if they feel you need something slightly different. This section is meant purely as an indication of likely treatments; it is not meant as a DIY guide to the medical uses of the different complementary therapies.

Orthodox methods of birth control may bring problems in their wake. Some of these respond to complementary therapies.

Clinical nutrition
The contraceptive pill pushes Vitamins B, C, E and K out of the body and may lead to increases in Vitamin A and iron. Vitamin B, C and E supplements are recommended. A folic acid supplement can help prevent Pill-induced deficiency of folic acid, which can create a pre-cancerous condition.

Prolonged use of the Pill increases the risk of blood clots and cardio-vascular problems in general – this can be helped by daily doses of Vitamin E. If the vagina loses its normal acid nature, it can lead to thrush and other fungal infections, plus increased risk of sexually transmitted diseases. Live yoghurt or diluted cider vinegar douches counteract this effect. Reduced sugar intake helps, too.

Homoeopathy
Homoeopathy can actually offer an alternative method of birth control – but only a very experienced homoeopath should be approached.

Medical herbalism
Problems caused by the Pill, such as altered nutritional status, infections due to altered

acidity in the vagina, and circulatory problems (such as varicose veins) respond well to herbal treatment. This may include advice on nutrition and other aspects of lifestyle, as well as herbal remedies. With acute infections, medical herbalism is most useful if it's combined with other, orthodox treatment. Douches and antiseptic washes for the vaginal area help cystitis sufferers.

Do not try to use herbal forms of birth control – qualified and experienced medical herbalists *never* recommend them.

Contraception helplines

Association of Community Health Councils
30 Drayton Park, London N5 1PB (071 609 8405)
Advice and support to patients who have worries or complaints about any doctor or
  member of the medical profession.

British Pregnancy Advisory Service
Austy Manor, Wooton Wawen, Solihull, West Midlands B95 6BX (056 42 3225)
This service offers counselling and assessment for fertility problems, including a total
  physical assessment for couples. They also offer sterilization reversal operations for
  men and women.

Brook Advisory Centre
HQ – 233 Tottenham Court Road, London W1P 9AE (071 323 1522)
Contact HQ for the centre nearest you.

Harmony
A mail order, budget priced condom service, run by women for women. Offer
  condoms (including some of the more exotic ones) at about half the retail price in
  shops. Call for information on (0242 252878).

Chartex (makers of Femidom)
Call (04834 89211) for details of where to buy them and how best to overcome any
  practical user problems they may initially present. Or alternatively ask one of the
  advice nurses or doctors at your local Family Planning clinic – or phone the
  PFA's HQ in London for advice.

Copper 7 Association
54 Firgrove Road, Farnham GU9 8LQ

Dalkon Shield Association
24 Patshull Road, London NW5

The Family Planning Association
27 Mortimer Street, London W1 (071 636 7866)
See GENERAL HELPLINES, page 480, for details.

British Society of Nutritional Medicine
This is a group of medical doctors with special extensive training in nutrition: can
    advise you if you are worried about how to prevent any nutritional problems the
    Pill may produce. Call Dr Alan Stewart on (0273 487003) for details of any
    BSNM members in your area: they are likely to be more clued up about this
    than an ordinary nutritionist, but may well be running a private rather than an
    NHS practice.

International Planned Parenthood Federation
18–20 Lower Regent Street, London SW1Y 4PW (071 486 0741)

Marie Stopes Clinics
108 Whitfield Street, London W1 (071 388 0662/2585)
10 Queens Square, Leeds (0532 440685)
1 Police Street, Manchester (061 832 4260)
See GENERAL HELPLINES, page 480, for details.

Margaret Pyke Centre
15 Bateman Buildings, Soho Square, London W1 (071 734 9351)
As they did some groundbreaking trials on both the progesterone ring and
    Femidom their advisory staff may well be able to help you with queries about
    these methods.

Menopause Collective
c/o WHRRIC, 52 Featherstone Street, London EC1Y 8RT

National Association of Natural Family Planning Teachers
NFP Centre, Birmingham Maternity Hospital, Birmingham B15 2TG (021 472 1377)
Trains teachers in natural family planning, aims to promote knowledge of fertility to
    parents, schools and other avenues of adult education. They have a national
    network which coordinates the work of natural family planning teachers.

National Association of Ovulation Method Instructors (NAOMI)
47 Heathhurst Road, Sanderstead, South Croydon, Surrey CR2 0BB
Teaches the Billings method of family planning – qualified teachers offer individual
    counselling or postal tuition service.

Natural Family Planning Service
Catholic Marriage Advisory Council, 15 Lansdowne Road, London W11
    (071 727 0141)
Clitherow House, 1 Blythe Mews, Blythe House, London W14 0NW (071 371 1341)
Teaches natural family planning to Catholics and non-Catholics.

Pregnancy Advisory Service
11–13 Charlotte Street, London W1 (071 637 8962)

Post-Abortion Counselling Service
340 Westbourne Park Road, London W11 1EQ (071 221 9631)

RELATE (formerly the Marriage Guidance Council)
Herbert Gray College, Little Church Street, Rugby CV21 3AP (0788 573241)

Woman's Health Information and Support Centre (Northampton Well Woman Centre)
Junction 7, Hazelwood Road, Northampton NN1 1LG (0604 89723)
Drop-in centre with discussions on all health and emotional problems. Advice, information, self-help groups, classes, pregnancy testing and counselling are available to anyone in the Northants area.

Specialist products and services
ASH (Action on Smoking and Health)
109 Gloucester Place, London W1 (071 935 3519)

The Association of Qualifield Curative Hypnotherapists
10 Balaclava Road, Kings Heath, Birmingham (021 441 1775)
See GENERAL HELPLINES, page 480, for details.

Roussel Labs
(0895 834343)
Makers of the new progestogen vaginal ring.

National Society for Non-Smokers (now called QUIT)
(071 487 2858)
Contact HQ for details of inexpensive stop-smoking courses countrywide.

Weight Watchers
HQ – Windsor (0753 856751)

Further reading
Sex and Your Health by Dr James Bevan (Mandarin)
The Billings Method of Family Planning by Dr Evelyn Billings and Ann Westmore (Thorsons)
The Complete Cervical Cap Guide by Rebecca Chalker (Harper and Row)
Natural Birth Control by J. and K. Drake (Thorsons)
Natural Family Planning by Dr Anna Flynn and Melissa Brooks (Unwin Hyman)
The Vasectomy Book by M. Goldstein and M. Feldburg (Tungstone Press)
Safer Sex: A New Look at Sexual Pleasure by P. Gordon and L. Mitchell (Faber)
The Bitter Pill by Dr Ellen Grant (Corgi)
The Pill by John Guillebaud (Oxford University Press)
Vasectomy and Sterilization: What You Need to Know by Suzie Hayman (Thorsons)
The Which? Guide to Birth Control by P. Kane (Consumers' Association)
The Pill Protection Plan by Gillian Martlew and Shelley Silver (Grapevine)
The Law and Planned Parenthood by J. Paxman (IPPF)
Contraception; A Practical and Political Guide by Rose Shapiro (Virago)
The IUD: A Woman's Guide by Robert Snowdon (Unwin Hyman)
'Contraception', Leaflet M11. Send 30p plus SAE to: Templegarth Trust, 82 Tinkle Street, Grimoldby, Louth, Lincs LN11 8TF

Cystitis

Nearly half of all women in the UK will get a painful attack of cystitis at some time in their lives – mild or severe. For some, it is a rare event. Others have four or five attacks or more in a year, for years on end. Every year, about 1.7 million women in the UK suffer cystitis.

While there is much you can do to relieve attacks, and strategies for avoiding them completely, the basic questions continue to baffle GPs and urologists: why do some women suffer attack after attack, while others remain free? Why do symptoms continue in cases where there isn't even an infection?

What is it?
Cystitis means inflammation of the bladder and/or urethra. It may be caused by (i) infection, or (ii) bruising, or (iii) irritation, or (iv) a combination of these. The urethra is the tube through which urine passes out of the body. It leads up to your bladder, where urine is stored. From the bladder, two more tubes (called ureters) go up to your kidneys.

The urethra is where you'll feel much of the pain of cystitis. If the attack does turn out to be caused by an infection, and it is not treated, it can spread up to the kidneys (via the bladder and the ureters) and produce more serious infection.

Men and children, usually girls, can also suffer from cystitis. Men do not often get it, but have the same risk as women of going on to develop a serious internal infection if they do. In a man's case, it is infection of the prostate gland.

Symptoms
Classic symptoms
Cystitis symptoms come on quite suddenly and can last a few hours or a few days. Whether the cystitis is infective or non-infective, the symptoms are similar. Women with recurrent cystitis come to recognize very early symptoms, and to take immediate action (see **Self help**, below).

These are the most common symptoms of cystitis:
* burning pain whenever you pass water;
* a frequent and urgent need to pass water, even though when you try there is hardly any (or no) urine;
* needing to get up often at night to pass water.

Other symptoms
You may also get some of these other symptoms:
* dragging pains in the lower abdomen and lower back;
* nausea and perhaps vomiting;

* a painful burning sensation at the outer end of the urethra, which may extend to the edge of the vagina;
* dark, sometimes bad-smelling urine, which may be pinkish or contain bright red blood;
* deep yellow or orangey urine, with a strong smell.

Urine colour can also be changed by being very concentrated (if you're not drinking enough) by vitamin supplements and by certain foods, e.g. asparagus.

These symptoms may indicate problems other than just cystitis, and should be checked out by a doctor.

Causes

YOUR BASIC ANATOMY. A woman's basic anatomy is one of the problems. The urethra is your urinary system's point of contact with the outside world, and so is a way in for irritants which can cause cystitis. It is thought that women have a built-in risk of infection here, too, and one of the reasons they get it so much more often than men is because they have a much shorter urethra than men – germs have a shorter distance to travel before they reach the bladder. Once there, they can form a reservoir of infection – sometimes using it as a staging post on the way to causing serious kidney infections.

Larrian Gillespie, an American urologist, is one specialist who disagrees. Women, she says, are 'built like a French bidet' and are meant to have a strong gush of urine which cleans the whole genital area every time they pee. The fault, she says, is in factors which restrict the flow. These include simply not drinking enough or fitting a too-large contraceptive diaphragm which presses against the urethra from the vagina next to it, narrowing the passage for urine to pass out.

Male and Female Urethra

Why women get cystitis – and men tend not to. It's our anatomy that's to blame . . .

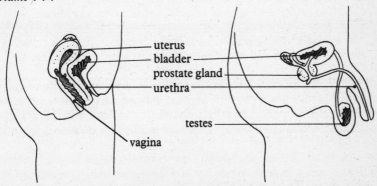

uterus
bladder
prostate gland
urethra
testes
vagina

The female urethra is short, allowing offending organisms easy access to the bladder and, in severe, untreated cases, to the kidneys.

INFECTION. Cystitis is infective (caused by an infection) in about 50 per cent of cases. If urine is infected, the bacteria found are usually those associated with faeces (Escherichia coli, most often). They have probably travelled the short way from the anus to the urethra and up the urethra, from there. Women who suffer frequent attacks are thought to have particularly sensitive linings to their urethras and bladders. If this is the case, the inflammation is more likely to be just in your urethra, rather than the bladder as well.

One expert, Angela Kilmartin, believes that often infection can't be found because by the time some laboratories get round to investigating the sample, the bacteria have died.

If there is really no infection antibiotics are useless and you'll need to look for other causes, such as:

CONTRACEPTIVE DEVICES: (i) being on the pill can produce hormone changes which may increase your sensitivity; (ii) spermicidal cream can irritate the urethra, if it reaches it; (iii) use of a diaphragm may cause problems.

SEX. The opening to your urethra is just above the opening to your vagina, and bruising can occur during sex, which can inflame it and make infection more likely. Cystitis is sometimes called 'the honeymoon disease' because a first attack often used to occur on or just after the honeymoon – when inflammation is brought on by the first sexual activities.

Particles of dust or dirt can be introduced to the urethral opening by fingers, or bits of sand and earth, if you make love out of doors. Inserting objects of any sort around the opening to your urethra may irritate it and cause inflammation.

CHEMICAL IRRITANTS, including toiletries – soap, bubblebath, shampoo, talcum powder and bath oils, especially the perfumed kind, and vaginal deodorants or wipes may be to blame. Also the chlorine in swimming pools and public whirlpool spa baths, and biological washing powder used on underwear.

VIBRATIONS. From abrasive sexual intercourse – and even a bouncy car, motorbike, badly sprung bike seat or tractor, might cause irritation.

CLOTHES: the warmth and abrasion caused by wearing all-in-one fashion bodies/leotards with pants and tights or under tight leggings or trousers.

DRINKING TOO LITTLE makes your urine very concentrated, which irritates, and also means the bladder is not properly flushed out and may be more prone to infection. Not emptying your bladder fully when you pass water, leaving a residue of urine containing bacteria which may multiply and cause infection.

TEMPERATURE: HEAT. Sitting on radiators, for example, won't help inflammation, and if you are hot enough to sweat you'll lose water, with the same result as from drinking too little. COLD. This irritates the bladder's nerve endings. The frequent urination which results makes things even worse, through loss of water.

FOOD IRRITANTS. If you're sensitive (or even allergic) to something, this can irritate the bladder's nerve endings, too. The most frequent culprits are: spicy foods, e.g. pepper, vinegar, pickles and curry powder, alcohol and strong coffee. Some cystitis sufferers are sensitive to onions, gluten, starch and lactose (found in milk).

REAL FRUIT JUICE, which is acid, produces acidic urine which irritates the urethra.

ANTI-CANCER THERAPY. Radiotherapy treatment can cause irritation and inflammation (see CERVICAL CANCER, CANCER OF THE OVARY, CANCER OF THE UTERUS, pages 78, 87 and 93).

PREGNANCY. Because the urethra is relaxed by the extra progesterone being produced by your body, infections can enter more easily and in late pregnancy, the enlarging womb can cause residual urine to remain squashed in the bladder (see PREGNANCY PROBLEMS).

THE MENOPAUSE. Hormone changes may lead to looser muscle tone, with similar effects to those caused by pregnancy, and to a drier, more easily irritated, vagina. (See MENOPAUSE, page 276.)

Who is at risk?
* Women who are pregnant, especially in the later months, or even earlier if the growing baby is 'sitting' on their bladder;
* Women who wear a diaphragm, especially if they have been given one that is a little on the large side 'for a snug fit';
* Women whose bladders and urethras are especially sensitive to irritation, anyway;
* Women who have had a very prolonged session of lovemaking – especially after not having one for a while, or not having done so before;
* Women who are on the Pill;
* Women who use chemical contraceptives (spermicides);
* Women who use perfumed soaps (or indeed, any soap) on their vulvas to wash them clean; who enjoy strongly perfumed baths; or use perfumed talc;
* Women who swim in chlorinated pools, or sit in even more heavily chlorinated (and hot) whirlpool spa baths (like Jacuzzis) for a long time;
* Women who eat a lot of spicy foods or drink strong-tasting drinks such as coffee, alcohol and fruit juices;
* Women who sit on very hot or very cold surfaces;
* Women who ride a poorly-sprung vehicle: on a boneshaker bicycle or in a rattler of a car;
* Women who drink little liquid;
* Women who are undergoing chemotherapy;
* Women who are menopausal or post menopausal;
* Women who are generally very tired, run down or who have been ill recently (less strong immune systems);

* Young girls get cystitis for the same reasons as women except, of course, for those resulting from the menopause, sex, etc. (Cystitis is occasionally a sign of sexual abuse, but it is also quite common in non-abused children.)

Treatment
Medical help
See a doctor if any of the following apply to you:
* it is your first attack;
* it is a recurrent attack, but self help isn't working;
* you have *any* of the symptoms listed above under Other Symptoms;
* you are pregnant;
* you have a temperature;
* pain is worse than in previous attacks (if any);
* you suspect you may have an STD (sexually transmitted disease) or vaginal thrush (see SEXUALLY TRANSMITTED DISEASES and VAGINAL THRUSH, pages 438 and 453).

You can visit your GP, STD clinic, family planning clinic, well woman clinic or a private gynaecologist.

The doctor needs to check whether you are really suffering from cystitis or from another condition with similar symptoms (a vaginal infection, kidney infection or endometriosis, for instance). Then, if it is cystitis, he should discover whether it is the infective or non-infective kind.

He should start by asking the history of your symptoms: what they are; when they started; whether you have noticed them before; whether any steps you have taken have helped. He should examine you physically, taking your blood pressure and feeling your stomach and kidneys.

He may also give you an internal examination. Many women dislike these, or find them painful. If you are one of them you should say so, giving the doctor a chance to be particularly gentle and to use an extra amount of lubricating jelly. Also, you can try relaxing yourself with slow, deep breathing (in for a count of eight, hold, out for eight). You can also choose to see a woman doctor or visit a well women's clinic.

The doctor should ask for a urine specimen. It is a good idea to bring a fresh one with you and present him with it (a useful reminder to him that he should require one).

How to take a urine specimen
1. Thoroughly clean a glass jar (with a tight screw-top lid) using detergent and a lot of hot water. Rinse it well. The presence of jam or soap in urine will confuse the bacteriologists who test it.
2. Write your name, your doctor's name, the date and 'MSU' (midstream speciment of urine) on a sticky label – but don't put it on the jar yet.
3. Wash your genital area thoroughly in plain warm water.
4. Sit on the loo and pass a little water, then tighten up the muscle and stop. Then hold the jar under the urine flow and continue peeing. Stop again, and look to ensure there is some in the jar. Remove the jar and put it carefully where it will not spill (or put on the lid). Finish your pee.

5. Wash your hands. Put the lid on the jar. Wash and dry the outside of the jar.
6. Stick on the label and put the jar into the refrigerator.

Urine testing
Your specimen will be sent off to the local laboratory to test for bacteria, pus and blood cells. In due course (time varies according to where you are, perhaps up to three weeks) your doctor will get a report on whether you have 'significant' numbers of bacteria likely to cause cystitis (all urine has some bacteria – 100,000 per 1ml of urine indicates infection).

The lab also tests out antibiotics which kill bacteria, and recommends what the doctor should prescribe for you. The doctor will then prescribe an antibiotic – and at the same time should advise you on how to take steps to avoid getting infected again.

If blood is present in the urine he or she will probably refer you to hospital, where you may have further tests to see if you have anything else which might account for your symptoms. Possibilities include: kidney disease, infection, bladder stones, growths (not necessarily malignant), abnormal physiology (kinks, bulges or pouches in your urethra or kidney which might harbour bacteria) or tumours. Do not immediately assume the worst. Very few cystitis cases are due to any of these.

Other tests
If you need other tests those available include blood tests, MSU, cystoscopy (for which you are given a local or general anaesthetic and a viewing instrument is passed into the bladder to enable the inside of it to be examined), ureteric catheterization (where a tiny tube is passed into each kidney to obtain a specimen of urine), and intravenous urogram (or pyleogram) which is a sort of X-ray of the kidney, ureters and bladder (see CANCER OF THE OVARY, page 87).

Treatment
For infections
Unless your cystitis symptoms are very mild, the doctor may prescribe antibiotics without waiting for the result of the test (sometimes these can take days, or weeks). If there is an infection it is best to start getting rid of it immediately.

He may do so even if there is a negative result, believing that it is better to play safe regarding possible kidney infection. If you have the slightest worry on this score, go straight to the local hospital's walk-in STD or genito-urinary (GU) clinic for speedy investigation of your urine and vagina (see SEXUALLY TRANSMITTED DISEASES, page 438, for full details).

What your GP should *not* do is continue to prescribe antibiotics for recurring attacks without examining you or sending specimens for investigation. If this happens, you should ask for further investigations to be made.

The bacteria most likely to be present in infected urine are uncomplicated ones, treatable by antibiotics. If anything unusual shows up, you'll probably need extra investigations by the GU specialist. The antibiotics prescribed may vary if the doctor knows about local resistance conditions, or if the laboratory suggests special types. For short courses (1 to 3 days) the antibiotics could include Mictral, Amoxil or a sulphonamide. For longer-term doses for recurrent infection the antibiotics could include Septrin, Chemotrim, Penbritin or Monotrim.

Finally, your doctor should ask you to return for a further check up after the course of antibiotics is complete, to ensure that the infection has gone. If he does not ask, go back anyway as soon as you finish the tablets.

* Remember that some antibiotics affect the effectiveness of oral contraceptives (the Pill), so other precautions should be taken. Your doctor should remind you of this – if he forgets, ask.

* Antibiotics can also make you more likely to develop thrush. Look out for itchiness, redness or a white discharge (see VAGINAL THRUSH). Try and get your doctor, for this reason, to give you a short rather than a long course, or ask for preventive anti-thrush pessaries, like Canastan, to use during antibiotic course.

* Do take the full course of antibiotics prescribed, even if your symptoms quickly vanish. Half-treated infections can become resistant to drugs.

* All Escherichia coli, Staphylococcus/Streptococcus/Klebsiella/Proteus infections of the urethra and bladder occur in faeces. Such bacteria comes from the patient's own back passage and nowhere else. (See **Self help**, below, for how to avoid these infections.)

If no infection is found

There is a 50-50 chance that your urine will be found not to be infected. Then your doctor (and you) will want to look for another cause for your cystitis, probably among the many possibilities suggested earlier. Your doctor should also advise you on how to prevent further attacks (see **Self help**, below).

Sadly, many women suffer from recurring non-infective cystitis even with these measures. In these cases they learn to judge which attacks need their doctor's attention and which they can manage themselves.

Self help

The woman who suffers recurrent attacks of cystitis may find her home, social and family life suffering as she can't go out during attacks. She can't leave the loo, feels too ill to go out and doesn't want sex. Also her working life can become difficult when she is feeling rotten so much of the time and is rushing to the lavatory every 5 minutes (this is especially difficult when on public view e.g. in assembly-line jobs, or in an open-plan office).

Although some causes of cystitis are not entirely preventable in some sensitive women, the precautions listed below should make attacks less frequent and/or milder.

Precautions against infection

1. Do not wear nylon pants (cotton is better), tights (stockings or nothing is better) or tight trousers (skirts are best). All these encourage sweating and thus provide a warm, moist environment for bacteria to flourish.

2. Always wipe your bottom from front to back. This gives less opportunity for bacteria from faeces to be wiped on to the opening of the urethra.

3. Try to avoid introducing faecal bacteria during sex:

* have a good wash of your anal region beforehand, with unscented soap and warm water, then pat dry;
* ask your partner not to touch your anal area with either his hands or his penis if it can be avoided;
* explain what you are trying to avoid, and enlist his help, pointing out that you are unresponsive during an attack, so that any assistance he gives you will be to his advantage in the long run;
* peeing after sex also helps to wash out bacteria but a mere trickle of concentrated or infected urine bathing your urethra can do more harm than good. So drink plenty of fluid before making love for a strong, well-diluted flow to flush out bladder and urethra;
* drink a glass of water after sex, too (to stimulate your urine flow, and to dilute it).
4. The dangling string of tampons can transfer anal bacteria to the urethral opening:
* consider changing to soft, slim sanitary towels;
* make sure you change them very regularly as they, too, make a good breeding ground for bacteria.
5. Wash effectively:
* wash – every day after passing a stool and after attacks of diarrhoea. Do it very gently, with unscented soap. Wash the anal area only and pat (don't rub) dry; wash the genital area with warm water only.
* wash thoroughly after passing faeces: (i) wipe with paper, front to back; (ii) with a soapy hand, cleanse the back passage only; (iii) then sit back on the lavatory. Pour a bottle of *warm* water down the perineum and make sure to remove all the soap from the back passage.
* in a public loo you should: (i) wipe; take some paper soaked in tap water into the toilet cubicle with you and wash your anal area with wet paper.
   Use any way you can think of, in fact, to keep the whole area (and especially the urethral opening) clear of bacteria.
6. Keep pubic hair cut short.
7. Unprocessed (but clean) honey has anti-bacterial properties and so does aloe vera gel, which is also anti-fungal. Apply gently – don't rub.
8. Reduce (better still, cut out) smoking, which damages your body's natural immune system.
9. Get plenty of rest, reduce stress in your life as far as possible, and eat a healthy diet – or consider also taking nutritional supplements (consult a qualified nutritionist – see HELPLINES) to help boost your immune system so you are less vulnerable to cystitis – and other infections too.
10. A new study from Youngstown State University in Ohio has shown that drinking cranberry juice is more effective than antibiotics in the early stages of cystitis. The juice seems to work by preventing the urine from sticking to the urinary tract.

Other precautions against cystitis
1. Contraception:
* if you use the Pill, spermicidal cream, a cap, a diaphram or the sheath, stop

for a few months to see if the cystitis stops as well (meanwhile use another type of contraception – (see CONTRACEPTION, page 155);

* if you use a diaphragm, check whether the flow of urine is less vigorous when you wear it. If so, discuss trying smaller size with your doctor.

2. Sex:

* ask your partner to wash his hands carefully before sex (and his penis too, if he's amenable to such a suggestion) – particles of grit or dirt may cause inflammation;

* avoid sex toys and anything else which may irritate the urethral opening;

* keep sex gentle – ensure the angle at which a male partner's penis enters you is not too 'steep', so it abrades the wall of your vagina (next to your urethra) less.

If all this is a bit difficult to explain to your partner, try also telling him he will benefit in the long run if you are free of attacks of cystitis.

* if sex seems to trigger your cystitis, 'cover' for it by drinking plenty of water to keep urine diluted (non-irritating) and to flush the urethra and bladder thoroughly;

* use a lubricating gel like KY, from the chemist;

* space lovemaking, and think twice about very prolonged lovemaking.

3. Irritating chemicals:

* don't put anything in your bathwater;

* use plain uncoloured soap; and don't use them directly on your vulva area;

* avoid vaginal sprays and wipes;

* try not to swim in chlorinated water for a while, to see if it helps;

* use a different washing powder for your underwear; try changing from a biological one to a 'green' one, perhaps.

4. Do not cycle, particularly if the bicycle is old, the seat uncomfortable and the ground bumpy.

5. Avoid sitting on cold or hot seats.

6. Avoid spicy foods, pickles, acid fruit juices and most alcohol. Also avoid foods to which you think you may be allergic or sensitive.

7. It is very important to drink enough fluid, as it acts to 'flush' the bladder: three or four pints daily of water, weak tea or coffee, fruit squashes (*not* real fruit juice – this is too acid) or milk. A couple of pints more than this will do no harm.

8. Pass water as soon as you can after you feel the urge. Do not try to hang on – and when you do go, make sure you empty the bladder. When you think you have finished, wait a few seconds, then see if any more will come.

9. Take precautions against thrush (Candida), which is not an infection but very irritating for the entire area (see VAGINAL THRUSH, page 453).

10. Long, very hot soaks in the bath bring on attacks in some women.

11. So can letting yourself get chilled – in particular, keep your back warm.

12. Keep up your general health with fresh air, exercise and a good diet (but don't overdo citrus fruit like oranges, which are acidic).

13. If you get an attack, note what you have been eating and drinking – you may discover a personal 'trigger' which you can avoid in the future.

14. You may want to check that you don't have the beginnings of a prolapse of the uterus, or vagina (see PROLAPSE, page 430). Slight displacements of any of the organs around the bladder and urethra may cause pressure which stops the free flow of cleansing urine.

15. Simple bad posture could also, possibly, distort your urine flow.

16. Stress can bring on frequency of cystitis attacks, so try yoga, relaxation or meditation if this is a problem for you, and/or get help with your personal problems (see HELPLINES).

What to do during an attack

The first indication that an attack of cystitis is coming on is a burning pain when urinating. Self-help measures should be started immediately – even if it is the middle of the night. Many women find the following can help stop an attack within three or four hours:

* Drink a pint of water immediately, then continue to drink half a pint of liquid every 20 minutes for three hours (tap or mineral water is best but something weakly flavoured will do).

* Make some hot-water bottles. One for your back and one for between your thighs.

* Take something to make your urine less acid, and thus less painful to pass. Bicarbonate of soda (1 tsp in a glass of water) is good (but do not use it if you have high blood pressure or a heart condition).

* Take 2 to 3 strong painkillers.

* Put your feet up as much as possible.

* Pass urine whenever you feel like it. The more you drink and the more you pee, the quicker you will flush out the bladder and help the cystitis to wear off. You might try coffee or tea as a diuretic but not if you've found, or suspect, that one of the causes associated with your cystitis is coffee/tea. Mildly diuretic herbal drinks and teas can help (ask a herbalist, or try a healthfood shop – see HELPLINES).

* Non-prescription treatments which alleviate the symptoms of cystitis are available from chemists (e.g. Cystopurin, Cymalon). You may wish to try one of them, but if you are suffering from heart disease or high blood pressure, diabetes, other kidney diseases or are pregnant, leave them alone until you have consulted your doctor.

* Drink cranberry juice.

* Take a clean urine sample to the doctor as soon as you can.

Do not try to struggle on with your life if you can possibly avoid it. Try and take some time out to deal with an attack.

Complementary therapy

Complementary therapies tailor their treatments very much to the individual: the precise nature of the treatment you receive will vary, depending on your medical history, symptoms, lifestyle, etc. The following information indicates the *sorts* of things a therapist is most likely to do or recommend. Do not be surprised if they feel you need something slightly different. This section is meant purely as an indication of likely treatments; it is not meant as a DIY guide to the medical uses of the different complementary therapies.

Complementary therapies can help alleviate many of the symptoms of cystitis and, if it is caused by infection, attack the bacteria causing it. However, if the cystitis is severe, or if the therapist – after careful consultation – suspects you have a kidney infection, it is best to combine therapy with orthodox medical help.

Acupuncture

Acupuncture can alleviate the symptoms of cystitis and help your body to produce anti-bodies, strengthening its resistance to infection and inflammation.

Aromatherapy

The bactericidal – anti-inflammatory and anti-infectious properties of essential oils, such as chemotyped eucalyptus, or Melaleuca – will clear infection fairly quickly if used correctly. A culture and sensitivity test must be undertaken before treatment.

Clinical nutrition

Propolis is a natural antibiotic which helps kill harmful bacteria. Vitamin C, from sago palm, supports your immune system. Kidney glandular tissue gives support to your kidneys and helps rebuild damaged tissue. Proteolytic enzymes are anti-inflammatory and help relieve discomfort. Vitamin E prevents scarring and shrinkage of your bladder.

Combined with all or some of these treatments, dietary advice is important. Eating plenty of meat, eggs, milk, cheese, breads and cereals provides a good supply of amino acids and helps control bacterial growth. Citrus fruits and juices should be avoided.

Homoeopathy

Causticum is one of the chief remedies for cystitis and it is often prescribed as a preventive measure for women with weak bladders who have to travel a long way! Apis and Cantharis are for frequent painful urination; Sarsparilla if the pain comes only at the end of urination.

For various kinds of coloured or strong-smelling urine there are matching remedies, including Belladonna, Benzoic acid, Berberis and Lycopodium.

And for classic 'honeymoon cystitis' in newly married women, Staphysagria is used.

Medical herbalism

In the initial stages, drinking plenty of fluids and infusions of diuretic or soothing herbs, such as chamomile, couchgrass or marshmallow may help alleviate your symptoms. Buchu, celery seed or bearberry are antiseptics for the urine, and they inhibit colonization by bacteria. To heal damaged tissue and improve resistance to future infection, buchu or Echinacea might be used.

Cystitis helplines

Angela Kilmartin
75 Mortimer Road, London N1 (071 249 8664)
Author and cystitis expert, Angela Kilmartin will offer a counselling service for
stubborn cystitis – but only to those who have read her books (see FURTHER
READING, below) and still failed to solve the problem.

The Family Planning Association
27 Mortimer Street, London W1 (071 636 7866)
A full-service organization that can offer advice on all aspects of cystitis care.

Women's Health and Reproductive Rights Information Centre (WHRRIC)
52–54 Featherstone Street, London EC1Y 8RT (071 251 6580)
A volunteer organization which can give useful advice and support on any aspect of
women's health care.

Women's Nutritional Advisory Service
PO Box 268, Hove, East Sussex (0273 487366)
Send SAE for dietary advice to relieve cystitis.

Specialist products and services
Relaxation for Living
HQ – 29 Burwood Park Road, Walton on Thames, Surrey
Countrywide relaxation classes designed to help health problems; contact HQ for
details.

Further reading
You Don't Have to Live with Cystitis by Dr Larrian Gillespie (Century)
Cystitis: A Complete Self-Help Guide by Angela Kilmartin (Hamlyn)
Sexual Cystitis by Angela Kilmartin (Arrow Books)
Understanding Cystitis by Angela Kilmartin (Arrow Books)
Cystitis: A New Approach by Caroline Shreve (Thorsons)
Cystitis: A Woman Doctor's Guide to Prevention and Treatment by Dr K. Schrotenboer
(Macdonald Optima)
'Cystitis', Leaflet P32. Send 30p plus SAE to: Templegarth Trust, 82 Tinkle Street,
Grimoldby, Louth, Lincs LN11 8TF

Ectopic pregnancy

What is it?

Ectopic pregnancy is any pregnancy that develops outside the uterus. Ninety-six per cent of all such cases develop in a Fallopian tube (although they can also develop in the ovary, cervix, or abdominal cavity).

Many ectopics cause no great problems – the embryo dies and is reabsorbed back into the mother's body, and the only sign that it happened may be a delayed period. This is, in fact, what happens in most ectopics – at about six to eight weeks.

But it is vital to pick up any signs of an ectopic pregnancy early. When things go wrong, ectopic pregnancy is dangerous. It accounts for 10 per cent of maternal deaths (88 per cent of them from bleeding).

How common is it?

'Tubal pregnancies' occur in about one in 200 pregnancies (often, unknown to the woman herself). Ectopic pregnancy seems to be on the increase. In the USA the reported number has risen fourfold, only partly due to better diagnosis. No UK figures are available, but it is generally accepted that it is happening more often. One suggested reason is that ectopic pregnancy is linked with PID (see PELVIC INFLAMMATORY DISEASE, page 322), which in turn is linked with chlamydia (see SEXUALLY TRANSMITTED DISEASES, page 438) – which is rising fast. It is also more common in first pregnancies.

Causes

In a normal pregnancy the ovum (egg) is fertilized by the sperm in the Fallopian tube; it travels down the tube and rests in its lower part. Here, it begins to grow, while the uterus lining thickens to prepare for its arrival. And it is here that things may start to go wrong.

If there are blockages in the tube, the new embryo cannot travel along it into the uterus, and it gets stuck. As a result, the embryo may implant and try to develop in the wall of the tube. Usually it does not survive beyond 14 weeks and this is very rare. (By then, it is still only a few millimetres long, because it can't grow at a normal rate.)

Symptoms

Many women develop the normal symptoms of pregnancy, since the same hormonal changes are occurring. These include morning sickness, tenderness and swelling of the breasts, softening and closing of the cervix, enlargement of the uterus and loss of periods.

As the embryo starts to develop in an ectopic pregnancy, the blood supply to the tubes increases and the tube stretches. What happens next will vary.

★ If the embryo dies early on, it may be completely reabsorbed by the mother's

194

body (especially if it implants near the ovary). You will have only mild symptoms – a dull ache in the abdomen and a few days' delay in your period. Normally there is no damage to your tubes.

* Light on-off bleeding may result if the embryo burrows through the wall of the tube and causes a slow leak from 6 to 9 weeks.

* Heavier bleeding will result if the embryo goes on growing. Eventually it will get so large that it will rupture the tube – usually between 10 to 14 weeks. This may happen gradually, with blood leaking over a few weeks into the pelvic cavity.

* Emergency symptoms are pain and/or a large loss of blood. This happens if the tube ruptures suddenly. It is most dangerous when the embryo implants near the uterus. This could damage the wall of the uterus, which could be fatal.

* Infection is possible and the symptoms are pain, vaginal discharge and fever. Once the embryo has died, the hormones produced to sustain pregnancy will disappear. Then the lining of the uterus, which has been building up as for a normal pregnancy, is shed in clots or as a whole. The dead embryo is left in the tube. If is not reabsorbed, it may become infected.

Symptom checklist
SWELLING:
* tender swelling on one side of the abdomen, caused by the Fallopian tube becoming swollen with blood or the embryo developing there;
* a swollen abdomen, caused by internal bleeding from the rupture of the tube.

UNEXPLAINED SUDDEN BLEEDING:
* this can be internal and/or external, the blood may be fresh (red) or old (brown), spotting or more profuse. If the pregnancy persists, one or two periods may have been missed before any bleeding occurs.

PAIN:
* abdominal (colicky) pain is often an early symptom of ectopic pregnancy, although some women experience only mild discomfort or no pain even though a ruptured ectopic pregnancy is later diagnosed;
* a slight soreness or a stitch-like pain may accompany early spotting or light bleeding;
* the pain is likely to come suddenly and sharply if the tube ruptures;
* the acute pain may subside, leaving a dull ache between attacks, if there is intermittent internal bleeding;
* pain may be the result of internal bleeding irritating the lining of the pelvis or peritoneum;
* 'referred pain' may be triggered in the shoulder if the diaphragm (which is close by) is affected.

SHOCK:
* if the blood loss is great, a state of shock may occur, with symptoms of nausea, hot and cold flushes and a rapid, irregular pulse.

A recent study looked at the experience of women who had had an ectopic pregnancy and found that:
* 97 per cent had pain even before the tube ruptured;
* 93 per cent had had missed periods, or abnormal periods;
* 50 to 80 per cent had irregular bleeding – usually mild and intermittent;
* 95 per cent had abdominal tenderness;
* 75 per cent had vaginal bleeding;
* 75 per cent had a uterus which was soft and of normal size;
* 33 per cent had an enlarged uterus – up to the size of an eight-week pregnancy.

Who is at risk?
Several factors have been linked with ectopic pregnancy. In some of these the reason is clear: it can cause blockages in the tubes, or delay the progress of the embryo through the tube in some other way. Such risk factors include:
* salpingitis (infection of the tubes);
* previous infection in the pelvis, perhaps after abortion, miscarriage or childbirth;
* an earlier ectopic pregnancy;
* tubal surgery;
* pelvic inflammatory disease (PID). Some researchers say it is a common cause, others not, but the recent increase in PID has coincided with a dramatic increase in reported cases of ectopic pregnancy;
* sexually transmitted diseases, which account for up to 80 per cent of tubal infections in women under 25 (often these infections have few or no symptoms);
* fibroids in the ovaries or tubes, which press on the tubes;
* endometriosis;
* sterilization (ectopic pregnancy is three times more common in women after sterilization).
    Other risk factors have different reasons for causing ectopic pregnancy:
* pregnancy induced with the help of fertility drugs has a higher risk of being ectopic, just as it carries a higher risk of miscarriage, because, for whatever reason, the woman has problems in having a normal pregnancy;
* test tube fertilization (for the same reason as fertility drugs);
* taking the Progesterone-Only Pill (pregnancy is possible because this Pill does not stop you ovulating, but if a pregnancy takes place, the hormone signals are confusing and it may not proceed normally);
* having an IUD. If you get pregnant while using an IUD (there is a 2 per cent risk) this sometimes seems to slow down the embryo, so that by the time it is ready to leave the Fallopian tube it is too big to get out).
    Ectopic pregnancy is also more common with first pregnancies, although the precise reason is not known.

Diagnosis
The list of risk factors gives you an idea of whether you might be at risk. If you think you are pregnant, take seriously any symptoms which seem like ectopic

196

pregnancy and see your GP immediately. If you cannot get an appointment for a day or so go directly to your local hospital's casualty department.

Do not rely on a negative result from a home pregnancy test to tell you whether or not you have an ectopic pregnancy. Though the tests' manufacturers say they are 99 to 100 per cent accurate, a study carried out in America by the National Medical Center and George Washington University found that their real error rate when used by ordinary people at home, rather than by trained lab technicians, was up to 12.5 per cent. As an ectopic pregnancy can kill you, if you suspect you have one, you need to be 100 per cent sure as to whether you have conceived, or not.

The big danger is that the embryo will go on growing, and the tube will rupture suddenly and violently, with heavy bleeding. If this happens, you are a top priority emergency as it is possible to bleed to death in minutes. Many women with ruptures arrive in emergency departments. But as women become more aware of ectopic pregnancy, doctors are seeing them at a much earlier stage. This makes it possible (in theory) to treat the problem before it becomes an emergency.

You should report any bleeding in pregnancy to your doctor anyway. Usually, minor bleeding has no effect on a normal pregnancy, but if it is an indication that you have got an ectopic pregnancy you need to know about it. If you shed any tissue along with the blood, save it for examination under microscope. If no foetal tissue is found, this will help to distinguish between a miscarriage and an ectopic pregnancy.

Going by symptoms alone, a doctor will have only a 50 per cent chance of picking up an ectopic pregnancy. Only specialized tests can do it more accurately. The symptoms are the same as those of many other gynaecological conditions (such as salpingitis, a ruptured cyst, threatened or incomplete miscarriage, endometriosis or a degenerating fibroid). Ectopic pregnancy may even mimic appendicitis.

A text-book case of ectopic pregnancy will have these symptoms:
* no periods for eight to ten weeks;
* severe abdominal pain or persistent pain to one side of your navel (around the ovaries and Fallopian tubes);
* abdominal tenderness;
* if the tube has ruptured, it may be possible to feel a lump in the abdomen – and there may be severe shock.

The tests
If an ectopic pregnancy is suspected, there are accurate techniques for diagnosing it, all of which involve either sending samples to a laboratory for testing or visiting the hospital yourself. They include:
1. A pregnancy test. This is the one most often used. An ectopic pregnancy produces less of the hormone human chorionic gonadotrophin (HCG) than a normal pregnancy. Rapid urine pregnancy tests (including home kits) often fail to pick up the difference, but the newer laboratory pregnancy tests that use monoclonal antibodies have greater sensitivity – between 90 to 96 per cent success in diagnosing ectopic pregnancy.

197

2. Serum radio-immunoassay. This new blood sampling technique for measuring HCG is more sensitive still, and spots 99% of ectopics.
3. Pelvic ultrasound. If a woman has symptoms of pregnancy but an ultrasound scan does not show an embryo in the uterus, the doctor may suspect an ectopic pregnancy. (A normal pregnancy rules out an ectopic pregnancy – they coexist in only one in 30,000 cases.) Ultrasound is said to be capable of showing the ectopic pregnancy in the tube in 75 per cent of all patients.
4. Laparoscopy. A slender probe with a light and a telescope is inserted into your abdomen while you are under anaesthetic. Through this, the doctor can view your pelvic and abdominal organs. This reveals the ectopic pregnancy in more than 90 per cent of cases.

Ectopic pregnancy will be diagnosed from the signs and symptoms you report, backed up by a combination of tests. If symptoms are not too bad, doctors usually try the human chorionic gonadotrophin test first, plus ultrasound to see if a normal pregnancy is present. If symptoms are severe, the doctor may decide to go straight ahead with laparoscopy; so if necessary they can detect and then deal with the ectopic pregnancy in one go.

Treatment
The aim of treatment is: (i) to remove the embryo, to prevent any danger to you; and (ii) if necessary, to deal with any damage already done. Most treatment for ectopics is surgical (latest methods use delicate lasers). But increasingly some units are adopting a wait and see approach, admitting the woman to hospital where they can monitor her, but giving the condition the chance to resolve itself without surgical intervention (which it sometimes does).

LAPAROTOMY. A laparoscope is inserted first, to view your pelvic organs and make the diagnosis (laparoscopy – see above). The laparotomy itself usually involves a 4-inch horizontal cut (bikini cut) just above your pubic hairline. Sometimes, if speed is vital, it is easier to do a vertical cut.

Once the abdomen is opened up, any remaining blood clots are cleaned out and the affected tube is identified. The other tube is checked to see if it is healthy.

It is not possible to transfer the ectopic pregnancy into the uterus and try to make it into a normal pregnancy. It has to be removed altogether. It is sometimes possible to 'milk' it out of the end of the tube, or to use microsurgery techniques to remove it (very rare in this country).

SALPINGECTOMY. Most often, unfortunately, the tube has been permanently destroyed by the pregnancy. In this case the tube itself has to be removed – in an operation known as salpingectomy. If the ovary has been damaged, that too may be removed. If the ovary on the same side as the affected tube is healthy, it is usually left. For young women, only the affected tube should be removed. In older women who do not want any more pregnancies, both may be removed.

HYSTERECTOMY. If a rupture has caused damage, even the ovaries and uterus may have to be removed. If both ovaries are removed, you will have all the symptoms of menopause (see THE MENOPAUSE and HYSTERECTOMY, pages 276 and 225).

Unless there is an emergency, it is vital to discuss what will happen with the surgeon before *any* of these operations. Some surgeons can still be a bit too casual about taking out body parts when it is not strictly necessary (especially if you are older and supposedly don't 'need' your complete reproductive system). So ask what the surgeon thinks he may have to remove.

Once you've signed the consent form, the surgeon is free to do what he thinks best. Signing it, on the other hand, gives you a golden chance to ask questions and make demands. Nobody can operate until you agree to sign, so this gives you a certain amount of power. Build on this and be confident. Think about what you want to ask *before* you see the gynaecologist, and take some notes with you so you don't forget anything.

After-care
The length of stay in hospital after a laparotomy and/or salpingectomy is about seven to ten days. You will need to convalesce for about a month. (See also HYSTERECTOMY, page 276, if that is what you have had, for further advice.)

There will be a follow-up appointment at the hospital, about six weeks after the operation. The scar is checked and you can discuss the reasons there might have been for the ectopic pregnancy, and any problems.

If the ectopic pregnancy did not cause major damage to the tube, it may be possible to repair it through delicate micro-surgery (see INFERTILITY, page 250). This is usually left for three to six months after the laparotomy, so that any inflammation has had a chance to die down.

Self help
Self help measures for an ectopic pregnancy are concerned with helping yourself recover as fully and quickly as possible rather than preventing the event in the first place. The latter is almost impossible, unless you count using barrier contraceptives to try to avoid sexually transmitted diseases that might lead to a pelvic infection and blockage of your Fallopian tubes; or getting checked out both regularly, and before you begin trying for a baby, to ensure you don't have an infection like chlamydia, which can lead to an ectopic pregnancy (see SEXUALLY TRANSMITTED DISEASES, page 438).
* Bleeding after an ectopic pregnancy: use pads not tampons, to reduce the chances of an infection. By the time your first period returns it is usually safe to start using tampons again.
* Periods are likely to come back after four to six weeks. But the first one might be heavier and more painful than usual, so consider taking aspirin (the most effective over-the-counter painkiller as it reduces the womb's contractions' strength – which is what is giving you the pain) and planning not to do much (even consider taking a day or two off work) when it occurs. Hot-water bottles and rest will also help.

Your second period is more likely to be normal.

* Sexual intercourse: it is best to avoid it for four to six weeks. An orgasm from either yourself or your partner stimulating you manually is also likely to be painful for a few weeks.
* Contraception: bear in mind that neither the IUD not the Progesterone-Only Pill are advisable after an ectopic pregnancy because they up the risk factor of another one.
* Will it happen again/why did it happen? Try and make sure you take advantage of your check-up appointment to fully discuss the reasons for your ectopic pregnancy, the likelihood of another one for you personally and any problems you may be having. Also ask about the condition of your ovaries, and the remaining tubes or tube, and your chance of becoming pregnant again in future.
* Your feelings: You have just gone through a physically, mentally and emotionally painful experience and have lost a potential baby. You are likely to feel upset and weepy, and these feelings are entirely natural. Don't try to suppress them – you will get even more upset in the end. It can help a lot to talk about your feelings with others who have had the same experience (see HELPLINES – there is no support group specially for ectopics, but many others, such as The Miscarriage Association, can help).
* If you become pregnant again and wish to keep the baby, it may be reassuring for you to be sure it hasn't 'happened again' by having an ultrasound scan as soon as possible to ensure the tiny foetus is in the right place – your womb – and not trapped in a Fallopian tube again. Ask your GP to refer you for one.

Future pregnancies
Having an ectopic pregnancy does increase your risk of having another. But your chances of a normal pregnancy are still 30:1 in your favour, says Fran Reader, honorary consultant to the well woman services in the London borough of Tower Hamlets. If both ovaries are still in place, you will go on producing eggs in the normal way. If one ovary has been removed, the remaining ovary will double up to produce the same amount of hormones each month as two ovaries would. Instead of the ovaries taking turns to ovulate month by month, ovulation will still occur each month from the one ovary. Your chances of pregnancy are normal.

If one tube has been removed, the remaining tube is capable of picking up eggs produced by either ovary – even the one which is on the opposite side of the body.

After an ectopic pregnancy you will probably be advised to wait three cycles before trying to conceive again, to allow the normal cycle to re-establish itself. Over and above that it is really up to you to decide when you feel ready. If you haven't conceived after a year, ask for an investigation of your tubes to see if they could benefit from surgical repair. Microsurgery is a far more successful technique for such a delicate operation than ordinary surgery.

If you find you are too badly damaged to conceive naturally, some infertility treatments may be able to help, such as IVF (see INFERTILITY, page 250 and INFERTILITY HELPLINES, page 272)

Complementary therapy

Complementary therapies tailor their treatments very much to the individual: the precise nature of the treatment you receive will vary, depending on your medical history, symptoms, lifestyle, etc. The following information indicates the *sorts* of things a therapist is most likely to do or recommend. Do not be surprised if they feel you need something slightly different. This section is meant purely as an indication of likely treatments; it is not meant as a DIY guide to the medical uses of the different complementary therapies.

If you consult a complementary therapist while the ectopic pregnancy is still inside you, you will be recommended to seek immediate help from an orthodox gynaecologist as ectopic pregnancies need prompt surgery.

Complementary therapies can, however, be of great value *after* surgery – when you are left to cope with post-operative pain, grief and, perhaps, depression and the possibility of future infertility.

Acupuncture

Acupuncture treatment can help considerably, both in alleviating pain and in lifting depression by stimulating your body to release pain-relieving and anti-depressant substances. Some acupuncture formulae also produce relaxation and a feeling of well-being.

Aromatherapy

An aromatherapist will use essential oils of lavender, rose or sandalwood, among others, in an individual blend to help your mental and emotional symptoms and alleviate feelings of grief, disbelief and numbness. The treatment – which should continue as long as you need it and include counselling – may consist of full-body massage, supplemented with bath oils and oils for use in a room vaporizer.

Ectopic pregnancy helplines

The Family Planning Association
27 Mortimer Street, London W1 (071 646 7866)
They can help and advise on virtually any pregnancy-related problems.

Foresight
28 The Paddock, Godalming, Surrey (0483 427839)
Association for the promotion of pre-conceptual care.

The Miscarriage Association
c/o Clayton Hospital, Northgate, Wakefield (0924 200799)

PID Support Network
c/o WHRRIC, 52 Featherstone Street, London EC1Y 8RT (071 251 6331)
Ectopic pregnancy is often the result of previous PID. See PELVIC INFLAMMATORY
  DISEASE HELPLINES, page 330.

The Templegarth Trust
82 Tinkle Street, Grimoldby, Louth, Lincs LN11 8TF
Send SAE plus 30p for information on most women's conditions.

Further reading
When Pregnancy Fails by S. Borg et al. (Routledge and Kegan Paul)
In Our Hands by S. Ernst et al. (The Woman's Press)
Surviving Pregnancy Loss by R. Friedman et al. (Little Brown & Company)
Hidden Loss – Miscarriage and Ectopic Pregnancy by V. Hey et al. (The Woman's
  Press)
What Every Woman Needs to Know by Penny Junor (Birthright)
Dealing with Depression by K. Nairne et al., (The Woman's Press)
Bereavement – Studies of Grief in Adult Life by C. Parkes (Penguin)
Our Bodies, Ourselves by A. Phillips and J. Rakusen (Penguin)
Miscarriage, by Oakley, McPherson and Roberts (Penguin)

Endometriosis

What is it?

The endometrium is the lining of the uterus (womb). Every month, hormones in the blood prepare it to support and nourish a fertilized ovum. If there is no pregnancy, the endometrium is shed during your period. It comes out through your cervix (neck of the womb) – but some also travels back up through the Fallopian tubes and spills into your abdominal cavity. This is quite normal and usually causes no problems. The stray endometrial cells are simply absorbed.

But with endometriosis, some of these cells implant, and start to grow. The result can be pain, scarring and infertility – although how this happens is not understood.

The problem it causes depends on where the endometriosis is. According to an Endometriosis Society survey of 800 women, it is very common in the peritoneum (the lining of the whole abdominal cavity). Sites include the ovaries (56 per cent), the outside of the uterus (36 per cent), the Fallopian tubes (31 per cent), bladder (13 per cent), bowel (13 per cent), cervix (6 per cent), and vulva (1 per cent). In fact, rare cases of endometriosis have been known to appear just about anywhere in the body (including the liver and eye).

The patches can look like blood blisters (often, bluish-black specks), or may be a chocolate-brown colour – these are called chocolate cysts. They may be the size of a pin-head, or as large as a walnut. You may have one or two, or up to a hundred. They may all be in one area, they may be scattered all round your pelvis – or all round your body. It is not cancer, and there is no association with cancer at all.

The endometriosis patches develop over months or years – exactly what happens varies a lot from woman to woman. Inflammation and scar tissues build up around the patches, especially on the very sensitive peritoneum. The scar tissue (called adhesions) may also make internal organs stick together and be unable to slide comfortably over each other as they should in the closely-packed pelvis. Ovaries may stick to the uterus, or the uterus to the bowel. All this may affect fertility – or hurt.

How common is it?

Estimates on endometriosis vary, from five to 20 per cent of all women. It never starts before puberty, and only very rarely persists after the menopause. One in 10 women in the UK suffers either severe period pains, painful sex or infertility problems – all of which can be signs of endometriosis.

It is the second most common problem in gynaecology wards (after fibroids) and is found (often in mild form) during a quarter of gynaecological operations. Thirty per cent of infertile women have it.

It may be on the increase: it is certainly being found more often than

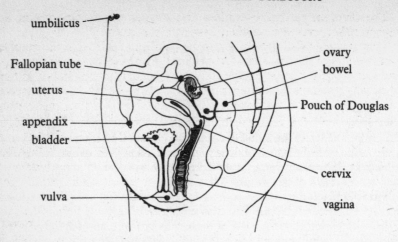

umbilicus

Fallopian tube

uterus

appendix

bladder

vulva

ovary

bowel

Pouch of Douglas

cervix

vagina

The usual sites of endometriosis

previously, but nobody knows if it is really more common, or whether doctors are simply better informed than they used to be, and so are looking for endometriosis more often.

Who is at risk?
It is almost impossible to say, until all women are screened for it, because endometriosis is found in all kinds of women.
* It was thought for many years to be a disease of white, middle-class career women. But this is a myth. It is just that they are diagnosed more often, probably because they are more persistent in getting help.
* Fewer black women than white are currently diagnosed, but this may also be because fewer seek, or get, help.
* There is some evidence that it runs in families, but no evidence that there's an actual genetic link.

Symptoms
The text-book symptoms include:
* infertility;
* painful periods (dysmenorrhoea);
* painful sex (dyspareunia);
* painful bowel movements or urination.
  In fact one in 10 of (diagnosed) sufferers has severe period pains, sub-fertility, and painful sex.
  Other symptoms described by sufferers include painful ovulation, a swollen abdomen, a loss of old brown blood, heavy periods, blood clots during periods, irregular periods, PMS, constipation, nausea, back pain, dizziness, diarrhoea, insomnia (from the pain) and – not surprisingly – depression and other psychological problems.

204

The site of the patches determines, to a great extent, the type of pain. Some women suffer severe pain. Others have no symptoms at all.

Strangely enough, the severity of the pain is not related to the number or even the size of the endometriosis patches. Mild cases can cause severe pain, and vice versa. But a scattering of tiny cysts can hurt more – and be far harder to detect – than the larger 'older' ones. Pain is probably the worst aspect. It can lead to tiredness, mood swings, a ruined sex life, conflict in relationships – especially if the real problem has not been diagnosed as even doctors are sometimes very ignorant about endometriosis. And the kind of symptoms caused by endometriosis can also be caused by other conditions, which makes diagnosis difficult.

What causes it?
The precise cause is not known, but there are plenty of theories.

* Retrograde menstruation bleeding upwards into the Fallopian tubes instead of downwards and out through the vagina. Ninety per cent of women have some degree of retrograde menstruation, and they don't all get endometriosis. But those who do, it is thought, are unable to clear it from the abdominal cavity in the normal way.
* Auto-immune disease – the body's defence mechanisms turning on itself.
* Misplaced cells – endometrial cells meant for the lining of the womb which were formed before birth and ended up in the wrong place.
* The lymphatic system sweeping endometrial tissue away from the uterus, so it ends up in other places.
* Metaplasia – other body cells converted into endometrial cells by hormone imbalance, infection or pollution.
* Reduced immunity to endometrial cells.

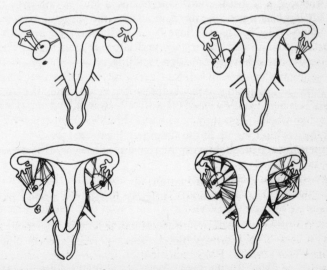

The advance of endometriosis on the ovaries and fallopian tubes.

All these theories need more research. The auto-immune theory is very popular among researchers at the moment.

A few things which are known *not* to cause endometriosis are: tampons; the contraceptive pill; IUDs (this is another discredited theory); stress (although it may make existing endometriosis worse); pregnancy; delayed child-bearing (although again this may make existing endometriosis get worse – the menstrual cycle never has a break, so the endometrial patches continue to build up, month by month).

Diagnosis
This can be tricky. The only sure way is for a doctor to see the patches. There is no quick and simple test. Diagnosis may take, literally, years.

EXAMINATION. After he has asked you about your symptoms, a GP can feel for suspicious lumps or enlarged ovaries, and can check the position of the uterus. (Unfortunately if sex is painful, the examination will be uncomfortable, too).

Medical research indicates that the best time for an examination is just before your period. The best method is probably a two-handed examination. Ask your GP just what is involved, before the examination starts.

All this should help the GP to rule out other possible problems which could be causing your symptoms (such as pelvic inflammatory disease, or various bowel and bladder disorders). This done, the next step should be to do a good test for endometriosis.

LAPAROSCOPY. The patches of endometrial tissue can't be seen through the vagina, so the only way to be sure is to go into hospital for a surgical procedure called laparoscopy, under anaesthetic.

A laparoscope is a slim tube with a light and a lens at one end. Inserted through a small incision near the navel, it enables the surgeon to look around the pelvic cavity. The cavity will have been gently pumped up with carbon dioxide gas to separate out the organs and allow a good view. The gas is removed afterwards, although some of it may linger.

A laparoscopy can be done in a day surgery unit, or it may require a stay of about two days. Try to arrange it just before your period, when the patches are easier to see. It is best to take a week off work afterwards, and avoid strenuous exercise for two weeks. You may have some shoulder pain, triggered by the remains of the gas building up in the abdomen. Scars are rare.

Tip: peppermint tea can help with the remains of the gas. But it clears very quickly.

For diagnosis, laparoscopy is not foolproof. Sometimes the patches are too tiny to see without a microscope. Early cysts may be colourless. And, of course, if the patches are outside the pelvic cavity they won't be visible. So a negative test still doesn't rule out a diagnosis of endometriosis – although some GPs are very reluctant to refer for a second laparoscopy. Sometimes, accurate diagnosis has taken several years.

If a diagnosis is made during laparoscopy, treatment might start then and there (see **Which treatment?** below).

206

The Future:

A NUCLEAR SCAN is an experimental method being developed at the John Radcliffe Hospital in Oxford. An antibody, labelled with a low dose of radioactivity, is injected and is attracted to the endometrial patches. These can then be shown up under a nuclear scanner. It has been tried on only a few women so far, but may prove useful.

Another method being tried at the John Radcliffe is based on the auto-immune theory. Levels of antibody to the endometrial cells are being measured in the blood of women with endometriosis. This may result in a simple blood test for endometriosis. But the research is still in its very early stages.

Difficult doctors

Not all GPs are up to date on endometriosis and not all GPs are keen to refer a patient for diagnostic surgery if they secretly suspect you are just a neurotic – even less keen if you've had one laparoscopy which found nothing (which is possible). After all, laparoscopy, and the anaesthetic used with it, may cause problems in themselves.

Unfortunately some doctors do think women with endometriosis are 'just neurotic'. It is difficult for patients to be persistent about problems which are very intimate, like the symptoms of endometriosis. The Endometriosis Society has found that GPs are most sympathetic towards women who complain repeatedly about painful periods or infertility, but they are not so responsive to complaints about painful sex. Some women are even told to 'wait for the menopause'.

If you want to be referred to a specialist and your GP refuses, remember that painful periods, painful sex and infertility are *not* normal and *not* something you should have to live with, so you can:

* ask your GP to arrange a second opinion for you (he is obliged to do this);
* change your GP (get advice from your local Community Health Council – find them in the phone book under 'C' usually, or ask Directory Enquiries);
* go to a family planning clinic, where doctors should be more clued up about women's health;
* ask the Endometriosis Society (see HELPLINES) for advice.

Infertility and endometriosis

Between 30 per cent and 40 per cent of women with endometriosis find they cannot conceive. Doctors are reluctant to conclude that endometriosis is the cause of the infertility because it is also found in women who have no trouble in conceiving. And both endometriosis and infertility are pretty common, so both might occur by coincidence in the same woman. But there does seem to be a link, especially if there are adhesions around the ovaries which impair the ripe egg's exit each month, or in the Fallopian tubes which means the egg cannot descend down them to be fertilized by a sperm.

Severe endometriosis can certainly cause infertility, but not all doctors agree that mild endometriosis can. So it is a matter of controversy whether treating mild endometriosis will improve things for women whose only symptom is infertility.

For moderate or severe endometriosis, there are various treatments – such as surgery or drugs – which can improve pregnancy chances. The choice depends on where the endometrial patches are, and how severe. See **Which treatment?** below.

The drugs available all offer much the same success rate, so it is a question of finding one that suits you.

Specific fertility treatment may be recommended: fertility drugs, IVF and GIFT (see INFERTILITY) are all suitable in theory for women with endometriosis. But they may not all be suitable in your particular case.

Pregnancy and endometriosis
Pregnancy is not a cure for endometriosis, although it can reduce the symptoms in some women. Young women with severe endometriosis may be urged to have a baby sooner rather than later, before the endometriosis has progressed too far and reduced their fertility further. This is a reasonable argument, but it might be a difficult decision.

If you have been treated with drugs, it is a good idea to use contraception for at least two months before trying to get pregnant, to let body systems settle down again. Previous drug treatment doesn't appear to affect the baby's health (except for babies conceived during drug treatment, when safety can't be guaranteed).

There is a widespread belief that women with endometriosis have more miscarriages. The evidence is conflicting, however – it may or may not be true.

Tip: watch your health, and stop smoking. For other ways to maximize your chances of a healthy pregnancy (see MISCARRIAGE, page 297).

Pregnant endometriosis sufferers may have pain and possibly bleeding, if the growing pregnancy is stretching an adhesion (see PREGNANCY PROBLEMS, page 360). If either symptom appears, it is essential to check with your doctor because these are also potential danger signs of miscarriage.

In general, there's not much information about endometriosis and pregnancy though there is no evidence that childbirth is any different. PMS is naturally relieved during pregnancy. Some women find that it never comes back but some find that afterwards it returns more severely. Most women don't experience a return of their endometriosis symptoms until their first period after the birth – so there may be something in the idea that breastfeeding, since it suppresses oestrogen production and thus delays the first period, is useful in extending the respite. Some women find that endometriosis symptoms disappear for good after a pregnancy.

Which treatment?
The choice of treatment depends on how many endometrial patches you have, how large they are, where they are, and how bad your symptoms are. The two options (often combined) are: (i) to remove the patches surgically and (ii) to shrink them with drugs.

It is your decision what treatment you have, if any. Most doctors now recommend that mild, pain-free endometriosis should be left untreated (with regular observation to see if it is getting worse).

Medical treatments on offer all involve drugs and/or surgery (sometimes, repeated surgery). So it is a question of deciding just how much your particular symptoms are damaging your life, and what you're prepared to do to get rid of them. No two cases are alike, and no two women are alike. Make sure your doctor knows this, and does not press you into treatments you don't want – or bar your way to treatments you do want.

What you decide will depend on many things, including: your age; your desire to have children; the site of the endometriosis; the degree of pain; and probably your consultant's assessment of the value of the newest treatments.

Surgery

One aim of surgery is to get rid of existing endometriosis patches or adhesions if they are causing trouble. Sometimes surgery is followed up by drugs.

Advantage: it is the only way to deal with large patches, or patches which are stuck on body organs.

Disadvantage: there may be an unavoidable risk of creating adhesions around the surgeon's cut, which could compromise your future fertility. Tiny, widespread patches cannot all be picked up by surgery alone.

LAPAROSCOPY. The simplest surgical treatment can be done during the laporoscopy examination which is used to diagnose endometriosis. Laparoscopes can have either surgical or (very rarely) simple laser attachments which the surgeon may plan to use to remove patches of tissue. Check this out with your GP or surgeon before you have the laparoscopy.

LAPAROTOMY is a more invasive form of surgery. It involves a stay of seven to ten days in hospital and an anaesthetic. An incision is made below the bikini line (the scar will be small, but may be visible) and the abdomen is opened up. Patches are cut out or cauterized (burned) away. The ovaries may be moved, to break up adhesions – which can bring dramatic relief for painful sex.

Advantage: laparotomy is a good way to deal with very large patches, or areas of adhesion.

Disadvantages: (i) the surgeon can treat only the patches he can see; (ii) some patches may be on areas that are too risky to touch (like the bowel); (iii) scar tissue may be formed, causing its own problems; and (iv) sometimes, according to recent research, adhesions are made worse by surgery.

It is not unknown for a woman to go into hospital for a laparoscopy examination and treatment, only to find when she wakes up that the surgeon decided to open her up and perform a full laparotomy. Make sure you discuss this possibility at the time you sign the consent form (which in practice covers both types of treatment).

MICRO-SURGERY. New developments include micro-surgery techniques (incisions are made with hot wires which seal wounds as they go, and loosened tissue is removed by suction).

Advantages: (i) it is a more delicate technique than ordinary surgery; and (ii) there are fewer problems with creating new, or worsening, adhesions.

209

Disadvantage: it is not widely available. Ask your GP to find out if local surgeons use it; or contact the Endometriosis Society.

LASER SURGERY uses expensive, specialized equipment. High energy light is used to destroy patches and separate adhesions without touching any nearby tissue. Two or three incisions may be made, to reach all the patches.

Advantages: (i) lasers can be used in delicate areas where a surgeon wouldn't dare use his scalpel; (ii) the laser seals as it cuts, so there is little bleeding and faster healing; (iii) endometriosis does not recur at the sites treated (but unfortunately in 50 per cent of cases it will reappear somewhere else); and (iv) the technique can be carried out in a day unit, with no overnight stay.

Disadvantage: it is available at a few hospitals in the UK (like St Luke's Hospital in Guildford, Farnborough Hospital and the Royal Northern Hospital in London); they have very long waiting lists; your GP can refer you, but you could wait up to two years – while the endometriosis gets worse all the time. Consider drug treatment as a 'holding' measure while you are waiting.

HYSTERECTOMY (removing the uterus) is sometimes advised for women who have tried all the other treatments with no success. It cannot, of course, help if you have a lot of endometriosis spread throughout your abdominal cavity. Hysterectomy is major surgery, so read HYSTERECTOMY, page 225, and discuss things fully if it is offered to you. Oophorectomy (removing the ovaries) used to be a treatment for endometriosis but is not now in use – it is too drastic (it brings on an early menopause) and it won't clear existing endometrial patches.

Drugs

The aim of all the drugs on offer is to interrupt the normal menstrual cycle and/or stop it encouraging the endometrial tissue. All of them have a contraceptive effect if the dosage is high enough.

The drugs control the symptoms of endometriosis while you take them, but they are likely to recur after you finish. It is a good idea to tail off the dosage gradually at the end of treatment, although not every doctor thinks of advising this.

Courses of drugs are given:
* before surgery, to shrink the patches and make them easier to deal with;
* after surgery, to keep patches under control once surgery has removed the worst;
* to control your symptoms enough to enable you to have a baby while the effects last;
* simply to give you a break from your symptoms, with a chance that they won't come back so badly – or at all.

The drugs include:
DANAZOL. This hormone treatment, first prescribed in 1971, is the most common drug used. It works by tricking the body into a fake menopause, by reducing oestrogen levels in the body. Without oestrogen the endometrial patches can't survive. Courses of six to nine months are given.

In about 40 per cent of cases the symptoms recur after the course of Danazol ends, but there is some evidence that the risk decreases with time. Recurrence may mean more treatment with Danazol, or it may mean that another treatment altogether is needed.

The dose is 200–800mg a day. Adjust your personal dose with your doctor, until you find the minimum dose which is effective. There is no general agreement or whether or not your periods have to be suppressed for the Danazol to work.

Advantages: (i) it is effective for pain (90 per cent of women report improvement in one American study); (ii) above 400 mg, Danazol doubles as an effective contraceptive; and (iii) lower doses may control endometriosis well enough to allow you to have a child.

Disadvantage: (i) Danazol causes side effects in 85 per cent of women. Some are mild, some too severe to be worthwhile – as always, it is your decision. Effects can include: deeper voice, smaller breasts, weight gain, dry vagina, hot flushes, acne, excess hair (face included), hair loss, oily skin, nausea and fatigue. Most of these effects disappear when you stop taking the drug; the deeper voice is pretty rare, but if you get it, it stays.

The effects of long-term hormone treatment are at present simply not known. Recent recommendations on long-term treatment include regular blood tests. The Department of Health says that Danazol should only be used as a last resort, for women with serious problems. But it is worth noting that when a trial of Danazol versus the contraceptive pill was made, side effects from the Pill led as many women to drop out as did those from Danazol.

OTHER HORMONES
* THE PILL – the ordinary combined contraceptive pill, taken continuously, can be used for mild cases of endometriosis (only for non-smokers under 35). (See CONTRACEPTION, page 155.)
* SYNTHETIC PROGESTERONE 'look-alikes' – Primolut N (norethisterone) and Duphaston (dydrogesterone) are both related to the female hormone progesterone, which is part of the menstrual cycle. Instead of tricking the body into a false menopause like Danazol, they trigger off a false pregnancy. The side effects are less severe – more like PMS than the menopause – but they are also less effective as treatment. Provera (medroxyprogesterone acetate) is a tablet form of the controversial contraceptive Depo-Provera (see CONTRACEPTION, page 155) – but it is used only rarely.
* NEW HORMONE ANALOGUES are GnRH (sometimes called LHRH) analogues, such as buserelin, nafarelin and goserelin: hormones which release gonadotrophin, which makes the body react as if the ovaries had been removed. In other words a 'medical oophorectomy' – which still gives menopausal symptoms but is at least reversible once you stop taking the hormone.

Also: Gestrinone, similar to Danazol.

Advantages: as effective as Danazol, but no masculinization/weight gain.

Disadvantages: (i) they seem to reduce bone marrow, by anything up to 6 per cent in six months, although the effect seems to be reversible; and (ii) it is not yet known whether endometriosis symptoms return after treatment or not.

They can cause some menopause-style side effects such as hot flushes, headaches, libido loss and vaginal dryness. However, some women, if given the choice, find even these preferable to Danazol's side effects.

Self help

Endometriosis is a long-term ('chronic') disease, but it can be controlled. It many cases, it can be cured. Self help will probably focus on coping with any symptoms which still remain after medical treatment, or in cases where you have decided that the treatment would be worse than the problem itself.

Sex
* Sex may be easier if you are on top of your partner as you can control the depth of penetration more easily, and you can move more easily if you feel pain.
* Drug treatment may lead to a dry vagina – use KY jelly.
* If fear of sex is putting you off forming relationships, the Family Planning Association is a likely source of advice and can tell you which family planning clinic near you has a psychosexual counsellor who can help you. (See HELP-LINES.)

Diet
A whole range of vitamins and minerals have been found useful by various women with endometriosis. They include:
* Vitamin B complex and B6 (also good for PMS);
* evening primrose oil (good for PMS and some of the side effects of drug treatment);
* Vitamins C and E and A (for pain and heavy bleeding);
* selenium (for pain);
* magnesium (for PMS);
* zinc (for PMS);
* Vitamin E (to help with the pain associated with adhesions) – but take care – it may interact with your own body's oestrogen and exacerbate the endometriosis;
* the Endometriosis Society can advise on various 'cocktails' of nutrients that have been found helpful;
* American doctors have found that treatment for Candida albicans (see VAGINAL THRUSH, page 453) can help women with endometriosis. This includes an anti-Candida diet, plus supplements. The reason it works is not understood. Its also a good idea to check the supplement amounts to take, with a trained nutritionist (see HELPLINES).

Pain
* Making a chart to show how your pain changes from day to day (rate it on a scale of 10) will help you establish its pattern, and the pattern of your self help strategies.
* Ideas worth trying are: warm baths, deep breathing, massage, exercise – for its general effects on health and wellbeing (e.g. walking or swimming), yoga, relaxation classes and a healthy diet. If you're constipated, it won't help with the pain so see CONSTIPATION, page 145, for how to help.

* Useful drugs you can buy for yourself include: aspirin, paracetamol, ibuprofen, Feminax (formulated for period pain) and some codeine mixtures (see PERIOD PROBLEMS, page 332). (Take care – codeine is part of the opium family and can be addictive, even in small doses, if you take it regularly.) Most painkillers, if taken continuously over a long period, can cause stomach ulcers. Herbal 'aspirin', made from willow bark extract, is an effective painkiller, but gentler on the stomach. Try Willow Complex from Ethical Products (0460 53699).

* If none of these works well enough for you, discuss with your doctor what he or she could prescribe – and don't be fobbed off or made to feel you are exaggerating. If you think it hurts too much, it hurts too much. Possibilities include: Ponstan, Synflex, codeine formulas (remember danger of addiction).

* Other drugs, such as anti-depressants, sleeping pills or tranquillizers, have their uses. But long-term use is a bad idea – the danger is that you will become addicted and/or the drugs will stop working for you. Use them for 4 weeks max.

* Another option is a TENS machine (transcutaneous electrical nerve stimulation), which blocks out pain by stimulating the nerves with electrical charges. (This is described more fully in CHILDBIRTH, page 109, with details on how to obtain one for hire or to buy. In fact, many methods useful in childbirth (e.g. relaxation, deep breathing) can help control endometriosis pain.

Complementary therapy

Complementary therapies tailor their treatments very much to the individual: the precise nature of the treatment you receive will vary, depending on your medical history, symptoms, lifestyle, etc. The following information indicates the *sorts* of things a therapist is most likely to do or recommend. Do not be surprised if they feel you need something slightly different. This section is meant purely as an indication of likely treatments; it is not meant as a DIY guide to the medical uses of the different complementary therapies.

In mild and moderate cases of endometriosis, some complementary therapies can be helpful. Complementary therapy is generally less helpful in severe cases, which would be treated by an orthodox practitioner.

Acupuncture

Acupuncture can offer valuable pain relief during menstruation and, for some women, can also help with pain during intercourse. However, acupuncture treatment alone is not helpful in shrinking or reducing the adhesions of endometriosis, nor can it help for sub-fertility. But the acupuncture continued with acupressure and Chinese Herbs can be very helpful in reducing adhesions and shrinking of endometriosis.

Aromatherapy

Cramping menstruation pains are relieved by gentle massage of your abdomen and lower back, with an individual blend of essential oils of clary sage, rose, melissa and others, which relax the muscle of the uterus.

The same individual blend can be used before intercourse by your partner for a gentle massage to relax your muscles and relieve spasm. Massage techniques should be taught by the therapist whenever possible. These techniques, if made a part of your lovemaking, ease the pain of intercourse.

The ability of essential oils to be absorbed by the body (such as rose, chamomile, lavender, jasmin, neroli and others) and their healing and anti-spasmodic action on muscles and connective tissue, may help to shrink or to reduce adhesions when regularly used in gentle massage. Their relaxing and hormone-balancing properties may also help to increase fertility. A medical trial using aromatherapy for endometriosis has been started, too.

Clinical nutrition
Because the precise cause of endometriosis has never been established, treatment is not certain. It has been suggested that excessive Candida in the system creates blockages in the fallopian tubes, thereby causing a leak of cells to the endometrium. Therapists assuming Candida is at the root of the problem, have achieved good results in the treatment of endometriosis patients. (See VAGINAL THRUSH, page 453.)

Homoeopathy
All these remedies are useful, and can be combined together, in low potencies, into one 'complex remedy': Apis Mellificia (for swelling, inflamed right ovary, nervousness), Crabro vespa (inflamed left ovary), Lilium tigrinum (painful periods), Platinum metallicum (pains which increase and decrease, heavy bleeding, mental change), Melliotus Officinalis (painful periods, painful ovaries), Viburnum Opulus (painful periods). Helonias dioica is extremely useful for adhesions, and for inflammation of the womb lining; Mercurious Sublimatus Corrosivus for inflamed ovaries, Fallopian tubes and, again, adhesions.

Medical herbalism
In the long term, herbal treatment for endometriosis is aimed at alleviating the problems by rebalancing your hormone levels and improving the function of your ovaries. Chaste tree or cramp bark, for example, relieve spasms and inflammation, and will help with pain during both menstruation and intercourse. Their effects on hormone levels also help reduce adhesions and improve fertility levels.

Osteopathy
Congestion of the uterus, giving rise to painful periods, can be helped by osteopathic techniques which encourage drainage through the veins. For some women, adhesions can be reduced by using osteopathic functional techniques through the vagina. Not all osteopaths practise in this way so it is important to ask the osteopath beforehand if they practise 'viscerae osteopathy'.

Endometriosis helplines

BABIE (British Association for the Betterment of Infertility Education)
PO Box 4TS, London W1A 4TS (071 224 0724)
This charity offers a full range of reduced-rate fertility treatments (including half-price IVF, if you have a note from your doctor confirming that you are suitable for, and would benefit from, this treatment), counselling and adoption advice to both members and non-members. Affiliated to the Fertility Advisory Centre, BABIE offers to members: free medical advice line, fact sheets on fertility problems and their treatments, and a newsletter.

British Nutrition Foundation
52 to 54 High Holborn, London WC1 (071 404 6504)
This centre can put you in touch with a trained dietitian.

British Pregnancy Advisory Service
Austy Manor, Wooton Wawen, Solihull, West Midlands B95 6BX (05642 3225)

CHILD

HQ – 367 Wandsworth Road, London SW8 2JJ (081 893 7110)
Advice and support group for people with fertility problems. There are local self-help groups who meet countrywide – contact HQ for details. They offer a wide range of fact sheets on fertility problems and treatments, adoption, up to date information on all fertility clinics (NHS and private), a newsletter, and price lists for fertility clinic services.

Endometriosis Society
35 Belgrave Square, London SW1 (071 235 4137)
Offers advice and support to women with Endometriosis, also a bi-monthly newsletter, and helpful books and publications. (Send SAE, ring only in evenings.)

Hysterectomy and Endometriosis Support Group
c/o Carol Naden, 28 Manvers Road, Liverpool L16 3NP (Carol: 051 722 5838; Geraldine: 051 727 3104; Linda: 051 727 1091) This society was formed by a group of women who now offer help, comfort, support and friendly listening for those who have had or are about to have a hysterectomy – or suffer from endometriosis. Meetings are held at the Woman's Hospital in Liverpool.

Hysterectomy Support Group
c/o Ann Webb, 11 Henryson Road, London SE4 1HL (081 690 5987)

RELATE
Herbert Gray College, Little Church Street, Rugby CV21 3AP (0785 73241)
A sexual advisory service is offered.

The Templegarth Trust
82 Tinkle Street, Grimoldby, Louth, Lincs LN11 8TF
See ECTOPIC PREGNANCY HELPLINES, page 201.

Further reading
Coping with Endometriosis by Dr Lyale Breitkopf and Marion Gordon Bakoulis (Grapevine)
Understanding Endometriosis by Carolyn Hawkridge (Optima)

If endometriosis has led to fertility problems for you, please see the INFERTILITY HELPLINES, page 272.

Fibroids

What are they?

They are round solid growths of extra tissue (muscle) on the uterus. They may be single, there may be several; and about half develop on 'stalks', and are very common; up to 20 per cent of women over the age of 30 have them.

The good news is that they are benign growths (their medical name is uterine leimyomata) and it is extremely rare for them ever to turn into cancer of the uterus – that only happens in 0.5 per cent of cases.

Further, though they can produce fertility problems this is by no means always the case. Many women with fibroids have no problems at all having babies.

What is more, up until recently they have been rather hard to treat as no one is quite sure what causes them to develop – other than the fact that the hormone oestrogen encourages them on. But lately specialists have been giving women a synthetic form of LHRH hormone (see **Medical treatment**, below) that is proving most effective at shrinking them – and sometimes getting rid of fibroids altogether, which, if nothing else, can provide relief from the heavy periods fibroids can produce.

Often they can be there for years and cause no problems at all, so the first a woman knows of her fibroids is when she is having, say, an internal examination for something else.

Less good news is that though they can be the size of a pea they can also grow up to the size of a seven-month pregnancy. Also, if you have fibroids they may cause you fertility problems, they will increase the likelihood of miscarrying a pregnancy and they might interfere with its delivery. They can also lead to heavy and painful periods.

Causes

Quite simply, nobody really knows for sure, but there are some clues:

OESTROGEN. Fibroids may grow larger when oestrogen levels are high (e.g. sometimes – but not always – in pregnancy when you may develop fibroids or when Hormone Replacement Therapy is given). They are very rare before puberty. After the menopause – if you can wait that long – they shrivel up, as your body runs down its oestrogen production. The link is obviously complex, though. Oestrogen may make some fibroids bigger, but it doesn't necessarily cause them.

One piece of research, however, quoted by Dr John Guillebaud of the Margaret Pyke Centre, suggests that taking the contraceptive pill (which raises oestrogen levels) can actually cut your risk of developing fibroids by about 17 per cent for every five years you take it. This disagrees with other evidence, so it is quite a controversial topic.

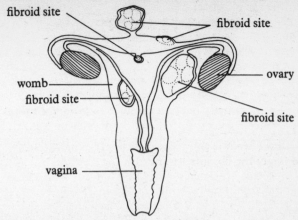

Fibroids, which can be as small as a pea or as large as a grapefruit, can develop in various places in the womb. Here are some common sites.

PROGESTERONE. A new (1989) study in the *American Journal of Obstetrics & Gynaecology* found that progesterone, the other female hormone, seems to inhibit fibroids. Since the Combined Pill has both hormones, this may explain the current confusion. Certainly, it seems that Combined Pills are a better protection if they have a high progesterone content.

YOUR WEIGHT. Another odd finding is that slim women rarely get fibroids (although not *every* study finds this). The connection between weight and fibroids may have something to do with oestrogen levels (oestrogen is stored in fat). But the link is not clear: women who weigh 11 stone or more are three times more likely to have fibroids than women who weigh 8 stone or less – but that remains true even if the heavier women are heavy because they are tall, not fat.

SMOKING seems to protect against fibroids. A study of 1,000 women in Milan found that current smoking lowered the risk by about 40 per cent, but that ex-smokers had no reduced risk. No explanation was attempted in the study, but again the link may be with oestrogen. ASH (Action on Smoking and Health) says there is plenty of evidence that smoking reduces your oestrogen levels.

GALLSTONES. A recent (1987) study confirms older research that found fibroids were more common in women who have gallstones (hard stone which develop in the gall-bladder). The authors suggest that the two may be 'associated diseases, probably sharing a common cause'.

Who is at risk?
At risk groups are thought to include:
* women who have not yet had the menopause;

* women over the age of thirty;
* women taking HRT for menopause symptoms;
* pregnant women;
* childless women (who are four times as likely to have fibroids as women who have had five or more children).

It is also widely believed that black women are more at risk than white women, but there are no actual studies which support this view.

Symptoms

In many cases there are no symptoms. Where symptoms develop, they vary, depending on where the fibroids are and how big they are.

The worst problems are usually caused by fibroids which grow at, or just under, the lining of the uterus (submucous fibroids). They bulge out under the lining (endometrium) and give it a bigger surface area – hence heavier, and maybe longer, periods and, if they are really bad, anaemia (low blood iron, leading to pallor and fatigue). Even quite small fibroids can cause heavy bleeding in this way.

If the fibroid grows out on a stalk, the uterus sees it as a foreign body and tries to expel it with painful, labour-like cramps. If it half-succeeds, it can get stuck in your cervical canal causing pain, plus bleeding.

Sometimes a fibroid growing on a stalk wraps round itself and cuts off its own blood supply. This is called 'red degeneration'. Symptoms are fever, abdominal pain, vomiting and general unwellness. Treatment just consists of managing the pain and fever. Then the pain goes, leaving behind a hard, dead, stone-like fibroid (womb stone) – detectable to the touch. This can sometimes happen in pregnancy, but it does not endanger the baby.

Fibroids which grow on (or very near) the cervic are quite rare (only 5 per cent of cases). But if you are having a baby, they may get in its way during the birth. Any kind of fibroid inside the uterus, but especially one on or near the cervix, can block the outflow of menstrual fluid resulting in, pain and a very light period.

Fibroids which grow under the endometrium, within the wall of the uterus (intramural fibroids) are the least trouble. If they are big, however, you get a bulging stomach.

Fibroids which grow on the outside of the uterus (subserous fibroids) usually cause no symptoms unless they are large. Then, they could press against other organs and cause quite severe pain, especially during menstruation. Pressure from them on the bladder can cause incontinence or, sometimes, stop the flow of urine completely (this is serious, so see a doctor at once).

All fibroids – particularly large ones – can distort the shape of any organ near them, or the uterus itself. So fibroids could be the explanation for all kinds of odd things, and luckily they are very easy to diagnose.

Symptom checklist
* Heavy periods
* Anaemia, caused by the heavy periods

* Painful periods
* Painful sex
* Bloated abdomen
* Backache
* Constipation
* Frequent peeing
* Sub-fertility or infertility. Fibroids alone are not a common cause of infertility; but if you have other problems in conceiving they may tip the balance between success and failure (this is called relative infertility). (See INFERTILITY, page 250.)

Pregnancy and fibroids

Fibroids alone probably won't stop you getting pregnant, if they are not too large or too numerous, although if you have other fertility problems they don't help. And, in about one in ten cases, they can make pregnancy more complicated. Fibroids can't be removed while you are pregnant, so if you have any which you suspect may cause trouble, get them treated before you plan a pregnancy. These are the main complications.

* Enlarged fibroids. In some women, the high levels of oestrogen produced in pregnancy may make fibroids grow larger.

* A study published in 1988 in the *British Journal of Obstetrics and Gynaecology*, followed 29 pregnant women with fibroids and found that in only 20 per cent of them their fibroids got bigger – and then only by a quarter. Another study, published in *Radiology* in 1987, found that smaller fibroids got larger and larger ones got smaller in the middle three months of pregnancy, and that all the fibroids got smaller again in the last three months.

An ultrasound scan, available just about everywhere now, is a harmless and accurate way to keep tabs on both foetus and fibroids.

* Miscarriage. There is an increased chance of miscarriage with fibroids, but not a large one. Fibroids outside the uterus are least likely to cause this and fibroids inside the uterus are found in only 2 per cent of pregnant women.

* Pain and fever. In mid-pregnancy you may get red degeneration (see above). It is alarming but, in fact, not serious. The treatment is bed rest and perhaps pain killers. The fibroid may shrink away after the baby is born.

* Early or difficult labour. At the end of pregnancy, fibroids can provoke early labour, or make labour more difficult – depending on where they are, and how big they are. The *Radiology* study quoted above (which looked at 113 women) found that fibroids in the lower part of the uterus gave an increased risk of Caesareans, and also of retained placenta after the birth (a potentially dangerous condition). Groups of fibroids were more likely to lead to premature labour than single ones.

* Caesarean. Sometimes an awkwardly placed fibroid can block the baby's exit from your uterus, and you have to have a Caesarean. If you have previously had a myomectomy, the cut in your uterus might have left a permanent weak spot. Again this may mean you have to have a Caesarean in case the weak spot breaks open under the pressures of labour – especially if labour is taking a long time.

Medical treatment

Your GP can diagnose fibroids – even small ones – quite easily, just by feeling your abdomen. You may not even need an internal examination. The problem most likely to send you to your GP is heavy bleeding (menorrhagia). Unfortunately, many of the drugs which are successful with other cases of heavy bleeding don't work for fibroids.

GENERAL HEALTH CARE. The least drastic treatment for heavy bleeding from fibroids is just to support your health while you go on bleeding. (See **Self help**, before.)

* Maybe a D&C (dilation and curettage), which will bring away the womb lining more easily. This is thought to make subsequent periods lighter, but the effect doesn't last for long (see PERIOD PROBLEMS, page 332).

* Hormonal Treatment: involves taking a synthetic form of the body's natural Luteinizing Releasing Hormone (LHRH) which stops your ovaries making the oestrogen that is 'feeding' your fibroids. This will shrink the fibroids over a period of approximately 6 months and often make them disappear altogether. Drawback: the drug produces a temporary menopause.

Only you can decide if these will do for your heavy bleeding. The GP is most likely to suggest this 'conservative treatment' if you're close to the menopause. When it comes, the fibroids will shrink in size quite a lot. Again, whether that is acceptable depends on you. How bad are the symptoms? How soon is the menopause likely to be? (If you knew the age when your mother started her menopause, it is a good clue). If you can't wait that long, say so. There are more drastic treatments available.

MYOMECTOMY is an operation. You are given a general anaesthetic, your abdomen is cut open and the fibroids are 'shelled out' through a cut in the uterus. Several can be removed at once. Then the surgeon does a 'nip and tuck' to get the uterus back to a normal shape. The operation may be straightforward or it may be tricky, depending on what the fibroids are like. A skilled surgeon is needed, and not every surgeon has the necessary experience. Ask your GP to check this out for you, and refer you elsewhere if necessary. If you need any support or advice, contact the WHRRIC (see HELPLINES). Fibroids can grow back after they've been removed – the chance is about 10 per cent.

There is about a 50-50 chance that you will still be able to have a baby after myomectomy, and it may well give you a much better chance than you would have if the fibroids were left in place.

However, the uterus or nearby organs can get damaged (for instance, if the fibroids are outside the uterus and very close to the Fallopian tubes, the tubes may be damaged). Myomectomy can also lead to complications in pregnancy – if, for instance, the wall of the uterus is weakened. It is less safe than hysterectomy because heavy bleeding may be set off which would mean you would have to have a hysterectomy straight away.

Sometimes, a surgeon sets out to do a myomectomy and finds that the fibroids (or the danger of bleeding) make it impossible. He will then want to do a hysterectomy at once (see below). Make sure you discuss this possibility fully with the surgeon before you sign the consent form for the operation. If a hysterectomy really is necessary, it is better to have it straight away so that you don't have to have a general anaesthetic twice. However, it may be a difficult decision for you to take, so don't allow yourself to be pressured or rushed.

HYSTERECTOMY. If the fibroids are very big or there are a lot of them, or if the surgeon thinks the danger of bleeding is too great, myomectomy may be impossible. In fact, because of the potential dangers, many surgeons are reluctant to use it and will urge you to choose the next option – hysterectomy (see HYSTERECTOMY, page 225).

This would mean that you are unable to have children in the future, and even if you have finished having children, it is quite a big step to take – physically and emotionally. All the same, if your fibroids are causing you real problems, a hysterectomy would solve the problem completely. It also means that you will never have to worry again about cancer of the cervix or uterus.

The future
Several new options are being explored for fibroid treatment, but none of these is widely available – if available at all – in the UK.

ANTI-OESTROGEN DRUGS. One idea is to use drugs which cut down the body's production of oestrogen (examples are buserelin and leuprolide) to make fibroids shrink and thus relieve the symptoms. However, the fibroids come back as soon as the drugs are stopped, the drugs suppress ovulation and, used long-term, they cause menopause-like side effects, like loss of bone mass.

Until a way is found to combine them with other drugs which stop these side effects, it is mainly an experimental option. Quite a lot of research is being done, and there are hopes of a breakthrough. It is being tried at one or two UK centres (e.g. the John Radcliffe Hospital in Oxford, and the MRC (Medical Research Council) unit in Edinburgh). If you want to join a trial, contact the Endometriosis Society (see HELPLINES), who are working with the researchers to find volunteers (the drugs can work for endometriosis, too).

Possible uses of drugs for women with fibroids would be:
* for women who badly need treatment but can't have surgery for some reason;
* as a one-off treatment to shrink fibroids and make them easier to remove when surgery is done – this results in an easier operation and easier recovery.

SURGERY. Another new treatment (found to be 90 per cent successful with submucous fibroids) is to remove the fibroids through the vagina by dilating the cervix and grasping them with surgical instruments. This removes the need for a hysterectomy, or even for cutting the uterus (myomectomy).

TRANSUTERINE OR TRANSCERVICAL RESECTION. The surgeon uses a special instrument called a resectoscope – a sort of telescope with various devices on the end (a knife-like curette, a laser or a diathermy – heat treatment – loop) which removes the fibroid and part of the whole womb lining for good.

This is such a simple operation that you could be in and out of hospital in a single day, and perhaps have only a local anaesthetic. You would also stop having periods completely but your ovaries would be left in place, so you wouldn't have a premature menopause. However, although it is much less drastic than a hysterectomy, losing your womb lining still means you can't have children. This treatment has, up until now, been experimental but is now becoming more widely available. If you feel it would help you, request to be referred to a surgeon who uses it.

Self help
There is nothing you can do to definitely prevent fibroids (there is no hard and fast advice like stopping smoking to lessen your chances of developing lung cancer, for instance) since nobody is sure of the cause of them. Some factors which *seem* to reduce the risk of them are hardly worth adopting – like taking up smoking, or having lots of babies. However, the risk of fibroids is yet another good reason for keeping your weight down.

If your symptom is heavy bleeding and/or pain, many of the ideas suggested in PRE-MENSTRUAL SYNDROMES and PERIOD PROBLEMS, pages 411 and 332 may help you to avoid the last resort of hysterectomy, though the new transuterine resection (see above) may be another option. Otherwise you could consider some of the following suggestions.
* If you are using another type of contraceptive, perhaps try changing to the Pill (but note that there is conflicting evidence about its effect on the fibroids themselves).
* Consider drug treatments for heavy bleeding (though these are not as effective for fibroids as they are for other causes of heavy bleeding).
* Ask about being referred for an endometrial resection.
* Follow a high iron diet and/or take iron supplements if your bleeding is causing anaemia.
Complementary therapies (see below) can also be very helpful.
Otherwise, you either have to cope with the bleeding, or get your fibroids treated.

Complementary therapy
Complementary therapies tailor their treatments very much to the individual: the precise nature of the treatment you receive will vary, depending on your medical history, symptoms, lifestyle, etc. The following information indicates the *sorts* of things a therapist is most likely to do or recommend. Do not be surprised if they feel you need something slightly different. This section is meant purely as an indication of likely treatments; it is not meant as a DIY guide to the medical uses of the different complementary therapies.

Certain complementary therapies can be of some use in alleviating the pain associated with fibroids and in restoring the function of the uterus.

Clinical nutrition
Uterine fibroids are nearly always benign, not cancerous. May cause heavy periods and

bleeding between periods, or bleeding after intercourse, so check up for anaemia is advisable. Some oral contraceptives, especially those high in oestrogen, have been linked with fibroids. You may need to consult a doctor or family planning. No special diet needed. Ask your nutritionist about the most readily absorbed iron.

Homoeopathy
A useful basic remedy is Calc. Iodide, followed up by Lachesis. Aurum Mur. is also good, given over several months. For a heavy 'bearing-down' type of pain, Sepia is used.

Medical herbalism
As with endometriosis, cramp bark or chaste tree remedies, among others, help spasmodic pain and improve hormone balance and uterine function.

Fibroids helplines

The Association of Chartered Physiotherapists in Obstetrics and Gynaecology
c/o The Chartered Society of Physiotherapy
14 Bedford Row, London WC1R 4DD (071 242 1941)

Hysterectomy Support Group
c/o 3 Lynne Close, Greenstreet Green, Orpington, Kent (081 856 3881)
This group can put you in touch with women who have had a hysterectomy or
  fibroids. (Send SAE with covering letter.)

Women's Health and Reproductive Rights Information Centre (WHRRIC)
52–54 Featherstone Street, London EC1Y 8RT (071 251 6332/6580)
A voluntary organization that can give useful information and support on any aspect
  of women's health care. Send 40p plus SAE for leaflet on fibroids.

The Women's Health Concern
PO Box 1629, London W8 (071 938 3932)
See GENERAL HELPLINES for details.

Specialist products and services
Weight Watchers UK Limited
Kidwells Park House, Kidwells Park Drive, Maidenhead, Berks SL6 8YT
  (0628 777077)

Further Reading
What Every Woman Needs to Know by Penny Junor (a Birthright book, published by Century) contains a small but helpful section on fibroids.

To our knowledge there are no books solely on the subject of fibroids; instead there are chapters in general women's health books such as:

Every Woman's Medical Handbook by Miriam Stoppard (Dorling Kindersley)
Experiences of Hysterectomy by Ann Webb (Optima)

Hysterectomy

What is it?

Hysterectomy is an operation to remove the womb (uterus) – and sometimes other parts of, or the rest of, your reproductive system. There are four basic types and the extent of surgery depends on the reasons for the operation.

1. SUB TOTAL HYSTERECTOMY removes the womb itself, but the rest of your reproductive system is left intact (i.e. the cervix, your ovaries and Fallopian tubes). This operation is rarely done now, as the cervix is seen as a potential site for cancer. You will still need regular smear tests if your cervix remains.

2. TOTAL HYSTERECTOMY removes all the womb, *including* your cervix. The ovaries and Fallopian tubes are left alone. This is the most common type.

3. HYSTERECTOMY WITH BILATERAL (TWO-SIDED) SALPINGO-OOPHORECTOMY removes your ovaries and Fallopian tubes, as well as the whole uterus.

This means that production of the female hormones by the ovaries will stop, which produces the same effect as the menopause, so if there is a choice (and often there isn't) surgeons may leave one ovary and tube. If both ovaries have to be removed, you may have a hormone implant put under your skin during the operation, or you may choose hormone replacement therapy (HRT) after the operation. Both these methods keep hormones circulating to help you avoid most of the menopause's unwelcome effects. (See MENOPAUSE, page 276.)

4. WERTHEIM'S OR 'RADICAL' OR 'EXTENDED' HYSTERECTOMY removes the uterus, cervix, Fallopian tubes and ovaries, plus the upper part of the vagina, the ligaments which support the uterus, the nearby lymph glands and some fatty tissue. This is pretty extensive surgery, and would be needed only for cancer in danger of spreading. May be combined with radiography.

Hysterectomy is the fifth most common operation performed in the UK, with some 64,000 done every year. Every woman has a one in five chance of hysterectomy, but your chances vary according to the policies of the GPs and surgeons in your health authority area, as some are readier to recommend and perform the operation than others.

5. TRANS CERVICAL RESECTION: increasingly being done if the problem is small fibroids or heavy periods only. A minimally invasive new technique involving lasers or heat to take the entire womb lining away but leave the muscular body of it in place. Recovery is a matter of a week or two.

Reasons for hysterectomy

There are several possibles, ranging from a potentially life-threatening gynaecological cancer to problems which won't kill you but may be ruining your life, e.g. heavy, painful periods. However, hysterectomy should be an option only when other, less drastic, treatments have failed. Possible reasons for hysterectomy include:

FIBROIDS, which are the most common reason. Hysterectomy (uterus only) may be suggested if the fibroids are growing very fast, or causing pain or heavy bleeding (see FIBROIDS, page 216).

ENDOMETRIOSIS. Again, your symptoms may be so bad that you choose hysterectomy as the sure way to end them. How much is removed during the operation will depend on the extent of your endometriosis. (See ENDO-METRIOSIS, page 203.)

PROLAPSE. Surgical repair removing nothing, is the first option in prolapse, but your surgeon may well advise hysterectomy to give a better result. (See PROLAPSE, page 430.)

PELVIC INFLAMMATORY DISEASE is the least common reason. But if PID can't be cleared up, it can lead to severe scarring of the Fallopian tubes and ovaries, which can then become attached to the uterus by scar tissue. This may cause pain, including painful sex. How much is removed during the operation will depend on the extent of the damage.

CANCER. Four types of cancer can lead to hysterectomy – cancer of the cervix, the uterus (or endometrium – womb lining), the ovaries and (very rarely) the Fallopian tubes. Cancer, if it hasn't been detected soon enough, is the usual reason for the most extensive types of hysterectomy.

MENORRHAGIA, which is heavy bleeding. If your periods are unbearably heavy, painful or unpredictable, and if nothing else helps, you may decide a hys-terectomy is well worth it. It removes the problem once and for all. Only your uterus will be removed. (See PRE-MENSTRUAL SYNDROME and PERIOD PROB-LEMS, pages 411 and 332.)

Is your hysterectomy really necessary?
If you have a life-threatening cancer, hysterectomy is a life-saving and very necessary operation. However, many other conditions which can be dealt with by hysterectomy can also be treated by less drastic means. Some women prefer to give as many other options as possible a chance before having surgery; others feel it is a sensible and straightforward solution that is perfectly acceptable to them.

The decision as to whether or not to have a hysterectomy is entirely your own (and not your doctor's) providing you have all the necessary information about your own condition, plus details of all the available treatment options. In the past, and before much of the current knowledge was available, some doctors unfortunately were rather too ready to suggest hysterectomy for mild cases of certain conditions (see above). Any operation today, however, is a compromise between doctor and patient after full and frank discussion of the pros and cons.

Heavy bleeding

According to Margaret Rees, research gynaecologist at the John Radcliffe Hospital in Oxford, 6 out of 10 women referred for hysterectomy to end heavy period are *not*, in fact, losing that much blood and don't need their womb removed at all.

A woman's average monthly loss is around 50–70ml – and doctors feel any thing up to 80ml is acceptable, says Dr Rees. She adds that, ideally, your blood loss should be measured before you undergo surgery to check that it really is as heavy as you had thought. But the technique used (leaching blood out of sanitary pads with caustic soda) is available only at one or two research centres, so it is not always possible to check whether your periods truly are heavier than the norm.

Stress can also bring on menstrual changes such as menorrhagia. So if the problem is recent, a hysterectomy might remove a symptom – but not the cause.

If you are in doubt about whether your periods are heavy enough to justify a hysterectomy, it may help to try all the other possible treatments for heavy bleeding, which include:

* the combined contraceptive Pill (which stops the menstrual cycle and gives you light withdrawal bleeds only);
* the progestogen-only mini-pill (now thought suitable for older women up to about 45 years old to take for years at a time – see CONTRACEPTION, page 155). This may, however, cause irregular bleeding;
* the drug Ponstan, which stops production of progersterone which, in the latter half of the menstrual cycle, helps maintain your womb lining (see PERIOD PROBLEMS, page 332);
* other drugs which reduce blood loss at the time of periods;
* removal of the womb lining only, by heat treatment, leaving the shell of the womb intact (see later in this chapter).

If you are having problems, you must insist on full discussion, and you must feel your point of view is the deciding factor. You have the right to ask your GP or surgeon to refer you for a second opinion. If you are still not satisfied, change GP and start again or (if you can afford it) contact a private gynaecologist (although this won't necessarily result in better treatment). If you are having trouble getting a satisfactory diagnosis, contact the Medical Advisory Service for the Hysterectomy Association for advice (see HELPLINES).

You have two main decisions to make. First, have you run out of non-surgical treatment options? If so, are your symptoms bad enough to justify major surgery? Hysterectomy is much safer and simpler than it used to be, but it does involve major abdominal surgery. So, like any other operation, it carries some risk, and you will need weeks of rest to recover from it.

Second, how important is your uterus to you? Even the least extensive hysterectomy (sub total) means that you lose your ability to have children. If you have not had children yet, this could be heart-breaking. Even if your family is complete, you may be worried that you will feel less yourself – perhaps even less female – without it. Your partner may have strong feelings about this, too.

There are some benefits to hysterectomy, though, apart from relieving the condition which is your reason for having one: no more worries about contraception; and no more periods (though if you had PMS before, you will still get it if your ovaries are intact).

So, unless you have cancer, you may want to take your time and explore your feelings – with help from professional counsellors, or other women who have either had, or considered, a hysterectomy themselves and who know from experience how you feel. (See HELPLINES.)

Fears and fallacies
Hysterectomy attracts a lot of old wives' tales, which don't help you cope with any fears you may have:
* 'I'll have an empty space inside me.' You won't. That part of your body is quite crowded. No matter how much is removed, other organs will move over to fill the gap. This won't feel odd; abdominal organs move about like this anyway, gap or no gap. If you had a swollen uterus (from fibroids, for example), organs would have been pushed out of place and will be able to get back in line again. If your cervix is removed (it probably will be) the surgeon will probably carefully stitch up the top of your vagina so it has an 'end', as it did before. It will make no difference to your ability to enjoy sexual intercourse (see **Sex after hysterectomy**, below).
* 'I'll get fat.' There is no physical reason why you should – unless you are feeling low and eating to cheer yourself up, and/or not taking exercise.
* 'I won't be feminine or sexy any more.' Again, there is no physical reason for this, even if your ovaries are removed. But your feelings (and your partner's) are powerful, and you may need help to work through them. Don't bottle them up; it just gives them more power in the end. Speak to a sex therapist or counsellor (see HELPLINES).
* 'I'll age prematurely, get hot flushes, dry up inside, etc.' Symptoms like these are not caused directly by the hysterectomy, but by the early menopause brought on if your ovaries are removed. You may have no problems at all, but if you do, you *don't* have to put up with them (see MENOPAUSE, page 276).
* 'I'll lose my figure.' You won't if you do the pre- and post-operative exercises (see right).

Self help before the operation
* Talk over your feelings. Top of the list of people to talk to, unless it is quite impossible, is your partner (if you have one). But families have their own fears and worries, so they may react with seeming indifference to protect them-selves; say 'Don't be silly', 'Don't worry' or give you lots of unwanted 'good' advice. Your main need is somebody who will actually listen, and let you off-load your feelings – it doesn't much matter who it is. If there really is nobody you want to talk to, a sympathetic-looking pet, a cushion to thump or an imaginary person can all be surprisingly useful. Or contact a local branch of a support group (see HELPLINES).
* Make sure you know exactly what is going on. Find out all you can about the operation planned for you – from your GP and, when you see him, from your

Before the Operation

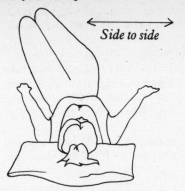

← Side to side →

Lie on your back with your knees bent up, one pillow under your head. Pull your tummy in. With knees together, slowly roll your knees first to one side and then to the other – a few inches at the beginning, increasing gradually. Repeat six times, three times daily.

Pelvic curl

Lying with your knees up, your head on a pillow, pull your tummy in, tuck your chin in and with your hands on your thighs, raise your head off the pillow to look at your knees. Hold and lower slowly. Repeat six times, three times daily.

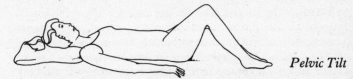

Pelvic Tilt

Lie on your back with one pillow under your head, and your knees bent. Pull your tummy in, tilt your bottom upwards slightly and try to press the middle of your back flat against the mattress. Do not push down on your feet or hold your breath. Then relax. Try this movement in a sitting position as well, to correct your posture.

surgeon. When you reach hospital, talk to the nurses on the ward. Raise *any* doubts you have. With any kind of surgery, it has been proved that you suffer less pain, have fewer side-effects, and recover more quickly, if you are kept informed. Again, consult books and support groups (see HELPLINES).

* Exercise to strengthen stomach muscles and pelvic floor muscles (see INCONTINENCE, page 239). You will need these to be as strong as possible. Take every chance you can, tightening all your abdominal muscles. Do it every time you think of it, standing, sitting, waiting in queues. Three other exercises you might try, are:

i) Pelvic tilt – lie down on your back, knees bent, pillow under neck and head. Pull in your stomach, keep breathing and tilt your bottom towards the ceiling to flatten your back against the floor. Don't lift off the floor. Do five a day, and more if you can.

ii) Pelvic curl – start in the same position as for the pelvic tilt. Tuck in chin and raise shoulders (nothing else) off the floor, curling head in towards knees. Start with five of these, then do more and more, day by day.

iii) Side-to-side – start in the same position as for the pelvic tilt, and then roll your your knees from side to side (imagine clock hands, going from 10 to 2).

* If you possibly can, give up smoking (or at least cut down) well before the operation, *not* within a few days of it. It is not helpful to anyone who is having an anaesthetic.

* In the days just before the operation, practise deep breathing (this will get you in the habit, and will help the anaesthetic wear off faster after the operation).

The Operation

Hysterectomies can be performed in two ways, through the abdominal wall or through the vagina.

1. VAGINAL OPERATION always used for hysterectomy for prolapse. The advantages are: no visible scar (although there will be internal stitching); and the surgeon can repair slack tissue in the vagina, making it tighter, at the same time. The disadvantages are: there is more danger of infection and bleeding; and the surgeon can't get a good view of your surrounding organs to give them the all clear.

2. ABDOMINAL OPERATION – the surgeon can cut horizontally along the top of the pubic hair (Pfannensteil incision or bikini cut) or cut vertically up towards the navel. In both cases, the scar will be six to eight inches long. The advantage of the vertical cut is that it allows the surgeon more room to manoeuvre if there are a lot of fibroids, or adhesions caused by endometriosis, or if you are very overweight. The disadvantage is that the scar is more obvious, and takes longer to heal.

If the cervix is removed, stitches are usually put in to close up the gap at the top of the vagina (sometimes a small opening is left to let fluid drain out, which closes up naturally in two or three weeks).

After the operation

(i) You will have vaginal discharge, probably brownish-red. It doesn't matter if:

* it's bluish (that will be the dye used to show up tissue during the operation);
* it has bits of thread in it (that will be the internal stitches, dissolving).

It does matter if:

* it's bright red (it could be internal bleeding – this happens in one in 1,000 hysterectomies);
* it has clots (internal bleeding, again);
* it's yellow or smells offensive (it could be an infection).

Report any of these three at once.

230

(ii) You will be urged to get up and walk from day one, to prevent blood clots forming in your legs (such clots could be fatal if they break away and block a vital artery).

* Signs of trouble are: leg pain, swollen ankles, chest pain, shortness of breath, a dry cough and/or blood-stained sputum.

Report any of these at once.

Self help
* Clear your system of anaesthetic by deep breathing and coughing. Keep your outer stitches protected by holding them with your hands and/or a pillow (after an abdominal operation) or a sanitary towel (after a vaginal operation) while you do this.
* Keep circulation in your legs going by flexing your ankles: legs straight, point toes then straighten, quickly and often.
* Learn the drill for getting out of bed safely: lie on your back, knees bent, roll

Getting out of bed

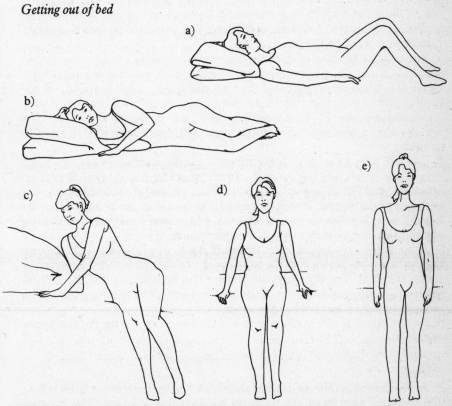

a) Knees bent; b) Roll to one side, knees together; c) Swing legs down, keeping your knees bent; d) Push up to sitting position and sit on the side of bed, feet flat on the floor; e) Stand straight up before beginning to walk.

on your side and swing your legs gently over the edge of the bed (knees together and still bent), sit on the side of the bed with your feet on the floor, stand up straight.

* Walk about gently. Stand up as straight as you can – it helps the wound heal correctly. Listen to your body. Make yourself do as much as you can; but at any hint of pain – stop.

* Do not cross your legs while in bed or sitting down.

Convalescence

* You may need a drip to replace lost body fluids and a catheter to drain urine from your bladder for a day or two. You might also need a drainage tube to remove any fluid trying to collect around the wound.

* Your stitches and/or clips will be removed after five or six days. All stitches inside you are self dissolving so they do not have to be removed but healing inside takes longer. Continue to watch out for any signs of internal bleeding.

* How soon you are discharged from hospital depends on that hospital's policy, the demand for its beds and how well you are recovering. It may well be as soon as five days after your operation. You may also go into a separate convalescent ward before you go home.

* You may get a period of the blues after your operation – it is a very normal reaction, but again, not everyone experiences it. It may be as a result of a physical reaction to the trauma of the operation itself, a need to grieve – either for the part of your body which has been taken away or for the end of your childbearing years. If you do get miserable, the feeling almost always disappears after a few days. If it doesn't, get help (see HELPLINES) as soon as possible.

* You will have a check-up appointment – usually after six weeks – to make sure the incision is healing properly. In the weeks leading up to your post-op check-up your GP (or, more likely, your district nurse) should be helping you with care of the wound. If they do not, and the area does not seem to you to be healing well, is weepy or has an offensive odour, don't wait for your 6-week appointment date, contact your consultant at once.

* At your check-up appointment there will also be careful checks to make sure that no tissue has grown over the top of your vagina (that is called granulation tissue, if it has). The doctor would remove this by touching it with a caustic solution – quite painlessly – and there may be further follow-up appointments to make sure that does not happen again.

* If your cervix is still in place, you will need to go on having regular smear tests.

Self help

* As soon as you get the medical go-ahead, start all the exercises you did before the operation (see above) to build up muscle support inside. The hospital physio therapist should come and teach you how, if necessary. If you have painful wind or backache, the pelvic tilt and side-to-side exercises are especially good.

* If you do have painful wind, do the exercises above to disperse it. Peppermint tea from the health shop can be helpful, too, as can tablets called 'Wind-cheaters', available from major chemists.

* Guard against constipation. The last thing you need is extra strain on your operation area so try drinking lots of fluid, and eating whole grains, vegetables and fresh fruit (the latter two may not be such a good idea if you are also suffering from wind). See CONSTIPATION, page 145, for other mild laxative ideas – those bought in chemists and found in foods.

* If your incision area feels sensitive and was around your bikini line (it may well do so for several weeks) try wearing a not-too-tight pantie girdle, preferably an old one softened by wear, to stop the wound area being irritated by clothes moving against it. Wear loose clothing – no tight trousers.

* You may be advised to take daily salt baths to help healing – but don't overdo it, as experts say one a day really is enough. If the area around your bikini line incision feels very uncomfortably dry try a little very bland moisturizing cream on it (e.g. E45 from the chemist).

* It is not uncommon to experience vaginal discharge for some weeks or months. See your GP at once if it contains any blood, smells offensive, seems highly coloured or particularly plentiful – enough to require a pad. You also have the right, up to a year after your operation, to go directly back to your consultant with any queries, without needing your GP's referral.

* Don't lift *anything*. For the first few days, don't even lift the kettle. Fill it with a cup and tip it to empty it. (There are aids for disabled people which do this safely – see HELPLINES.)

* Rest, as much as possible, for at least two weeks. You will probably want to. Daytime naps are a good idea, and don't stand for more than a few minutes. Never mind the housework or the job. You have had major surgery, which is tiring – and you must protect your internal stitches until everything has healed.

Organize your friends and family to help. If you know you won't get much chance to rest at home, ask if you can be sent to a convalescent home on the NHS or at least get a home help (ask your GP, hospital social worker or local authority social worker – in the phone book under Social Services).

* Then – get walking. This aids recovery and helps prevent weight gain – just a few gentle minutes a day at first (keep standing straight). Work up to more, as and when you can.

* When you're ready to do more, do it right. Do some housework, but sit. Use the vacuum cleaner, standing upright with your feet apart. Lift only small objects, and using the correct technique: hold things close to your body, keep your feet apart, hold in your stomach and pelvic floor muscles, bend your knees and *not* your back.

* Continue to get back to normal life gently.

* Swimming is a good all-round exercise which imposes no strain.

* Don't drive a car for 6 weeks.

Sex after a hysterectomy

In most hysterectomies, the vagina stays intact and is usually stitched closed at the top if the cervix has been removed, but you may miss the sensation of thrusting against your cervix. The uterus contracts during orgasm, so you won't feel that any more, either. Otherwise things should feel very much the same, for both of you. You will still feel the vaginal contractions from orgasm, as you may have done before. How much these things affect you depends on your individual sexual make-up. Some women report better orgasms after hysterectomy. Others report less sensation from a climax.

If you had a Wertheim's (extensive) hysterectomy you will probably have lost the top part of your vagina. You may have a new set of sensations to get used to; you will need especial loving care and support from your partner and/or need extra advice (see HELPLINES). But your clitoris is still there, and that's what gives the main pleasure, even during intercourse, when it is massaged by the penis's movements in the vagina, and the part of the vagina which you still have is the most sensitive part. Also, vaginas have plenty of spare capacity and so will stretch slowly, and get even longer during sexual arousal over time. So it is unlikely that your vagina will be too short to accommodate a penis.

See also CERVICAL CANCER, CANCER OF THE UTERUS, pages 78 and 93, and HELPLINES.

Self help
* Make sure you leave hospital knowing exactly what has been done to you, and what physical effects it will have on your sex life. Write it down – most people find they don't remember some of what they are told by doctors, and forget even more if they are anxious. Start with whichever member of staff it is easiest to talk to – your GP, surgeon, junior doctor, nurse, social worker, or physiotherapist.
* Wait for the six-week check before having sexual intercourse again. You need to be sure you have healed internally. Also, in the early days after the operation, orgasm may be painful – it sets off contractions in muscles which may still be sensitive. If this happens, it can put you off trying again and set up a vicious circle. It can put off your partner, too.
* Meanwhile, it helps to keep in sexual contact by kissing, cuddling and so on. If your partner is not usually much into foreplay, this could be a golden opportunity to re-educate him.
* Start gently. As you become sexually aroused the vagina lengthens; and a gentle start also relaxes you, so the soft folds of extra skin in your vagina loosen and help to lengthen it even more. If you have doubts about your partner in this respect, do call in whichever professional has the best relationship with him to have a word (see HELPLINES).
* If there is any bleeding when you do start again, report it. It is probably granulation tissue (see above), and easily dealt with.
* You may find you have doubts about starting again – neither of you is sure how it will feel, and you will both be worried about doing damage. If you have followed the suggestions there should be no actual physical problems – but you might still have emotional reservations.

There may be deeper-seated emotions, too. You may feel the real purpose of sex is children so there is no longer any point in it; you may feel 'empty' and less of a woman; if your marriage or sex life is less than perfect anyway your hysterectomy might have made it worse.

Your partner may feel that your condition is somehow his fault or that he is less of a man now he can't make you pregnant; he might be afraid of what he'll find 'in there' now. If he seems selfish or unsympathetic, the cause might be some hidden emotion.

All these things may be very hard to talk about – or even to think about. But they are very natural. If you get no sympathy, or useful advice, from a professional, there is something wrong with *them* – not you. Go elsewhere, to a well-woman clinic, a support group, a counsellor (see HELPLINES).

Complementary therapy
Complementary therapies tailor their treatments very much to the individual: the precise nature of the treatment you receive will vary, depending on your medical history, symptoms, lifestyle, etc. The following information indicates the *sorts* of things a therapist is most likely to do or recommend. Do not be surprised if they feel you need something slightly different. This section is meant purely as an indication of likely treatments; it is not meant as a DIY guide to the medical uses of the different complementary therapies.

Complementary therapies can help to control or to alleviate in their early stages conditions which, if untreated, may lead to a later need for hysterectomy. These conditions might include fibroids, endometriosis, heavy uncontrollable menstrual bleeding, other period problems, and chronic pelvic inflammation (PID).

It is certainly worth consulting a reputable, qualified practitioner if you are anxious to avoid hysterectomy. If the condition is too far advanced or if the therapy will not help, you will be referred back to orthodox medicine.

After hysterectomy, complementary therapies are valuable to control any unpleasant side effects. Menopausal symptoms brought about by hysterectomy are discussed in MENOPAUSE (see page 276).

Acupuncture
A small fibroid caused by hormonal imbalance may respond to early acupuncture treatment, avoiding the need for hysterectomy. Hysterectomy for other reasons cannot usually be prevented by acupuncture.

Post-hysterectomy abdominal pain or excessive tiredness can be alleviated by acupuncture, combined with dietary advice.

Depression and negative feelings about a hysterectomy may also respond to acupuncture.

If you have difficulties with sexual enthusiasm and enjoyment after hysterectomy, acupuncture can help to stimulate hormonal production and increase your energy.

Aromatherapy
If hysterectomy is suggested because of heavy periods (if disease is not present), fertility reasons or endometriosis, it can sometimes be avoided by using aromatherapy.

If an operation is necessary, a post-operative, very gentle massage – with healing oils such as lavender, everlasting and geranium, among others – helps to prevent infection and enhances the recovery process, thus lessening pain and discomfort.

Massage with oils of bergamot or sandalwood helps to relieve tiredness after the operation and, combined with other individually blended oils, can also help you to readjust and to cope with feelings of depression and loss.

Sexual enjoyment and libido may be depressed after hysterectomy, especially if your ovaries have also been removed. An individually prepared blend of oils, to be applied by your partner in a gentle massage before intercourse, can be a valuable source of relief.

Chiropractic
The position in which you have to lie during the hysterectomy operation sometimes results in damage to your lower spine and pelvis, which in turn leads to back pain. This can be alleviated by chiropractic therapy.

Clinical nutrition
Whether clinical nutrition can help depends on the reason for hysterectomy. If it is for fibroids, endometriosis, or ovarian cysts, it is possible that a nutritionist might help to avoid hysterectomy.

Complications might ensue if iron-deficient anaemia is present, or heart or lung disorders. So dietary changes and nutritional supplementation might help here. Consultation is essential before treatment.

Homoeopathy
Hysterectomy is sometimes suggested by orthodox practitioners as a cure for heavy uncontrollable periods, even if no disease is present. Successful treatment can avoid the need for hysterectomy. (See PMS and PERIOD PROBLEMS.)

A single dose of high-potency phosphorus, given a day before the operation, will help prevent nausea and other distress after the operation. Post-operative infection and other problems also respond to homoeopathy. In convalescence, China is good for wind pain and Calc. fluor for adhesions.

Medical herbalism
Early herbal treatment for hormonal imbalance, pelvic congestion leading to flooding, or chronic pelvic inflammation can relieve problems which might otherwise lead to a suggestion of hysterectomy.

After hysterectomy, herbal remedies might include chamomile to relieve inflammation and spasm, dandelion to retone your bowel, and garlic to aid your resistance to infection. Treatment to improve feelings of tiredness during convalescence is likely to be combined with dietary advice.

Long-term treatment – such as ginseng or cola – and counselling to improve your overall vitality and help your body cope with the stress of post-operative changes are valuable aids to recovering your sexual enjoyment, and readjusting to normal life. St John's wort can help depression.

Osteopathy
After hysterectomy, osteopathic work on the abdominal muscles helps restore tone and alleviate pain and discomfort.

Hysterectomy helplines

Association of Community Health Councils
30 Drayton Park, London N5 1PB (071 609 8405)
Advice and support to patients who have worries or complaints about any doctor or
  member of the medical profession.

The British Association for Counselling
(0788 78328)
A directory of therapists and helpful organizations who counsel couples countrywide,
  and can let you know where your local counsellors are located.

Cancer Link
17 Britannia Street, London WC1X 9JN (071 833 2451)
This is not an alternative/holistic centre, but provides general information and can put
  you in touch with supportive groups and sources of practical help.

Endometriosis Society
35 Belgrave Square, London SW1 (071 235 4137)
Offers advice and support to women with endometriosis, plus a bi-monthly
  newsletter and helpful books and publications.

Hysterectomy and Endometriosis Support Group
c/o Carol Naden, 28 Manvers Road, Liverpool L16 3NP
See ENDOMETRIOSIS HELPLINES PAGE 214, for details.

Hysterectomy Support Group
c/o 3 Lynne Close, Greenstreet Green, Orpington, Kent (081 856 3881)

Menopause Collective
c/o WHRRIC, 52–54 Featherstone Street, London EC1Y 8RT (071 251 6332/6580)

RELATE (formerly the Marriage Guidance Council)
HQ – Herbert Gray College, Little Church Street, Rugby CV21 3AP (07885 73241)
Contact HQ for details of your nearest branch.

SPOD (Sexual and Personal Relationships for the Disabled)
286 Camden Road, London N7 0BJ (071 607 8851/2)
Though you are most certainly *not* disabled if you have had a hysterectomy, this
  organization can give some very sensitive and helpful advice on the easiest way to
  enjoy intercourse and other forms of lovemaking following a hysterectomy –
  especially if the cervix or part of the vagina needed to be removed too, perhaps
  because the hysterectomy was a treatment for cancer.

Women's Health and Reproductive Rights Information Centre (WHRRIC)
52–54 Featherstone Street, London EC1Y 8RT (071 251 6580)
A voluntary organization that can give useful information and support on any aspect
of women's health care. They can put you in touch with a local hysterectomy
support group.

Specialist products and services
ASH (Action on Smoking)
5–11 Mortimer Street, London W1N 7RN (071 637 9843)
Contact ASH for advice on how to give up.

Further Reading
The Menopause: Coping with the Change by Dr J. Coope (Dunitz)
No Change by Wendy Cooper (Arrow)
Hysterectomy: The Positive Recovery Plan by Ann Dickson and Nikki Henriques
(Thorsons)
Women on Hysterectomy (or How Long Before I can Hang-Glide?) by Ann Dickson and
Nikki Henriques (Thorsons)
Hysterectomy and Vaginal Repair by Sally Haslett and Molly Jennings (Beaconsfield)
Hysterectomy by Suzie Hayman (Sheldon)
You Can Avoid a Hysterectomy by Dr V. Hufnagel (Thorsons)
Hysterectomy by E. Phillipp (BMA)
Experiences of Hysterectomy by Ann Webb (Optima)
Hysterectomy: Your Questions Answered by Pat Webb (Haigh and Hochland,
Manchester)
'Hysterectomy' leaflet, send 40p plus SAE to WHRRIC (address above)
'Hysterectomy' leaflet, send 30p plus SAE to: Templegarth Trust, 82 Tinkle Street,
Grimoldby, Louth, Lincs LN11 8TF
'Hysterectomy Support Group Advice' booklet, send £2.50 plus SAE to
Hysterectomy Support Group (address above)

Incontinence

What is it?

Incontinence is passing water when you don't want to. It can vary from a few small drops to the entire contents of your bladder. It is very common, too, so if it is troubling you you are most certainly not alone. One in three women develop some degree of incontinence after childbirth, one in five women over the age of 65 find they have it and there are some three million people in the UK who are wrestling with it – three quarters of whom are women. One way and another, says consultant Linda Cardozo of King's College Hospital, London, up to a third of us experience some form of incontinence at least twice a month.

The good news is that in nine out of ten cases the problem can be completely cured – sometimes within a matter of weeks. Incontinence is not a disease, nor is it something that you just have to grin and bear for good. It is just a sign that there is a problem relating to your bladder (often a very small and simple one) that needs sorting out.

Causes

Essentially it is the female anatomy that is to blame. Our means of stopping a flow of urine, and of keeping urine inside our bladder until it is convenient to empty it, is not as efficient as a man's. It is not always strong enough to withstand the stresses of vigorous exercise, pregnancy and childbirth, nor the way we lose tone from *all* our muscles (including the one which keeps the neck of the bladder closed) after the menopause.

To understand the causes and cures for incontinence it is necessary to know a bit about the way the bladder operates when it is working properly. Urine is made in the kidneys. and then flows down two tubes called ureters into the bladder, where it is stored until we urinate. The bladder is basically a muscular balloon, which expands as it fills with urine.

To get from the bladder and out of the body, the urine has to go down another tube called the urethra. This is much shorter in women than in men (which may be one reason why we get bladder infections such as cystitis more often than they do). This flow of urine is controlled by small muscles called bladder sphincter muscles. These tighten round the urethra tube, closing it shut – or relax, allowing it to open.

We usually get the signal to open our bladders and empty them every 2 to 3 hours when they have accumulated about ¼ pint's worth. If necessary, an average bladder can hold on until there is ¾ pint there. The feeling of wanting to urinate is called bladder urgency.

Incontinence happens when:
* the sphincter muscles around the urethra tube cannot remain tightly shut;
* the bladder is contracting abnormally and forcing out urine even past the closed bladder sphincter muscles;

239

* a combination of both.
    Incontinence always has a cause. It is not something that 'just happens', nor is it by any means an inevitable part of being a woman, or becoming older.

A BLADDER INFECTION (like cystitis) can cause temporary incontinence (see CYSTITIS).

CONSTIPATION. If there are a lot of hard faeces packed into your bowel, this can cause extra pressure on your bladder or urethra neck (see CONSTIPATION).

CERTAIN MEDICATIONS prescribed by your doctor can have this effect, including: some sleeping pills and tranquillizers or sedatives; certain types of antihistamines; some drugs prescribed to treat stomach spasms; and diuretics prescribed for water retention (pre-menstrually or for heart or blood pressure problems). Ask your GP if you think any of these may be the cause.

SOME MEDICAL CONDITIONS such as diabetes, and especially those that affect the nervous system (such as multiple sclerosis and Parkinson's disease).

PSYCHOLOGICAL PROBLEMS (such as depression, anxiety or recent bereavement) can cause incontinence, too.

PREGNANCY. As the weight of the baby presses down on your pelvic floor this can weaken bladder control in the later months. It may also happen in the earlier months if the child is lying against the neck of your bladder (see PREGNANCY PROBLEMS, page 360).

CHILDBIRTH. The physical effort of labour can damage the pelvic floor muscles and even affect the nerves controlling the bladder (see CHILDBIRTH, page 109).

THE MENOPAUSE. As the body produces less and less oestrogen, this affects the tone of all our muscles, including those of the bladder sphincter (see MENO-PAUSE, page 276).

BEING OVERWEIGHT. Additional bodyweight can cause additional pressure on the pelvic floor and bladder.

Symptoms and diagnosis
If you suffer from any of the following problems it probably means you do have an incontinence problem:
* If you leak urine when you cough, laugh or sneeze.
* If you leak urine when you are exercising, or lifting.
* If you leak urine when you are making love.
* If you have little warning of needing to pass water, perhaps sometimes not quite reaching the lavatory in time.
* If you need to pass water increasingly often, and perhaps even have to get up at night when you never needed to before.

* If you find that because you need to pass water more often, you are wary of going out for long, or find yourself checking where to find public toilet facilities, or are not happy about travelling unless there is a lavatory to hand.
* If you wet the bed at night.
* If you find yourself dribbling urine without having realized it.

The cure for your incontinence depends on whether it is very mild, or more severe, and on what type you have.

URGE INCONTINENCE is a very strong need to pass water, followed quickly by actually doing so involuntarily. Ninety per cent of the time this is caused by a bladder weakness. But in the other 10 per cent of cases it may have a more serious underlying cause (such as a bladder infection, kidney stones, a local tumour, a stroke or disease of the spinal cord). It is very important to be properly checked out by a doctor (who may refer you to a specialist at the local hospital) in order to make sure you are getting the *right* treatment, just in case. If you need urgent treatment for a nervous problem or it's a kidney stone that is causing your incontinence, it is no use being given pelvic floor exercises to do.

STRESS INCONTINENCE is when you pass water involuntarily when sneezing, laughing, coughing, exercising, making love, bending or lifting. This is also sometimes called 'partial incompetence of the urinary sphincter' (i.e. the ring of muscles whose job it is to keep the urethra closed and the urine shut in the bladder). Causes include pregnancy, labour and the menopause.

REFLEX INCONTINENCE is when you pass water involuntarily without having had any feeling at all that your bladder was full. This could be caused by diabetes or anything which affects the nervous system such as multiple sclerosis or a spinal cord injury.

OVERFLOW INCONTINENCE is involuntarily passing water because your bladder has become too full. This happens when something dams up the flow of urine until it builds up to such an extent that it can force open the sphincter muscles. It is very rare in women.

FUNCTIONAL INCONTINENCE happens when you just cannot get to a lavatory fast enough. Your urinary system will be working quite normally, but the incontinence happens because you are unable to move soon enough, perhaps due to disability. Pelvic floor exercises could help.

The treatments
Pelvic floor exercises
These are internal exercises which you can do anytime and anywhere, to strengthen the pelvic floor (the sling of muscle which holds up all the organs of your abdomen – bladder, womb, intestines). (See **Self help** below for how to do active pelvic floor exercise for the best effect.)

INTERNAL WEIGHT TRAINING exercises these internal muscles using small weights covered in perspex and weighed down inside by aluminium, for a sort of pelvic weight training (see HELPLINES, as these are available at some hospitals and can also be bought in small discreet consumer sets from Colgate Medical Ltd). You start off holding one of the lighter ones inside your vagina with your pelvic muscles for half an hour a day and work up to holding the heavier ones for longer. Check with your doctor or continence advisor before using these.

Suitable for: stress incontinence.

Success rate: approximately 80 per cent.

Time taken to be effective: improvements begin within weeks.

PASSIVE PELVIC FLOOR EXERCISES are for the more severe pelvic floor problems; most hospital physiotherapists have passive exercisers which use electrical impulses to tone up the muscles intensively (using exactly the same principle, and similar looking equipment, to the Slendertone machines in a beauty salon). It is also possible to buy smaller versions for your own use at home, from a company called Medinco (see HELPLINES). This form of toning up is intensive and has rapid results, but must be combined with doing active pelvic floor exercises yourself. You must also keep doing the active exercises, or you will lose your new-found muscle tone fast. Check with your doctor or continence advisor before using this machine at home.

Suitable for: stress incontinence.

Success rate: 80 per cent.

Time taken to be effective: for younger women with slight problems, you will begin to see an improvement from active exercises or weight training within a month, and within a week or two with passive electrical exercises. For women with more marked pelvic floor problems, it would be nearer two to three months before they started seeing a major improvement from active exercises. *It is important to do the exercises as often each day as you can, and to persevere* (see **Self Help**, below).

Where to get it: your GP, local continence advisor (see HELPLINES), or help association like the Association of Continence Advisors and the Continence Helpline or the Association of Obstetric and Gynaecological Physiotherapists (see HELPLINES), your midwife, health visitor or the practice nurse at your health centre. For details of weight training equipment and passive exercise speak to the physiotherapy department of your hospital and see addresses in HELPLINES.

Drug treatment

Medication can get rid of a bladder infection (like cystitis) which may be causing incontinence. Drugs such as Propantheline can help if the problem is down to the bladder's nerve supply. If your incontinence is due to the deterioration of your bladder sphincter muscle because of lack of oestrogen following the menopause, you would probably be prescribed Hormone Replacement Therapy (see MENOPAUSE page 276) to correct this, as well as pelvic floor exercises.

Suitable for: urge incontinence cause by infections; incontinence cause by

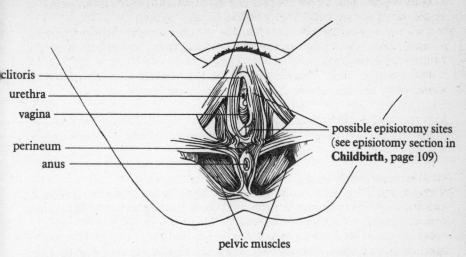

clitoris

urethra

vagina

perineum

anus

possible episiotomy sites
(see episiotomy section in
Childbirth, page 109)

pelvic muscles

These are the muscles which form your pelvic floor, the sling of muscle which holds up your bladder, womb, intestines and other pelvic organs. These muscles are strengthened when you do pelvic floor exercises.

the menopause; or reflex incontinence caused by nerve problems, such as diseases which affect the nervous system; and incontinence due to diabetes. Also for many other types of urge incontinence, some types of stress incontinence and reflex incontinence.

Success rates: there is about a 60 per cent chance of improvement if the problem is related to the nervous system. A 90 to 100 per cent chance of improvement if it is for a bladder infection. And, when HRT is coupled with pelvic floor exercises, up to a 50 per cent improvement if the cause is lack of oestrogen and the menopause.

Time taken to be effective: most drugs are effective within a few days if there is going to be an improvement, and within two to three months with HRT.

Where to get it: your GP, who may refer you to the obstetrics and gynaecology, genito-urinary or uro-dynamics departments of your local hospital. You may be referred to a menopause clinic if you require HRT. If you feel you need expert HRT treatment but your GP seems unwilling to refer you, contact Women's Health Concern (see HELPLINES).

Surgery

Surgery can lift the neck of the bladder, including the bladder sphincter muscles, to a higher position inside your body. This may involve correcting any sagging of the pelvic floor, or prolapse (dropping down) of your womb. Surgery would also be used to remove any obstructions in the urinary tract, and kidney or bladder stones.

Suitable for: severe stress incontinence (e.g. following childbirth) and overflow incontinence (to remove whatever is damming up your urine flow).

Success rate: up to 95 per cent for certain conditions, especially in young to middle-aged women who have never had surgery before.

Time taken to be effective: an operation to repair a pelvic floor or correct a prolapse takes about eight weeks to convalesce from, but its effects on the bladder are immediate.

Where to get it: your GP needs to refer you to a hospital, to the obstetrics and gynaecology, genito-urinary or uro-dynamics departments.

THE FUTURE: A new treatment gaining popularity in America involves surgically replacing tired sphincter muscles with a mechanical valve, for around £4,000.

Bladder retraining techniques

These teach your body to recognize the subtle early signals of needing to urinate – and training yourself to empty your bladder at longer and longer intervals, until you are back to normal.

METHOD ONE: Keep a strict diary of when you urinate (day and night). Then widen the intervals gradually between each time. Say, for instance, that after keeping your diary for two days you notice you are usually urinating every half hour (even if it is only a little bit at a time). The next step is to make yourself urinate every half hour on the dot, whether you want to at the time or not. Then widen the gap to every 40 minutes. Then every 50 minutes. Then every hour. Continue until you are up to a more acceptable frequency (two to three hours) which will mean you can go where you want, without having to worry about being near a lavatory. It would help to have the support of your GP, specialist or continence advisor during your retraining period.

Suitable for: urge incontinence.

Success rate: 60 to 80 per cent.

Time taken to be effective: three to four months.

METHOD TWO is called Biofeedback. It involves using electronic equipment to see and feel exactly when your bladder neck is beginning to open prior to letting out its urine, and training yourself to control that process.

At the moment it is only carried out at St George's Hospital in London. It involves inserting a slim catheter with a tiny electrode by your bladder neck. This will be connected safely to a small meter whose needle flicks upwards as the electrode detects your bladder neck beginning to open. Then you can see exactly when it is happening – and pinpoint how it feels. Once you have identified that small physical signal in your bladder you will be asked to practise keeping the needle back down (indicating that your bladder neck is staying closed). This is done by concentrating, deep breathing, and clenching muscles. It takes six to eight half-hour training sessions to master, and you will be helped by a sympathetic doctor or continence nurse, in a private room.

Suitable for: urge incontinence.

Success rate: 80 per cent.

Time taken to be effective: can be as little as two months.

Short-term interim measures
* Vaginal ring devices or ring pessaries help lift up the bladder neck if it is dropping down. They are available from your GP, continence nurse or specialist hospital department (obstetrics and gynaecology, genito-urinary or uro-dynamics). They are often lent out by the NHS, but to keep one you would need to buy one for about £100.
* Protective pads and pants are available from the chemist, your district nurse or continence adviser (see **Self Help**, below).
* Ordinary vaginal tampons, of the sort used during a period (see **Self Help**, below).

Self help
The following measures will help prevent incontinence in the first place.
* Do pelvic floor exercises every day as part of your health routine – just for a couple of minutes while brushing your teeth, watching TV, ironing, washing up, waiting in a queue, sitting in a car, travelling on public transport, sitting down at work. As they are internal no one can see you are doing them so you can carry them out literally anywhere. They are particularly important when you are pregnant, so do them right from the start.
* Do ante-natal exercises, including pelvic floor exercises, religiously after childbirth.
* Ask your doctor about HRT treatment during and after menopause, and suggest he refers you to a specialist menopause clinic if possible. (See MENO-PAUSE, p. 276.)
* Do not let yourself become overweight. This can cause extra bladder pressure and lead to, or worsen, continence problems.

Self-help treatment
PELVIC FLOOR EXERCISES mean:
Finding the right muscles to exercise, which is not always easy. You need to isolate three sets of muscles:

i) the sphincter muscle, which controls the neck of your bladder;
ii) the muscles which control your anus;
iii) the muscles which control the tone of your vagina.

To detect i) try stopping the flow of urine next time you are passing water. The muscle you squeeze to do that is your bladder sphincter.

To detect ii) pretend that you badly want to void your bowels, but are having to hang on. Or, next time you are voiding on the lavatory, stop halfway through. The muscles you flex to do this are the ones controlling your anus.

To detect iii) flex the muscles you use in your vagina when you squeeze your partner's penis while making love. If you are not entirely sure you are flexing the right ones, slide a clean finger or a cardboard tampon applicator into your vagina and try squeezing it.

2. Doing the pelvic flex, when you practise squeezing each of these sets of muscles in turn until you are able to do so readily. Then do the following simple exercise as often as you can each day:

i) tighten your anal muscles and hold for a slow count of four, then release;
ii) tighten your vaginal muscles, hold for a slow count of four, then release;
iii) tighten your bladder sphincter muscle, hold for a slow count of four, then release;
iv) now tighten all three one after the other, 'pulling up' the entire sling of muscle in your pelvic floor until all three muscles are tight, hold for four, then release. Get into a slow easy rhythm doing this, saying 'First Floor', 'Second floor', 'Third floor', 'Pull UP' (all three).

PADS AND PANTS. One survey suggested that up to 60 per cent of women are using ordinary sanitary towels to catch involuntary urine flows. But they are not the best thing to use, unless it is only a matter of a couple of drops or so. There are over 100 companies making products to help people with continence problems and their special pads are now very slim and discreet and far more absorbent than STs. They often contain special gels to neutralize any potential urine odour, too.

They are available in major chemists like Boots. If you are wondering which would be the best one for you, ring the free Continence Line (see HELPLINES), which is staffed by sympathetic trained continence nurses. They can also advise you how to claim some money back, as can the Association of Continence Advisors (see HELPLINES).

As nine out of ten continence problems can be cured, pads and pants are usually just an interim measure – you will not have to use them for long.

WEIGHT CONTROL. Keep your weight down. If you would like extra motivation to help you lose extra weight and keep it off, clubs like Successful Slimming and Weight Watchers can be very helpful (see HELPLINES).

CHECK YOUR MEDICATIONS with your GP, as some (especially diuretics) can have an effect on your urine output or on the nerve supply to your bladder.

DRINKS. Avoid diuretic drinks like coffee, tea, colas and alcohol, but do not restrict your fluid intake overall – that can actually make your incontinence worse, and produce other problems of its own for your kidneys. You need to drink about seven to eight mugs of fluid a day.

While you are sorting out a continence problem, however, it may help not to drink for two hours before you go to bed, or before an exercise class. Avoid drinking fluid for a couple of hours before making love, too, if you can, and empty your bladder before you do so.

AVOID CONSTIPATION by eating plenty of fibre (it bulks out faeces and traps water, so it is softer and easier to pass). Best sources of fibre are wholemeal bread, cereals and pasta, and fruit and vegetables (see CONSTIPATION, page 145). Avoid lifting heavy things by yourself too.

CLOTHES. While you are dealing with continence difficulties, it helps to wear clothes that can be adjusted rapidly so you can pass water without delay when you reach a lavatory: loose skirts, trousers without complex fussy fastenings, and French knickers. Wearing leotards, teddies or pantie girdles is not a good idea.

TAMPONS. Inserting a tampon into your vagina has a similar effect to surgery for weakened pelvic floors and prolapses – it raises up the bladder neck. This can be useful when you are going out, or exercising, as a temporary measure. But it is not a good idea to wear tampons all the time, nor to leave them in for more than a couple of hours without changing them.

SEEK PROFESSIONAL HELP. Continence tends to get slowly worse rather than better. It is not going to go away on its own if you ignore it. It is such a common problem, and often so very easy to cure, that many women are now visiting their local continence nurse in the same matter of fact way as they would go to the health centre nurse to get a sprained wrist strapped up.

So do get help as soon as you can, and stop incontinence in its tracks. If you feel at all embarrassed about discussing it, make a gentle start by ringing up to speak to one of the nurses who run the Continence Line (see HELPLINES). You can do so anonymously and in complete confidence. They will be able to offer you a great deal of very helpful advice and encouragement.

Other professionals who will be only too glad to help include: GPs, health visitors, practice nurses at the health centre, your local continence nurse (see HELPLINES), help organizations like the ASA (see HELPLINES), physiotherapists, midwives and gynaecologists.

Complementary therapy
Complementary therapies tailor their treatments very much to the individual: the precise nature of the treatment you receive will vary, depending on your medical history, symptoms, lifestyle, etc. The following information indicates the *sorts* of things a therapist is most likely to do or recommend. Do not be surprised if they feel you need something slightly different. This section is meant purely as an indication of likely treatments; it is not meant as a DIY guide to the medical uses of the different complementary therapies.

Acupuncture
By strengthening the muscle tone of the pelvic floor, acupuncture or electro-acupuncture, perhaps combined with Chinese herbs or acupressure, can help this problem. If you suffer from an 'irritable bladder' you may be helped by acupuncture intended to produce a proper yin-yang balance.

Clinical nutrition
Emotional problems often play an important role in this problem, and treatment may need to include counselling or psychotherapy. Kidney glandular tissues give renal and bladder support, and potassium lost through over-frequent urination also needs to be replaced. Avoiding high-oxalite foods – beans, coffee, chocolate, carrots, celery, rhubarb, tea, spinach, and Swiss chard – will help soothe your bladder. Smoking does not help.

Homoeopathy
One of the most useful remedies for incontinence with dribbling, general bladder

weakness and involuntary loss when laughing or coughing is Causticum. When pain and irritability are associated with incontinence of the dribbling kind, Nux Vomica can help. Ferrum Phos is for inability to control the flow of urine. Equisetum is used when there is associated infection.

Medical herbalism
Pelvic-floor muscle exercises are very helpful, combined perhaps with hot/cold compresses or sitz baths to stimulate your circulation, and improve your muscle tone and co-ordination. Horsetail strengthens and astringes the bladder muscles and membranes, and marshmallow soothes and heals the bladder lining.

Osteopathy
In certain specific cases, usually after childbirth, certain osteopathic techniques (cranio-sacral work) may indirectly help strengthen the fascia, which supports your ligaments and muscles. Not all osteopaths practise in this way and it is therefore important to ask the osteopath concerned *before treatment* if he/she practises cranial osteopathy.

Incontinence helplines

Association of Chartered Physiotherapists in Obstetrics and Gynaecology
c/o The Chartered Society of Physiotherapists, 14 Bedford Row, London WC1
  (071 242 1941)
Offers advice and information on exercises to help correct continence problems. They
  can also advise on ante-natal and post-natal exercise.

British Diabetic Association
10 Queen Anne Street, London W1 (071 323 1531)
Advice and support for diabetics on all sorts of matters, including continence.

Continence Line
(091 213 0050)
A helpline run by trained continence nurses who can advise you, in total confidence,
  about the best way to tackle your particular continence problem.

ERIC (The Eneuresis Resource Information Centre)
(0272 264920)
If incontinence is proving a problem at night, call them for confidential advice and
  help.

Marie Stopes Clinics
In London, Manchester and Leeds. (See GENERAL HELPLINES, page 480, for details)

Multiple Sclerosis Society of Great Britain and Northern Ireland
25 Effie Road, London SW6 (071 736 6267)
Advice and support for MS sufferers on all aspects of the condition, including
  continence.

Parkinson's Disease Society
22 Upper Woburn Place, London WC1H 0EP (071 383 3513)
Advice and counselling for people with Parkinson's Disease (on all aspects of the
  disease, including continence), and their families.

The Women's Health Concern
See GENERAL HELPLINES, page 480, for details.

Specialist Products and Services
Colgate Medical Limited
1 Fairacres Estate, Dedworth Road, Windsor, Berks (0753 860378)
Manufacturers and suppliers (by mail order) of small sets of vaginal weights for
  pelvic toning. Available in discreet packages from £24 for 3.

Continence Nurses
See Continence Line, above, for details. Also, many health centres and hospitals
  now have a specially trained continence nurse (ask at reception – by phone or in
  person – for details).

Midd Valley Micro Products
(0423 866375)
Distributes passive pelvic-floor exercise machines for use at home. They cost
  approximately £140.

Slimming Magazine clubs
(071 255 1711)

Weight Watchers UK Limited
Kidwells Park House, Kidwells Park Drive, Maidenhead, Berks SL6 8YT
  (0628 777077)

Further reading
Managing Incontinence by Cheryl Gartly (Souvenir Press – Human Horizon Series)
Overcoming Urinary Incontinence: A Self-Help Guide by Richard J. Millard (Thorsons)
*Understanding Incontinence: A Guide to the Nature and Management of a Very Common
  Complaint* by Dorothy Mandelstam (Chapman and Hall)

Infertility

What is it?

Infertility in its strictest definition means 'failure to reproduce'. Doctors reckon that if a couple has been trying to conceive a baby for 18 months without success, having regular unprotected sex two or three times a week, they should go to their GP and ask to be referred to a specialist unit to find out why. Some specialists recommend couples take action sooner than that: Dr Jack Glatt, director of the Infertility Advisory Centre at Solihull and London, suggests that couples over the age of 30 should only wait a year before seeking advice, and that if a woman is over 36 she should only wait six months. Female fertility peaks between 24 and 27, then declines slowly but surely thereafter.

But how quickly do most couples conceive? About 15 to 20 per cent do so within the first month of trying, about half of all fertile couples have done so within six months and around 85 per cent will have conceived within the year. The remaining 15 per cent – one in six of all couples – may find they have a fertility problem to deal with.

You may also hear the terms 'primary' or 'secondary' infertility. The former is used when the couple has never had a child together, the latter if they have had one or two children with no problems, but seem unable to do so again.

However, Professor Robert Winston, head of Europe's largest infertility unit at the Hammersmith Hospital in London, says 'Today couples stand a better chance than ever before of conceiving a baby, even if they are having difficulties.'

Causes

If anything goes wrong at *any* stage of the conception process there will be no baby. Conception is the successful fertilization of the egg by a sperm, but pregnancy will only result if the fertilized bundle of cells implants properly in the womb. Looked at in detail, the process appears so complicated and precise it begins to seem a wonder anyone ever gets pregnant at all. Successful conception will follow these steps:

1. The man must produce enough normal, healthy sperm and ensure they are placed near the entrance of his partner's womb (cervix). From here the sperm need to be able to penetrate the mucus barrier which protects the cervix's entrance from bacteria and viruses. The mucus is usually quite thick, but around the middle of a woman's menstrual cycle it becomes more plentiful – and more watery, so the sperm can swim through it.

2. The woman needs to have produced a ripe and healthy egg cell from her ovary. This is released into her Fallopian tube and stroked down its length by tiny finger-like projections (cilia). The egg can only live for around 24 hours, so the sperm has to get to it during this time. Sperm cells, however, survive longer

– up to three days. So it is possible to have intercourse two or three days before you ovulate and still become pregnant.

3. The sperm needs to be able to break into the egg to fertilize it.

4. Once sperm and egg have come together, they spend the next 3 days travelling down through the Fallopian tube until they arrive at the womb. They float freely here for a couple more days. Then what is by now the tiny developing embryo, a growing bundle of cells, embeds itself comfortably in the rich womb lining and starts growing. (It's thought that about 40 per cent of fertilized eggs are lost at this stage, because they don't implant themselves properly in the womb.)

5. The womb lining has to be kept in place by extra progesterone, produced by the woman's ovaries – and not shed as is usual at the end of the menstrual cycle about ten days or two weeks later.

The whole process, which can be made to look so easy by couples who have accidental pregnancies, or conceive quickly, is finely balanced throughout, and successful fertilization and implantation are not the end of it. In fact, according to fertility expert Professor Beard of St Mary's Hospital in London, 15 to 20 per cent of early embroyos which do implant in the womb lining are not maintained and conclude in what seems to be a late period.

'Infertility is not a disease,' says Professor Winston, 'It is a symptom, often a treatable one, of something that is not working properly in you or your partner's body. And at least half all couples with fertility difficulties can be helped. In around 30 per cent of cases, the problem lies with the male partner, in 30 per cent with the woman, and 40 per cent of the time the cause is either a mutual problem or a case of 'unexplained infertility', where the doctors aren't sure what is wrong, or with whom.

Female fertility problems and their treatment
Contraception
THE PILL. If a woman has been taking it for a few years, and then stops and switches to another form of contraception or uses no contraception, her cycles can be erratic for up to four or five months. There is anecdotal evidence (only) that a small number of women may find conception difficult after a long period of Pill taking.

IUDs can increase a woman's chances of pelvic infection threefold. This can affect fertility if the infection reaches the Fallopian tubes and is severe enough to block them with scar tissue. (See also CONTRACEPTION page 155.)

Smoking
This can affect a woman's (and a man's) fertility by causing constriction of the blood vessels, including those supplying the reproductive organs, thus inhibiting their proper function. It can also act directly on the tiny cilia lining the Fallopian tubes, inhibiting their action too.

Pelvic infections
Infections such as chlamydia and gonorrhoea, or those resulting from a

miscarriage or abortion, can affect the Fallopian tubes, which are delicate structures. Their insides are only the width of a piece of cotton as they lead from the womb, widening to the width of the lead in a pencil further up towards the ovaries. Scar tissue from infections can easily block them. A laparoscopic investigation, or passing a liquid dye through the Fallopian tubes and watching its progress on an X-ray, can show if there are any blockages.

The best method for correcting blockages is microsurgery – fine, precise surgery in which the surgeon uses a microscope (far more accurate than ordinary surgery). In suitable patients, microsurgery has a 30 to 60 per cent chance, depending on the skill of the surgeon, of unblocking the tubes sufficiently for the woman to become pregnant. Ordinary surgery has a success rate of about 20 per cent.

Another very new way of keeping tubes open if they are partially blocked is by inserting a tiny surgical balloon, which is blown up once it is in the tube, pushing its walls apart again. This treatment was adapted from a heart surgery technique, and no one is sure how successful it is yet.

(See also PELVIC INFLAMMATORY DISEASE, page 322.)

Abortion

This carries a very small risk of infection (about 1 per cent) due either to the operation itself or to a small amount of material from the pregnancy left behind in the womb (see **Pelvic Infections**, above).

Later abortions and multiple abortions carry a slightly higher risk of damaging the os (entrance to the womb) and stretching it so it is no longer able to remain tightly shut as it should in future pregnancies, to keep the developing foetus safely inside. A surgical stitch in the os after a woman conceives may help solve this problem. (See HELPLINES, ABORTION, page 12, and MISCARRIAGE, page 297.)

Womb problems

According to Professor Winston, women with womb problems often have no difficulty becoming pregnant, but they tend to miscarry within the first month. These problems account for up to 10 per cent of female infertility, and come in different forms. Adenomyosis, for instance, is a condition where small pockets of womb lining become embedded in the womb's walls, bleeding and forming scar tissue. This makes it difficult for fertilized eggs to implant themselves in the lining of the womb. It can be treated with drugs like Danazol, to help shrink the pockets of material.

Other problems could come from an unusually shaped womb, for example, or from polyps (small fibroids, which may stop an egg implanting in the same way as an IUD would).

Endometriosis

Pieces of womb lining can migrate to other places in the pelvis such as the Fallopian tubes or around the ovaries. Like the rest of the womb lining, they are still under the control of your hormones, so they continue to shed blood every month wherever they are. This can occasionally block the tubes or, more often, clog the area around the ovaries so the ripened egg cannot get out. The Endometriosis Society feels that endometriosis is a problem in up to half the infertile women in the UK. (This figure might be a bit high, other estimates say 25 per cent of infertile women have endometriosis mildly, and 10 per cent severely.)

Laparoscopy is the only sure way to detect endometriosis, though doctors may be able to make a guess from other symptoms which a woman may report, such as painful heavy periods and pain when she has intercourse. It can be treated with drugs such as Danazol or LHRH analogue (a man-made drug chemically identical to luteinizing hormone releasing hormone), or removed surgically or treated with surgical lasers. (See also ENDOMETRIOSIS, page 203.)

Fibroids

Many women have fibroids to some degree but it is not often that these benign growths of muscle can affect fertility. When they do, it may be because there are too many of them, or some large ones, which are distorting the womb's cavity and preventing the embryo implanting. Alternatively it may just be that the presence of something 'extra', like fibroids, in what should be an empty womb interior, makes it harder for an embryo to implant, in the same way as the presence of an IUD might.

If they are causing a problem they can be treated with drugs to shrink them, or be removed surgically. (See also FIBROIDS, page 216.)

Narrowed or scarred cervix

This is unusual, but an operation to remove pre-cancerous or cancerous cells from the cervical area can narrow or scar it. It must then be dilated gently by a doctor, more than once, over a period of a few months.

Operations like a cone biopsy could also destroy some of the cells around the cervix which make the thin, watery mucus which helps the sperm reach the womb by providing a good swimming environment.

Ovulation problems

No ovulation means no ripe egg to join up with a sperm, and no baby. There are many factors that affect ovulation, and ovulation problems are the reason why about 30 per cent of infertile couples cannot have a baby. According to Professor Winston the good news is that in nine out of every ten cases doctors are able to stimulate ovulation with drugs. As one of the commonest causes of infertility it also has the best chance of being treated successfully.

There are three basic reasons why a woman might not be ovulating:
1. the ovaries are damaged, or have been abnormal from birth (this accounts for 10 to 15 per cent of cases);
2. the ovaries are not working in a cycle, which can happen if, for example, someone is emotionally upset (this can happen in 10 to 15 per cent of cases);
3. the cause is hormonal or chemical (this accounts for 70 per cent of women who are not ovulating).

OVULATION SIGNS include:
* tender, full breasts;

253

* pain, felt to one side of your abdomen about half way down (a marker for 30 per cent of women);
* slippery, colourless vaginal discharge – like raw egg white;
* a slight drop in temperature, which tends to occur just before ovulation. If you go to see your GP because you are having no luck in becoming pregnant, the first thing he may suggest is keeping a temperature chart to work out if and when you are ovulating, and trying to have intercourse around that time. Unfortunately a lot of things can affect temperature besides ovulation, so these charts can be a poor predictor. They also remind you every day, as you fill in the chart, that you have a fertility problem, and they may put pressure on you to make love 'to order' when the chart says the time is right.

Many women, however, have none of the signs but still ovulate regularly.

OTHER WAYS TO CHECK IF YOU ARE OVULATING include:
* Home ovulation kits like Clearplan, which test your urine with a dipstick for traces of luteinizing hormone (LH) – the one that causes an egg to ripen and be released from one of your ovaries each month. The amount of LH in your urine rises 12 to 36 hours *before* you ovulate. The kits are fairly expensive, from £18 to £28 for between six and ten days' worth of tests. Like home pregnancy testers, their instructions need to be followed very precisely to avoid mistakes.

Another thing about these kits is that they do not always detect whether you have ovulated or not. The reason for this is that they are designed to spot the 'average' LH rise, but in some women the amount may be lower than the norm and the kit will not be able to detect it even though that woman has indeed ovulated. (See Natural Family Planning in CONTRACEPTION, page 164.)
* Blood tests, carried out by your GP or a specialist. One of these can check the hormonal cause of failure to ovulate. A blood sample is taken about a week after you feel ovulation either should, or does, take place. This shows if you are producing the right amounts of the hormones which are either made by your ovaries (e.g. progesterone) or are made by another gland in the body, but affect your ovaries (e.g. Prolactin).
* Ultrasound scanning: some fertility clinics check ovulation this way.
* Taking an endometrial biopsy (removing a tiny piece of your womb lining) a few days before your period is due. To do this, a doctor would insert a small tube into your womb via your cervix, to remove a scrap of the womb's lining, without the need for an anaesthetic. It can then be checked in the lab to see if your hormones have made it ready to receive an embryo. If it is ready, it means you have ovulated.
* Laparoscopy uses a tiny surgical telescope, usually inserted under general anaesthetic via a small cut in your navel, to take a close-up look at your ovaries and seek signs of ovulation.

TREATING OVULATION PROBLEMS. This is usually done by using drugs. (Dr Glatt explains this as 'setting the fertility thermostat to "High"'.)
* Clomiphene is taken for five days near the beginning of your menstrual cycle, stimulating the pituitary gland to work harder, thus stimulating the ovary to encourage eggs to ripen.

INFERTILITY

* Tamoxifen or Rehibin has a similar effect.
* HCG (Human Chronic Gonadotrophin) may be given in addition to the above drugs if the ripened eggs do not seem to be escaping from the ovary.
* Pergonal is a powerful drug, a mixture of LH and FSH (follicle stimulating hormone). It is given by injection in the first half of your menstrual cycle and will often be suggested if Clomiphene is unsuccessful. You would have blood and urine checks during this treatment to make sure all was going well, as people respond in different ways to Pergonal. Ultrasound may also be used to keep a watch on your ovaries.
* FSH, also given by injection, can be useful for women with polycystic ovaries (see below).
* Pump Therapy. Hormones called GRH – Gonadotrophin Releasing Hormones – are made by the tiny hypothalamus gland, and make our bodies produce LH and FSH, needed to ripen eggs. The pump releases small amounts of GRH every hour or so to 'trick' the pituitary gland into producing the FSH and LH in the normal way. The pump is a small object, about the size of a cigarette packet. Usually it is strapped to your upper arm, with a tiny needle going into a vein.
* Bromocriptine. This hormone affects your pituitary gland, and stops it from making too much Prolactin – a hormone that helps you produce milk, and which is also produced when we are under stress. Prolactin suppresses ovulation and can interfere with embryo implantation. This is why mothers who breastfeed regularly, about once every two or three hours, have up to 98 per cent contraceptive protection (see CONTRACEPTION and BREASTFEEDING, pages 155 and 52).
* Progesterone. Injections or pessaries of pure progesterone may help if you are ovulating all right, but not making enough progesterone to thicken the womb lining to be ready to receive the embryo afterwards.
* Corticosteroids. All women produce a certain amount of testosterone (the male sex hormone), but if you are producing a bit too much – and a blood test will show this up – this can stop you ovulating. Corticosteroids, which are usually prescribed to calm inflammation, can cut down the amount of testosterone you are making.
* Carotene. Vitamin A, found in orange and green fruits and vegetables, may stop periods and ovulation. According to Dr Michael Collins, formerly of Canada's McMaster University, there is a connection between high levels of carotene in the blood (which can be detected by a simple serum test) and the workings of the pituitary gland, which masterminds, among other things, ovulation. If this is the case, cut down on Vitamin A-rich foods, like spinach, oranges, carrots and dark green cabbage.

Polycystic ovaries
Repeated or multiple cysts on your ovaries can affect fertility. They can be treated with GRH and FSH (see above) or by an operation which removes a small wedge of the affected ovary.

According to the women's health research charity Birthright, around 20 per cent of infertile women may have polycystic ovaries. Initial work on diet, at St

255

Mary's Hospital in London, suggests the problem might be linked to a high-calorie, high-fat diet.

Cervical mucus

According to Professor Winston, it is thought that around 5 per cent of all fertility problems in women can be traced to the sort of mucus produced by the cells around their cervices. If, for instance, it is too thick and sticky, your partner's sperm may not be able to get through it to reach the egg. If your mucus contains antibodies which are hostile to the sperm, it will kill them before they can progress very far – this accounts for about 3 per cent of the problems.

If you have a small cervical infection, this too can affect the mucus quality (but can easily be corrected with drugs). Cervical damage, due perhaps to an operation which involved the removal of part of the area, may mean that the mucus is not of quite the right sort – but again this is usually easy to treat.

There is a test, called the Post Coital Test, which can tell you:
i) if your mucus is producing antibodies hostile to your partner's sperm;
ii) if you are producing the right sort of hormones needed for good mucus production;
iii) if your partner is producing enough normal sperm.
It is done by taking a small sample of the mucus from your cervix a few hours after you have had intercourse, for analysis. This is called a Post Coital test. The doctors may also want to do a sperm invasion test, by taking a sample of your cerivcal mucus and a sample of your partner's fresh sperm. They are placed together on a slide and looked at under a microscope to see if the sperm can swim quickly into the mucus. If they stop or become stuck together, this may mean your mucus is hostile to your partner's sperm. (This is one reason why a woman may be unable to become pregnant with one fertile male partner, but finds she can do so easily with another partner with a more compatible sperm output.)

TREATMENT. One or more for the following may help.
* Drugs to stop you producing antibodies to your partner's sperm, such as corticosteroids (but are very rarely effective).
* Placing your partner's sperm directly into your womb to by-pass the cervix and its mucus. However, it is possible that any antibodies present in your mucus might also be in your Fallopian tubes and womb.
* 'Taking-a-break' therapy. Avoiding any direct contact with your partner's sperm for about 6 months (making love using a sheath, perhaps) can sometimes make hostile antibodies decrease (temporarily); just as avoiding contact with *any* allergen (such as a food) can end any other sort of allergic reaction. If you're using a sheath, however, you are unlikely to become pregnant in the meantime, so this may be stressful for a couple who are very anxious to conceive.

Couples who are experiencing this problem may also benefit greatly from techniques like IVF and GIFT (see **Fertility technology**, page 261).

Nutrition

Many clinical nutritionists (doctors who are specially trained in nutrition), such as Dr Alan Stewart, information officer of the British Society of Nutritional Medicine, believe that being short of certain vitamins and minerals can make a difference to a woman's – or a man's – fertility. According to Dr Stewart: 'There is no question that a bad diet, clinical nutritional deficiencies and being underweight can lead to infertility. But less extreme cases, where there is a marginal (slight) deficiency in certain vitamins, like B6, and minerals like zinc, and in certain proteins, it can also compromise fertility by upsetting a woman's hormonal cycle, which reduces her chances of becoming pregnant.'

Speak to a professionally trained nutritionist (see HELPLINES) about this. Get them to check on what you eat to see whether you might be suffering from slight deficiencies which could be affecting your fertility, and ask for advice on supplements to take, or alterations to make in your diet or lifestyle.

Stress
Some UK doctors are starting to take the link between stress and infertility problems more seriously, although most still feel the connection is rather minimal.

However, Paul Entwistle, a Liverpool University fertility scientist and researcher, explains that the sort of hormones released when you are under stress (such as adrenalin and prolactin) most certainly do have a concrete, observable physical effect on the reproductive system. It has been shown that the levels of certain stress hormones do indeed rise before, during and after treatment, and that there are high levels present in the bloodstream of people who are stressed by the worry of not being able to conceive. According to Mr Entwistle:

Stress can make the Fallopian tubes go into spasm, so the egg cannot travel down them and be fertilized. It can affect the lining of the womb so that it is not 'rich' enough for a fertilized embryo to implant in there. It can cause ovulation to move around to different parts of the cycle – so if a couple are trying to time their love-making for when ovulation usually occurs, they will keep on missing it. It can also inhibit egg implantation and diminish sperm count. A person may even have subconscious psychological barriers which are preventing pregnancy, such as early sexual problems, a former miscarriage or abortion, childhood illness or separation. Hypnotherapy can help them explore and overcome these.

To bring down stress levels, Entwistle uses hypnosis for both partners 'to make the trying to have a baby process a lot less trying'. He also measures the levels of hormones in their blood before and after hypnosis, and is able to show they have improved. In one series of tests, 40 per cent of couples with 'unexplained fertility' who continued for at least four treatment cycles conceived.

Why should stress affect us in this way? Entwistle thinks this is not surprising:

The pituitary gland – the master gland at the base of the brain, which controls the body's entire hormonal output – is closely linked to the hypothalamus, which in its turn helps control the brain's emotional centres. So it follows that emotional upsets like the stress of infertility and its treatments could well affect hormonal output – and thus upset fertility systems even further.

Hypnotherapy can be a useful adjunct to other treatments such as artificial insemination, IVF and GIFT. Couples may find all of these invasive and stressful in themselves, as they involve a good deal of intimate contact with the hospital staff, invasion of privacy and anxious waiting to see if the treatment has worked.

It can also give back to the couple some measure of control over a process which can become very much dominated by hospitals, drugs and doctors. It can give you some steps to take on your own account, when in every other respect you are a passive receiver of treatment – things are being done *to* you.

He explains that a relaxation technique like hypnotherapy 'can give couples who are having fertility difficulties a way to have a positive effect on their situation *themselves*, adding:

Stress is not a vague term, even though it is often used in a woolly way. Stress is an actual biochemical state, produced by fright or anxiety, and relaxation is not a matter of simply sitting down with a glass of wine and watching TV for a while. Relaxation to help alleviate stress, when used as an adjunct to fertility treatment, is a more specific, disciplined routine. Couples deliberately use a specific calming regime to relax and clear their minds, then when the mind is in a quiet and receptive state, they can tell it things – a bit like gently programming a computer – which may help their situation: 'I will be calm and happy during my next treatments'; 'I will ovulate normally next cycle'; 'I am perfectly fertile and can easily become pregnant'; and so on.

While this type of treatment is still in its infancy in the UK, in some major American hospitals, such as the famous Beth Israel in Boston, anti-stress regimes have been a mandatory part of their fertility programmes for the past ten years. (See HELPLINES for information on hypnotherapy.)

Male fertility problems and their treatment

As one third of fertility difficulties lie with the male partner, no discussion on infertility would be complete without it. But work on male infertility has not achieved the same degree of success as that with female infertility.

Note I: there are several problems with quoting percentage figures for women's fertility problems. A new drug for a specific disease, for instance, will result in a rise in the number of diagnoses of that disease due to an increase in awareness of it. Also, different specialists quote different figures in relation to their own areas of expertise.
Note II: not all diagnosed problems mean you are definitely infertile; they could just be contributing to difficulty in conceiving. (For example, it is possible to conceive with fibroids.)

Low sperm count

Professor Cooke of the Jessop Hospital for Women in Sheffield estimates that 30 per cent of male infertility problems are due to this. The average number of sperm in a man's ejaculate is 300 million or so. But the quality is far more important, from the point of view of conception, than the actual numbers. So the 'lower end of the range' may be as little as 20 million but good results can still be achieved.

A sperm count can check on the number of sperm – and on their quality. The lab will check to see that they are swimming rapidly and strongly in a straight line. (As a senior embryologist from the London Bridge Hospital put it, 'the sperm's journey from the vagina to the Fallopian tubes to reach the ripe egg is the equivalent of a man swimming the Atlantic through treacle'.)

In fact, healthy mobile sperm can reach the tubes within minutes of being ejaculated. This may be partly because a woman's orgasm contractions in her womb, produced by contact with the prostaglandins in the seminal fluid, create a partial vacuum, which sucks the sperm rapidly inwards and upwards.

If only a few normal sperm are found it is best to do two or three counts on different occasions, as they can vary. If it is consistently low, it could be due to one of the following.

HORMONE PROBLEMS, which might be treated successfully with drugs or hormones (including testosterone and hormones from the pituitary gland).

A VARICOCELE, which is an enlarged vein (there may be several), rather like a varicose vein, around the testicle. It may be overheating the testes and reducing sperm production. A more recent theory is that the varicocele is secreting a chemical that impairs sperm production. However, removing the vein does not always improve a man's fertility, and many men who have these veins are perfectly fertile. So it is rather controversial as to whether varicoceles have much effect on sperm values or not.

Checks for varicoceles include visual examination, Doppler ultrasound, to check the bloodflow to the area, and thermography (a picture of heat variations between specific areas).

'LIFESTYLE FACTORS' such as smoking, drinking, extreme stress and poor diet can all affect fertility (see **Self Help**, below).

Poor sperm quality

If there are enough sperm, but not many of them (fewer than 40 per cent) are swimming straight and strongly, the problem may lie here. Sperm mobility problems can be caused by:

AN INFECTION IN THE SEMEN, which may have been there for some years at a low level. It may be possible to clear this up with antibiotics;

TESTES NOT PRODUCING ENOUGH NORMAL SPERM. Again, factors like smoking, drinking and environment at work or home can be the culprits. These are in your own control to a great extent. Certain drug treatments may also help.

259

A very small amount of ejaculate fluid
If there is less than the usual 1.5 to 6mls there might be a problem. It could be due to an inflammation of the glands which produce the seminal fluid. If so, it can be treated with antibiotics. Retrograde ejaculation will also produce a low volume (see below).

No sperm seen at all
This might mean the testes are not making any. If this is the case, treatment is unlikely to be successful. But it may mean there is a blockage in the tubes bringing the seminal fluid down from the testicles. Or it could mean that there is an ejaculatory problem – perhaps 'retrograde ejaculation' is taking place, when semen passes back into the bladder.

These are only a few of the many possible reasons for lack of sperm, and getting to the root of the problem would mean careful and thorough investigation.

Blocked tubes:
The tubes transporting semen are tiny (the epididymis has an inside thickness like a cotton thread; the vas deferens is wider but still pretty minute), so if an area has been blocked, perhaps by some past infection which left scarring, microsurgery is the best course.

Professor Robert Winston estimates that around 8 per cent of infertile men have a blockage like this, but that up to a third of them will produce normal sperm after an operation.

Sperm stuck together in clumps
This stops them moving freely so they cannot swim off and fertilize an egg. The problem may be due to an infection (which can be treated with antibiotics). Or the man may have antibodies to his own sperm (this will cause sperm to survive very poorly in his partner's mucus), in which case corticosteroid drugs may be helpful, taken intermittently for several months in fairly large doses. It is thought that about 20 per cent of men with antibody problems (about 4 per cent of infertile men) can be helped in this way. Some doctors however have reservations about steroid treatment for infertility problems, as it can be associated with damage to the bone at the neck of the femur.

Sperm which cannot penetrate into an egg
When sperm cells reach the egg something called an acrosome reaction happens – the sperm head sheds its outer membrane and releases an enzyme which enables it to break through the egg's protective barrier. It is thought, though, that for some men's sperm, either this reaction is weak or it may not take place at all, and that could be the cause of fertility problems.

Work is currently going on at King's College in London to develop a reliable test to check whether this reaction is taking place. Scientists are also hoping that 'washing' sperm (by placing it in a medical centrifuge) will help maximize this reaction so that the sperm cells have the best possible chance of fertilizing the egg.

Stress

According to Entwistle (see above), chronic stress associated with muscle tension can restrict the blood flow all around the body in general – including the blood flow to the testicles. This is, in turn, thought to reduce the transport of hormones from the pituitary gland to the testicles, resulting in a gradual, long-term reduction in sperm cells.

Fertility technology: treatment

Artificial insemination by partner (AIP/AIH – H standing for husband)

Centres usually require that the partner be your husband, but some do not (such as the British Pregnancy Advisory Service – see HELPLINES). Your partner provides a sample of fresh semen by masturbating, and catching the fluid in two test tubes. Clinics can provide a quiet and private environment to do this, but catching the fluid precisely may require a bit of practice.

The semen is collected on the day the woman ovulates – she may do so naturally or be given ovulation-stimulating drugs. Using a speculum (the instrument used in standard vaginal examinations) to hold the walls of the vagina slightly apart, the semen will either be injected into the cervix using a syringe, or, if the doctors feel it is wise to bypass the cervix (perhaps there are cervical mucus problems), it can be passed into the womb via a slim tube.

Neat semen cannot be used, as it can cause an allergic reaction. It needs to be prepared in the lab first, either by a 'wash' technique or by a 'swim up' method to isolate the healthiest and most mobile sperm.

Suitable for:
* couples with immune difficulties – such antibodies to the sperm found either in the woman's mucus or the man's own body;
* men with poor quality or few sperm;
* couples with other cervical mucus problems (perhaps the cells around the cervix are not producing enough, or it is too thick to allow the sperm through);
* couples with 'unexplained infertility';
* men who suffer from retrograde ejaculation.

Not suitable for:
* couples where either partner has a tubal problem;
* women who have ovulation problems;
* women where there is a difficulty with the shape of the womb;
* women with endometriosis, fibroids or polycystic ovaries.

If not done on the NHS it will cost from about £30 at a charitable organization like BABIE (see HELPLINES), or £40 at the British Pregnancy Advisory Service, to between £50 and £100 a time (sometimes even more) at private clinics.

Number of tries reasonable: between six and twelve cycles.

Success rate: depends on the fertility of the man's sperm, so it is difficult to say.

AID (Artificial Insemination by Donor)

The procedure is the same as for insemination by your partner. This is also an option for gay women who wish to have a baby. BPAS is happy to help in these cases – other organizations are often not, though.

is happy to help in these cases – other organizations are often not, though.

Donors usually remain anonymous, though you can ask to be matched for race, and are chosen because they have a good and healthy sperm count. All are carefully screened for hepatitis B, and should be for AIDS if the samples are to be frozen, but it is not possible to do this for sperm which is to be used fresh.

Frozen sperm *can* produce results almost as good as those achieved with fresh sperm samples, but in practice most centres report that if sperm is frozen it can reduce its effectiveness by as much as half. However, the Fertility Sub Committee of the Royal College of Obstetricians & Gynaecologists recommends fresh anonymous donor semen is not used because of the risk of AIDS.

Suitable for: fertile women whose partners are infertile because of a problem which is not likely to respond to treatment (e.g. a vasectomy which has not responded to reversal techniques).

Not suitable for: women who have tubal problems, ovulation difficulties, an abnormally-shaped womb, endometriosis, fibroids or ovarian cysts.

Number of tries reasonable: between 6 and 18 cycles.

Success rate: up to 90 per cent for fertile women over one year of trying with frozen sperm. The costs are similar to those for artificial insemination by your partner.

GIFT (Gamete Intra Fallopian Transfer)

This is a method of bringing the sperm together with an egg. The eggs are collected by laparoscopy under general anaesthetic, after the woman has probably been given an ovulation stimulating drug to encourage her to produce several eggs rather than the usual one. They are mixed with a fresh sample of semen in a test tube or glass dish then around four are replaced straight back into the Fallopian tubes with the sperm, so fertilization has a maximum chance of occurring. Usually no more than four to six eggs are used because of the risk of multiple pregnancy. GIFT uses either your partner's sperm or donor sperm. GIFT costs about the same as IVF treatment, see below.

Suitable for:
* couples with 'unexplained infertility';
* couples with problems with the cervical mucus;
* women with endometriosis (at least one Fallopian tube needs to be free from blockage).

Not suitable for: women whose tubes have been damaged or who have had a previous ectopic pregnancy (in case this leads to another).

Number of tries reasonable: up to six.

Success rate: clinics' estimates vary from 20 to 35 per cent per completed treatment cycle, but many cycles have to be abandoned without any eggs being introduced (overall success rate is about 15 per cent).

IVF (In Vitro Fertilization)

The process is similar to GIFT except that once the eggs have been collected they are placed with a washed sample of sperm, one egg plus sperm at a time, in a series of glass test tubes or dishes ('in vitro' – glass). The lab technicians check each one 48 hours later to see if it has fertilized and an embryo has begun. If it

In Vitro Fertilization and how it works

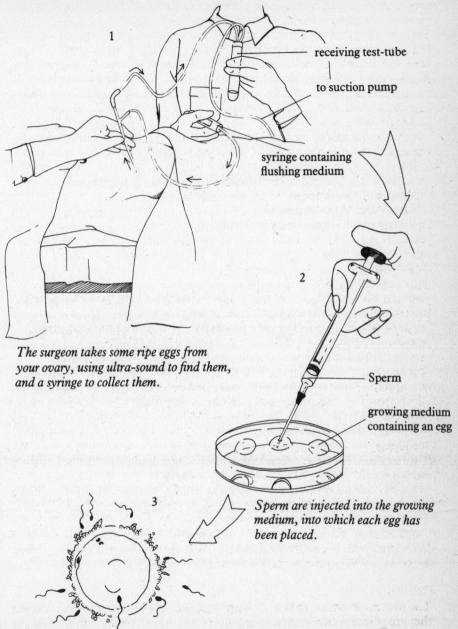

1

receiving test-tube

to suction pump

syringe containing
flushing medium

The surgeon takes some ripe eggs from
your ovary, using ultra-sound to find them,
and a syringe to collect them.

2

Sperm

growing medium
containing an egg

3

Sperm are injected into the growing
medium, into which each egg has
been placed.

*Right on target – a sperm (bottom right) has broken through an egg wall and
fertilized it.*

has formed it will have divided into four cells and be the size of a speck of dust. Any embryos will be replaced directly into the woman's womb, using a syringe and plastic tubing inserted gently through the cervix, and left to see if any of them implant themselves in the womb lining.

Many women are a bit nervous of what they can and can't do immediately after this. Doctors usually advise that they stay off work for a couple of days and rest, and avoid sexual intercourse for a couple of weeks. Most of the embryos will not implant themselves, but are shed. To check if a pregnancy is developing many clinics can do a sophisticated hormone test a week or so after the transfer.

Suitable for:
* women with Fallopian tube problems (e.g. they have been so severely damaged by an infection that IVF has a better chance of success than tubal surgery);
* couples where both tubes are damaged and the partner's sperm count is low;
* 'unexplained infertility';
* certain types of endometriosis;
* couples with cervical mucus problems.

Also, if the male partner's sperm count is low, or there are few normal sperm, at least with IVF you will know for sure whether the egg is being fertilized or not.

Not suitable for:
* women with such badly scarred tubes, or ovaries which have had so many cysts, that the eggs cannot be retrieved by laparoscopy;
* women who do not ovulate even when given ovulation stimulating drugs;
* women over 40;
* women with a scarred, abnormally-shaped uterus or large fibroids.

Success Rates are improving year by year. At the best fertility units, says Nottingham University's NURTURE embryologist, the 'take home baby rate' is up between 30 and 40 per cent – it was nearer 10 per cent five years ago.

Number of tries reasonable: up to four or five times. If there is still no luck, it may be best to discuss the situation with the clinic, especially if you are going privately – this treatment is expensive and costs can really mount up. Some clinics suggest that if you can afford it and the eggs seem to be being fertilized properly by the sperm, up to eight or even nine tries would be reasonable.

Few IVF clinics are run by the NHS, and the waiting lists for them are up to three or more years in some centres. At others the lists have been closed until further notice because they are so over-subscribed. Costs vary from approximately £1,500 to £3,500 at private clinics, but the fertility charity BABIE offers members a far lower price of approx. £1,000 per cycle. Some universities' obstetric departments also offer GIFT or IVF at subsidized rates.

The future
1. There is an experimental technique being tested out at the moment whereby embryos (at the four-cell stage) are coated in a nutrient-rich gelatin capsule to try and maximize their chances of survival and implantation in the womb. No success ratings are given as yet – the method is too new.

Other variations include Trans Cervical GIFT – mixing sperms and egg together outside the body then injecting them straight into the womb via the cervix. As this is done without general anaesthetic it's less expensive than ordinary GIFT. No reliable success rate levels available.

Another method being tried is nicknamed POST: Peritoneal Oocyte (egg) and Sperm Transfer. Ripe eggs, and sperm, are collected and injected together into an area called the Pouch of Douglas just behind the womb, so it can easily reach to the fallopian tubes.

New Sperm Techniques:

The most exciting advances though, are currently being made in the field of male fertility help. Having had very little successful research done on male fertility techniques for the past 40 years or more – partly because experts felt it was easier to manipulate a single (comparatively large) egg than millions of sperm, the area is now coming into its own and some of the biggest breakthroughs are being made in andrology, rather than obstetrics and gynaecology.

In fact, so great are the advances that according to the director of ISSUE, John Dixon, low sperm count, once the greatest bar to male fertility, doesn't matter any more: 'all it takes is one healthy one'. And that single one can be manipulated into the right place – at the right time.

The new techniques are called Micro Fertilization. They are not yet (1993) widely available. The only four centres currently offering them to the public are the Hallam Clinic and Bridge Fertility Centre in London, Bourne Hall in Cambridgeshire (all are private clinics) and the NHS fertility research centre in Nottingham University Hospital, NURTURE.

So fertilization of an egg can take place, the sperm has to break on through the two fairly tough barriers surrounding that egg. They are called the cumulus cells and zona pellucida. Micro Fertilization methods make it easy for the sperm to do so. One method called PZD (Partial Zona Dissection) involves collecting ripened eggs from the man's female partner and then treating them with a naturally occurring chemical which removes the cumulus layer round the egg. Then a tiny hole is made in the zona itself using a special glass needle – making the perfect entrance for a sperm to get through with no trouble.

There is another similar technique called SUZI (Sub Zonal Insemination) which makes things even easier for sperm, because they are injected into the inside of the egg itself – they don't have to do a thing to get there. This is used to help men with sperm which are barely moving of their own accord – or indeed, alive but not moving at all.

To find out which clinics are going to be offering this in the future – the number is slowly growing – contact CHILD (HELPLINES) or see 'Choosing a Clinic' (see reading list).

Defective sperm function is the largest known cause of human infertility, and the new computerized semen analysis is useful here. There are also new treatments for antisperm antibodies (which can cling to the sperm themselves and impede their progress). Sperm penetration tests, new drug combinations to stimulate sluggish sperm, and electro-ejaculation for men with severe neurological problems (spinal injuries, MS) are also achieving success.

Getting treatment

One of the most upsetting aspects of fertility problems is the delay in getting help. Claire Brown, of the support and advisory service CHILD, says: 'Waiting is the most usual experience for infertile couples. First you may be told you can go to an NHS clinic which will begin doing tests on you. They may – or may not – be able to identify the problem, but first you have to join a waiting list in your area that is probably a year to 18 months or more long. Meanwhile, you have to sit and watch other friends getting pregnant.

You start the tests, wait in between each one for their results, do more tests, wait for their results. This can take years in hospitals with stretched resources, and inadequate facilities. And many centres do suffer from this because fertility care is not a Department of Health priority. Then you wait to get treatment, wait to see if it has worked – and wait again to have another try if it has not.'

Available figures show waits of up to 30 weeks or more before a GP can refer couples for their first fertility clinic visit, and waits of up to three or four years before treatment starts. Yet, according to Dr Glatt of the Infertility Advisory Centre, in a well-organized and adequately funded NHS clinic the relevant tests really need only take a couple of months.

How to get the right help faster

How long should you wait before seeking help? Many GPs say 18 months, but fertility experts like Dr Glatt suggest a year – if the woman is over 36, six months. The following steps might save you time and money in your search.

1. Ring the NAC or CHILD (see HELPLINES) to find the name and address of the best specialist clinic in your part of the country. Be prepared to travel, if necessary, in order to go to the best one, rather than simply the nearest one.

2. Telephone the clinic's administrator and ask what their waiting lists are for seeing new patients. If they sound very long to you, check with CHILD or NAC as to whether this is usual. If it is not, ask if they can suggest another good clinic which may not have quite such long queues.

3. When you feel confident about your choice of clinic, make an appointment to see your GP. Explain that you are very concerned, that you have been trying to conceive for about a year with no results and do not wish to wait a further six months or so with temperature charting, but would like to be referred to the specialist centre you have chosen. Suggest the name of the senior consultant of the clinic, so you can present the information necessary to your GP 'on a plate'. Do it all in one breath to give the GP little opportunity to attempt to talk you out of your decision.

If your own GP seems unwilling to refer you on, change to a more sympathetic GP within the same practice – or go to another doctor in a different practice.

4. If all the clinics suggested by the advisory organization seem to have unacceptably long waiting lists and you do have some money, consider saving time by paying to have the basic initial tests done by one of the following:

i) a charity such as the BPAS – their fees are very reasonable (see HELPLINES);
ii) a charitable organization such as BABIE (see HELPLINES), which also keeps its fees as low as possible;
iii) privately, if you can afford it. Again, CHILD could advise on the best centre and give you an idea of their fee levels. Paying for the necessary tests and investigations will save a great deal of time.

Privately or at a charitable fee-paying clinic, it could take a couple of months to identify your problem and to start treating it – instead of two or three years on the NHS.

5. Having identified the problem quickly, it should then be possible to explain to the NHS clinic whose waiting list you are still on that:
i) you have had certain tests (say which) at such and such a private clinic (state which). Make sure you get a copy of your results to show them, or ask the private clinic to send them direct;
ii) the clinic's conclusions are 'X'.

Ask them if it would therefore be possible to begin the treatment suggested by the results of these tests as soon as it is your turn to be seen, rather than going through the same tests again over a long period of time. Your only problem might be that the NHS clinic might still wish to repeat tests you have already had, to make sure of the results, in which case you can either accept that and the delay, or pay for treatment if you can afford it. When looking for a clinic initially, and checking their waiting lists (2 above), it might be worth asking about their policy on accepting tests carried out by other clinics.

The following table will give you some idea of the cost differential for some of the more usual infertility tests, and for one of the infertility treatments. (The figures are for 1990.)

Tests	Charity	BABIE	Private London clinic
First consultation		£50	
Revisit		£25	
Mucus hostility	An all-in investigation,	£25	Mucus hostility and
Semen analysis	including all these tests, is	£20	semen analysis, £50
Sperm survival	£250	£45	
Blood tests to check hormone levels		£15 each, five for £75)	£17.50 each (five for £77.50)
Sperm concentration and wash		£30	£48.50 (done with AIP)
Laparoscopy	£220	£250	£500 approximately
Total:	£470	£415	£676
IVF treatment	Not available	£850	£1,400

Selp help

The following recommendations and observations apply to both partners in the couple seeking help with infertility.

GIVE UP SMOKING tobacco and recreational drugs, like marijuana, at least three months before you start trying to conceive. Some studies suggest that cigarette smoking may induce sperm abnormalities and therefore increase male infertility. One study done in 1985 at the US National Institute of Environmental Health Sciences suggests that women who smoke are 3.4 times less likely to conceive within a year than non smokers, and that women smokers are only three quarters as fertile as non smokers.

GIVE UP DRINKING ALCOHOL at least three months before you begin trying to conceive. According to recent research by Professor Kaufman, head of Edinburgh University's Anatomy Department, the alcohol you drink before you conceive – or very shortly afterwards – could well be a greater danger to the foetus than the alcohol you drink during the subsequent weeks and months of the pregnancy. Up to 50 per cent of foetuses miscarry sometime between conception and the twelfth week of pregnancy, and about half of them probably do so because they have abnormal chromosomes. 'Eggs ripening in the ovary are particularly vulnerable to having their chromosomes damaged by harmful substances like alcohol just before or right at the time of conception,' explains Kaufman. Abnormal chromosones would result in an abnormal foetus – which the body would usually recognize, and spontaneously miscarry.

EAT A HEALTHY DIET with as much fresh food (like raw fruit and vegetables, fresh fish and meats) and wholefoods (such as brown rice, wholemeal pasta and wholemeal bread) as you can. This will help make sure you both get plenty of vitamins, essential fatty acids and minerals like zinc.

If you feel you need specific mineral or vitamin supplement treatment (i.e. that you may be short of one or two specific things and are not sure what they are), or have a suspicion that part of the problem could be the effect of toxic pollutants from food, air and water, contact a good clinical nutritionist, or the preconceptual care organization, Foresight (see HELPLINES).

DATE OF CONCEPTION. October to March appears to be the most successful time for conception. (Studies have found that the highest number of conceptions happen at this time of year, not just in the UK but also in America, Nigeria, Norway and Egypt.) The most recent report on the subject, from the Jessop Hospital for Women and the North Manchester Hospital, suggests this may be something to do with the quality of the woman's eggs and the fact that her womb lining may be more receptive to a foetus implanting in it at this time of year.

AGE. A woman's fertility does drop as she gets older – as does a man's, though his declines more slowly. This may be worth bearing in mind if you are planning to have a family at some point in the future. According to the London Independent Hospital there is a 70 per cent chance of conceiving within a year until you are 30 years of age, a 60 per cent chance from the ages of 31 to 35, and a 45 per cent chance of doing so within a year at 35 plus. There is good news for women who delay having their first child until well into their thirties. A recent American study indicates that apart from chromosomal abnormality (which can largely be screened for by amniocentesis), first-time mothers in their mid-thirties have just as good a chance of having a normal, healthy baby as those in their early twenties (according to research at New York's Mount Sinai Hospital).

RELAXATION can help both male and female fertility (see **Stress**, above). Relaxation classes and exercises and learning hypnotherapy to practise on yourself for regular deep relaxation (see HELPLINES), taking physical exercise, or going on holiday can all go some way towards relieving the very natural anxiety you may be feeling – but which may be part of the problem.

MAKING LOVE 2 or 3 times a week regularly will help maximize chances of conceiving, too. Having intercourse around the time you ovulate each month will help – but you do not have to make love right on the exact day of ovulation. For one thing, this can result in mechanical 'baby-making' sex and a rigid attention to the calendar, which can be stressful and sometimes upsetting in its own right.

For another, sperm can, in fact, live for up to 3 days, and a ripe egg (which lives for 24 hours) may take two or three days to travel down the Fallopian tube, where it needs to be fertilized. So, in fact, whether you ovulate on day 7 or day 23 of your menstrual cycle (it is not always on the conventional day 14, and remember your ovulation day may not always be the same one in your cycle) you will still have up to 3 or 4 days on which to try and conceive. (See **Ovulation**, above, for how to check when you have done so.)

The following advice is relevant for the male partner.

KEEPING TESTICLES COOL. They should be two to three degrees cooler than the rest of the body anyway. If the temperature is raised this may affect sperm production (hence the stories about tight trousers being linked with infertility in men). Wear:
* baggier underpants like boxer shorts instead of tight briefs;
* looser trousers instead of skin-tight jeans and shorts.
* A flabby stomach, which overhangs the waist and perhaps the penis and testicles to some extent, can make a difference:
  reduce it by exercise and diet.

Other options
Adoption in the UK
Adopting a baby or child to bring up and love as your own can be a very happy and rewarding experience for all three of you. And many couples do think of adoption if they are having fertility problems, as:
* waiting lists for NHS infertility clinics are up to three years long;
* private fertility care is expensive, £1,800 to £3,500 per IVF attempt;
* techniques like IVF have often been made to sound dramatically successful by the media. But in reality, although they *can* have excellent results, they are time-consuming, can be stressful and invasive of a couple's sexual privacy and have a final 'take-home-baby rate' of around 10 per cent per attempt. Higher success figures quoted (up to 35 per cent) relate to the pregnancy rate rather than the birth rate and in *completed* cycles.

On hearing that a couple are having trouble conceiving, friends and family may say in a well-meaning fashion: 'Oh well, you can always adopt.' But it is not such a simple option as many believe.

For one thing the number of British children now available to be adopted by non-relatives has dropped. Many are currently adopted by their natural mother, father, or both. According to the Parent to Parent Information Network (see HELPLINES), there were some 24,000 in 1967 but only an estimated 8,000 in 1989. And only about 1,000 of these are babies.

According to the Parent to Parent Information Service (see HELPLINES), there are about 20 eligible couples waiting to adopt every baby. Further, you are not in practice eligible to adopt a baby if either you or your partner are over 30, which is often about the age when you might realize you have fertility difficulties.

Adoption agencies are best contacted locally. At present there are 47 registered in England, Wales and Scotland (ask the BAAF for the ones in your area). They will be trying to place children of all ages, races and abilities. The BAAF's book *Adopting A Child* has details of all the existing adoption agencies, either charitable ones like Barnardo's, state-run ones or church-run ones like the Mission of Hope. There is also a computerized database which social workers can tap into to try and match up children of all ages with the sort of parents who might suit them best, and a book which social workers have called *Be My Parent* gives details and photographs of children who are hard to place.

If you decide to go ahead a social worker will need to interview and counsel you and your partner very fully and to explain the legal procedure. He will also do a 'home study' report on you. If you are eligible for adoption, you will be placed on an area waiting list, which may be two or more years long. Charities and church adoption organizations have their own social workers.

Foreign adoption
Difficulties with adoption in the UK have led some couples to adopt children from abroad. The Parent to Parent Information Service estimates that perhaps as many as 400 couples a year are adopting young babies from countries such as South America and Korea. Though the practice is frowned on by the BAAF, other organizations (such as the PPIS, the National Association for the Childless and CHILD, see HELPLINES) do try to give couples who wish to adopt in this way what information they can. The most helpful thing usually is to be put in touch with other couples who have followed a similar route (see HELPLINES).

There are two ways to adopt a foreign child:
1. Legally, which involves applying for adoption in the usual way in this country, and having a home study report and so on to obtain the necessary official papers, before going to the country of your choice to try and contact a lawyer and an adoption agency. This usually takes many months, and can even take years.
2. Illegally, which means far less waiting – for the right price. (Currently up to a £30,000 fee in Brazil, which has rapid inflation so this figure may already be outdated. This sum does not include lawyers's fees, travel and accommodation abroad, and loss of earnings while you wait for a baby.)

270

There are an estimated sixteen 'baby gangs' in Brazil alone who will undertake to obtain a baby for a couple if they pay enough. However, how they may come by the babies is open to question. There have been many reports of newborn babies being taken from hospitals, and of mothers being offered a very small 'maternity fee' (some £10) to hand over a new baby they simply cannot afford to keep. The baby is then 'sold' to its new adoptive parents at a very high price, most of which will go into the organization's own pocket.

Surrogate mothers
A surrogate mother is another woman who bears your child for you, having been fertilized by your partner (either by sexual intercourse or via AID), on the understanding that the child will be yours when it is born. (See COTS and TRIANGLES in HELPLINES.)

The British Medical Association (BMA) have recently produced a selection of ethical professional guidelines for doctors regarding surrogacy and infertility. Doctors have been informed that they can now advise couples about this option whereas previous to these guidelines, such practice was deemed unethical.

Complementary therapy
Complementary therapies tailor their treatments very much to the individual: the precise nature of the treatment you receive will vary, depending on your medical history, symptoms, lifestyle, etc. The following information indicates the *sorts* of things a therapist is most likely to do or recommend. Do not be surprised if they feel you need something slightly different. This section is meant purely as an indication of likely treatments; it is not meant as a DIY guide to the medical uses of the different complementary therapies.

Depending on what is causing the infertility, some complementary therapies can be helpful.

Acupuncture
Acupuncture can help to improve hormonal balance. Stimulating the appropriate acupuncture point can also promote *chi* in your body, thus balancing your body's biochemistry to alleviate such problems as over-thick cervical mucus.

Stress resulting from infertility (or its orthodox treatment) also responds to acupuncture.
(See also ENDOMETRIOSIS *and* FIBROIDS, pages 203 and 216).

FOR MEN
Acupuncture treatment can be helpful in improving the sperm count and the quality of sperm, when used in conjunction with Chinese herbs. Hormonal problems also respond to acupuncture treatment, as does the mental stress resulting from infertility (and its treatment).

Aromatherapy
Low oestrogen may be restored by massage with essential oils such as clary sage, which acts directly on the hypophiso-ovarian axis. The same treatment may also be useful for those whose cervical mucus is scanty.

Pelvic infection, leading to blocked tubes, may be improved by massage with essential oils such as rosemary, tea tree or lavender, prepared individually for you.

Full-body massage with oils to calm and relax will help you cope with the stress of infertility and its treatment.

(*See also* ENDOMETRIOSIS, page 203.)

FOR MEN

Distilled essential oil of rose, in association with a balanced diet, Vitamin E and mineral supplements, helps increase sperm-cell production. Stress associated with infertility can be alleviated by full-body massage with relaxing oils.

Clinical nutrition

Hormonal imbalance may be due to individual glands (pituitary, thyroid, adrenals and ovaries), so treatment with the appropriate glandular tissue concentrates helps restore the balance.

Too much cervical mucus is usually caused by excessive production of oestrogen. Anterior pituitary glandular tissue regulates this. Vitamins A and E also help regulate your mucus production. Pantothenic acid, supported by adrenal glandular concentrate, will help you to handle stress.

(See also ENDOMETRIOSIS, page 203.)

FOR MEN

Deficiency of Vitamin E or B6 can lead to a low sperm count. Zinc deficiency can result in decline of the prostate gland. All these can be helped by dietary supplements. Production of sex hormones is stimulated by increased protein, essential fatty acids, Vitamin E, Vitamins B5 and B6, and orchic glandular concentrate.

Homoeopathy

The homoeopathic remedy known as 'the constitutional remedy' is initially most useful. This is chosen to suit your individual nature – mental, emotional and physical. Possibilities include Conium (women with painful breasts, scanty periods, ovary problems), Iodum (women unable to put on weight but always hungry), Aurum (women with no identifiable physical problem, but scanty periods and frequent depression), Phosphorus (slim, vivacious, outgoing women with heavy periods), Natrum Mur. for nervous women (tearful, anxious and basically insecure), Sepia (for irregular periods, constipation and a white vaginal discharge). A good general remedy is Silica and, for obstinate cases, Natrum-carb.

Medical herbalism

Two widely used remedies for hormonal imbalance are false unicorn root, which improves the function of the ovaries and is used especially in the first half of the menstrual cycle, and chaste tree, which improves *corpus luteum* function and is used in the second half of the cycle if progesterone levels are inadequate.

Treatment of cervical mucus problems is aimed at overall health and the proper function of the reproductive system. Douches may be combined with internal medication. To help you cope with stress, nerve restoratives, such as oats, ginseng, or rosemary, may be offered.

FOR MEN

Remedies like Damiana and Saw Palmetto have hormonal effects. They stimulate and tone the male reproductive system, while also acting as nerve restoratives. Widely used for all kinds of male reproductive problems, prostate disorders, and sexual problems, they may be prescribed in the medium to long term, as appropriate.

Infertility helplines

BABIE (British Association for the Betterment of Infertility Education)
PO Box 516, London E1 4NP (071 224 4500/021 711 1360)
This charity offers a full range of reduced-rate fertility treatments (including IVF if you have a letter from your own doctor to confirm you would be suitable for, and benefit from, the treatment), counselling and adoption advice to both members and non-members. Affiliated to the Fertility Advisory Centre. Available to members are: a free medical advice line, fact sheets on fertility problems and their treatments, and a newsletter.

British Nutrition Foundation
15 Belgrave Square, London W1 (071 235 4904)
Answers questions for the public on various aspects of nutrition.

CHILD
HQ – (081 893 7110)
Advice and support group for people with fertility problems. Newsletter, a wide range of fact sheets on fertility problems and treatments, and adoption, plus up-to-date information on all fertility clinics (NHS and private) with approximate price levels, are available to anyone with fertility problems or queries. Contact HQ for further information and a list of self-help groups nearest you.

Endometriosis Society
35 Belgrave Square, London SW1 (071 235 4137)
Offers advice and support to women with endometriosis. They also supply a bi-monthly newsletter, helpful books and publications, and a network of local support groups countrywide. Contact HQ for details.

Foresight (Association for the Promotion of Pre-Conceptual Care)
28 The Paddock, Godalming, Surrey (0483 427839)
This association will recommend specific pre-conceptual care programmes to maximize the chances of successful conception for couples, as well as supplying a newsletter, leaflets and booklets. Send SAE and letter.

Marie Stopes Clinics
In London, Manchester and Leeds. (See GENERAL HELPLINES, page 480, for details.)

The Pregnancy Advisory Service
11–13 Charlotte Street, London W1 (071 637 8962)
One of the very few organizations which will offer artificial insemination to single women and to lesbians who wish to have a baby without the help of a male partner.

NURTURE: Dept of Obstetrics and Gynaecology, East Block, University Hospital, Nottingham (0602 709490)
Non profit-making, pioneering fertility unit, specializing in, amongst other things, male fertility problems and their treatment.

Miscarriage Association
c/o Clayton Hospital, Northgate, Wakefield (0924 200799)
Contact this association to find your local group or volunteer. They will offer
  support for women – and their families – who are undergoing, or have
  undergone, a miscarriage.

ISSUE (Formerly the National Association for the Childless)
318 Summer Lane, Birmingham B19 3RL (021 359 4887)
Provides support, via self-help groups and information, to people with fertility
  problems. May be able to put you in touch with other couples who have adopted
  a baby from abroad, if you are considering this option.

National Childbirth Trust (NCT)
Alexandra House, Oldham Terrace, London W3 6NH (081 992 8637)

Paul Entwistle
HQ – 35–37 Rodney Street, Liverpool L1 9EN (051 709 3505)
Clinics in Liverpool and London. Write to HQ, enclosing SAE, for details.

Pelvic Inflammatory Disease Support Network
c/o WHIRRC, 52 Featherstone Street, London EC1
Offers support to PID sufferers. They publish a newsletter, collect information and
  data on PID, and recommend sympathetic doctors and hospitals.

RELATE (formerly the Marriage Guidance Council)
Herbert Gray College, Little Church Street, Rugby CV21 3AP

Adoption
British Association for Adoption and Fostering
HQ – 11 Southwark Street, London SE1 1RQ (071 407 8800)
Offers advice, information and leaflets/books on the adoption of children of all ages
  in the UK. Can also put you in touch with your local adoption agencies. Contact
  HQ for further details.

The Overseas Adoption Helpline
(071 226 7666)

The Parent to Parent Information on Adoption Services
c/o Philly Morrall, Lower Boddington, Daventry, Northants (0327 60295)
Offers self-help support and information on adoption services for existing and
  prospective adoptive parents. May be able to put you in touch with couples who
  have adopted a child abroad, if you are considering this option. A newsletter and
  information leaflets are available.

Surrogacy
COTS (Childlessness Overcome Through Surrogacy) and TRIANGLES
Laondhu Cottage, Lairg, Sutherland (0549 2401)
Offers support to couples and anyone else involved throughout a surrogate
  pregnancy. Following the birth, advice and guidelines on both the emotional and
  legal aspect of the surrogacy option are available. All services are free.

Puts couples in touch with some who may be willing to help them by acting as surrogate mothers. All services are free. COTS will advise when a willing surrogate mother is found.

Note: Official BMA guides are now available so doctors may be more willing to help and advise couples seeking the surrogacy option.

Specialist products and services
ASH (Action on Smoking and Health)
5–11 Mortimer Street, London W1N 7RN (071 637 9843)

Alcohol Concern
(071 833 3471)
Offers helpful advice, practical tips and plenty of information about low alcohol and alcohol-free drinks, including lagers and wines. They can advise the best route to giving up or drinking less alcohol throughout the pregnancy/conception.

The Association of Qualified Curative Hypnotherapists
10 Balaclava Road, Kings Heath, Birmingham (021 444 5435)
Teachers can instruct on self-hypnosis for relaxation – usually within two sessions. Prices range from £15–£40 per session.

British Wheel of Yoga
HQ – 1 Hamilton Place, Boston Road, Sleaford, Lincs (0529 306851)
Contact HQ for details of teachers and classes in your area.

National Federation of Spiritual Healers
Old Manor Farm Studio, Sunbury on Thames, Middlesex (0932 783164)
May be able to offer help and comfort – and even show you visualization and mediation techniques which may be useful. Some healers charge nothing, others may charge from £8–£40 per session.

National Society for Non-Smokers (now called QUIT)
(071 487 2858)
Has a list of inexpensive courses countrywide. Contact HQ for details.

Relaxation For Living
HQ – 29 Burwood Park Road, Walton on Thames. Surrey KY12 5LH
Contact HQ for information about relaxation classes countrywide. Send large SAE.

Further reading
The New Fertility by Graham H. Barker (Adamson Books)
The Fertility Handbook by Joseph Belling and Josleen Wilson (Penguin)
Trying for a Baby? by Maggie Jones (Sheldon Press)
Getting Pregnant by Robert Winston (Anaya)
Infertility: A Sympathetic Approach by Robert Winston (Optima)
Choosing a Clinic: published by CHILD (up to date listing of the services of all clinics – both private and NHS – offer: GIFT, IVF, egg donation, AID etc.) and sperm freezing.

The Menopause

There are two ways of looking at the menopause. One is as the next natural stage in a woman's physical development – the ancient Greek philosophy was that in terms of all our lifetime's natural phases (puberty, menstruation, pregnancy, childbirth) the menopause was just an entry into the next calmer stage, where women were relieved of the burden of childbearing and rearing to concentrate on themselves, and on what they wanted to do for a change.

The other way of looking at it is that the inevitable physical changes it causes in our bodies can bring new problems and discomforts.

There is truth in both. But while the menopause or change of life is not necessarily straightforward it is not inevitable that all menopausal women are going to have a hard time. In fact, according to the US National Institute of Health, 80 per cent of women will experience only mild symptoms, or none at all. Around 20 per cent will have some menopausal symptoms severe enough to need medical help. More good news: for every unwelcome symptom, there is a solution.

What is it?
The menopause is the gradual slowing, then stopping, of oestrogen production in your body. Periods become heavier or lighter, less frequent, and eventually stop altogether. It usually happens during your mid to late forties or early fifties – but menopause can begin naturally as early as 35. If for any reason your ovaries are removed, it will happen then, all at once, rather than gradually. (See CANCER OF THE OVARY and CANCER OF THE UTERUS, pages 87 and 93.)

The slowing down or changing nature of your monthly periods is a symptom of a parallel winding down of your body's production of female hormones:
i) ovaries slow down, then eventually stop, producing oestrogen, which results in erratic periods and all the menopause's physical symptoms;
ii) at the same time the body increases its production of LH (Luteinizing Hormone), the hormone that causes an egg to be ripened and released from your ovaries each month.

These two changes can happen so slowly and subtly and the transmission be so smooth that you barely notice it happening and get few, if any, awkward side effects. The change-over time can also have dramatically unpleasant effects (see **Symptoms**, below), lasting from a few months for some women to 10 years for others. The menopause's 'official' beginning is a full year after your last menstrual period. Continue using contraception for a full year after your last period or you might still become pregnant. (See 'contraception' in **Treatments**, below.)

This gradual slowing down and stopping of oestrogen production (in particular) can have quite an effect as the hormone plays some very important roles in our body:

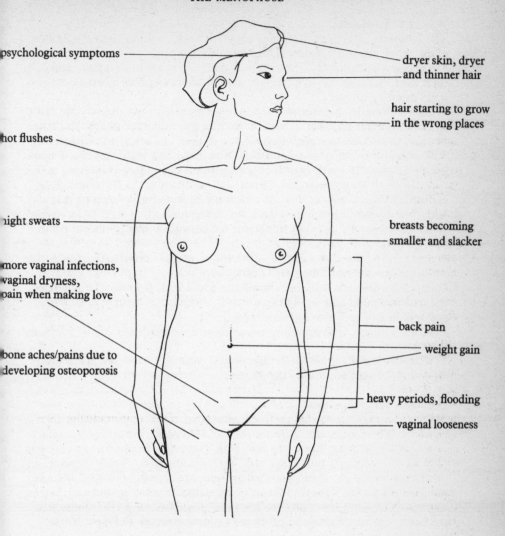

psychological symptoms

dryer skin, dryer
and thinner hair

hair starting to grow
in the wrong places

hot flushes

night sweats

breasts becoming
smaller and slacker

more vaginal infections,
vaginal dryness,
pain when making love

back pain

weight gain

bone aches/pains due to
developing osteoporosis

heavy periods, flooding

vaginal looseness

* maintaining your womb lining so you have periods when you shed it
(progesterone is also involved in this process);
* preventing calcium being lost from your bones and so keeping them strong
and solid;
* helping to lubricate skin, and keeping the inside of the vagina moist and
supple;
* maintaining the collagen in the skin (body, facial and vaginal) so it keeps its
suppleness and spring; and helping maintain the tone of our muscle fibres.
* prevention of heart disease and strokes.

Who is more at risk?

The following categories of women are more likely to suffer from one or more of the problems associated with the menopause:

* Anyone who has little calcium in their diet, or has had low calcium intake all their lives, because they are thought to be more susceptible to osteoporosis – bone-thinning disease.

* Thin women, as their bodies contain fewer reserves of oestrogen. (You make and store it in fat deposits, as well as producing it from the ovaries. The fatter you are, the more oestrogen you have; the thinner you are, the less you have.)

* Women who suffered from PMS, who may find that they have more problems going through their menopause and may be more vulnerable to the psychological symptoms (like depression and anxiety). Dr Diana Riley, consultant psychiatrist at St John's Hospital in Aylesbury, suggests that – as with Post-Natal Depression, which also has a connection with PMS – some women may simply be more vulnerable to changes in their hormonal balance than others.

* Smokers, because smoking can affect the oestrogen output of the ovaries (its connection with infertility is well documented).

* Excessive drinkers, because alcohol can have a bad effect, too. (For women, the recommended limit is 14 units a week – a unit being a half of beer, a single pub measure of spirits or a glass of wine.)

* White women, who are more prone to osteoporosis than Afro-Caribbean women.

* Women who have an early menopause whether it occurs naturally or following surgical removal of the ovaries.

Problems and symptoms

Many specialists say that as the problems associated with the menopause are caused by a hormone deficiency (shortage of oestrogen), the best way to treat it is by replacing what has been lost with Hormone Replacement Therapy (HRT). It is thought that HRT can deal with just about every menopausal symptom, from a dry vagina and skin to osteoporosis and depression. If you do not wish to take HRT, or are advised by specialists that you should not, there is also much that can be done to tackle individual symptoms. Complementary medicine, too, can be very helpful – see **Complementary Therapy**, below.

It is possible to spend a fortune on 'rejuvenating' facial creams and serums which promise to restore the skin elasticity and muscle tone your face loses around the menopause and soon afterwards. Generally, they can temporarily tighten the surface of the skin and moisturize, but their other claims are questionable.

You cannot replace the skin's elasticity, but you can tone up the muscles which act as the scaffolding under the skin of your face and give it its contours. You do exercises to tone up a loosening pelvic floor – why not a loosening face? Done daily, they can help a great deal. You may notice a difference within about ten weeks – so keep at it.

 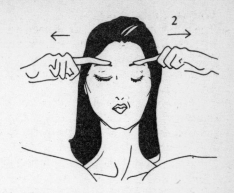

1 Good for muscles around jaw, mouth, cheeks. Make the vowel sounds:
'A, E, I, O, U' in a slow, exaggerated fashion, opening mouth as wide as
possible. Repeat five times.

2 Good for cheeks, chin, forehead muscles. Put two fingers firmly on ends of
eyebrows. Hold skin still by pressing in gently but at the same time try to push them
up and out with your brow muscles. Hold for the count of six. Repeat four times.

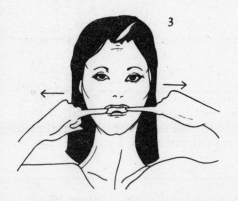 

3 For muscles around cheeks, mouth, nose, chin. Placing little finger inside
corner of mouth on either side, pull fingers outwards towards the sides, resisting
the tug with your mouth muscles. Hold for count of six. Repeat four times.

4 For the muscles that give you defined cheekbone contours. Put index finger and
longest finger together on each hand as if pointing them at someone. Insert one
over the top of the other into mouth. Suck inwards hard, holding for the count of
four. Repeat twelve times.

279

Problems, symptoms and causes

BACK PAIN is largely due to the effect of lack of oestrogen on your ligaments and joints – and, much later, to loss of calcium from bones, including the spine.

Medical help

You should be able to stand for long periods: if you are more comfortable lying down than standing or sitting, get checked out for bone loss by asking your GP to refer you to a menopause clinic or the radiology department of a large hospital which has suitable equipment (see OSTEOPOROSIS, page 311). HRT will help.

Self help

* Practise gentle stretching exercises to keep the ligaments and muscles supporting the back as supple as possible.
* Avoid long periods (more than an hour) of sitting. Get up for a five-minute break. Sitting puts pressure of around 100 kilograms on your back, compared with about 70 kilograms standing and only about 30 kilograms lying down.
* Consider investing in a Swedish 'Balans' chair – a tilted low stool with knee rests, which encourages your body to sit in the best possible position (thighs at a 135° angle to your body, as if you were riding a horse).
* Strengthen your stomach muscles: they are the 'guy ropes' that help keep your back supported.
* Hot-water bottles, warm baths or ice packs (make your own from a large packet of frozen peas or corn, wrapped in a clean tea-towel) may help temporarily.
* Yoga may help strengthen the back, as will regular swimming.
* Avoid very hard beds. 'Orthopaedic' beds are not always designed by orthopaedic specialists unless this is specifically stated. If they are too hard the curve of the lower back is not supported properly but is stretched like a shallow arch over the hard surface, with nothing holding it up except your already aching muscles and ligaments.
* Enjoy regular weight-bearing exercise (e.g. brisk walking, not swimming).
* A diet rich in calcium (see OSTEOPOROSIS, page 311).
* Stop smoking and avoid excess alcohol. (See HELPLINES.)

BREAST SHRINKAGE AND SAGGING. This is caused by loss of muscle and skin (collagen) tone, reduction in hormones and wear and tear due to ageing.

HRT can make breasts fuller. Surgery (small silicone gel implants and tightening the fan of skin supporting the breasts) is an option, but costs around £2,500 to £3,000 and is unlikely to be available on the NHS.

* Bust exercises to improve tone in the muscles supporting the breasts and to make them look firmer and trimmer.
* Swimming – four times a week – is very good.
* A really well-shaped, well-fitting supportive bra helps and it is worth getting it professionally fitted, free, at a major department store like John Lewis, as your cup size may have altered, and so may your chest measurement.

DECREASED SEX DRIVE. Some women may find their sex drive and sexual response increases; others that it diminishes. Lack of oestrogen can cause a drop in sex drive, and a dry vagina can make intercourse painful.

HRT can help boost sexual drive (though it is not a magic aphrodisiac) and alleviate vaginal dryness. Hormone cream applied locally will also relubricate a dry vagina far better than an ordinary lubricant.

It now takes longer to become sexually aroused, and more foreplay is needed. If you have any pain on intercourse, it will naturally put you right off.

* Check with your GP that there are no underlying physical causes that need treating with something more than oestrogens, such as Pelvic Inflammatory Disease or a recurrent low-level infection (see VAGINAL THRUSH, page 453, and PELVIC INFLAMMATORY DISEASE, page 322.

* Massage is a gentle and sensual way to re-establish sensory contact. It is only sexual if you want it to be, and can also just be caring, affectionate touch. It might be interesting to go on a short course with your partner.

* Time alone with your partner, or a holiday away from your usual environment (somewhere warm?) may help you both.

* A talk with a professional, or some counselling, may also help (especially if you are finding it hard to talk to your partner about how you feel). Relate (formerly the Marriage Guidance Council) has waiting lists of only a week or two for daytime appointments. Waiting times are longer for evening appointments – several months in some areas. (See HELPLINES for other relationship counselling organizations.)

DRY HAIR, THINNER HAIR. Due to lack of oestrogen, hair may become thinner.

Your GP will check for diseases or stress events which may have affected hair follicles. (It takes them up to six months to replace themselves, but in healthy women this is a continuous process.) There are certain preparations for male baldness (like Minoxidil) which doctors may prescribe for you. HRT can also help.

* Careful styling and use of hair pieces can disguise thinning hair.

* A daily scalp massage for two minutes will encourage the blood capillaries in the scalp to bring nutrients to the hair roots. Golden Millet supplements help.

* Use good protein conditioners – Redken and Lancôme's Fluence are both effective.

* Use hair thickener rinses (which act a bit like blow dry lotion, coating the hair to make it look thicker).

* Use a home-made protein conditioner. (A good one, tried and tested, is to mix 2 tablespoons of shampoo with 1 tablespoon (one packet) of powdered gelatin and one beaten egg and use it as a shampoo. Leave it on for five to ten minutes before washing it off in cool water.)

Problems, symptoms and causes	Medical help	Self help
DRY SKIN. This is due to lack of oestrogen again and can cause a 'skin crawling' sensation.	HRT can help alleviate the problem.	* Avoid excessive sun exposure. Cover up with a good sun screen (this will also help prevent the proliferation of dark skin spots, enlarging moles and skin tags). If you get any moles appearing suddenly, increasing rapidly in size, or with a varigated brown/black colour, or which seem weepy or sore go and see your GP to check it is not a skin cancer beginning. * Try not to smoke (it dries out skin even further). (See HELPLINES for stop-smoking courses.) * Use non-drying soaps, either glycerine-based or oat-based (like the Aveeno range from chemists, often suggested for psoriasis sufferers, or a gentle wash cream like Aqueous Cream from Boots pharmacy counters). * Use a rich but non-greasy facial and neck moisturizer under morning make-up or after your morning face wash – and at night. A cheap moisturizing lotion like Vaseline lotion can be used all over the rest of the body after baths and showers. * Avoid very hot baths (they are drying on skin, and help destroy collagen, which keeps skin springy). * Control spots (which some women get, thanks to increased levels of male hormones in the body) with spot creams from the chemist. * Exfoliate skin once a week (face and body). This helps speed up the process of cell renewal, which in menopausal women slows down naturally.
LESS FIRM FACIAL CONTOURS. Due to lack of oestrogen affecting their muscle tone.	HRT can help alleviate the problem.	* Daily facial exercises (see diagram ii) help tone up facial muscles below your skin to keep facial contours firmer. Otherwise they will tend to sag, as will the muscles in the rest of the body, thanks to lack of oestrogen. * Facial contours respond especially well to exercise as they are the only muscles in the body which are directly attached to the skin itself.
FLOODING (very heavy periods). Your periods may start becoming irregular around your late thirties, stopping altogether around the	Although the menopause is by far the likeliest cause, get thoroughly checked out by your GP to ensure there is no other reason. Heavy bleeding may sometimes be a sign of fibroids,	* Take iron and a B-group complex vitamin (as well as Vitamin C to absorb the iron), to offset possible anaemia. * Try to bring down your own oestrogen level by losing any excess weight. (Oestrogen is responsible for building

early fifties. During this time they may get lighter, heavier, longer or shorter.

HOT FLUSHES. Recent research links these to oestrogen lack, too. (They were formerly thought to be due to an increase in luteinizing hormone (LH), which helps ripen an egg from our ovaries each month).

polyps, or overgrowth (hyperplasia) of the womb lining, which can sometimes lead to pre-cancerous cell changes there, which may go on, if not checked, to be endometrial or womb cancer. So keep your cervical smear tests up to date.

Danger signs are continual spotting, haemorrhage, spotting, after intercourse.

Flooding cannot usually be helped with a small D&C operation; in extreme cases, if the blood loss is very excessive and shows no signs of an improvement, a hysterectomy will be suggested. New techniques (Endometrial Resection) can remove the womb lining while leaving the womb itself in place (see HYSTERECTOMY, page 225).

HRT is often effective, whether the flushes takes the form of drenching night sweats, an increased sensitivity to temperature (so you tend to feel hotter or colder than everyone else in the room) or the light blushes on your face, neck and chest which pass quickly. Dealing with night sweats can also combat the fatigue and depression that broken sleep patterns may bring.

up the womb lining: the more it builds up, the more there is to shed when you have a period.)
* Use heavier sanitary protection: super absorbent soft pads and high absorbency tampons, perhaps used together (especially at night). Always carry a supply in your bag (a number of brands now come in discreet, attractive, individual packages).

* Layer your clothing (blouses and jumpers or jackets give you more flexibility than a woollen dress).
* Get a desk-top fan and/or a small portable battery-operated fan to carry in your handbag.
* Handbag-sized water sprays, like the Evian sprays, can be useful.
* Learn deep breathing techniques, to help restore your control.
* Visualization exercises will all help (see HELPLINES). A hypnotherapist, healer or yoga instructor could teach you these: two simple but effective ones are to imagine you are sinking (naked) into a huge powdery snow-field or being rubbed all over with large cloth bags full of ice cubes. (These work better than you might think.)
* Keep your weight down. Fat acts as an insulator and prevents your body radiating off heat – which will make hot flushes worse.
* In bed wear an absorbent material like cotton next to your skin, and have cotton duvet covers or sheets.
* Natural fibres – especially cotton – worn next to the skin and as outer clothes may be helpful. They are cooler and although they keep in heat they allow skin to 'breathe' more than man-made fibres, which can aggravate sweatiness and over-heating.

Problems, symptoms and causes

INCONTINENCE. This is certainly one of the common menopause problems. Thanks to the combination of female anatomy – a short urethra (the tube from the bladder to the opening for urination), upright posture and loss of muscle tone – due to wear and tear, childbearing, possible obesity and some loss of muscle tone due to lack of oestrogen – the pelvic floor muscles are not as strong as they were and may leak urine when stressed by coughing, sneezing or exercising.

OSTEOPOROSIS. Following the menopause oestrogen deficiency leads to rapid loss of bone mineral for about five years, then a more gentle slide downhill will continue for the rest of your life. (See OSTEOPOROSIS, page 311 for details of treatments available and self help suggestions.)

Medical help

If self help pelvic floor exercises (see INCONTINENCE, page 239) have proved unhelpful and your GP has checked you over for any obvious reasons why you are not improving, ask to be referred to a hospital to see a urologist. He will assess your kidney and bladder (see INCONTINENCE for tests and treatments available).

HRT can help restore some skin and muscle tone to relieve incontinence due to thin bladder tissues and an irritable bladder. Fitting and prescribing a ring pessary.
* Irritable bladders can be helped by drugs, which relax the bladder tone.
* Surgery can improve muscle tone in the urethra and the sphincter muscle, or put any sagging sections of bladder and urethra back to their right positions.

HRT can stop the loss of bone, as well as supplying oestrogen to protect the bones from further damage.
Painkillers might be prescribed for very painful joints.

Self help

* Ring pessaries are vaginal support devices you can insert yourself that will return the bladder and urethra back to their correct position if they have 'dropped down'. You need to have one prescribed and fitted by a doctor first. (See INCONTINENCE, page 239, and HELPLINES, page 239, for the easiest and most effective way to do pelvic floor exercises.)
* Active pelvic floor exercises are very important. (See INCONTINENCE, page 239, and HELPLINES, page 239, for the easiest and most effective way to do pelvic floor exercises.)
* Look for good continence pads, which are so slim and discreet now that they differ little in bulk from ordinary sanitary towels, but are very absorbent and contain a gel which neutralizes odour. Your local continence advisor, a specially trained nurse working at the hospital or health centre will be able to help you. (See HELPLINES.)
* Passive pelvic floor exercises must be done in conjunction with the active exercises (see INCONTINENCE, page 239).
* Recent studies indicate that magnesium may be as important as calcium for maintaining bone density in women who have passed their menopause. High magnesium foods include nuts, beans and grains. Or try magnesium supplements.
* See OSTEOPOROSIS, page 311, and HELPLINES.

PSYCHOLOGICAL SYMPTOMS: agoraphobia and other phobias, anxiety, confusion, depression, feelings of unreality, inability to concentrate, irritability and poor memory.

Seek professional counselling from a good menopause clinic or well woman clinic (see HELPLINES for how to find one). HRT may help for some women. So might mild tranquillizers (for acute problems and only in the short term – no more than four weeks – as they are addictive and should only be used for short term 'emergency' situations).

* Deep breathing exercises (in for eight, hold for eight, breathe out for eight, saying 'Calm IN' as you inhale and 'Stress OUT' as you exhale). This sounds too simple to be helpful but it does very soon slow the heartbeat and breathing rate, and is a very useful trick.
* Visualization exercises (see HELPLINES).
* Talking to other women who feel as you do, via the self help and support groups (see HELPLINES).
* Talking to a counsellor, to see in which areas of your life you can reduce stress (see HELPLINES).
* Regular (preferably daily) gentle exercise.
* Trying to get a comfortable balance between home and work.
* Meditation or yoga classes (see HELPLINES).

UNWANTED HAIR GROWTH. Increased facial and body hair is due to male hormones we produce called androgens. Either they increase slightly or, as our oestrogen production drops, their effect is more noticeable, producing hair in 'male' places such as the face, stomach or chest.

This can sometimes be helped with drugs such as Cyproterone Acetate and Spironolactone, which stop the male hormones acting on the hair follicles to produce strong 'male' hairs where before there were only unnoticeable fine 'female' ones. Unfortunately the symptoms may recur when the drugs are stopped, and they have side effects, such as tiredness and depression. They should only be given by a specialist, such as an endocrinologist, who is a hormone therapy expert.

* Waxing can be done in a beauty salon or at home. But if the problem area is around the mouth and face this is very sensitive, so consider having the hair waxed away professionally for the first few times, and ask a beautician about the best way to do 'maintenance' waxes at home. Hair removed by this method stays away for about 2 weeks or so before it begins to grow back.
* There are also quality facial depilatory creams (the active ingredient – the same chemical as is in perming solution – dissolves the hair above skin level). The effect is short-lived though: only a few days before regrowth begins.
* Electrolysis is the only permanent method of removing unwanted hair. If hair has been plucked out before, this will have twisted the hair root, so the electrolysis needle – which is passed down the hair follicle to the root to kill it with a tiny electric shock – may need more than one attempt to reach and erradicate it for good. Sessions cost from about £7.50 for 15 mins, and a skilled electrolysist can deal with one or two hairs per minute. It is essential to get a properly qualified electrolysist (go to a good general hair and beauty salon or to a specialist clinic like one of the Tao outlets – see HELPLINES).

Problems, symptoms and causes	Medical help	Self help
		Some people find electrolysis rather uncomfortable. There is, however, one technique which is less so than the conventional method: developed by an electrolyist called Sylvia Lewis with the help of University College in London, there are practitioners trained in it countrywide – see HELPLINES. * Do not try any electrolysis DIY kits: they may scar, in unskilled hands.
VAGINAL INFECTIONS AND IRRITATION. The vagina is more prone to infections if it is dry; despite repeated treatment they may keep returning. You may also have continuous itching or irritation, which make intercourse uncomfortable, even painful.	HRT can help and so can hormone cream, containing oestrogen. It is very useful as a localized form of HRT. Use sparingly, as some will be absorbed into the bloodstream via the blood vessels close to the surface of the vagina's skin.	* (See also **Self help** in CYSTITIS, PELVIC INFLAMMATORY DISEASES and VAGINAL THRUSH, pages 193, 330 and 461.) * Avoid drying soaps and scented bath preparations. * Wear loose cotton underclothes and, if possible, stockings rather than nylon tights. Avoid tight, crotch-biting trousers. * Natural yoghurt, used on the vaginal area, helps restore the healthy, acidic environment which may have been destroyed by the drying-out of tissues. This makes it more resistant to infections, especially yeast organisms like thrush. Lactobacillus tablets taken orally may also help to restore the acid/alkaline balance (from major health food shops). * A little lubrication gel (like KY) on the outside of the vagina and labial and around the entrance to your vagina and up into it, can help lubrication for intercourse. (You could get your partner to put it on your labia area, and surrounding areas for you as part of foreplay, if you both like the idea.)
VAGINAL LOOSENESS. Sometimes women notice a feeling of slight slackness or of something 'sticking out' into the vaginal passage. This is partly loss of muscle tone (due to oestrogen lack) and partly wear and tear due	* Your doctor may prescribe and fit a pessary for you as an interim measure. Pessaries are devices made of plastic or rubber which support the vaginal walls and uterus in their proper place. They come in different shapes and sizes, such as rings, cubes or bell shapes. Some need to be inflated and	* Pelvic floor exercises (see INCONTINENCE, page 239). * Weight loss (if overweight). * Exercise – choose an activity which does not put downward pressure on your pelvic organs and the pelvic floor which holds them up (e.g. cycling or swimming, rather than jogging or tennis). * Try and stop smoking – apart from anything else,

to ageing and to childbirth. The protrusion that may be felt might be a section of the urethra, bladder or rectum dropping downwards slightly, or displacement and dropping down of the uterus (see PROLAPSE, page 430) due to years of pressure and wear on the pelvic floor, the sling of muscle that usually holds these organs in place.

WEIGHT GAIN is not inevitable, but around the menopause many women do put on more weight around their stomach and hips. This may be because some women's metabolic rates (the rate at which calories from food are burned) slow down, so you put on weight even if you are still eating the same amount. Some lucky women may get a rise in their metabolic rate and easily stay the same weight, or even lose a little.

Another reason for weight gain may be water retention (under hormonal control) or fear of exercise because of stress incontinence, or a hysterectomy.

deflated. Some need to be inserted by a doctor; others by the woman herself. It may take a few tries to find one which suits. Remember that sexual intercourse is not possible when pessaries are in place (except for ring devices), so any sexually-active woman needs one that she can put in and take out herself.

Pessaries can make you more prone to small vaginal infections and irritations, but they have few side effects and can help avoid surgery.

* Surgical repair removes sections of tissue from the back and front walls of the vagina, with or without a hysterectomy (depending on whether your womb has dropped down out of place or not). Possible complications include scar tissue in the vagina, vaginal shortening and infection.
* HRT can help, if part of the problem is atrophy of the vaginal walls.

Certain appetite suppressant drugs taken *short term* under careful medical supervision may be prescribed, but this is not very often the case. Appetite suppressants can be addictive.

coughing makes things worse. (See HELPLINES.)
* Avoid constipation – straining to pass stools makes things worse, too. (See CONSTIPATION, page 145.)

* Cut down on what you eat and alter your diet to include more fresh fruit and vegetables (which are especially filling and unfattening). Go for low-fat milk and cheeses, top puddings with yoghurt rather than cream, grill meats and consider joining a weight control club (see HELPLINES).
* Do any sort of exercise you feel happy with at least three or four times a week to improve muscle tone. Large toned bodies look a lot better and more inviting than large flabby bodies – or even slim flabby bodies, come to that.

Treatments

Hormone replacement therapy (HRT)

What is it? HRT replaces the oestrogen your body has lost with low doses of oestrogen (and usually progesterone, too). In the early days of HRT women were only given oestrogen ('unopposed') HRT. Studies in the 1970s found a link between cancer of the womb and HRT, but they were assessing the effects of oestrogen-only HRT, not the modern oestrogen plus progesterone – 'opposed' – HRT.

How taken? You can take oestrogen as an oral pill, an implant in the abdomen underneath the body fat or from a patch that sticks to your skin and releases oestrogen into it. (See also **Taking HRT**, below.)

Advantages. HRT can deal with most – but not all – menopausal symptoms, including hot flushes, dry vagina, body and facial skin and hair. It can improve muscle tone to a certain extent (and is partially helpful for problems associated with this, such as vaginal slackness, and the type of incontinence where the bladder tissues get thin and 'irritable'). It can improve your sex drive (although it is not a cure-all aphrodisiac by any means) and often helps deal with some psychological symptoms like irritability, mood swings, depression and anxiety or lack of concentration. HRT can also prevent further calcium loss from bones and, may replace some lost bone mass to make your skeleton stronger, and also offers protection against heart disease.

Disadvantages. There are drawbacks to HRT.

* Unopposed HRT (oestrogen only) increases the rate at which the womb lining (endometrium) thickens, and can cause over-thickening or 'endometrial hyperplasia' – a condition that can produce cell changes that are the forerunners of endometrial cancer. But this does not happen if progesterone is taken, too (Opposed HRT). More recent medical surveys suggest, in fact, that today's 'Opposed' HRT has a protective effect against endometrial cancer.

* A possible link with breast cancer. The evidence is still conflicting, but it seems there is a small risk, if HRT is taken for more than 10 years. Extra oestrogens may tend to enhance existing pro-cancer conditions, rather than being a direct cause of cancer, as oestrogen does stimulate breast tissue growth (see BREAST CANCER, page 68, and BREAST PROBLEMS, page 41). Some women taking HRT have regular mammogram checks as a peace of mind precaution.

Contraception. Continue using contraception for a full year after your last period or you might still become pregnant. You might prefer one of the lighter barrier method such as the diaphragm, spermicidal pessary, or the Today sponge (which does not provide enough protection for a younger, more fertile, woman but would for an older one).

Side effects (which mean that about one in five women cannot tolerate HRT). The most common unpleasant ones are nausea, irritability, abdominal cramps and breast enlargement (though this may be welcome for some). It is usually possible to deal with some of these problems by prescribing a slightly different balance of HRT hormones – there are many to choose from – but you need to be seen by a specialist at a menopause clinic for this. See HELPLINES (Women's Health Concern) for how to find one if your GP seems unable or unwilling to refer you.

* Period-style bleeds each month. HRT causes withdrawal bleeds, like the 'periods' you get on the Pill. Many older women find this unwelcome, especially if they were glad to have got their periods over and done with after their menopause.

But there is a period-free type of HRT, called the continuous combined method, brands include Livial and Organon. (Again, contact the WHC for details of where to find other centres offering it). This involves taking oestrogen plus just a little bit of progesterone *every* day, instead of taking it the usual HRT way – oestrogen continuously, with a larger amount of progesterone for 12 of those 28 days (which causes the withdrawal bleed 'period').

HOW LONG CAN YOU TAKE IT FOR? Theoretically, some experts say, you can take HRT indefinitely if you feel well on it and have regular health check-ups (see **Health checks and screening tests**, below). It is thought that you need to take it for about five years to have a good protective effect against osteoporosis, the loss of calcium from bone which accelerates fast when you stop making oestrogen and your menopause comes to an end.

Unfortunately, some GPs who are not experts in HRT but are alarmed about reports concerning its connections with cancer, are nervous of letting their female patients take HRT for longer than a few months, and have often stopped their dosage suddenly. This means HRT's protective effects – against heart disease and osteoporosis etc. – are minimal and that any troublesome menopause symptoms it was helping with will come straight back.

HOW TO GET HRT. Unless your GP has specialist training in this area – and some (not many) now do – it is important to get referred to a proper menopause clinic or a gynaecologist specialist in this area, either at a major family planning clinic, privately, or at a large hospital, in order to get seen and treated by the experts. (Ask WHC – see HELPLINES – for your nearest clinic. There are not many so it may mean travelling, but after initial visits to ensure all is well, you need only go back for check-ups and new supplies every 6 months or so, so it would be worth it to get expert treatment.)

GETTING TREATMENT FROM EXPERTS is important because:
i) there are several types of HRT, in the same way as there is one more than one brand of Pill. Different ones suit different women, and a doctor needs to know exactly what he is doing in order to find the best one for you personally. Too often, women have been put on the most popular form – or the cheapest – by their GPs, then not felt well on it, become discouraged and had to discontinue it when perhaps more knowledgable prescribing would have made all the difference;
ii) many GPs are still nervous about putting women on HRT because of the studies linking it with cancer. A specialist menopause clinic would be well up on all the latest medical evidence in this area and would have the facilities to keep careful checks on women taking HRT to ensure no problems developed.

IT IS NOT SUITABLE FOR women who are heavy smokers (smoking is not advisable at all, in fact – try and stop; see HELPLINES), or women with:
* a history of breast cancer;
* kidney disease – patients may need special advice;
* a history of womb cancer (endometrial or uterine);
* a history of gall bladder or liver problems;
* deep vein thrombosis, especially if it appeared out of the blue, or to a lesser degree, happened when you were on the Pill. If you still want HRT it is best to be monitored very carefully and regularly if you have had DVT;

Women with diseases that worsened during pregnancy (e.g. diabetes, high blood pressure, epilepsy) need to be very carefully and frequently monitored on HRT, and may be offered a patch (which can be easily removed).

TAKING HRT. You should take it for at least five years to get the protection you need for your bones. It is important to have regular health checks – see **Health Checks and Screening Tests** below – while you are receiving HRT. There are several different ways of taking it.

Patches on the skin are given in packets of eight; you change them twice a week. Their advantages are that they are under your control (you can remove them at once if they do not agree with you). They give a steady, smooth oestrogen supply, which bypasses the liver and puts no strain on it. However, they may irritate your skin and you have to remember to keep changing your patch.

Implants are inserted into the fatty layer under the skin of your abdomen, where they release oestrogen into your body. Each one lasts about 6 months and you can forget about it once it is there. But should it not agree with you, your doctor is unlikely to be able to find it again to remove it. There is a slight possibility of infection.

Pills are easy to take and you can stop taking them if HRT does not agree with you. But the pills have to be processed by the liver, which puts extra strain on it.

Cream is only used locally in the UK, in the vagina, to deal with menopausal dryness. In France there is a cream which can be rubbed onto the skin surface as an alternative way of taking HRT.

HEALTH CHECKS AND SCREENING TESTS. While taking HRT you should report to your doctor any of the following:
* migraine headaches;
* any unusual bleeding, apart from withdrawal bleed 'periods' if you are having them;
* any side effects of HRT with which you are unhappy (see if they can alter your HRT programme slightly to alleviate them);
* any lumps, skin dimpling or thickening, discharge, or anything unusual at all around your breasts and underarms (self-check your breasts each month – see BREAST CANCER, page 68).

In addition you should have regular check-ups with your doctor or clinic while taking HRT:

1. Three months after first assessing and prescribing HRT (sooner if there are problems).
2. Every 6 months after that: for blood pressure, weight, etc.
You should also ask for the following clinical screening tests.

* *A mammogram* is a sort of breast X-ray that can detect small or deep lumps which cannot be felt by hand examination. It is preferable to have one every 18 months after the menopause. Unfortunately, mammograms are only being offered every three years to women between 50 and 64 years of age, so if you want a more frequent check on your breast health (besides examining yourself every month) you will probably have to pay for it yourself, if you can afford it. Done privately they cost between £55 and £150. Contact the WNCCC (see HELPLINES) for your nearest screening centre, and be sure the results are given to you promptly and fully explained. If you are not sure about the explanation given, contact the WNCCC for clarification with a copy of the results to hand. If there are any abnormalities make an immediate appointment with your GP.

* *Cervical smears* should be done every 18 months after the menopause, too. They are free on the NHS every 3 to 5 years if you ask for them, but payment for private ones starts from about £8. Again, ask the WNCCC for the nearest screening centre, chase up the results (which should be given to you within 10 days) and ensure they are fully explained to you. If there are abnormalities, and you do not understand the explanation completely, contact the WNCCC for clarification and make an immediate appointment to see your GP.

* *Bone density measurements* are available at a few of the major menopause clinics on the NHS. (Contact the National Osteoporosis Society – see HELPLINES – for details of where to go. You can ask your GP to refer you there even if it is not local.) These tests give an idea of your risk of osteoporosis, and of the extent to which you have already developed it (see OSTEOPOROSIS, page 311).

Complementary therapy
Complementary therapies tailor their treatments very much to the individual: the precise nature of the treatment you receive will vary, depending on your medical history, symptoms, lifestyle, etc. The following information indicates the *sorts* of things a therapist is most likely to do or recommend. Do not be surprised if they feel you need something slightly different. This section is meant purely as an indication of likely treatments; it is not meant as a DIY guide to the medical uses of the different complementary therapies.

Complementary therapies can be very valuable in helping you to continue with your normal everyday life during the menopause, by alleviating some or all of the unpleasant symptoms you may have.

Acupuncture
Acupuncture or acupressure, perhaps combined with Chinese herbs, can stimulate your body's natural production of substances which reduce anxiety, depression and

irritability. Acupuncture to improve the mobilization of *chi* to your nervous system helps poor memory.

Hormonal imbalance during the menopause often gives rise to symptoms such as hot flushes, heavy periods or flooding, and back pain, due to oestrogen deficiency. Acupuncture can improve the balance of the hormones, thus alleviating the symptoms.

Acupuncture can also relieve other problems associated with the menopause, such as breast shrinkage and sagging, by increasing muscle and skin tone. Headaches and migraines can be relieved by treatment to produce natural pain-relieving substances; weight gain be helped by acupuncture to encourage your body to produce appetite suppressants.

Women suffering from osteoporosis associated with the menopause may also find acupuncture helpful.

(See OSTEOPOROSIS, page 311.)

Aromatherapy
Essential oils, blended for the individual patient, and used in full-body massage or in the bath, can be helpful in calming and relaxing your mind, relieving feelings of anxiety, depression, irritability, confusion and memory loss.

Very gentle self-massage with a blend of oils may help breast shinkage and sagging. Dry hair and skin will respond to moisturizing lotions prepared individually for you.

The aromatherapist can prepare an individual blend of oils for use by your partner in gentle massage (using techniques explained by the therapist) to increase libido. Symptoms caused by hormonal imbalance, such as hot flushes, heavy periods and back pain, may respond to massage with essential oils which help balance the hormones.

A blend of analgesic and calming oils, such as lavender and chamomile, used in specialized massage treatments of your head, neck and shoulders, removes tension and improves circulation, alleviating headache and migraine symptoms.

Vaginal dryness may make you prone to vaginal infection; this may be helped by using vaginal douches containing antiseptic oils, like tea tree.

Chiropractic
Back pain due to an oestrogen deficiency or the beginnings of osteoporosis responds well to spinal manipulation and soft-tissue work. While you should also have orthodox treatment for osteoporosis, chiropractic therapy can help alleviate the pain – even if you have spontaneous fractures – by reducing muscle tension and spasm.

Chiropractic therapy has been found very effective in reducing headache and migraine caused by tension or neck problems. It restores normal joint flexibility, and reduces nerve pressure and muscle tension.

Clinical nutrition
The loss of ovarian hormones, common at menopause, inhibits the sympathetic nervous system and causes a disturbance of calcium metabolism. Also, there can be a break in the feedback loop between the anterior pituitaries and ovaries, resulting in a reduction of the luteinizing and follicle-stimulating hormones. Whole pituitary glandular tissue will help re-establish this loop and wheatgerm oil acts as an anti-oxidant, helping to reduce inflammation.

This rebalancing of the system will help reduce many of the symptoms associated with menopause, and relieve pain.

At the same time, the nutritionist will discuss your diet, and probably advise you to avoid pepper, mustard, vinegar, sugar, tobacco, caffeine, while reducing your intake of oil, margarine and salt.

Homoeopathy
Several homoeopathic remedies are available to treat the unpleasant symptoms of menopause. After careful and in-depth consultation and discussion of your individual problems, the homoeopath will prescribe an appropriate treatment or combination of treatments. These include Cimicifuga (irritability, depression, restlessness, headache, sinking feeling in pit of stomach); sanguinara (headaches, hot flushes); veratum viride (hot flushes); Pulsatilla (hot flushes, mood changes and weepiness in fair, placid women); Bellis Perennis (backache and fatigue); and Graphites (obesity during the menopause).

Lachesis, for example, is a most helpful remedy if you are suffering from hot flushes, headaches, sweating and vertigo; tension and anxiety may be treated with Caulophyllum.

Medical herbalism
Probably one of the most useful aspects of herbal medicine is its effectiveness and relative safety over long periods of use. This makes it a good bet for the problems of menopause, which may last for months or years.

Appropriate remedies depend on the individual patient, and the particular combination of problems. Symptoms of anxiety, confusion and irritability respond to long-term treatment with nervous restoratives.

Other remedies might include herbs (such as sage) which have an effect on oestrogen levels and are useful for problems associated with hormone imbalance, such as breast shrinkage, decreased libido, and increased hair growth.

Dry hair and skin respond to long-term treatment with applications of herbal oils, together, perhaps, with Vitamin E supplements taken internally. Vein irritability leading to hot flushes can be helped with such nerve restoratives as life root. Loss of vaginal tone and dryness of the vagina respond to healing and astringent infusions – such as marigold or comfrey – applied locally.

Advice on diet and exercise is important at this time. Maintaining an active lifestyle can help reduce the calcium loss associated with menopause, and is helpful in reducing back pain and for those suffering osteoporosis. Indeed, the medical herbalist is likely to offer advice on both diet and exercise – to be continued throughout and after the menopause – to help maintain peak health, both physically and mentally.

Menopause helplines

Age Concern
HQ – Astral House, 1268 London Road, London SW16 4EJ (081 679 8000)

Association of Chartered Physiotherapists in Obstetrics and Gynaecology
c/o Association of Chartered Physiotherapists, 14 Bedford Row, London WC1
   (071 242 1941)
Has leaflets and advice on continence exercises.

Association of Continence Advisors: is now called Continence Line
2 Doughty Street, London WC1N 2PH (091 213 0050)
Advice on how to restore continence, as well as exercise leaflets, books, practical
   advice (by telephone), and services to put you in touch with your nearest continence
   advisor.

British Association for Counselling/RELATE (formerly the Marriage Guidance
   Council)
37A Sheep Street, Rugby, Warwickshire (0788 578 328)
Both associations can put you in touch with trained counsellors in your area, who
   can help with any relationship or sexual difficulties.

British Nutrition Foundation
52 to 54 High Holborn, London WC1 (071 404 6504)

Cytoscreen
(081 868 2423)
Inexpensive smear test service run by the president of the British Cytologist
   Association – see page 105.

The Family Planning Association
See GENERAL HELPLINES, page 480, for details.

Hysterectomy Support Group
11 Henryson Road, London SE4 (081 690 5987)

Institute of Marital Studies
The Tavistock Institute of Marital Studies, Tavistock Centre, 120 Belsize Lane,
   London NW3 5BA (071 435 7111)

Marie Stopes Clinics
In London, Manchester and Leeds. (See GENERAL HELPLINES, page 480, for details)

National Osteoporosis Society
Barton Meade House, PO Box 10, Radstock, Bath BA3 3YB (07614 32472)

Women's Health Concern
PO Box 1929, London W8 (071 938 3932)
Trained nurse counsellors in London and Cardiff (and their panel of medical experts)
   can answer your queries on all aspects of menopause, including HRT and where to
   obtain good HRT treatment in your area.

Women's National Cancer Control Campaign (WNCCC)
1 South Audley Street, London W1 (071 499 7532)
Can answer queries on cancer screening and tests, and put you in touch with your
   local screening facilities.

Women's Nutritional Advisory Service
PO Box 268, Hove, East Sussex (0273 771366)
Advice on how to alleviate both menopause and PMT (it was formerly the PMT
   Advisory Service), via careful attention to your daily eating habits, and mineral and
   vitamin supplementation.

Specialist products and services
Alcohol Concern
(071 833 3471)
For advice on cutting down on drinking, contact this service.

Aquacise
82 Cherry Tree Avenue, Clacton on Sea, Essex CO15 1AS
(0255 436 932)
Exercises in water devised by local GPs, physiotherapists and a former swimming
    instructress. Suitable for pregnant, post natal, elderly, and young and fit alike.
    Ring for details of over thirty venues across the UK.

Association of Qualified Curative Hypnotherapists
(See GENERAL HELPLINES, page 480, for details)

British Wheel of Yoga
1 Hamilton Place, Boston Road, Sleaford, Lincs (0529 306851)
Can put you in touch with a professionally qualified teacher in your area. Yoga can be
    a helpful relaxation method and the teachers can also show you effective
    visualization techniques.

Health and Beauty Exercise (formerly the Womens League of Health & Beauty)
(071 243 6384)
Classes held by properly trained teachers countrywide, which can help with general
    fitness levels, suppleness and weight control. Contact HQ for the class (very
    reasonably priced) nearest you.

National Federation of Spiritual Healers
Old Manor Farm Studio, Sunbury on Thames, Middlesex (0932 783164)
Many women have found healing is very helpful and soothing for just about any
    health problem, including those associated with menopause (and its psychological
    effects). The NFSH can put you in touch with a registered healer in your area.
    Charges vary (see COMPLEMENTARY THERAPIES, page 462, for details).

National Society for Non-Smokers
(071 487 2858)

Nature's Best
PO Box 1, Tunbridge Wells, Kent TN2 3EQ (0892 34143)

Relaxation for Living
(0932 836355)

Pil-Food
Lake Pharmaceuticals (081 997 8247)
Extract of golden millet in capsule form. Taken over a period of three months it can

make thinning hair thicker, as it affects the hair follicles, so that more hair stays in the growing stage. Approx £24 for 6 weeks' worth.

Sterex Advisory Bureau
PO Box 182, Exhall, Coventry
A free advisory service set up by a major manufacturer of electrolysis equipment, which can put you in touch with a local salon with professional therapists.

Slimming clubs
(071 255 1711)
Groups countrywide which provide support in the form of weekly meetings, menu plans and discussions for anyone who wants to lose weight.

Sylvia Lewis Salon and School
108 New Bond Street, London W1 (071 491 4919)
Ms Lewis is an experienced electrolysis therapist who has developed, with University College, a method which is less uncomfortable (and therefore suitable for treating sensitive, or larger, areas of unwanted hair). Contact her school for your nearest therapist.

Tao Electrolysis
Enquiries to 5 Sloane Street, London SW1X 9LA
(071 235 9393)

Weight Watchers UK limited
(See GENERAL HELPLINES, page 480, for details)

Further reading
The Menopause: Coping with the Change by Dr Jean Coope (Optima)
No Change by Wendy Cooper (Arrow)
Understanding Osteoporosis: Every Woman's Guide to Preventing Brittle Bones by Wendy Cooper (Arrow)
Menopause: The Natural Way by Anne Dickson and Nikki Henriques (Thorsons)
Menopause the Natural Way by Dr Sadja Greenwood (Optima)
Menopause: 40+ The Best Years of Your Life by Ada Khan and Linda Hughey Holt (Bloomsbury)
The Menopause – A Guide for Women of All Ages by Jill Rakusen (A Health Education Authority Publication)
Overcoming the Menopause Naturally by Dr Caroline Shreeve (Arrow)
The Menopause Send £2.50, plus P & P to Women's Health Concern (see above for address).

Miscarriage

What is it?

'Miscarriage' is the name for the spontaneous loss of a pregnancy before the 24th week. After that, the death of a baby is called stillbirth. Sometimes, a miscarriage is a 'missed' one, where the foetus dies but is not immediately expelled from the womb.

The medical term for a miscarriage is 'spontaneous abortion', but women who have suffered a miscarriage don't usually like the term. It sounds too much like 'induced abortion' – the name used for pregnancy termination, when a woman comes to a decision deliberately to end the pregnancy.

A miscarriage happens against the will of the woman who is carrying the baby. She is likely to feel a great sense of loss, and it is important to recognize this.

Miscarriage is thought to be the single most common complication in pregnancy, and is the reason that brings young women into hospital most often. Very early miscarriages may affect up to one in two pregnancies (the miscarriage may show up as a late, heavy period or not be noticed at all). Among women who have had a positive pregnancy test, it is estimated that roughly one in six will have a miscarriage. Up to half of 'threatened miscarriages' can be prevented, but many can't because the pregnancy simply isn't viable and your body has recognized the fact.

Causes

One of the first things someone who has had a miscarriage will ask is why it happened. In about 60 per cent of cases, there is an explanation: the lost foetus had something abnormal in the make-up of his or her chromosomes. Chromosomal abnormality can be caused by increasing age, excessive or, in some cases, moderate drinking and smoking, intake of certain recreational drugs, environmental pollution (e.g. a water supply containing too much aluminium) or polluted air – all can contribute. Often there is no known certain cause for a 'bad' egg or sperm cell which carries faulty DNA material.

But that leaves a large number of miscarriages which just can't be explained. Doctors simply don't know the cause of the other 40 per cent of miscarriages. And that, unfortunately, means that they can't suggest anything you could have done differently – or any treatment, either. This is frustrating for everyone. You are bound to wonder if it was somehow your fault, or your partner's fault. But it almost certainly isn't anyone's 'fault'.

However, research is now showing you can do quite a lot for yourself (both of you) to make the most of your future chances, and the vast majority of women who have miscarriages do go on to have a healthy baby with no further trouble.

Where the cause of the miscarriage is established there is nearly always something that you, or your doctor, can do to reduce the risk of further miscarriages: see **Your next pregnancy: medical help** and **Your next pregnancy: self help**, below, for details of possible causes, future risks and how to deal with them.

Who is at risk?

Some pregnancies have a slight built-in risk of miscarriage which is difficult to overcome by medical or self help means (see below). These risks are more likely among the following.

* Older women – although they are not at major risk. According to Dr Richard Aubry, professor of obstetrics and gynaecology at the State University of New York, Syracuse, the chance of a woman under 35 having a miscarriage is about 10 to 12 per cent; at 35 to 40, it goes up just to 15 per cent. In women over 40, however, it may be as high as 25 per cent. These are likely to be early miscarriages, caused by a defect in the ovum (egg). Women are born with their lifetime's supply of ova ready-made. In time, they age and are slightly more likely to develop into an abnormal foetus, which miscarries – usually within the first 12 weeks of pregnancy. There is now a blood test available for Down's syndrome called a Fetacheck. Developed by St Bart's Medical School in London, this test is only 60 per cent accurate at the present time, but is a helpful screening process which, used in conjunction with ultra sound and other blood tests, can help to avoid the need for amniocentesis in older women. They are working to improve this figure.

* Women who get pregnant as a result of fertility treatment have a higher chance of miscarriage. This is logical, since problems in maintaining a pregnancy are often the reasons for having fertility treatment in the first place.

* Daughters of women who took the synthetic hormone DES – diethylstilboestrol – (prescribed to prevent miscarriage) have a higher than usual miscarriage rate themselves.

* Women who started their periods at an early age may have more miscarriages, although the danger diminishes after the first pregnancy.

* Twin pregnancies, or other multiple pregnancies.

* Pregnancies where the placenta fails to develop well enough to support the growing foetus. This is usually the result of faulty eggs – the placenta develops from the egg, as does part of the embryo. Occasionally an impaired maternal circulatory system, which means insufficient oxygen and nutrients going to the developing placenta and foetus, is to blame. Sometimes no explanation can be found and it is difficult to give *any* reason for certain without extensive post-miscarriage lab tests – which is not usual.

* Parents with a chromosome abnormality. This is rare, but a blood test called a karotype can reveal these. It is usually arranged when a previously miscarried foetus has been found to have chromosomal abnormality, or if there is a family history of it in either parent. Then, the couple needs genetic counselling.

Most other at-risk groups can be treated by medical or self help (see below).

Types of miscarriage

Threatened miscarriage

The symptoms of a threatened miscarriage are:

* bleeding from the vagina, especially clots;
* mucus in the vaginal blood;
* abdominal pain;
* back pain;
* cramp-like pains, rather like period pains.

Not all bleeding in pregnancy is a threatened miscarriage. It is common to 'spot'. Sometimes the extra progesterone being produced to maintain the womb lining for the growing embryo implanted in it is not quite enough to suppress the shedding of some of the womb lining – but it produces a healthy baby all the same. This is why some women will not know they are pregnant, as they continue to have what seem to be light periods for the early months after conceiving (see PREGNANCY PROBLEMS, page 360). Spotting during the first four weeks after a missed period, and especially at the time the period was due, is also not at all uncommon. If the cervix stays tightly closed the pregnancy will continue.

At least 50 per cent of women who threaten to miscarry will actually do so. Nothing can be done about it, in the vast majority of cases. And nothing should be done either, say midwives and (more recently) doctors – the pregnancy is very probably being 'aborted' for a good reason. (See **Suspected miscarriage**.)

Inevitable miscarriage
A threatened miscarriage will end in inevitable miscarriage if:
* the cervix opens, and bleeding continues – 'inevitable abortion';
* everything empties out of the uterus, the cervix closes and the bleeding stops – a 'complete abortion' (in practice this is rare);
* the uterus partly empties, the cervix remains open and bleeding continues – 'incomplete abortion'. Many miscarriages are 'incomplete', and treatment is needed to clear the uterus.

It is often advisable to have a surgical clearing (D & C or D & E) of the uterus, under general anaesthetic (see ABORTION, page 12). Most doctors recommend this for any lost pregnancy which was more than six weeks old.

In late pregnancy, a miscarriage will feel very like labour.

Missed abortion
If there is a 'missed abortion' (the foetus is dead, but still in the uterus) you may or may not know about it. If the foetus has been old enough (16-plus weeks) to be felt moving, it will stop. Otherwise, there is no obvious way to tell if a foetus is alive or dead without an ultrasound scan. Many women just feel that they are no longer pregnant, by the cessation of various pregnancy symptoms. This is less likely in a first pregnancy, when you don't yet know what your personal pregnancy signs are.

If you don't recognize the missed abortion at once, you will sooner or later notice some bleeding, feel abdominal pain or signs of infection (fever, etc). Again, you will need a D & C or, in late pregnancy, one of the treatments used to induce abortion (see ABORTION, page 12). This may be very traumatic. It can also be very distressing to have to wait for a D & C appointment. It is worth explaining your feelings to the doctor (or getting your partner to do so) and pressing for an immediate one. If you can afford it, and don't want to wait, consider going privately. (See HELPLINES in ABORTION.)

Suspected miscarriage

If you are pregnant and have any of the symptoms of miscarriage (see **Threatened miscarriage**, above), call your GP. The symptoms don't necessarily mean you will miscarry. Your GP will assess the situation.

* By asking questions – especially about the type of bleeding: bright red/fresh blood may mean threatened miscarriage; dark/old blood may mean missed abortion; extreme abdominal pain with or without bleeding may mean ectopic pregnancy; also about how long you have been bleeding for; and, if you have any pain, where and what sort of pain it is. Blood clots passed can indicate real trouble.
* By doing a manual examination of the cervix to see if it is open or closed.
* By doing a urine pregnancy test.
* By referring you for an ultrasound scan.

Until you can see the doctor, you might want to rest. This may encourage the nourishing blood flow to the placenta and foetus and slow down your vaginal bleeding; more likely, it just makes you feel more comfortable and that you are doing something to help. GPs often advise bed rest.

Some doctors give progesterone for threatened miscarriage. Women with low levels of this hormone in pregnancy are more likely to miscarry. But, says John McGarry, consultant at North Devon District Hospital, there is no evidence that it works. In fact, he says, there is no possible medical treatment of any kind which will prevent a 'threatened' miscarriage going all the way, if that is what it is going to do.

Medical help: during a miscarriage

You may be taken into hospital for observation, where you may also be put on a drip to deliver progesterone or HCG (Human Chorionic Gonadotrophin hormone) into your body. (Progesterone is the hormone which helps maintain a pregnancy and miscarriages can be caused by a shortage of it being produced when pregnant.)

You will be given total bed rest there, including bed pans from the nurses instead of being allowed to visit the toilet; and blanket baths if necessary instead of a bath or shower.

Self help: during a miscarriage

* Total bed rest (get up to go to the loo only).
* Lie in bed and keep warm: but do not put a hot-water bottle on your abdomen – don't do anything at all to the area, leave it strictly alone. Put a hot-water bottle on your back if you have backache, if you like.
* Do not take painkillers if you can help it.
* Relax as much as you are able to: e.g. with deep breathing, relaxation training, visualization.
* Think positively if you can – again, visualizing (perhaps visualizing everything being just as it should be, the foetus safe, healthy and secure, your cervix closed) may help.

* Distract yourself from worrying by watching TV if you can have it in your bedroom, or by reading.
* Call on a close friend or partner for encouragement and support – and make sure someone is there to look after you (bring your meals etc.) so you can remain strictly in bed. (Note: With bed rest, bleeding should stop, if it's going to, within 24 hours.)

WHEN TO GO TO HOSPITAL. Most doctors feel that a threatened miscarriage is a case for bed rest, but a miscarriage that is showing physical signs such as bleeding should be taken to hospital via the casualty department. So when bleeding does begin, ask to be taken to hospital straight away if you have been told a miscarriage is inevitable. If you have been advised that it might go either way, and to rest and see what happens, phone up the gynaecology ward of your local hospital if bleeding does begin and ask their advice. They will probably tell you to come in for admission so you can be looked after by the right trained medical staff.

A miscarriage can be over in a matter of hours, or it may take several days to occur naturally.

Medical help: after a miscarriage

* You may bleed until your first period. Call the doctor if you have blood clots or any fever. These might indicate an infection, which will need speedy treatment.
* Many hospitals offer follow-up appointments, especially after a late miscarriage. These give a chance to discuss the results of any tests on foetus or parents, and also to talk through the emotional distress of the experience. Future treatment may be planned.
* See ABORTION, page 12, for details of a D & C and how you will feel afterwards.

Self help: after a miscarriage

* Don't use tampons for post-miscarriage bleeding – they encourage infection. After your first period it should be safe to use them again, though.
* You may produce colostrum (early, watery breast milk). Resist the temptation to squeeze it out, as this will only stimulate you to make more. It may stain clothes with a watermark, so put tissue in your bra. The milk will die away, although it can be suppressed with hormones if necessary.
* Avoid sexual intercourse for at least two weeks – again, the danger is infection. Other forms of sexual pleasure, including masturbation, are fine if you feel ready for them but don't be surprised if you do not feel like sex. This feeling will pass and is quite normal.
* Take at least a few days off work to recover physically.
* Give yourself a chance to grieve. According to the Miscarriage Association, talking can help a lot. Miscarriage can be a very private kind of loss – it is something of a taboo subject, for one thing. Few people realize how common it is – so those who suffer it feel they must be abnormal and that their future chances of a healthy pregnancy are poor. Neither of these things is true.

Some people can be surprisingly unsympathetic, too. They may unconsciously protect themselves from other people's unhappiness by making light of what has happened. It may well be true that 'you can always have another one', but that misses the point for a woman who has carried a baby inside her, and perhaps felt it move. The baby was an individual, and should be mourned as an individual.

Especially difficult times are: a few days after the miscarriage, when hormone levels are dropping and you feel distressed and weepy; and months later, on the day the baby would have been born. Try to let your partner know about this, and arrange support from your own friends or a support group (see HELPLINES).

Some women may find they feel they want to know as much as possible about the foetus, especially if it was a later miscarriage – its sex, for instance. You might want to see it, spend some time alone with it, or even have a photograph taken. Whether you want to do any of these things, or none of them, is entirely up to you, but be assured that none of these requests is abnormal or unreasonable. So ask.

For a late miscarriage, you might also want to arrange a proper burial. Details depend partly on the age of the foetus – ask the hospital chaplain to help you. A foetus of less than 24 weeks has no legal status and does not have to be registered, named or buried. You may like to give it a name yourself.

Since miscarriage is often thought of as a slightly embarrassing 'female problem', the male partner can feel particularly helpless and left out, or may refuse to express any emotions about it at all.

You need to be able to talk, as much as you want to, to somebody who will actually listen. It could be anyone – if you're desperate, talk to an imaginary person in your head (whoever you'd like to talk to in person). A self-help group like the Miscarriage Association can certainly put you in touch with someone who has been through it herself, and will understand. It helps to know that miscarriage is *very* common – it just isn't talked about much. If you can get talking to other women, you'll be surprised how many have had experiences like yours.

Trying again
In theory, if your miscarriage had no complications, such as an infection for instance, doctors advise that you can start trying to conceive again after you have had two normal periods.

Many will positively encourage a woman to do so, feeling that to become pregnant again as soon as possible is the best thing a woman distressed by a miscarriage can do, as it restores her peace of mind that she is still fertile and that a new pregnancy can help 'make up' for the lost one.

However, this is not right for all women, many of whom need time to get over their miscarriage from an emotional point of view first, and though they may be physically ready for pregnancy again they may not feel psychologically ready for many months. If this is the case it might be helpful to take as much time as you feel you need to adjust, and perhaps use those months to get into peak physical condition to have a baby: plenty of good nutrition, rest and exercise (see HELPLINES) to help maximize their chances of a happy, successful pregnancy next time around – rather than simply aiming to conceive again as fast as possible.

Will it happen again?
Because miscarriage is so common, one miscarriage is not seen as medically 'significant'. Statistics show that a woman who has had one miscarriage has exactly the same chance of a successful pregnancy as a woman who has never had a miscarriage. For this reason – and because very often there is no known cause for the miscarriage, anyway – medical treatment probably won't be offered until a woman has had three miscarriages. Her problem is then classified as 'recurrent miscarriage', and investigations begin.

It is very unlikely that you will get earlier help on the NHS, where services are being heavily cut. You have more chance if you are older (over 35) and/or there is a proper infertility clinic locally. Ask your GP or the Miscarriage Association. If you don't want to wait for a possible three miscarriages you may have to go privately. Again, ask your GP or the Miscarriage Association to recommend someone, or enquire through friends and/or a local private hospital.

After three miscarriages, the chances of a healthy pregnancy are still something like fifty-fifty, dropping to 40 per cent after four or more.

Your next pregnancy: medical help
There are certain medical conditions, or medical tests, which always carry a risk of miscarriage:
* Some optional tests done in pregnancy to detect abnormalities can themselves carry a small risk to the foetus: amniocentesis (carries a 1 per cent risk of miscarriage) and chorion villus sampling (a 2 to 3 per cent risk). Ask for a full discussion about the risks if you are offered these. Risk varies with the skill of the technician.
* Certain medical disorders, including diabetes, lupus, kidney disorders and a severely under- or over-active thyroid gland. Just make sure you get proper medical supervision, which can make your chances of a successful pregnancy very good indeed. You could also contact the relevant self-help group for your condition (see HELPLINES).
* Rubella (German measles) during pregnancy. You should always check your immunity before you get pregnant, and even if you have had a rubella vaccination in the past, ask your GP to get your immune status checked and, if necessary, to revaccinate you. Sense, the rubella charity (see HELPLINES) says that immune status does disappear in some vaccinated women.
* Uncontrolled high blood pressure is a risk, but this will be routinely monitored at ante-natal appointments in *every* pregnancy, and treated or managed as necessary. Miscarriage is a possible outcome if it is not controlled. (See PREGNANCY PROBLEMS, page 360, and contact PETS – the Pre-Eclamptic Toxaemia Society – see HELPLINES.)
* High dosage X-rays are bad news in pregnancy, but only in the abdominal area (don't panic if they need to X-ray your leg as your abdomen can be protected by a special shield). And it's standard radiotherapy practice to safeguard all women of child-bearing age, whether they think they're pregnant or not.

Other medical conditions may not become apparent until after you have had one or more miscarriages and your 'recurrent miscarriage' problem has been investigated. Once they have been diagnosed, however, most can be successfully treated.

* An 'incompetent cervix' is one unable to close up tight enough to hold in the pregnancy. A miscarriage for this reason is most common in the second three months (trimester) of the pregnancy. Possible causes of an incompetent cervix include: a previous D & C; a previous cone biopsy (to check for, or treat, cervical cancer); and repeated termination of pregnancy. But it can also occasionally happen in women with none of these risk factors.

If you have any reason to suspect that this is your problem, insist on an examination from your GP or a referral to a specialist. Don't let anyone make you wait until you've had three miscarriages, because it can be treated.

A stitch (a sort of ring-shape round the cervix), or actual surgical stitches, can be inserted to help the cervix stay closed. It is sometimes inserted between pregnancies, but more usually around the fourteenth week of pregnancy. It must be removed about two weeks before the birth. If you go into early labour, make sure the midwife knows you've got a stitch – it shouldn't be a problem then. (See also ABORTION, page 12, for more information about cervical stitches.)

However, inserting one can actually cause a miscarriage, as can any other interference with the cervix and there is some debate about how useful these stitches are. Discuss this with the relevant support group (see HELPLINES).

* Women who have had several previous pregnancies may have an over-stretched uterus (womb), which leads to too-early labour. Make sure this is discussed at your ante-natal sessions.

* Incompatible rhesus factors in you and your partner. Eighty-five per cent of the population is rhesus positive; the rest are rhesus negative. If a mother is rhesus negative and the partner is rhesus positive there may be a problem. Therefore it is a good idea to check blood before pregnancy is contemplated. All women's blood groups are checked at the first ante-natal clinic and should the mother be rhesus negative she will be monitored throughout her pregnancy for rhesus antibodies that may affect her baby. They are unlikely to be a problem in a first pregnancy and at the birth of a baby or at the time of a miscarriage treatment is always given to avoid the production of these antibodies. Therefore it is always a good idea to remind your doctor or midwife that you are rhesus negative, if this is so.

* Abnormalities in the father's sperm may be a factor in recurrent miscarriage. Some of these can be corrected, but not all (see INFERTILITY, page 250).

* Immunological problems might also cause recurrent miscarriage. The body is supposed to recognize that a pregnancy is not a 'foreign body' which needs to be fought, despite the fact that it is partly formed of 'foreign' tissue – your partner's. But the signals don't always work.

Research at St Mary's Hospital, London, is starting to show this problem may be more common than had been thought, in women who have repeated miscarriages. Good results are being had at the six UK centres doing trial treatments (a 70 per cent success rate in women who are found to have this problem). If you qualify, they might help you (see HELPLINES). Blood tests on you and your partner will show if you do have an immunological problem. If you do, treatment is by 'vaccination' with blood cells from your partner.

* Low progesterone levels in early pregnancy (levels of these hormones should always rise during pregnancy) lead to miscarriage. This problem can be tested for, and women with previous miscarriages caused by this have done well when given extra progesterone. Further studies, however, say this treatment may just be having a placebo effect (i.e. the extra attention made things better). Even if that is the case, the important thing is that it helped.

* A misshapen uterus might result in miscarriage, but there are no rules here – perfectly successful births have emerged from some very odd uteri. Surgery can repair many abnormalities.

* There is mixed evidence about the effects of stress on pregnancy, but if you've had a previous miscarriage you are bound to be worried and to need reassurance. Ask for an early ultrasound scan at six to eight weeks. If the foetus is seen to be alive and all right at this stage, there is only a 5 per cent chance of subsequent miscarriage. This is very reassuring. Also, if you had a previous miscarriage, ask for an ultrasound scan a week or so after the point in the pregnancy when it happened last time. Again, seeing that the foetus is alive is very reassuring.

* Some other conditions where there is a risk are dealt with in detail elsewhere in this book. They include: fibroids (which can often be successfully removed, though the chances of subsequent scar damage affecting future pregnancies must be assessed) distorting the shape of the uterus (see FIBROIDS, page 216); an IUD still being in place when you get pregnant (see CONTRACEPTION, page 155); endometriosis 'gumming up' Fallopian tubes (see ENDOMETRIOSIS and INFERTILITY, pages 203 and 250); and ectopic pregnancy (see ECTOPIC PREGNANCY, page 194).

Your next pregnancy: self help
Many of these self help recommendations apply to any pregnancy, whether it follows a miscarriage or not, and the dangers they cover could result in a damaged baby as well as in miscarriage. (The advice about drinking, smoking or cat faeces, for example, is relevant to all pregnancies.) But if you have had one or more miscarriages you will feel particularly keen to minimize the risks of another one, and all these precautions will help reduce those risks.

* Sudden emotional shocks (despite the old wives' tales) hardly ever cause miscarriage – but research does now show that emotional support is a positive factor in pregnancy. A Swedish study (published in the American *Journal of Obstetrics & Gynaecology*) shows that when a research study provided 'optimal psychological support' and a weekly check-up to women who had no identifiable abnormality, their miscarriage rate dropped sharply with no medical treatment at all. Take all the psychological support you can get, including frequent check-ups in early pregnancy with a sympathetic doctor. (If necessary, consult HELPLINES.)

* Quite small amounts of alcohol can increase the likelihood of miscarriage in some women by causing chromosome abnormality in the egg. If you are one of

THE WELL WOMAN'S SELF HELP DIRECTORY

these, the USA Academy of Paediatrics estimates that even 1 to 2 drinks a week can increase your risk. Drinking at the time you conceive or sometime before, can also damage the chromosomes in a ripening egg, says Professor Kaufmann of Edinburgh University's anatomy department. Any damaged chromosomes in the egg mean an abnormal foetus, which will be miscarried. So give up if you can (see HELPLINES).

* Smoking could almost double your risk of miscarriage (and can damage your baby). The ideal is to give up completely, but if you can't – cut down (see HELPLINES).

* Unwanted hormones can damage your pregnancy and cause miscarriage. If you have been on the Pill, use some other form of contraception for six months to clear out any residues, says Foresight (see HELPLINES).

* Cat faeces may contain a harmful organism called toxoplasma gondii which can result in toxoplasmosis. This can damage your baby or cause miscarriage. Wear gloves to clear out the cat's tray, and for gardening too. Wipe down surfaces that cats have been sitting on before preparing or eating food there – better still, do it somewhere cat-proof.

* Raw meat may also contain toxoplasma gondii (see above). Use similar precautions – handle with gloves and wipe down surfaces which might contaminate other food, and cook food (specifically meat) well.

* Food poisoning is also a danger. Salmonella and listeriosis can cause miscarriages. In 1988, there were 291 cases of listeriosis in the UK – 115 of them in pregnant women, of whom 26 lost their babies.

Foods most often implicated are: pâté, soft unpasturized cheeses, ice-cream and instant cook-chill convenience meals (for listeriosis); and chicken and eggs (for salmonella). Careful refrigeration and very thorough cooking are supposed to kill these bacteria, but there is growing evidence that you can't be sure you have done so. (Microwave ovens, in particular, may have 'cold spots' that don't cook thoroughly, and you don't always know about storage conditions in the shop before you bought the food, either.) The safest thing is to avoid all the foods listed.

* A few drugs, prescribed or bought at the chemists can cause miscarriage. If getting any drug, remind your doctor or the pharmacist that you are pregnant. If you are still unsure about its safety, check with the WHRRIC (see HELPLINES), and, if possible, take no drugs without consulting your doctor.

* Complementary therapies are powerful, and some techniques and substances used can increase the likelihood of miscarriage. If you are having any complementary therapy, tell the practitioner you are pregnant and discuss the treatment with your GP or midwife.

* Some viral infections, including flu, herpes and syphilis, might lead to miscarriage. If you suspect any of these, contact your GP immediately. (Syphilis is routinely tested for at ante-natal clinics.)

* Heavy physical effort is associated with miscarriage. Cut down on heavy housework or gardening etc. as much as you can. In particular, avoid lifting heavy weights and standing for long periods.

* Lack of rest might encourage miscarriage ('bed rest' is sometimes recommended for a threatened miscarriage – see above). One of the pieces of advice

given in a successful Swedish project (published in 1984) which helped 86 out of 100 women who'd had previous miscarriages, was to retire to bed at the point in the pregnancy when the previous miscarriage had happened. This might be worth trying unless you know that your miscarriage resulted from an abnormal foetus.

* Miscarriage has also been associated with long hours spent working on VDU computer terminals. The issue is hotly debated – there is no widely accepted proof either way. The official UK line (from the Health & Safety Executive) is that there is no risk.

The VDU Workers Rights Campaign (see HELPLINES) says: 'The link has been established between intensive VDU work and miscarriage. Women who work more than 20 hours a week on VDUs are twice as likely to miscarry, according to a major USA research review in 1989.'

If you can't change job, switch off your VDU whenever possible, and don't sit in front of it when you are not using it (while eating lunch, etc.). Get away from the VDU at least once an hour. Better still, contact your safety rep and/or trade union branch and ask for a change of job within the company, or a special protective screen (this is not the same thing an ordinary anti-glare screen). If you work at home, get your own. Advice: the London Hazards Centre (see HELPLINES)

There is no evidence yet that working with a VDU at the time you conceive is an added hazard – but you may want to play safe.

* There are other work hazards for pregnant women. Various substances are dangerous – for example, solvents, heavy metals, pesticides, various laboratory chemicals (such as the mercury used in dental fillings), plastics ingredients, anaesthetic gases, hormone preparations and radioactive materials. You have the right to ask your employer if you are using anything that could cause miscarriage. Get your safety rep, personnel officer or trade union to help. If you work on a farm avoid lambing (sheep carry listeriosis and chlamydia) and intensive farming pig and chicken houses (which might be low in oxygen). On all this, get more details from the Health & Safety Executive (see HELPLINES).

* Poor nutrition can be a miscarriage risk. A basic, healthy diet is obviously important in pregnancy – ask for advice from your GP, midwife or ante-natal clinic if it is not offered. If you can't afford the recommended diet, get advice on benefits (see HELPLINES). Be aware that it is common for applications for benefits to be refused the first time round, but granted on appeal. So don't lose any time – persist.

Some women have special nutritional needs. Consult Foresight (see HELPLINES) for advice. They can advise you where to get skilled hair mineral analysis to see if you have high levels of any harmful substances (there are 'cowboy' companies which give unreliable results, so don't shop around yourself). Foresight also run clinics which give detailed advice on vitamins and general nutrients. An ordinary multi-vitamin and mineral supplement is all right, but do not experiment with high doses of single nutrients without consulting your GP, midwife, nutritionist or ante-natal clinic.

Complementary therapy

Complementary therapies tailor their treatments very much to the individual: the precise nature of the treatment you receive will vary, depending on your medical history, symptoms, lifestyle, etc. The following information indicates the *sorts* of things a therapist is most likely to do or recommend. Do not be surprised if they feel you need something slightly different. This section is meant purely as an indication of likely treatments; it is not meant as a DIY guide to the medical uses of the different complementary therapies.

Some therapies can be helpful for women who have a history of spontaneous abortion – used either before conception is attempted or during the early months of pregnancy. If you know or suspect you are pregnant, it is extremely important to tell your therapist, even if the consultation is for something quite different.

Some of the substances and techniques used by complementary therapists can induce miscarriage and must be avoided. The physical and emotional effects of miscarriage respond well to complementary therapy.

Clinical nutrition

For women with a history of miscarriage, wheatgerm oil is an anti-miscarriage ingredient, and it improves circulation. Chlorophyll helps stabilize your hormone output. Calcium helps avoid cramping, and raspberry tea relaxes the pelvic muscles. Multi-vitamin and mineral supplements are important to ensure an adequate level of nutrients from the very earliest stages of pregnancy.

WARNING: Most nutritional treatments can be carried on throughout pregnancy. The exception is any treatment which detoxifies the body. While this is usually safe within the first four months of pregnancy, seek your therapist's advice if you are trying to get pregnant, or think you may already be pregnant.

Homoeopathy

If you have a tendency to recurrent miscarriage, there are preventive remedies to match various symptoms: in the third month Apis (dragging pains, loss of bright red blood with clots), in early months Secale (frequent pains, pallor, dark black blood), Cimicifuga (flitting, 'colicky' pains), Sepia (a 'bearing down' sensation, plus constipation).

If a miscarriage threatens, remedies are given according to each case: Secale (cramping pains, possible premature labour), Arnica (possible premature labour associated with trauma), Chamomilla (threat associated with excessive nervous excitement), Viburnum Op. (threat associated with spasmodic colicky pains in lower abdomen and thighs), Cinnamomum (associated with strain or a fall, little pain but considerable bleeding), Belladonna (profuse bleeding, back-ache, head-ache), Sabina (in the twelfth week), Aconite (fever, thirst, restlessness, anxiety, fear). Veratum Alb. is a good general-purpose stabiliser for the pregnant uterus.

Physical and emotional problems following miscarriage also respond to homeopathic treatment; for instance, a retained placenta is treated with Pulsatilla.

Medical herbalism

Preventive treatment to help reduce muscular spasm and to regulate the function of the ovaries are sometimes useful before you try to conceive, if you have a history of miscarriage.

After miscarriage, astringent and anti-spasmodic remedies may be of value, to reduce bleeding and discharge and to lower muscular tension. Hormone balancers and anti-inflammatory agents may also be used.

WARNING: A number of plants carry some risk of inducing miscarriage and should be avoided. Ask your medical herbalist for details.

Miscarriage helplines

AIMS (Association for Improvement in Midwifery Services) 21 Iver Lane, Bucks (0753 652 781).

Association for Spina Bifida and Hydrocaephalus
42 Park Road, Peterborough PE1 2UQ (0733 555988)

CHILD
(081 893 7110)

COTS (Childlessness Overcome Through Surrogacy)
(See INFERTILITY, page 272, for address.)
Offers support throughout the entire pregnancy, and afterwards, giving guidelines on both the emotional and legal aspects of the surrogacy option for women considering it, including those who have experienced repeated miscarriages and are unable to carry a pregnancy to term.

CRUSE
Cruse House, 126 Sheen Road, Richmond, Surrey (081 940 4818)
Counselling service for the bereaved.

The Debendox Action Group
(0332 517896)
For women who were given this drug (relating to morning sickness) during their pregnancies and had subsequent problems.

Foresight
28 The Paddock, Godalming, Surrey (0483 427839)
Provides a wide range of booklets and information of private pre-conception clinics.

Listeria Support Group
2 Wessex Close, Faringdon, Oxon SN7 7YY

Marie Stopes Clinics
In London, Manchester and Leeds. (See GENERAL HELPLINES, page 480, for details)

The Toxoplasmosis Trust
61 to 71 Collier Street, London N1 (071 713 0599)
Advice on avoiding toxoplasmosis (carried in cat faeces) and the treatment of it for both women affected, and the unborn children they are carrying. Support for parents of older children affected by the disease too.

The Miscarriage Association
c/o Clayton Hospital, Northgate, Wakefield (0924 200799)

ISSUE
318 Summer Lane, Birmingham B19 3RL (021 359 4887)

National Childbirth Trust
HQ – Alexandra House, Oldham Terrace, London W3 6NH (081 992 8637)
Publishes leaflets on miscarriage and runs support groups.

PETS (Pre Eclamptic Toxaemia Society)
Ty Iago, Carmel, Caernarvon, Gwynedd (0286 880057)

SANDS (Stillbirth and Neonatal Death Society)
28 Portland Place, London W1 (071 436 5881)
Local groups are often willing to help miscarriage sufferers.

Cervical Stitch Network
Fairfield, Wolverton, Norton Lindsey, Warwickshire.

TAMBA (Twins and Multiple Births Association) TWINLINE
PO Box 30, Little Sutton, South Wirral L66 1TH (051 348 0020)

The London Hazards Centre
(071 837 5605)
Charitable organization with large resource database on all aspects of health and
    safety at work – including protection against any harmful emissions from VDU
    screens.

Specialist products and services
ASH (Action on Smoking and Health)
5–11 Mortimer Street, London W1N 7RH (071 637 9843)
Can help you quit smoking for your pregnancy.

Health and Safety Executive
Baynards House, 1 Chepstow Place, Westbourne Road, W2 (071 229 3456)
Responsible for enforcing law which limits exposure to hazards at work. The
    executive will supply a large number of information leaflets.

Natural Therapeutics
25 New Road, Spalding, Lincs PE11 1DQ
Suppliers of the protective No Rad Shield, for VDU users.

Nature's Best
PO Box 1, Tunbridge Wells, Kent TN2 3EQ (0892 34143)
Mail-order nutritional supplements.

Relaxation for Living
29 Burwood Park Road, Walton-on-Thames, Surrey KT12 5LH

Further reading
Hidden Loss: Miscarriage and Ectopic Pregnancy by Valerie Hey et al. (The Woman's
    Press)
Miscarriage by Wendy Jones (Thorsons)
What Every Woman Needs to Know by Penny Junor (A Birthright book, published by
    Century)
Miscarriage by Margaret Leroy (Optima)
Miscarriage by Anne Oakley, Ann McPherson and Helen Robert (Penguin)
Infertility by R. Winston (Optima)
VDU Terminal Sickness, by Peggy Bentham (Green Print/Merlin).

Osteoporosis

What is it?
Osteoporosis is a condition where the bones become increasingly fragile and prone to fractures because the total amount of bone making up a formerly strong skeleton is decreasing. Someone with really bad osteoporosis can have her ribs cracked by an affectionate bear-hug or a violent sneezing fit. It is a condition that affects one in every four women past their menopause.

Symptoms
Osteoporosis is often called the 'silent killer' because it betrays itself by very few symptoms – until it becomes so far advanced that your bones start cracking and breaking easily. It is possible to have it for 15 to 20 years without noticing anything. However, there are a few signs to watch out for.
* Back pain, which is possibly due to early, tiny fractures in the vertebrae. There may also be joint rather than bone pain, as our ligaments (along with muscle fibre) lose some of their elasticity when the body stops making oestrogen around the time of the menopause.
* Loss of height – any loss, even a quarter or half centimetre, suggests that your backbone may be losing mass thanks to osteoporosis (providing it is not your posture that has changed).
* The beginnings of curvature in your upper back suggest that the problem may be fairly well advanced. This later develops into the 'little old lady with a hump' look, if not checked.

Causes
You lose bone as you get older (both the cortical bone – the outside part of bones that looks hard and solid – and the trabecular bone – the spongy-looking bone on the inside). This is partly because the bone-making cells (osteoblasts) get less efficient, something common to both men and women. For women, it is also because the oestrogen we produced until the menopause protected us against bone loss. After the supply stops, there is a five-year period after the menopause – start counting from one year after your last period – where bone, as one specialist put it, 'can literally melt away, it is lost so rapidly'. Loss after that will continue steadily, but less rapidly.

Who is at risk?
* Thin, lightly boned, small women (especially those under 5ft 2in and weighing less than 7½ stone). This is because women usually form oestrogen in their fat deposits, so those also have a protective effect against bone loss. Thin women have less fat to use as an oestrogen factory.

* Women who started their periods late (15 years old or more) because they will have had fewer years making oestrogen.
* Caucasian women. Black women are seldom affected by osteoporosis. Their bones are strong and dense, as are their teeth.
* Women who have had anorexia (important minerals and vitamins lacking from the diet prohibit normal hormone production and the build-up of healthy bone matter).
* Smokers and alcohol drinkers (oestrogen in the body is depleted).
* Women who have had little calcium in their diets (e.g. those who don't like dairy products, or who had a poor diet when they were young).
* Women who take little exercise, especially weight-bearing exercise (like tennis or walking) which exerts a gravitational stress on bones that actually strengthens them.
* Women whose mothers or grandmothers had osteoporosis. They may have inherited a similar type of skeleton, fat deposit pattern, rate of normal bone replacement and age of menopause. Women who've had their ovaries removed (perhaps for anti cancer treatment).
* Women who start the menopause early. This means the protective effect of oestrogen starts falling away earlier. (And women who smoke can get their menopause up to two and a half to three years earlier than those who don't.)
* Women on certain oestrogen-depleting medications. If you regularly take steroids, for example (for asthma, or any other condition), or if you have been treated with thyroid hormones or had an over-active thyroid gland.
* Women who've never been pregnant, taken the Pill – and regular dieters.

Detection

If you fell into any of the above at-risk categories, you may well benefit from anti-osteoporosis treatment to keep your skeleton strong. Once it has degenerated past a certain point, there is little that can be done.

To tell if you need treatment, you will need to have a scan to see just how strong and dense your bones are. Ask your GP to refer you for one at your menopause, and then maybe another one, two years later to see how much bone you've lost, depending on results from the first scan. If it seems that you have a lost a fair bit and are likely to continue doing so, you will need to consider the available treatments. If you are already taking Hormone Replacement Therapy to alleviate other symptoms of the menopause (see MENOPAUSE) you won't need it. HRT can prevent osteoporosis going any further – and may even replace small amounts of bone, to help restrengthen your skeleton.

Tests for bone loss
1. X-RAY is widely available, but not very sensitive.

2. CAT SCAN (computerized axial tomography) is quite widely available. It can assess how dense and strong the spongy part of the bone is – the part that is most susceptible to treatment, so it is good for catching the beginning of the disease. However, it gives a relatively high dose of radiation and is expensive, so it may be more difficult to get. The scan itself can be a bit intimidating.

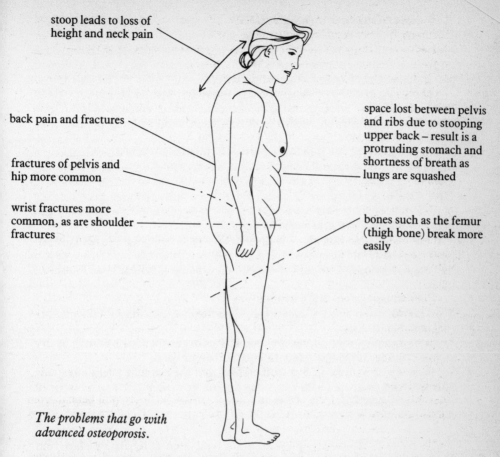

stoop leads to loss of
height and neck pain

back pain and fractures

fractures of pelvis and
hip more common

wrist fractures more
common, as are shoulder
fractures

space lost between pelvis
and ribs due to stooping
upper back – result is a
protruding stomach and
shortness of breath as
lungs are squashed

bones such as the femur
(thigh bone) break more
easily

*The problems that go with
advanced osteoporosis.*

3. SINGLE OR DOUBLE PHOTON ABSORPTIOMETRY detects very early bone loss in your spine (a key place for osteoporosis). It only uses a low dose of radiation but there are few machines available.

4. BIOCHEMICAL TESTS such as analysing urine, for example. If too much calcium is being lost from your skeleton you will be getting rid of it through your urine.

5. DEXA (Dual Energy X-Ray Absorption) is the latest way of scanning bones. It is similar to Photon Absorptiometry, but does not take so long.

If your GP does not know where to send you for one of the more accurate sorts of bone scan, information on local specialist units can be obtained by joining the National Osteoporosis Society (£5 fee only).

The treatments
These treatments can be used singly, and some can be used together.

1. Hormone Replacement Therapy (HRT)

Hormone Replacement Therapy replaces the bone-protecting oestrogen your ovaries were making before your menopause (see MENOPAUSE, page 000). It can be given as a pill, an implant (embedded in the skin and fat of your abdomen) or as a skin patch that looks like a round plaster.

There is an increased risk of cancer of the womb with oestrogen-only HRT (the earliest form it was prescribed in, sometimes called 'unopposed HRT'). So unless you have had your womb removed, you should be given progestogen, (opposed HRT) too.

The progestogen will mimic the part of the menstrual cycle which causes the lining of the womb to be shed each month, so this causes withdrawal bleeding, like the return of light periods. This may be unwelcome so there is a variety of HRT (called Continuous Combined HRT) which does not produce any period-style bleeds. This form is at a fairly early stage of development, and many women get breakthrough bleeding on it.

It has been found that not only does HRT stop bone loss, it can actually put bone mass back into a weakened skeleton. (A Swedish study in 1988 has shown that regular exercise puts back about half the amount HRT can) (see **Exercise**, below).

Other advantages of HRT include:
* extra protection against heart attacks (oestrogen offers this naturally before the menopause, too);
* relief of many other unpleasant side effects of the menopause, such as dry vagina, bladder problems, incontinence and depression.

However, about one in five women find that they cannot tolerate the side effects it can produce (such as tender breasts or nausea), or that because of other health problems (e.g. a family history of breast cancer) it is inadvisable for them to take it.

WHEN TO TAKE IT. Have a good accurate bone scan immediately after your menopause finishes (that is one year after your very last menstrual period). If your bones are found to be weak already it would be sensible to discuss taking HRT then and there to prevent further loss.

HOW LONG TO TAKE IT FOR? Theoretically you could take (HRT) indefinitely, as its bone-protecting effect will cease when you stop using it. But you should take it for at least 5 years, and preferably for 10 years. Discuss this fully with a specialist HRT or menopause clinic, rather than a non-specialist GP. Find one for your GP to refer you to (if they will not you can, often, in practice, 'refer yourself' – see HELPLINES).

If you are on HRT it is vital to have six-monthly check-ups, to make sure your body is still tolerating it well and no problems are developing.

HRT is often used *with* calcium supplements and an exercise regime as well as on its own.

Calcium

Build up your bones as much as you can as they reach 'peak bone mass at around 30 to 35 years'. Denser bones stay fracture-free longer. One good way to guard against getting osteoporosis later in life is to build up your bones and to protect them from calcium loss when you are younger. That means taking extra calcium when you are pregnant (or you'll lose some from your own bones to make your baby's) and when breastfeeding (making milk depletes your reserves). Children and adolescents, whose bones are still growing, need more. Adults should *all* ensure they are getting enough, as should women going through their menopause as well as women who have already done so.

The following table shows the UK government's and the National Osteoporosis Society's recommended daily allowance (RDA) of calcium in milligrammes.

Categories	Age	Allowance
Babies	0 to 1	600
Children	1 to 8	600
Teenagers	9 to 14	700
Older teenagers	15 to 17	500
Adult women	18 to 40	500 (the National Osteoporosis Society says this is too low and suggests 1,000mg)
Adult men	18+	500
Pregnant women		1,200
Breastfeeding women		1,200
Post-menopausal women (not on HRT)		1,500 (recommended by the NOS)
Postmenopausal women (on HRT)		1,000 (recommended by the NOS)

WHERE TO GET IT

* Supplements are available on prescription or over the counter in health food shops and chemists, or in calcium-enriched milks (like Calcia). It is important to remember that taking straight calcium is not good enough. In order for it to be absorbed and used by the body you need vitamin and mineral co-factors as well – sodium, magnesium and Vitamin D. (Good ways of getting Vitamin D are taking cod liver oil and letting sunlight fall on your bare skin.) Otherwise the calcium is likely to go straight through you without being used – or even to deposit itself in the soft tissues of your body, like your kidneys. What is more, according to some of the country's leading osteoporosis clinics, such as the one at Guy's Hospital in London, calcium may be what osteoporotic bones are lacking, but that is because there is no more oestrogen being produced to keep the calcium *in* the bones.

They add that just giving calcium on its own (or even with the right extras like sodium/magnesium) is not good enough if you already have osteoporosis because without oestrogen it is just not going to get put back into your bones. They recommend that it ought to be given along with HRT instead, to help 'fix' the mineral back into a weakening skeleton.

* Food is the best way to get your calcium as all the necessary co-nutrients for

315

proper absorption are already in it. But beware of eating lots of extra full-fat diary products like cheese and full-cream milk or Greek strained yoghurt as this will help pile weight on you – and weight gain is often enough of a problem during and after the menopause anyway. Go for fat-reduced versions: semi-skimmed milk (tastes as nice as full cream, though totally skimmed milk can seem very watery), fat-reduced cheeses, plain low fat or ordinary yoghurts. But if you don't like dairy products, don't worry. There are plenty of other good calcium food sources to choose from as the table below shows.

Source	Quantity	Calcium present
Whole milk	⅓ pint	230mg
Semi-skimmed milk	⅓ pint	240mg
Skimmed milk	⅓ pint	250mg
Yoghurt	5oz/150g	270mg
Cheddar cheese	2oz/60g	440mg
Cottage cheese	4oz/120g	60mg
Diary ice cream	6oz/180g	68mg
Tinned sardines	2oz/60g	220mg
Tinned salmon	2oz/60g	46mg
Prawns	2oz/60g	75mg
White bread or brown bread	2 big slices	60mg
Green leafy vegetables, e.g. cabbage, broccoli	4oz/120g	30 to 80mg
Baked beans	4oz/120g	45mg
Red kidney beans	4oz/120g	140mg
Peanuts	4oz/120g	68mg

(Figures courtesy of Dr Allan St John Dixon and Dr Anthony Woolf, respectively chairman and treasurer of the National Osteoporosis Society, from their book *Avoiding Osteoporosis*, Optima)

PROS

* calcium can build up your bones all through your life so when depletion does start there is more to lose before you have any problems;
* extra calcium can slow down the rate of calcium loss from bones, but only well after the menopause has finished, says the Royal College of Physicians. And it is the five years immediately after your menopause finishes that most damage is done;
* it is easy to take more of and is present in good quantities in the foods that you'd be eating in a healthy diet anyway, so it is not too much trouble to take;
* it is a drug-free treatment, which may be important if you prefer not to take drugs or medicines.

CONS

* there is little evidence that calcium supplements (in food or tablet form) are much help when your bone loss will be at its worst (the five years immediately after your menopause finishes) and the greatest amount of damage is done;
* the Royal College of Physicians' report points out that giving calcium on its own is only half as effective at stopping bone weakening as giving HRT;
* many calcium supplements (especially commercial ones) are calcium only.

You need magnesium, sodium and Vitamin D, too, for them to be used properly by your body.

As a treatment, calcium may be used with HRT, with exercise or with Calcitonin, or alone.

Exercise

Tennis, badminton, brisk walking or playing frisbee and dancing (anything from ballroom to jazz and low-impact, gentle aerobics) are weight-bearing exercises, and are better from a bone-strengthening point of view than swimming, where your weight is supported by water, or cycling.

Several studies have shown the benefits of exercise to osteoporosis sufferers: one by a Swedish team (of Drs Munk Jensen, Nielsen, Erikson and Obel) in 1988, showed that an hour's brisk walk twice a week for eight months actually managed to put back bone into spines affected by osteoporosis, to the tune of 3.5 per cent (half the effect oestrogens can achieve). By then, the women in the study who weren't exercising had lost another 2.7 per cent of bone.

Exercise may be used with HRT, calcium supplements or Calcitonin, as well as being recommended on its own. Why not discuss options with both the National Osteoporosis Society counsellors and your own GP?

Fluoride

This treatment is accepted in France, Italy and Germany, but not yet in the UK because of its side effects, which can include sickness, gut irritation and, for some, an arthritic-type pain. It works by stimulating the osteoclast cells which make bone to increase the density of the hard, solid bone on the outside of the skeleton. It is given in tablet form (available over the counter) and must be used with a gramme (1,000mg) of calcium a day.

There is also a question over the *sort* of new bone fluoride produces. Some experts are still not sure whether it is laid down in a natural pattern or not. There is also a possibility of tiny microfractures of the new bone later on, which may be what causes the arthritis-like pain some women experience on this treatment.

Calcitonin

Studies using Calcitonin are going on worldwide, directed from Fort Washington, USA (home of the head office of the company which makes it). Calcitonin is a hormone that occurs naturally in the body. For treatment purposes it can be given in a synthetic form which is either injected or taken by nasal spray (this way of dosing up is still experimental). It interferes with cells called osteoclasts which reabsorb bone matter from the bones themselves, back into the body.

Usually used to treat osteoporosis rather than to prevent it, Calcitonin can stop further loss but cannot replace lost bone.

Magnesium

Dr Guy Abraham, former professor of obstetrics and gynaecology at Los Angeles School of Medicine suggests that magnesium may be as important as calcium for maintaining bone density in women who have passed their menopause, and in treating osteoporosis. High-magnesium foods include nuts, grains and beans. And there are supplements available in health food shops, but make sure they have calcium and phosphorous included in the tablets.

Anabolic steroids

These are rarely used, because they have a masculizing effect on many (such as deepening the voice and encouraging hair growth in unwelcome places). They build up muscle and bone but are expensive and the effect wears off when you stop taking them.

Diphosphonates (e.g. Etidronate)

These inhibit bone reabsorption, too, but their use is only at the experimental stage. Again, they act on the osteoclast cells which would usually eat up bone.

Boron

This is the latest addition to the nutritional weapons for combatting osteoporosis. It is a natural mineral, found in small quantities in many foods and in the human skeleton. Supplements are available by mail order (see HELPLINES). It is thought to help because it is involved in the metabolism of calcium, magnesium, and phosphorous and early studies suggest small Boron supplements help prevent these vital bone minerals being lost from our bodies during the menopause and afterwards. It is used with calcium treatment.

Self help

There are a lot of things you can do yourself, without drugs or expensive supplements, to protect yourself against osteoporosis.

* Exercise regularly at something you enjoy doing, and that fits in easily with the rest of your life. (Try half an hour's *brisk* walk a day and perhaps link it in with things you have to do anyway, like shopping or travelling to work – why not walk to the next bus or tube stop rather than the nearest one?)

* Keep your weight as near to your 'ideal' level as possible by exercise and sensible eating.

* Avoid excess alcohol.

* Cut down or stop smoking (see HELPLINES).

* Bare skin (adequately screened) to sun – it helps produce Vitamin D in your skin.

* Make sure you've got enough calcium in the food you eat; some experts feel the ideal is the US level of 1,500mg a day after the menopause and 1,000gm before, not the UK RDA of 500mg a day.

* Consider taking a small Boron supplement along with your extra calcium.

* Have a bone scan to find out your bone density status in the first year after your menopause finishes. If you have lost a fair amount of bone already, get another two years later at the same place, so your doctors can compare the two.

If bones are already weak discuss with them bone-preserving tactics such as more exercise and HRT immediately.

* If you are prescribed HRT make sure you are in the best possible hands: there are few expert HRT centres around the country. If you are not sure about the centre treating you, or if you are having problems which they seem unable to resolve, contact a specialist centre for a second opinion (see HELPLINES).

If you are on HRT ensure you have mammograms every two years and check your breasts each month yourself to make doubly sure no early breast lumps develop. While the risk is small, it is better to be on the safe side. (See MENOPAUSE for further information on HRT.)

Complementary therapy

Complementary therapies tailor their treatments very much to the individual: the precise nature of the treatment you receive will vary, depending on your medical history, symptoms, lifestyle, etc. The following information indicates the *sorts* of things a therapist is most likely to do or recommend. Do not be surprised if they feel you need something slightly different. This section is meant purely as an indication of likely treatments; it is not meant as a DIY guide to the medical uses of the different complementary therapies.

Age, general health and diet are all important considerations in osteopathic treatment. Complementary therapists will take these into account and offer advice on exercise, general nutrition and calcium supplements, as well as suggesting specific treatments.

Acupuncture

Acupuncture or acupressure, in conjunction with Chinese herbs, help in many cases to diminish the loss of calcium and increase absorption of essential substances needed to replace healthy bone.

Chiropractic

Soft-tissue work, ultrasound and heat/ice therapy can help alleviate pain by reducing muscle strain and tension due to bone damage.

Homoeopathy

Phosphorus helps prevent the loss of calcium from your bones, and calcium phosphoricum helps disordered calcium metabolism. Several treatments for bone pain might be prescribed, including Hecla lava, Kalium jodatum (for night pain and sciatica) and Asafoetida (stabbing pain).

Medical herbalism

Many herbal remedies contain oestrogen-like substances – for example, hops and sage – and may be of value as part of a treatment programme, to encourage calcium intake by your bones. In dietary terms, magnesium and Vitamins A and D encourage better calcium absorption.

Pain remedies with anti-inflammatory or analgesic properties include willow, devil's claw and wild yam.

Calcium can also be lost gradually if your diet is high in acid-forming foods, e.g. proteins, grains, dairy products and pulses. By nature we're alkaline and in order to alkalinize the tissues again we use up our mineral reserves – including calcium. Correct this by eating lots of leafy green vegetables: supplements of calcium lactate and potassium chelate may help – ask your nutritionist.

Osteoporosis helplines

Age Concern
HQ – Astral House, 128 London Road, London SW16 4EJ (081 679 8000)
Advice and help for all older people, on subjects including any disability due to
  advanced osteoporosis, and exercise for the older person.

Amarant Trust
80 Lambeth Road, London SE1 7PW (071 490 1644)

Anorexia and Bulimia Nervosa Association
Tottenham Woman's and Health Centre, Annexe C, Tottenham Town Hall, London
  N15 4RX (01 895 3936)

British Nutrition Foundation
15 Belgrave Square, London W1 (071 235 4904)
Answers questions for the public on various aspects of nutrition, including the
  calcium question – and eating to beat osteoporosis.

Eating Disorder Association
44 to 48 Magdalen Street, Norwich, Norfolk (0603 621414)
For advice and support for those with eating problems such as anorexia (a
  predisposing factor in osteoporosis).

Food Watch International
4 Butts Pond Industrial Estate, Sturminster Newton, Dorset DT10 1AZ (0258
73356)

Margaret Morris Movement
Suite 3/4, 39 Hope Street, Glasgow G2 6AG
Send SAE.

The National Osteoporosis Society
PO Box 10, Radstock, Bath BA3 3YB (0761 32472)
For a small membership fee of about £5, answers to all queries, including medical
  enquiries (which it sends off to its board of medical consultants for detailed replies),
  information on specialist treatment and scanning centres for osteoporosis, and
  newsletters, are available. Information on the latest treatments, fund-raising events
  and details of information centres and support groups are also provided.

Women's Health Concern
PO Box 1629, London W8 (071 938 3932)
Advises women on how to seek treatment for a whole range of obstetric and
  gynaecological problems – of which osteoporosis is one. Also offers information on
  HRT and the specialist centres at which it is available.

Specialist products and services

Alcohol Concern
305 Gray's Inn Road, London WC1X 8QF (071 833 3471)
For cutting down on drinking – ways to do it, alternative drinks, information on very palatable low- and no-alcohol drinks – contact this service.

Aquacise
82 Cherry Tree Avenue, Clacton on Sea, Essex CO15 1AS
(0255 436 932)
Exercises in water devised by local GPs, physiotherapists and a former swimming instructress. Suitable for women and men of every age – including pregnant women and post-natal or elderly women. Ring for details of thirty venues across the UK.

Nature's Best
PO Box 1, Tunbridge Wells, Kent TQ2 3EQ (0892 34142)
Mail-order nutrition supplements company which makes and supplies Boron supplements. (Boron supplements are also available in selected health food shops, by Solgar and Lifeplan.)

Extend
Penny Copple, 3, The Boulevard, Sherringham, Norfolk NR26 8LJ (Sherringham 822 479)
Send SAE for details of excellent exercise classes for older people, available countrywide.

The National Dairy Council
5–7 John Princes Street, London W1M 0AP (071 499 7822)
Has plenty of material on the calcium content of all kinds of different foods (including those other than dairy products), which will be sent out upon request.

National Society for Non-Smokers (now called QUIT)
(071 487 2858)
Runs courses in conjunction with health education departments countrywide. Five consecutive evening classes, plus two follow-up evenings costs approximately £25.

Further reading
Understanding Osteoporosis: Every Woman's Guide to Preventing Brittle Bones by Wendy Cooper (Arrow)
Avoiding Osteoporosis by Dr Allan Dixon and Dr Anthony Woolf
Calcium: Beat the Osteoporosis Epidemic by Leonard Mervyn (Thorsons)

Pelvic inflammatory disease

What is it?

PID is pelvic inflammatory disease, an umbrella term for infections and inflammations which have penetrated deep into the reproductive system – the ovaries (oovaritis), Fallopian tubes (salpingitis) and/or uterus (endometritis).

Salpingitis is the most common form of PID. Left untreated, it is a serious condition, which can lead to chronic ill-health, and may even be fatal. It can also cause scarring which blocks the Fallopian tubes, leading to infertility and a greater chance of ectopic pregnancy. (Swedish studies suggest that one severe attack results in a one in eight chance of infertility. Two attacks and the odds rise to one in three. Three or more attacks, and three out of four sufferers become infertile.)

PID can be acute (one sharp attack) or chronic (long-lasting). If the root cause is not dealt with – or is treated incorrectly – attacks can come and go for years on end. The infection may become more difficult to treat. Some cases are proving almost impossible to clear up.

Symptoms can be very severe. Sometimes, however, they can be so mild that they are missed, or are just accepted as 'one of those things'.

How common is it?

No one knows how many sufferers there are – but all forms of the disease seems to be on the increase worldwide. For example, PID caused by chlamydia (see below) can pose a special threat to fertility, so women with this form of PID show up in the figures collected by infertility clinics. For instance, one survey of 212 women wanting IVF showed that 176 had had salpingitis. Of those, 100 showed some evidence of past chlamydia infection.

In the UK, salpingitis is estimated to run at about 83,000 cases a year. This may be an underestimate – the figure covers only hospital admissions, and there are no figures for diagnoses by GPs or outpatients' departments. The true figure is probably nearer 100,000.

Causes

According to Dr Caroline Bradbeer of St Thomas's Hospital, London, Swedish and American studies show that even the best doctors misdiagnose PID a surprising 60 per cent of the time, as the causes of pelvic pain are so many and varied. There are a few clearly established facts:

* not all PID is caused by infection;
* no single infection is to blame for all cases of PID which *are* caused by an infection;
* in some women there may also be more than one infection at once;
* the chief infection causing PID may even vary from country to country;

* PID is not always caused by an STD (sexually transmitted disease). (See **How do infections become PID?**, below.)

There are two ways to look for causes: first, which organism (if any) is causing the PID? Second, how did it get the chance to penetrate so far?

Which organism?

GONORRHOEA. This sexually transmitted disease is blamed by Dr Pat Munday, consultant venereologist at London's Praed Street Clinic, for most cases of PID in countries where gonorrhoea is not controlled.

* CHLAMYDIA. In most western countries, studies show that when PID is caused by an infectious disease, two in five cases are down to chlamydia (see SEXUALLY TRANSMITTED DISEASES, page 438). This is bad news – chlamydia is now quite common, and frequently goes untreated because it may show no symptoms unless it has had the chance to develop into full-blown PID. In the USA between three and ten million people a year now get chlamydia (and PID is thought to kill about 900 women a year). It is estimated that by the year 2000, a quarter of North American women will have had it. UK trends in STDs tend to follow American ones.

Actual numbers of women affected by PID, and how they came to develop it, are very difficult to obtain. However, the very latest ones from an overview of PID in the *British Medical Journal* (1990), are that chlamydia infections are behind up to half the cases of PID in Europe, and that the peak time for getting PID is between fifteen and twenty-four (when one in fifty women is thought to have it). In general, about one per cent of women of reproductive age are affected.

* OTHER POSSIBILITIES: (i) various viruses (most of them rare); (ii) the normal, usually harmless 'flora' found in the vagina; (iii) cystitis, caused by the bacteria normally found in faeces (see CYSTITIS, page 000, for advice on keeping these away from your vagina); (iv) infections acquired after a gynaecological operation like a D&C, or abortion, or an event like childbirth or miscarriage.

How do infections become PID?

* Infections can reach the innermost reproductive organs because of almost anything which involves stretching the cervix: childbirth; abortion; or a D&C operation.

* Surgery of any kind on the reproductive system can allow a lurking infection to travel further.

* Other pelvis surgery, like appendicitis, can cause tissue damage which allows infection to get a hold.

* An IUD is considered a prime cause by some experts. Reports at an international Symposium on PID in 1980 showed that IUD users were three to five times more likely to get PID than Pill users, and about four times more likely than users of the sheath or cap.

If a woman has any infection on the cervix (e.g. chlamydia), inserting an IUD can push it inside the uterus; and the dangling IUD thread may also act like a ladder for all kinds of organisms, such as bacteria, to climb (see

CONTRACEPTION, page 155, for news of a threadless IUD now being developed).

The Dalkon shield IUD was withdrawn in 1975 because it caused a lot more PID than other IUDs. In 1987 the Copper 7 IUD was withdrawn for seven months because of doubts on this score, but it has now been cleared. For more information on these, see HELPLINES.

* There is confusion about the possible role of the Pill. Swedish studies show that the Pill helps protect against PID; but American evidence seems to show that Pill users have an increased risk of PID.

Who is at risk?

PID is more common in women who:
* use an IUD;
* have had a previous pelvic infection;
* have undergone surgery or injury in the pelvic area;
* have had an abortion or a miscarriage;
* have acquired an infection following childbirth;
* have had more than one sexual partner;
* have suffered from an STD;
* have a partner who has had an STD (maybe, unknown to them).

The last three points are by no means proved. Drs Warren Newton and Louis G. Keith, in the *Journal of Reproductive Medicine*, say: 'Some good evidence suggests that multiple sexual partners are a significant risk factor for the development of PID.' Toni Belfield of the Family Planning Association says: 'Where a woman is in a mutually faithful sexual relationship, the risk of her suffering PID is very small.' But no authority has said that all cases are caused by an STD; yours could be different, and the result of one of any of the other causes above. Women more at risk of contracting an STD may, therefore, be more at risk of contracting PID (see SEXUALLY TRANSMITTED DISEASES, page 438).

Symptoms

PID may happen as one short attack, which you can't help noticing even if it is mild. It may be mistaken for flu, period pains and so on. If it is not dealt with, PID can turn into a long-term (chronic) condition, with symptoms – sometimes severe – which can happen at any time, with no apparent trigger.

If you have two or more of the symptoms listed below together – get a check-up. It is important.

Acute (sudden) symptoms
1. Fever with a temperature of 38°C (100.4°F) or more, with occasional chills (normal temperature is 36–37°C, 97–98°F).
2. Painful sex (dyspareunia).
3. Vaginal discharge which is different in any way from your usual discharge at the time of the month when it happens.
4. Vaginal bleeding after sex or between periods, or any abnormal vaginal bleeding at all.

5. Severe, low stomach pain in the centre and/or both, or either, sides (this could also indicate chronic PID).
6. Back pain.
7. Attacks of shaking (caused by the fever).

Chronic (ongoing) symptoms
1. Backache.
2. Weight loss.
3. Nausea/diarrhoea.
4. Tiredness or lethargy.
5. Pain on passing urine.
6. Low stomach pain to the centre and/or both, or either, sides.
7. Infertility or reduced fertility.

Getting treatment
Your GP
You may have a GP who is knowledgeable about PID, and you may, in any case, decide it is easiest to start off seeing your GP, or that he knows your medical history and lifestyle well and is a trusted advisor. Your GP will probably prescribe a short course of antibiotics to relieve the symptoms (see **Treatment**, below).

If this doesn't help, it is important that he should refer you to a genito-urinary (GU) physician. Make sure this happens – you can't afford to keep on trying different antibiotics prescribed by a non-expert, hoping for the best.

PID is a specialist subject and GPs aren't specialists. Some women have had problems convincing their GP that they are not neurotic or malingering when they complain of feeling unwell. If that happens to you, simply go to your local GU clinic. You don't need a referral from your GP.
Note: The experts feel that your first visit should be to a Genito-Urinary Clinic.

The special clinic
With any infection that affects your reproductive system, the real experts are in the specialist clinics in hospitals (usually called STD or GU – genito-urinary – clinics). For more details about these clinics see SEXUALLY TRANSMITTED DISEASES, page 438. You can walk straight in without being referred by another doctor. Get the telephone number and address from the phone book or local hospital switchboard.

The specialist will do an internal examination and sometimes a blood test. He will be feeling for swelling and tenderness of the abdominal and pelvic organs. Swabs will also be taken: tiny samples of cell tissue from the vagina, cervix, the inside of the urethra (the tube through which urine leaves the body) and, ideally, the anal canal, to check all possible sites of bacterial infection.

The speed with which test results come back varies from area to area depending on available manpower in the laboratory, and the type of test used. Many GU clinics have lab facilities on the premises. So your waiting time could vary from 30 minutes to two or three weeks.

It only takes 30 minutes to get results from the fluorescent stain used in the

Direct Immunofluoroescence (DIF) method. This shows up chlamydia under a special microscope. An alternative technique called Enzyme Immunoassay (EIA) takes about five hours. Older style – but very accurate – tissue culture techniques need a minimum of two days for analysis.

The treatment

* DRUGS. Your GP or GU clinic will usually prescribe in the first instances up to three weeks' worth of antibiotics: a cocktail of erythromycin or tetracycline (unsuitable for pregnant or breastfeeding women) often with metronidazole (Flagyl). These will combine to kill off all bacteria, and symptoms usually disappear within 48 hours.

Dr Tim Moss at Doncaster Royal Infirmary, who specializes in PID, stresses that the key is to use the *right* antibiotic (penicillin alone, he says, is no good). The drugs mentioned above are more successful than penicillin – so ask what is being used on you. Also, it is vital to treat (appropriately) every infection present. There may be more than one, and some organisms can go piggy-back on other infections to penetrate your system.

* BED REST, until symptoms are completely cleared.
* NO SEX until you are given the all-clear. (Don't be too shy to ask about this.)
* INTRAVENOUS ANTIBIOTICS (injected into the vein) treatment. Some patients with severe PID are hospitalized for one or two days for this treatment. They may be given 'take-away' antibiotics to use should symptoms recur after they have been discharged.

* LAPAROSCOPY. If the PID persists, a gynaecologist should perform a laparoscopy to see what is going on inside you. Under general anaesthetic, a slit about the size of a little finger-nail is made in the abdomen. Then gas is pumped into the abdominal space to separate the organs and give a clear view of them, and a fine, bendy tube with a light and a telescope (the laparoscope) is inserted.

The gynaecologist will be looking for adhesions and any reddening, swelling or discharge from the Fallopian tubes. He may be able to tell if the real culprit is not PID but another cause of pain, such as an ovarian abscess – a painful problem requiring aspiration (sucking out pus, fluid or air via a fine needle).

It may well be a bad idea to go on trying different antibiotics, if the first attempt doesn't clear your symptoms. Dr Munday, at Praed Street Clinic, says: 'There is increasing agreement between surgeons that early laparoscopy is better than continued courses of antibiotic treatment. If you take people with classic PID symptoms and laparoscope them, 80 per cent will have PID. With milder symptoms, only 20 per cent are found to have PID. So you can reassure 80 per cent of these that they are all right – and treat the other 20 per cent properly.'

* YOUR SEXUAL PARTNER should also be treated, to rule out the risk of reinfection when you resume sex. Some people can be carriers of infection without suffering any of the symptoms. Caroline Bradbeer, GU consultant at St Thomas's Hospital, suggests that some cases of recurring PID may be happening because the woman's sexual partner has another sexual partner. He gets treated; his other sexual partner does not. He gets reinfected; you get reinfected. This can be tricky, of course. You may not be keen for your sexual

partner to suspect you could have an STD. You have to trust the 'contact tracer' at the clinic to handle it for you. These people understand the problems very well, and have ways of getting round them. He doesn't have to be told that the story starts with you, for instance. The clinic is not prying – they just want to do everything it takes to cure you: PID is potentially very serious.

The future
Research into the diagnosis and treatment of PID is still going on.

* At the Margaret Pyke Centre (family planning clinic) every woman wanting an IUD fitted is routinely tested for chlamydia beforehand, and counselled according to the results. This would appear to be basic ideal practice for any family planning clinic.

* Better ways to diagnose chlamydia will help many PID cases. John Janes, marketing manager of Oxiod Ltd, a supplier of microbiology products to hospitals and clinics, says that his company is 'not the only one' working on a new dip-stick urine test for chlamydia. This will be like a do-it-yourself pregnancy test – in the presence of chlamydia, the chemicals in the test will change colour. GPs would be able to do the test as a matter of routine.

Self help
Prevention
* Don't ignore unusual abdominal symptoms, especially pain. If the pain level is low, it might still be serious if it is PID.

* Consider your contraception (see CONTRACEPTION, page 155). If you feel you are at risk of PID, your best bet is a 'barrier' method – cap or sheath – now being recommended by experts as protection against all infections, including chlamydia. The new female condom should be equally effective if it comes on the market, and you might like to consider being one of the users in the current trials at the Margaret Pyke Centre (see HELPLINES).

* Don't neglect any possible signs of any infection. Get treatment (see SEXUALLY TRANSMITTED DISEASES, page 438).

* Make sure your partner receives treatment, too.

* Make sure your personal hygiene, is scrupulous – see CYSTITIS, page 182.

* Your contraception: a 1990 study by an Oxford family planning clinic found the Pill/diaphragms/sheath protect against it; IUDs increased risk.

Managing PID
If you've got PID, these suggestions will help reduce your symptoms and fight the infection.

* When you have an attack, get into the habit of noticing anything unusual you have been doing, eating or drinking. Some women find they have individual 'triggers' for PID attacks, which can range from alcohol to sugar, or from stress to lack of sleep.

* Take the full course of any drugs you are prescribed during an attack. If any infection is only half-treated, it can become resistant to the drug, and very hard to treat.

* For the same reason, go back to your doctor or clinic after 48 hours if your symptoms do not seem to be getting better. A different drug, or mix of drugs, may be needed. (Note: Flagyl may take up to 4 or 5 days to work through.)
* If you have recurring attacks of PID, make sure you know what drugs you are being prescribed. If you are offered something which did not work well the last time – say so, and insist on having something else. You should not waste time on possibly ineffective treatment which might give the PID time to get worse.
* Also, be wary that constantly taking antibiotics may make you dependent on them – with flare-ups of PID every time you stop. Shop around for a sympathetic GP who will explore your case thoroughly, try new approaches and be willing to refer you for specialized help. Get advice on this from the PID Support Group (see HELPLINES).
* If you are taking antibiotics, consider the possibility of developing thrush – which may thrive in the vagina when antibiotics are taken. One do-it-yourself safeguard is natural, plain 'live' yoghurt which contains the helpful bacterium called acidophilus (available in some ordinary shops or supermarkets and from most health food shops – check the label to make sure you are not getting a pasteurized, 'dead' yoghurt). It replaces healthy gut bacteria killed by the antibiotics and gets your digestive system and vagina back into balance. It works in two ways: you can eat it, and you can apply it inside the vagina. If you use yoghurt in or around your vagina, apply it on clean skin and make sure the yoghurt is from a clean, newly purchased pot that you're not using for anything else. Otherwise, you could introduce yet more infection. Using anti-thrush pessaries, like Canastan, preventatively, may also be helpful. (see also VAGINAL THRUSH, page 453.)
* An alternative to yoghurt in your vagina is taking acidophilus tablets, from health food stores or by mail order from Nature's Best (see HELPLINES).
* During an attack – rest! This is very important, and can make all the difference between full recovery and grumbling infection, say the WHRRIC (see HELPLINES). Rest helps to keep infection from spreading, and allows inflammation to heal without more trauma being caused by jarring. The rule is: bed rest (complete) until your temperature has been normal for two days. If this works for you, use bed rest every time you have an attack.
* Avoid sex during bouts of PID. If you have a bad attack, it is probably the last thing on your mind anyway, but be cautious with even mild symptoms.
* Apply heat to the abdominal area (it opens up the pelvic veins and relaxes your muscles. Try hot-water bottles or heating pads (you can get them in all shapes and sizes from camping shops and some chemists). Or try sitz baths: you sit almost up to your waist with your legs sticking out over the top – in a bath of hot, soap-free water.
* Look at your diet. The PID Support Group suggests a high protein diet with extra Vitamins E, A and C and a zinc supplement. All these nutrients build up the immune system and also promote tissue healing.
* Cutting out dairy products may help, apart from some 'medicinal' live yoghurt. Doing this tends to reduce the body's production of mucus in general, including the kind produced by inflammations.

* Reduce, or stop, smoking (for the same reason).
* Some women have found acupuncture and homoeopathy particularly useful (see **Complementary therapy**, below).
  If you've got PID, you also need support.
* You need to be at ease with whoever is treating you. Don't let an infection drag on – if PID doesn't clear up from your GP's treatment, move on quickly (no matter how nice he is). If you are not happy with your GU clinic, refer yourself to another – maybe one doing specialist work on PID (see HELPLINES).
* You need to talk to other women who know what you are going through. A local women's group will sympathize. Better still, contact the PID Support Group. They can give treatment tips as well as sympathy (see HELPLINES).
* You may need help with your relationships (see HELPLINES): it can be hard for your partner, friends and employers to understand how wretched it can be to suffer continuing illness, and (maybe) continuing attempts at treatment.

Complementary therapy
Complementary therapies tailor their treatments very much to the individual: the precise nature of the treatment you receive will vary, depending on your medical history, symptoms, lifestyle, etc. The following information indicates the *sorts* of things a therapist is most likely to do or recommend. Do not be surprised if they feel you need something slightly different. This section is meant purely as an indication of likely treatments; it is not meant as a DIY guide to the medical uses of the different complementary therapies.

Acupuncture
Acupuncture can help any inflammatory condition by promoting anti-body production, increasing your body's resistance to inflammatory organisms, increasing the production and effectiveness of white blood cells, and promoting your recovery processes.

Aromatherapy
Twice-daily, massage of your lower abdomen and back, with essential oils of, say, rosewood and palmarosa, helps destroy the infectious agents, strengthen your immune system, and aid your recovery from infection. Other anti-infectious oils can be individually prescribed for you, after culture of the infectious agent and an aromatogram.

Clinical nutrition
Symptoms of PID can indicate a high level of toxins in your body, caused by a sluggish lymphatic system or constipation. These afflictions cause toxins to be reabsorbed into your body. Various detoxification programmes can be devised, including herbals, vegetable juices, enemas, colonic irrigation, or a diet high in leafy green vegetables and fruit.

Homoeopathy
To help reduce penetration of acute inflammation deeper into the pelvis, Mag-sulph is used. Aesculus Hippocastanum is for dragging pain and hip pain when walking, plus white discharge. Sepia is for a 'bearing down' sensation, common in PID.

329

Medical herbalism

Almost a standard treatment for this problem is the herb Echinacea, taken internally, often for months. Echinacea improves the capability of your immune system to clear up the infection. Other remedies, both internal and external, depend on the extent of the problem and the exact symptoms involved.

Pelvic inflammatory disease helplines

British Pregnancy Advisory Service
Austy Manor, Wooton Wawen, Solihull, West Midlands B95 6BX (056 42 3225)
This service offers counselling and assessment for fertility problems, including a total physical assessment for couples. They also offer sterilization reversal operations for women and men, artificial insemination by partner, husband or anonymous donor.

College of Health Healthline Tapes
(081 980 4848)
Confidential telephone information service available from between 6–10 p.m. each evening. Ring and ask for tape numbers 151 (PID) and 113 (Chlamydia).

Copper-7 Association
54 Firgrove Road, Farnham GU9 8LQ

Dalkon Shield Association
24 Patshull Road, London NW5 (071 485 7743)
No longer a pressure group but will still advise you.

Doncaster Royal Infirmary
Armthorpe Road, Doncaster DN2 5LT (0302 66666)
Offers same-day treatment in emergency.

Family Planning Association
25–35 Mortimer Street, London W1N 7RJ (071 636 7866)
Advisory service only. They can put you in touch with family planning clinics and/or well women clinics (staffed by women) nationwide.

Institute of Optimum Nutrition
5 Jerdan Place, London SW6 1BE (071 385 7984)
Can put you in touch with a nutritionist in your area.

Marie Stopes Clinics
In London, Manchester and Leeds. See GENERAL HELPLINES, page 000, for details.

Margaret Pyke Centre
15 Bateman Buildings, Soho Square, London W1 (01 734 9351)

PID Support Network
c/o WHRRIC, 52 Featherstone Street, London EC1Y 8RT (071 251 6850)

PID Support Group
c/o 52–54 Featherstone Street, London EC1Y 8RT (071 251 6850)
Puts sufferers throughout the UK in touch with one another, for mutual support.
  Send large SAE and £2.00 for details.

RELATE (formerly The Marriage Guidance Council)
Herbert Gray College, Little Church Street, Rugby CV21 3AP (07885 73241)

University College Hospital
Department of Genito-Urinary Medicine, Gower Street, London WC1E 6AU
  (071 388 9294)
Offers routine chlamydia screening. Ring between 9–12 p.m. and 1–5 p.m. for an
  appointment. Emergency day service is available.

Specialist products and services
ASH (Action on Smoking and Health)
5–11 Mortimer Street, London W1N 7RH (071 637 9843)

Nature's Best
PO Box 1, Tunbridge Wells, Kent TQ2 3EQ (0892 34143)
Mail-order nutrition supplements company which carries acidophilus tablets.

Further Reading
Hidden Loss: Miscarriage and Ectopic Pregnancy by Valerie Hey, et al. (The Woman's
  Press)
Below the Belt: A Woman's Guide to Urino Genito-Urinary Infections by Denise Winn
  (Optima)

The PID Support Network (see above) also provides a great deal of useful
  literature. Contact their HQ for details.

If your infection has resulted in blocked Fallopian tubes, please see INFERTILITY and
ECTOPIC PREGNANCY HELPLINES.

Period problems

The main problem areas for periods are: painful ones, very heavy ones or no periods at all. Self help can do a lot to help you cope – but remember it is also true that period problems might be symptoms of some underlying medical condition which needs treatment so make sure you get checked out. And, if there is no medical cause to be found, medical treatment may still help with the symptoms.

Medical help
For any kind of period problem, these are your options when you go for help.

* Your GP – if there is a female doctor at your GP practice and you'd rather see a woman, you can, even if you are not registered with her. Ask the receptionist.

* The practice nurse at the GP surgery – you can start by talking to her, and she will know at what stage to bring in a doctor. Again, ask at reception.

* A well woman clinic. Some health authorities run these, and there may even be one at your GP practice. Ask your GP, or GP receptionist, or ring your local Community Health Council (look in the phone book). There are also some well woman clinics run by the Family Planning Association and Marie Stopes (contact HQ in both cases to find if there is one local to you see HELPLINES).

* A family planning clinic. These deal with all kinds of women's health problems, and you can ask to see a woman doctor if you want. FPCs are run by health authorities (track them down in the same way as well woman clinics, and see HELPLINES).

* A specialist menstrual problems clinic. These are rare, but ideal. See HELPLINES for a list of main ones; contact The Premenstrual Society (send SAE), or The National Society for PMS (NAPS), for a full list.

* A hospital gynaecologist. If your GP can't help, he can (and should) refer you for tests to see if there is some underlying medical problem. If he refuses, you have a right to demand a second opinion. Just ask. If you can't face it, change GP (go and register with another one, explaining the problem – all the paperwork about transferring will be done for you – or ring the local Family Practitioner Committee and ask for a transfer).

* Women's help groups, such as the Medical Advisory Service and Women's Health Concern can advise you on how and where to get treatment (see HELPLINES).

* A psychologist, counsellor or psychiatrist. Don't be fobbed off by anyone who says your period problems are 'all in the mind' – physical period symptoms can, however, be caused by stress and emotional problems. If you suspect this is so in your case ask your GP to refer you or consult HELPLINES for ideas.

* A private gynaecologist. If you can afford it (it cost from £35 for a first

332

consultation), you can at least be surer you'll be taken seriously. A local private hospital can give you some names if you don't know of anyone good, or try researching (start with the phone book) until you find a practice that feels right for you. Or ask your friends if they can recommend anyone. If you are stuck, call the Medical Advisory Service or the WHC (see HELPLINES) for advice as to how to find a reputable specialist.

Painful periods (primary dysmenorrhoea)
Symptoms
* Sharp, cramping pains and or a dull dragging ache, in the lower abdomen and/or lower back.
* The pain can also spread to your thighs.
* Sometimes you will have headaches, sweating, diarrhoea and a need to pass water frequently.
* In severe cases you might have fainting and/or vomiting.
Symptoms occur usually a day or so before a period is due and perhaps for the next couple of days. These symptoms:
* start after your first few periods – within the first three years of beginning menstruation.
* usually get less severe during your twenties, and generally go away in your thirties.
* They are often 'cured' by the birth of a first baby.
* Sometimes, the symptoms get worse after the first baby, so don't be satisfied if you are told: 'It will all clear up when you have a baby'.

Causes
Women with dysmenorrhoea get more, and stronger, contractions of the uterus muscles than the normal ones used by the uterus to expel its lining as a period. The contractions themselves are caused by prostaglandins, hormone-like substances which are produced as part of the normal cycle to stimulate the contractions – women with dysmenorrhoea seem to produce more prostaglandin and/or to be more sensitive to it.

Also, during contractions the blood flow to the uterus is reduced, so you get sharp pains (like the pain of angina, which is caused by poor blood flow to the heart).

Occasionally an abortion can lead to period pains, due to hardening of the os (the channel through the cervix which lets the blood flow out during a period) (see ABORTION, page 12).

Medical help
If self help (see below) fails, go and see your doctor. Make sure he examines you before prescribing anything. He should: (i) check whether you've got primary or secondary dysmenorrhoea; (ii) take a full history of your symptoms – when they started, what they are like, what helps – if anything; and (iii) give you a pelvic examination to check for other medical problems (primary dysmenorrhoea itself can't be detected by examination).

Once he has diagnosed the problem, he might prescribe any of the following:

333

* a stronger painkiller, like ibuprofen (this also counteracts prostaglandin);
* drugs to counteract the effect of prostaglandin (mefenamic acid or flufenamic acid);
* synthetic progesterone (usually Duphaston) which changes the general hormone environment;
* the Pill, which alters the endometrium (where prostaglandin is produced) and myometrium – muscle tissue of the uterus – (where the contractions take place);
* a D & C (dilatation and curettage), which is dilation of the cervix and scraping away the top layer of womb lining under general anaesthetic. It is rarely used these days, except perhaps as a last resort when other remedies have failed. It reduces heavy periods for a month or two, but is short term at best.

Self help
* Aspirin (helps with pain and also lowers the prostaglandin levels slightly – though not enough to help in more severe cases).
* Ibuprofen (sold as Nurofen) is a stronger painkiller and also lowers prostaglandin levels.
* Go to bed with a hot-water bottle.
* Exercise, taken regularly in small doses, may help in the long term. Sedentary women are more prone to period pains, so take up a form of exercise you would enjoy regularly, like walking, running or swimming.
* At the time when you are in pain, there are some specific exercises that can help, so try to make yourself have a go – take them slowly and gently:
(i) Lie on your back, leave one leg stretched out and bring the other knee up towards your chin. Grasp it with your arms to ease the strain and stay like that for a few minutes.
(ii) Lie on your back with your legs propped up against the wall so they are higher than your head. Stay there for five to ten minutes.
(iii) Get down on your knees and stretch out your head and arms so that your elbows are on the floor in front of you, your head between your arms.
* If you are constipated, this may make the pain worse. Drink plenty of fluid, eat lots of fibre-rich food (beans, whole grains, high-bran breakfast cereals, fruit and vegetables) and see also CONSTIPATION, page 145.
* Check your diet: (i) A high-protein, low-sugar diet in the week before your period is due can help; (ii) so can avoiding spicy food and salt.
* Calcium tablets, taken in the ten days before your period, are worth trying, too (calcium, with oxygen, is needed by the uterus to make the contractions which aid menstruation).
  To help relieve sharp cramps when they occur:
* try chamomile or mint tea;
* try taking Vitamin E capsules – these, like aspirin, inhibit the action of prostaglandins and will help make the cramps less sharp. They also help increase the blood circulation, and therefore the amount of blood carrying oxygen to the womb (poor blood flow to the womb means sharper pains).

Painful periods (secondary dysmenorrhoea)

Symptoms

These are the same as for primary dysmenorrhoea, but secondary dysmenor-rhoea starts later in life – maybe in your twenties or thirties. Certainly, if pain starts after you have had periods for three years you should treat it as secondary dysmenorrhoea.

Causes

Unusual period pain could be a symptom of many problems, so secondary dysmenorrhoea should always be treated seriously. Most likely causes are:
* endometriosis;
* fibroids;
* infection in the pelvis (PID).

So don't try self help first: make sure, instead, that there is no underlying problem by going to your GP. You should be given an internal examination and a cervical smear test. Other tests and treatment will depend on the likely cause of the problem. If necessary, press to be referred to hospital. (See also ENDOMETRIOSIS, FIBROIDS and PELVIC INFLAMMATORY DISEASE, pages 203, 216 and 332.)

No periods (primary amenorrhoea)

Symptoms

Primary amenorrhoea just means that you never start your periods. It can be very distressing to see all your friends 'start' while nothing happens to you, but medically there is nothing to worry about until you are 18 or so.

Late onset of menstruation tends to run in families. So if your mother started late, the likelihood is that you will be a late starter, too. In which case, there is nothing wrong with you.

Causes

* Low weight – periods usually start when a girl reaches what is known as a critical weight (approximately 48kg), at the time the childhood spurt of growth begins to slow and fat deposits are laid down in 'female' places like breasts and hips. These deposits are one of the body's factories for making oestrogen (involved in the menstrual cycle). Girls who have not reached this weight may not start their periods because they are short of the oestrogen needed to begin their menstrual cycle.
* There are also a few rare inherited conditions which prevent menstruation and these must be diagnosed medically.

Medical help

If you reach the age of 18 and you still have not started your periods, the GP is your first port of call. He will take your history and ask when your female relatives started their periods (so make sure you know), and he will check your weight and height and so on.

If no obvious reason for your lack of periods becomes evident, you should be referred for hospital tests to ensure that there is no genetic basis for it (it is very rare). Most cases can be treated easily by a doctor, by inducing periods/ovulation through drugs, such as Clomid.

No periods (secondary amenorrhoea)

Symptoms

Secondary amenorrhoea is when your periods stop after having previously been normal.

Causes

* The most obvious reason for the cessation of periods is pregnancy. This must be ruled out before any other treatment is considered, because it might endanger the foetus. You may have been scrupulous about contraception, but even the most effective methods have a tiny chance of failure.

* Low weight (weight loss), as with primary amenorrhoea. Anorexic women often cease to menstruate or, if they have not reached their critical weight, never start at all, when they get down to around 48kg and, occasionally, so do super-lean elite athletes or very slim professional dancers. In a case like this, the cure may simply be to put on weight. Also, excess Vitamin A.

* Starting oral contraceptives. Periods may return to normal, in the form of 'withdrawal' bleeds, after four to five months when your hormones have regained balance, or may never reappear while you take the Pill. Stopping the Pill will usually cause the periods to return to normal in a few months – sometimes much sooner.

* A severe shock can stop ovulation (which starts the build-up of the womb lining which will be shed as a period). Continuing stress – has the same effect as a shock.

* Anaemia (your body decides it can't afford to waste blood).

* Thyroid disease, or trouble with other gland systems (e.g. the pituitary), can upset the hormone cycle which controls your periods.

* A fibroid (a growth of excessive, non-cancerous tissue) in your uterus can block the flow of blood. You will have pain, too, so it is a sign that you shouldn't wait to see if the problem solves itself.

* Also factors: polycystic ovaries, endometriosis, too much prolactin and Asherman's Syndrome (where front/back walls of womb are stuck together).

Medical help

Your GP should check for pregnancy. If that isn't the cause, the usual advice is to wait for a few months to see if your periods return of their own accord. If they don't, it is time to start running through the possible medical causes, and to treat them as appropriate.

Don't assume that no periods means that you can't possibly get pregnant. You can. Don't stop using contraception.

Self help

Your priority is to get the medical cause identified and treated. But, depending on the cause, there are things you can do yourself, too.

* If stress is involved, you will need to look at your whole lifestyle and see what is stressing you, perhaps with professional help, and then eliminate as much of it as you can and learn ways of coping with things you can't change, including by relaxation. See HELPLINES.

* If you are anaemic, see the self help ideas listed under **Heavy periods**, below.

* If you are seriously underweight through anorexia, it can be hard to accept that you should do something about it. But please do consider talking to someone who really understands. (See HELPLINES.)

Heavy periods

Women vary considerably in the amount of blood that is lost during a period. 'Light flow' is approximately 2 teaspoonfuls of blood; 'medium flow' can be 4 tablespoons; and 'heavy flow' is up to a half teacupful or so, though it probably looks like more. Heavy for some women may be light for others. In other words, the 'norm' varies from woman to woman – but there probably is a 'norm' for you, as most women tend to lose the same amount each month.

MORI's 1990 poll found that half the women in the UK between sixteen and forty-five had either very heavy or painful periods at some time.

The bottom line is: (i) if your normal periods are heavy enough to interfere with your life, it is worth doing something about them; and (ii) if your periods *suddenly* become heavy you should certainly seek medical advice immediately. There may be something wrong.

Symptoms
Heavy periods are difficult to define on an individual basis (see above). Doctors define 'heavy' as any loss greater than 80ml per month, but not all of the liquid lost is blood, anyway, so this is rather a crude measure.

Causes
1. Heavy bleeding can be caused by various medical conditions (so it is important that a change from light or medium to heavy bleeding is investigated by a doctor):
* fibroids (see FIBROIDS, page 216);
* polyps (non-cancerous growth in the womb, which are harmless but very fragile structures which bleed easily);
* PID and any infection in the reproductive tract (see PELVIC INFLAMMATORY DISEASE and SEXUALLY TRANSMITTED DISEASES, pages 332 and 438);
* various problems with the endometrium (the lining of the uterus), including endometriosis (see ENDOMETRIOSIS, page 203), endometrial hyperplasia (an overgrowth of cells in the endometrium) and endometrial cancer (but rarely cancer of the cervix);
* hypothyroidism (too little thyroid hormone being produced) and various other hormone imbalances;
* disorders of the mechanisms which make blood clot.
2. Two forms of contraception can cause heavy bleeding (see CONTRACEPTION, page 155):
* the IUD;
* injectable contraceptives like Depo-Provera.

3. For over 50 per cent of women with heavy periods, however, no medical cause can be found. For some of these, stress might be the root cause, since it interferes with the production of various hormones linked with menstruation. Heavy periods with no medical cause are a clear message that it is worth taking a look at your whole lifestyle and seeing what you can do to change it. If the problems can't be solved, you may choose to seek treatment for the symptoms.

Medical help

* If you suspect the cause of your bleeding is a new form of contraception you have been put on, go to whoever prescribed it. Don't wait for your next routine appointment.
* Otherwise, go to your GP, who should check to see if there is any treatable medical cause (there may be none). You will be asked for a full medical history and probably have an internal examination and cervical smear. If a cause is found, treatment will obviously vary to suit it.
* If no cause is found, but heavy periods are something new for you, ask to be referred to a gynaecologist, who may be able to pick up something the GP has missed.

If still no cause is found, after having had a second opinion, decide whether you can cope on your own with the problem or whether you want medical help to cope with the symptoms. Possibilities include:

* the contraceptive pill (see CONTRACEPTION, page 155);
* Danazol – a drug with quite a lot of side effects (see chapters on ENDO-METRIOSIS and PRE-MENSTRUAL SYNDROME, pages 203 and 411, for further information;
* drugs which reduce levels of prostaglandin, which is part of the menstrual cycle (e.g. aspirin, mefanamic acid – brand name Ponstan). You take it during your period and it reduces bleeding for about 50 per cent of women;
* drugs which directly act on bleeding mechanisms (e.g. Epsikapron, Cyclo-kapron, Dicynene). You take them during your period, but they may have side effects: headaches, dizziness, nausea, diarrhoea and rashes;
* iron tablets, to make sure the bleeding doesn't make you anaemic. (It is important to take these with Vitamin C, either as orange juice or as a Vitamin C tablet or combined iron and Vitamin C tablet, as the body does not absorb iron very well without it);
* a D & C – which involves scraping out the womb lining under anaesthetic. This makes later periods lighter, but only for a while. It works best for heavy bleeding which is caused by polyps or endometrial hyperplasia, and sometimes for some women where a cause can't be found for the bleeding. However, Professor Stephen Smith, University of Cambridge, suggests that D & Cs do *not* solve heavy periods. He explains that the myth arose because the first period after a D & C is usually lighter, and a woman's post-operative checkup is six weeks later, when she's had one, not two periods. Subsequent post-D & C periods are generally as heavy as ever.
* a hysterectomy – removing the whole uterus. There is also a new method of doing a hysterectomy called Endometrial Resection, which removes the lining only using heat treatment. It can be done on a out-patient basis and it leaves the

rest of the womb intact (see HYSTERECTOMY, page 225). This obviously stops your periods for good, but it does mean you can't have children. Quite a few women who have had their children and are exhausted by heavy bleeding have found it an acceptable option (see HYSTERECTOMY, page 225). Because the operation is 'minimally invasive' recovery is only a matter of a week or so.

Self help
* Use stronger forms of protection – a tampon and a towel, and train yourself to change them both more often. Towels with side 'wings' are useful.
* Make sure your diet in good, and especially rich in iron to replace what is lost. Iron deficiency is common in all women who have periods, so take the risk seriously is you bleed heavily. Good sources of iron are eggs, meat, liver and dark green vegetables. Foods containing Vitamin C (e.g. citrus fruits) should also be eaten at the same meal to help the absorption of the iron.
* Get iron and Vitamin C tablets from the chemist, but don't overdo it – constipation may follow.
* If you suspect you are deficient in iron, get your GP to check with a simple blood test. The usual symptoms are: pallor and fatigue.
* Bioflavonoids have helped a lot of women, says the WHRRIC (see HELP-LINES). These nutrients are found in foods which also have Vitamin C (citrus fruits – especially the pith, strawberries, cherries, green peppers, apricots, tomatoes and broccoli) and can also be bought as supplements – try 250mg per day or more, and persist for at least three menstrual cycles to see if they work for you. There has been no scientific research on humans, but bioflavonoids are thought to help by making tiny blood vessels less fragile. Also ask a nutritionist about a suitable dosage for you. (See HELPLINES.)
* It may also help to take Vitamin A supplements, and make sure that you eat plenty of food that is high in Vitamin A (like liver, margarine, butter – and, best of all, Halibut Liver Oil, which you can get in capsule form from health food shops). No one is quite sure how the Vitamin A/heavy periods connection works, but it has been shown that women's levels of Vitamin A fluctuate with their menstrual cycle, suggesting a stong link between the vitamin's levels and female hormones. A South African study done at Johannesburg General Hospital by Doctors Lithgow and Politzer found that women suffering from heavy periods did indeed have a Vitamin A shortage (but beware of too much).

It is probably best to take Vitamin A with some Vitamin E (which helps improve its storage and utilization) and some zinc (needed to move Vitamin A from the liver, where it is stored). Speak to a nutritionist about the best dosage and the most effective way to take it first (see HELPLINES).

Complementary therapy
Complementary therapies tailor their treatments very much to the individual: the precise nature of the treatment you receive will vary, depending on your medical history, symptoms, lifestyle, etc. The following information indicates the *sorts* of things a therapist is most likely to do or recommend. Do not be surprised if they feel you need something slightly different. This section is meant purely as an indication of likely treatments; it is not meant as a DIY guide to the medical uses of the different complementary therapies.

1. PAINFUL STOMACH CRAMPS

Acupuncture
Acupuncture and/or acupressure can relax the muscles of your stomach and help your body to produce natural analgesics.

Aromatherapy
Gentle massage of your abdomen with anti-spasmodic oils, such as clary sage, cypress, marjoram and lavender, among others, helps to relax the muscles of your uterus.

Clinical nutrition
Both calcium and Vitamin B6 deficiencies can cause cramps, and can be remedied with supplements.

Homoeopathy
The exact nature of your cramps must be discussed with the homoeopath before a remedy can be offered.

Medical herbalism
Your hormone balance should be examined, and corrected if necessary. Remedies such as cramp bark act as a muscle relaxant. For mild cramps, a hot infusion of chamomile or lemon balm, perhaps with a little ginger added, can give relief.

Osteopathy
Abdominal massage of your abdomen, together with work on pressure points, helps muscle relaxation and relieves pain.

2. HEAVY MENSTRUAL FLOW

Acupuncture
Acupuncture or acupressure will promote hormone balance, improve the muscle tone of your uterus, and promote contraction of your blood vessels to reduce bleeding.

Aromatherapy
Gentle abdominal massage with geranium, rose or cypress helps lessen the bleeding.

Clinical nutrition
Thyroid deficiency, which may be the cause, can be improved with the use of kelp or dulce. Hormone imbalances can be rectified with anterior pituitary tissue supplements, and calcium deficiency by calcium tablets.

Homoeopathy
Various remedies are available, depending on your exact symptoms – the presence or absence of clots, for example. For instance, if you lose bright red blood you could be treated with Ipecacuanha if you have nausea; Belladonna, if you have a red complexion. If you have blood clots and cannot tolerate pain, chamomilla might help, but if the pain is severe and you are also irritable and have hot flushes, Lachesis might be better.

Medical herbalism
Treatment depends on the cause of your heavy flow – for instance, fragile capillaries, hormonal imbalance or pelvic congestion. Ladies' mantle has an astringent effect, reducing excessive bleeding. Yarrow improves blood flow and helps regulate menstruation.

3. BAD LOWER BACKACHE
Acupuncture
Acupuncture initiates the relief for all forms of back pain.

Aromatherapy
Lower back massage, or a hot compress with essential oils, individually blended for you, is enormously beneficial.

Chiropractic
Spinal manipulation and work on your soft tissue and muscular trigger points makes a significant difference.

Clinical nutrition
Calcium, magnesium and Vitamin B complex reduce muscle tension, which is a common cause of menstrual backache.

Homoeopathy
Sepia can help with backache, which is accompanied by 'bearing down' feelings.

Medical herbalism
Backache during menstruation is often related to congestive menstrual problems, and remedies like white deadnettle are helpful in this area. Herbalists will offer individual help and treatment.

Osteopathy
Work on spinal tissues and reflex arcs helps to relieve the pain.

4. VERY LONG PERIODS
Acupuncture
Acupuncture can be used to promote hormonal balance and, combined with Chinese herbs, to constrict the blood vessels in your uterus, thus reducing bleeding.

Aromatherapy
Massage with a hormone-like oil – for example, clary sage – may help.

Clinical nutrition
Very long periods may be caused by an overly high oestrogen level or by a Vitamin B12 deficiency. Normal cycles can be restored by treatment.

Medical herbalism
Treatment will be similar to that for the relief of a heavy menstrual flow (see **Heavy menstrual flow** in this section, page 337). The herbalist will also consider the possible effects of heavy bleeding, such as anaemia, suggesting remedies for these side effects as well; for example, nettles.

5. IRREGULAR PERIODS
Acupuncture
Acupuncture can help to adjust your hormonal balance and restore a normal cycle.

Aromatherapy
Oestrogen-like oils, such as clary sage or sage, used under careful supervision, may help regulate your cycle.

Clinical nutrition
Kelp and dulce elevate your thyroid function. *Dong quai* root aids hormone balance.

Homoeopathy
Remedies will take into account other physical conditions and symptoms as well, following careful consultation. For instance, Conium may be used if you also have painful breasts; Pulsatilla if there is also a pale, watery discharge; China if the periods are long and heavy with dark clots.

Medical herbalism
It is important to find out the cause – stress, over-exercise, hormone imbalance – before prescribing. False unicorn root is often helpful as a tonic for ovaries and the uterus, with other remedies as appropriate.

6. BREAST PAIN
Acupuncture
Selected acupuncture points stimulate the production of natural pain-killers in your body.

Aromatherapy
Locally applied cold compresses of lavender oil, together with relaxing baths with essential oils, increase your circulation and relax your tissues, relieving soreness.

Clinical nutrition
Dietary advice, centring on omitting pepper, mustard, vinegar, sugar and caffeine from your diet, gives useful results.

Medical herbalism
Remedies to regulate hormone levels are the most likely approach, as well as stimulants for your lymphatic system, such as marigold or cleavers.

Osteopathy
Osteopathic soft-tissue massage of your breast tissue and supporting tissue can, in some circumstances, be very helpful for swollen pre-menstrual breasts, by encouraging an increased lymph flow.

7. AMENORRHOEA
The first and most important step is to ensure that pregnancy is not the reason why your periods have stopped.

Acupuncture
A hormonal imbalance, for whatever reason, can be restored by acupuncture – with or without Chinese herbal remedies.

Aromatherapy
Once pregnancy has definitely been ruled out, daily massage of your lower abdomen and lower back, with a blend of clary sage and fennel, should continue till the start of a period. The oils help to regulate the general ovarian hormonal balance – but only under the supervision of qualified practitioner.

Clinical nutrition
Amenorrhoea is common in anorexia nervosa, and in women who jog or run long

distances regularly. It is also associated with ceasing to take the Pill, protein deficiency, glandular fever or ME. Glandular tissue concentrates are a fast and effective way of restoring health and normal function to glands which may be out of balance. A therapist's advice is essential – you must not treat yourself.

Homoeopathy
A remedy can be prescribed only after a consultation to find out the cause of the period stoppage. For instance, Ignatia may be suggested for grief, Bryonia for chill or shock, calc-carb or Ferrummet for anaemia.

Medical herbalism
Treatment and advice will depend on the cause of your amenorrhoea, following a full consultation. A tonic for the uterus, such as false unicorn root, encourages re-establishment of your menstrual cycle.

Period problems helplines

There are very few clinics dealing specifically with menstrual problems. If there isn't one in your area, a well woman clinic or your nearest family planning clinic should help. You can find these through your local library or by telephoning the Community Health Council: Association of Community Health Councils, 30 Drayton Park, London N5 1PB (071 609 8405)

British Pregnancy Advisory Service
Austy Manor, Wooton Wawen, Solihull, West Midlands B95 6BX (0564 793 225)
See GENERAL HELPLINES, page 480, for details.

The Brook Advisory Centre
HQ – 153A East Street, London SE17 (071 708 1234)
See GENERAL HELPLINES, page 480, for details.

Eating Disorders Association
Sackville Place, 44 to 48 Magdalen Street, Norwich (0603 62414)
For all sufferers of anorexia and other eating disorders – and their families. Send SAE for details.

The Family Planning Association
HQ – 25–35 Mortimer Street, London W1 (071 636 7866)

Marie Stopes Clinics
In London, Manchester and Leeds. (See GENERAL HELPLINES, page 480, for details.

National Association for Pre-Menstrual Syndrome (NAPS)
PO Box 72, Sevenoaks, Kent TN13 3PS (0227 763133)
Strong believers in regular carbohydrate snacks and progesterone therapy; not keen
  on vitamins/minerals. They offer a helpline, support and campaign group.

The Linbrook Clinic, Woking (04384 89211) or 144 Harley Street (Dr Michael
  Collins)

Pre-Menstrual Society (PREMSOC)
PO Box 102, London SE1 7ES
Helps women who suffer from PMS. Aims to promote research and educational
  courses on PMS and to support individuals and organizations. £5 per year
  membership fee.

RELATE (formerly The Marriage Guidance Council)
Herbert Gray College, Little Church Street, Rugby CV21 3AP (07885 73241)

Women's Health Concern
PO Box 1629, London W8 (071 938 3932)
Advice on the telephone by nurse counsellors. Useful leaflets, including one on PMS.
  Please enclose SAE if you write. They can help you find someone locally who can
  treat you.

Women's Health and Reproductive Rights Information Centre
52–54 Featherstone Street, London EC1Y 8RT (071 251 6580)
Telephone advice, or send for their PMS fact sheet and the politics of PMS fact sheet
  (20p each, plus SAE). They also have a good library on women's health.

Women's Nutritional Advisory Service
PO Box 268, Hove, East Sussex (0273 487 366)
Advice and help for women suffering from PMS, using nutrition to combat the
  problem. Can advise on exercises to help relieve painful periods: various
  publications are available, as are diet analysis and counselling by detailed
  questionnaire through the post (full fee £50). They will also question you and advise
  over the telephone, and will put you in touch with a clinical nutritionist (doctor
  specially trained in nutrition). For full, face-to-face consultations and accurate tests
  to check which vitamins and minerals you need, contact the WNAS to arrange an
  appointment.

Specialist products and services
Association of Qualified and Curative Hypnotherapists
See GENERAL HELPLINES, page 480, for details

British Wheel of Yoga
1 Hamilton Place, Boston Road, Sleaford, Lincs NG34 7ES (0529 306851)
Can put you in touch with a professionally qualified teacher in your area. Yoga can be
helpful for stress relief, and the teachers can also show you effective visualization
techniques.

Ecofem
c/o Ganmill Limited, 38–40 Market Street, Bridgewater, Somerset TA6 3EP (0278
423037)
For those concerned about the effects of sanitary products on the environment, there
is a modern, washable towel called Ecofem, designed with advice from the
Women's Environmental Network. It is made of soft, unbleached cotton, and
packs are available in a discreet carrying purse for about £1 each.

Nature's Best
PO Box 1, Tunbridge Wells, Kent TQ2 3EQ (0892 534143)
Mail-order nutrition supplements company which carries evening primrose oil,
among other natural treatments for period problems and PMS.

Relaxation for Living
(0932 836355)

Further reading
Why Suffer? Periods and their Problems by L. Birke and K. Gardener (Virago)
Understanding PMT by Dr Michael Brush (Pan)
Curing PMT the Drug-Free Way by Moira Carpenter (Arrow)
Once a Month by Dr Katharina Dalton (Fontana)
The Premenstrual Syndrome and Progesterone Therapy by Dr Katharina Dalton
(Heinemann)
Evening Primrose Oil by Judy Graham (Thorsons)
Self Help With PMS by M. Harrison (Optima)
Seeing Red: The Politics of PMT by Valerie Hey, et al. (Hutchinson)
Lifting the Curse by Beryl Kingston (Sheldon Press)
The PMT Solution by Dr Ann Nazzaro, et al. (Adamantine Press)
Coping With Periods by Dr Diana Sanders (Chambers)
The Wise Wound by Penelope Shuttle and Peter Redgrove (Fontana)
Beat PMT Through Diet by Alan and Maryon Stewart, et al. (Ebury Press)
Pain-Free Periods by Stella Weller (Thorsons)
Female Cycles by Paula Weideger (The Women's Press)
'Heavy Periods', a leaflet produced by the WHRRIC (see above for address). Send
40p plus SAE. They also produce leaflets entitled 'Not All In The Mind' and
'Women's Health and the Politics of PMS' (40p each).

Post-natal illness (PNI)

What is it?
Depression following childbirth can vary enormously in severity, from 'baby blues' (which last only a few days), to post-natal depression (PND, which can last several months), to the rare, but most severe form, puerperal psychosis (which may require hospital admission).

Between 50 and 80 per cent of women go through the blues after childbirth; 10 to 15 per cent develop post-natal depression; and an unlucky one or two new mothers in every thousand experience puerperal psychosis. The good news is that women nearly always recover completely, and that a mixture of counselling, practical support and drug therapy can alleviate the symptoms while they are doing so.

Post-natal illness of any kind is not some vague psychological sickness which comes seemingly from nowhere. If you get it you are not mentally unbalanced or somehow inadequate. It can, and does, happen to anybody. And as the Association for Post-Natal Illness points out: 'It is a physical illness, not a mental weakness. And like any other illness it has physical, social and psychological causes behind it.'

Symptoms
How do you watch out for it developing within yourself, or perhaps recognize when a friend or relative needs some help? You need to know someone quite well to spot it. Different women show different signs of the three types of post-natal illness – or even none at all, because (consciously or unconsciously) they are trying to keep them hidden, so that they can still be seen to be managing, to be being good mothers, to be competent. No one wants to admit that she cannot handle her new baby or that the child which everyone expects should be making her happy has made her miserable instead.

The consensus of the experts seems to be that PNI is not generally caused by one thing, but more by several contributing factors – some physical, some social. However, most do agree that the two most likely culprits are hormones (as your body tries hard to adjust to the drop in levels of oestrogen, progesterone and other hormones) and plain tiredness and stress, which almost always accompany the birth and first months of caring for a new baby. (See also **Who is at risk**, below.)

Baby blues
Baby blues are characterized by weepiness, irritability, mild depression, nervousness and anxiety, fears about being responsible for the baby and managing at home, and feeling very vulnerable.

They generally occur around the third or fourth day after the baby is born and last from a day or so to a few days.

346

Post-natal depression (PND)

About 750,000 babies are born every year in the UK, which means, if you have post-natal depression, that there are up to 100,000 other women all over the country feeling very much as you do. It is characterized by feeling miserable all the time, feeling that you just cannot cope, feeling guilty or inadequate, a loss of interest in sex, difficulty eating and sleeping, feeling permanently exhausted and worrying excessively and obsessively about your new baby (if it is all right, whether you are doing things right), or being afraid that you should not really be taking care of it in case you harm it in some way.

Such symptoms tend to steadily get worse rather than better and if you find that at your six-week post-natal check-up you feel less able rather than more able to cope – say so. Ask your GP or health visitor to help you before the situation deteriorates further and causes you any more distress.

Post-natal depression usually starts some time in the first weeks after the baby is born, but may not for up to a year afterwards for some women. Research done by Dr Peter Cooper shows that 27 per cent of new mothers who develop PND will feel it in the first month after the birth; 40 per cent within three months, and 27 per cent in the last six months of the first year.

According to PND expert Dr Kumar, who is a consultant at the Institute of Psychiatry, it usually lasts between three months and a year. Without treatment it can persist for as long as two years in severe cases, and if untreated can even produce what seems to be a permanent personality change for some women – 'she just hasn't been the same since the baby was born'.

With prompt treatment you can start to feel better fast – within a few weeks. Recent research (Holden and Cox, University of Keele, 1989) suggests that about 70 per cent of sufferers recover completely in just three months, if they have good support from friends and partners and good counselling from their health visitor or GP.

Puerperal post-natal or post-partum psychosis

Puerperal psychosis is characterized by a psychotic breakdown, where the new mother's reaction will be one of the three listed below, or a mixture of symptoms:

* manic – she will seem very high, hyper-active and unnaturally euphoric;

* depressive – she may feel terribly unhappy and dejected – even suicidal – all the time, spending much of the day in floods of tears. She may feel fits of panic, and also of inadequacy – fearing that she cannot look after the baby properly. Other signs include exhaustion and insomnia;

* schizophrenia-like – she might start experiencing hallucinations, hearing or seeing things which aren't there at all.

It begins around one month after the birth and usually lasts for one to three months. Recovery is typically complete but the illness can recur, especially after a subsequent birth. If the new mother gets good treatment promptly she can start feeling better within a few weeks.

Who is at risk?

There is quite a bit of argument about some of the factors that may make one person more likely to develop some form of PNI; but generally any of the following may be risk factors:

* Sheer exhaustion: having your sleep patterns disturbed; no longer getting enough sleep; having too much to do during the day.
* Having suffered PMS in the years before the birth of your baby.
* Past sensitivity to other times of hormonal upheaval, such as: a difficult puberty and adolescence; problems adjusting to taking the Pill (and also perhaps, when coming off it, after long-term use).
* A family history of similar hormone-related problems (perhaps a mother who had PNI herself, or a difficult menopause).
* Becoming anxious, depressed or very euphoric during pregnancy.
* A first pregnancy (unfamiliarity can cause nervous tension, and your body's inability to deal with the flux of hormones).
* Being a very young, first-time mother.
* Lots of stress in your life during your pregnancy, such as: a demanding job (if you have got one, don't go back too soon); taking on a lot of new work; moving house or making troublesome alterations to your home in the few months before the birth, or immediately afterwards.
* Too little practical help at home when you bring the new baby back.
* A difficult labour – perhaps a long, tiring and painful one or one that was intensively managed and required a lot of intervention from medical staff.
* A previous history of PNI.
* A very different sort of labour and delivery from the one you had hoped for, that has simply not lived up to your expectations. Perhaps you worked and practised very hard for a natural childbirth, but needed an emergency Caesarean when the time came.
* Being prone to other sorts of depression.
* Relationship problems before the birth, which the stress of a new baby can intensify. Dr Kumar points out: 'The root of the trouble may lie in the relationship which you and your partner have together – but it is the woman who shows the depression after the birth of a baby.'
* Having a difficult baby who cries a lot, has a good deal of colic, is demanding and sleeps little.
* Breastfeeding problems (see BREASTFEEDING DIFFICULTIES, page 52).
* Breastfeeding itself. Dr Beth Alder of Queen Margaret College, Edinburgh and psychiatrist John Cox found that, despite the huge advantages and emotional satisfaction many women got from breastfeeding, mothers who breastfed their babies (with no bottle supplements) for up to 3 months were twice as likely to develop symptoms of PND than mothers who did not. Breastfed babies feed more often, so their mothers lose more sleep and breastfeeding mothers suffer more hormonal disturbance.
* Being without a partner to share the work and responsibility of childcare.
* Isolation – finding yourself at home alone with the baby all the time, with no support from health visitors, local mother and baby groups, friends or family.
* A partner who does not support you, either emotionally or practically.
* Sudden, and unwelcome, change in your life – perhaps from a satisfying full-time career to being at home alone all the time.

Medical help: preventing PNI

Doctors, scientists and psychiatrists are all investigating some possible measures to help prevent PNI developing after childbirth.

Vitamin B6

Dr Diana Riley, consultant psychiatrist at St John's Hospital in Aylesbury, has noted the connection between PMS and PNI (many of the symptoms are similar, PMS often follows PNI, both happen at times of hormonal imbalance, and there is an apparent connection between suffering severe PMS and the likelihood of developing PNI). For mild cases – if you had slight PNI the last time you had a baby, for instance – she suggests 20mg of B6 (available over the counter) a day in the final month before giving birth, and 100mg a day for four weeks after the birth.

Evening primrose oil

Take evening primrose oil for the last month of pregnancy, and for two months afterwards. You can buy it from a chemist. Trials to see how effective this is are currently going on at London's Royal Free Hospital.

Zinc

Professor Bryce-Smith, head of Reading University's organic chemistry department, says: 'The majority of depressed people are zinc deficient.' He feels that new mothers may tend to be short of zinc, and therefore vulnerable to depression, because of the trauma of birth (stress depletes our zinc reserves), plus the loss of the placenta (itself a rich source of zinc) and depleted nutritional reserves after nourishing a foetus in your womb.

One way to find out if you are short of zinc is the Zincatest taste test. If you can taste the liquid in the test it is thought that you are not zinc deficient. If you cannot, there is a good chance that you are, explains Bryce-Smith, who developed the test for Nature's Best (see HELPLINES). Otherwise your GP would refer you to hospital for clinical blood analysis and a sweat analysis if he suspects you were short of zinc. A clinical nutritionist (a doctor with extensive training in nutrition) could do this for you too, though generally on a private, fee-paying basis (see HELPLINES).

If you are low on zinc, consider taking some gentle zinc supplementation for a few months during late pregnancy and for a couple of months following the birth – around 25mg to 40mg a day is often recommended for anyone who is not severely short of this mineral. (White spots on your nails can be an indication of lack of zinc.) If you feel you may need more, ask your community dietitian (via your GP) or consult a nutritionist (see HELPLINES).

Progesterone

Given preventatively via suppository and/or injection, progesterone is a natural hormone, and one which does not interfere with breastfeeding. Progesterone treatment can help redress a hormonal balance which has been thrown badly out of kilter following childbirth.

Dr Katharina Dalton, whose methods have not been proven in strict medical trials, but who has pioneered this treatment for PMS and PNI for many years, made a study in 1985 of 94 women, all of whom had previously experienced post-natal depression that was bad enough for them to seek medical help. She found that treating them with natural progesterone meant that only 10 per cent got the problem again, compared with 'an expected recurrence rate of 68 per cent'.

Contact the National Association for Pre-Menstrual Syndrome (NAPS) (see HELPLINES) for details of other doctors who offer this treatment.

When a pregnant woman or her doctor asks Dr Dalton for preventative PNI measures, the woman is advised to take the progesterone ampoules into hospital with her. Her obstetrician receives a letter asking for his co-operation. The treatment consists of a week's daily injections of progesterone, followed by suppositories twice daily until the woman's periods return.

Dr Dalton explains that during pregnancy the amounts of oestrogen and progesterone – and other hormones – circulating in our bloodstream build up gradually to high levels but they drop suddenly and sharply after birth. It is this sudden drop which can cause women problems and for which the progesterone is prescribed.

Eating the placenta

Some women, who believe strongly that childbirth should be as natural as possible, and that we could learn a good deal from the way animals behave when they give birth, recommend that eating the placenta may help to prevent PNI. It is rich in the hormones which would otherwise be very suddenly depleted, and also in vital minerals such as zinc.

Though there have never been any proper scientific studies to back this recommendation, there is a certain amount of anecdotal evidence from women who have tried it, to suggest this does indeed help. If you want to try it yourself, discuss the idea first with your obstetrician so that the placenta can be kept clean and not disposed of in the usual way. You can either eat raw chunks, a little at a time (keeping the placenta refrigerated), or cook it (perhaps in the same way as you might cook liver, using onion and seasoning, which are said to make it perfectly palatable).

However, medical experts such as Dr Diana Riley and Dr Katharina Dalton feel that the hormones in the placenta, if eaten, could well prove to be little use, as they might be broken down by the digestive system. They also point out that the body would not be able to absorb large quantities of minerals all at once, because it tends to excrete any excess amounts it gets.

Medical help: treating PNI

As puerperal psychosis is far more severe than the blues or post-natal depression, it has different treatments. Care for a woman with puerperal psychosis is usually in hospital. Help for PNI is usually from your GP, health visitor, support groups, friends and family. The blues, on the other hand, doctors regard as very mild. As it gets better on its own in a few days, you don't usually get any treatment for it.

Hormone treatment

'We know in our bones that hormonal imbalance is a major cause of PNI, but it is hard to prove,' says Dr Diana Riley.

'Hormonal imbalance is undoubtedly one of the major factors in PNI – along with others such as social and psychological ones,' explains Dr Kumar. 'But how to treat PNI by altering or trying to redress the balance between powerful hormones such as prolactin, oestrogen and progesterone is so very complex, and so little understood, that for the time being we feel it is safer to treat mothers with counselling and anti-depressants.'

What is more, the connection between PNI and hormonal imbalance following childbirth may not be as clear cut as we think. Dr Beth Alder and Dr John Bancroft of the Medical Research Council, tried a very detailed study, regularly and repeatedly checking the hormonal levels in the bloodstream of 25 women over six months. They were surprised to find that the mood changes the women were going through seemed to bear no resemblance to which hormones were in their blood, and in what amounts.

Hormones can be given orally, or as suppositories, but the latest way of delivering hormones as a treatment for PNI is via a patch (in the same way as HRT can be given – see MENOPAUSE, page 276) on the skin. The patches release oestrogen gradually into the bloodstream while they are worn (either on the buttock or stomach) for up to six months, being changed every three days. This method was pioneered at the Dulwich Hospital in South London, was found to be helpful, and is now becoming more widely available. Ask your GP or health visitor about this.

Anti-depressants

These are used to help lift depression and to calm feelings of distress and anxiety. They are given to PND sufferers to tide them over their period of depression by providing their minds with a 'breathing space' from PND's symptoms. As medication is helping to reduce these it gives the body its chance to help adjust to the new demands being made on it, and for any hormonal balances to settle naturally and in their own time.

Anti-depressants should always be used together with good counselling and support to help tackle the other contributing reasons for the depression, such as extreme tiredness, feeling isolated.

Many anti-depressants have side effects, such as a dry mouth, and sleepiness (though the latter, if you are having trouble sleeping and are feeling 'hyper', might actually be helpful). Different anti-depressants have different side effects. Ask your doctor about the side effects of the drug he has given you, so you can be better equipped to deal with them.

You will not feel better immediately (they usually begin to help after a couple of weeks). If you are feeling no better after six weeks go back to the doctor and say so, asking for another variety. If necessary, take a friend or partner to back you up, or write down the points you want to make. Not all brands are suitable for everyone, and it may be a case of finding the one which suits you best. You can often cease taking them after three months or so.

Make sure, too, that you are on the full dose. Some doctors give half doses to

THE WELL WOMAN'S SELF HELP DIRECTORY

try and minimize the drugs' side effects, but unfortunately, instead of having half the effect, half doses tend to have none at all. It's not wise to breastfeed while on anti-depressants.

Tranquillizers (like Librium or Valium)
Unless you are in hospital with your PNI, a doctor should offer you these only if you have serious insomnia and a lot of anxiety. He may do so on the basis that getting enough sleep can be a huge help in itself. But they are only emergency measures, and should not be taken for longer than four weeks because they are addictive. However, some strong tranquillizers (like Chloropromazine) can be invaluable if a woman has severe psychosis. These can be given under careful supervision, as she is likely to be in hospital.

Counselling
Proper support and back up help enormously. Your GP will be able to put you in touch with a group like MAMA or the Association for Post Natal Illness (see HELPLINES), who can keep in regular sympathetic contact, and sometimes come and visit you.

For women who do need a spell in hospital it is very important that they are not separated from their babies. There are only a few Mother and Baby units in the UK, where mums can keep their babies with them. So even if you don't have a PNI problem, push your local Community Health Council for one in your area, too. (Find them in the phone book under 'C' and write to them.)

ECT (Electro Convulsive Therapy)
Electro Convulsive Therapy has got itself a bad name – in the past it has been misused and overused. But if used properly, and with informed consent from the patient and her family, it can turn around a really serious psychiatric post-natal illness within weeks, says Dr Kumar. It might be used for pueperal psychosis where depression is very severe, but not for PND.

If you are concerned about being given ECT, but your doctors feel that your illness is severe enough to warrant it, ask to speak to other patients who have experienced it for puerperal psychosis. The doctor should be willing and able to put you in touch with them promptly, so that you and your family can ask questions of someone who has had a positive experience of ECT. If you feel ECT treatment is simply not necessary, ask for a second opinion. If you have a problem getting a second opinion, contact the Association for Post-Natal Illness for advice (see HELPLINES).

Where to get help from
Your GP is the best person to help if you get on well with him. Your health visitor (who will keep in close personal contact by regular visits) will also help. If you do not seem to be getting better on the treatment you are given, but your GP seems reluctant to help further, ask to change doctors, or ask for a referral to hospital, where you can get a second opinion. Take a partner or friend to support you while you explain this is necessary – the last thing you may feel like

352

with PNI is asserting yourself and applying pressure. You could also contact the Association for Post Natal Illness (see HELPLINES).

According to Dr Kumar, only two or three per cent of post-natally depressed women get to see a psychiatrist. And Dr Riley points out that 'as psychiatrists are usually dealing with major psychiatric illnesses, post-natal depression (classified as "mild" depression by the medical profession) may seem to them a relatively trivial illness which is going to get better on its own anyway – unlike most of the other patients they are dealing with. So you may get rather short shrift – even though PND can affect a woman's relationships, the rate at which her baby develops mentally, and her entire family. Unless she gets good professional help, it may be a very long time before she recovers.'

Recurring PNI
Estimates vary for the number of cases of recurring post-natal illness. But a study of 413 women by Dr Dalton suggests that:
* mild PND has a nearly 60 per cent chance of coming back after future pregnancies;
* moderate PND has a nearly 80 per cent chance of returning in future pregnancies.

Other estimates are lower, suggesting as little as a 20 per cent chance, but it is generally thought that:
* severe Post-Natal Illness (psychosis), which needs hospital admission, has more than a 20 per cent chance of coming back with future pregnancies.

Self help: avoiding and managing PNI
Reduce stress
According to a major study (in 1988, involving 286 women) by the International Health Foundation in Brussels and the University of Melbourne, staying happy and calm during pregnancy is the most effective way of avoiding PND. Also helpful is anything at all that you can do or arrange before your baby is born to help take the load off you and reduce stress in any area of your life, leaving your energies free to concentrate on the baby so consider the following anti-PNI measures:
* arrange temporary help in the house;
* accept a relative's or neighbour's offer to bring in a cooked meal every day;
* ask your partner to arrange a couple of weeks holiday so that he can help you immediately after the baby is born;
* sort out any relationship problems before the birth;
* track down local mother and baby support groups;
* find out what financial aid you are entitled to and how to obtain it.

All these can help make life less stressful when your energy is in short supply. Plan ahead to make things as easy on yourself as possible, and ensure as much help and support as you can for the weeks after you bring your new baby home from hospital.

Exhaustion
Broken sleep patterns can play hell with your emotional resilience and energy.

According to Dr Jim Horne, director of the sleep research laboratory at Loughborough University, it is a major factor in long-haul jetlag (with its attendant feelings of disorientation, malaise, irritability and tiredness). He reckons it may also be a factor in PNI. It may help to:
* arrange with another mum to take each other's babies regularly for a couple of hours, so each of you can sleep;
* arrange with your partner, before the birth, exactly what he will do each day to help you with the baby or the housework;
* join a local mother and baby group, even temporarily, so that you don't ever feel that everyone else is somehow managing better than you;
* arrange temporary cleaning help, if only once a week (ask the social services; or pay for the odd few hours, at least for major things like cleaning floors and cookers) until you get your energy back. Let your household know it cannot expect a clean and tidy house for a bit.

Going back to work
Try not to put yourself under extra pressure by agreeing (in a fit of enthusiasm, loyalty or guilt) to go back to work as soon as humanly possible – unless that is what you really want and can manage. It may take longer to adjust and recover than you think – so give yourself the longest 'time out' possible. (You can always score brownie points with your boss by going back earlier than you'd arranged, if you feel up to it.) For help and advice contact the Working Mothers Association (see HELPLINES).

Your labour
A distressing or disappointing labour can sometimes prey on your mind for many weeks or even months afterwards, particularly if you had an especially difficult birth, if your wishes for minimal intervention were – or had to be – disregarded or if you needed an emergency Caesarean or a forceps delivery after planning and practising hard for a natural childbirth.
* Discuss the way you feel with the teacher who took your ante-natal classes.
* See the consultant or senior registrar at the hospital to find out why certain things were done or not done during your labour. It might be helpful to register your feelings officially with the person responsible – and to try and get an explanation (there may have been very good reasons you were not told of).
* Discuss the way you feel at the six-week post-natal check-up. If no one seems to be taking any notice, send a letter to the consultant who was in charge.
* If a Caesarean experience is upsetting you, the Caesarean Support Group may be able to help (see HELPLINES).

Your relationship
If there has been a problem of any sort brewing for some time – perhaps you don't feel your partner is pulling his weight in the house or is supportive enough, or perhaps a sexual problem is bothering you – try to do something about it in the months before you have your baby. Afterwards, for a while, you will both have far less energy for solving difficulties. Depending on what is wrong, talking it over fully together, seeking counselling or even reading

helpful literature, are all options to help prevent trouble developing (see HELPLINES).

Alone at home
Local support groups can be useful for mothers feeling isolated. Ideas include: Meet A Mum (MAMA) and NCT groups (see HELPLINES) or mother and baby groups (advertised in your GP's surgery or local library perhaps). Or try asking if anyone in your ante-natal class lives near you and would like to take occasional turns with you at sharing childcare, to give you each the odd break (for catching up on sleep, or just having time to yourself).

Breastfeeding problems
See BREASTFEEDING DIFFICULTIES, or HELPLINES, for the many organizations who can give practical help and encouragement. A number have counsellors who will come to your home. Ask your health visitor or local hospital whether it has an infant feeding advisor, or someone similar, who might help.

Sexual problems
A slowly-healing or badly-stitched episiotomy, or other vaginal or labial tears, can cause pain on intercourse and put a woman right off sex until it is better. In addition, as Dr Beth Alder of Queen Margaret College in Edinburgh points out, most women are less sexually active towards the end of their pregnancies and it may take a year to get back to their previous level. Additional vaginal dryness because of breastfeeding, or a readjusting oestrogen balance, might mean that sex can be a problem for a while. Discuss any problems fully with your doctor – and your partner – so that you get the support you need, and any treatment that may help. (See also BREASTFEEDING DIFFICULTIES, page 52, POST-PREGNANCY PROBLEMS, page 393 and HELPLINES.)

Checklist
Keep an eye out for any danger signs of PND developing. If you continue to feel less able rather than more able to cope, seek help from your GP or health visitor, or one of the support associations (see HELPLINES) before the problem can become established. Do not wait for it to clear up on its own.

THINGS TO TRY AND AVOID:
* moving house or making last-minute major alterations to create more room for the baby;
* being inflexible about the sort of birth you want;
* being Superwoman and doing everything.
* trying to deal single-handed with 'babyshock'. (How am I going to look after it? How can I cope with this major responsibility? Who am I now?) Contact a support group; this is just what they are there to help with.

Complementary therapy

Complementary therapies tailor their treatments very much to the individual: the precise nature of the treatment you receive will vary, depending on your medical history, symptoms, lifestyle, etc. The following information indicates the *sorts* of things a therapist is most likely to do or recommend. Do not be surprised if they feel you need something slightly different. This section is meant purely as an indication of likely treatments; it is not meant as a DIY guide to the medical uses of the different complementary therapies.

Acupuncture

Acupuncture or acupressure can be used both to produce and release anti-depressive substances from your body and to promote hormonal balance if the depression is due, as it often is, to hormonal disturbance.

Aromatherapy

To help alleviate fatigue and the stress of adjustment to coping with a new baby, the therapist uses blends of essential oils selected specially for you. Such oils, which can be used in whole-body massage, in the bath, or in room vaporizers, include clary sage, bergamot, sandalwood and jasmin, amongst many others.

The oils do not make you drowsy or confused, not do they interfere with your milk production or affect the baby.

Clinical nutrition

Because you have had to supply vitamins and minerals to the foetus, you may become deficient in Vitamin C, B-complex vitamins, calcium, iron, magnesium, or potassium. Replacement therapy is valuable if this is the case, but careful consultation with a nutritionist is necessary first.

Supplements of phenylalanine, tryptophan and tyrosine, all amino acids, help to ease depression.

Homoeopathy

Homoeopathy is very much concerned with the mind and emotions – and the relationship these have with physical symptoms. Help for PNI would involve a detailed consultation to build up a total picture of your individual problems. For some examples of how these might work, see ABORTION.

Medical herbalism

Advice on diet, exercise and rest, combined with counselling, are important aspects of general treatment for post-natal illness. To restore your hormonal balance, chaste tree is very effective, encouraging *corpus luteum* function and progesterone secretion. Nerve restoratives, such as St John's wort and wild oats, help reduce the effects of stress and improve your ability to cope with it.

Post-natal illness helplines

The Association of Breastfeeding Mothers
131 Mayow Road, Syndenham, London SE26 (081 659 5151)
A counselling service for mothers, with local support groups. Membership is £4 per
   year.

The Association for Post Natal Illness
25 Jerdan Place, London SW6 (071 386 0868)
Holds a register of women who have had and recovered from PNI of all types, and
   who can stay in telephone contact with mothers who are currently depressed. Some
   may even be able to visit your home. The association also answers letters on getting
   treatment, backed up by an eminent board of obstetricians and psychiatrists – and
   there is a selection of helpful literature that can be sent to sufferers. As well as
   providing non-professional support, the association can advise how and where to
   get good counselling and medical treatment.

The British Association of Counselling
(0788 578 328)
Has a directory of therapists and helpful organizations who counsel couples
   countrywide. They will supply details of the counsellor nearest you.

British Nutritional Medicine Society
Dr Alan Stewart, Bio Lab, 9 Weymouth Street, London W1
Professional association for doctors. Can put your GP in touch with a clinical
   nutritionist.

Caesarean Support Network
2 Hurst Park Drive, Huyton, Liverpool L36 1TF (051 480 1184)
Support from a contacts network.

The Catholic Marriage Advisory Council
Clitherow House, Blythe Mews, Blythe Street, London W14 (071 371 1341)
It is not necessary to be a Roman Catholic (or married) to be counselled.

Cry-sis
BM Crysis, London WC1N 3XX (071 404 5011)
Has volunteers offering support and advice to mothers whose babies cry excessively
   or won't sleep. Call between 9.30 a.m. and 5.30 p.m. only.

Dr Katharina Dalton
100 Harley Street, London W1 (071 935 2146)
Dr Dalton, who pioneers preventative treatment using natural progesterone, can be
   contacted for information at her surgery. (Your GP should also be able to help.)

The Institute of Marital Studies
The Tavistock Institute, Tavistock Centre, 120 Belsize Lane, London NW3
   5BA (071 435 7111)

Institute of Optimum Nutrition
5 Jerdan Place, London SW6 (071 385 7984)

The Jewish Marriage Council
23 Ravenshurst Avenue, London NW4 4EE (081 203 6311)

La Leche League of Great Britain
B 3434, London WC1 (071 242 1278)
Breastfeeding advice and help.

MAMA (Meet-A-Mum Association)
26A Cumnor Hill, Oxford OX2 9HA
Runs self-help groups for mothers, with the emphasis on tackling the isolation they
   may feel – which often results (or be part of) PNI. They are casual, informal
   meetings in members' houses.

Marce Society
c/o Dr Beth Alder, Queen Margaret College, 36 Clerwood Terrace, Edinburgh
Contact Dr Alder for further details of PNI.

Maternity Link
The Old Co-op, 42 Chelsea Road, Easton, Bristol BW5 6AF (0272 541487)
Offers support, interpreting – and if required, English tuition to ante-natal and
   post-natal women who do not speak English.

The Maternity Services Liaison Scheme
Brady Centre, 192 Hanbury Street, London E1 5HU (071 377 1064)
A network of community health workers who will accompany women of ethnic
   minorities to ante-natal clinics and hospital, to give birth. Offers ante-natal and
   post-natal care via parent education classes in hospitals and health centres.

National Childbirth Trust
HQ – Alexandra House, Oldham Terrace, London W3 6NH (081 992 8637)
Offers support for new mothers in the form of local branches and group meetings,
   coffee mornings, tea-time meetings, etc. Both mothers and babies are very
   welcome. They can also offer advice, information and practical help from
   counsellors.

National Children's Home Careline
(071 226 2033) (HQ)
Telephone for your local branch number. This careline is for all parents experiencing
   family problems – including problems with babies.

NSPCC
Look in the Yellow Pages, or phone directory enquiries for your local branch)
All branches have a 24-hour helpline service, run in the strictest confidence, for
   anyone who is under such physical or mental stress that they fear they are in danger

of harming or neglecting their child/baby – or are already doing so. The NSPCC prefers whenever possible to keep families together and to leave children with the parents.

Parentline
Raysa Ho, 57 Hast Road, Sundersley, Essex SS7 3PD (0268 757077)
Ring and you will be put through to a 24-hour answering service, which can give you a local volunteer's telephone number. Parentline is a network of organizations giving advice and counselling to parents trying to manage the stresses of bringing up children. Most groups are run by parents for parents.

Parents Anonymous Lifeline
6–9 Manor Gardens, London N7 (071 263 8918)
Offers a confidential service run by volunteers for parents who are having problems with children or babies of any age.

RELATE (formerly The Marriage Guidance Council)
Herbert Gray College, Little Church Street, Rugby CV21 3AP (0788 78341)
Can put you in touch with your nearest branch.

Specialist products and services
Aquacise
82 Cherry Tree Avenue, Clacton on Sea, Essex CO15 1AS (0255 436932)
Exercise in water classes for men and women of every age.

The British Nutrition Foundation
52 to 54 High Holborn, London WC1 (071 404 6504)
This service can put you in touch with a nearby, professionally trained nutritionist.

Nature's Best
PO Box 1, Tunbridge Wells, Kent TN2 3EQ (0892 534143)
Mail-order service for nutritional supplements. Zincatest is available from Nature's Best. They can also refer you to the nearest retail outlet.

Working Mothers Association
77 Holloway Road, London N7 8JZ (071 700 5771)
Gives practical advice on coping with returning to work.

Please see POST-PREGNANCY PROBLEMS and BREASTFEEDING DIFFICULTIES HELPLINES.

Further reading
Towards Happy Motherhood by Maggie Comport (Corgi)
Surviving Motherhood: How to Cope with Post-Natal Depression by Maggie Comport (Ashgrove Press)
Depression After Childbirth by Dr Katharina Dalton (Oxford University Press)
The New Mother Syndrome by Carol Dix (Allen and Unwin)
Breastfeeding Your Baby, by Sheila Kitzinger (Dorling Kindersley)
Your Body, Your Baby, Your Life by Angela Phillips, with Nicky Leap and Barbara Jacobs (Pandora)
Caesareans by E. Phillips (Sidgwick & Jackson)

Pregnancy problems

Some women sail through pregnancy, never having felt better in their lives. Some have a few discomforts, but nothing lasting. Others are unlucky enough to be plagued with one thing after another for the entire nine months. No two pregnancies are exactly alike. They differ as much as the women who are experiencing them differ from each other.

However, the common problems you may temporarily develop will generally not be treated medically by your doctor, unless they become very troublesome, as they are caused by the very things which are helping you to maintain a successful pregnancy:

1. A huge rise in the amount of oestrogen and progesterone in your body. This is responsible, amongst other things, for water retention, morning sickness, and the relaxation of muscle tissue and ligaments, which can result in all sorts of problems – from varicose veins and heartburn to back trouble.

2. Up to double the usual amount of blood and fluid in your body. This produces fluid retention, the possibility of varicose veins, a need to pass water frequently, night sweats, and finding that you seem to get hotter than other people – especially in summer.

3. The increasing weight of your growing baby and the enlarging size of your womb. These contribute to incontinence (a need to pass water frequently and passing water when you do not want to), breathlessness (as your womb grows and takes up space under your diaphragm, squashing your lungs) and to a type of pain called round ligament pain.

The problems list is long, but the symptoms may be very mild. And out of the apparently huge litany of possible discomforts, you personally may only experience one or two – or none at all.

These so-called 'minor' pregnancy problems are seen as such because they are not threatening the health of your growing baby. But they may well be making *your* life a misery. So the good news is that there is always something you can do yourself to alleviate the discomfort they are producing.

Being told 'it is normal and it will pass' when you have chronic morning sickness is cold comfort at the time. And seeing varicose veins as an 'inevitable' side effect of pregnancy, or being informed that a certain amount of incontinence (both before and after giving birth) as in some way a woman's lot, is neither sympathetic nor true.

Prevention of problems

The more serious maternal potential problems of pregnancy, like gestational diabetes or Pre-Eclampsia, can be prevented by keeping a regular check on: a) your weight; b) your blood sugar levels; and c) whether there is protein present in your urine or not. So go to *all* your ante-natal appointments, and make sure you never miss one, where the medical staff at your clinic, GP surgery or hospital will check up on all these points – and more – for you.

You will be asked to go for a clinic visit once a month from when you are three months pregnant until your seventh month. After that your visits will usually be every two weeks (depending on the health district you are in) and in your final month you will go each week.

Ante-natal visits include routine checks on:

* your urine (from a sample you take with you) to see if there is any protein present in it – which could indicate the beginnings of pre-eclampsia – and also to check it for too much sugar – which could indicate diabetes;

* your weight, because excess weight gain can cause many problems in pregnancy (including varicose veins, additional strain on the heart and extra stress on the pelvic floor);

* the size of your womb, to ensure the baby is growing at roughly the rate it should;

* your blood (you will have a test two or three times during your pregnancy) to make sure you are not becoming anaemic (and to establish your blood group and test for syphilis and rubella immunity).

There are other advantages for expectant mothers as far as the health service goes: you are entitled to free prescriptions and, very importantly, dental care, while you are pregnant and for up to a year afterwards. You can get the relevant form from your doctor.

For full details of what you are entitled to and how to get it, send a sae to the Maternity Alliance (see HELPLINES) with a covering note for a leaflet called 'Money for Mothers and Babies'.

There follows a summary of the more common pregnancy problems. Most of them would be seen as minor by many doctors. But they include the potentially far more serious pre-eclamptic toxaemia, which ante-natal staff check for at every clinic visit, and gestational diabetes, which can affect up to one in 20 women, too. Details of the problem, what causes it, what you can do to make it less troublesome or to avoid it altogether and, where appropriate, what your doctor may do, are all set out in chart form to make the information as quick and easy to scan as possible.

NOTE. If you feel your male doctor, your partner, or childless workmates of either sex are distinctly lacking in sympathy for the discomfort you may be feeling and seem surprised that you cannot sit down for too long in one position without getting backache or are totally out of breath after climbing a flight or two of stairs, consider the Empathy Belly!

You fill it with water (full up it weighs 35lbs – 2½ stone – which one can easily put on during pregnancy). Strapped round a sceptical person's stomach, it will produce an instant bulging abdomen, bring on backache, shortness of breath and potentially uncomfortable changes in posture. Then all they have to do is imagine the morning sickness, heartburn, varicose veins . . . (Empathy Bellies are available from Birthways – see HELPLINES.)

Pregnancy problems and what to do about them

Problem, symptoms and causes	Medical help	Self help
ANAEMIA – see POST PREGNANCY PROBLEMS, page 393.		
BACKACHE. The baby may be lying with its head pressing on your sacrum (the base of the back). Also there are posture changes to accommodate the extra weight of the baby. Ligaments grow more flexible and softer, which means the bones of the back and pelvis can slip out of alignment more easily.	You may be recommended to see an osteopath, physiotherapist or chiropractor.	* Don't put on too much weight. * Pay attention to posture. * Wear sensible footwear (no high heels that push posture out further). * Swim regularly to strengthen back. * Sleep on a firm mattress, or put a board under your part of it. * Take care with lifting and bending (ask a physiotherapist for the best way). * Balance shopping bags, and avoid carrying toddlers or babies on your hip too much. * Put a small cushion in the small of your back while sitting and/or driving. (Maternity pantie girdles may give extra support too.) * Sit with a large Yellow Pages Directory (or thick books) under your feet, or under the front two legs of your chair (tipping it back slightly) if working at a desk. * Try the frog stretch or lying on your back, legs over a chair (as diagrams show), to relieve an aching back.
BLEEDING DURING PREGNANCY. 1. Continuing your periods while pregnant may happen for several reasons, most of which pose no threat to the pregnancy. Occasionally the amount of progesterone the body produces is enough to maintain a healthy pregnancy but *not* enough to completely suppress menstrual	Any medical help will depend on the reason for the bleeding. As well as the reasons opposite, this could include: a bit of the placenta coming away from the wall; a vaginal or cervical infection like thrush; something knocking against the 'ripe cervix' (i.e. the penis, during intercourse); ectopic pregnancy; hydatidiform mole pregnancy; the loss of one embryo early from a twin pregnancy; and, miscarriage.	* Report any bleeding to your doctor or midwife immediately. * Rest up completely in bed. * If blood is red, less than for a normal period, no clots and no pain, it is usually OK. Bleeding will stop – if it's going to – within 24 hours. * If bleeding continues, becomes heavier, or if you have back/abdominal pain, it could mean a problem. Call your doctor or midwife straight

bleeding. A woman may have lighter, shorter periods, though pregnant, for the first few months. (It is very unusual, but not unknown, for this to continue all through pregnancy.) This does not seem to harm the foetus at all.

2. Intermittent or sudden bleeding. If early in pregnancy, this may indicate that a small piece of the chorionic villus membrane surrounding the early developing foetus (later to become the placenta) has broken off; such bleeding is probably quite harmless. However, doctors usually treat any bleeding in pregnancy with caution lest it herald a possible miscarriage (see MISCARRIAGE, page 297).

BLEEDING GUMS. Hormonal changes, such as extra oestrogen, cause thickening and softening of the gums so they bleed more easily, and food can collect in the soft margins where bacteria rots them. This may lead to gum disease (a symptom of which is bleeding) – see below.

Have regular dental check-ups – which are free while you are pregnant.

Always book the first dental appointment of the day, so the air contains no toxic mercury vapour from previous filling drillings. Cover your nose and eyes and ask for a mouth suction tube to clear debris. The foetus is vulnerable to damage (of the brain and eyes) through toxic mercury vapour released when old amalgam fillings are drilled out. Note that female dentists have rates of infertility, stillbirth and miscarriage three and a half times the national average.)

* Use a softer toothbrush, but brush after each meal for at least 2 minutes (try an electric toothbrush unit).
* Use an anti-plaque mouthwash like Plax (from Boots) or rinse out after cleaning with warm salt water.
* Floss regularly.
* Go to the dentist for regular dental hygiene check ups (free in pregnancy).

BREATHLESSNESS. As the uterus grows, it takes up more room and pushes the other organs in your abdomen up against your diaphragm, leaving less room for your lungs to expand.

Nil

* Take slow deep breaths.
* Sit up as straight as possible (slumping will restrict the lungs even more).
* Prop up your head and shoulders with plenty of pillows in bed.
* Kneeling on all fours, belly hanging downwards, also helps relieve the pressure.

Problem, symptoms and causes	Medical help	Self help
CONSTIPATION. Extra progesterone relaxes all the muscles and ligaments in the body to help prepare it for labour – including the ones in the bowels. This means slower bowel movements; waste may become hard-packed and more uncomfortable to pass. Also, the expanding womb squashes your intestines, which slows the passage of food through your bowel.	Your doctor may suggest laxatives, which stimulate nerves to relax the bowel. But overuse may mean your own nervous signals stop working so well, which means you need ever higher doses.	★ Eat plenty of dietary fibre: fruit, raw vegetables, bran cereals, wholemeal bread and pasta, even add extra bran in small amounts to cereal. Fibre absorbs water and bulks out stools (it is not digested itself), to make them bulkier and softer. ★ A small bowlful of prunes every morning is a good natural laxative too. ★ Iron is 'binding' (if you are taking it as a supplement, but a bit less so if taken from natural sources like foods). ★ Avoid 'binding' foods (like eggs) in large quantities. (See CONSTIPATION, page 145)
CRAMPS. Pain in your feet, calves and thighs, often at night, is partly due to poorer circulation (veins and capillaries relax under the influence of extra progesterone, like the rest of the body's muscular tissue, and also have much more blood and fluid to pump round the body, so the circulation system is not so efficient). Cramps may also be partly due to calcium deficiency (the baby is taking much of yours for bone building – you need more in your own diet).	Your doctor may try calcium gluconate tablets.	★ Massage the affected area. ★ Try foot flexing, (legs straight out in front, pull toes gently back towards you). ★ Get plenty of calcium in your diet (see the calcium chart in OSTEOPOROSIS, page 315, for the best sources. Consider calcium supplements (see OSTEOPOROSIS, page 311).
CRAVINGS. These are connected to changes in progesterone levels, but usually cravings are quite mild: you may go off favourite foods and tastes can seem to alter. Craving for very unusual substances like wall plaster and coal *may*, it is thought, be due to anaemia. Extra sex hormones currently in the body affect your insulin's control of blood sugar and may make you crave sugar more (especially	Ask your doctor if it is worth being checked for anaemia if your cravings are peculiar.	★ Eat little and often, with plenty of complex carbohydrates like bread and pasta, also fresh fruit (bananas are very useful) and dried fruit, to stop the blood sugar level dropping. ★ Avoid sugary food and sweets.

mid-afternoon), to correct any drops fast. But sugar is fattening and *not* a long-lasting glucose supply (it *is* soon used up, so you get another blood sugar drop and need more sugar).

FAINTING. The lowering of your blood pressure (blood vessels relax under the influence of extra hormones) means blood may 'pool' in the lower part of your body. This, plus an increased demand for extra blood to the womb, means your brain sometimes goes temporarily short. Also, due to your baby's nutritional demands, your blood sugar drops more quickly than usual and can cause 'mid-afternoon crash' featuring sugar craving and faintness at around 3 p.m.

Nil

* Avoid prolonged standing.
* Avoid wearing tight clothes or underwear.
* Do not lie on your back, as the weight of the womb will press against a major artery called the venae cavae, cutting off the blood supply to the brain.
* If you feel faint lie on your side with your feet slightly raised or sit with your head down between your knees for a moment.
* A protein snack (e.g. nuts) or a complex carbohydrate snack (e.g. a small banana) around 3 p.m. can help avoid the mid-afternoon crash effect.

FEET. Your arches may fall a bit and your feet expand up to a half a size bigger, thanks to the general relaxation of all the body's muscles and ligaments under hormonal control from the progesterone. Excessive weight gain will also have an effect on your feet.

Your doctor may suggest a visit to a chiropodist for advice.

* Do not wear arch supports (they can weaken the foot's own muscles): try Scholl exercise sandals whenever possible.
* Do foot exercises: clenching toes (bare) across the carpet as if picking up a pencil with them is a good one, done twenty-four times morning and evening.
* Watch your weight.

FLATULENCE. The intestines' smooth muscle relaxes under hormonal control (from the extra progesterone) so it moves digesting food and waste along more slowly – and wind can build up.

Your doctor may suggest charcoal tablets.

* It also helps to eat fewer refined and sugary foods (they can make it worse) and fewer carbohydrates.
* Digestion-aiding drinks like peppermint tea may help, as might peppermint tablets.
* Avoid 'flatulent' foods like beans and cabbage.
* Exercise is probably beneficial, too.

Problem, symptoms and causes	Medical help	Self help
FLUID IN THE VAGINA. The sudden appearance of a gush of profuse, thin watery fluid (like urine only colourless), as opposed to the usual thicker vaginal discharge of pregnancy, *may* mean your waters (the sac of amniotic fluid surrounding the baby) have broken, so it is less protected from infection.	You will need to be seen straight away to check if the cause is early labour. If it is, go into hospital (or call the midwife right then, if you are having a home birth).	In case this is a sign of early labour, consult your doctor or midwife immediately.
FLUID RETENTION (swelling in legs, hands, ankles and feet); also called OEDEMA. The hormonal changes of pregnancy affect the levels of albumen in your cell tissues. This upsets the salt and potassium balance of cells so they retain more water. The extra oestrogen in the body during pregnancy particularly encourages water retention. Further, your overall blood volume rises and the pressure of your growing baby on certain major blood vessels can contribute to swelling.	Your doctor may prescribe mild diuretics if the problem is very troublesome.	* Raise your feet whenever you can (especially for 15 minutes each evening). * Avoid long periods of standing, and very salty foods. * Massaging the affected areas helps. * Try also lying down on your left side (this keeps the weight of the baby off your major blood vessels).
FREQUENT URINATION may be caused partly by the baby lying against the bladder, or neck of the bladder, (and irritating the nerves there, so you keep thinking you want to open the bladder neck and urinate). This happens particularly in the first 14 weeks, and *late* in pregnancy. Also, the blood flow to the kidneys is doubled during pregnancy, so they remove twice as much water as usual from the blood, which needs to be excreted via the bladder. If lying against the bladder neck, the baby may move off in its own time; if squashing of	Nil	* Avoid diuretic drinks like coffee and tea (especially at night). * Keep drinking plenty of other fluids so as not to concentrate the urine (otherwise infections like cystitis more likely). * Always empty your bladder fully when urinating – lean forward.

the bladder is due to the baby's increasing size, pressure will be off when it moves higher up in the pelvic cavity under your ribs, then return as it drops down again late in pregnancy. (See also **Incontinence**, below.)

GUM DISEASE. Gums, like other tissue in your body, are swollen with extra blood and fluid; extra progesterone in the body makes them softer. This makes them much more vulnerable to gum disease – which can mean lost teeth.

Prevention is better than cure, although dentists can reverse early gum disease by removing build-up of plaque. (See also **Bleeding gums**, above.)

* Clean your teeth often, and always after eating or drinking sugary or starchy things.
* Use a soft brush and don't brush hard but brush long – a full 3 minutes at least twice a day.
* Try an electric toothbrush if wrist gets tired.
* If you can't brush, chew sugar-free gum, which stimulates saliva to neutralize mouth acids.
* Make sure of enough Vitamin C, which protects gums.
* Eat enough protein – if you're deficient, the baby will draw its supplies from the vulnerable area between gum and base of tooth.
* Plaque-removing mouthwashes (like Plax) used with brushing, can be very useful and reduce brushing time.

HAEMORRHOIDS (PILES). Itchiness or pain around the rectum is caused by varicose veins, caused in turn by blood vessels relaxing under the influence of extra progesterone so blood flow through them is not so efficient.

Piles can be made worse by pushing and straining if you are constipated (see CONSTIPATION, page 145).

Also, pressure of the baby's head in later pregnancy can obstruct major blood vessels and stop them returning blood back from the pelvic area, meaning veins balloon out.

Some anti-haemorrhoid creams are on prescription from your GP. Piles can also be treated by minor surgery if not better within three months of having your baby. If, during pregnancy, a vein has clotted (thrombosed) it can be lanced by your doctor there and then for immediate relief – without having to wait until after delivery.

* Have plenty of fibre in your diet and drink lots of fluids to help keep your stools loose, moist and easy to pass.
* Avoid very hot baths which encourage all blood vessels to enlarge to radiate off the extra heat.
* Try ice packs on the affected area, and soothing creams from the chemist; or cold compresses soaked in Witch Hazel Lotion (from major chemists) and held against the area for 10 to 15 minutes.
* Soaking in a *warm* (not hot) bath can be comforting.

Problems, symptoms and causes	Medical help	Self help
HAIR AND SKIN. Lank hair and greasy skin (even spots) can be due to extra male hormones being produced. The problem usually clears after the third or fourth month.	Nil	★ Follow a regular cleansing/toning routine, using antiseptic cream on the worst spots (on your back, face or chest). ★ Wash your hair regularly in mild shampoo; rinse well in cool water, and condition the ends only.
HEARTBURN is a burning sensation in your upper chest, plus a sour taste in your mouth. Due to high levels of progesterone during pregnancy the muscle between your food pipe and stomach relaxes (like all the other muscle tissue in the body), slowing the passage of food from stomach to gut. Also, the enlarging womb presses on the digestive organs in late pregnancy. Both mean the stomach's food-digesting acidic juices may rise up your throat, causing a burning sensation.	Your GP may prescribe anti-acid preparations.	★ Eat little and often, so your stomach does not get too full but a flow of nutrients is maintained. ★ Avoid very fatty foods, spicy foods and too many carbohydrates. ★ Try anti-acid tablets or liquids e.g. Milk of Magnesia from the chemist to neutralize the stomach acids, or Tums, which are high in calcium, too. ★ Raise your head and shoulders when lying down in bed but do not lie flat for a few hours after eating. ★ Limit the amount of liquid drunk *with* meals (it will make your stomach fuller).
HIGH BLOOD PRESSURE. The action of extra progesterone on the muscular walls of the blood vessels relaxes them so the heart has to work harder to pump blood around your body – this leads to higher blood pressure for all pregnant women, and too-high blood pressure for some.	Doctors tend to advise bed rest rather than giving medication.	★ Bed rest followed by much reduced activity. ★ Get your blood pressure monitored very regularly (check with your doctor how often would be necessary in your own case)
INCONTINENCE. Urine leaking when you laugh, cough, sneeze or lift something heavy may be due to the baby sitting against the neck of the bladder and irritating it, so it wants to open	Nil	★ Do pelvic floor exercises as often as possible (see INCONTINENCE page 239). ★ Empty your bladder often. ★ Avoid lifting, or a very full stomach, as this increases internal pressure.

more often and more easily. Sometimes the baby also squashes the bladder, so there is less room for urine than usual. Also, more urine is produced (up to twice as much) when you are pregnant. The muscles of the bladder neck and pelvic floor may be relaxing, like other muscles, too, due to extra progesterone. (See also **Frequent Urination**, above.)

INSOMNIA. You may sleep less in the last three months, because you are more uncomfortable due to the increasing size of the baby. You will tend also to sleep more fitfully and be more sensitive to noise, in possible preparation for new sleeping patterns after the baby's arrival. Also, though the baby will kick and move all the time, day and night, it is more noticeable at night.

Nil. Sleeping pills are not given unless it is an emergency and they are for short-term use.

* Have a warm, relaxing pre-bed bath (possibly using a sedative essential oil like cedarwood).
* Try a hot milky drink, relaxation exercises or calming music.
* Do not watch exciting TV films, or work late, and then go to bed without unwinding.
* Wear cotton in bed to avoid overheating, and use cotton bedcovers.
* If feeling big and bulky, sleep with a pillow supporting your stomach, and put one in the small of back and one between your knees for support and comfort.

ITCHING SKIN. Your skin may itch, as the body does not metabolize bile salts so well when you are pregnant; they can be deposited under your skin and cause irritation.

Nil

* Drink plenty of non-diuretic fluids to help elimination of waste products like bile salts.
* Calamine Lotion helps.
* Half a cup of bicarbonate of soda in the bath helps soothe itching (avoid your face), as does a cupful of oats in the bath or oat-based emollient soaps like Aveeno, or Aqueous Cream (instead of soap), which help stop skin drying – and itching – even more.

Problems, symptoms and causes	Medical help	Self help
MORNING SICKNESS can occur at any time of day – or all day. It is usually limited to the first three months, but some unlucky women get it all through their pregnancy. It may be directly related to an increase in progesterone, oestrogen, and – in the first three months – Human Chorionic Gonadotrophin.	If there is a real problem with vomiting (and resulting dehydration and weight loss) an anti-sickness drug may be given.	★ Small increases in blood sugar help, so try a drink (if you can face it) of Lucozade or another sweet drink (e.g. sweetened tea) with some digestive biscuits before rising (then get up slowly). ★ Ginger drinks, tablets, capsules and tea help (see HELPLINES). ★ Try Sea Bands (elasticated wristbands with a plastic stud pressing on each wrist at the Nei Kwan Chinese acupressure point (also good for seasickness and worsened car sickness in pregnancy – see HELPLINES). ★ Eat small, frequent meals (an empty stomach makes things worse). See HELPLINES for product addresses.
NIGHT SWEATS. Your increased blood supply causes vessels to dilate, and radiate warmth.	Nil	★ Wear natural fibres. ★ Do not rush around and expend too much energy just before retiring for bed. ★ Get up and shower if you wake up hot and sweating in the middle of the night.
NOSE PROBLEMS. The increase in oestrogen means all the body's membranes (those in the vagina, mouth, nose, etc) become softer and thicker. This may lead to extra mucus in the nose, and a stuffy blocked feeling. Also, the increased blood supply plus softening of the membranes, means noses, like gums, bleed more easily.	Nil	★ Avoid nasal sprays (decongestants, if used often, can eventually have a rebound, e.g. the opposite effect, or cease to be effective). ★ Try inhaling steamy infusions (e.g. eucalyptus oil and boiling water steam). ★ Avoid heavy nose blowing (which could trigger a nose bleed). ★ Prevent any drying out of the nasal membranes (leading to cracking and more bleeding inside your nose) by smearing on a little Vaseline, especially in hot, dry environments like air-conditioned, centrally-heated offices.

PELVIC PAIN felt in the groin, or down the inside of your thighs when walking, is due to the baby's head pressing on the pelvic nerves, especially towards the end of pregnancy. There is also the small possibility that it might be early labour pains.

Nil, unless the cause is early labour, in which case you will be admitted to hospital for total bed rest, plus careful monitoring (urine tests each day to check for protein, your blood pressure taken every four hours). Such total rest usually stops the contractions. If not, drugs (such as sedatives for lowering blood pressure) will be given. If they are still not effective and the baby is well developed enough, you may have labour induced, or a Caesarean section. If it is too early for either, you'll be kept in hospital until it is time for the baby to be born.

Some experimental work using aspirin as a preventative measure for premature labour is also being done in some centres.

* Rest with your body supported on pillows.
* Gentle rocking will ease the discomfort (the pain is too sporadic for painkillers).
* If your lower abdomen is going hard to the touch repeatedly (rather than the usual Braxton Hicks contractions occurring all through pregnancy), it may be premature labour pains. Contact your doctor or the labour ward of the hospital you are booked into, or your midwife, immediately.

RASHES. If you become too heavy, rashes may develop below your breasts and in the groin flesh folds (a warm, damp, enclosed environment). You may also become more sensitive to allergens (see homoeopathy and medical herbalism, below).

Your doctor may prescribe hydro-cortisone cream if the problem gets very persistent.

* Keep your skin folds clean and well dried. Dust with plain zinc talc – not perfumed talc, as that could irritate further.
* Watch your weight.
* Try HC45 from the chemist.

RIB PAIN. You may feel a sharp pain under one breast ('costal margin pain') as your womb pushes the ribs upwards towards the end of your pregnancy. The pain will disappear around the 36th week as the baby drops down into the pelvic cavity before delivery.

Nil

* Sit up as straight as you can, or propped up, so your ribs are not compressed.

ROUND LIGAMENT PAIN. This is the name given to the sharp, stabbing, pulling pains that you may feel (usually in the first three months of pregnancy) when the ligaments suspending the uterus from the abdominal walls start stretching, as your womb gets bigger and heavier. You may feel the pain in your groin, too.

If the pain becomes insistent and continuous see your doctor as soon as possible to make sure there is no other cause for your discomfort, such as a premature labour or threatened miscarriage. Your GP is unlikely to do anything for the pain unless he suspects an early labour or miscarriage, in which case he would probably arrange for you to be admitted to hospital for observation (see MISCARRIAGE, page 297).

* Have warm baths and warm hot-water bottles.
* Lie down with a soft pillow supporting your stomach.
* Try gentle massage, over and around the abdomen.

Problem, symptoms and causes	Medical help	Self help
SKIN COLOUR CHANGES. Your body makes more melanocyte-stimulating hormone, so the 'skin around the nipples darkens, a darker line (linea nigra) appears from the pubic area to the navel, your skin may tan more easily and there is a possibility that you may develop the 'butterfly mask' of pregnancy: a darkened area of skin around the brows, cheeks and chin in a 'butterfly' shape. Pigmentation fades after the baby is delivered.	Nil	★ Avoid strong sun and much sunbathing. ★ Use a good sunblock.
STOMACH PAIN, see **Round Ligament Pain**, above.		
STRETCHMARKS are fine red lines on the abdomen, breasts and thighs caused by skin stretching, due to weight gain and the expansion of your breasts or stomach. Lines fade to silvery marks a few months after delivery.	Nil	★ Watch your weight. ★ Some women say rubbing oil on these areas, right from the second month of pregnancy, helps (see also **Aromatherapy, Clinical nutrition, Medical herbalism** and **Homoeopathy**, below). ★ If very bad, and the abdomen skin is very stretched, you could consider abdominoplasty cosmetic surgery (see HELPLINES). This removes some areas of stretched skin, though not all. Results are usually a bit disappointing.
THRUSH. Up to a third of women experience thrush in pregnancy, usually in last three months, thanks to the increased glycogen (sugar) content of the cells and the fact that high hormone levels interfere with insulin's usual control over sugar levels in the body. Extra oestrogen in the body predisposes the vagina to thrush, too. (See also VAGINAL THRUSH, page 453.)	You might get fungicidal creams, pessaries etc. from your GP.	★ Use a fungicidal pessary like Canestan preventatively a couple of times a month if you know you are prone to thrush (ask your GP). Canestan cream does not need prescription. ★ Keep the vulva area cool and do not let it get damp and sweaty (wear cotton underwear and stockings rather than nylon pants and tights; skirts rather than trousers).

TIREDNESS. In early pregnancy you will probably feel the desire to sleep a lot (often in the early afternoon) and find it hard to resist. Go with it if you can. It stops around the third month, returning later when the excess weight you are carrying makes movements harder work.

Nil

* Rest as much as you feel you need to, if you have the opportunity.
* Ask for a place to rest up at work and take an afternoon nap if you can. See if your GP will give you a note to say you need this.
* Delegate as much work and as many house chores as possible.
* Eat little and often to keep up your blood sugar level (if it drops you'll feel tired).

VAGINAL DISCHARGE increases during pregnancy under the influence of extra hormones, in the same way as all the mucus membranes of the body (including the gums and nasal membranes) thicken and soften. Discharge should usually be thickish and white. If brownish or bloodstained, it is probably cervical erosion (very common in pregnancy and harmless – see POST-PREGNANCY PROBLEMS, page 393). But see a doctor to make sure.

Nil, unless it is due to an infection, in which case your doctor would give appropriate medication.

* Always wipe your bottom from front to back (sometimes a reservoir of the thrush fungus, Candida albicans, is in the bowel).
* A saline wash is helpful for temporary relief if you get an attack while waiting to see your GP (see VAGINAL THRUSH, page 453).
* In hot weather and after love making, gently wash your vulva with cool water from the shower spray.
* If discharge is heavy, wear pantie liners.
* Wear cotton knickers, changed up to twice a day.
* Wash the area twice a day in warm water using toilet paper.
* Do not use scented vaginal sprays or douches.

Problem, symptoms and causes	Medical help	Self help
VARICOSE VEINS, in the legs, are due to the relaxation of the muscular walls of the blood vessels (because of extra progesterone in the body). Blood does not get returned to the heart so efficiently and can 'pool' in certain areas, distending the blood vessels. They are also due to the fact that the amount of blood in the body increases by up to 50 per cent. Also, they may be due to the baby's head pressing on certain major blood vessels.	Your doctor may suggest an operation to remove them if they have not cleared up 3 months after delivery.	* Wear support stockings or tights from six or seven months onwards (earlier if your legs ache). Keep them under your pillow in bed and put them on before setting a foot on the floor to get up. (See HELPLINES.) * Put your feet up at intervals during the day, especially for 15 minutes each evening. * Avoid long periods of standing or wearing anything that constricts the blood flow in the leg (e.g. hold-up stockings, pop socks). * Do not sit with your legs crossed or pressing on a hard chair lip. * Do foot-circling exercises and elevate your feet whenever sitting down. * Regular swimming helps blood circulation, too (see HELPLINES).
VARICOSE VEINS, in the vulva are caused by the same reasons as varicose veins in the legs. They may be especially itchy and uncomfortable – but fortunately they are rare. They should disappear after delivery within three months.	As for varicose veins in the legs.	* Sleep with a cushion under your bottom to elevate it; watch TV like this, too, lying down on the sofa or floor. * It may help to wear soft sanitary pads pressing against the veins.
VISUAL PROBLEMS. Additional oestrogen in the body may affect vision, and albumen loss from cells affects the amount of water retained in the tissues. The eyeball may retain more, too, and consequently change its shape slightly. This can make contact lens wearing a problem.	Nil	* Try glasses instead of contact lenses until after delivery – or new contact lenses (ask your optician).

These next two conditions, Diabetes and Pre-Eclampsia, can be dangerous if not treated, so take special care about them. The warning signs will be picked up at your routine ante-natal visits, but it is as well to know them for yourself.

DIABETES (gestational diabetes). Hormones produced by the placenta interfere with the body's handling of glucose in the bloodstream, so women with a slight predisposition to diabetes may find pregnancy can tip the balance. It is *not* common, but happens in 3 to 5 per cent of all pregnant women (according to the British Diabetic Association).

Another problem with gestational diabetes is that the baby may be put on a lot of weight and become uncomfortably large to deliver – possibly making a Caesarean necessary.

If a high-fibre diet does not work, doctors will prescribe insulin tablets. It is also possible to have the insulin 'delivered' into your body by small pumps, by injections or by pen-style cartridges (not always available on the NHS).

* Eat a high-fibre diet with a substantial fixed calorie intake – get a menu plan to follow strictly from the hospital.
* Have very regular ante-natal check-ups.
* If you start to feel odd in between visits, call your doctor for an immediate appointment.

PRE-ECLAMPSIA. Potentially a serious condition, as it is the forerunner of full blown Eclampsia (which threatens the life of both mother and baby). PE usually develops after the fifth month – the symptoms are raised blood pressure, weight gain, swelling (oedema) from water retention in the hands, ankles, face and feet, and protein in your urine (detected by a test done at the ante-natal clinic).

Full Eclampsia can produce fits and unconsciousness in the mother, bloating of her body, stomach pain, irritability, very high blood pressure, migraine-like headaches and visual disturbances. It can also affect the blood supply to the placenta so the baby is starved of both food and oxygen.

Some doctors feel it is caused by lack of high quality proteins (meat, fish, eggs, cheese, lentils) in your diet, so will suggest dietary change. If PE is getting worse, they will suggest total bed rest for a while, possibly in hospital.

* Eat a very good healthy diet (with plenty of protein, fresh fruit and vegetables). Get further details from the Pre-Eclamptic Toxaemia Society (PETS) – see HELPLINES).
* Try not to put on too much weight.
* Go for *all* your ante-natal check-ups.
* Contact your doctor if you notice swelling in hands, feet or face.
* Exercise is another preventative measure (e.g. swimming three times a week for as long as you feel you can manage it; walking (daily) also reduces the risk of high blood pressure.
* Can monitor own urine at home every few days with a test called Albusticks from the pharmacist.

Complementary therapy

Complementary therapies tailor their treatments very much to the individual: the precise nature of the treatment you receive will vary, depending on your medical history, symptoms, lifestyle, etc. The following information indicates the *sorts* of things a therapist is most likely to do or recommend. Do not be surprised if they feel you need something slightly different. This section is meant purely as an indication of likely treatments; it is not meant as a DIY guide to the medical uses of the different complementary therapies.

Many of these problems also occur outside of pregnancy. It is important to tell the therapist that you are pregnant at the start of a consultation – even if you think it is obvious! The role of clinical nutrition in pregnancy is mainly to ensure a good all-round diet to nourish the foetus (and you) and perhaps to prescribe supplements if it's found that you are deficient in a certain nutrient. This is not a case for self-prescribing or for guesswork, because too much of a certain nutrient, or imbalance between different nutrients, can be as dangerous as deficiencies. Some supplements, however, are often specially useful. These include: calcium, multivitamins and minerals, chlorophyll, wheatgerm oil, multi-amino acids and rutin.

The need for calcium doubles during pregnancy so calcium is needed for that reason and also to prevent muscle cramping. A good multi-vitamin and mineral maintains a good level of nutrients, chlorophyll is a sex hormone precursor, and gives good support to the intestines. Wheatgerm oil helps blood circulation and also acts as an anti-miscarriage factor. Multi-amino ensures a complete protein (amino-acid) pattern. Rutin helps prevent spontaneous abortion and premature labour.

1. STOMACH PAIN
Caused by stretching of ligaments supporting the womb.

Acupuncture
Acupuncture can enhance the body's production of pain-relieving substances.

Aromatherapy
Very gentle massage with oils of lavender, mandarin, geranium or chamomile, blended professionally in apricot kernel and wheatgerm oil, relaxes the abdominal wall, and improves and nourishes the mother's skin (thereby preventing stretch marks).

Medical herbalism
Light massage over the lower abdomen and back with oil of lavender, diluted in vegetable oil, can be helpful.

Osteopathy
Pelvic manipulation to the pelvic joints and the joints supporting the structures causing the pain will help them to function correctly. Furthermore, consultation with a registered osteopath at regular intervals throughout the pregnancy can help stretch the supporting tissues in anticipation of the increased weight-bearing demand – thereby preventing back pain and joint tenderness.

Osteopathic treatment can also be helpful later in the pregnancy to make the birth process easier and less painful. A post-natal check of mother and baby is also a good idea to ensure that any problems which have arisen during the birth are sorted out at an early stage.

A good position to help relieve backache when you are pregnant: stay like this for as long as you feel comfortable.

Another good one for backache – taught in Active Birth Classes. You can rest on your elbows, or, if it feels comfortable, slowly stretch out your arms in front of you into position b). This is the Frog Stretch. Stay there for a minute or two and come up slowly. Be careful in either one not to arch your back.

2. BACKACHE

Acupuncture

Acupuncture and acupressure will help by producing pain-relieving substances in the body, thereby balancing the muscle tone of the back and strengthening the muscles of the back area where the pain occurs.

Aromatherapy

Massaging your back with oils of lavender, mandarin, sandalwood or rose helps to relax the muscles and thus relieve pressure on the spine and alleviate pain by freeing the muscle fibres. Treatment may need to be continued for several weeks.

377

Chiropractic
Spinal manipulation and soft-tissue work, continuing throughout pregnancy, reduces the stress on the spine and pelvis by restoring normal joint flexibility and motion.

Homoeopathy
Backache associated with weakness and dragging in the loins responds to Kali-carb. Severe pain before or when passing fæces is treated with sarsaparilla.

Medical herbalism
Massaging with oil of lavender, for example, helps muscle tone. Using hot compresses with lavender or rose oils relaxes and eases muscle tension.

Osteopathy
A full postural and structural examination and a complete case history are necessary to enable the osteopath to diagnose the reason for an individual's pain. Your basic posture can change up to three times during pregnancy if the body has the ability to adapt. The osteopath will assess your capability for change and treat accordingly.

3. CHANGED POSTURE
Acupuncture
Acupuncture and acupressure help balance the muscle tone, strengthen the muscle structure and readjust poor posture.

Aromatherapy
Massage with relaxing and soothing oils helps ease muscle tension, which alleviates the pressure on the spine.

Chiropractic
Altered posture can lead to lower back strain and increased muscle tension in the lumbo sacral area. Chiropractic treatment throughout pregnancy would aim at reducing strain and tension in the soft tissues and joints.

Medical herbalism
The medical herbalist may well recommend remedial exercises such as yoga and/or the Alexander Technique.

Osteopathy
Soft-tissue manipulation, stretching the ligaments and mobilizing the joints would aim to correct the problem as far as possible for each individual patient. Initial treatment lasts for an hour, further treatments half an hour.

4. BLEEDING GUMS
Aromatherapy
A hydrosol mouthwash with oils of lavender and thyme may be offered to help prevent infection of the gums.

Medical herbalism
The herbalist might suggest a mouthwash of myrrh or Calendula, supplemented with dietary advice, e.g. taking more Vitamins B and C, together with iron and zinc to help build up the strength of the capillary walls. The mouthwash is astringent, so it helps prevent bleeding or infection and helps healing.

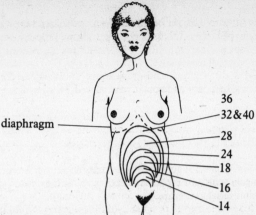

diaphragm

36
32 & 40
28
24
18
16
14

This is the size of your womb at each stage of pregnancy. As it grows bigger, it begins to constrict your breathing by taking up space under your diaphragm (hence breathlessness becomes a problem), and its increasing weight may squash the major blood vessels in your pelvis, if you lie flat on your back. This is one reason why it is more comfortable to sleep propped up on pillows towards the end of your pregnancy.

5. CONSTIPATION

Acupuncture
Acupuncture would be combined with advice on diet and general care.

Aromatherapy
Clockwise self-massage of the abdomen with a blend of chamomile and lavender oils helps increase intestinal movements. Full-body massage by an aromatherapist with an individual blend of essential oils may also be effective.

Chiropractic
A side effect of spinal manipulation for a low back problem may be relief of constipation.

Clinical nutrition
Dietary changes would probably help; added fibre suits some people and not others. A consultation is necessary to ascertain the cause of your constipation.

Homoeopathy
Remedies vary according to your individual problem, the consistency of your faeces, and your habits – all of which would be discussed during a consultation. Possible remedies include Sepia or Opium.

Medical herbalism
The main advice would probably be dietary, including increased fibre intake, together with discussion of posture and exercise to improve your abdominal and bowel tone. Gentle aperients, such as dandelion root, might be prescribed to encourage normal bowel action without harsh stimulation by strong laxatives (most of which also stimulate the muscle of the uterus.

Osteopathy
Direct work on your intestines might be undertaken, combined with dietary advice, to increase the movement of faeces. Work on the spine allows reflex pathways to work on the bowel and encourage normal emptying. You should ask the osteopath beforehand if they have trained in 'visceral osteopathy'.

6. CRAMPS IN FEET, THIGHS AND CALVES
Acupuncture
Acupuncture and acupressure can both help, combined with advice on diet, exercise and general care.

Aromatherapy
Full-body massage with a blend of geranium, rosemary and either lavender or bergamot should improve muscle tone and blood circulation, as well as your lymphatic circulation, to give resultant relief of cramps.

Clinical nutrition
Stress plays a part in most types of cramp, as do certain nutritional deficiencies, i.e. potassium, sodium, calcium, magnesium and pantothenic acid. Adrenal exhaustion can also cause cramps. Consultation is essential to determine the underlying cause. Cramps can be caused by insufficient stomach acid, thus preventing adequate absorption of calcium.

Homoeopathy
Four-hourly doses of Veratrum Album may be suggested.

Medical herbalism
External application of products like cramp bark, together with internal treatment, dietary advice and, perhaps, massage, help relax muscle spasm, while an overall balance of nutrition and improved circulation are achieved.

Osteopathy
Direct work on the affected muscles, coupled with dietary advice to improve your general well-being, may provide relief.

7. FOOD CRAVINGS
Acupuncture
Activating the appropriate acupuncture points will improve your willpower and suppress hunger.

Aromatherapy
A relaxing bath oil – or blend of oils – helps provide a good night's sleep and prevents night-time cravings. Dietary advice may also be offered.

Clinical nutrition
Food cravings usually result from allergies or food intolerances, low blood sugar, intestinal parasites/blockages, adrenal exhaustion, low thyroid function, a glandular imbalance, or chronic candidiasis.
    Symptoms might include any of the following: bloating/flatulence, mood swings/ irritability, sugar/chocolate cravings, excessive weight gain, dizziness, nausea, premenstrual tension (symptoms often appear worse before a period).
    The hypothalamus (part of the forebrain) is the body's appetite regulator. One part

380

sends out signals which compel eating in order to supply the body with much needed fuel, while another part inhibits the desire to eat. Sometimes this mechanism acts abnormally, and a good nutritional clinician should be able to help you correct this abnormality.

Homoeopathy
Chelidonium helps prevent overwhelming cravings for unusual foods.

Medical herbalism
Cravings are sometimes linked to low blood sugar levels. The use of bitter foods (endive or chicory, for example) or mildly bitter herbal medicines (such as artichoke), can help to improve liver, pancreas and digestive functions and restore balance. Advice on general diet and supplementation will also help, alongside herbal treatment.

8. FAINTING
Acupuncture
Fainting has many different causes – anaemia, poor sleeping patterns, anorexia, hunger, dehydration, pain, nervous shock or poor ventilation – so the acupuncturist will first try to find the reason before considering an appropriate treatment.

Aromatherapy
Inhaling essential oils, such as lavender or rose, when you feel weak may help.

Clinical nutrition
Sudden decrease in blood pressure can temporarily deprive the brain of adequate blood supply. Causes of this can be any of the following: prolonged bouts of coughing, straining to produce a bowel movement, emotional disturbances, heartbeat abnormality, low blood sugar (usually after eating or drinking), or rising from a chair or bed too quickly. In any event, a thorough examination is necessary before dietary advice can be given.

Medical herbalism
The medical herbalist will first try to discover the reason for fainting, and will monitor your blood pressure and perhaps your haemoglobin levels. Recovery from fainting is helped by using essential oils of lavender or rosemary as smelling salts.

9. FLATULENCE
Aromatherapy
Peppermint or chamomile herb teas may help. Gentle massage of your abdomen with anti-spasmodic/digestive oils (such as lavender or chamomile) may reduce your production of excessive gases through the digestive processes.

Chiropractic
A side effect of spinal manipulation may be a lessening of flatulence.

Clinical nutrition
Everyone's gut contains gas, often caused by the action of bacteria on food residues in the colon. Certain types of food, e.g. pulses (beans, lentils, etc.) in particular may lead to excessive gas production.

Belching is commonly caused by air being swallowed with food or drink. Carbon dioxide is released when stomach acids react with alkaline foods or pancreatic juices in the duodenum. Many people can be cured by the simple realization that they might not be creating excessive gas but simply sucking it in. However, a nutritionist may determine whether enough stomach acids or digestive enzymes are being produced, and whether intestinal flora is adequate. Treatment in each of these cases can be simple and quickly effective.

Homoeopathy
Several remedies are possible, including Pulsatilla, Colocynth, Lycopodium, China and Carbo-Veg. The choice depends on where the flatulence is felt – whether it passes upwards or downwards, and how it makes you feel emotionally, as well as physically.

Medical herbalism
Advice on exercise, rest, posture and leg elevation, to assist drainage of the fluid back towards the heart, may be supplemented with a careful use of diuretic remedies. Couch grass or chamomile may be offered for a short period (up to one week), and perhaps repeated later if necessary.

10. FLUID RETENTION
Acupuncture
Acupuncture can block your water-retention mechanism; acupressure will stimulate your body to expel retained water.

Aromatherapy
Massaging your legs with essential oils of rosemary, geranium, or individual blends incorporating bergamot, juniper and cypress will increase circulation and the return of blood to your heart. This prevents fluid retention caused by sluggish circulation.

Clinical nutrition
Fluid retention can be restricted to local conditions, e.g. hands, ankles, knees, abdomen or other parts, or can occur in many parts of the body simultaneously. Causes can be varied, including kidney disease, sluggish or blocked lymphatic system, poor circulation, adrenal dysfunction, protein deficiency, low thyroid function, premenstrual syndrome, anaemia, liver disease, excess salt in diet, constipation, and many other causes. Clearly, the underlying cause needs to be determined before dietary guidance can be given, but certainly a nutritionist can be very helpful in overcoming this distressing problem.

Medical herbalism
Advice on exercise, rest, posture and legs elevation to assist drainage of the fluid back towards the heart, may be supplemented with the careful use of diuretic remedies. Couch grass or chamomile may be offered for a short period (up to one week), and perhaps repeated later if necessary.

11. OVER-ACTIVE SEBACEOUS GLANDS
Aromatherapy
Effective skin toners and moisturizing lotions are those made with essential oils of orange flower blossom, rose, lavender or chamomile.

Clinical nutrition
This usually leads to acne, where cebum (made from excess fatty acids and waxes) causes a blockage in the gland's duct, leading to infection. A newly discovered derivative of Vitamin A is particularly helpful in reducing the production of sebum, helping to quickly eradicate acne. Unfortunately, it is not to be taken when pregnant, so see your nutritionist for alternatives.

Medical herbalism
Local applications of diluted, distilled witch-hazel for the skin, or rosemary, birch or pine infusions for the hair, all act as cleansing astringents to reduce gland activity.

12. THE NEED TO PASS WATER MORE FREQUENTLY
Acupuncture
The acupuncturist would need to discover the cause of the condition before offering advice or treatment.

Aromatherapy
If the cause of the condition is bladder inflammation, essential oils of lavender, sandalwood, juniper berry and bergamot – alone or in combination – massaged into the abdomen, or in a sitz bath, may help.

Clinical nutrition
Again, there are so many possible causes that consultation before treatment is essential. May be due to infection of urinary tract, adverse reaction or side effect of drugs, food intolerance, a prolapsed colon pushing down on the bladder can create a constant urge to urinate, poor nutrition leading to a deficiency of B vitamins, or the result of sudden or prolonged stress. Without determining the underlying cause, treatment could be futile.

Homoeopathy
Sepia or Causticum may be suggested to help this condition.

Medical herbalism
If there is no accompanying discomfort, the medical herbalist may offer advice on exercise and posture to relieve pressure on your bladder. Inflammation or irritation of the bladder may be helped by marshmallow tea, which has a soothing effect.

13. HAEMORRHOIDS
Aromatherapy
Aromatherapy can be helpful, combined with other forms of treatment. Lower back massage with oils of lavender and chamomile helps improve circulation and decrease pressure in your lower abdomen.

Clinical nutrition
Haemorrhoids are commonly caused by straining as a result of constipation; the nutritionist will want to help you overcome any difficulties with bowel movements. This may necessitate dietary changes, including an increase in dietary fibre where this appears to be lacking (not everyone benefits from increased fibre, so consult), usually through taking more fruit and vegetables.

Very often the constipation is caused by liver toxicity, and a secondary problem may be congestion of the veins and/or capillary engorgement. The nutritionist would probably give rutin for this, together with adrenal glandular tissue to support the capillary system. The ileo-cecal valve should be checked, and manipulated if necessary.

Medical herbalism
Advice on diet and internal treatment is helpful (see CONSTIPATION). Local application of astringent remedies such as witch-hazel or horse chestnut, constricts the swollen blood vessels and prevents bleeding.

14. HEARTBURN
Aromatherapy
Dietary advice will be given to restore balance, but herbal teas of chamomile and peppermint may help in the meantime.

Chiropractic
If the heartburn is judged to stem from a spinal problem in the chest area, chiropractic treatment can restore normal joint flexibility and reduce irritation in your stomach, through changes in your nervous system.

Clinical nutrition
Usually caused by hiatal hernia, or irritation/ulceration of the oesophagus. The former can be ameliorated by a simple manipulation of the diaphragmatic valve. Irritation/ulceration of the oesophagus might be improved with Vitamin E supplementation. Important to avoid food and drink that cause regurgitation of stomach contents, e.g. coffee, chocolate, fatty foods, spices. May be stress related, so Vitamin B complex and calcium levels should be checked.

Homoeopathy
Heartburn caused by acidity responds to Calc-carb, while heartburn without acidity is treated with Pulsatilla. Gastric pain, plus bringing up wind, can be treated with Lycopodium and Calc-fluor is good for digestive problems in general.

Medical herbalism
Remedies such as meadowsweet or lemon balm will reduce the discomfort. Advice on exercise and posture improvement will aim to reduce pressure on your stomach.

Osteopathy
Direct work on your diaphragm and rib margins, and work on your spinal reflex pathways, will help prevent gastic reflux. Advice on sitting and sleeping posture will also be provided.

15. INCONTINENCE
(See POST PREGNANCY PROBLEMS.)

16. INSOMNIA
Acupuncture
Acupuncture combined with acupressure would increase more effectively the treatments of the various causes of insomnia by stimulating the body system to cause sedation and a calming effect to the nervous system.

Aromatherapy
A relaxing pre-bed bath, containing a blend of lavender and Roman chamomile oils, may help. So may drops of lavender or chamomile on your pillow.

Chiropractic
Spinal problems, especially at the top of the spine, can affect sleep. Spinal manipulation restores normal soft tissues and joint mobility, and reduces stress, thus helping to ensure sleep.

Clinical nutrition
Caffeine, alcohol, overeating, food allergies/intolerances, nutritional deficiencies, low/high thyroid function are just a few of the possible underlying causes. As with all health problems, the nutritionist will try to establish the nature of the problem and treat accordingly. Supplementation may include Myo-inositol, niacinamide, B complex vitamins and calcium.

Homoeopathy
Various remedies are available according to the reason for – and the timing of – attacks of sleeplessness. General remedies include Coffea and hycopodium. Insomnia due to pain or cramps can be eased by chamomile, while waking in the middle of the night after a short sleep calls for sulphur or Pulsatilla.

Medical herbalism
Gentle relaxants such as lemon balm or lime blossom may be used. The general rule is to use the gentlest method first, increasing dosage or changing to a stronger remedy only if necessary.

17. MORNING SICKNESS
Acupuncture
Acupuncture can suppress morning sickness.

Aromatherapy
Fennel tea may help digestion for some patients. Ginger oil may also help.

Clinical nutrition
A term used for a nauseous feeling or actual vomiting that frequently occurs within or throughout the first three months of pregnancy. Basically, it is caused by the body cleaning itself out and preparing for the foetal growth and development. Thus, the object should be to mildly encourage the detoxification process. Every effort should be made to avoid smoking, caffeine-containing drinks and alcohol during pregnancy. Enemas or colon cleansing may be beneficial. As always with pregnancy, professional advice should be sought.

Homoeopathy
A number of homoeopathic remedies are available, according to the severity of your problem and any side effects it has caused. If the feeling of sickness is severe and accompanied by an aversion to food, Symphoricarpus is of great value. If the problem is severe and persistent, Cerium Ox may be used. For less severe cases, there is Sepia (nausea, together with exhaustion, backache, constipation and irritability), Nux Vom (retching without vomiting), Anacardium (when eating relieves the nausea), Natrum Phos (sour-tasting vomit, followed by great hunger), and Carbolic acid (nausea with headache and irritability).

Medical herbalism
Ginger tea, sipped little and often, reduces nausea and seems to stabilize both digestion and sugar levels. (Morning sickness has a strong correlation with low blood sugar.)

18. EXCESSIVE MUCUS – CAUSING NASAL PROBLEMS
SUCH AS NOSEBLEEDS
Acupuncture
Appropriate stimulation of acupuncture points can relieve this condition.

Aromatherapy
Inhaling essential oil of chamomile and lavender may help, especially if it's combined with a tobacco- and alcohol-free diet, low in saturated fats.

Medical herbalism
In the short term, remedies such as ribwort, ground ivy, yarrow or perhaps elderflower

are helpful. They reduce mucus secretion and catarrh, relieving pressure on your nasal passages to prevent nosebleeds. Natural astringents, they check the mucus production and tone up the membranes.

19. PELVIC PAIN
Acupuncture
Acupuncture is ideal for pain relief. Acupressure is often combined.

Aromatherapy
Gentle massage with lavender, rosemary and geranium oils, singly or blended according to individual needs, relaxes and tones the muscles, bringing pain relief.

20. SKIN PIGMENTATION CHANGES
No appropriate therapy has been suggested by any of the therapists. Consult your orthodox physician for advice.

21. ITCHY SKIN
Itchy skin can be caused by a blood disorder, fungal infection, parasites, the effects of chemicals, new clothing or an irritating fabric, or a side effect of some drugs. Some cosmetics and even jewellery can cause itching. The nutritionist will test for all of these potential underlying causes and treat accordingly.

22. RASHES IN SKIN FOLDS
Aromatherapy
Local massage with a blend of neroli, chamomile and lavender essential oils in a carrier vegetable oil, is excellent for sensitive skin, serving to relieve itchiness and help the skin regain its healthy texture. Other blends may also be prescribed for individual needs.

Medical herbalism
You may be given creams or ointments containing anti-inflammatory and soothing herbs such as chamomile, marigold or lemon balm – together with advice on diet and hygiene to avoid perspiration build-up.

23. RIB PAIN
Acupuncture
Acupuncture for pain relief may help.

Aromatherapy
Local massage with a blend of lavender oil and melissa or jasmin – or an individually blended oil – relieves aches and pains at local level.

Chiropractic
Spinal/rib joint adjustment by manipulation may help by relieving stress in the rib area and restoring joint mobility.

Medical herbalism
Local applications of lavender or peppermint, which are analgesics, may reduce discomfort in the short term.

Osteopathy
Work on the ribs, the intercostel muscles, the diaphragm and posture can relieve pain and prevent rib problems from occurring.

24. STRETCH MARKS

Aromatherapy

A blend of essential oils of lavender, neroli and mandarin – in wheatgerm and apricot kernel carrier oils – massaged into your lower abdomen, breasts and upper thighs twice daily, is most effective. The oils nourish the skin and increase circulation and elasticity.

Clinical nutrition

Slightly higher protein diet, combined with pantothenic acid (250mg/day) and Vitamin E (400IU/day) increases skin elasticity and should help to avoid stretch marks. In many cases, this combination has eradicated stretch marks from former pregnancies.

Medical herbalism

Rubbing in wheatgerm oil, and perhaps essential oil of rose, is very helpful – improving the elasticity of your skin; allowing it to expand and (after the birth) to contract more easily and effectively; and healing damage to your skin layers caused by these changes. The herbalist may also give advice on posture and exercise, to avoid adding to the problem.

25. NIGHT SWEATS

Acupuncture

Acupuncture, combined with Chinese herbal remedies, can help.

Aromatherapy

A blend of essential oils of lavender and chamomile, used in a tepid bath before you go to bed, helps to cool and relax you.

Clinical nutrition

Apart from fever, night sweats are commonly caused by the body's need to eliminate excess sodium (salt). The body controls its water content partly through the skin (sweating reduces water, the colon conserves water), and also reduces overheating by sweating. A nutritionist may suggest increased potassium foods, e.g. cantaloupe melon, bananas, kidney beans, asparagus, baked potatoes, etc.

Medical herbalism

Although this is chiefly a hormonal effect, which a medical herbalist would be reluctant to treat in pregnancy, lemon balm or oats to restore balance to the nervous system might be helpful. The nerve fibres supplying the blood vessels would become less irritable and therefore less likely to swing between the dilation and constriction causing sweats.

26. EXCESSIVE TIREDNESS AT THE BEGINNING AND END OF PREGNANCY

Acupuncture

Acupuncture, plus dietary advice, can be most useful, depending on the cause of the condition.

Aromatherapy

At the beginning of pregnancy, full-body massage with essential oils of lavender, neroli and chamomile will calm and relax you, and should be carried out regularly. Other carefully selected oils, professionally chosen and blended for a pregnant woman, may also be used.

If swollen limbs at the end of the day is a problem in the final weeks of pregnancy, oils such as rosemary – blended with geranium and lavender – may be used in full-body massage or in the bath.

Clinical nutrition

Pregnancy requires an increase in blood volume, thereby raising a need for increased iron (500 to 1000mg of iron is donated to foetal growth and storage). Thus, any deficiency in iron is going to result in increased tiredness and fatigue. This often creates non-food cravings, e.g. ice, clay or starch. Stomach acid and ascorbic acid (Vitamin C) are essential for iron absorption. For about three months after pregnancy, there is an increased demand for iron (50mg/day). Failure to provide this will result in fatigue.

Medical herbalism

Dietary advice, combined with advice on both exercise and rest, is valuable. Remedies in the short term might include wild oats, vervain or rosemary. A vitamin supplement, especially Vitamin B may be suggested. Gentle tonics and restoratives to the nervous system help build up your energy without over stimulation.

27. EXCESSIVE VAGINAL DISCHARGE

Acupuncture

Acupuncture, with dietary advice or combined with Chinese herbal medicine, is often very helpful.

Aromatherapy

If the discharge is mucous or serous, then essential oils such as Rosemarinus officinalis var verbenone in a hydrosol may be used to help eliminate or lessen the discharge.

Clinical nutrition

About 50 per cent of all excessive vaginal discharge (yellow-green, frothy) is caused by a microscopic parasite called Trichomonas, and only normally presents a problem when the vaginal area becomes alkaline (blood is slightly alkaline, so the problem is often at its worst during and after menstruation). Treatment might include Vitamin A (as beta carotene, up to 50,000IU/day) Riboflavin (50mg/day), Vitamin B6 (100mg/day), and pantothenic acid (100mg/day).

Candida albicans (thrush) is responsible for about 25 per cent of cases, and can be helped by douching with live yoghurt or diluted (6:1) cider vinegar and warm water. Discharge is thick and cheesy.

The remainder are called non-specific vaginitis – usually a thin greyish colour. Treatment as for Candida.

Homoeopathy

According to the nature of the discharge, homoeopathic remedies can be prescribed – Calcrea for milky-white discharge, for example, Sepia if it's yellowish-green, or Platina for a watery discharge with marked itching. China is appropriate when there is also a feeling of itching.

Medical herbalism

Tinctures of marigold or ladies' mantle can be very helpful. Their astringency tones the membranes and reduces the discharge. The tinctures, diluted in salt water, are used as a wash or external (only) douche. They must not be taken internally.

28. VARICOSE VEINS IN LEGS

Aromatherapy

Essential oil of cypress in the bath is a helpful remedy. Careful massage (above the varicose area only) with cypress, lavender or juniper improves the tone of the vein walls.

Homoeopathy
Pulsatilla, followed by Lachesis or Nux Vomica, may be suggested by the homoeopath, if there is also constipation, haemorrhoids and irritability.

Medical herbalism
Advice on exercise, including frequent leg elevation, is likely to be combined with dietary advice and the use of Vitamin E to help maintain the elasticity of the vein walls. A local application of astringents like Calendula or witch-hazel would be beneficial.
   Full internal treatment may have to wait until after pregnancy.

29. VARICOSE VEINS IN VULVA
Homoeopathy
(See **Varicose Veins in Legs**, above.)

Medical herbalism
Treatment, combined with pelvic floor muscle exercises, is the same as for varicose veins in the legs.

30. VISUAL PROBLEMS
Due to the normal retention of water throughout pregnancy, the eyeball shape may change, causing interference to your vision.

Acupuncture
Acupuncture, in combination with the use of Chinese herbs, is often helpful.

Medical herbalism
Advice on exercise and rest is most important, but very mild diuretics such as couch grass or chamomile may be offered for a short period (up to one week).

Pregnancy problems helplines

The Active Birth Centre
55 Dartmouth Park Road, London NW5 (071 267 3006)
Preparation classes for you and, if you wish, your partner, to help your body prepare
   for labour and cope with the changes it goes through in pregnancy.

Caesarean Avoidance and Support Scheme (For Norfolk and Suffolk, but willing to
   help others as well)
Poplar Farm, Silverlys Green, Halesworth, Suffolk 1P19 0QJ
Offers advice, encouragement and information for those wishing to avoid a Caesarean
   delivery. It is also a befriending organization which can put women in touch with
   other mothers who have successfully had a vaginal delivery following a previous
   Caesarean birth.

389

Caesarean Support Network
2 Hurst Park Drive, Huyton, Liverpool L36 1TF (051 480 1184)
Support for women who are going to have, or have had, a Caesarean delivery; advice
and information for women who want to try for a vaginal delivery after having had
one C-section previously. Has support groups countrywide, one-to-one contacts,
plus publications and information leaflets.

Continence Line
(091 213 0050)
Advice on remaining continent during pregnancy and afterwards. They offer
literature, information over the phone and can put you in touch with your nearest
continence advisor (such as a specialist nurse working at a health centre of hospital).

Diabetics Care Department
British Diabetic Association, 10 Queen Anne Street, London W1 (071 323 1531)
Advice for pregnant diabetic women.

Maternity Link
The Old Co-op, 42 Chelsea Road, Easton, Bristol BS5 6AF (0272 558495)
Offers support, interpreting – and if required, English tuition to ante-natal and
post-natal women who do not speak English.

The Maternity Services Liaison Scheme
Brady Centre, 192 Hanbury Street, London E1 5HU (071 377 1064)
A network of community health workers who will accompany women of ethnic
minorities to ante-natal clinics and hospital to give birth. Offers ante-natal and
post-natal care via parent education classes in hospitals and health centres.

Miscarriage Association
c/o Clayton Hospital, Northgate, Wakefield (0924 200799)
Gives information, and support, from members who themselves have experienced
miscarriage via a countrywide network of 120 support groups. Has a newsletter and
information leaflets.

National Childbirth Trust
HQ – Alexandra House, Oldham Terrace, London W3 6NH (081 992 8637)
Advice and information for pregnant women and mothers on all aspects of maternity
and childbirth. Also have a catalogue of high-quality, inexpensive maternity and
nursing bras; plus details of childbirth preparation classes run by NCT teachers all
over the UK.

Osteopathy Clinic for Expectant Mothers
The British School of Osteopathy, 1 Suffolk Street, London SW1 (071 930 9254)
The only clinic in the UK designed specifically for pregnant women and the
prevention/treatment of back and posture problems which may develop during
pregnancy. Treatment is by senior students/recent graduates under the direction of
senior osteopath tutors. It is therefore cheaper than going to an osteopath's own
practice (approximately £15 for the first visit, then £11 thereafter – as opposed to
£20–£40 normally charged).

Specialist products and services

Aquacise

82 Cherry Tree Avenue, Clacton on Sea, Essex CO15 1AS (0255 436932)

Exercises in water devised by local GPs, physiotherapists, and a former swimming
  instructress. Suitable for pregnant women.

ASH (Action on Smoking and Health)

5–11 Mortimer Street, London W1 (071 637 9843)

Advice on how to cut down and stop smoking – important during and before
  pregnancy.

Boots

Check the telephone directory for the branch nearest you. Boots stock 'Sea Bands'
  (ask at the pharmacy counter). Sea Bands can also be purchased direct from the
  manufacturers.

Holland & Barrett health shops

Check your telephone directory for the shop nearest you. H & B stock a number of
  essential oils – look for their own brand, as these are made by a good aromatherapy
  company called Tisserand. They cost about £4 for a small bottle. H & B also stock
  numerous nutritional supplements and homoeopathic supplies.

Independent Professional Therapist International

(0777 700383)

There are masseurs who can help with water retention and relaxation at all good
  beauty salons, plus most of the salons in major department stores (for example,
  Glemby). To try to find one who will come to your home – a more relaxing and
  often more beneficial treatment – contact the IPTI, which has a register of all
  professionally qualified masseurs and beauticians.

Lastosheer Support Stockings

Their Class I variety in black, and two beige shades, are on prescription from your
  GP, if you specify Lastosheer by Kendall. Class I look like ordinary fashion tights
  or stockings, unlike most proper brands of support hose, which can look very thick
  and unattractive. You can also order them from the pharmacy at your chemist,
  without prescription, but they will cost you about £11 per pair. These are the only
  prescription hosiery available in fashionable black.

McCarthy's Medical Supplies

(0708 746033)

Makers of ginger capsules, which can help banish morning sickness. You can get
  them on prescription from your GP or obstetrician, or order them privately
  through the pharmacy of a chemist (in which case you have to pay for them –
  upwards from £20 for 100 capsules). The usual dosage is one, three times daily
  before meals, or, if the sickness is very bad, two, three times daily.

National Society for Non-Smokers

Latimer House, 40–45 Hanson Street, London W1 (071 636 9103)

Nature's Best
PO Box 1, Tunbridge Wells, Kent TN2 3EQ (0892 34143)
Manufacturers of ginger pills, which they say are primarily for travel sickness. They are worth trying, as they are substantially cheaper than most morning sickness tablets.

QUIT (Stop Smoking Classes)
National Society for Non-Smokers, Latimer House, 40–48 Hanson Street, London W1P 7DE
Courses are £25 for five sessions in the London area. They will supply lists of contacts countrywide who run similar courses based on a behavioural, habit-breaking approach and follow-up support. **Stopping smoking is one of the most important things you can do if you are pregnant, or trying to become pregnant. Yet the largest survey on the subject, at Queens Medical Centre in Nottingham, in 1989, found that 37 per cent of pregnant women were smoking and only one in four managed to stop during their pregnancy. The study also found that in half these cases, the women's GPs had never said anything to them about quitting while pregnant, nor how to go about it.**

The Society of Chiropodists
53 Wellbeck Street, London W1 (071 486 3381)
Can put you in touch with your nearest, qualified chiropodist.

Ultrasound information
(0753 672781)
Not everyone thinks regular ultrasound scans are necessarily a good thing. For the other side of the argument read, 'Ultrasound? Unsound' by the Association of Independent Midwives, £5.

Further reading
Pregnancy After 30 by Mary Anderson (Faber)
Active Birth by Janet Balaskas (Sidgwick & Jackson)
Natural Pregnancy by Janet Balaskas (Sidgwick & Jackson)
New Life by Janet and Arthur Balaskas (Sidgwick & Jackson)
Who's Having Your Baby? A Health Rights Handbook to Maternity Care by Beverley Beech (Camden Press)
Pregnancy by Gordon Bourne (Pan)
Childbirth for Men by Herbert Brant (Oxford University Press)
Sex During Pregnancy and After Childbirth by Sylvia Close (Thorsons)
Diabetes and Pregnancy by Anna Knopfler (Optima)
Birth Over 30 by Sheila Kitzinger (Sheldon Press)
Pregnancy and Childbirth by Sheila Kitzinger (Sheldon Press)
Birth Reborn by Michel Odent (Fontana)
Your Body, Your Baby, Your Life by Angela Phillips, with Nicky Leap and Barbara Jacobs (Pandora)
Caesareans by E. Phillips (Sidgwick & Jackson)
Being Pregnant by Ruth Steinberg (Anaya)

Post-pregnancy problems

Just as no two pregnancies are ever exactly the same, no two recoveries from childbirth are the same either – and nor are the resulting babies. Everyone's experience of labour is different, just as every woman's powers and rate of physical and mental recovery vary.

But for all the more common problems associated with childbirth and getting back to normal afterwards, there is plenty you can do to speed the process yourself. Your doctor or obstetrician can make things easier for you, too, and help you deal with any possible difficulties which do not seem to be resolving themselves.

And if it seems that everyone from your ante-natal class is springing back to normal faster than you – don't believe them. It is perfectly normal for a woman to take anything up to a year after delivery to get completely back to her former self.

When can we make love again?
Because everyone's experience of childbirth is different, and so are their rates of recovery and their libidos, there are no hard and fast rules about when you 'should' resume sex. Some women find their sexual desire doesn't really return for a year or so, others feel back to normal after a very few weeks.

As soon as you and your partner wish to you can make love, although doctors recommend waiting until after your six-week post-natal check-up before you resume having full intercourse again, because of the possible risk of infection. Doctors would also advise you to avoid tampons and use pads as sanitary protection for that six weeks, for the same reason. If you feel loving before the six weeks has elapsed there's no reason whatsoever why you cannot both enjoy oral or gentle manual stimulation together.

Other women find six weeks far too soon. However, psychosexual counsellors do suggest that you both have some level of sensual contact (such as gentle caressing or stroking) before the six-week post-natal check-up to 'give yourself permission' to become a sexual person once again, because sometimes the longer this resumption of sexual contact is left, the more difficult it can seem. Many women also find they want to wait for a while in order to re-establish the privacy of their bodies, having had a birth experience where they felt they and their most private areas were on view and 'shared' by all and sundry.

The information for problems you might meet after pregnancy and childbirth is given in chart form to make it as quick and easy to scan through as possible. For the relevant help and support associations, see HELPLINES.

Post-pregnancy problems and what to do about them

Problems and causes

ANAEMIA. This could be caused by anaemia during your pregnancy or by excessive bleeding during delivery.

ABDOMEN BADLY STRETCHED. This is due to the growth of the baby and womb and will be made worse by excessive weight gain.

BREAST SHAPE AND SIZE. Your breasts may be less upstanding, or less firm, due to an increase in size. 'Dropping' may have been caused by size increase without sufficient support.

CAESAREAN DISCOMFORT. Though it is now a very safe operation, a Caesarean is still regarded as a major procedure as it involves making a cut in, then carefully restitching, both the abdominal wall and the womb. It may well cause discomfort for many weeks afterwards, especially if you are breastfeeding

Medical help

You will need a blood transfusion if the problem is acute enough. Otherwise you will be given iron tablets, which can take a long time to help build up your iron reserves, and are not a fast route to anaemia improvement.

If you are not intending to have any more children, you may want to consider an abdominoplasty surgery operation. Approximately about £3,500 to have done privately, as it is hardly ever available on the NHS.) (See HELPLINES.)

Cosmetic surgery is an option if you don't intend to have any more babies (see HELPLINES). (About £2,000 for an uplift done privately; it is not available on the NHS if it is for cosmetic reasons.)

Nil, unless your stitches are infected.

Self help

* Take iron tablets with folic acid (just iron alone is not well absorbed by the body). A linctus called Floradix from health shops is a very good source.
* Follow an iron-rich diet: ask to see the hospital nutritionist for advice before you leave.
* Ensure the hospital does a check on your blood.

* Exercises may help to tone up the muscles underneath the skin, so they support it better.
* Try not to put on too much weight.

* If they are much larger, wear a good bra day and night from about the sixth month, and all the time while breastfeeding.
* Exercises help, e.g. pressing the palms of your hands together, elbows out at right angles at breast height, if done as often as possible.
* Swimming, especially breast stroke, is a great help too.

* To ease breastfeeding, use soft pillows to support the baby or a light 'Snugglesac' (see HELPLINES).
* To help recovery do the post-natal exercises shown to you by the hospital physiotherapist or midwife religiously – and make sure they do give you advice.

(which causes the womb to contract – and the baby is lying across the area which has been stitched).

You will be allowed home in 5 to 8 days. Any bloody discharge should cease in 3 to 5 weeks, but soreness may remain for much longer.

CERVICAL PROBLEMS. Many women develop ulcers or small erosions on their cervix during pregnancy (responsible for some of the heavier discharge). About half heal spontaneously; others may become infected.

Cervical erosion is the shedding of some soft ripe cells on the outer layer of your cervix which have a richer blood supply when you are pregnant. This can produce a blood 'spotting' effect, or a slightly blood-stained discharge.

CONTRACEPTION. Many unplanned pregnancies happen in the first few months after a birth. Fear of pregnancy can also cause sexual difficulties for both partners. Safe contraception will help both problems.

If you are breastfeeding fully (see BREASTFEEDING DIFFICULTIES, page 52) this is about 98 per cent effective at preventing pregnancy, due to suppression of oestrogen production.

* Mention any problems to the doctor at your six-week post-natal check-up.
* Contact one of the Caesarean support groups for detailed advice and, if you wish, contact with other women who have had a Caesarean (see HELPLINES).

Nil, but if you notice any discharge that's unusual for you, see your GP to check there is no infection.

Infections will be treated by your GP with the appropriate medication.

Ask your doctor or family planning clinic about the choices of contraception available.

* Many couples find the sheath convenient for a while, even if they did not use one before.
* Your six-week post-natal check is a good time to have an IUD fitted. There is a greater risk of it being expelled if it's fitted earlier.
* If you prefer the Pill, opt for a low-dose progesterone-only or mini Pill if you are breastfeeding. (The oestrogen of the Combined Pill will interfere with your milk supply.)
* If you want to use a cap or diaphragm get properly fitted for one either by a GP who has had special family planning training or at a family planning or well woman clinic. If you used one before you will have to be refitted as your vagina and cervix will have changed shape a bit after delivery. You may prefer to wait a few months, however, as the tension in the tissues around the cervix may make wearing a snugly-fitting cap with a spring in its rim quite uncomfortable.

Problems and causes

EPISIOTOMY TEAR OR CUT. This may be made to make more room for the baby's head to get past your perineum (the muscular area between your anus and vagina). Average tears heal more readily than larger cuts. Any larger cuts or larger tears will need stitching up afterwards, and can be most uncomfortable when healing.

Medical help

Episiotomy cuts are currently made in an average of 50–60 per cent of births – but this rate varies from hospital to hospital, and from consultant to consultant. If they do not heal well and are lumpy and uncomfortable you can have the excess growth removed surgically.

If it grows back lumpy again, the scar is what is known as 'keloid' and may be helped by steroids injected directly into it. If it healed badly and causes you discomfort it may be necessary to have a small operation to open the scar again and stitch it up very carefully once more, so it heals smoothly.

Episiotomies should be feeling better by your six-week check-up after the birth – if yours is not, mention it forcibly to your doctor.

Self help

* It may help to sit on a child's plastic swimming ring or a foam rubber ring, of the sort used in geriatric wards, to reduce the pressure on your stitches.
* Keep the area very clean (rinse in a bidet or with the showerhead, from front to back, after urinating or emptying your bowels).
* Dry thoroughly ('soggy' stitches become more easily infected) with a hairdryer on a cool setting, not with a potentially abrasive and less than sterile towel. Soothing cold compresses help: try taking six wet mens' cotton handkerchiefs, laying plastic in layers between them (a cut up supermarket plastic carrier bag would do) and freezing the cotton and plastic 'sandwich' in the fridge freezer compartment. Use them one at a time, twisted into a slim, flexible – and very cold – pad, on the episiotomy area. Ice packs help.
* Also bathe in salt baths (add a handful of salt to each bath) or in herb infusion baths (using equal measures of comfrey, uva ursa and shepherd's purse from a herbalist – see HELPLINES).
* If you are breastfeeding your baby, lying down or standing up are the most comfortable positions for a few days.
* When urinating, if the stitches sting, pour a glass of water or cold comfrey tea (keep some in a big container by the lavatory, and make some fresh every day) over the perineum area as you do so to reduce the sting and help the area heal.
* See also CHILDBIRTH, pages 137–8

FLATTER FEET. The ligaments of the foot, including the arches, soften during pregnancy – as do other ligaments in your body. Excess weight gain exacerbates this problem. Feet may get a half size bigger for the same reason.

See a chiropodist (ensure he is state registered).

* Practise foot exercises: picking up imaginary pencils with your toes 24 times a day; or standing with your feet together, trying to turn your knees outwards while still pressing ankles together (this sounds unlikely but you will feel this pulling on your foot arches and buttocks).
* Exercise sandals help; so does any sensible footwear.

HAIR LOSS. Your hair becomes sparser, and may seem thinner and more brittle. This is partly due to hormonal changes after the birth (your body no longer has all the extra oestrogen and progesterone it has had for nine months, which might have had the effect of making your hair glossier).

Also, hair has a 6 to 9 month cycle – growing, resting, falling out. During pregnancy the hormones ensure that all hair goes into a growing phase, so it seems to get thicker. The hair follicles pass into a resting phase after the delivery, then the hairs begin to fall out, so it seems thinner.

Your doctor will reassure you that the hair thinning is temporary. A trichologist may be able to help (see HELPLINES) if you are really worried.

* Massage your scalp to bring nutrient-rich blood to the hair follicles to encourage new growth: do it every time you wash your hair.
* Use good-quality salon protein and home-use treatments (e.g. Redken).
* As a stop-gap, use a cosmetic hair-thickening product to make hair look fuller (ordinary blow-dry lotion also has a similar effect, and it is cheap).
* A good homemade protein shampoo which strengthens hair and makes it look fuller is: 2 tablespoons of ordinary shampoo, 1 packet of powdered gelatin and one egg. Mix together and use as an ordinary shampoo, leaving it on for 5 to 10 minutes.

INCONTINENCE. Leaking a little when you cough, laugh, more vigorously, etc, is due to the stress of the baby's growing weight pressing down during pregnancy on the sling of muscle that forms your pelvic floor. Afterwards the stress of the delivery itself can also affect the muscle tone of the pelvic floor. One in three women develops a continence problem following pregnancy and childbirth.

Requesting delivery by Caesarean section can help avoid pelvic floor stress during delivery. However most obstetricians would not carry out a C section just for this reason – although it is now very safe it is still classed as a major operation.

Pelvic floor surgery may be suggested if the problem is still there, despite exercises, six months or so after delivery (see HELPLINES).

* Do pelvic floor exercises religiously before, during and after pregnancy.
* Other methods of controls such as pelvic cones, passive pelvic exercises, etc, also help.
* See INCONTINENCE page 239.

Problems and causes

LABIAL TEARS. The delivery of the baby may cause small tears in the labia (the soft fleshy lips around your vulva leading to your vagina). They do not usually need to be stitched as they are quite small, and should heal pretty fast.

Birthing stools and birth cushions may produce more of these small labial tears *but* they make an episiotomy less likely, as the sitting/squatting position helps the coccyx swing backwards and widens the pelvic area and its soft tissues to create a little more vital room for the baby's descending head.

LACK OF PHYSICAL DESIRE. Sheer tiredness during your physical and mental recovery, and the fact that your sleep patterns are being shattered, are enough to put any woman off sex.

Also, you may not want to be touched because your breasts are sore from breastfeeding or your episiotomy site hurts.

MENTAL SHARPNESS. Many women complain that they seem to have lost their mental 'edge' after the birth of a baby, and never quite get it back. The extra hormones produced in pregnancy help keep you calm, and you may even find your memory is slightly affected while pregnant. But experts suggest that although any loss of mental edge afterwards

Medical help

Nil, unless they are big enough to need stitching. Your doctor may suggest certain anaesthetic or antiseptic creams.

If you lost a lot of blood during delivery or your iron intake was not very high during your pregnancy, you might be anaemic. Ask your GP for a blood test.

If you are anaemic, ask about having a small blood transfusion to boost your haemoglobin count – iron supplements can take a long time to do so.

Your doctor would encourage you to get the extra help you need at home, and would also speak to your partner on your behalf if you wished it.

Self help

* Keep the area very clean to help them heal.
* Use any gentle antiseptic your midwife or GP recommends.

* Try and get as much rest in cat-nap form as you can.
* Get your partner to take over a night feed.
* Get help from friends and family during the day so you can sleep.
* Eat iron-rich foods in case you are anaemic, and consider iron supplements.
* Give yourself time to recover physically and emotionally, and explain your feelings to your partner.
* If you are worried about this problem, or it is affecting your relationship, perhaps it would help to talk things through. If you want the help of a counsellor – see HELPLINES.

* If you are feeling increasingly less able rather than more able to cope, tell your GP, midwife or health visitor at once. The way you are feeling may be a warning sign that you are developing post-natal depression (see POST-NATAL ILLNESS, page 346) and need extra help and support for a while so it does not get worse.

may possibly be due to hormonal adjustment it is more likely to be due to tiredness. Breastfeeding, however, may make a difference. The hormone prolactin, which produces milk, also temporarily suppresses oestrogen production. And as many menopausal women find, lack of oestrogen can, amongst other things, affect memory and mental agility. (See BREASTFEEDING DIFFICULTIES and MENOPAUSE, pages 52 and 276.)

PERIODS RETURNING. If you do not breastfeed your periods should return within six to eight weeks. They may be rather heavier than before. You might experience a slightly different type of period pain, which some women describe as being sharper than before, as the blood vessels constrict more. Some women, however, find their periods become easier.

* If you are being made very uncomfortable by your periods now, and you never were before, go back and see your doctor. (See also PERIOD PROBLEMS.)

PERSISTENT PILES. Piles are haemorrhoids – veins like varicose veins which have relaxed under hormonal control to become distended. If around the anus, they can itch and be most uncomfortable. The haemorrhoids should disappear by about 3 months after your delivery, as your vascular system returns to normal.

Nil

If they have not gone 3 months after your delivery, your doctor may suggest minor surgery to remove them. A GP can also prescribe strong, local anaesthetic creams to tide you over current discomfort.

* Haemorrhoid creams take away the itch and sting temporarily, and are available at the chemist.

Problems and causes

PMS (Pre-menstrual syndrome). Some women develop PMS after their second or third baby, although they never had it before. One explanation is that they are more vulnerable to hormonal changes than others and their hormonal systems never quite 'click' back into place after a birth. Another reason is the tiredness and stress that looking after a new baby, with little sleep, can cause. The baby may also have depleted some of your nutritional reserves so that you are now short of certain nutrients (like zinc and magnesium) which can help prevent PMS.

POST-NATAL DEPRESSION (PND) is *not* all in the mind. Though recognized as a psychiatric illness, its causes are physical (hormonal upheaval, which some women may be more vulnerable to than others, tiredness from the birth and the demands of a new baby) and social (feeling isolated, needing help and company, not getting any support). (See also POST-NATAL ILLNESS, page 346.)

VAGINAL DRYNESS. If you are breastfeeding, your vagina may still be rather dry as breastfeeding suppresses oestrogen production

Medical help

Clinical nutriton could help (see a doctor trained in nutrition); as could a good gynaecologist specializing in PMS (see HELPLINES).

Treatments include hormones, tranquillizers and anti-depressants to tide you over until you begin to feel better naturally; also counselling and group support, and better nutrition.

Your doctor may consider offering you short-term hormone treatment to help hormone balance; or oestrogen creams to use

Self help

* Reduce stress and tiredness (if you can).
* Eat more healthily.
* Take supplements or hormonal treatments if necessary. (See also PRE-MENSTRUAL SYNDROME, page 411.)

* Contact your midwife, GP, the PND Advisory Service or your health visitor *as soon as* you realize that you are feeling less, rather than more, able to cope.
* Some doctors feel mild PND may be prevented with Vitamin B6 and Evening Primrose Oil, taken for six weeks before until three months after the birth (see POSTNATAL ILLNESS, page 346).
* Women who developed PND previously can be helped with the right care and support to prevent it happening again.
* Organize as much help as possible, in the home and with your new baby, and avoid stress (such as demanding work or moving house) before the birth.

* KY jelly helps a good deal if your vagina feels dry all the time. Keeping it lubricated also helps avoid any infections which could

(see BREASTFEEDING DIFFICULTIES, page 52). Another reason for dryness may be that your hormonal system is not yet back to normal and so you may be short of oestrogen anyway.

WEIGHT LOSS DIFFICULTY. Your body lays down fat supplies during pregnancy as part of its biological programming to have enough 'put by' for breastfeeding. If you do not breastfeed, or do not do so for long, this extra fat can be hard to shift. There may also be a hormonal connection with cellulite formation – which is even harder to lose than fat cells which are arranged in the usual way.

EXTRA INFO: Mood swings: see PND. Evening Primrose Oil and zinc supplements may help, as can Rescue Remedy (A Bach Flower remedy from Holland & Barrett stores and good health shops: acts as a mild tranquilizer). Thrush: can be a problem if you still have bleeding and discharge. Regular cool water washing there plus a few drops of tea tree oil in bath water help – see Thrush chapter too. Slight prolapse: of vagina, womb or rectum may be a problem if delivery very rapid or problematic: pelvic exercises, faradic pelvic stimulation from hospital physio dept and if necessary after 6 months, a 'tuck' in the area can all help (see Prolapse chapter).

locally on your vagina. Also ask him to check you thoroughly for any possible vaginal infections (you may have developed one after delivery).

None, unless you are dangerously overweight and may have heart problems because of it. Your doctor may advise you on a good diet, refer you to a community nutritionist or advise a very low calorie diet for up to four weeks if you are breastfeeding.

arise in tiny cracks in the dry skin.
* If you are not breastfeeding and the problem persists, go back and see your obstetrician – mention this at your six-week post-natal check-up.

* Try and keep your weight down in pregnancy.
* Do not 'eat for two': you only need approximately 200 to 250 extra calories a day.
* The best time to lose fat deposits is in the 8 weeks after delivery – they seem to shed more easily then, so again watch what you eat (follow a diet high in proteins, low in sugars and saturated fats).
* Breastfeeding helps – it can use up to 1,000 calories a day if you are doing so fully (see BREASTFEEDING DIFFICULTIES, page 52).
* If you find you need more food go for complex carbohydrates, e.g. bread, rather than sweet foods.
* Try and exercise each day: a brisk walk for half an hour with the baby each day will help.
* Do not actually *diet* (i.e. calorie count) *while* breastfeeding. But try afterwards.
* If you have put on a lot of weight and cannot seem to get rid of it, ask your doctor about a very low calorie diet for 10 days, e.g. The Cambridge Diet (see also HELPLINES) to get your weight loss off to a flying start. After that go for a healthy eating regime, to maintain weight loss. Joining a weight loss and maintenance organization like Weight Watchers will also help. (See HELPLINES.)

Complementary therapy

Complementary therapies tailor their treatments very much to the individual: the precise nature of the treatment you receive will vary, depending on your medical history, symptoms, lifestyle, etc. The following information indicates the *sorts* of things a therapist is most likely to do or recommend. Do not be surprised if they feel you need something slightly different. This section is meant purely as an indication of likely treatments; it is not meant as a DIY guide to the medical uses of the different complementary therapies.

1. INCONTINENCE
(See INCONTINENCE, page 247.)

2. POORLY HEALED PERINEAL OR VAGINAL TRAUMA
Acupuncture
Acupuncture may help, but you *must* have a consultation with a qualified and experienced therapist.

Aromatherapy
An individual blend of essential oils of lavender, chamomile or everlasting flower (Helycrismus) in apricot or peach kernel oil, which you can apply yourself, will encourage healing and avoid secondary infection, leaving a neat, pain-free scar.

Clinical nutrition
Vitamin E supplements will help.

Homoeopathy
A slow-healing, painful wound usually needs Hypericum. For infected wounds, Echninacea tincture may be applied, or alternating doses of Ars-Alb and Hepar-Sulph.

Medical herbalism
Preparations from herbs such as comfrey or calendula will soothe inflammation and aid healing. These are applied on the outside, not taken internally.

3. WEIGHT GAIN
Acupuncture
Acupuncture, combined with dietary advice, may be helpful if the reason for the weight gain can be found.

Aromatherapy
Dietary advice is important. If fluid retention is the problem, lymphatic drainage massage may help. If you are 'comfort eating', relaxing bath treatments will help relieve stress and aid relaxation.

Clinical nutrition
A careful diet – consisting of one meal a day and two protein drinks with psyllium husks and guar gum for your bowels, multi-vitamin and mineral tablets, and evening primrose oil – will help. In addition, pituitary gland extract regulates the endocrine glands.

Homoeopathy
The homoeopath will want to discover the underlying emotional cause of weight gain

and advise on correct diet and regular exercise. *Natrum mus* will help if fluid retention is a cause. Phytolacca berry, used daily as the mother tincture, helps to reduce cravings for food. Calc-Carb helps if appetite is unpredictable (or bizarre) and you feel chilly and depressed.

Medical herbalism
Advice on a nutritionally sound diet at a correct level, and on exercise, is of great importance. Hormonal imbalance can be corrected, and mild diuretics (such as cleavers or fennel) may be used to encourage fluid expulsion. Kelp can be of value as it provides iodine for your thyroid gland, which helps increase your metabolic rate.

4. ANAEMIA
Acupuncture
The underlying source of the anaemia must be found before treatment can be offered.

Clinical nutrition
Iron tablets or liquid with liver glandular tissue are helpful to relieve iron deficiency anaemia. For pernicious anaemia, Vitamin B12 lozenges are more easily absorbed. Tahini (sesame seed paste) greatly enhances iron absorption in your normal diet as does Vitamin C, taken with iron.

Homoeopathy
If the anaemia is due to fluid loss (such as bleeding or breastfeeding) cinchona is usually the choice remedy. But a full consultation is vital before any treatment can be considered.

Medical herbalism
Dietary advice is very important, as the problem is often faulty absorption rather than just inadequate intake of iron – supplements are notoriously constipating and disturbing to the bowels. Remedies may include yellow dock to improve your digestion and absorption, or nettle or parsley, which are rich in iron.

5. HAIR LOSS
Acupuncture
Many cases are due to hormonal imbalance. Acupuncture is successful in over sixty per cent of cases, by balancing your hormones. It may be combined with the use of Chinese herbs and acupressure.

Aromatherapy
Daily scalp massage with a blend of oils of lavender, rosemary or chamomile in apricot kernel oil or jojoba increases scalp circulation and nourishes your hair follicles.

Clinical nutrition
The chief causes of hair loss are lack of protein or an underactive thyroid. The first step is to check your normal diet and seek improvements. Thyroid glandular concentrate can be offered if your thyroid gland is unproductive.

Homoeopathy
Advice on diet and nutritional supplements should be combined with an individual prescription by a qualified homoeopath. Some of the remedies used are Nat. Mur., Sepia, Carbo-Veg and Lycopodium.

Medical herbalism
Dietary advice and treatment for poor digestive function and circulation are valuable. Infusions of rosemary, juniper or nettle, applied to your head, help to stimulate your scalp and encourage the follicles to regrow hair.

6. STRETCH MARKS
(See PREGNANCY PROBLEMS, page 376.)

7. BADLY STRETCHED SKIN ON MUSCLES AND BREASTS
Acupuncture
Treatment for three to six months will increase your muscle tone and improve the elasticity of your muscles and skin.

Aromatherapy
A long period of regular massage with essential oils of lavender, sandalwood or frankincense may help to improve tissue vitality, if it's used in conjunction with a balanced diet.

Clinical nutrition
Vitamin E and pantothenic acid strengthen the elasticity of your skin, which may become damaged in pregnancy due to lack of protein. Supplements of these vitamins will also help avoid stretch marks. If your muscles are slack after pregnancy, calcium and magnesium supplements help build them up.

Homoeopathy
Slack muscles, combined with a tendency to become easily fatigued, respond to Gelsemium.

Medical herbalism
Advice on exercise and posture, combined with massage, can help to tone up tissue and improve circulation to your muscles and skin.

8. VARICOSE VEINS
(See PREGNANCY PROBLEMS, page 376.)

9. DEVELOPMENT OF EROSIONS OR ULCERS ON CERVIX
Homoeopathy
Careful consultation to discover the type of ulcer you have, must be undertaken before a remedy can be recommended.

Medical herbalism
Douches with Calendula or comfrey promote healing, and may be used with internal remedies like Echinacea to stimulate your immune system and help prevent infection.

10. MORE PAINFUL PERIODS (WHEN THEY RETURN)
Acupuncture
When the cause is hormonal imbalance, acupuncture can be beneficial. General period pain also responds well to acupuncture. (See also the PMT and PERIOD PROBLEMS, pages 422 and 339.)

Aromatherapy
(See PMT and PERIOD PROBLEMS, pages 422 and 339.)

Clinical nutrition
To restore glandular balance, anterior pituitary glandulars, ovary glandulars and *dong quai* all help. Painful periods may be due to calcium loss. A calcium supplement, with or without evening primrose oil, can be very helpful.

Homoeopathy
(See PMT and PERIOD PROBLEMS, pages 422 and 339.)

Medical herbalism
Chaste tree and false unicorn root have powerful beneficial effects on the cycle. The first tends to encourage progesterone secretion, whole the second benefits the first part of the cycle, when oestrogen secretion is more important. (See also PMT *and* PERIOD PROBLEMS, pages 422 and 339.)

Osteopathy
Osteopathic treatment may increase drainage from a sluggish pelvis via spinal manipulation and pressure-point work.

11. LOSS OF LIBIDO (NOT RELATED TO FATIGUE)
Acupuncture
Many cases can be helped by either acupuncture or acupressure, combined with Chinese herbal medicine, over a period of three to six months.

Aromatherapy
The aromatherapist can blend a selection of relaxing oils – including, for example, clary sage, ylang ylang, rose or sandalwood – to be used by your partner in a quiet and private atmosphere.

Clinical nutrition
Histadine deficiency can cause loss of libido and should, therefore, be replaced. Chlorophyll, which helps build up sex hormones, can also be helpful.

Homoeopathy
Sepia is a good remedy.

Medical herbalism
Tonics for your ovaries (such as false unicorn root) and stimulants can be effective. A short course of ginseng helps to improve general energy and well-being.

12. MENTAL SHARPNESS
Acupuncture
Acupuncture promotes *yin-yang* balance, both mentally and physically.

Aromatherapy
Essential oils such as basil and rosemary improve your concentration and mental capability, clarify your thoughts, and increase mental agility.

Clinical nutrition
This condition may be caused by low blood sugar or low oxygen blood. A diet lower in sugars, refined carbohydrates, coffee, tea and alcohol, supplemented with brewer's yeast, will counteract low blood sugar. Chlorophyll tablets and Vitamin B15 attract

oxygen to the blood. Manganese, magnesium or protein deficiency all decrease alertness. Supplements can be provided.

Medical herbalism
Specific remedies for hormone imbalance may be prescribed, together with tonic and restorative remedies such as rosemary, vervain or (in the short term) kola. Extra Vitamin B can also be helpful.

13. POST-NATAL DEPRESSION
(See POST-NATAL ILLNESS, page 356.)

14. SEX AFTER PREGNANCY
Pain around the site of an episiotomy scar, and anaemia are discussed in the chapter on Post-Pregnancy Problems (page 393).
   Sore breasts in newly breastfeeding mothers can often be helped by complementary therapy.

Acupuncture
Pain and inflammation respond well to acupuncture.

Aromatherapy
Compresses of lavender and chamomile increase your blood flow and ease tender breasts. Massage of your nipples with essential oil of lavender in apricot kernel oil helps nipple soreness and, if carried out by your partner, can also be sexually stimulating.

Clinical nutrition
Vitamin supplements of A, C and E, combined with a Vitamin E cream massage, ease inflammation of cracked nipples or blocked milk ducts.

Medical herbalism
Local applications with remedies such as marigold, lavender, marshmallow or comfrey help reduce soreness and heal cracked nipples.

Post-pregnancy problems helplines

The Association of Breastfeeding Mothers
ABM Order Department, Sydenham Green Health Centre, 26 Holmshaw Road, London SE26 (081 778 4769)
See BREASTFEEDING DIFFICULTIES, page 52, for more information.

The Association for Post-Natal Illness
25 Jerdan Place, London SW6 (071 386 0868)
Advice and support for mothers with post-natal illness of all degrees. They offer advice on obtaining correct treatment and puts you in contact with other former sufferers, by phone. Helpful literature is supplied.

The British Association for Counselling
37a Sheep Street, Rugby, CU21 3BY
(0788 578 328)
Has a directory of therapists all over the country, and of helpful organizations.
  They can tell you where to find a local counsellor who can help if you find you
  have a sexual or relationship problem after the birth of your baby.

British Society for Nutritional Medicine
Dr Alan Stewart, Bio Lab, 9 Weymouth Street, London W1
The information officer, Dr Stewart, can put you in touch with a clinical
  nutritionist.

Caesarean Support Group
Isle of Man coordinator Yvonne Williams (0624 620 647)
Offers information and support to women who have had a Caesarean – and to their
  partners.

Caesarean Support Network
2 Hurst Park Drive, Huyton, Liverpool L36 1TF (051 480 1184)
Support, advice, contact mums, meetings and literature – for all aspects of
  Caesarean delivery.

Continence Line
(091 213 0050)
Gives advice, information and literature on all aspects of regaining and maintaining
  continence. Can also put you in touch with your nearest Continence Advisor
  (specially trained nurses working at health centres and hospitals).
Please see INCONTINENCE, page 239, for further information.

Cry-sis Support Group
BM Cry-sis, London WC1 3XX (071 404 5011)
Advice, support and information for mothers whose babies cry excessively

The Family Planning Association
See GENERAL HELPLINES, page 480, for details.

The Harley Medical Group
6 Harley Street, London W1 (071 631 5494)
Private clinic (probably the best-known one) specializing in all types of cosmetic
  surgery. Has a free advice line – ask to speak to one of their nurse counsellors
  (trained SRNs), who can give basic advice, explain what is involved in certain
  cosmetic operations, and estimate likely costs.

La Leche League
BM 3424, London WC1 (071 242 1278)
See PREGNANCY HELPLINES, page 390, for details

MAMA (Meet-A-Mum Association)
26A Cumnor Hill, Oxford OX2 9HA
Runs self-help groups for new mothers to meet other mothers in their area, to try to
  help tackle the isolation of being at home all day alone with a young baby.

Marie Stopes Clinics
HQ – Marie Stopes House, 108 Whitfield Street, London W1P 6BE (071 388 2585)
Marie Stopes Centre, 10 Queen Square, Leeds LS2 8AJ (0532 440685)
Marie Stopes Centre, 1 Police Street, Manchester M2 7LQ (061 832 4260)
Have counsellors who can also help you with any sexual or relationship difficulties
    developing after the birth of a baby. (See GENERAL HELPLINES, page 480, for details)

The Maternity Alliance
15 Britannia Street, London WC1 (071 837 1265)
Advice and information on legal rights and benefits for new mothers.

Medical Advisory Service
10 Barley Mow Passage, Chiswick, London W4 (081 994 6477)
Advice on how to get the right sort of medical treatment for a whole range of
    problems, including pregnancy related ones – and cosmetic surgery – both on the
    NHS and privately. A charity run by trained nurse counsellors.

National Association for Pre-Menstrual Syndrome
(0483 572806)
Help and advice for PMS sufferers, treating the problems from a hormonal angle with
    natural progesterone.

National Childbirth Trust (NCT)
HQ – Alexandra House, Oldham Terrace, London W3 6NH (081 992 8637)
Advice on all aspects of pregnancy, childbirth and post-pregnancy problems.

NIPPERS
PO Box 1553, Wedmore, Somerset

Parents Anonymous Lifeline
6–9 Manor Gardens, London N7 (071 263 8918)
Confidential service run by volunteers for parents who are having problems with new
    babies or older children.

RELATE
Herbert Gray College, Little Church Street, Rugby (0788 573241)
Can put you in touch with your nearest branch, which will counsel you and your
    partner if you find you have any sexual or relationship difficulties which develop
    after the birth of your baby.

TAMBA (Twins and Multiple Births Association)
TWINLINE: PO Box 30, Little Sutton, South Wirral L66 1TH (051 348 0020)
Advice, information and support groups for parents of twins.

Woman's Health Concern
PO Box 1629, London W8 (071 938 3932)
Help and advice from trained nurse counsellors for all types of women's health
    problems, including those relating to pregnancy and childbirth.

Women's Nutritional Advisory Service
PO Box 268, Hove, East Sussex (0273 771366)
Advice and help for women suffering from PMS, using nutrition to combat the
   problems. (Please see PMS and PMS HELPLINES, pages 411–426, for details)

Specialist products and services
Very Low Calorie Diets:
Always check with your GP, whether or not a Very Low Calorie Diet would be suitable
for you. Do not go on a low-calorie diet when breastfeeding, or too soon after delivery,
as you will need all of your energy to recover fully and quickly.

   Very Low Calorie Diets are nutritionally complete meals in powdered form (mix with
water) or diet bar form, which give you all of the vitamins, minerals and protein you
need each day, but at less than 500 calories per day. It is not recommended that you use
these diets as a regular form of dieting – or that you go on them for longer than two
weeks without a doctor's supervision.

   Diets are sold by private distributors with no specialist nutritional training, not via
shops. For your nearest contact call:

Ainsworth Homoeopathic Pharmacy
38 New Cavendish Street, London W1M 7LH (071 935 5330)
Stockists and mail-order suppliers of homoeopathic remedies

G. Baldwin and Company
173 Walforth Road, London SE17 (071 703 5550)
Herbalist health foods.

Culpeper Ltd
21 Bruton Street, London W1 (071 629 4559)

The Cambridge Diet (0603 760777)
Uni Vite (0296 630900)

Culpeper Ltd
21 Bruton Street, London W1 (071 629 4559)
Herbalists – call for details of branches and mail order.

Institute of Trichology
288 Stockwell Road, London SW9 (071 733 2056)
Can put you in touch with a professional trichologist in your area if your GP cannot
   recommend one.

Neal's Yard
(0865 245 436)
For herbal preparations and whole food. Mail order.

Slimming Magazine Clubs
HQ – 071 225 1711
Contact HQ for details of approximately 550 slimming clubs nationwide. Diets are
   chosen to suit slimmers' lifestyles and weaknesses.

Society of Chiropodists
53 Wellbeck Street, London W1 (071 486 3381)

The Working Mothers Association
77 Holloway Road, London N7 (071 700 5171)
Sensible advice about how to cope with the sort of problems working mums and new
   mums returning to work may face.

Weight Watchers UK Limited
See GENERAL HELPLINES, page 480, for details.

Further reading
Natural Pregnancy by Janet Balaskas (Sidgwick & Jackson)
Surviving Motherhood: How to Cope with Post-Natal Depression by Maggie Comport
   (Ashgrove Press)
Towards Happy Motherhood by Maggie Comport (Corgi)
The New Mother Syndrome by Carol Dix (Allen and Unwin)
Depression After Childbirth by Dr Katharina Dalton (Oxford University Press)
Breastfeeding Your Baby by Sheila Kitzinger (Dorling Kindersley)
Your Body, Your Baby, Your Life by Angela Phillips, with Nicky Leap and Barbara
   Jacobs (Pandora)
Caesareans by E. Phillips (Sidgwick & Jackson)
Breast is Best by Dr Andrew Stanway (Pan)

Pre-menstrual syndrome (PMS)

Almost all women suffer, sooner or later, from some sort of problem associated with menstruation. Working out just what is wrong is the beginning of coping.

Many of the problems are classed as PMS (pre-menstrual syndrome). This used to be called PMT (pre-menstrual tension), but has been renamed because it can involve a lot more than tension. It is estimated that 75 per cent of all women suffer from some degree of PMS at some time in their lives, and 10 per cent suffer disabling symptoms.

Other menstrual problems (see PERIOD PROBLEMS, page 332) are not classed as PMS, but are troublesome all the same. Sometimes they are menstrual problems pure and simple. But a lot of disorders and emergencies (such as fibroids, endometriosis, miscarriage and ectopic pregnancy) can produce menstrual symptoms. For instance, pain in the early teens and twenties is unfortunately quite normal, but a later onset may indicate an underlying problem.

So it is vital that you do not bottle up your problems, but visit your GP – especially if the symptom is new, for you. It is also important to remember:
1. you are not alone, and not a freak, no matter how strange or extreme your symptoms may seem;
2. trouble with periods may be common but it is not 'woman's lot', and you should not be expected to put up with it;
3. there is a lot of potential help available from: doctors, other professionals, other women and your own family.

What is PMS?
PMS is a blanket term covering a wide number of symptoms which occur, singly or in combination, regularly every month. More than 100 different symptoms are now recognized as being linked with PMS (for the main ones see **Symptoms**, below).

Some are psychological (emotional), some physical and some behavioural. The symptoms occur *only in the phase of the menstrual cycle between ovulation and the first day of your period*.

Different PMS problems have different causes, so the way you deal with them depends on finding that specific cause. That is why what works for one person may not necessarily help another. If your PMS is due to a lack of certain nutrients it won't really tackle the problem if you take hormones – and if your problem is a hormonal one, taking, say, Vitamin B6 tablets will prove disappointing.

What causes PMS?
Basically it can have two causes:

411

1. Hormonal imbalance (produced by anything from gynaecological disorders to childbirth).
2. Nutritional deficiencies: generally very marginal ones (called sub-clinical deficiencies, whereas a shortage of say, Vitamin C, which is large enough to cause a specific disease like scurvy, is called a clinical deficiency).

Marginal nutritional shortages of certain minerals and vitamins – especially things like magnesium, zinc and Vitamin B6, and certain nutrients such as essential fatty acids, can affect your hormonal balance – which in turn affects your likelihood of getting PMS.

This may sound odd, but if you are short of the things which your body needs to make the hormones oestrogen and progesterone you won't be able to manufacture them in the right quantities. Therefore you will be relatively short of one and have relatively 'too much' of the other – thus creating a hormonal imbalance, and therefore the right conditions for PMS. Vitamin and mineral deficiencies also affect a variety of other functions, including influencing the proper production of mood-controlling substances in the brain.

If for instance, you end up with too much oestrogen (a 'stimulating' hormone, produced in increasing amounts in the first half of your menstrual cycle then tailing off after you ovulate) in your system and not enough progesterone to balance it out, this is likely to produce symptoms like nervousness, irritability, mood swings and anxiety. If you end up with too much progesterone (the 'calming' hormone, produced in increasing amounts during the *last* two weeks of your menstrual cycle up until the time you menstruate) without the right amounts of oestrogen to balance it you are likely to feel, amongst other things, miserable and depressed.

Another thing that happens when the delicate oestrogen/progesterone cycle's balance is disturbed is that the production of yet another hormone, insulin, is upset. This is the one that is responsible for regulating the amount of sugar in your bloodstream. If it is not doing its job properly you will get sudden 'highs' when lots of sugar material is suddenly released from the liver where it is stored; then rapid 'lows' when the sugar runs out and you start to crave carbohydrates and sweets to raise the level again, and feel shaky, grumpy and faint.

Theories about the role of hormones in PMS are still very controversial. Some think that the hormones are mainly triggering underlying metabolic problems from ovulation onwards to the period.

The other common set of symptoms PMS sufferers have are due to too much water retention (bloated stomach, swollen ankles, feet and fingers, swollen tender breasts). One theory is that it is produced by too much oestrogen, causing the body to make too much of yet another hormone called Aldosterone which affects the kidneys' ability to correct your salt/water balance. In fact the Women's Nutritional Advisory Service, who advocate treating PMS – and menopausal symptoms – with nutrition reckon PMS falls roughly into four categories (which type are you? Many PMS sufferers fall into two or even three categories):
* Type A: for 'Anxiety' (includes nervous tension, irritability, mood swings).
* Type H: for 'Hydration' (the bloating and water retention).

* Type D: for 'Depression' (including crying fits, feeling pessimistic and sad, confusion, thoughts of suicide even).
* Type C: for 'Carbohydrates and Cravings' (including wanting sweet foods like chocolate, jams and cakes; feeling weak and shaky if you don't get them).

Why do some people get PMS and not others?

Fifteen years ago most doctors weren't sure why and, as most felt that women who thought they had PMS symptoms were somewhat neurotic, merely concluded that some of us were therefore more neurotic than others.

Thankfully, PMS has now been recognized as a *physical* disorder (i.e. brought about by physical causes – hormonal imbalance and nutritional deficiency affect the production of certain chemicals affecting the brain, including hormones). And it is now thought that women who get PMS do so either because their hormone levels fluctuate more noticeably than the levels of those who don't get PMS, or that some of them simply have systems which are more sensitive to hormonal changes than others.

This may also explain why some women seem to sail through the menopause and others do not, why some women recover from childbirth faster than others and why some develop post-natal depression and others escape it.

How do I know if I've got PMS?

Almost any symptom – physical or mental – can be part of PMS. The problem is diagnosed not so much by what it is, but simply by *when* it happens. If you are wondering whether you really suffer from PMS, or whether it is in fact something else, keep a diary to record days when you feel cross, bloated, ill, hungry, etc.

Most women with genuine PMS are fine for the first week after menstruation. Troubles which occur between ovulation and before the start of the period are usually PMS. To ascertain whether or not you have PMS, your symptoms – whatever they are – should happen in the 10 to 14 days leading up to your period, end when the period starts, or within 48 hours of the start of the period, and not happen at any other time of the month.

If this is your pattern, you have almost certainly got PMS. If it isn't, you haven't. About half of all women who suspect they have PMS turn out not to have it – but months and years are sometimes wasted because nobody has suggested this simple test. If you find your symptoms are not PMS, your way is now open to find out what they really are, by checking all the other chapters in this book.

Who is at risk?

Almost everyone is at risk: PMS can strike any woman, at any age before the menopause. PMS occurs across all age groups, all races and all socio-economic classes – and even in women who have had hysterectomies, provided their ovaries are still intact. There do, however, seem to be some factors which can predispose you to PMS or which suggest you are more sensitive than is usual to hormonal changes in your system, and are therefore more likely to have

413

Menstrual chart PMS

*Indicate on the chart the days on which symptoms trouble you, using the appropriate letter or letters from the key below. Also mark the days of the menstrual flow (**M**). Please punctuate carefully to avoid any confusion.*

Fill in months (e.g. May)

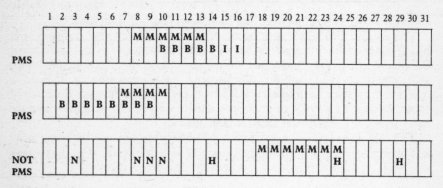

Days of the month

Key to symptoms

Depression = **D**	Swollen ankles or fingers = **F**	Loss of sex drive = **LS**
Irritability (tension) = **I**	Headache = **H**	Period pains = **PP**
Lethargy (tiredness) = **T**	Increased appetite = **AP**	Nausea = **N**
Breast discomfort = **B**	Lack coordination (clumsiness) = **C**	Menstrual flow = **M**
Swollen abdomen = **A**	Backache = **BA**	

problems with the monthly fluctuations of oestrogen and progesterone which occur during the menstrual cycle. They include:

* stressful life events (illness, marital discord, overwork, etc.);
* childbirth, though not necessarily after the first baby – especially if your process was complicated by pre-eclampsia (see POST-PREGNANCY PROBLEMS, page 393);
* post-natal depression (see POST-NATAL ILLNESS, page 346).
* recent gynaecological operations can also upset your hormonal balance, as can a miscarriage and abortion;
* using alcohol and tobacco, which stimulate your entire system artificially;
* pollution (of any kind: air, water etc., as dealing with it depletes the body's stores of PMS-fighting nutrients);
* having a gynaecological disorder such as endometriosis, or ovarian cysts can also upset hormonal balance.
* underlying psychiatric disorders (such as depression, mania, or a family history of mental illness);

Many of the factors listed above are linked with hormonal upsets. Others include:

414

* a negative attitude to menstruation (shame, embarrassment, feeling 'unclean'), as the mind has very powerful affects on the body (see **Self help**, below – this is, however, just one theory);
* lack of exercise;
* a diet high in refined (especially sugary) foods;
* long-term use of the Pill – this can sometimes cause small deficiencies in your nutritional stocks, which can build up unnoticed because the Pill stops ovulation, but which will give you sudden PMS when you finally come off the Pill. Also, as the Pill flattens out the 'peaks and troughs' of rising and falling levels of oestrogen and progesterone, it can mask any developing PMS until you stop taking it – and then you suddenly appear to develop PMS out of the blue;
* your age – PMS symptoms can get worse as the years go by which can be masked by the influence of the Pill if you are taking it.

Symptoms
Remember that the main question used in the diagnosis of PMS is not 'What are the symptoms?' but 'When do they happen?' PMS symptoms (mostly negative – but some positive ones – see **The up side of PMS**, below) are always immediately relieved by the onset of the menstrual period, which is followed by at least seven symptom-free days. Similar symptoms which appear all the time may indicate a different problem which requires different treatment (e.g. anaemia, depression or thyroid deficiency). There are over one hundred medically recognized symptoms, but the most common ones reported for PMS can be divided into three groups.

1. Physical symptoms:
* breast tenderness or swelling;
* abdominal bloating;
* swollen hands and feet;
* weight gain;
* headaches and migraines (menstrual and midcycle migraine can also be a separate problem requiring different treatment);
* pelvic discomfort – pain at different times than dysmenorrhoea (see PERIOD PROBLEMS, page 332). Any pelvic discomfort should be checked by your GP, regardless;
* changes in bowel habit (either constipation or diarrhoea);
* food cravings (especially for sweet things);
* spots;
* lank, greasy hair and skin;
* being prone to cystitis (rare);
* disturbances in vision (very rare, this should be checked out separately to eliminate the possibility of a more serious condition);
* reduced tolerance to alcohol;
* increased or unusual appetite;
* tiredness.

Other physical conditions may be aggravated by PMS, such as epilepsy or skin disorders. They are not PMS as such and must be treated separately from, and in addition to, the PMS.

2. Behavioural symptoms:
* clumsiness;
* lack of concentration;
* poor coordination (being accident prone);
* violent tempers;
* violent behaviour.

3. Psychological symptoms:
* tension and anxiety (90 per cent of sufferers experience this);
* irritability;
* depression;
* tiredness;
* confusion;
* disturbed sleep;
* decreased libido;
* suicidal thoughts.

Once again, women already suffering from psychiatric disorders (mania, depression etc.) may find these are aggravated by PMS, but these conditions should be treated separately from, and in addition to, the PMS.

The combination of symptoms, and their severity, will differ from woman to woman – or from cycle to cycle in the same woman. Intensity also differs and can range, for example, from mild annoyance with family and colleagues to unrestrained and quite irrational anger – even violence.

Tension and irritation are very common symptoms. Dropping glasses and shouting at the children may not matter too much, but while suffering PMS women are also more prone to road accidents, accidents at work, baby battering and marital problems – even marriage breakdowns.

UK law courts recognize the existence of PMS, and it has been successfully pleaded as the reason for diminished responsibility in crime, but only where there is a clear history of PMS prior to the crime.

The up side of PMS
Yes there is a positive angle. This is partly because, once recognized, PMS can now be dealt with very effectively if you get the right treatment for you personally (see HELPLINES for how to go about it if the treatment you are receiving does not seem to be helping much or has unacceptable side effects). And partly because (as suggested by a study in 1989) it seems that many women report some *positive* symptoms in their pre-menstrual phase. These include more energy (18 per cent), more imaginative creative ideas at work (11 per cent), increased confidence (6 per cent), increased enjoyment of sex (31 per cent) and increased interest in sex (37 per cent). Twenty per cent also find their breasts fuller, rounder and more attractive and 29 per cent reported more of a tendency to 'get things done'.

Altogether that is nearly seven out of ten women who reported at least one good thing about their pre-menstrual phase, says Dr Donna Stewart, associate professor of psychiatry at University of Toronto in Canada, who carried out the research on 102 consecutive women at Canadian well woman clinics.

Medical help

The logical thing to do, if you are suffering from PMS, is to start with easy self help ideas like diet and lifestyle (see **Self help**, before) and, if they don't work, go on to explore treatment with specialized nutrition advice or with hormones.

Certainly, if your menstrual problems are affecting your life to the extent that you are unable to carry on as 'normal' (for you) during particular times in your cycle, then you should consult a sympathetic doctor at once, instead of beginning with self help measures.

If you believe your GP will be unsympathetic, or if he is a man and you simply cannot bring yourself to talk to him, ask the local Community Health Council (look in the phone book) or local health centre if there is a local PMS or menstrual problem clinic, well woman clinic or family planning clinic (see also HELPLINES for a comprehensive list of PMS clinics).

The doctor should ask you for:
* a list of symptoms and *when* they appear;
* details of your menstrual pattern;
* your gynaecological, obstetric and contraceptive history.
  He should also ask you the following questions:
* have you noticed any relationship between your symptoms and your periods?
* did the symptoms start after a change of contraceptive method?
* did they start after childbirth?
* did you have post-natal depression?
* how long have your symptoms been troubling you?
* have you tried any self-help methods?
* if so, what were they and how successful were they?
* what about your general lifestyle (diet, stress, alcohol consumption, exercise, etc.)?
* have there been any major changes in your life recently?
* have you any other physical symptoms? (These should be investigated to rule out diseases which are not PMS, e.g. endometriosis.)
  If you are not asked any of these questions, volunteer the information.

You may also have an internal examination. If the idea of it worries you, say so. The doctor should understand and be specially gentle. But he or she cannot know if you don't tell them. You can also ask for a woman doctor – if there isn't one at your GP practice and this bothers you, go to a well woman or family planning clinic where there are more female doctors (see HELPLINES).

If you have not previously kept a diary of symptoms, the doctor should suggest that you start one. Then he can tailor his advice to your particular set of problems. If self help, diet and relaxation are not enough (see below) he can offer other treatment, taking your patterns into account.

FIRST-TRY TREATMENTS include:
* Vitamin B6;
* evening primrose oil (a rich source of essential fatty acids; as is borage oil and also blackcurrant seed oil – ask your local health food shop);
* a multi-mineral or vitamin formula specifically for PMS such as Optivite or Magnesium OK, available from major chemists and health shops;
* diuretics (for water retention);
* tranquillizers (for tension).

Diuretics and tranquillizers treat the symptoms of PMS and not the causes, so they are best not used for long. Tranquillizers, in particular, are highly addictive and you could end up with two problems instead of one. They are for short-term 'emergency' use only.

If these treatments are not successful, your doctor might suggest hormone treatment.

HORMONE TREATMENT is a rather more drastic solution, but it can be very effective – especially in severe cases which haven't responded to anything else. Every woman is different, so you and the doctor will have to experiment with different drugs and doses.

Hormone treatments include natural progesterone suppositories, pessaries, implants or injections; progestogen pills (a synthetic form of progesterone which can be taken by mouth); the Pill; Danazol; and Bromocriptine.

How they work:
* *Natural progesterone* is given in the form of a suppository, an implant under the skin or an injection. It may be necessary to administer the suppositories yourself, up to two or three times a day in the few days before your symptoms usually begin until you menstruate. Injections can be given by a doctor every other day. An implant will stay in, releasing progesterone, for some months. In comparison with oestrogen implants, progesterone implants are very rarely used and are often very unsatisfactory. Progesterone injections are usually tedious and unpleasant. They are reserved for some exceptionally difficult cases.

If your doctor feels that your PMS is due to lack of the 'calming' hormone progesterone he may try this. Some experts, including the doctor who pioneered this treatment and still runs clinics using it, Dr Katharina Dalton, feel that *natural* progesterone is far more effective than the artificially produced form of it, progestogen. However, the drawback of natural progesterone is that it has to be administered direct into the bloodstream (i.e. by suppository, implant or injection), as taken by mouth it gets broken down by your liver and rendered useless.
* *Artificial progesterone, progestogen* can be taken easily in pill form (e.g. Duphaston) and is thought to have a similar effect to progesterone.
* *The Pill* is given because it levels out the naturally occurring peaks and troughs of our hormonal changes each month, and therefore protects us from the effects of excessive swings in either too much oestrogen, too much progesterone, or too little of either.
* *Danazol* is a powerful drug which is not in itself a hormone. But it acts upon

the pituitary gland, which then cuts down on our ovaries' production of sex hormones, again supressing the highs and lows we would otherwise experience and their side effects, which appear as PMS.

* *Bromocriptine* (often in the form of a particular brand called Parlodel) might also be used. This works by inhibiting the production of a hormone called prolactin, which all women produce naturally (that is the one that we produce in larger quantities when we are breastfeeding a baby to encourage a supply of milk). However, too much prolactin can produce symptoms like headaches, mood changes and breast discomfort.

* *The pros and cons of hormonal treatments. Natural progesterone* has a few non-dangerous side effects, including weight gain, local irritation and a tendency to thrush. *Artificial progestogens* like Duphaston are more convenient as they are taken orally but like natural progesterone, may produce weight gain, and mild nausea and breast tenderness.

The Pill may help some PMS symptoms, but it can also make others, like depression, worse. *Danazol* has some beneficial effect on PMS but also produces unpleasant side effects for many women, including greasy hair and skin, a facial hair growth, deepening of the voice and nausea. *Bromocriptine* can help with symptoms like tender breasts, but very few women's PMS is due to excessive prolactin so it is not tackling the cause of PMS, just one of the symptoms. The side effect of nausea is almost inevitable; all the side effects of Danazol are closely related to the doses given.

If your symptoms persist or get worse, go back to your doctor. If you are still unhappy, ask tactfully to be referred to a PMS clinic (sadly there are not very many PMS clinics in the whole country). Ask the Women's Health Concern, the National Association for Pre-Menstrual Syndrome or the Pre-Menstrual Society (see HELPLINES) if there is one near you. Or get help from one of the other organizations listed in HELPLINES.

Self help
* Look at any negative feelings you have about menstruation and start seeking some of its positive angles. See **The up side of PMS**, above, and HELPLINES.

Talk about PMS
* Tell your family you are suffering from PMS. Show them some books, and perhaps your diary, or ask the doctor to back you up.
* Explain your symptoms – especially the psychological ones like irritability.
* Ask for their understanding – and their patience for bad days.
* Tell them what you are doing about PMS – patience and understanding wear thin if there is no apparent improvement, or hope of it.
* Even quite little children will understand that you're having 'an off day' if you tell them in advance that they have to be extra nice to you.
* Emphasize that the problem is you and not them.
* Stress that you still love them, even when you are impatient and angry.
* Remind them in the good times that not-so-good times are coming later, and vice-versa.

419

* If children can cope with all this, men certainly should be able to, so use the same tactics with your partner.
* You might have to explain lack of libido (if that is one of your symptoms). Make sure your partner knows that you still find him sexually attractive – fragile male egos can cause reactions just as irrational as your PMS.
* Women can often feel very sexy once menstruation begins, so consider making the most of it to compensate for the other times.
* Try to open the subject with your women friends. You will get a sympathetic response, and you will almost certainly find that many of them suffer, too.
* PMS can explain why close friends are sometimes ratty and sometimes delightful. You can then make an inter-friend pact: you make allowances for them and they make allowances for you, and both of you have the relief of not having to strain to be nice to everybody, all the time.
* Friends may be able to share some useful hints with you. The mutual support is important, and very useful.
* Contact one of the PMS help groups by phone, when you feel bad. They will know exactly what you are going through and be able to give a very sympathetic ear as well as good advice (see HELPLINES).

Problems at work
PMS at work can be a real problem. You won't much want to draw attention to your PMS but on the other hand, you may not be able to work at your best, or you may be at a greater risk of industrial accident.
* If you can, plan your workload around your good and bad times.
* Some larger concerns now recognize the problem and make allowances. Investigate. Is there a helpful personnel officer, occupational health nurse or safety officer you can confide in?
* If the problems are widespread, try talking to other women and see if you can bring about changes in management attitude. Recognition of the problem is half the battle.

Diet
Improving your diet can often help: follow the well-known rules of low fat, high fibre, low sugar and lots of fruit and vegetables. You will benefit from the general improvement in your health. Special points to note are:
* a high intake of processed food and saturated (mainly animal) fats interferes with production of the helpful substance prostaglandin E-1. So cut them down;
* also cut down on tea, coffee, alcohol and cola drinks – these will encourage mood swings;
* a simple, cheap idea that can work wonders is to eat small, regular meals or snacks (about every three hours) which include lots of unrefined carbohydrate (wholemeal bread, rice, pasta etc). Fresh fruit will also help and bananas are especially good, quite convenient to carry around as emergency supplies. This gives you a steady level of blood glucose which helps control cravings and mood swings;
* carry with you complex carbohydrate snacks, e.g. wholemeal baps, bags of

unsalted nuts and bananas, to top up your body with foods that release their glucose steadily, thus avoiding 'glucose gaps';
* avoid sweets and sugary snacks: the brief rise in blood sugar soon swings down to low again.
* if you suffer especially from a pre-menstrual craving for sweet things – chocolates, sweets, biscuits, cakes and heavily sweetened 'health' bars, taking a supplement of chromium may help. So can eating foods high in chromium which include molasses, dried Brewer's Yeast (although some people are allergic to Brewer's Yeast, so take care) and egg yolk.

This is because chromium is linked to our insulin levels, and insulin is what controls the amount of sugar in our bloodstream feeding the brain (and other body cells). Too little chromium means not enough insulin produced – so you get sharp sweet craving before your period, which has led many women to consume several Mars bars or four packets of biscuits in one go. Chromium supplements are available (although they are expensive and their connection to PMS not fully proven). There is one called Sugar Factor from Nature's Best (see HELPLINES).

Vitamins and minerals
* Vitamin B6 (pyridoxine) can be helpful. It is a good starting point because it is cheap: (i) start with 50mg twice daily; (ii) increase the dosage if the symptoms persist, to a maximum of 150mg daily (some researchers think you could overdose on more – too much Vitamin B6 can cause nervous problems; (iii) start two days before your symptoms begin, and stop after two days of menstruation.
* If Vitamin B6 alone is not working, try adding evening primrose oil (more expensive, but often very effective): (i) the usual dosage is 4 to 6 500mg capsules twice daily after food; (ii) begin two days before you expect symptoms; (iii) finish two days after the start of menstruation. A few women suffer from diarrhoea and mild gastric upset with evening primrose oil, and you shouldn't use it if you have temporal lobe epilepsy. In severe cases of PMS it may be worth taking it without break all month. (see BREAST PAIN pp. 42).
* Other supplements that have worked for some women include Vitamin E. But always get proper advice first (see HELPLINES), because you have to take care with supplements, vitamins and minerals, as they all work together in complicated ways. Too much of one will cause imbalances of the others.

Relaxation and exercise
Anything that reduces stress is helpful to PMS symptoms. Daily doses of exercise and/or relaxation (yoga or other techniques) is far better than longer irregular bouts.
* Try to organize your life as much as possible to avoid stress during PMS times: do not arrange to take the children on a huge outing, embark on a difficult report for work, or play in a doubles squash tournament. The outcome is likely to be a disaster and you will end up feeling worse.
* Exercise releases the body's natural opiates or 'happy chemicals', endorphins, which have a calming effect on you.

* Hot baths have the same effect as exercise.
* Try the Rescue Remedy – a Bach Flower Remedy, distilled from wild British flowers. Put four drops in a glass of water (you can get it from health food shops). It takes about 20 minutes to begin to work and the effects are not dramatic, but you suddenly realize you are not feeling quite so jittery.
* Hypnotherapy can teach you deep, calming relaxation techniques (see HELPLINES).
* Relaxation techniques with visualization (see HELPLINES).

Complementary therapy
Complementary therapies tailor their treatments very much to the individual: the precise nature of the treatment you receive will vary, depending on your medical history, symptoms, lifestyle, etc. The following information indicates the *sorts* of things a therapist is most likely to do or recommend. Do not be surprised if they feel you need something slightly different. This section is meant purely as an indication of likely treatments; it is not meant as a DIY guide to the medical uses of the different complementary therapies.

Of the many symptoms of PMS, the ones listed here are the most common. You may suffer from some or all of these – or from others – every month. It is sensible to start a PMS diary and to list your symptoms before visiting a therapist, because an in-depth consultation and discussion is necessary for correct individual treatment.

1. BLOATING AND WATER RETENTION
Acupuncture
Acupuncture, possibly combined with Chinese herbs, can help control bloating by aiding the elimination of excess fluid.

Aromatherapy
Lymphatic drainage massage with a blend of geranium and rosemary helps improve your lymphatic circulation and prevents toxins and fluid from building up.

Clinical nutrition
Vitamin B6 acts as a diuretic, as does dandelion root coffee. Fenugreek tea or adrenal glandular tissue stimulate the flow of lymphatic fluids. Besides prescribing these, the nutritionist will advice you to avoid foods containing salt – such as cheese, salted butter, bacon and some tinned foods – which encourage fluid retention.

Homoeopathy
Lachesis and Natrum Mus, prescribed according to any other symptoms you may have, can help reduce fluid retention.

Medical herbalism
A medical herbalist will be concerned with your hormone levels (keeping a special look out for poor progesterone secretion, as this may be responsible for many PMS symptoms), and offer remedies accordingly. Dietary advice is also important, particularly to counteract hypoglycaemia, or low blood sugar levels. Couch grass may also be suggested as a diuretic.

2. CRAVING SWEET OR CARBOHYDRATE FOODS

Acupuncture

Acupuncture at appropriate sites can suppress your appetite and increase your will power, to resist temptation.

Aromatherapy

Oils such as geranium, cypress, bergamot or lavender, used in the bath or in a room vaporizer, help you to relax and to resist cravings. Dietary advice may also be offered.

Clinical nutrition

Hypoglycaemia is a major cause of many PMS symptoms, creating a glandular imbalance by stressing the adrenals. The clinical nutritionist will test for hypoglycaemia and/or diabetes. If the glucose tolerance test is positive, your clinical nutritionist may suggest that you cut down protein and refined carbohydrates, while eating more unrefined carbohydrates. This will reduce cravings, as will a supplement of brewer's yeast, adrenal glandulars or pancreas glandulars. The same treatment may be offered for other PMS symptoms such as mood swings, lethargy, tiredness and clumsiness.

Medical herbalism

Bitters, such as gentian, improve digestion and control your blood sugar levels.

3. MOOD SWINGS – ANXIETY OR DEPRESSION; FEELINGS OF VIOLENCE AND ANGER

Acupuncture

Acupuncture and acupressure are used to calm your nervous system and to reduce and suppress depression.

Aromatherapy

Blends of essential oils – prepared individually for you and used for self-massage – help re-establish emotional calmness by balancing your hormones.

Clinical nutrition

The same clinical nutrition treatment for **Craving sweet or carbohydrate foods** (see above) is applicable here.

Homoeopathy

Mood swings take many forms and the homoeopath will need to find out your particular problems before prescribing. For instance, if you are irritable, Causticum might be used if you are also pessimistic, Kreasote if you are restless and Lycopodium if you are also sad.

Medical herbalism

After checking your hormone levels and acting accordingly, the medical herbalist may also offer nerve restoratives such as wild oats or scullcap. Chamomile tea is also a suitable prescriptive.

4. HEADACHES

Acupuncture

Acupuncture therapy has general pain-relieving effects.

Aromatherapy

Head, neck and shoulder massage, with lavender, sandalwood and chamomile oils, helps relieve tension and relax the muscles in your scalp and the back of your neck.

Clinical nutrition
Moods are normalized by balancing the ratio between the hormones oestrogen and progesterone. To restore hormonal balance, a calcium supplement, together with evening primrose oil and glandular concentrates, is helpful.

Medical herbalism
Peppermint, rosemary or feverfew reduce tension levels and improve circulation through your head.

Osteopathy
Manipulation of your neck reduces muscle tension and increases blood flow.

5. PAINFUL BREASTS
Acupuncture
General suppression of pain by acupuncture can be supplemented by acupressure to control any inflammation.

Aromatherapy
Cold lavender compresses together with relaxing bath oils, increase your circulation and relax the tissues, thereby reducing soreness.

Clinical nutrition
After checking for hormonal imbalance, the therapist may also prescribe a diuretic.

Homoeopathy
Conium may relieve sore breasts, but you must have a full consultation to find out exactly what the cause of the problem is – several remedies could be used, including Calc-carb and Pulsatilla.

Medical herbalism
Cleavers are helpful as a mild diuretic and lymphatic stimulant, and may be combined with a herbal remedy to restore your hormone balance.

Osteopathy
Osteopathy can encourage the flow of water from your breasts, reducing tissue tension, both by direct massage in that area and by an indirect massage through your spine.

6. LACK OF SEXUAL DESIRE
Acupuncture
Increased sexual desire can be achieved by acupuncture or acupressure, combined with the use of Chinese herbs, to increase hormone production in your body.

Aromatherapy
An individually mixed blend of oils for use by your partner will stimulate desire for both of you.

Clinical nutrition
Histadine deficiency can result in lack of libido; so can adrenal stress. Dietary supplements of histadine or adrenal glandular tissue will help.

424

Homoeopathy
Lowered libido, combined with irritability and depression, responds well to Sepia.

Medical herbalism
Restoring your hormones to a normal level is the first aim. Ginseng or Chinese angelica act as overall tonics, improving your energy levels.

7. LETHARGY AND TIREDNESS
Acupuncture
Acupuncture or acupressure promote the activity of *chi* to attain a proper yin-yang balance. This will improve your mobilization of *chi* energy.

Aromatherapy
Individual blends of geranium, bergamot, rosemary and others, used for massage and in the bath, will diminish fluid retention and act as an uplifting mind stimulant, helping to establish a holistic balance.

Clinical nutrition
(See **Craving sweet or carbohydrate foods** in this section, page 421.)

Medical herbalism
Many women find Vitamin B of specific value for this condition, along with revitalizing herbal remedies.

8. CLUMSINESS, LACK OF COORDINATION
Therapists feel that this condition is part of a more general manifestation of PMS symptoms and consider that treatment of the root cause will improve coordination.

9. BACKACHE
Acupuncture
Acupuncture and acupressure for pain relief will help.

Aromatherapy
A full-body massage with individual blends of oils – paying special attention to your lower back – will relax your muscles and relieve back strain.

Chiropractic
Spinal manipulation for backache is usually combined with another complementary therapy to treat PMS.

Clinical nutrition
Backache is often caused by kidney, liver or colon problems. The cause must be ascertained before treatment can be offered.

Medical herbalism
Exercises are important. Chaste tree or white deadnettle improve circulation and reduce congestion and pressure.

Osteopathy
Once the tissues which are causing pain have been identified, direct manipulation will help.

10. SPOTTY SKIN AND LANK, GREASY HAIR

Aromatherapy

The therapist can provide creams and lotion to help your skin and hair, but best results are experienced in combination with a carefully controlled diet.

Clinical nutrition

Evening primrose oil and choline help your body to metabolize fatty acids more efficiently. Bile production can be regulated with tablets.

Medical herbalism

Regulating your hormone levels is an important first step. Burdock is helpful as it is a valuable blood cleanser, improving cellular nutrition and waste matter removal.

Pre-menstrual syndrome helplines

There are very few clinics dealing specifically with menstrual problems. If there isn't one in your area, a well woman clinic or your nearest family planning clinic should help. You can find these through your local library or by telephoning the Community Health Council: Association of Community Health Councils, 30 Drayton Park, London N5 1PB (071 609 8405)

Action Against Allergy
Greyhound House, 23–24 George Street, Richmond, Surrey

The Allergy Shop
PO Box 196, Haywards Heath, W. Sussex (0444 414290)
   Shop and free counselling service.

Association for Post-Natal Illness
25 Jerdan Place, London SW6 (071 386 0868)

The Brook Advisory Centre
HQ – 233 Tottenham Court Road, London W1P 9AE (071 323 1522)
See GENERAL HELPLINES, page 480, for details.

The Eating Disorders Association
Sackville Place, 44 to 48 Magdalen Street, Norwich (0603 62414)
For all sufferers of anorexia and other eating disorders – and their families. Send
   SAE for details.

Marie Stopes Clinics
In London, Manchester and Leeds. (See GENERAL HELPLINES, page 480, for details)

Migraine Trust
45 Great Ormond Street, London WC1N 3HD (071 278 2676)

National Association for Pre-Menstrual Syndrome (NAPS)
PO Box 72, Sevenoaks, Kent TN13 2PS (0227 763133)
Strong believers in regular carbohydrate snacks and progesterone therapy; not keen
   on vitamins/minerals. They offer a helpline, support and campaign group.

National Breast Pain Clinics
Breast pain (before your period, i.e. about 10 days before) a real problem? If your
   GP's not helping ask them for referral to one of the few specialist benign (i.e. not
   associated with cancer) breast pain clinics in the country: they include The
   University Hospital of Wales; the Withington Hospital, Manchester; Nottingham
   City Hospital; and the Edinburgh Breast Unit at the Western General Hospital.

Pregnancy Advisory Service
11–13 Charlotte Street, London W1P 1HD (071 637 8962)

National Association for Pre-Menstrual Syndrome (PREMSOC)
PO Box 72, Sevenoaks, Kent TW13 3PS (0732 459 378)
   Helps women who suffer from PMS.

Pre-Menstrual Support Group
21 Dalcruin Gardens, Moddlesburn, Chryston, Glasgow G69 0NQ
Meets monthly, supporting the theory of controlling PMS through diet. A telephone
   support network has been set up, too.

Pre-Menstrual Tension Advisory Service (now the Women's Nutritional Advisory
   Service)
PO Box 268, Hove, East Sussex BN3 1RW (0273 771366)
Strong believers in a nutritional approach. Various publications are available, plus
   postal counselling/diet planning (£68). Telephone advice is also available – and
   they can also put you in touch with a clinical nutritionist (doctor specially trained
   in nutrition) who can give you a very full face-to-face consultation, and the
   necessary tests (i.e. blood and sweat analyses) to ascertain precisely what minerals
   and vitamins your body is deficient in. They can also determine – and to what
   extent – this has caused your PMS; then advise appropriate individual
   supplementation, dietary change and action.

The Breast Care Helpline
(0628 481 333)
   Advises on cyclicly painful breasts – associated with PMS – amongst other
   things.

PMS Society
PO Box 102, London SE1 7ES
A new group of doctors, nurses and lay people aiming to improve and coordinate
  knowledge and contacts. Send large SAE for pertinent leaflets.

RELATE (formerly The Marriage Guidance Council)
Herbert Gray College, Little Church Street, Rugby CV21 3AP (0788 73241)

TRANX (Tranquillizer Recovery and New Existence)
Ms Joan Gerome, 17 Peel Road, Wealdstone, Middlesex (081 427 2065)

Women's Health Concern
83 Earl's Court Road, London W8 6EF (071 938 3932)
Advice on the telephone by nurse counsellors. Useful leaflets, including one on
  PMS. Please enclose SAE if you write. They can help you find someone locally
  who can treat you.

Women's Health and Reproductive Rights Information Centre (WHRRIC)
52–54 Featherstone Street, London EC1Y 8RT (071 251 6580)
Telephone advice, or send for their PMS fact sheet and the politics of PMS fact sheet
  (20p each, plus SAE). They also have a good library on women's health.

Specialist products and services

Phobic Action
Greater London House, 547 to 551 High Road, Leytonstone, London E11 (081 558
  6012)

Association of Qualified and Curative Hyponotherapists
See GENERAL HELPLINES, page 480, for details.

British Wheel of Yoga
1 Hamilton Place, Boston Road, Near Sleaford, Lincs (0529 306851)
Can put you in touch with a professionally qualified teacher in your area. Yoga can be
  helpful for stress relief, and the teachers can also show you effective visualization
  techniques.

Nature's Best Health Products Limited
PO Box 1, Tunbridge Wells, Kent TN2 3EQ (0892 534143)
Mail-order nutrition supplements company which carries evening primrose oil, chromium, optivite, among other natural treatments for period problems and PMS. EPO can work out expensive; remember it's now available from your GP on prescription for breast pain only (not PMS in general) as a brand called Efamast: (you could always suggest you have breast pain as a PMS sympton even if it's not a problem, if you feel EPO could help your PMS as a whole, to save money).

Further reading
Why Suffer? Periods and their Problems by L. Birke and K. Gardener (Virago)
Understanding PMT by Dr Michael Brush (Pan)
Curing PMT the Drug-Free Way by Moira Carpenter (Arrow)
Once a Month by Dr Katharina Dalton (Fontana)
The Premenstrual Syndrome and Progesterone Therapy by Dr Katharina Dalton (Heinemann)
A Manual of Natural Family Planning by Dr A. Flynn and M. Brooks (Unwin)
Evening Primrose Oil by Judy Graham (Thorsons)
Self Help With PMS by M. Harrison (Optima)
Seeing Red: The Politics of PMT by Valerie Hey, et al. (Hutchinson)
Lifting the Curse by Beryl Kingston (Sheldon Press)
The PMT Solution by Dr Ann Nazzaro, et al. (Adamantine Press)
Beat PMT Through Diet by Maryon Stewart, et al. (Ebury Press)
Female Cycles by Paula Weideger (The Women's Press)
Pre-Menstrual Syndrome: Diet Against It by Dr Robert C. D. Wilson (Foulsham)
'Heavy Periods', a leaflet produced by the WHRRIC (see above for address). Send 40p plus SAE. They also produce leaflets entitled 'Not All In The Mind' and 'Women's Health and the Politics of PMS' (40p each).

Prolapse

What is it?

Prolapse is the term used when the uterus and/or vagina slip downwards because the structures designed to keep them in place have weakened or stretched. (Another name for it is 'pelvic relaxation'.) Prolapse of the vagina is the more common of the two.

Either kind of prolapse can be mild or – if it is neglected – more serious. A prolapsed uterus may just mean that the cervix is lying a bit lower than normal. Left without treatment, however, this can get worse and worse. Something very rarely seen these days is the last stage of prolapse of the uterus, where the whole of the uterus has been allowed to work its way down through the vagina. It could even end up right outside the body.

Prolapse of the vagina means that the vagina's walls get weak and allow other organs (the bladder and the rectum) to push into them. This, again, can be quite mild, but can turn into serious displacement if you neglect it. So if you do think things might be slipping, remember prolapses don't go backwards, and get treatment while it's still a minor problem.

Your abdomen is full of assorted organs – stomach, bladder, uterus, digestive tract, and so on. They are tightly packed together and, influenced by gravity, are under pressure to move downwards. They are mostly kept in place by the pelvic girdle – a sort of bowl-shaped bone at the base of the abdomen. But it can't do everything. Both sexes need a gap in it (about 5cm for men) to let the bowel contents through and out. Women also have to be able to get a baby through – so their gap is about 10 centimetres. Everything above the gap is supported by a sling of muscle called the pelvic floor, and 10 centimetres is a long distance to bridge with muscle alone. So the uterus always has the potential to start bulging through, and the vagina may prolapse as well.

The uterus and vagina both have structures to support them, however, so prolapse won't happen unless these start to fail.

THE UTERUS is kept in place by a band of tissue (the transverse ligament), which keeps it at the right level and at the right angle. (Most women – about 70 per cent – have a uterus which points forwards; about 20 per cent have one which points backwards; the rest have an in-between angle.)

The front end of this transverse ligament also runs under the bladder, and supports that, too; the back end circles round the rectum and supports it. So there are several stress points where it can be strained and stretched. If there is added weakness in your pelvic floor muscle, you are likely to be in trouble.

THE VAGINA. The transverse ligament is attached to the top end of the vagina, too, and supports it. About two thirds of the way down the vagina, there is also a muscle (the levator ani) which supports the lowest third of it. Damage to

430

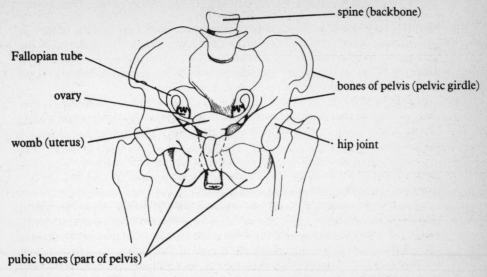

spine (backbone)

Fallopian tube

bones of pelvis (pelvic girdle)

ovary

womb (uterus)

hip joint

pubic bones (part of pelvis)

Female front view showing gap in bone structure which has to be bridged by muscle, which in turn has to support the contents of the abdomen.

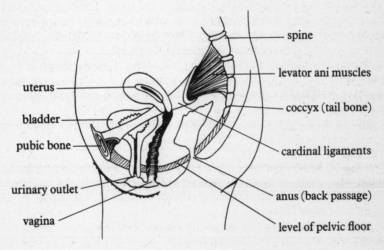

spine

levator ani muscles

uterus

coccyx (tail bone)

bladder

pubic bone

cardinal ligaments

urinary outlet

anus (back passage)

vagina

level of pelvic floor

Side view of female pelvic area, showing pelvic organs and pelvic floor muscles.

either of these supporting structures will make your vagina liable to move downwards (maybe to start turning inside out), even if the uterus is still safely in place.

Causes
There are two basic causes: difficult or problem childbirth and gravity.

431

1. Childbirth

Normal childbirth does no harm to the ligament which supports the uterus. It moves aside as the cervix dilates, to let the baby through. But if the labour is very rapid, and the baby is pushed through the cervix before it has had time to dilate out fully – or if it's a forceps delivery (which can also cause damage) – this may lay the foundations for a prolapse later on.

One difficult birth – or a lot of births, which may or may not be difficult – can also cause small rips in the ligament, which are repaired by weaker scar tissue. So can a very long labour or heavy physical work during the last stages of pregnancy.

Usually, damaged as it is, the ligament holds up until around the menopause. Then all the muscles tend to lose tone anyway, and this is often the last straw for the already-strained ligament.

Even normal childbirth, on the other hand, is bound to cause major stretching of the vagina – and perhaps to the structures designed to support it, which get pushed aside to let the baby through. A weak place may be left behind permanently. If it is in the front wall of the vagina, the bladder may start bulging into it (cystocele). If it is in the back wall, the rectum may do the same (rectocele).

2. Gravity

You don't have to have had a baby to suffer a prolapse. The normal forces of gravity create constant downward pressure, which may in the long term prove too much for the ligament and muscles. Chances of this are higher if you have:
* a chronic cough, which creates surprisingly high pressure, day after day;
* chronic constipation, which will make you strain downwards while on the loo; and while you're opening the rectum muscles you can't keep the vaginal ones tight – both factors combine to stretch the vagina and push the uterus down into it;
* a weight problem – obesity puts pressure on the supporting structures, too.

Who is at risk?
* Women who have experienced difficult, long or rapid childbirth (especially if forceps were used), or who have had a lot of babies.
* Women who suffer from a chronic cough or chronic constipation. (See CONSTIPATION, page 145.)
* Women who are overweight (see HELPLINES, page 153).
* Women who have reached the menopause.

Symptoms
Either type of prolapse – of the uterus or vagina – can cause:
* a feeling of 'something coming down';
* a dragging feeling around your lower abdomen;
* backache;
* fatigue.
Prolapse of the vagina has some symptoms of its own. Cystocele can cause:
* an urge to pass water frequently;

432

* leakages of urine when you cough, laugh or move quickly (this is called stress incontinence, see INCONTINENCE, page 239);
* possible urinary infections.
Rectocele can cause:
* difficulty in opening your bowels;
* vaginal discharge;
* an aching or dragging feeling around the perineum (the area between the vagina and anus).
Both cystocele and rectocele can cause:
* a slight bulge which you can feel with a finger gently placed in the vagina.

Treatment
Your GP will do a manual examination. Prolapse, whether of the uterus or vagina, is straightforward to detect. Treatment depends on how far it has progressed. It can include pelvic exercises you do yourself, electric stimulation plus exercises from a hospital physio or corrective surgery.

Strengthening the supporting muscles
If your symptoms are basically those of stress incontinence, you might ask to be referred for advice from an expert on incontinence (see HELPLINES). If the problem hasn't progressed too far, pelvic floor exercises (see INCONTINENCE, page 239, for details on how to do them) may be enough to solve it. You will have to do them faithfully, and progress will take weeks rather than days. It helps to keep a diary about how often you leak, and how much, so that you can see the improvements, however small at first.

Wearing a pessary
If things have gone too far for pelvic floor exercises, the first step (for prolapse of the uterus only) will probably be for your GP to fit a pessary, which is placed at the top of the vagina. This is a ring of plastic which fits around the cervix and holds the uterus back, while the cervix protudes, untouched, through the hole in the middle and menstrual blood can flow out normally. The traditional pessary shape is a sort of ring bent into an S-shape (the Hodge pessary), but this is now rare. The usual shape today is a simple ring (about 1 centimetre thick) made of soft, rubbery plastic. It should be fitted by a doctor (many GPs prefer to refer you to a hospital out-patients department for this – family planning clinics don't do it). It stays in until it needs replacing, so good fitting is important – there is a range of sizes. It protrudes into the vagina a little, because it is so thick, but you should not be able to feel it. Your sexual partner will, but this should not be a problem if he is gentle at first – your vagina has plenty of extra capacity and when you are sexually aroused it becomes longer.

The pessary *must* be changed regularly, as there is always a danger of infection setting in. Doctors' opinions vary on this – some leave one pessary in place for up to six months, some suggest changing it every three. Do check regularly for signs of infection (the main one is an offensive discharge) and report them at once.

With luck, you won't have to wear the pessary for more than three months. It is really only used as a temporary measure while you wait for surgery to correct the problem once and for all. Surgical and anaesthetic techniques have improved so much that very few women are too old or frail for surgery. Pessaries, on the other hand, almost always cause a certain amount of vaginal inflammation. This might turn into an ulcer, caused by the constant pressure on the delicate tissues, and they don't always completely relieve the symptoms of prolapse anyway.

Surgery

Unless you have a serious illness which rules out surgery (e.g. tuberculosis or heart disease) there is only one good reason to delay surgery. That is when (rarely) the uterus prolapses in a young woman who wants more children. Surgery could damage the uterus, or future childbirth could undo the prolapse operation. Pregnancy after a successful prolapse operation may be an indication for a Caesarean delivery. Surgery would still be strongly recommended once you have completed your family. (See **Self help**, below, for advice on extra care to be taken in the meantime.)

Surgery for prolapse involves a general anaesthetic and a stay in hospital of around 10 days. Exactly what is done depends on what is wrong in each case. The simplest treatment is to tuck and tighten up whichever muscle or ligament has been over-stretched – basically by cutting it and stitching it together again. If you have a uterine prolapse (the least common kind) most gynaecologists feel they can do a better repair by removing your uterus – unless you particularly wish it to remain. (See HYSTERECTOMY, page 225.) The earlier you seek treatment, the less drastic the cure will be.

AFTERCARE

* Stick strictly to the advice you are given about resting, or the interior stitches will come undone and the operation will have to be done again. Ask your GP, hospital social worker or local authority social worker to arrange a home help for you and/or get friends and family to rally round and help out. If you have a job, make sure you get a letter from your GP to ensure you have enough time off.

* Follow a really good diet, with lots of Vitamin C and zinc to help the healing process.

* Do your pelvic floor exercises (see INCONTINENCE, page 239, for instructions). They it will make you sore, but there is no alternative – you should not delay until they are completely comfortable, says Dr Peter Mansfield, a practising GP with long experience in complementary therapies who has set up the Templegarth Trust health education service. It will help if you practise the exercises in advance of the surgery, and get the hang of them.

* For comfort and for toning muscles, try making daily use of cold water around your vagina – splash or spray it on or use a bidet. If you haven't got a bidet fill a bowl with cold water and sit in it every day for about 30 seconds, or long enough to get past the first shock and feel a tingling sensation that tells you that muscles, nerves and circulation around the vagina are being toned up.

* If you *have* had a hysterectomy you will face the problems associated with that (an early menopause, for example). See HYSTERECTOMY, page 225 for advice.

* See below for how to help yourself prevent another prolapse.

How to prevent prolapse

Unless all you have is mild cystocele, which may be cured by pelvic floor exercises, self help is a matter of prevention – not cure. The following advice applies even if you have never had a prolapse, and also if you have had a prolapse which has been repaired by surgery (it is possible to have a repeat prolapse, if you are still at risk from what caused the first one).

* If you are pregnant, work regularly to stretch the entrance to your vagina to make it as flexible as possible, by massaging the perineum with a finger in the vagina.

* Before you go into labour determine to take your time delivering the baby's head through your vagina – unless you are advised at the time that the baby will be in danger if it is not born quickly.

(i) Tell the midwife or doctor in advance that this is your intention, and have it written into your birthplan. (ii) Avoid, if possible, artificial means of accelerating your labour, and induction (because some hospitals do this routinely if you are a bit overdue) which can also mean a more rapid labour. (See CHILDBIRTH, page 109.)

Health professionals are generally well aware of the dangers of prolapse, so you can be confident they will support your plans.

* When you are in labour and the midwife or doctor tells you to curb your urge to push – try to do so. It may help to kneel, with your forehead touching the floor or bed, and knees apart, bottom high up in the air (a strategy taught by the Active Birth Movement – see CHILDBIRTH HELPLINES, page 141). Pushing before the cervix is far enough open does no good, and can start off a prolapse.

* Practise your pelvic floor exercises religiously every day before and after the birth, starting as soon as possible.

* In fact, make pelvic floor exercises a lifelong habit even if you haven't had a baby. Do them every day. One way to remember is always to do them when you carry out certain regular routines, such as cleaning your teeth or putting the kettle on. Or just do them any time you have a minute to fill – standing in queues, sitting at a desk, watching TV, driving. They are quite invisible, so nobody will know you are doing them (see INCONTINENCE, page 239).

* Don't suffer with chronic constipation. (See CONSTIPATION, page 145, for ways to deal with it once and for all.)

* If you have a chronic cough, you should see your GP to find and treat the cause. Meanwhile, make a point of tightening pelvic floor muscles when you cough.

* If you have put on a lot of weight (especially if you are older) don't squeeze into corsets, or even tight clothes – they increase the risk of prolapse. Wear loose, attractive clothes or, better still, lose some weight.

How to manage a prolapse

If you are waiting for surgery for a prolapse, you may have to learn to manage one for several months. Apart from using a pessary on the doctor's advice, there are other things you can do.

* If you have backache (i) try to keep your posture good, (ii) sit and drive with

a cushion to support the small of your back and (iii) avoid standing for long.

* If prolapse is making sex a problem, think about other ways you and your partner can give each other sexual pleasure without actual penetration of your vagina, e.g. by oral or manual stimulation (see HELPLINES).

* Wear light sanitary towels or pant-liners to catch any unexpected drops of urine. If the leaks are very bad, try the special continence pads and pants (pretty, slim and discreet these days). Your GP can put you in touch with the local continence adviser or district nurse, who can help you choose and may be able to get supplies for you on the NHS; or ring the Continence Advisory Service (see HELPLINES) for confidential advice.

* Avoid constipation: All-bran for breakfast is mundane but very helpful.

Complementary therapy

Complementary therapies tailor their treatments very much to the individual: the precise nature of the treatment you receive will vary, depending on your medical history, symptoms, lifestyle, etc. The following information indicates the *sorts* of things a therapist is most likely to do or recommend. Do not be surprised if they feel you need something slightly different. This section is meant purely as an indication of likely treatments; it is not meant as a DIY guide to the medical uses of the different complementary therapies.

Acupuncture

For early and mild cases, acupuncture and acupressure can help strengthen the tone of the muscles supporting your womb.

Clinical nutrition

Uterus glandular tissues give support to your uterus; Vitamin E increases your tissue's response to stress; and phosphorus thins out thick, sticky blood. The therapist would also examine you for circulatory and cardio-vascular problems, offering exercises to help strengthen your muscles.

Homoeopathy

Sepia is used for a pressing, 'something coming out' feeling; aloe for a long-standing prolapse associated with a feeling of fullness, and perhaps morning diarrhoea.

Medical herbalism

Internal remedies to tone the muscle of the uterus, such as motherwort, life root and ladies' mantle, are likely to be combined with pelvic floor exercises to help you regain muscle tone.

Prolapse helplines

The Association of Chartered Physiotherapists in Obstetrics and Gynaecology
c/o The Chartered Society of Physiotherapy, 14 Bedford Row, London WC1R 4ED
  (071 242 1941)

British Nutrition Foundation
52 to 54 High Holborn, London WC1 (071 404 6504)
Can put you in touch with a private nutritionist in your area, who can prepare a diet
   with special features.

The Colonic Irrigation Asociation
26 Sea Road, Boscombe, Bournemouth BH5 1DF

Association of Continence Advisors
Is now called Continence Line (091 213 0050)
Can offer advice on treatment and management of all kinds of continence, and will
   supply helpful books, leaflets and exercise sheets. Will advise where to contact your
   local continence nurse.

RELATE (formerly The Marriage Guidance Council)
Herbert Gray College, Little Church Street, Rugby CV21 3AP (07885 73241)

The Templegarth Trust
82 Tinkle Road, Grimoldby, Louth, Lincs LN11 8TF
An independent charity, publishing a wide range of literature representing the
   professional experience of its directors, a doctor and a teacher. A leaflet on prolapse
   is available. Send 30p and SAE.

Women's Health and Reproductive Rights Information Centre (WHRRIC)
52–54 Featherstone Street, London EC1Y 8RT (071 251 6332/6580)
A voluntary organization that can give useful information and support on any aspect
   of women's health care.

Specialist products and services
National Childbirth Trust (NCT)
HQ – Alexandra House, Oldham Terrace, London W3 6NH (081 992 8637)
Offers exercises for pregnant women (and post-pregnant women or women with
   weakened pelvic muscles) to strengthen pelvic floor and help avoid a prolapse.

Weight Watchers UK Limited
See GENERAL HELPLINES, page 480, for details.

Further reading
We couldn't locate any books which deal solely with prolapse; however, several
chapters in general women's health books cover prolapse, some more fully than others.
Two helpful books are:

Hysterectomy and Vaginal Repair by Sally Haslett and Molly Jennings (Beaconsfield)
Experiences of Hysterectomy by Ann Webb (Optima)

Sexually Transmitted Diseases

These days, more than ever, women (and men) are vulnerable to a whole range of different infections in their reproductive systems. Some are quite trivial, and easily put right; others are more serious (see below, page 441, for details of the different infections).

There is very little point in trying to separate 'ordinary' infections affecting the genital and reproductive areas from sexually transmitted diseases (STDs) which affect the same places – for the simple reason that, with one or two exceptions, infections can be caught both sexually *and* in other ways.

So try not to jump to hasty conclusions if you (or your partner) catches an infection. It might not have been through sex.

Who is at risk?
Every woman is at risk. Even infections which are basically STDs can be caught through poor hygiene, among other things. Although sex does not cause all infections, you are most definitely at risk if:
* you have more than one sexual partner;
* you have only one partner, but your partner has one or more other partners (whether you know about them or not).

Medical help
The best place to go with any mysterious gynaecological infection is the nearest STD clinic. (They used to be called VD – venereal disease – clinics, and now a lot of them are called GU – genito-urinary – clinics). You don't need to be referred by a doctor; you can just walk in.

Alternatives to the GU unit are your GP, a well woman clinic, your family planning clinic or (for under-25s) the Brook Advisory Centre (see HELPLINES).

Why a GU clinic?
* GU clinics are the experts on all types of infection, and they have the necessary testing facilities on tap so they can both diagnose, and treat, your problem more accurately, quickly and more efficiently than anyone else. This is important: many infections are hard to identify; many, too, need specialist knowledge both to identify and to treat.
* If you go first to your GP or family planning clinic, they may well refer you on to the GU clinic anyway.
* Most district general hospitals have an STD clinic. Find it by ringing the switchboard, or ask at reception, or ring your local Community Health Council (or just look in the phone book under 'C' for community).
* GU clinics are convenient. You can usually drop in without an appointment.
* If you need supplies of tablets or creams for treatment they are free – there is no prescription charge.

438

* You will find that clinics are very discreetly sign-posted. They also may well have tactful but confusing names like 'Mary Smith Ward'.
* Staff make a point of being pleasant and tactful, because it is their job to stop STDs from spreading, and they won't do that if they put off potential patients.
* You can ask to see a woman doctor.
* Because of the AIDS crisis more funds have been channelled into GU clinics. So they are generally much nicer, and better equipped, than they used to be even a couple of years ago.
* You can be diagnosed and treated with minimum delay. Many infections have very uncomfortable symptoms – and a few need urgent treatment, so fast, expert help can be important.

What happens at the clinic?
You will find yourself in a waiting room – some clinics now have women only waiting areas, others still have mixed ones, even for separate clinics – and then you'll see a doctor (or perhaps a nurse) who is quite likely to be male. If this bothers you, ask to see a woman.

WHAT YOU WILL BE ASKED. You will be asked for some fairly intimate details before any tests are done, including who you've been sleeping with (if this is relevant in your case) and what kind of things you did with them. For instance, they may well need to know if you practised oral sex or anal sex. This 'interview' won't be as bad as it may sound. The doctor often reads out a list of sexual activities and all you have to say is 'yes' or 'no'. Everything you say is absolutely confidential. You can be sure that no matter how exotic – or ordinary – your sex life may be, the doctor has heard it all before, and will not make any unwelcome comments. Staff who disapprove of people who have unusual sexual practices or lots of sexual partners don't apply for jobs in STD clinics. If they did, they would not last long. If, by any chance, you don't like the doctor's attitude, try and pluck up courage and say so to somebody else at the clinic. The fault is with the doctor – not with you.

The tests
Any tests done depend on what infection you might have. Some can be detected just by a blood test; others need an internal examination, or a swab taken from your vagina. However, it is quite common to have more than one infection at once, and the symptoms of one infection may mask the symptoms of the other. So a conscientious doctor might give you all the tests.
* The doctor will almost certainly need to take a swab from your vagina, and possibly from your cervix (higher up), or (rarely) from your rectum, even if you haven't been having anal sex. This is exactly like having an ordinary smear test. You will be asked to part your legs, and maybe to put your feet into stirrups to keep your legs in place. You will feel very little physically, but it will be more difficult if you are tense and your vaginal or rectal muscles get tighter. Deep, slow breathing (in for a count of eight, hold it for eight, let it out slowly for a count of eight) will help relax you as they do the examination. Another advantage of going to a specialist STD clinic is that the skilled staff there take

439

swabs all the time so they can do so as gently as possible, and can also put people at their ease while carrying them out.

You may also be asked to give a blood sample and, again, frequent practice tends to mean the staff are skilled and gentle. A handful of clinics are now testing their blood samples routinely for the HIV virus (anonymously) as part of a national survey to monitor the spread of the disease. It is not known which clinics are doing this and the results are secret (i.e. patients are not informed). If you dislike the idea of unwittingly taking part in such a survey, you are within your rights to refuse permission for a blood sample to be taken. (See AIDS, page 27).

Now what?
All the samples taken from you will be sent for analysis. How long this takes depends on the local laboratory facilities, and on what the tests are looking for. You may get the results at the end of your first clinic visit, before you go home. But it is more likely that you will be notified a week, two weeks or even three weeks later. If you are waiting to find out if you have a contagious infection, it is best to abstain from sex until you get the all-clear.

Your results will be sent to you (in a plain envelope – it will not be stamped with indiscreet wording like 'VD Clinic'). However, if it would be awkward for you to get them by post, say so at your first appointment and you can arrange to ring up instead. At many clinics you can arrange to return and get your results given to you in person by a doctor. This is quite usual, so do not be afraid to ask.

If you do have an infection, you need to return to the clinic for treatment. Usually this just means taking tablets (see below for details of the different treatment).

The treatment
Do:
* follow instructions (make sure you understand them before you leave – write them down somewhere private);
* finish the *whole* course of tablets, even if your symptoms disappear very quickly. An infection which is only half-treated may become resistant to the drug that's been used, and be much harder to clear;
* turn up for the follow-up appointment. Some infections are trickier to clear than others and you must be sure it has gone. Otherwise the infection can go on developing, perhaps leading to serious illness or infertility;
Don't:
* have sex again until you get the all-clear. You could pass on your infection to somebody else – and, indeed, get it back again from that person after you have been cured.

Contact tracing
Meanwhile, you may have been asked to see the 'contact tracer'. The clinic's job is to stop STDs from spreading. No one will be making judgements about your sex life – they just want to do their job, so they will want to make sure your

sexual partner(s) gets treated too, especially if your infection is a potentially serious disease like gonorrhoea.

If you feel unable to break the news yourself to your sexual contacts the clinic will be happy to help. If you don't really know how to trace some of your partners, contact tracers who are skilled detectives and can work from quite small clues.

A contact tracer (sometimes called a health adviser) is a specially experienced professional, probably a nurse or health visitor, with a clear code of ethics. Part of that code is total confidentiality. They can get in touch with your sexual partner(s) in a way that doesn't reveal that the story started with you – if that's what you would prefer. They will also find a way to contact your sexual partner without notifying his (or her) other sexual partner (if they have one), if necessary. Then they'll work out a way to notify *that* sexual partner, in turn, without causing trouble.

Contact tracers are very sympathetic, and do understand that STD can cause havoc in delicate webs of relationships. While nobody can guarantee that every single staff member at an STD clinic is friendly and helpful, with contact tracers the guarantee is 100 per cent. They are also very resourceful, and can probably find a way round any difficulty.

The infections

Most people, when they think of sexually-transmitted infections, think of gonorrhoea and syphilis (VD) the two traditional STDs, which have been around for centuries. But there are many others which are much more common. Here they are, listed in alphabetical order. Do take note that while these infections can all be caught from a sexual partner through intercourse, there are almost always other far more 'innocent' ways of getting them, too.

Chlamydia

WHAT IS IT? A bacterial parasite called chlamydia trachomatis. It is very common – thought to be the most common STD worldwide today (apart from the mixture of conditions classified together as NSV, see below). It may affect up to 10 per cent of all sexually active women but until there is routine screening of all women, nobody will really know.

SYMPTOMS: there is no irritation, but a discharge – sometimes a little, sometimes a lot. Often, it isn't noticed at all. Occasionally there is a frequent need to go to the loo. If a swab is being taken from the cervix, it will bleed. Untreated, chlamydia spreads deep up into the whole reproductive system and the most common symptom then is pain.
* Untreated chlamydia is a common (maybe the commonest) cause of PID, which is serious and can lead to chronic illness and infertility. Chlamydia is to blame in at least 50% of all cases (see PELVIC INFLAMMATORY DISEASE, page 322).
* chlamydia can pass to a baby while it is being born, causing eye infection, which is sometimes serious.

DIAGNOSIS: The main problem with chlamydia is not in treating it, but in knowing it is there in the first place. It usually shows up from a swab test, but in 10 to 20 per cent of cases it doesn't – and anyway, women with no symptoms have little reason to go for swabs.

Dr Owen Caul, microbiologist at Bristol's public health laboratory, has developed a simple urine test which is more reliable – but for men, not women. Further work on this might give a simple method of testing which could be the basis of nationwide routine screening – the best hope of stopping chlamydia.

Another hope for the future is on trial at the Boston Medical Center, where they have identified cell changes in the cervix which are 98 per cent accurate as indicators of chlamydia. If the trials are a success, screening for these cell changes could become part of the routine cervical smear test.

TREATMENT: by antibiotic – usually oxytetracycline or erythromycin taken two or four times a day for 14 days; or doxycycline which you take as one large starter dose, then three times a day for 14 days. There are no side effects.

Genital herpes

WHAT IS IT? Caused by a virus called herpes simplex (HSV) – one of four herpes viruses which can affect humans. There are two HSVs, called I and II, which lead to cold sores and other skin infections, including the genital kind. It used to be thought that only HSV II could cause genital herpes, but these days it is accepted that both of them can. It is one of the 'newer' diseases – in its STD form, anyway. But it isn't just an STD. You can even give genital herpes *to yourself* – by letting the virus from a cold sore get to your genital area, for instance. It is spread by contact with sores, when they're infectious. In 1990 there were around 17,000 new cases a year. NOTE: if your partner gets a herpes attack, don't automatically assume infidelity: it could be an old infection flaring up (the intervals can be long).

SYMPTOMS: Fifty per cent of cases may have no symptoms; 40 per cent have mild ones; 10 per cent have severe symptoms (mainly women). The main symptom is blisters, which then become sores and later heal. They are found around the vagina and/or anus (usually cervix, too). They are very painful, expecially during sex or when you are going to the loo.

You may have warning signals first: sensitivity, tingling, burning or aching. In 40 per cent of cases you will have flu-type symptoms, too.

The first attack is the worst, and lasts up to three weeks in women (less in men). Then the virus lies dormant. In about 50 per cent of cases with symptoms, there are no more attacks (although the virus stays in the body for life). For the other 50 per cent (nearer 80 per cent if it's HSV II) it becomes active again from time to time, with new sores. You are only infectious during these attacks.

There may be complications, although they are rare:
* viral meningitis (which cures itself without treatment);
* very severe attacks in people with weak immune systems (e.g. people with AIDS, or on immunity-suppressing drugs like those used for leukaemia).

TREATMENT: Alas, they may not help, but are worth a try.
* The sores can be painted with a special paint (5 per cent idoxuridine), which has some limited effect.
* The drug Acyclovir (an anti-viral agent) can help control acute attacks. Given orally for a first attack of HSV it helps shorten the attack. It is not prescribed if you're pregnant, but otherwise is very safe. Acyclovir cream is sometimes prescribed, but may be of little help.
* There is no sign of a long-term cure.

SELF HELP
* Painful attacks can be helped by painkillers, salt baths and ice packs on the sores.
* Keeping sores dry (expose them to the air, if and when you can, and dab them with witch hazel from the chemist).
* Avoiding sunlight and sunbeds, which seem to make sores more painful.
* Although you can't get rid of herpes for ever, you can work round recurrent attacks (if you have them) and be confident, also, that they will get milder.
* Between attacks, you are not infectious. When you have no sores, sex is safe.
* To reduce the pain of urinating over a sore apply Lignocaine jelly (which you can get from the clinic) before passing urine.
* For more advice, contact the Herpes Association (see HELPLINES).

Genital warts

WHAT ARE THEY? Just like the warts you might get anywhere else on your body and, like them, caused by a whole family of viruses with the group name of human papilloma virus (HPV). The genital kind, however, are a distinct sub-group, so you can't get genital warts by contact with 'ordinary' warts.

They are quite common, and getting more so. The number of people in GU clinics found to have warts doubled (from 18,000 to 36,000) in the ten years up to 1983, and had more than doubled again (to 75,000) by 1987.

Until about ten years ago, genital warts were seen as no more than a nuisance. There is no clear evidence yet, but experts are beginning to think there may be a link between genital warts and the cell changes on the cervix which are not cancer, but might, without treatment, lead to it (see CERVICAL CANCER, page 78). The link seems stronger with some types of genital wart virus than with others.

SYMPTOMS: These can usually be seen and/or felt anywhere around or inside the vagina, cervix or anus. Men get them on the penis (often, under the foreskin). Some warts are flat and almost invisible. But even these are easily spotted by an experienced professional. (If they are inside you, they can be seen with a magnifying instrument called a colposcope.)

Sometimes, the warts itch. If they are in the urethra they can cause a burning feeling (like cystitis) when you go to the loo.

Vaginal discharge may be another pointer – not because it is caused by warts, but because it makes warts more likely to flourish.

TREATMENT: There are lots of choices here, and they all work – but, unless you have a very mild case, treatment can be a long and sometimes painful business. It can take 16 clinic visits – or more – to clear them, says the Women's Health and Reproductive Rights Information Centre (WHRRIC), and it may take a few tries to find which treatment works best for you.

* Painting the warts with a natural substance called podophyllin (extracted from a root) burns them off. The surrounding skin must be protected with Vaseline, and it must be done in the clinic for safety (2 to 3 times a week, for up to six weeks). With stubborn warts, an even more caustic chemical (trichloracetic acid) may be used as well, or instead. Neither of these treatments can be used on your cervix, if you have warts there.

* Other treatments: there are various other ways of destroying the warts, which can be used on your cervix: diathermy (high-frequency electric current); electrocautery (red hot wire); cryocautery (freezing); laser treatment (available only in gynaecology departments, not GU clinics); and, for bad cases, surgery (you'll be given local anaesthetic for external warts; a general anaesthetic for warts inside you). Laser treatments were pioneered for cervical cell change problems. They are effective but can be painful. Check that you're being given a local anaesthetic, and request painkillers after.

* A new drug treatment (Immunovir) is being tried out.

SELF HELP

* You will need to get regular and frequent cervical smear tests every 12 to 18 months in case there really is a link with pre-cancerous cell changes. (See also CERVICAL CANCER, page 78.)

* Any sexual partners with warts (male or female) must be treated too. You may need persistence: the WHRRIC (see HELPLINES) reports cases when men with warts had to insist on treatment because doctors didn't appreciate the possible risk to their sexual partner.

Gonorrhoea

WHAT IS IT? One of the oldest STDs, possibly mentioned in the *Bible*.

It may be found in the urethra, the Bartholin's glands nearby, the cervical canal and sometimes the rectum (even if you don't practise anal sex). Almost any infection may reach the Bartholin's glands. These are tiny glands next to the entrance to your vagina, whose main job is to produce lubricating fluid when you get sexually aroused. If one or both swell up and/or hurt, they are infected. Treatment depends on the cause. Occasionally, the only remedy is a minor operation to drain out the pus or (very rare) remove the whole gland.

Gonorrhoea can't survive for long in an adult's vagina, but it can in a child's – sometimes children can be infected if they have contact with a gonorrhoea sufferer (not necessarily sexual contact – it is much more likely to be passed on through poor hygiene).

It has an incubation period of 2 to 10 days. There are about 25,000 cases a year.

SYMPTOMS: There is a mild, non-irritating discharge but if gonorrhoea is untreated, it can spread into the uterus and Fallopian tubes, causing abdominal pain and fever. Men may have pain when they urinate, or an offensive-smelling discharge. If untreated in them, it can spread to the testicles, causing swelling and pain.

* Untreated, gonorrhoea can spread a long way and cause PID and infertility. It can also infect a developing foetus, or a baby during birth, and cause eye problems – even blindness. In men, it can cause permanent damage, including stricture (narrowing) of the urine passage which makes if difficult or imposs-ible to urinate – a dangerous condition which needs urgent treatment.

TREATMENT: Generally antibiotics, usually penicillin. If you are allergic to penicillin there are alternatives. Also, there are many different strains of gonorrhoea, and some of them are resistant to certain antibiotics, so it is important to get the right one – a mix of more than one may be used. It is absolutely vital, therefore, to attend follow-up appointments (the first one is usually within a week of treatment starting) to make sure that the treat-ment is succeeding, and to change it if necessary.

The usual procedure is to give you a high dose at once, and sometimes more tablets to take away with you – dosage instructions vary. Sometimes the first dose is given by injection, with a built-in painkiller. There are no side effects.

SELF HELP
* While treatment is going on, don't drink alcohol.

NOTE: The fabled 'lavatory seat' story: the truth is that gonorrhoea bacteria are tougher than the organisms producing the other form of VD – syphilis – and can survive for a while, just, on towels and in paper waste. There are, however, no reliable records of the infection being passed on this way.

NSV, NSU and Gardnerella Vaginalis
WHAT ARE THEY? If you have irritation or discharge, it may be written on your case notes as non-specific urethritis (NSU) – this is when your urinary tract is infected; or – when your vagina is the infected place – as non-specific vaginitis (NSV), bacterial vaginosis, or anaerobic vaginosis. With men, the term most usually used is NSU (typical male symptoms classed as NSU are pain on passing urine, or a discharge from the penis).

All these mean that there is an infection but no one is sure what it is.

In either sex, these problems can arise without having been sexually transmitted. The most common culprit for a non-specific infection, in women, is gardnerella vaginalis. This is a type of bacteria which naturally lives in the vagina, but can get out of hand if the vagina loses its normal acidity.

NSV is by far the most common STD amongst women – 132,000 infections were put down as NSV in 1987. Gardnerella often coexists with other infections, which is why it gets mixed into the general statistics for NSV.

SYMPTOMS: NSV just means any kind of discharge and/or irritation. Gardner-ella doesn't cause irritation, but a particularly smelly discharge ('foul and fishy', say some women), which could be grey and frothy or thick and pasty.

445

TREATMENT. There is lots of choice. Drug treatments include various anti-biotics. But the most usual treatment is Flagyl (metronidazole) – as for trichomonas, see below, and with the same drawbacks. A more comfortable way of administering metronidazole is being tried out in a large study covering Europe and the USA (in the UK, it is in the hands of the GU Department at the Royal South Hants Hospital, Southampton). Sponges are impregnated with the drug and placed in the vagina. The results of the English trial so far show it to be effective in nine out of ten women – and to have no side effects.

Surface treatments include sulpha cream or povidone-iodine pessaries (tablets to go in your vagina), but these are less successful than Flagyl.

Syphilis

WHAT IS IT? One of the oldest STDs, caused by an organism called treponema pallidum. The incubation period can be up to 90 days but is usually 3 to 4 weeks. It is not always passed on through sexual activity – it can be inherited from an infected mother.

It is much rarer than gonorrhoea, although it is often found with it. There are about 1,500 cases a year in the UK.

SYMPTOMS: First there will be an ulcer (called a chancre) somewhere near your vagina. It is not painful, but very infectious. There may also be swelling of nearby glands. The chancre heals by itself in a few weeks, but the syphilis continues to spread inside you. The second stage, a few weeks later, is fever, sore throat and/or skin rashes. Again, these clear up by themselves – but the syphilis is still spreading. The third stage could be years later, and could have a wide range of symptoms, mimicking the effects of almost any disease, mental or physical, usually very nasty ones. (One of the final effects is vividly called 'general paralysis of the insane'.)

Syphilis can be passed on to an unborn baby, and go all the way to the third stage if it is not treated. Ante-natal clinics do a routine test for it.

TREATMENT is most successful at the first (chancre) stage. The usual treatment is penicillin by injection, with a built-in painkiller to make sure the injection doesn't hurt. If you are allergic to penicillin, another drug will be used, and this will be equally effective. You may also get tablets. There are no side effects. It is important to get the dosage right, so you must keep follow-up appointments. Inadequate doses will only mask the symptoms while the disease progresses quietly on to the next stages.

Trichomonas vaginalis

WHAT IS IT? A parasite, usually (not always) transmitted through sex. It lives in the deep folds of the vagina. Its incubation time is 7 to 21 days.

At least 20 per cent of women are likely to get it at some time during their child-bearing years. There are about 11,000 cases a year (10,000 of them in women) and it's thought to be on the increase.

SYMPTOMS: Often, there are none. Changes in the vagina's acid balance make trichomonal vaginalis flourish, and then you get actual infection with swelling and a frothy green, unpleasant-smelling discharge, sometimes bloodstained. The infection may then spread to your urinary tract, or to the glands around the entrance to your vagina, causing swelling and perhaps pain.

In bad cases there is severe swelling, pain, and sometimes pain when you urinate. Male partners often have no symptoms, but they may have painful urination and a slight discharge.

Trichomonas seems to have a friendly relationship with the much more serious STD gonorrhoea (one STD specialist says: 'Put it this way – I'm never surprised to find the two together'), so you'll probably be tested for gonorrhoea too just in case.

TREATMENT: Flagyl (metronidazole) tablets, three times a day for a week. If you can't be sure of taking the tablets so frequently, you may be given a higher dose to take every 12 hours but this will mean more side effects. The main side effects are nausea, a metallic taste in the mouth and stomach upsets.

Go back for a checkup after six weeks – and, ideally, again at three months to make sure the trichomonas has been killed.

SELF HELP
* Avoid alcohol during treatment – it speeds up excretion of the drug, making it more diluted in the body and less effective. It may also react with the drug and cause even more nausea, and vomiting.

Other infections
Miscellaneous
There are many other, much rarer, infections which affect women's vaginas and reproductive systems. Since barrier methods of contraception (the sheath, cap and diaphragm) are the best all-round protection against infection the boom in the use of other methods (like the IUD and Pill) has made the way clearer for all kinds of infections like chancroid, lymphogranuloma vereneum and granuloma inguinale. However, these are *very* rare in the UK. There is also thrush, which affects your sexual organs and can be passed on by a partner, but it arises on its own very often, and is very common, so see VAGINAL THRUSH, page 453.

Annual figures for all these (except for thrush) are in tens rather than thousands (which is another good reason for choosing a specialist clinic to investigate you – you might have something your GP has never even heard of).

Little creatures
Sometimes you might scratch, investigate and see what looks like a little insect (more likely, several of them) in your pubic hair. These will be either scabies or pubic lice (sometimes called 'crabs'). They aren't infections in the usual sense of the word, but they *are* passed on from person to person. Usually they are sexually transmitted, but sometimes they can be passed on through sharing clothes, towels, bedding and so on.

You may be horrified, but treatment is quite straightforward, and it works fast. There is a lotion for each of them (benzyl benzoate for scabies, gamma benzene hexachloride for pubic lice).

Self help: prevention

Prevention is much better than cure. These are the basics on how to protect yourself.

* Keep clean. Even if you never have sex, you can still get infections. Wash at least daily. Take care when you go to the loo to wipe yourself from front to back – normal bacteria from the faeces can cause havoc if they get into your vagina. If you use tampons, change them often – and do remember to take out the last one at the end of your period.

* Try not to upset the acid/alkali balance of your vagina. It is, in fact, designed to cope with many minor irritations and infections. Its normal chemical balance is acid, which can deal with quite a few invaders. (See VAGINAL THRUSH for more information and advice.) If you use natural yoghurt to prevent or treat upsets in your vagina, make sure the yoghurt is very clean, plain not flavoured, and not from a container you have already been using in the kitchen.

* Use a 'barrier' form of contraception – sheath, cap or diaphragm (see CONTRACEPTION, page 155). This prevents infected semen (and other secretions) from touching you. The Pill gives no such protection, and an IUD puts you at more risk of infection, anyway. (Gay women don't have to worry about contraception, but they can still get STDs.)

* If you feel you might be at risk of an STD, have a regular check-up at a GU clinic. This is a sensible precaution because many infections have no symptoms at all, or very minor ones, but they could be quite serious all the same. If they are left untreated, they get a chance to spread and cause a lot of damage, including PID (see PELVIC INFLAMMATORY DISEASE, page 322). GU clinics will not think you are wasting their time if you go for a test and nothing is found.

Good times to make a visit even if you have no symptoms are: when you have any doubts about a lover, or former lover; when you know such a person has an infection; when you're starting a new relationship; when there is a media scare about some disease, and it's worried you; when you plan to get pregnant.

* Always go for a check-up if you have any suspicious symptoms. Again, infections can become serious if they are not caught in time. Watch for any discharge from your vagina which is unusual for you – more than usual, a different smell, a different colour. Any smell you find unpleasant or unusual for you is a warning. If the discharge makes you itchy or causes any other kind of irritation, that's a warning sign, too. Don't forget that your normal discharge changes during the monthly cycle. For instance, when you ovulate the discharge may increase, and it will always become clearer and more slippery – like raw egg-white. Make a point of noticing what is normal for your body. Perhaps get into the habit of keeping a check, especially if you have more than one sexual partner.

* Other warning signs are any unusual pain, anywhere in your abdomen. Often, infections may cause pain when you urinate.

* Be warned if your male sexual partner has symptoms, such as pain on urination, or a discharge from his penis.

* Don't assume that a male partner is 'safe' if he has no symptoms. It is a fact of life that men get far fewer symptoms than women – often, none at all.
* If one sexual partner has an STD, both partners always have to be treated. Otherwise the treated partner just gets reinfected. This can be particularly tricky if there is a chain of sexual partners. If a single person remains untreated, then everyone else will be reinfected. STD clinics have contact tracers (see above) – and they must be told the truth.
* Most STDs have an incubation period (usually a week or two – sometimes up to three months) when they are present but have not become active. So if you have been infected by somebody else, you won't see any signs straight away. Some infections take a long time to show symptoms, so even when they become active you still won't see symptoms for a long time – and by then, they will have spread further and/or be harder to treat.
* Some infections can cause serious damage to a developing foetus, or infect it while it is being born. Take special care if you are pregnant: don't neglect any hint of infection, and think carefully about having several sexual partners during this time.

If you are in a high-risk job, press your obstetrician to screen you (it is done by blood test). You may have a fight on your hands – only a few realize the danger. Try quoting an expert to back up your point: Dr Darrel Ho-Yen, consultant microbiologist at Raigmore Hospital in Inverness, strongly believes screening is vital, and has written his views in the medical press.
* If you suspect an STD, or have had one diagnosed, always get expert treatment. There are too many potential risks in doing otherwise. All the same, there are special networks of support for certain infections where the problems may not all clear up as soon as you are treated, and these can be very useful (see HELPLINES).

Complementary therapy
Complementary therapies tailor their treatments very much to the individual: the precise nature of the treatment you receive will vary, depending on your medical history, symptoms, lifestyle, etc. The following information indicates the *sorts* of things a therapist is most likely to do or recommend. Do not be surprised if they feel you need something slightly different. This section is meant purely as an indication of likely treatments; it is not meant as a DIY guide to the medical uses of the different complementary therapies.

It is illegal for anyone other than a registered medical practitioner to treat sexually transmitted diseases. However, in combination with orthodox treatment, complementary therapies are helpful in strengthening resistance to infection and coping with the symptoms of the disease.

1. HERPES SIMPLEX
Clinical nutrition
Herpes cannot cause lesions until the body fluids have lost their calcium base, so it is essential to replace calcium; evening primrose oil acts as a calcium carrier. Propolis and Vitamin C, derived from sago palm, fight viral infections. Glandular concentrates support, and deficiencies of lysine should be replaced.

449

Homoeopathy
According to your symptoms, Mercsol, Nitric Acid or Natrum Mur may be used. Phytolacca can be applied locally.

Medical herbalism
General improvement of your immune system and health, through both diet and remedies such as Echinacea, is valuable. Local use of marigold or tea tree is often effective against the virus.

2. GENITAL WARTS
Clinical nutrition
Treatments include: dulse or kelp to purify your blood and provide iodine; spleen glandular concentrate to support your immune system; thymus glandular tissue to help drain your lymphatic system; evening primrose oil, which acts as a calcium diffusor; and, rutin to dilate your veins.

Homoeopathy
There is a celebrated trio for this condition: Thuja, Stappisagric and Nitric acid.

Medical herbalism
Treatment is the same as for herpes, perhaps supplemented with local application of tree of life, which is highly effective in killing the virus responsible.

3. GONORRHOEA AND SYPHILIS
The occurrence of either of these viruses should be referred directly to a registered practitioner, although homoeopathy is among the therapies which can help with advanced symptoms.

4. CHLAMYDIA
Clinical nutrition
Colonic irrigation with lactobacillus implant helps flush out the parasitic bacteria at its source, establishing an acid environment in which Chlamydia cannot survive.

Homoeopathy
All of chlamydia's symptoms can be treated according to your individual needs.

Medical herbalism
Often an acute attack calls for antibiotics; however, these rarely clear the problem entirely. Herbal remedies can be very helpful over a period of time. Advice on diet and health is important to deter the spread of symptoms. Good vaginal hygiene and the practise of emptying your bladder after intercourse are also helpful. Your partner's health and hygiene will need to be discussed.

5. TRICHOMONIASIS
Clinical nutrition
An examination should be made to establish whether you have adequate protein intake and the right hydrochloric acid levels in your stomach. Treatment then consists of replenishing nutrients depleted by the presence of the parasite; riboflavin, pryridoxine, Vitamin A and Vitamin E are suitable prescriptives.

Homoeopathy
Symptoms can be treated according to your individual needs.

Medical herbalism
Treatment would follow the same lines as that for Chlamydia.

6. PUBIC LICE
Homoeopathy
Staphysagria is a suitable remedy.

Medical herbalism
Local rashes may be treated with tree of life, wild indigo and other parasite-killing herbs. Otherwise, treatment follows the general principals with other STDs.

7. THRUSH
(See VAGINAL THRUSH, page 461.)

Sexually transmitted disease helplines

The British Association of Counselling
37A Sheep Street, Rugby CV21 3BX (0788 578 328)
A directory of therapists and helpful organizations who counsel couples countrywide. They will let you know where your local counsellors are based.

The Brook Advisory Service
HQ – 233 Tottenham Court Road, London W1 (071 580 2991)
Can offer support, advice and medical treatment for various sexually transmitted diseases. Ring HQ for details of the branch nearest you.

Herpes Association
41 North Road, London N7 9DP (071 609 9061)
Advice and information leaflets for herpes sufferers, plus a telephone helpline.

Marie Stopes Clinics
In London, Manchester and Leeds. (See GENERAL HELPLINES, page 480, for details)

Medical Advisory Service
10 Barley Mow Passage, Chiswick, London W4 (081 994 6477)
Advice and information on many health matters.

PID Support Network
c/o WHRRIC, 52 Featherstone Street, London EC1Y 8RT (071 251 6331)
If your sexually transmitted disease causes a pelvic inflammation, contact the PID support group, which offers support to other PID sufferers. They publish a newsletter, collect information and data on PID, and try to identify sympathetic doctors and hospitals.

Women's Health and Reproductive Rights Information Centre (WHRRIC)
52–54 Featherstone Street, London EC1Y 8RT (071 251 6332/6580)
A voluntary organization that can give useful information and support on any aspect
of women's health care.

Further reading
The Herpes Manual by Sue Banks and Carole Woddis (Wigmore)
Sex and Your Health edited by Dr James Bevan (Mandarin)
Sexually Transmitted Diseases and VD by Duncan Catterall (BMA – a Family Doctor
   publication)
Safer Sex: A New Look at Sexual Pleasure by P. Gordon and L. Mitchell (Faber)
What Every Woman Needs to Know by Penny Junor (A Birthright book, published by
   Century)
Herpes and Other Sexually Transmitted Diseases by D. Llewlyn-Jones (Faber)
Stop Herpes Now by B. North and P. Crittenden (Thorsons)
Herpes: The facts by J. Oakes (Penguin)

Vaginal thrush

What is it?

Vaginal thrush is a very common condition which seven out of every ten women will get at some time in their lives. It is caused by the fungus Candida albicans. This lives naturally in the vagina (it can also be found in the mouth, bowel and, to some extent, on the skin). It only becomes a problem when there is an overgrowth of it.

It is not a sexually transmitted disease in the same way as, say, a venereal disease like gonorrhoea because, although it may very occasionally be passed to you by a male partner, it is far more likely to break out of its own accord, triggered by other conditions in your body (see **Causes**). People who are not sexually active can also get thrush.

Symptoms

Symptoms for thrush can include:

* vaginal discharge. Some women have a lot of discharge quite normally, even when they do not have thrush, others have very little. So it is a case of deciding what 'a lot' of discharge is for you personally. It may be white, thick and lumpy looking or it may be watery;
* a sore, dry, red, itchy vulva;
* a stinging pain when you pass water, as the urine passes over the inflamed vulva's skin surface;
* soreness and discomfort when you have sexual intercourse;
* a red rash which may extend down the inside of your thighs, or round to your anus;
* tiny, sore cracks in the vulva's skin, if it is very dry.

Men can carry thrush, but because their penises offer little of the enclosed, warm, damp membrane areas that thrush likes (unlike a woman's vulva and vagina) men tend not to get symptoms. If you are getting repeated attacks, however, it is worth asking your partner if he has any rash or itching around the glans (head) of his penis or suggesting he has a test for the infection.

Causes

There are many different theories about the causes of thrush, and not all specialists agree with every one of them. Basically anything can do the trick if it changes the conditions in the vagina to make it an easier place for Candida to grow. This includes any factors that change its pH (acidity), or cause irritation (either chemically or by abrasion and rubbing). It also includes anything that increases the amount of glycogen in the body's cells (including the ones in the vaginal tract walls) because Candida, being a yeast, feeds off sugars, and the more food it gets the faster it will multiply.

Causes of a Candida overgrowth, and thus an infection, can include any of the following.

PREGNANCY. The body's higher than usual hormone levels mean more changes in the vagina and its cells, especially in months seven to nine. Hormones might also have a direct effect on the Candida itself.

THE PILL. Taking higher oestrogen brands could have a similar effect to that of pregnancy. However, since the phasing in of safer, lower dose pills, the high oestrogen varieties are less common. If you are still on one, ask your doctor why and request a change.

PRE-PERIOD RECURRENCE. Many women say that recurrent thrush tends to flare up in the third or fourth week of their menstrual cycle. Dr Glyn Evans, thrush expert and senior lecturer in medical mycology at the University of Leeds, suggests this may be because certain hormones peak in the second half of the menstrual cycle and these influence the environment in the vagina and the vaginal cells or have a direct effect on the yeast. This triggers a thrush attack – which shows up the following week.

BEING PHYSICALLY RUN DOWN. If you have an illness, have just recovered from an illness, or are under psychological stress, these can all affect your immunity status. If it is low, you will be less capable of suppressing a threatened Candida overgrowth. Changes in the balance of your sex hormones can also affect the immune system.

ANTIBIOTICS can cause thrush as a side effect. Broad spectrum antibiotics, such as tetracycline, ampicillin and cephalosporins are the worst offenders. It is thought that antibiotics reduce the normal protective bacteria, such as lacto-bacillus (the sort found in plain live yoghurt) so the Candida is left with more of a free rein to multiply.

DIABETES can produce additional sugars in the vagina's secretions if it is not controlled; this can lead to overgrowth of Candida.

SEXUAL PARTNER. Candida can be passed on in the same way as other infections, but this is uncommon.

ALLERGIES. If there is swelling and soreness already in the vagina this may make it more vulnerable to Candida. It is thought some women may even be allergic to Candida itself.

PHYSICAL TRAUMA, which means any sort of abrasive or rubbing action on the vulva or vagina such as rough sexual intercourse or intercourse before the woman's vagina is sufficiently lubricated. Even riding a narrow, hard-seated racing bicycle or a very long horseback ride, if you are not used to it, could have this effect.

DAMAGE TO THE VAGINA'S PROTECTIVE MUCUS LAYER can be caused by chemicals in vaginal deodorants, perfumed soaps, heavily disinfected baths, heavily chlorinated and disinfected swimming pools or whirlpool spa baths.

TIGHT FITTING CLOTHES. Avoid densely-woven or nylon-based underwear and tight trousers or leggings that encourage a warm, damp vaginal/vulval environment.

CROSS INFECTION. If you have Candida elsewhere in the body – under your fingernails, in the mouth or in your bowel, for instance, it can be transferred to the vagina.

CHANGES IN THE VAGINA'S PH. The vagina is normally acid (pH 4.5) and is kept that way by bacteria (which naturally live there) such as the lactobacilli. Again, deodorants, soaps, perfumed baths or heavily disinfected and chlorinated spas and pools can change the vagina's pH.

Why do you get recurrent attacks?
There are many different theories about recurrent attacks and they include the following.
* A new idea from Leeds University's recent research, which is that a former Candida overgrowth might be leaving a residue behind after it has been treated. The residue could be toxins secreted by the Candida – or even bits of cell wall left behind by the fungi cells themselves. These may still irritate the vagina, causing inflammation – redness and itching – which seems like yet another bout of full blown thrush. They could also be maintaining 'pro thrush' conditions in there.
* 'Recolonization' or infection from your bowel, or other parts of the body which still carry the thrush fungus.
* Reinfection by your sexual partner, who may have no symptoms at all himself and so be unaware of the fact that he is carrying it.
* The fungus might be getting deep into the lower layers of the vagina's skin cells. For a while, as the top layers of vaginal membrane are treated with a cream or pessary, it seems that the infection has gone. Later, the lower layers of skin cells rise to the top, as the upper ones are gradually shed (just like skin on the outside of the body). As the Candida-bearing cells reach the surface, the redness and itching begins again.
* A minor defect in your immune system could make you more prone to thrush, in the same way as some people are more prone to flu. If your immune system is temporarily weakened (say after an illness like bad flu, or if you are under a good deal of stress – and stress hormones have been shown to affect the immune system's efficiency) this might make you more vulnerable to thrush, too. Patients taking corticosteroids, or undergoing chemotherapy will also suffer a depressed immune system.
* With recurrent, persistent thrush attacks it often turns out that there is another infection there too, such as chlamydia, also causing inflammation. This makes the vagina vulnerable to yet another thrush attack.
* Your recurrent redness, itching and discharge may not be caused by thrush

after all. This might not have been realized if you have not had comprehensive tests to check for other sorts of infection. A single test to check for thrush alone is not really good enough if you get recurrent attacks: you need the full battery of tests which can only be done at a hospital's genito-urinary department, or at a clinic specializing in sexually transmitted diseases (usually called the STD clinic or special clinic). Ask you GP to refer you – or you can refer yourself to an STD clinic.

* There could be a possible excess of sugars in your diet. This might be enough to raise the level of glycogen in all the cells in your body – including those in your vaginal wall – thus creating a helpful environment for Candida to multiply. Some nutritionists blame an excess of yeasts, too (e.g. in bread, vinegar). But according to Dr Caroline Bradbeer of St Thomas' Hospital, the yeasts in the foods which are often excluded by 'anti-Candida diets' are not the same as any of the many strains of Candida albicans yeast, so they should make little difference anyway.

The treatments
Where to go
Your GP, family planning clinic, well woman clinic, STD clinic or a gynae-cologist. You could start by asking your GP to refer you to a gynaecologist, or better yet, a genito-urinary physician, on the NHS at the local hospital, or refer yourself to one who has a private practice, if you are prepared to pay. You can also refer yourself, on the NHS, to the STD clinic – ask your local health centre for the telephone number of the nearest one. It will be called the Genito Urinary, GU Medicine, Special Clinic or STD Clinic.

What will they do?
They should *all* take a vaginal swab and send it away to be extensively tested, to ensure that you really have thrush and not another infection with similar symptoms. You will probably be given anti-fungal preparations in the mean-time, and be contacted if the infection turns out to be another sort that needs different treatment.

Anti-fungal drugs come in three different forms: oral – pill form; creams to smooth on the vagina and vulva; or pessaries – to place inside the vagina where they melt slowly in your body heat, coating the vagina and cervix. Generally, all offer a cure rate of between 80 and 90 per cent.

If you have not heard from your GP or clinic after two weeks and the infection does not seem to have cleared up, telephone them and chase up the results.

To check up on repeated infections, you will probably need a cervical smear (this can often pick up signs of infections such as trichomaniasis) and tests for other infections, such as trichomaniasis, chlamydia and gardnerella (see SEXUALLY TRANSMITTED DISEASES), which may be causing or compounding the problem.

ORAL TREATMENT is usually in the form of a one-day treatment. This is often prescribed for recurrent thrush, as the drug can enter the body's cells and act from within. This is useful if the Candida has also penetrated the lower layers of the vagina wall's skin cells, where creams cannot reach it all. Names of drugs include Diflucan and Sporanox.

CREAMS AND PESSARIES will soothe a thrush attack but not always stop it returning. They can be applied to a sore, inflamed vulva for almost immediate relief, or inserted into a syringe-like applicator and deposited high in the vagina near the cervix to tackle the source of the infection itself. If you just put cream on the vulva, it will become reinfected by the Candida living further up the vagina and cervix quite rapidly.

Canesten comes as a white cream and a pessary, which should be used together, either in a one-day treatment or treatment over six days. You can buy the cream over the counter, but you need a prescription for the pessaries. Nystan also comes in creams and pessaries to be used together for up to two weeks – it is yellow and can stain pants, so wear a pants shield. Gyno-Daktarin is a waxy white cream and pessary, which again can be used as a one-off treatment. You might also be given Betadine pessaries. These may be effective against thrush and bacteria, but dissolve into a messy brown discharge which, again, stains clothing – and they need to be used for two weeks.

Self help
There are several self help measures you can take both to prevent thrush and help stop it from returning.

* CLOTHES. Avoid clothes which make you feel hot, damp and sweaty in the crotch area: tight jeans, tight nylon knickers, plastic 'sauna' exercise trousers, tight high-cut leotards or swimsuits. Go for looser cotton underwear which allows any perspiration to evaporate properly, and for clothing which does not constrict you.

* SANITARY PROTECTION. If you have a period during a thrush attack or when you still feel thrush symptoms may be lurking, avoid tampons. They may create friction at the entrance to your vagina and inside it. As they are designed to absorb moisture efficiently, tampons may also draw the extra moisture which you need to keep your vaginal skin lubricated, especially if your period is starting, finishing or very light. This makes you more vulnerable to thrush attacks. Consider using soft sanitary towels instead.

* SEX. If you are making love with a male partner (without a condom) the sperm (a little of which may remain around the cervix and in the vagina) can provide the sort of warm, damp, glucose-rich environment Candida likes, suggests Dr Elisabeth Scott, an Edinburgh GP.

Another recent idea is that there may be a component in sperm that can stop the immune defences in a woman's vagina working properly, again making the area more vulnerable to thrush. Some consultants disagree with this, arguing that sperm is alkaline, while thrush likes an acid medium, and that in any case sperm does not stay in the vagina but trickles out again after intercourse. Even so, Dr Scott reckons that if a woman has a long vagina, or one with very strong muscle walls, it will not always drain out completely, and if she is sitting or lying in bed after intercourse the vagina tends to 'cup' its contents (the same happens to menstrual blood during a period).

Another sensible preventative measure, therefore, if you are prone to thrush, is to wash soon after intercourse (just by splashing with cool water or by spraying gently with a showerhead on low power). Ensure also that your vagina is well lubricated for intercourse to avoid any abrasions; either naturally with your own secretions or with KY jelly.

* AFTER A PERIOD. Wash the vagina out, as after intercourse, to get rid of any remaining blood which, if left there, can also provide the perfect environment for Candida to develop. When you change your pad or tampon during your period wash your vulva and vagina gently in warm water (do not use a powerful spray of water).

* SALINE BATHS. Get a washing-up bowl and half fill it with warm water and salt (1 teaspoon of salt to one pint of water). Sit in it for a while after your bath or shower, swishing it around. This is also very useful for providing temporary relief when your vulva is at its itchiest from a thrush attack. Do not just pour salt in your bathwater – you will probably get the proportions wrong, and it will dry the rest of your skin.

* SWIMMING POOLS AND WHIRLPOOL SPAS (like Jacuzzis). If you are prone to thrush, avoid any that are heavily chlorinated or disinfected. They may irritate your vulva and vagina making them more prone to another attack.

* PERFUMED or COLOURED BATH ADDITIVES. Avoid additives in your bath, vaginal sprays or perfumed sanitary pads. They, too, may irritate and make you more prone to a thrush attack. They may also alter the vagina's own pH, which would have a similar effect. For the very thrush-prone, Dr Robert Wilson, Director of Preventative Medicine for BUPA suggests you beware of coloured loo paper, too, or white bleached loo paper: the dyes or bleach used may, in some very sensitive women, be enough to reduce the skin's natural immunity to thrush colonization by causing a mild allergic or chemical reaction. Use white *unbleached* loo paper instead.

* PERSONAL HYGIENE. Because of the possibility of reinfection from Candida living in your bowel, always wipe your bottom from front to back after emptying your bowels.

* REBALANCING YOUR BACTERIA. You can try and deal with an overgrowth of Candida in your bowel (which may be a major source of reinfection) by taking supplements containing the right sort of bacteria, such as acidophilus and lactobacillus (the ones found in plain, live yoghurt). For advice on the best sort – because many of the products sold in health shops are of little use, despite what they claim on their packaging – contact the Institute for Symbiotic Studies or the Candida Clinic which specialize in this area (see HELPLINES). The question of bacteria supplements remains controversial, as many specialists

argue that the small bowel is sterile – so by the time any beneficial organism has passed through it will have been killed.

It is also possible to buy pessaries containing these beneficial bacteria, which have been freeze-dried (again, contact the above organizations). Or you can anoint the vulva and insert into the vagina some cold, live plain yoghurt. This also contains these bacteria, though not in concentrated form like the supplements and pessaries.

* YOUR CONTRACEPTION. The contraception you choose can also help – and IUDs are not usually recommended while you are suffering from thrush.

Condoms will catch the sperm and stop them providing any material on which Candida can feed and multiply. But make sure the condom is properly lubricated. If you fear you may be allergic to the latex they are made of, or the spermicides most are impregnated with, try a Durex Allergy Sheath.

IUDs: Candida can possibly climb up the long nylon string 'tails' to infect the upper part of the vagina and the cervix, so if you have an IUD and recurrent thrush attacks, it may be worth considering whether part of the problem is the device. A tailless coil is also being developed (see CONTRACEPTION, page 155).

A diaphragm must be kept in place for six to eight hours after making love, but it might be a good idea to rinse the vagina when you do remove the cap.

The Pill may make the body's cells richer in glycogen (which thrush thrives on) if it is one of the higher oestrogen brands. Consider changing to as low an oestrogen dose as possible, or opting for a different form of contraception. Speak to your family planning clinic or GP. If your GP is not very helpful and you do not already go to a clinic, call up the Family Planning Association (see HELPLINES) and ask for the address of your nearest one.

* WASHING POWDER. Use a non-biological (enzyme-free) powder which has as few irritants in it as possible for washing your knickers. One of the ecology-friendly brands like Ecover may be helpful – again, to avoid the possibility of an allergic reaction to any biological washing powder residue left on the clothing, weakening your vagina's resistance to a thrush infection, or slightly altering the vagina's pH.

* PREVENTATIVE PESSARIES. If you know that you get regular thrush attacks before every period (and have had all the necessary tests to show it really is thrush and not another infection, or not thrush *and* another infection), ask your GP for a supply of anti-thrush pessaries and use one or two preventatively a couple of days before your attacks usually begin. They will not cure the problem permanently, or tackle the underlying cause, but they will control it.

* CREAMS: Femeron and Canesten now available without prescription with an internal applicator. This means the cream can be inserted right up by your cervix to get rid of the infection, rather than just temporarily soothe it.

* SEXUAL ACTIVITY. It is possible that oral sex can affect the likelihood of thrush, for a woman who is very sensitive to pH changes in her vaginal environment. According to Dr Robert Wilson, if a woman's partner cleans his or her teeth with strong toothpaste or washes their mouth out with mouthwash

before performing cunnilingus, that may be enough to alter the vaginal pH sufficiently to make it more prone to thrush infection.

Complementary therapy

Complementary therapies tailor their treatments very much to the individual: the precise nature of the treatment you receive will vary, depending on your medical history, symptoms, lifestyle, etc. The following information indicates the *sorts* of things a therapist is most likely to do or recommend. Do not be surprised if they feel you need something slightly different. This section is meant purely as an indication of likely treatments; it is not meant as a DIY guide to the medical uses of the different complementary therapies.

Complementary therapy can be most valuable in dealing with thrush – in the short term by alleviating the symptoms, while dealing with the immediate infection, and in the long term by offering advice on nutrition and lifestyle, and treatment to prevent recurrence.

Acupuncture

Acupuncture therapy for general inflammation and discomfort can be useful throughout thrush attacks. Stimulation will improve antibody production and your acid-base balance, thereby helping to ward off future attacks.

Aromatherapy

Vaginal douches of essential oils of rosemary or tea tree in hydrosols help alleviate the symptoms, while also acting on the infection. Dietary advice, combined with this local treatment, encourages greater acidity of your vagina's mucus and prevents the growth of Candida.

Clinical nutrition

Foods which create an ideal alkaline breeding ground for the yeast fungus should be avoided. These include: dairy and dairy-based products (cheese, yoghurt and butter, etc.); yeast products (beer, wine and fermented foods); fats; oranges, orange juice and other canned or frozen fruit juices; apple cider vinegar, hops and malt; peanuts and peanut butter; mushrooms; fried foods and pre-cooked meats; refined sugars; eggs and egg substitutes; and coffee, tea, chocolate and other stimulants.

Colonic irrigation with lactobacillus implant washes out the fungus and generates production of the flora, which control micro-organisms.

To alleviate the soreness and itching, live yoghurt douches, cider vinegar in the bath and sponging with tea tree oil help kill infection and create an acid environment.

Homoeopathy

Advice on dietary control, to regulate the bacterial flora and maintain correct acidity in the bowel, can be combined with appropriate homoeopathic remedies for distressing symptoms. These include: Bacteriuni-Coli, Echinacea, Mercuris Solubilis Hahnemann; used as a lotion, Calendula in olive oil is good for dryness and itching.

Medical herbalism

Local applications, ranging from live yoghurt to essential oil of tea tree, garlic, and Calendula, are all valuable in either altering the environment to render it hostile to fungal infection or to directly creating anti-fungal activity. Advice on clothing, hygiene and so on are all helpful.

Internal remedies such as Echinacea or garlic help boost your immunity and encourage your natural defences, while live yoghurt and salt water douches soothe itching and dryness.

Vaginal thrush helplines

The Richmond Clinic (private)
129 Sheen Road, Richmond TW9 (081 332 6685)

Dr Harry Howell (private)
56 Harley House (off Euston Road), London W1 and at the Candida and ME
   Clinic, The Lodge, Sherborne Road, Henstridge, Templecombe, Somerset (0963
   63957)
Telephone for details of clinics, which are run one day per week.

The Institute of Symbiotic Studies
5 Fairlight Place, Brighton, Sussex EN2 3A8
Organization which treats illnesses by rebalancing the 'good' and 'bad' bacteria in the
   gut. They regard most diseases, including thrush, as being the result of an
   imbalance of these different bacteria. Have trained many nutritionists and some
   doctors in this manner of treating illness. Write to the Institute for details.

Angela Kilmartin
75 Mortimer Road, Islington, N1 (071 249 8664)
Offers counselling to assist desperate sufferers from cystitis and thrush. Will speak to
   groups, and has written three books on the subject (read one before contacting her).

Marie Stopes Clinics
In London, Manchester and Leeds. (See GENERAL HELPLINES, page 480, for details)

Thrush and Candida Albicans North London Support Group
5 Chaseside Place, Enfield, Middlesex EN2 6QA (081 363 8615)
Telephone from 9.30 a.m. to 5.30 p.m., Monday to Friday. Eight-week courses
   include information on diet, allergies, skin complaints, fatigue and environmental
   health control. Take care of your body and learn how to control your infection.
   Individual counselling is available.

Further reading
Coping With Thrush by Caroline Clayton (Sheldon Press)
Sexual Cystitis by Angela Kilmartin (Arrow)
Victims of Thrush and Cystitis by Angela Kilmartin (Arrow)
Below the Belt: A Woman's Guide to Urino-Genital Infections by Denise Winn
   (Optima)
Candida Albicans: Yeast and Your Health, Gill Jacobs, (Optima – has a list of
   practitioners experienced in treating stubborn candida infections).

A beginner's guide to complementary therapies

What is complementary therapy?
There are many different kinds of complementary therapies. But they tend to share the same basic principles.
* They work on people – not diseases.
* They believe that the body has its own healing ability (or energy), and that the therapist's job is to get the individual back into balance and release that energy.
* They look at people as a whole – not just their bodies – and believe that health is strongly affected by lifestyle and attitudes.
* They don't just treat a set of symptoms, but take time to find out about the individual patient as well.

Complementary therapy and ordinary medicine
Good complementary therapists work alongside (complementing) orthodox (ordinary) medicine and are trained to recognize when conventional medicine would be more appropriate. In turn, many conventional doctors are happy to refer their patients on to therapists. In fact, many progressive doctors now take courses, usually short, some full, themselves in therapies such as homoeopathy or acupuncture.

Complementary therapies can be very helpful for 'women's problems'. Some of these have no identifiable 'medical' cause, and little or no known medical treatment as such (i.e. unexplained infertility), so even the most sympathetic conventional doctor may not be able to help.

Finding a good practitioner
* By word of mouth – good reputations get around.
* Some practitioners band together in 'natural health' clinics. This is useful, because you can then get advice on which of a number of therapies available might be helpful for you.
* If you see a promising advert (perhaps in a health food shop or magazine) check the advertiser's qualifications with one of the national organizations listed below or with the ICM (Institute for Complementary Medicine).
* Some therapies require a long training period – herbalists, osteopaths and chiropractors all study for over four years, for instance – and reputable training colleges keep a list of their graduates.
* The Institute for Complementary Medicine says that several therapies are now standardizing their training requirements and developing a registration system, so it will be easier to sort out the good therapists from the quacks. The

national organizations listed here can give you a list of qualified practitioners in your area, as can the ICM itself, which holds registers of approved complementary therapists around the UK.
* When you go to visit a therapist, check that the premises are clean and professional looking.
* Check the therapist's qualifications with the relevant national organization.
* If the fee quoted alarms you, check it with the therapist's national organization. Don't book in advance for a *course* of treatment (especially if it's long or expensive) and distrust a therapist who tries to sell you one.
* Avoid practitioners who blame you for your disease.
* Avoid practitioners who offer unrealistic advice (like early morning meditation if you have young children).
* Avoid practitioners who promote their therapy as the only one likely to help you, or who emphatically offer a total cure.
  If you have difficulty finding a good local practitioner, contact:
The Institute for Complementary Medicine
PO Box 194, London SE16 1QZ (071 237 5165)

The fees
Many of the national schools listed have cheaper rates for those who are willing to be treated by supervised senior students. Most complementary practitioners have a personal sliding scale of fees, though they don't advertise the fact. If money is a problem for you, discuss it with them before they treat you. Some private insurance shemes will now pay for certain therapies, check with your insurers. In certain cases, the DHSS may reimburse for homoeopathic treatment if your GP refers you to one of the five homoeopathic NHS hospitals in the country (see **Homoeopathy**, below). Recent statutory changes now also mean that osteopathy and chiropractic treatments may be claimed from certain insurers. As the governing bodies of the other major complementary therapies standardize professional training, it is hoped that this will extend to the other major therapies in Britain too by the end of the century.

Which complementary therapy?
All the different therapies, in their different ways, work to strengthen and balance you as an individual. The focus of attention is on you – not your symptoms. So you might find several therapies equally helpful. For those which can help most with specific women's health problems, see **Complementary therapy** in each chapter.
  Listed below are the major therapies, with some suggestions about the kind of problems they may be able to help. Pick out the ones which attract you – this in itself will mean something. Then find a good practitioner (see above), describe your problem and ask if he or she can help. If they can't you'll be recommended to somebody else who can.

Acupuncture
What is it?
Acupuncture is an ancient Chinese theory, still used widely in China today.

Acupuncturists believe that certain pressure points on the body are linked with particular organs or functions of the body by invisible paths of energy (called 'meridians'). Along them travels the life force some describe as electromagnetic energy (Ch'i or *Chi*). If they get blocked, the flow of energy gets out of balance and illness results in the areas they 'supply'.

An acupuncturist inserts thin sterilized needles at specific 'energy points' to unblock and redirect the body's own healing electromagnetic energy. Sessions can last from 20 minutes to one and a half hours and will cost from around £15 to £40. Acupressure (or Shiatsu), often used with or instead of acupuncture by therapists, works on the same principles but uses finger pressure, not needles. An acupuncturist may also use Moxibustion (sticks of healing herbs, whose heat and smoke are directed over certain pressure points) or Cupping (glass cup shapes which create a vacuum over certain pressure points).

The needles
The needles don't hurt at all, if the therapist is doing a good job – they are thin, and usually lightly inserted. Many people report a 'tingling', like a very slight electric shock. Afterwards, the client should feel relaxed, maybe elated, or possibly sleepy.

The acupuncturist decides where to put the needles after taking a detailed case history, and by physical examination and Chinese pulse taking (this is more detailed than ordinary pulse taking – acupuncturists can detect up to sixteen different pulses flowing through different body systems).

Is acupuncture safe?
Reputable acupuncturists have to follow strict sterilization procedures. The safest of all are those who use disposable needles. There is no need for you to worry about AIDS with a reputable therapist, and you can request they use disposable needles.

What is acupuncture useful for?
It is useful for many conditions, including bronchitis, asthma, digestive problems (such as colitis and ulcers), pain (including headaches, migraines, muscular and back problems), 'nervous conditions' (such as depression and anxiety), circulatory problems, smoking and drug addiction. For women: menstrual problems (including PMT, painful or heavy periods), ovulation difficulties, menopausal problems, speeding recovery after miscarriage – and many more.

Contact: British Acupuncture Register and Directory
34 Alderney Street
London SW1V 4EC 071 834 1012
(for a Registered Practitioner's list send £1.50, plus p&p)

Aromatherapy
What is it?
Aromatherapy goes back to the ancient Egyptians, and has undergone a major

revival in the last decade – a body of research has now been built up, and the therapy is even practised in some NHS hospitals.

Aromatic 'essential oils' or essences are extracted from flowers, plants, trees or spices, blended with vegetable oil and massaged into the face and/or body, sometimes referred to as vegetable hormones. Through massage, the small amounts of oils can reach the bloodstream, where they affect (in particular) the nervous and hormonal systems. They can also be treated in the form of steam from scented water, where the rich blood supply near the surface of the skin in the nose will take small amounts of the active ingredients into the blood. Aromatherapy is quite a powerful treatment – not just a pretty scent.

Different oils are selected for their different effects on the system (calming, revitalizing, infection-fighting and so on). The massage adds to the effect. Afterwards, you feel relaxed and have a sense of wellbeing. A session, which lasts about an hour or an hour and a half, costs from around £12 to £45.

Can I use the oils myself?
Oils can be bought for self use in baths and for massage and steam inhalation from health food stores. They have to be stored very carefully to preserve their qualities and need to be pure (not synthetic, and not adulterated) – so they can be expensive and cost from £4 per 15ml.

Reliable brands include: Holland & Barrett, Tisserand, Shirley Price, Body Treats, Daniele Ryman, Michele Arcier.

You can get them by mail order from: Aroma Therapy Services Ltd, Unit 3, Knoll Bus Centre, Old Shoreham Road, Hove, Sussex, 0273 412139. (Tisserand oils.) The oils from the Body Shop smell nice, but most therapists feel they are not strong enough to be of much therapeutic use.

What is aromatherapy useful for?
It is helpful for many things including respiratory, and stress- and tension-related, problems, muscle aches, headaches and digestive problems. The massage part of a treatment eases tight muscles, increases circulation and helps the body rid itself of toxins. As aromatherapy has a beneficial effect on the skin, it can be used for shingles, acne and healing scars and burns. For women: anything relating to hormonal problems or imbalances, e.g. PMT, menopause, recovery from miscarriage and childbirth.

For a list of practitioners contact the International Federation of Aromatherapists
Dept of Education
The Royal Masonic Hospital
Ravenscourt Park
London W6
081 846 8066
or The Tisserand Aromatherapy Institute
10 Victoria Grove
Second Avenue
Hove
East Sussex BN3 3WJ 0273 206640 (Tisserand is a teaching college and also publishes a quarterly journal).

or The London School of Aromatherapy 071 267 6717 (for a list of their own graduates).

It is also worth checking health clubs, beauty salons and even local authority swimming pools, as some now run aromatherapy sessions. But do make sure the practitioner has a proper aromatherapy qualification (check with the ICM) – not a two- or three-day course diploma.

Chiropractic
What is it?
Chiropractors believe that much illness originates in a misaligned spine. Back, head, neck, arm and shoulder pains, for instance, are often caused by tightened muscles trapping and inflaming a nerve can be traced to one or two vertebrae which are out of line.

Treatment is based on the manipulation of mainly the neck and spine. This can consist of gentle pulling, twisting, or sometimes a series of short sharp thrusts of great precision to get the neck and spinal vertebrae back in their proper position, so that tendons, nerves and muscles connected with the back also fall back into line. Some chiropractors use heat treatment and many use X-rays to study the spine in detail. All have to undergo at least four years of intensive training.

A chiropractor decides which joints to manipulate through taking a detailed medical history, by feeling the spine and joints, or by X-ray. It should never hurt, although you may be a bit stiff or sore for a day or so afterwards. A session costs from around £16 to £45 and lasts between 30 minutes and an hour.

A chiropractor or an osteopath?
They both seem to deal with backs and there are many similarities, but some of the differences are that a chiropractor may be more likely to use X-rays in diagnosis (both use them to exclude disease). (See below for **Osteopathy**.) There are also subtle differences in the way they manipulate; and an osteopath may rely more on his hands to detect small changes in connective tissue, joints and muscles. Whereas a chiropractor uses direct pressure/manipulation on a troublesome joint or vertebrae, osteopaths use more leverage.

Is it only useful for back complaints?
Chiropractic can relieve anything to do with the spine and its nervous system – low back pain, slipped discs, sciatica, neck shoulder and arm pains, some arthritis and rheumatism. It can also relieve migraines, asthma, digestive disorders and some neurological conditions; and help certain women's problems such as painful periods and the postural problems associated with pregnancy, childbirth and osteoporosis.

Send £1 for a registered practitioners list from The British Chiropractic Association
Equity House
29 Whitely Street, Reading
0734 757557

Dietary therapy (Clinical Nutrition)

What is it?

Diet has long been neglected as an element in health, but it is now coming into its own. GPs themselves are not routinely trained in nutrition (about three days of medical school training is devoted to this area) but there are specialist doctors who are, called clinical nutritionists.

There are also some specialist training courses in nutrition – some better than others – whose graduates set up as independent practitioners.

Many complementary therapists also have specialist knowledge of diet or nutrition. In particular, naturopaths (all-round practitioners of several natural therapies), medical herbalists, and some acupuncturists.

A good practitioner will:

* go through your whole diet with you, and suggest improvements;
* use tests (a questionnaire, hair mineral analysis, 'Touch for Health' muscle testing, maybe blood or sweat analysis) to determine whether you are low in certain minerals and vitamins.

The advice you get may involve taking vitamin and/or mineral supplements for a while as well as a change in your eating habits. A session will cost from around £20 to £50 (plus the cost of the supplements, if recommended) if you go privately. It is free on the NHS if recommended by your doctor.

Few people have signs of outright vitamin deficiency – such as scurvy – but it is now widely accepted that many people have slight shortages of minerals or vitamins called 'sub-clinical deficiencies' which show up as mild ill-health, tiredness, susceptibility to colds, 'flu and other infections, and so on. Certain people are quite likely to eat a less than balanced diet, anyway, including those who can't afford (or don't have time to buy) fresh fruit and vegetables or people who rely on refined and junk food. Women are often too busy to look after their own needs, and women who menstruate are sometimes short of iron in particular. Those who have had a baby recently or who are breastfeeding may also be a bit short of everything, as their bodies are nourishing the baby's growth.

A better diet rather than supplements might do the trick, but if you are seriously short of a certain nutrient, it may take an awful lot of food to replenish it. People's nutritional needs also vary widely, so your nutritionist may find that you have an unusually high requirement for a certain nutrient. But do be wary of any practitioner who suggests your problems can be dealt with purely by taking supplements, and is not interested helping you change your diet for the better.

Is a good diet expensive?

Not necessarily. It is quite likely to be cheaper than a poor diet. Few people, for instance, need to eat expensive things like meat every day (vegetable protein like lentils and tofu are cheap in comparison) and fresh foods are always much cheaper than ready-prepared refined foods. Your main problem may be finding the time to buy fresh food several times a week, then to cook and eat properly, but that can be overcome too.

467

What conditions can dietary therapy help?
Almost anything, since food is the basis and the fuel of all the chemical processes that take place in your body. Very good results can be obtained with rheumatism and arthritis, high blood pressure, fatigue, constipation and other digestive troubles, wound healing, skin problems, and many apparently psychological and behavioural problems. If you turn out to have a food allergy, a nutritionist can help you to identify it, and eliminating the guilty food could solve all kinds of health problems. For women: anaemia, PMS, menopausal symptoms, constipation and often thrush especially.

To find a practitioner, contact
The Dietary Therapy Society
33 Priory Gardens
London N6 5QU 081 341 7260
or The Women's Nutritional Advisory Service
PO Box 268
Hove
East Sussex BN3 1RW 0273 487366

To find a doctor trained in clinical nutrition get your GP to write on your behalf to
Acorns
Romsey Road
Cadnam
Southampton 0703 812124

To find a dietitian or nutritionist trained in conventional, state-regulated nutrition contact the British Nutrition Foundation
52 to 54 High Holborn
London WC1
071 404 6504

Homoeopathy
What is it?
Homoeopathy was mentioned by Hippocrates, but was put on to a systematic basis by a nineteenth-century German doctor called Hahnemann.

It is based upon the principle that 'like treats like'. Minute quantities are given of a substance which, in a healthy person, would produce the symptoms of the illness we are trying to cure, for instance, minute amounts of flower and grass pollen may be given to a hay fever sufferer. Homoeopathic remedies aggravate symptoms very minutely, and this stimulates the body's own defences to get well.

Instead of simply suppressing the symptoms of illness, as conventional medicine does, the assumption of homoeopathy is that the body knows what it is doing and the symptoms are, in fact, indications that it is working to try and deal with the root cause of the trouble, and that this process should be encouraged – not suppressed. For example, conventional treatment for bron-chitis would suppress the cough, whereas a homoeopath would see the cough as a healing mechanism and prescribe a remedy which might aggravate the cough slightly at first.

Another remarkable thing about homoeopathy is that the doses used are very very low. Sometimes they are diluted tens of thousands of times – so diluted, in fact, that no trace of the active substance can be found by conventional analysis. It was Hahnemann who found that the more he diluted homoeopathic remedies, the stronger their effect became. Nobody really knows how such small doses work. Some people believe it concerns the electromagnetic fields of the individual cells in the body. Whatever the reason, homoeopathy does indeed work for many people.

Is it safe?
Homoeopathy is so safe it can be used on babies. The doses are so low that in conventional terms they should have no effect at all.

Is there only one specific remedy for each illness?
No – a homoeopath will prescribe for you individually. A remedy may work for one person, but not for someone else with the same symptoms. When you first visit a homoeopath, you will be asked seemingly strange questions to establish which remedies to use for you personally like: 'Do you prefer the mountains or the seaside?' 'Do you get cold easily?' 'Do you dream vividly?'

Homoeopaths should always explain what they are giving you, if asked. If your practitioner won't, find another.

Treatment
It is best to see a homoeopath at first because a treatment prescribed for you personally is likely to be more effective than a general one bought in a health shop, although homoeopathic remedies can be bought for self use at health food shops. Also, homoeopathy is the only complementary medicine recog-nized in law like other medical disciplines. There are NHS homoeopathic hospitals in London, Bristol, Glasgow, Tunbridge Wells and Liverpool, where, if you are referred by a doctor, the treatment is free on the NHS and the price varies for private homoeopaths depending on their location, from around £15 to £60 for the first one-hour session, to half that for a second hour-long consultation.

What is it useful for?
Many chronic, i.e. long-term, 'grumbling' conditions such as asthma, diges-tive problems, nervous and psychological disorders are treated by homoeopathy. Also acute conditions such as post-operative shock, coughs, colds and allergies. It is not usually suitable for conditions that need surgery. For women: menstrual and menopausal problems, anaemia, morning sick-ness, breast disorders, preparing the body for childbirth and a swift physical recovery from it.

Send SAE for a free list of medically qualified homoeopaths to
The British Homoeopathic Association
27A Devonshire Street,
London W1N 1JR 071 935 2163.

For a lay homoeopath (not medically qualified), contact
The Society of Homoeopaths
2 Artisan Road
Northampton NN1 4HU 0604 21400 (send SAE for list).

Or contact the Hahnemann Society
071 837 3297

Medical herbalism
What is it?
Herbalism is an ancient healing art. Remedies may take time to work and are
gentle but effective. Herbalists believe it is safer to use the whole (or part of the
whole) of a plant, rather than extracting and synthesizing the 'active' part, as
conventional medicine does.

Herbs are prescribed for particular symptoms. Remedies may be in the form
of an infusion (like a tea), a tincture (herbs suspended in alcohol), a lotion or
liquid, tablets, capsules, or a poultice (to apply to affected parts). Often a
combination of different herbs is used.

A registered herbalist will be well aware of the toxic side effects of some
plants, or of conditions when certain herbs should not be used (e.g. during
pregnancy). Some herbs *can* be dangerous, especially if taken regularly or in
large doses, e.g. some herbs produce uterine contractions in pregnant women.
Common helpful remedies can be bought in health food shops (e.g. chamomile
for inducing sleep or Calendula ointment for cuts, but if you are thinking of
trying anything other than, say, an ordinary herb tea from a health food shop,
go to a trained herbalist or a reputable specialist herbalist shop. If you are
pregnant, treat herbs with exactly the same caution as you would treat
conventional medical drugs – they can be just as powerful.

A herbalist takes a detailed medical history and notes any allergies before
recommending any treatment. It costs around £15 to £25 for the first consultation – one hour – and usually half of that for the next hour-long session.

What is herbalism useful for?
It can be used for hay fever, colds and respiratory disorders, digestive disorders
(such as ulcers and constipation), headaches, anxiety, depression, recurrent
infections, rheumatism, arthritis, skin problems, and many more conditions.
For women: menstrual and menopausal problems, morning sickness, anaemia
and many others respond well.

Contact The Secretary
National Institute of Medical Herbalists
9 Palace Gate
Exeter
Devon EX1 1JA 0392 426022

Osteopathy
What is it?
Osteopathy is one of the most widely accepted therapies. With back pain so common and causing so much absence from work, many orthodox doctors refer patients to an osteopath.

Osteopaths believe that if the spine is wrongly aligned it can cause muscle and sometimes nerve problems in other parts of the body. They treat abnormalities in the skeleton and muscles by adjustment and manipulation, restoring bones, muscle ligaments and nerves to their proper alignment. Osteopaths use more of a leverage technique than chiropractors, and also deal with 'peripheral' joints that are giving trouble, such as knees and shoulders. They only occasionally use X-rays as diagnosis. They take a detailed medical history, observing the way you walk, sit, stand.

It will cost from around £14 to £45 for the first consultation (lasting an hour or more), and subsequent sessions will cost from £11.

It shouldn't hurt, although the treatment is very physical and it may involve you in a variety of postures while the osteopath manipulates the head, arms, legs or back.

The osteopath will also give postural advice and may recommend exercises to correct bad habits.

Is it only useful for back complaints?
It is obviously useful for back and neck injuries, but it can also help things like asthma, bronchitis, constipation, digestive problems and headaches. For women: menstrual troubles, help with the pregnancy problems (e.g. backache from softening of bones and ligaments, caused by hormonal changes, in particular).

Cranial osteopathy
In this very gentle treatment the slightly mobile skull bones are adjusted, which influences the pressure and flow of the cerebro-spinal fluid which flows around the brain and spine. It is useful for migraines, headaches, birth injuries, whiplash injuries, tinnitus and facial neuralgia. Only qualified osteopaths can take the course to qualify them to practise this.

Contact the British School of Osteopathy
Little John House
1 Suffolk Street
London SW1Y 4HG 071 930 9254
or British College of Osteopathy and Naturopathy
6 Netherhall Gardens
London NW3 5RR 071 435 7830

For a list of registered osteopaths, send £2.20 to
The General Council and Register of Osteopaths
56 London Street
Reading
Berkshire RG1 4SQ 0734 576585

Complementary therapies helplines

Auckenkyle Clinics
Southwoods Road, Troon, Ayrshire, Scotland KA10 7EL (0292 311414)
Run by naturopath Jan de Vries.

British Acupuncture Register and Director
34 Alderney Street, London SW1V 4EU (071 834 1012)

The British Chiropractic Association
Equity House, 29 Whitely Street, Reading (0734 757557)

British Council for Complementary and Alternative Medicine
(see The Council for Acupuncture, below)

British Homoeopathic Association
27A Devonshire Street, London W1N 1RJ (071 935 2163)

British Naturopathic and Osteopathic Association
1–4 Suffolk Street, London SW1Y 4HG (071 435 8728)

British Nutrition Foundation
52 to 54 High Holborn, London WC1 (071 404 6504)

British School of Osteopathy
Little John House, 1–4 Suffolk Street, London SW1Y 4HG (071 930 9254/8)

Friends of the Earth Limited
26–28 Underwood Street, London N1 7JQ (071 490 1555)

The Institute for Complementary Medicine
PO Box 194, London SE16 1QZ (071 237 5165)

Institute for Optimum Nutrition
5 Jerdan Place, London SW6 1BE (071 385 7984)

Institute of Psychosexual Medicine
11 Chandos Street, Cavendish Square, London W1M 9DE (071 580 0631)

International Federation of Aromatherapists
Dept of Education, The Royal Masonic Hospital, Ravenscourt Park, London W6
  (081 846 8066)

The National Institute of Medical Herbalists
9 Palace Gate, Exeter, Devon EX1 1JA (0392 426022)

Natural Pregnancy Oils
Active Birth Centre, 55 Dartmouth Park Road, London NW5 1SL (071 267 3006)

School of Herbal Medicine
148 Forest Road, Tunbridge Wells, Kent TN2 5EY (0892 30400)

Shiatsu Society
Elaine Liechti, 19 Langside Park, Kilbarchan, Renfrewshire PA10 2EP (05057 4657)

The Society of Homoeopaths
2 Artizan Road, Northampton NN1 4HU (0604 21400)

Tyringham Clinic
Newport Pagnell, Buckinghamshire MK16 9ER (0908 610450)
A cross between a health farm and a naturopathic residential clinic.

Further reading
Healing Without Harm by E. G. Bartlett (Eliot Right Way Books)
The Handbook of Alternative Medicine by Stephen Fulder (Coronet)
The Alternative Health Guide by Brian Inglis and Ruth West (Michael Joseph)
Alternatives in Healing by Simon Mills (Macmillan)
The Good Health Guide by Patrick Pietroni (Bloomsbury)
Journal of Alternative Medicine by Robert Tisserand
Alternative Healthcare for Women by Patsy Westcott (Grapevine)
The National Directory of Alternative Aid by Michael Williams (Health Farm
  Publishing)

Setting up your own support group

In the past few years, women's self help groups have mushroomed. Women join self help groups when they would never dream of joining more formal groups set up by health professionals.

But they don't work by magic. And, while they can be rewarding and sustaining, they are hard work to set up, and can take over your life if you are not careful. There can be problems: with finance, organization and the pecking order. We have drawn on the real-life experience of three women who are (or who have been) members of self help groups to illustrate the rewards and the problems: Milly, who founded a miscarriage support group in London; Sarah, who was one of five co-founders of an endometriosis group in Kent; and Jane, who attended a Manchester endometriosis group for several months.

What is self help?
Self help, often, means a group of people who come together to give mutual support for a common problem – usually after they have looked in vain for support or information elsewhere. You can meet together, several of you, in person; on a one-to-one basis – or often, just talk down the phone to a sympathetic person, if that is what you would prefer.

The problem can be almost anything. It might be a chronic complaint (like endometriosis), where women may continue in the group for a long time, or a medical 'event' (like miscarriage), which can have long-term emotional, mental and perhaps physical effects.

Advocates of self-help emphasize that it should not be used to patch up scanty provision by the state. The idea should be to complement existing services, offering women a different perspective.

Support can come through regular meetings, or over the phone (particularly for people in isolated rural areas, or where sufferers can't face going to meetings). Group members are usually willing to take some responsibility for their own problem, instead of leaving all the decisions to professionals – indeed, they may be desperate to find out more about it.

One of the best things about a self help group is being able to talk, and share experiences, with other women who know *exactly* how you feel, because they've had, or have, the same problem. They can often offer extremely practical advice about how to cope which a doctor cannot, because of their personal experience. Many people feel an enormous sense of relief when they first meet others with the same condition. Jane says: 'It is great to sit in a room with 12 or 15 women who know what you're talking about – know the severity of the disease, and know that when you say you didn't want to get out of bed that morning, you mean just that. For me, it was quite empowering to see other women who did hold down jobs. With endometriosis you tend to feel you can't do anything.'

Milly says: 'You feel so alone after a miscarriage – other women who haven't been through the experience often don't want to talk about it. I wanted a space to air our feelings and experiences, without feeling guilty.'

Group members are usually willing to share information, and work together with others. One great advantage of a group is that you are neither a patient, being ministered to, nor a volunteer, ministering to others. You can assume either role at different times – sometimes you need support yourself; sometimes you have energy to give to others.

Why self help?

There may already be a more formal group, administered by health professionals, in your area. What in particular has a self help group got to offer?

Sarah says: 'A lot of our meetings might consist of moaning about the treatment women get from doctors. If health professionals were present, or running the group, we wouldn't be able to do it.' Milly says: 'If a group is set up by professionals, women can feel intimidated. In a self help group we can be relaxed, give tips, comfort each other. We're more able to talk because we're meeting in our own houses rather than in centres. We'd be more at ease to break down if we needed to. We wouldn't feel uncomfortable.'

How to start a group

First steps

First, be aware that a group can take up much more time than you bargained for. It is important to be clear what (and who) the group is for, what commitment you yourself can offer, and what, realistically, the group can achieve. The answers to these questions will help you pin down some details.

* Do you want it to be just a mutual support group, or do you want to campaign, or do research?
* Would you like to stay small, or expand?
* When and how often will you meet?
* Do you want publicity?
* Do you want to apply for large-scale funding, or rely on members paying small subs?
* Will you be able to answer queries and give information to people who can contact you (e.g. over the phone), who have the problem, and aren't members?

It is worth checking with the national organization for your problem (if there is one) before you start. For instance, the National Endometriosis Society publishes a newsletter which gives local contacts. There may already have been a group in your area, now no longer active, from which you can salvage a few members. Or there may be single contacts willing to participate in a group.

Check with general local organizations, too. The phone book is the place to find them:
* the local authority's self help directory, if there is one;
* the local authority information department, if there is one;
* the social services;
* the social worker at the local hospital;
* community centres, women's centres, and so on;

* the local Community Health Council (CHC);
* the local Council for Voluntary Service (CVS);

Also check national information resources listed in HELPLINES, especially in the book *The Self Help Guide*, which lists the names and addresses of many of the self help organizations in the country, to see if a national group exists – if it does, ring them up for advice about starting a local branch.

Setting up a group

If you've checked with local and national organizations, and there is *nothing* local which meets your needs, how do you begin?

Milly says: 'I started one group mainly on my own. I got information from the National Miscarriage Association and the local SANDS (Stillbirth and Neonatal Death Society) were also very supportive. One of my miscarriages was at 20 weeks, with full labour, so I'd classed it as a stillbirth, even though the doctors didn't, and I felt there were a lot of issues where we crossed over.

'I gave my name as a contact to the national association and I started going round hospitals, trying to explain to student midwives how we felt. I began to get enquiries through the national organization, and from hospitals and health centres. I made posters telling women when the meetings were and took them round to women's centres and health centres.

'When I got a contact, I would talk to her on the phone first so that she felt easier about coming to a meeting. I wanted it very much to be a local group, even though we were affiliated to the national organization.'

Sarah says: 'We started off as four women in our thirties who all had endometriosis. Our aim was to provide support to each other. Then we put an advert in the National Endometriosis Society newsletter. We got four or five phone calls and it went on from there. We were going to have an article in the local paper to increase publicity, but in fact we didn't need it.' (This group now has about 22 members, and regular meetings every six weeks.)

Where to meet?

A big problem, always, is finding somewhere to meet. Both the Kent and London groups solved it by meeting in each other's houses, with informal arrangement for lifts home.

But there are problems to this approach. Jane, who eventually left her Manchester endometriosis group, felt uncomfortable: 'After going to one of the meetings, in one of those five-storey posh jobs up on the heath, I thought – there's no way I can invite them back here. [Jane lives on her own in a less smart part of town.] 'I suggested the local women's centre near my flat, but they said – we're not going down there, it's too rough.'

So, if you decide to meet in each other's houses, it is important to check that it is convenient and comfortable for everyone. People might prefer to opt for a more 'neutral' meeting place. If they do, start by seeing if there are any free rooms available locally. (But bear in mind that sometimes it is well worth paying for a room, if you can. It is hard to insist on even basic good service if you're getting a free room.)

Places to try include: the CVS, the CHC, the Citizens Advice Bureau, the local authority information department, libraries, the health education unit, health centres, community centres, women's centres, schools, adult education institutes, pubs, churches or day centres. In some areas there are specific 'Self Help Support Centres', with workers who help groups to get off the ground – contact the CVS to find out if there is one.

Judy Wilson, author of a helpful book (see HELPLINES), says that you should consider the seven Cs when choosing a place to meet: character, comfort, continuity, chairs, car parking/public transport, coffee and caretakers.

Above all, your meetings should be welcoming – people will overlook shortcomings if they feel welcome: Jane went to – 'three hours in somebody's house discussing things, without being offered a cup of tea!'

And think carefully about the timing of meetings – when is late-night shopping night? When are the school holidays? What about the weekend? Or the middle of winter?

Finance

Milly points out: 'Money is always needed for something – transport for visiting people or the hospital, postage, stationery, posters. I got a grant for £500 one year from the local women's committee and £400 the next year. With that I bought a desk and some equipment, and paid for postage and transport.'

Sarah's group took the opposite tack: 'We went to all kinds of meetings on how to get a grant, but in the end we decided to keep our group small. We charge 50p per meeting, which covers tea or coffee and postage.' Jane's group tried a third way – and it didn't work too well: 'There was no money, so we all put in what we could. So those with more money ended up putting in more, and ended up feeling resentful, I'm sure.'

There are, of course, small-scale fund-raising events like jumble sales and sponsored swims, but if you want to expand you often need grants for capital and running costs. If you want to be more than a local mutual support group, read some of the books on the HELPLINES list, or contact national organizations such as the Directory of Social Change.

Ask your local authority switchboard how to contact the women's committee (if there is one) and the grants unit (again, if there is one). With a little ingenuity, you may also be able to track down a local business which wants to get a good name locally (American-owned companies are much more clued up about this kind of thing), or a manufacturer of relevant drugs or products (hormone tablets? tampons? baby foods or baby equipment? makers of nutritional supplements targetted at women?) who would benefit PR-wise by being associated with you.

Always remember to ask people to send an SAE when you publicize any offer of information or leaflets. Otherwise, you could be sunk by the cost of stamps and the chore of addressing envelopes.

Publicity

Your publicity needs depend on the level of membership you want, and what you want to achieve. Be realistic. You can start small, using word of mouth, hand-drawn or photocopied posters, notices in appropriate centres, e.g. health centres, doctors' surgeries, local hospitals, maternity wards and gynaecology wards or at patient clinics, and free ads in the 'community' sections of local papers. Or you can push for articles in local papers and spots on local radio and regional TV. Or you might just want extra publicity for specific events.

If you do want to get a lot of publicity, read some books (see HELPLINES), learn how to write a press release, decide which radio spots you want to go for and cultivate local journalists. But beware – publicity can sometimes be too successful, and you might not be able to cope. Lay on extra people and telephone contact numbers if you know you are going to get some media attention, or women who seek your help will be put off by jammed telephone lines or delays in getting mail answered.

Sarah says: 'We would be worried if we had more publicity. We might get inundated. It's nice to think there are people out there we could help, but we've had to recognize that we only have so much energy, especially as many of us are not well at times.'

Keeping going

After the group has been going for a while, you might come up against different problems.

* Keeping people interested, for instance. It's important to recognize that people use different groups in different ways. Milly comments: 'Some members might come to the group straight after a miscarriage, and then might not come again for a long while. They use it according to need.'

* You might have to check that your group really does welcome all the people you think it does. Milly says: 'I made sure that I put on the posters that all nationalities were welcome. I wanted the group to be accessible to young black women like myself, not just middle-class couples.'

Sarah adds: 'As we were all in our thirties, we worried that we might end up as a group of women all the same age, going on about childlessness. But in fact we have all ages, from seventeen to women in their forties.'

Some groups toy with the idea having members other than 'sufferers' themselves. Sarah's group found it didn't work: 'We had some husbands at the beginning, but it wasn't as good for the women, so now we just invite partners to Christmas socials.'

* Is the group open to different ways of dealing with the problem? Jane, for instance, says: 'I was the only one going to a homoeopath – all the others were very much into conventional medicine. I felt a bit out of it.' Contrast this with Sarah: 'It can be a real help hearing about all the different methods of treatment.'

* Key members – founding members especially – can get exhausted. Milly (who has recently had a baby) says: 'I don't get drowned in it, but it does get a bit much. Like now, for instance. I'm supposed to be having a break, but if a woman phones up in distress, I have to listen. If you're thinking of setting up a group, it's important to get some support for yourself – co-counselling, or something.'

Setting up your own support group helplines

College of Health
St Margaret's House, 21 Old Ford Road, London E2 (081 983 2225)
Provides information on a wide range of health topics, including self-help.

Health Education Authority
Hamilton House, Mabledon Place, London WC1H 9TX (071 383 3833)
A wide range of resources on health, for consultation at the centre and for
borrowing.

Health Rights
(071 274 4000)
A health-campaigning organization which also publishes a quarterly magazine
looking at health issues.

National Council for Voluntary Organizations
Regents Wharf, 8 All Saints Street, London N1 (071 713 6161)
Provides information on councils for voluntary services, and rural community
councils, plus literature. They will provide lists upon request.

Nation Self-Help Support Centre
(071 713 6161)
Provides information on self-help and produces bulletins.

The Patients Association
18 Victoria Park Square, Bethnal Green, London E2 (081 981 5676).

Women's Health and Reproductive Rights Information Centre (WHRRIC)
52–54 Featherstone Street, London EC1Y 8RT (071 251 6580)
Computerized records of many women's health groups, support groups, voluntary
  organizations and individuals. They also have a large library of books, news
  clippings and pamphlets. Information is given by telephone, in writing, or in
  person. Send SAE for publications list.

Further reading
Get it On by Jane Drinkwater (Pluto)
Lobbying by Alf Dubbs (Pluto)
The Self-Help Guide by Sally Knight and Robert Gann (Chapman and Hall)
Using the Media by Dennis MacShane (Pluto)
Directory of Self-Help Support Centres published by NCVO, the Patients Association
  and the College of Health. Send 50p plus SAE.
Getting the Message Across by Su Ward (Pluto)
Self-Help Groups: Getting Started and Keeping Going by Judy Wilson (Longman)

Self-Help OK (VIDEO) from NACAB vision, Middleton House, 115–123 Pentonville
  Road, London N1 9LZ (01 833 2181)

Note: If you have difficulty obtaining the Pluto Press books, telephone the publishers
on 081 348 2724.

General helplines

ASH (Action on Smoking and Health)
109 Gloucester Place, London W1 (071 935 3519)

Association of Qualified and Curative Hypnotherapists
8 Balaclava Road, Birmingham (021 444 5435)

British Association for Counselling
37a Sheep Street, Rugby CV21 3BX (0788 578 328)

British Association of Cancer United Patients (BACUP)
121–123 Charterhouse Street, London EC1M 6AA (071 608 1785)

British Association of Plastic Surgeons
Royal College of Surgeons, 35–43 Lincoln's Inn Fields, London WC2A 3PN
  (071 831 5161)

British Diabetic Association
10 Queen Anne Street, London W1M 0BD (071 323 1531)

British Foundation for Age Research
49 Queen Victoria Street, London EC4N 4SA (071 236 4365)

British Heart Foundation
102 Gloucester Place, London W1H 4DH (071 935 0185)

British Holistic Medical Association
179 Gloucester Place, London NW1 6DX (071 262 5299)

British Library of Tape Recordings for Hospital Patients
12 Lant Street, London SE1 1QH (071 407 9417)

British Medical Association (BMA)
BMA House, Tavistock Square, London WC1H 9JP (071 387 4499)

British Nutrition Foundation
15 Belgrave Square, London W1 (071 235 4904)

British Pregnancy Advisory Service
HQ – Austy Manor, Wooton Wawen, Solihull, West Midlands B95 6DA
   (0564 793 225)

British Society for Nutritional Medicine
PO Box 3AP, London 3AP 1NN (071 436 8532)

British United Provident Association (BUPA)
Provident House, Essex Street, London WC2R 3AX (071 353 5212)

British Wheel of Yoga
1 Hamilton Place, Boston Road, Sleaford, Lincs (0529 306851)
Can put you in touch with a professionally qualified teacher in your area. Yoga can be
   helpful for numerous conditions.

The Brook Advisory Centres
HQ – 233 Tottenham Court Road, London W1P 9AE (071 580 2991)
There are five centres in London and affiliated organizations in other cities (e.g.
   Coventry, Birmingham, Bristol, Cambridge, Liverpool and Edinburgh). Will
   advise on all contraception, sexual and emotional matters for under-25s.

Citizens' Advice Bureaux
(071 833 2181)
Has bureaux nationally offering free information or referral to specialist agencies;
   addresses from local phone books, town hall, or from head office.

Family Planning Association
HQ – 27 Mortimer Street, London W1N 7RJ (071 636 7866)
Most family planning clinics are now run by AHAs, but the FPA itself still runs about
   25 clinics, offering advice on vasectomy, sub-fertility, counselling, contraception
   and emotional matters. Contact HQ for details.

Health Visitors Association
50 Southwark Street, London SE1 1UN (071 378 7255)

The Institute for Complementary Medicine
PO Box 194, London SE16 1QZ (071 237 5165)

The Institute for Optimum Nutrition
5 Jerdan Place, London SW6 1BE (071 385 7984)

Marie Stopes Clinics
HQ – Marie Stopes House, 108 Whitfield Street, London W1P 6BE
   (071 388 0662/7585)
Marie Stopes Centre, 10 Queen Square, Leeds LS2 8AJ (0532 440 685)
Marie Stopes Centre, 1 Police Street, Manchester M2 7LQ (061 832 4260)
Marie Stopes is a registered charity which offers services and runs clinics across the
   country (and in many cases the world) for virtually every female complaint. Contact
   HQ for details of an affiliated clinic near you, and specialist advice for your
   condition. They specialize in family planning, but are equipped to deal with many
   other aspects of women's health.

National Childbirth Trust
HQ – Alexandra House, Oldham Terrace, London W3 6NH (081 992 8637)

National Federation of Spiritual Healers
Old Manor Farm Studio, Church Street, Sunbury on Thames, Middlesex
   TW16 6RG (0932 783165)

National Association for Pre-Menstrual Syndrome
PO Box 72, Sevenoaks, Kent TA13 1XQ

Patients Association
18 Victoria Park Square, Bethnal Green, London E2 (081 981 5676)

The Premenstrual Society
Verona, Hare Hill, Addlestone, Weybridge, Surrey KT15 1DT

RELATE (formerly the Marriage Guidance Council)
Herbert Gray College, Little Church Street, Rugby CV21 3AP (0788 573 241)
Offers counselling for women of any age, with their partners or families.

Weight Watchers UK Limited
HQ – Kidswell Park House, Kidswell Park Drive, Maidenhead, Berkshire SL6 8YT
   (0628 777077)

Women's Alcohol Centre
254 St Paul's Road, Islington, London N1 2LJ (071 226 4581)

Women's Health and Reproductive Rights Information Centre (WHRRIC)
52–54 Featherstone Street, London EC1Y 8RT (071 251 6580)
A voluntary organization that can give useful information, support and advice on
any aspect of women's health.

Women's Health Concern
PO Box 1629, London W8 (071 938 3932)
For advice and information on all aspects of women's health.

Women's National Cancer Control Campaign (WNCCC)
1 South Audley Street, London W1Y 5DQ (071 499 7532/4)
Promotes measures for early detection and treatment of cervical and breast cancer,
providing leaflets, posters, films and breast-screening details.

Women's Nutritional Advisory Service (WNAS)
PO Box 268, Hove, East Sussex BN3 1RW (0273 771366)
Advice on coping with many women's problems, by changing the food that you eat
and by taking mineral and vitamin supplements.

Helplines for Australia, New Zealand and Canada

Australia
Abortion Access
237 Lutwyche Road, Windsor, Queensland 4030

Abortion and Contraception Advisory Service
116 Wellington Parade, East Melbourne, Victoria 3002 (03 419 1686)

Airlie Women's Clinic
1 Airlie Avenue, Prahran East, Victoria 3181 (03 525 1941)

Breast Cancer Support Service
32 St Georges, Perth, Western Australia 6000 (09 325 9620)

Changing Shape
24 Arundel Crescent, Surrey Hills, Victoria 3127 (03 830 4531)

Childbirth and Education Association of Victoria
761 Burwood Highway, Ferntree Gully, Victoria 3165 (03 758 7813)

Childhood and Parenting Association of Victoria
49 Taylors Road, Croydon, Victoria 3136 (03 725 4832)

Family Planning Association of Queensland
100 Alfred Street, Fortitude Valley, Queensland 4006 (08 252 5151)

Family Planning Association of Victoria
259 Church Street, Richmond, Victoria 3121 (03 429 1868)

Health Commission of Victoria
555 Collins Street, Melbourne, Victoria 3000 (03 616 7777)

Health Department of Western Australia
70–74 Murray Street, Perth, WA 6000 (09 221 1122)
Aids screening services, and sexually transmitted diseases centre.

Health Issues Centre
148 Lonsdale Street, Melbourne, Victoria 3000 (03 662 1766)

In Focus
308 Malvern Road, Phrahran, Victoria 3181 (03 525 1833)

Mid-life and Menopause Support Group
Room 6, Agnes Walsh House, KEMH, Bagot Road, Subiaco, Western Australia 6008
  (09 380 4444)

Multicultural Women's Health Centre
114 South Street, Beaconsfield, Western Australia 6162 (09 335 8214)

Natural Birth Control Centre
20 Brunswick Street, Fitzroy, Victoria, 3065 (03 419 6355)

Nursing Mothers Association of Australia
Western Australia Branch (09 447 0137)

Nursing Mothers' Association of Australia
49 Carew Street, Nundah, Queensland 4012

Nursing Mothers' Association of Australia
5 Glendale Road, Nunawading, Victoria 3131 (03 878 3304)

Premenstrual Support Group of Victoria
9 Quixley Grove, Wantirna, Victoria 3152 (03 801 2001)

Queensland Aids Council
546 Stanley Street, Mater Hill, Queensland 4101

Queensland Cancer Fund
553 Gregory Terrace, Fortitude Valley, Queensland 4006

Stillbirth and Neo-Natal Death Support Group
G9 Agnes Walsh House, KEMH, Bagot Road, Subiaco, Western Australia 6008
  (04 382 2687)

Support Groups for Mastectomy
42 Ord Street, West Perth, Western Australia 6005 (09 321 6224)

Victorian Aids Council
117 Johnstone Street, Collingwood, Victoria 3066 (03 417 1759)

Western Australia Aids Council
107 Brisbane Street, Northbridge, Western Australia 6000 (09 227 8355)

Western Institute of Self Help (WISH)
30 Railway Street, Cottesloe, Western Australia 6011 (09 383 3188)
Addictions, health, sexually transmitted diseases are all dealt with at the institute, and
  they carry a complete index of self help groups and resources.

Women's Healing Centre
East West Acupuncture Centre, 45 Temple Street, Victoria Park WA 6100
  (09 361 9511)

Women's Health Care Association
100 Aberdeen Street, Northbridge, Western Australia 6000 (09 335 8214)

Women's Health Centre Brisbane
86 Stephen's Road, Highgate Hill, Queensland 4101

Women's Health Resource Collective
653 Nicholson Street, Carlton North, Victoria 3054 (03 380 9974)

Women's Information Services
280 Adelaide Street, Brisbane, Queensland 4000

Women's Service for Health
60 Droop Street, Footscray, Victoria 3011 (03 689 9588)

New Zealand
Auckland Women's Health Collective
Women's Health Centre, 63 Ponsonby Road, Ponsonby, Auckland, New Zealand
  (765173)

Auckland Women's Health Council
10 Carlton-Gore Road, Auckland 1, New Zealand

Christchurch Homebirth Association
PO Box 2806, Christchurch, New Zealand

Community Health Nursing Services
Community Service Centre, Wellington Hospital, Wellington, New Zealand (04
  897069)

Community Services
Otago Area Health Board, Dunedin, New Zealand (024 777740 x 811)
Can deal with continence, among other women's conditions.

Continence Advisor
PO Box 4091, Christchurch, New Zealand

Continence Advisor
PO Box 9238, Newmarket, Auckland, New Zealand

Dunedin Homebirth Association
PO Box 6124, Dunedin, New Zealand

Home Birth Association New Zealand Limited
PO Box 7093, Wellesley Street, Auckland, New Zealand (5202396 or 761986)

Lower Hutt Woman's Centre
52 Laings Road, Lower Hutt, New Zealand (692711)

Ministry of Women's Affairs
Braemar House, 32 The Terrace, Private Bag, Wellington, New Zealand (04 734112)

National Collective of Independent Woman's Refuges
PO Box 6386, Te Aro Wellington, New Zealand (856768)

National Collective of Rape Crisis and Related Groups of Atoearoa Inc.
PO Box 6181, Te Aro Wellington, New Zealand (856768)

National Network of New Mother Support Groups
PO Box 9600, Courtney Place, Wellington, New Zealand

New Zealand AIDS Foundation
PO Box 1004, Dunedin, New Zealand

New Zealand AIDS Foundation
PO Box 6663, Wellesley Street, Auckland 1, New Zealand
Note New Zealand's toll free AIDS Hotline is based in Auckland and can be reached
   on AUCKLAND 395560.

New Zealand AIDS Foundation
PO Box 21258, Edgeware, Christchurch, New Zealand (03 793353)

Pacific Island Woman's Health Project
510 Richmond Road, Grey Lynn, Auckland, New Zealand

St George's Hospital
Maternity Office, Private Bag, Christchurch, New Zealand
The only private hospital in New Zealand. You might wish to arrange to have your
   baby here.

The Health Alternatives for Women Inc. (THAW)
PO Box 884, Christchurch, New Zealand (796970)

Wellington Homebirth Association
PO Box 9130, Wellington, New Zealand

Wellington Woman's Health Collective
10 Kensington Street, PO Box 9172, Wellington (856383)

West Auckland Woman's Centre
111 McLeod Road, Henderson, Auckland, New Zealand (8366381)

Women Against Violence Centre
PO Box 13-476, Christchurch, New Zealand

Women for Sobriety
PO Box 6399, Dunedin, New Zealand (737896)

Womanline
Women's Health Centre, 63 Ponsonby Road, Ponsonby, Auckland, New Zealand
(765173)

Women's Health Collective
Student Union Building, Otago University, Dunedin, New Zealand

Canada
Acupuncture Foundation of Canada
7321 Victoria Park Avenue, Unit 18, Markham, Ontario, Canada L3R 2ZB (416 474
0383)

Alcoholic Anonymous Toronto
Intergroup Office, 234 Eglinton Avenue East, Suite 502, Toronto, Ontario, Canada
M4P 1K5 (416 487 5591)

Association of Parent Support Groups in Ontario
11 Nevada Avenue, Willowdale, Ontario, Canada M2M 3N9 (416 223 7444)
Contact this number for nationwide referral.

Bellwood Health Services, Inc.
1020 McNicoll Avenue, Scarborough, Ontario, Canada M1W 2J6 (416 495 0926)
Pioneers in the treatment of chemical addictions and dependencies. They will also
offer pre-conceptual care, based on physical and spiritual well-being. One of
Canada's only sleep disorder clinics is based here.

Canadian AIDS Society
267 Dalhousie Street, Suite 200, Ottawa, Ontario, Canada K1N 7E3 (613 230 3580)

Canadian Cancer Society
77 Bloor Street West, Suite 702, Toronto, Ontario, Canada M5S 3A1 (416 961 7223)

Canadian Society of Homoeopathy
87 Meadowlands Drive West, Nepean, Ontario, Canada K2G 2R9 (613 723 1533)

Family and Children's Services Division
Department of Community Services, PO Box 696, Halifax, Nova Scotia, Canada
B3J 2T7 (902 424 3202)

Health League of Canada
PO Box 4000, Station B, Scarborough, Ontario, Canada M1N 4C6 (416 261 3636)

Healthy Horizons
PO Box 1674, Fort Qu'Appelle, SK, Canada S0G 1S0

International Childbirth Education Association
8207 10 Street Southwest, Calgary, Alberta, Canada T2Y 1M7

Ministere de la Sante det des Services Sociaux
Programmes Communante famille, jeunesse
1075 CH, Ste-Foy, 6e Etage, Quebec, Canada G15 2M1 (418 643 4031)

National Institute of Nutrition
1565 Carling Avenue, Suite 400, Ottawa, Ontario, Canada K1Z 8R1 (613 725 1889)

Natural Family Planning Association
3050 Yonge Street, Suite 205, Toronto, Ontario, Canada M4N 2K4 (416 481 5465)

Non-Smokers' Rights Association
344 Bloor Street West, Suite 308, Toronto, Ontario, Canada M5S 3A7 (416 928 2900)

Ontario Coalition for Abortion Clinics
PO Box 753, Station P, Toronto, Ontario, Canada M5S 2Z1 (416 969 8463)

Planned Parenthood Federation of Canada
1 Nicholus Street, Suite 430, Ottawa, Ontario, Canada K1N 7B7 (613 238 4474)

Pre-Menstrual Suyndrome Centre
1077 North Service Road, Applewood Plaza, Mississauga, Ontario, Canada K0A 3G0
  (416 273 7770)

United Family Court
55 Main Street West, Hamilton, Ontario, Canada L8P 1H4 (416 525 1550)

Index

piles, 367, 383, 399
The Pill, 168–74
  after abortion, 21
  and breast cancer, 69
  and endometriosis, 211
  and infertility, 251
  and pre-menstrual syndrome, 418, 419
  side effects, 170–2
  and thrush, 454, 459
placenta, 134, 350
polycystic ovaries, 255–6
positions, childbirth, 129–33
post-natal illness, 346–59, 400
pre-eclampsia, 375
pregnancy: abortion, 12–26
  and AIDS, 31–2
  childbirth, 109–44
  constipation, 148
  and cystitis, 185
  ectopic, 167, 194–201
  and endometriosis, 208
  and fibroids, 219
  and incontinence, 240
  miscarriage, 12, 297–310
  post-pregnancy problems, 393–410
  problems during, 360–92
  tests, 13–14
  thrush, 454
pre-menstrual syndrome (PMS) 278, 400, 411–29
private medicine, 11, 71, 112–13
progesterone, 349–50, 418, 419
prolapse, uterus, 226, 430–7
psychological problems, menopause, 285
pubic lice, 447–8, 451
puerperal psychosis, 347, 350

radiotherapy, 67, 68
  breast cancer, 75
  cervical cancer, 85
  ovarian cancer, 92–3
  self help, 99–100
  uterine cancer, 96–7
rashes, in pregnancy, 371, 386
relaxation, 101, 269, 421–2
religion and contraception, 156–7
rhythm method, contraception, 164–6

safe sex, 35
salpingectomy, 198
salpingitis, 19, 322

scabies, 447–8
sedatives, in childbirth, 123–4
segmentectomy, breast cancer, 74, 75
self help groups, 10, 98–102, 474–80
sexual intercourse: after abortion, 21
  after cervical surgery, 84–5
  after childbirth, 355, 393, 398, 405, 406
  after hysterectomy, 96, 233–5
  after ovarian surgery, 91
  and cystitis, 184, 190
  and endometriosis, 212
  and infertility, 269, menopause, 281
  in pregnancy, 117
  pre-menstrual syndrome, 424–5
  safe sex, 35
  and thrush, 457–8, 459–60
sexually transmitted diseases, 323, 326–7, 438–52
shaving, before childbirth, 122
sheaths see condoms
skin: menopause, 282
  in pregnancy, 368, 369, 372, 382–3, 386
  pre-menstrual syndrome, 426
sleep problems, 61–2, 369, 384–5
smear tests, 79–82, 291
smoking, 217, 251, 268, 278
sperm, 259–61, 457–8
spermicides, 163–4
spiritual healing, 102
sponges, contraceptive, 162–3
sterilization, 176–8
stillbirth, 297
stitches, episiotomy, 137–8
stomach pain, in pregnancy, 371, 376
stress, 257–8, 261, 353
stretch marks, 372, 387, 404
support groups, 10, 101, 474–80
surgery: breast cancer, 74–5
  cancer, 67
  cervical cancer, 84–5
  ectopic pregnancy, 198–9
  endometriosis, 209–10
  fibroids, 220–2
  hysterectomy, 230–3
  for incontinence, 243–4
  ovarian cancer, 90–1
  for prolapse, 434
  uterine cancer, 95–6
surrogate mothers, 271
syphilis, 446, 450